ECONOMICS UNCUT

Economics Uncut

A Complete Guide to Life, Death and Misadventure

Edited by

Simon W. Bowmaker

Academic Associate in Economics, University of Edinburgh, UK, Adjunct Lecturer in Economics, Florida State University and Visiting Lecturer in Economics, State University of New York at Buffalo and University of Colorado at Denver, USA

Edward Elgar
Cheltenham, UK • Northampton, MA, USA

Published by
Edward Elgar Publishing Limited
Glensanda House
Montpellier Parade
Cheltenham
Glos GL50 1UA
UK

Edward Elgar Publishing, Inc.
136 West Street
Suite 202
Northampton
Massachusetts 01060
USA

A catalogue record for this book
is available from the British Library

ISBN 1 84376 362 1 (cased)
      1 84542 580 4 (paperback)

Printed and bound in Great Britain by MPG Books Ltd, Bodmin, Cornwall

Acclaim for *Economics Uncut*

'Sex, drugs, rock and roll and so, so much more – there is enough here to persuade even the deepest skeptic of the analytical power and breadth of economics. The material is presented with careful attention to the evolution of economic ideas, as well as state-of-the-art economic theory and empirical analysis. Many strands of economic thought are represented. Any class would be enriched by examples drawn from this expansive collection.'

– Alan B. Krueger, Bendheim Professor of Economics and Public Affairs,
Princeton University, USA

'If you thought you could hide your secrets from the prying eyes of economists, think again. From sex to drugs to gambling to crime, this book will show you how the tools of economics can be used to understand just about any human behavior. This book will assuredly be the unofficial economist's guide to vice for the foreseeable future.'

– Steven D. Levitt, Alvin H. Baum Professor of Economics,
University of Chicago, USA

'This exciting book shows that economics can explain a dizzying array of real world phenomena and that economics can be great fun. I recommend this book to anyone who wants to see the progress that has been made in using the tools of neoclassical economics to understand a wide range of seemingly irrational behavior.'

– Edward L. Glaeser, Professor of Economics, Harvard University, USA

'For students who care about how the world works, microeconomics should be one of the most relevant and exciting subjects they study. Yet many students view microeconomics as some kind of abstract theory, and fail to understand how it relates to the real-world decisions made by firms, consumers, and governments. It is therefore essential that students be shown detailed examples of the application of microeconomics to practical problems – studying the theory alone is simply not enough. This outstanding book provides those examples, and would make a perfect supplementary text for any intermediate microeconomics course. The topics and examples covered are extremely timely and interesting, and are explained with great clarity. Instructors take note: students will find this book fascinating, and reading it will give them a much deeper understanding and appreciation of microeconomics.'

– Robert S. Pindyck, Tokyo-Mitsubishi Professor of Economics and
Finance, Massachusetts Institute of Technology, USA

'Those who think economics has little to say about the real world will change their minds after reading the essays in this splendid collection. Well written and authoritative, they show how the economic way of thinking can shed light on an unexpectedly diverse range of issues.'

– Robert H. Frank, Professor of Economics, Cornell University, USA

'Who said that academic economists need to get out more? This book will certainly shatter the illusion that economic analysis has little to say on topics of everyday interest.'

– Evan Davis, Economics Editor, BBC, UK

'This wonderful new volume shows that economic tradeoffs influence all of the decisions that we make. The book both educates and provokes its readers by using the rational actor model to explain seemingly pathological human behavior like suicide, drug addiction, and prostitution.'

– David Laibson, Professor of Economics, Harvard University, USA

'This is an important book that showcases the strength of economics for understanding human behavior and provides a convincing case for why economics should be reckoned as *the* social science. The chapter on prostitution provides the most comprehensive discussion of the topic to date.'

– Lena Edlund, Associate Professor of Economics,
Columbia University, USA

'Sex, drugs, suicide, murder, football – instead of a "dismal science", this book makes economics seem popular, or rather notorious. A rational analysis of these topics contains something to offend everyone. You may not agree with these papers but they will challenge you to think more deeply.'

– Robert Cooter, Herman Selvin Professor of Law, University of
California, Berkeley, USA

'Economics is most useful – and most provocative – when the spotlight of its intellectual rigour is trained on social issues. This book demonstrates how economists think about sex, drugs, and rock 'n' roll. This is an illuminating approach to subjects usually obscured by woolly thinking and conventional platitudes. It should be compulsory reading for anybody devising or legislating public policy.'

– Diane Coyle, author of *Sex, Drugs, and Economics* and
Paradoxes of Prosperity

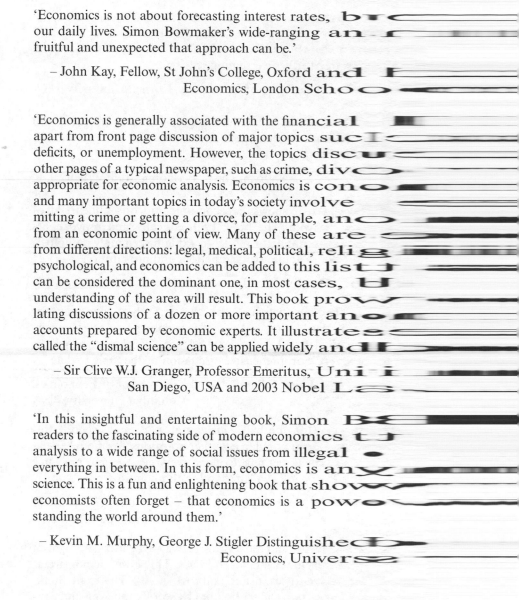

'Economics is not about forecasting interest rates, b...
our daily lives. Simon Bowmaker's wide-ranging an...
fruitful and unexpected that approach can be.'

– John Kay, Fellow, St John's College, Oxford and...
Economics, London Scho...

'Economics is generally associated with the financial...
apart from front page discussion of major topics suc...
deficits, or unemployment. However, the topics discu...
other pages of a typical newspaper, such as crime, div...
appropriate for economic analysis. Economics is cono...
and many important topics in today's society involve...
mitting a crime or getting a divorce, for example, an...
from an economic point of view. Many of these are...
from different directions: legal, medical, political, reli...
psychological, and economics can be added to this list...
can be considered the dominant one, in most cases,...
understanding of the area will result. This book pro...
lating discussions of a dozen or more important an...
accounts prepared by economic experts. It illustrate...
called the "dismal science" can be applied widely and...

– Sir Clive W.J. Granger, Professor Emeritus, Uni...
San Diego, USA and 2003 Nobel L...

'In this insightful and entertaining book, Simon B...
readers to the fascinating side of modern economics t...
analysis to a wide range of social issues from illegal...
everything in between. In this form, economics is an...
science. This is a fun and enlightening book that sho...
economists often forget – that economics is a powe...
standing the world around them.'

– Kevin M. Murphy, George J. Stigler Distinguishe...
Economics, Univers...

Acclaim for *Economics Uncut*

'Sex, drugs, rock and roll and so, so much more – there is enough here to persuade even the deepest skeptic of the analytical power and breadth of economics. The material is presented with careful attention to the evolution of economic ideas, as well as state-of-the-art economic theory and empirical analysis. Many strands of economic thought are represented. Any class would be enriched by examples drawn from this expansive collection.'

– Alan B. Krueger, Bendheim Professor of Economics and Public Affairs,
Princeton University, USA

'If you thought you could hide your secrets from the prying eyes of economists, think again. From sex to drugs to gambling to crime, this book will show you how the tools of economics can be used to understand just about any human behavior. This book will assuredly be the unofficial economist's guide to vice for the foreseeable future.'

– Steven D. Levitt, Alvin H. Baum Professor of Economics,
University of Chicago, USA

'This exciting book shows that economics can explain a dizzying array of real world phenomena and that economics can be great fun. I recommend this book to anyone who wants to see the progress that has been made in using the tools of neoclassical economics to understand a wide range of seemingly irrational behavior.'

– Edward L. Glaeser, Professor of Economics, Harvard University, USA

'For students who care about how the world works, microeconomics should be one of the most relevant and exciting subjects they study. Yet many students view microeconomics as some kind of abstract theory, and fail to understand how it relates to the real-world decisions made by firms, consumers, and governments. It is therefore essential that students be shown detailed examples of the application of microeconomics to practical problems – studying the theory alone is simply not enough. This outstanding book provides those examples, and would make a perfect supplementary text for any intermediate microeconomics course. The topics and examples covered are extremely timely and interesting, and are explained with great clarity. Instructors take note: students will find this book fascinating, and reading it will give them a much deeper understanding and appreciation of microeconomics.'

– Robert S. Pindyck, Tokyo-Mitsubishi Professor of Economics and
Finance, Massachusetts Institute of Technology, USA

'Economics recently has developed an imperialistic policy. Economists now write on many, many things which were not included in the traditional economic curriculum. This book is an example, but the reader may think that it should have been included in the traditional curriculum. All the activities analyzed have economic implications and the study is a good example of applying economics in new areas. The reader may be a bit shocked by applying economics to such things as prostitution, but I think he will conclude that economics has something to say and that practical people trying to organize government controls in many areas would gain by reading this book.'

– Gordon Tullock, Professor of Law and Economics,
George Mason University, USA

'Who would not be curious to know what economics can tell us about drugs, crime, sex, religion and sports? So read this book – it demonstrates convincingly how much standard economics provides us with great new insights.'

– Bruno S. Frey, Professor of Economics, University of Zurich,
Switzerland

'Economics is all around us, and this terrific collection highlights the role of economic forces even in domains where the reader may not expect it. As a collection, the book's chapters make the case forcefully that economic incentives are embedded in all domains of life, and that even sex, drugs and rock 'n' roll are amenable to economic analysis. A collection that showcases modern economics as the lively discipline it is. It would be hard to be a student and not be excited by the possibilities.'

– Justin Wolfers, Assistant Professor of Economics, University of
Pennsylvania, USA

'This fascinating book shows that economics can be used to understand almost every aspect of human behavior: the consumption of addictive goods, divorce, pornography, sports, religion, suicide, criminal behavior, abortion, and rock 'n' roll. The conventional wisdom is that these behaviors should be studied by sociologists and psychologists. Simon Bowmaker and his collaborators demonstrate the fallacy of this proposition with great insight and clarity. Their analysis is provocative, penetrating, profound, and always entertaining. The reader is quite likely to conclude that there is only one social science. All in all a most remarkable book. Bravo!'

– Michael Grossman, Distinguished Professor of Economics,
City University of New York Graduate Center, USA

'Those who think economics has little to say about the real world will change their minds after reading the essays in this splendid collection. Well written and authoritative, they show how the economic way of thinking can shed light on an unexpectedly diverse range of issues.'

– Robert H. Frank, Professor of Economics, Cornell University, USA

'Who said that academic economists need to get out more? This book will certainly shatter the illusion that economic analysis has little to say on topics of everyday interest.'

– Evan Davis, Economics Editor, BBC, UK

'This wonderful new volume shows that economic tradeoffs influence all of the decisions that we make. The book both educates and provokes its readers by using the rational actor model to explain seemingly pathological human behavior like suicide, drug addiction, and prostitution.'

– David Laibson, Professor of Economics, Harvard University, USA

'This is an important book that showcases the strength of economics for understanding human behavior and provides a convincing case for why economics should be reckoned as *the* social science. The chapter on prostitution provides the most comprehensive discussion of the topic to date.'

– Lena Edlund, Associate Professor of Economics,
Columbia University, USA

'Sex, drugs, suicide, murder, football – instead of a "dismal science", this book makes economics seem popular, or rather notorious. A rational analysis of these topics contains something to offend everyone. You may not agree with these papers but they will challenge you to think more deeply.'

– Robert Cooter, Herman Selvin Professor of Law, University of
California, Berkeley, USA

'Economics is most useful – and most provocative – when the spotlight of its intellectual rigour is trained on social issues. This book demonstrates how economists think about sex, drugs, and rock 'n' roll. This is an illuminating approach to subjects usually obscured by woolly thinking and conventional platitudes. It should be compulsory reading for anybody devising or legislating public policy.'

– Diane Coyle, author of *Sex, Drugs, and Economics* and
Paradoxes of Prosperity

'Economics is not about forecasting interest rates, but about how we live our daily lives. Simon Bowmaker's wide-ranging analysis illustrates how fruitful and unexpected that approach can be.'

– John Kay, Fellow, St John's College, Oxford and Visiting Professor of Economics, London School of Economics, UK

'Economics is generally associated with the financial pages of newspapers apart from front page discussion of major topics such as inflation, budget deficits, or unemployment. However, the topics discussed in many of the other pages of a typical newspaper, such as crime, divorce, or sport, are also appropriate for economic analysis. Economics is concerned with decisions and many important topics in today's society involve taking drugs or committing a crime or getting a divorce, for example, and so can be examined from an economic point of view. Many of these areas can be considered from different directions: legal, medical, political, religious, sociological, or psychological, and economics can be added to this list. No single viewpoint can be considered the dominant one, in most cases, but together a deeper understanding of the area will result. This book provides deep and stimulating discussions of a dozen or more important and interesting areas in accounts prepared by economic experts. It illustrates how what has been called the "dismal science" can be applied widely and usefully.'

– Sir Clive W.J. Granger, Professor Emeritus, University of California, San Diego, USA and 2003 Nobel Laureate in Economics

'In this insightful and entertaining book, Simon Bowmaker introduces readers to the fascinating side of modern economics that applies economic analysis to a wide range of social issues from illegal drugs to religion and everything in between. In this form, economics is anything but the dismal science. This is a fun and enlightening book that shows readers what many economists often forget – that economics is a powerful tool for understanding the world around them.'

– Kevin M. Murphy, George J. Stigler Distinguished Service Professor of Economics, University of Chicago, USA

Contents

List of contributors   xi
Preface by Simon W. Bowmaker   xiii
Acknowledgements   xvi
Bend it like Becker by Simon W. Bowmaker   xvii

Introduction   1
David D. Friedman

PART I   SINS AND NEEDLES

1   Economics of drug addiction   11
    Simon W. Bowmaker and Frank Heiland
2   Economics of drug prohibition   44
    Jeffrey A. Miron
3   Economics of drug liberalization   68
    Mark Thornton, Bruce L. Benson and Simon W. Bowmaker

PART II   GUNS AND ROSES

4   Economics of crime   101
    Bruce L. Benson and Simon W. Bowmaker
5   Economics of marriage and divorce   137
    Leora Friedberg and Steven N. Stern

PART III   BODY AND SOUL

6   Economics of pornography   171
    Samuel Cameron
7   Economics of prostitution   193
    Peter G. Moffatt
8   Economics of suicide   229
    Samuel Cameron
9   Economics of religion   264
    Robert J. Stonebraker

PART IV   CONCEPTION AND REJECTION

10   Economics of assisted reproduction   291
      Sherrie A. Kossoudji
11   Economics of abortion   315
      Leo H. Kahane

PART V   FUN AND GAMES

12   Economics of sport   345
      John Goddard and Peter J. Sloane
13   Economics of gambling   367
      Robert Simmons
14   Economics of rock 'n' roll   389
      Simon W. Bowmaker, Ronnie J. Phillips and Richard D. Johnson

Index   423

Contributors

Bruce L. Benson, DeVoe L. Moore Professor of Economics and Distinguished Research Professor of Economics, Florida State University, USA

Simon W. Bowmaker, Academic Associate in Economics, University of Edinburgh, UK and Adjunct Lecturer in Economics, Florida State University, USA

Samuel Cameron, Professor of Economics, University of Bradford, UK

Leora Friedberg, Assistant Professor of Economics, University of Virginia, USA

David D. Friedman, Professor of Law, Santa Clara University, USA

John Goddard, Professor of Economics, University of Wales, Bangor, UK

Frank Heiland, Assistant Professor of Economics, Florida State University, USA

Richard D. Johnson, Associate Professor of Finance, Colorado State University, USA

Leo H. Kahane, Associate Professor of Economics, California State University, Hayward, USA

Sherrie A. Kossoudji, Associate Professor of Social Work and Adjunct Associate Professor of Economics, University of Michigan, USA

Jeffrey A. Miron, Professor of Economics, Boston University, USA

Peter G. Moffatt, Reader in Econometrics, University of East Anglia, Norwich, UK

Ronnie J. Phillips, Professor of Economics, Colorado State University, USA

Robert Simmons, Senior Lecturer in Economics, Lancaster University, UK

Peter J. Sloane, Professor of Economics, University of Swansea, UK

Steven N. Stern, Merrill Bankard Professor of Economics, University of Virginia, USA

Robert J. Stonebraker, Associate Professor of Economics, Winthrop University, USA

Mark Thornton, Senior Fellow, Ludwig von Mises Institute, USA

Preface
Simon W. Bowmaker

This book applies microeconomics to social issues. From drugs to divorce, pornography to prostitution, sport to suicide, and religion to rock 'n' roll, we show that economics can reach into the strangest of places and shed light onto the occasionally dark side of human nature. Most importantly, we establish that with every issue of society the economist has a right to speak, and can do so usefully.

The idea to put together this book originated at the University of Edinburgh, where I first taught in 1999. I quickly discovered that students have a surprisingly healthy appetite for a diet of sex, drugs and economics. My experiences in the United States, including spells lecturing at Florida State University and the State University of New York, Buffalo, convinced me that they (and their instructors) would appreciate such a volume. However, I am also aware from discussions with wider social contacts that people are interested in the issues we cover, but are still in search of an analytical framework for clarifying their opinions and decision-making. The chapters that follow will be of great value to these individuals.

To motivate the various topics, our starting point is a conversation with Gary Becker, the economist who has pioneered the application of microeconomics to whole areas of life that conventional wisdom may deem either inappropriate or inaccessible. I sought his views on a broad range of contemporary social issues, including drug legalization, same-sex marriage, capital punishment and suicide bombing.

We then proceed as follows. Part I, 'Sins and Needles', is a three-chapter examination of illicit drug use and policy. In Chapter 1, Frank Heiland and I analyse theories of addictive behaviour, the price elasticity of demand for illicit drugs, and the welfare economics of drug prohibition. Next, in Chapter 2, Jeffrey Miron shows that the unusual features of drugs markets result from their legal status, not from the mind-altering and addictive properties of drugs themselves. Finally, in Chapter 3, Mark Thornton, Bruce Benson and I examine the economics of drug liberalization, including the alternative policies of government monopoly, regulation, sin taxes and the free market.

Part II, 'Guns and Roses', looks at the contribution economists can make to understanding crime and marriage and divorce. In Chapter 4, Bruce Benson and I investigate the economic theory of the supply of criminal offences, the demand for crime prevention and law enforcement services, the allocation of resources within the criminal justice system and the possible reasons for the decline in crime rates in the USA in the 1990s. In Chapter 5, Leora Friedberg and Steven Stern then examine the gains from marriage versus living together and develop an economic model to help explain why people marry, the nature of decision-making within marriage and the nature of the decisions to marry and to divorce.

Part III, 'Body and Soul', begins with two chapters on the economics of sex. In Chapter 6, Samuel Cameron looks at research outcomes on the effects of pornography, the characteristics of the industry, Amartya Sen's argument about Paretian liberals as applied to porn, the nature of demand for porn, government approaches to its regulation, the impact of the Internet and the positive externalities arising from the consumption and production of porn. Next, in Chapter 7, Peter Moffatt considers the economics of prostitution. He examines theoretical models that seek to explain, among other things, how equilibrium earnings are so high in a profession with only rudimentary skill and capital requirements, analyses the empirical evidence relating to prostitution and discusses the issue from a policy perspective, including a description and evaluation of various models of legalization. In Chapter 8, Samuel Cameron turns to the economics of suicide. He discusses Emile Durkheim's socio-economic contribution to the subject, examines economic models of suicide and the empirical work undertaken by economists, investigates the potential economic cost of suicides, including those of celebrities, and shows how an anti-suicide bureau might operate. Finally, in Chapter 9, Robert Stonebraker examines the economics of religion. He considers the demand for religion, supply-side issues such as how providers of religious goods and services cope with free-riders, the problems of risk and uncertainty in religious choice and how competition and government regulation shape the structure and content of religious markets.

Part IV, 'Conception and Rejection', focuses upon the controversial economics of assisted reproduction and abortion. In Chapter 10, Sherrie Kossoudji provides an introduction to the markets for assisted reproduction, discusses the economics of the demand and supply of children, explores the development and size of markets in assisted reproduction, examines the economic issues in the markets for eggs, sperm and surrogacy, and undertakes a discussion of the ethics of assisted reproduction markets. Next, in Chapter 11, Leo Kahane looks at the demand and supply of abortion services and demonstrates how these fundamental tools of economic analysis can be used to understand the workings of the market. He reveals how the availability of abortion services and their legality has had ramifications for other related issues such as teen pregnancy rates, the propensity for pre-marital relations and fluctuations in crime rates across time.

Finally, Part V, 'Fun and Games', examines the economics of sport, gambling and music. In Chapter 12, John Goddard and Peter Sloane consider the objectives followed by team and league owners in sport, investigate the nature of product demand, the sports league's role as a cartel and issues relating to the efficacy and desirability of revenue-sharing, salary caps and collective selling of broadcasting rights. In Chapter 13, Robert Simmons examines the fundamental economic question of why people gamble and considers the economic reasons why US states and governments across the world may opt to legalize forms of gambling. He also looks at some contemporary policy issues involved in regulation and deregulation of gambling, including the social benefits and costs, the use of state government revenues from gambling for particular purposes and the threat to government tax revenues and government regulation posed by the growth of Internet gambling. In Chapter 14, Ronnie Phillips, Richard Johnson and I provide a brief history of the music industry, examine the complex relationships between the major record companies and the independents, and analyse the economics of recording contracts. We also show how technological change is affecting the relationship between record label and artist, investigate the presence of the 'superstar phenomenon' in music and discuss the economics of copying music.

So, various dimensions of social behaviour and interaction are discussed in every chapter, but this has only been possible because extensive use is made of economic analysis. Indeed, long-standing economics concepts are shown to have continued potency throughout. Marginal utility and price elasticity of demand are crucial to the analysis of illicit drug addiction. Traditional demand and supply analysis still has a lot to offer to the criminologist and to the student of abortion. Old and new economic theories jostle to provide a framework for analysis. The sturdy theory of the firm is useful in examining sport, prostitution and rock 'n' roll, while game theory helps the analysis of suicide and marriage and divorce.

Of course, inevitably linked to the presentation of a social problem is consideration of a policy response. Some of the issues discussed come into conflict with the criminal law, for example, sale of particular drugs, so the economics of enforcement and prohibition are given weighty consideration. Long-established policies such as competition policy have relevance in fields such as sport. Taxation policy is used to examine the economics of drug liberalization, and a variety of forms of regulation are dissected, even in unusual matters such as religion. First and foremost, this is a book about economics.

Acknowledgements

Many people have provided assistance during the preparation of this book. First, of course, I would like to thank the authors of the chapters for all their hard work and commitment to the task. My colleagues in Economics at the University of Edinburgh have also been tremendously helpful, particularly Stuart Sayer who supplied the initial encouragement to undertake the project. I am very grateful for all his advice. In addition, Simon Clark, Richard Holt, Colin Roberts and Donald Rutherford have been a source of some excellent ideas and invaluable input.

At Florida State University, I would like to thank Jim Cobbe from the Department of Economics for the opportunity to teach economics in the United States. During my first visit to Florida State, Bruce Benson, Gary Fournier, Carlos Garriga, Frank Heiland and Tim Salmon were very kind colleagues and a lot of fun to work with. They also spent a significant amount of time helping me with this book.

My gratitude to the following who provided constructive comments on various chapters: Farasat Bokhari, Andrew Burke, Samuel Cameron, Richard Caves, Dhaval Dave, Isaac Ehrlich, Rodney Fort, Donald George, Barry Hirsch, Ed Hopkins, Gary Koop, Ziggy MacDonald, Dave Marcotte, Patrick Mason, Jeffrey Miron, Robbie Mochrie, Stephen Platt, David Rasmussen, Jószef Sákovics, Tim Sass, John Sawkins, Robert Wright and Artie Zillante. David Friedman was extremely generous in providing extensive comments on the entire manuscript. I recommend that readers visit his highly entertaining website at www.daviddfriedman.com. Of course, I would also like to thank Gary Becker for kindly agreeing to an interview and for his subsequent time and care in answering my questions.

At Edward Elgar, I am grateful to Francine O'Sullivan for her patience and good humour throughout the whole process.

A special note of thanks goes to Cornelia for her help and support, and for the very best of times. Finally, I am greatly indebted to my parents for everything that they have done for me over the years. This book is dedicated to them.

Bend it like Becker
Simon W. Bowmaker

Gary Becker is University Professor of Economics and Sociology at the University of Chicago and a Senior Fellow at the Hoover Institution, Stanford University. He is best known for his work on microeconomic issues including human capital, economics of the family, economic analysis of crime, discrimination and population. His books include, *A Treatise on the Family* (1981 and 1991), *The Economic Approach to Human Behavior* (1976), *The Economics of Discrimination* (1957 and 1971), *Human Capital* (1964), *Accounting for Tastes* (1996) and *The Economics of Life* (1997). In 1992, he was awarded the Nobel Prize in Economic Science, 'for having extended the domain of microeconomic analysis to a wide range of human behaviour and interaction, including nonmarket behaviour'.

I interviewed Gary Becker on Friday, 12 March 2004 in his office at the Hoover Institution, Stanford University.

Early discrimination
This book applies microeconomics to social issues. I understand that when you were first introduced to economics as a Princeton undergraduate the subject did not help you understand such issues. Why was this and what made you change your mind?

Well, I didn't believe it helped me understand social issues because of the way price theory and economics was taught, particularly in those days. I had a very respectable teacher, but it was taught like a series of simple formal propositions with no connection with real world problems. That bothered me a lot. I did well on the courses, but I felt there was a disconnect with what I was interested in and what was being taught in economics.

Now, I changed my mind really when I went to Chicago to Graduate School. There is no doubt the major influence on me was Milton Friedman because Friedman taught in those days a first-year price theory sequence and he taught it as a field where the theory was useful in explaining all types of phenomena. He had many examples, it was rigorous, and became the basis for a book he put out called *Price Theory*. That really convinced me that, yes, this could be a powerful tool to understand the problems I was interested in.

Once you began to apply economics to social issues such as discrimination you received a fair degree of criticism. Were you confident that your approach would eventually be accepted?

Well, confident is maybe a little too strong [*laughs*]. I did believe that what I was doing on discrimination and subsequently later on other issues was a useful way of looking at it. And it was important to me that I had the support of some of the professors at Chicago who I admired the most, including Milton Friedman, Greg Lewis, Theodore Schultz, to mention a few, two of whom subsequently won the Nobel Prize in Economics. If they had confidence that what I was doing was significant, my own belief made me not confident that it would win out but more willing to take the risk that this was a good way of looking at it and ultimately the profession would come around. It took a while, but that was my belief. I needed that support from the people I mentioned. That was very important.

Happy families
We devote chapters in this book to economic behaviour of the family, specifically marriage, divorce and assisted reproduction. Why do you think your work in this area has been the most controversial?

Well, it probably was the most controversial. I hesitate a little in agreeing with that statement. Certainly, discrimination was very controversial for I would say ten years before economists began to take these issues seriously and merge into the field. At that time, when I mention anybody working on discrimination, including eminent economists, they didn't think that was economics. Some of the people at Chicago required a sociologist on my committee to keep me in line because they were sceptical.

Even the Nobel Committee in 1992 mentioned discrimination, crime and human capital with approval, but when it came to the family, it was still considered controversial. It's changed a little since '92, but not enormously, although an increasing number of economists are using a similar approach to marriage and divorce. There's actually a kind of mini-boom in that area and not long ago *The Treatise on the Family* was considered in the top 20 books in sociology over the last 50 years. I think it's had some impact.

The reason it remains controversial is that one is dealing with very intimate questions when one talks about the family. There is a belief that economics is a cold discipline. How can you talk about marriage, love, having children, divorce – issues of that type – which are emotional decisions at a certain level, with this cold calculus? I try to tell people that it's not cold calculus, it's a theoretical way of looking at people's behaviour, which has a lot of common sense to it. People want to do as best they can, and when I restate some of the language, I find many begin to agree. But then they say, 'that's kind of obvious', and so the question is to show them certain implications of the theory that surprise them, such as who is most likely to divorce and why birth rates may have gone down.

Do you believe changes in divorce laws account for the relatively high divorce rates in the USA and Europe?

No. In *The Treatise on the Family*, I did a little calculation for California and some theoretical analysis which suggested that the movement toward no-fault divorce would have basically no effect on the divorce rate. That discussion produced a fair number of subsequent papers that are still continuing. On the whole I think it fair to say that even among those people who say there was an effect on the divorce rate believe it was a small part of the total increase in the divorce rate. There is nobody to my knowledge who has studied this question empirically who has concluded that the change in the divorce laws was the major reason for the increase in divorce rate. I believe if it was a factor, it was a very *small* factor and there are other forces such as the increased labour force participation of women, the lower birth rates, the higher earnings of women compared to men and a bunch of other factors that one could mention that are far, far more important.

I understand you are in favour of marriage contracts. How exactly would these work?

Well, I am in favour of marriage contracts. I think it would give families more flexibility. I have often said that the best way to do it is to obligate that the family has the contract prior to getting married so that suggesting a contract to your potential wife or husband would not look like you didn't have confidence in the marriage. That's a bad signal. The contract is a requirement, everybody has to do it. What it would do I think is enable people to tailor what they have in their contract to their particular circumstances. Circumstances vary a lot. In the present system, we have to rely on courts and judges to make adjustments to take account of circumstances. Since the people and their children are the most involved, they are the ones that should make the contract.

The main provisions would be the custody of children because there are third parties to this arrangement. The provisions would be flexible such as how to allocate property, for instance, and you could re-open the contract every three years to look at changes in circumstances. You would give people much more flexibility and I think it would reduce the role of the courts and judges. Let the people involved be the deciders of the type of marriage they want. They could have a contract which can't be broken (you can't divorce), and others can have a contract which could be broken by either party under certain penalties or whatever, like a business contract. That's what I think it should be. It would reduce a lot of the problems we face under the current system.

What are your views on the same-sex marriage controversy in the USA?

I don't see what all the fuss is about to tell you the truth. I'm generally sympathetic. If you had a contract as the rule, well, gay couples can already write contracts, they can already adopt children. People say, 'well, that's adoption', but adopting children is legal by same-sex couples as far as I know in the overwhelming majority of, if not all, states in the US. I have known a number of couples who have not only adopted children but had them through various ways. Let's say there are two lesbians living together. One of them would be the host of the child and they would have a sperm bank at some other place.

You know, the jury is yet out on whether there are significant effects on children brought up by same-sex parents. One could maybe argue that issue and I don't know the answer to that. I don't think anybody does. We don't have enough experience.

The marital issue seems to me to be a much less important step. We already allow people of the same sex to live together. We already in many respects have moved to make them eligible for a lot of the benefits in companies and so on. So, I'm not sure why this has hit a button someplace in the so-called Right. Maybe you don't want to call it marriage and everybody would be happy but basically we are allowing it to happen today in terms of contractual arrangements. If we went to a marital system, I would say, yes, people of the same sex should be allowed to enter into that kind of relationship. I don't see why not from my point of view. If there is a controversy, it is over the children issue. That I don't have a strong opinion on because I don't think we really know enough about that. It seems to me there is a mis-emphasis someplace in the discussions.

How do you see the family (and its economics) evolving over time?

Well, it's changed enormously in the last 50 years, no doubt more rapidly over the last 50 years than in the previous 500 years. I think we understand not all of the reasons, but a lot. It will continue to evolve, although at a slower pace. Let's say 40 per cent of first marriages now break up. I don't expect we will ever get into a situation where 80 per cent of first marriages break up or anything like that. You will see the increase slow down dramatically in that regard.

Birth rates have come down a lot. They have low replacement levels throughout Western Europe and much of Asia. I estimate that almost half of the world's population are in countries with below replacement fertility. It's been a remarkable change. Are birth rates going to go lower? They could, but it is hard to believe they could go much lower in countries like Italy without immigration. In 25 years, they are going to have a much smaller population, in 50 years, an even smaller one. So I don't expect much evolution in terms of those countries. I do believe that birth rates will come down in countries that have high birth rates like India and some in Latin America and Africa. That will be an important step.

I think divorce rates will not rise much more radically, and more women will come into the labour force. These are the directions in which I think the family will evolve. We will get a much more complicated structure of families with people in second marriages and stepchildren mixing together. One may or may not like that, but I think that is a clear response to basic forces that, in a broadly defined sense, are economic in nature.

Are we likely to see, particularly in the USA, more inter-racial marriages?

Probably, but that's been slow to pick up. We have very low rates of inter-racial marriages, although they are perfectly legal.

Do you know why might that be?

Well, it's not difficult to understand why. I have studied that question although I haven't written or published anything on it. It's still true that blacks are considered in a lower-level position in the United States than whites. And typically they are. So, for a white person to marry a typical black person – I say *typical* because there are many blacks who are extraordinarily successful – they have the feeling they need some compensation for that. If you look at inter-racial marriages, you will find that the white person marrying the black person will get some compensation. When they are marrying a black man, they (the black man) will be more educated than the man a woman of her characteristics would get if they married a white person. It's a compensating differential if you like. I say compensating not for any intrinsic inferiority but because the social perceptions in the United States of blacks are at a lower level.

Now, to the extent that this weakens, and it has weakened a lot in the last 30 or 40 years, you would expect to see an increase in inter-racial marriages and we have had some increase. And we have had them by inter-religious marriages and so on. That has increased a lot. How far will it go? I don't know. It has been a slow process, and I think it will continue to move in that direction. Will we ever get to the point where we are as likely to have an inter-racial marriage as a marriage within the race? Not in my lifetime, but who knows what the more distant future will bring.

We've changed a lot. There is still discrimination in different areas against blacks but it is totally different to what it was when I wrote the economics of discrimination. When I was growing up, I remember the attitudes we had as boys. We just didn't know anything about blacks and there was tremendous segregation. They weren't in schools. When I was at Princeton it was not until my second or third year that the university accepted their first black undergraduate. It's hard to believe now, but they just wouldn't accept any. So, things have changed enormously – for the good. And I think they will continue to change. That will affect inter-racial marriages. How rapidly those will increase, I don't know. I don't think it will be something that will be very rapid in the next decade or so.

Crime and the fear economy
This book's chapter on crime examines some of the factors that may have led to the fall in crime in the USA in the 1990s. Do you place more importance upon police enforcement and punishment efforts relative to the strength of the economy?

Yes, I think if you look at victimization studies, crime actually started going down in the early eighties. So, I put a lot of emphasis on increased enforcement of the laws, increased conviction of criminals and the growing number of people in prison. One of the unfortunate by-products of all this is that we have around two million men and women in prison in the United States. That's a huge number, a larger fraction than the other Western countries as far as I know. But I think it has cut crime rates in the United States. I would say that is one factor.

One of my colleagues at Chicago, Steven Levitt, has written an interesting and controversial paper that I think is in the right direction on the effect of allowing abortion on the crime rate. He claims – he is a very good empirical analyst – that the effects of the seventies show up in the nineties, 20 years later when these kids get born and don't get born. That was really what he was arguing. I think that was a factor.

The prosperity was a factor, but I don't think it was a dominant factor in the United States. We've had countries like Britain that have been pretty prosperous where the crime rate has been going up, not down – very different from the US. I think it is because they have adopted a different policy in terms of treatment of criminals. The US change-around in about

1980 was very crucial. We were also, so I recall, soft on crime in the sixties and seventies and crime rates skyrocketed. People said it was due to changing morals and cultures. I argued against that position and for once I think I was right [*laughs*]. It wasn't changing morals. Criminals adapted to what we were allowing.

The intellectual view that punishing criminals was unjustified was itself the crime. Once we got away from that view and tightened up and toughened up, we brought our crime rates down enough so that in all areas of crimes of violence, we are considerably below Britain per capita now. On property crime, we are below quite a number of Western European countries. We still lead on violent crime, but even that is narrowing somewhat compared to Western Europe. So, I think we showed it can be done and I don't believe that prosperity was the major contributing factor in my judgement.

Are you in favour of capital punishment?

Well, that's obviously a very controversial issue. I think the discussion of it is often greatly obfuscated. I certainly would be strongly in favour of capital punishment the more convinced I was that capital punishment reduced murders. That's the main issue, not whether the state has a right to take people's lives. That's a mis-statement of the issue because if capital punishment did reduce murders, by not using it the state is indirectly taking people's lives by allowing innocent people to be murdered.

So, I think the issue is can we cut down murders significantly with capital punishment? I believe we can. To the extent I felt I was right about that, I would support capital punishment. If somebody could convince me that the evidence shows strongly that we can't, then I go against capital punishment.

It's something you don't want to have to use for lots of reasons. You don't want to take people's lives if you don't have to. You don't want to go to war if you don't have to. But if you have to go to war, most people are willing to. If you believe that capital punishment would reduce murders, I think most people would come along. But people have been convinced that the evidence shows that capital punishment has no effect. I think that is a mis-reading of the evidence. I would be willing to accept the view that the evidence is mixed. If it is mixed, then maybe you want to take the minimal view and not use it. I don't have any problems with that. I'm not a crusader on the capital punishment issue, but I believe – you asked me what I really *believe* – that it does deter and as a result of that we should use it. But I also believe one cannot demonstrate that conclusively with the evidence available.

What was your response to the papers on capital punishment produced in the 1970s by one of your former students, Isaac Ehrlich?

I think Isaac did some very important, pioneering papers. He didn't work only on capital punishment. He worked in general on deterrence, but he did come out with a very large number on capital punishment. Other people have criticized them. The debate is still continuing. There are at least two dozen papers or so on that subject since then. I've just read one recently that reaffirms, if you want, again that capital punishment has a significant effect. Others claim it doesn't, so it's an ongoing discussion, but Ehrlich was the one who got that discussion going.

His number that every execution reduces seven or eight murders is probably too high in my judgement, but I don't know what the number is. I think it's positive. It may well be more than one, although it doesn't have to be more than one to be in favour of capital punishment. When you are punishing people who are murderers, the lives you are saving are often innocent lives. Somehow you have to weight those differently in my judgement.

In recent years, we have seen a rise in international terrorism. Do you think there is something we can refer to as the economics of fear?

Yes, actually I have a paper in process on that with an Israeli economist. They know a lot about terrorism. I think terrorists almost by definition operate by spreading alarm and fear. That's their purpose and they succeed often in doing it. We're looking at people's willingness to ride buses in Israel after a suicide bombing on a bus. We find big falls and some permanent effects. We have a bunch of other evidence on people's willingness to go to restaurants and, from the United States, evidence on people's willingness to ride airlines. So, I think we can use an economic model to understand that. That's what we are doing in this paper. We've developed an investment model where people invest in trying to control their fear and those who are doing an activity the most have the biggest incentive to make that investment.

Look at mad cow disease in Europe. A study of that by a French economist showed that people eating meat the most were least likely to reduce their consumption. Now, that seems surprising, but our view is that it is the right view because most of the reaction to mad cow disease was excessive. It was a lot of fear. I think in England there were 150 cases documented, in Europe there was hardly one, yet there was a big decline in French and other European consumption. If you are eating a lot of meat you have more incentive to try to make that investment to control your fear. While if you are just an occasional meat eater, you might as well just give it up and not try to associate with it.

We find that with terrorism too. Those people who ride buses regularly are less likely to cut their bus use than those people who ride it occasionally. We have a bunch of evidence consistent with this interpretation. So, I guess there is an economics of fear. They (terrorists) operate by fear and I think understanding the type of responses people make can maybe help us in reducing the negative effects of terrorist attacks.

What criminological insights or perspectives have you found stimulating or interesting in recent years?

Well, I think (Steven) Levitt has been one of the leaders in this, two of his papers in particular. The one which better documents that putting people in prison in the United States has a positive effect and the abortion paper, although I don't think that was a major effect. I think it was a very interesting piece of work and convinced me that was a factor involved in it (the fall in crime in the US in the 1990s) which I wouldn't have thought of beforehand, I must say. So, I think those papers by Levitt were good.

Controversies over the use of guns have been interesting. I don't think we have any clear-cut answers yet on the controversy over whether gun-control laws reduce crime or raise crime. I'm pretty familiar with the main papers in the literature, although it's confusing because people reach some very different conclusions about it. My own belief is that gun control laws probably do raise crime. I have a very simple argument. Most people who use guns to commit crime get their guns illegally, so gun control laws don't affect their access to them. But the people who would legally use them to defend themselves would have a tougher time doing it. So, I have tended to favour a different approach: we punish those who use guns in committing crime much more severely than those who don't use such weapons in committing crime. I think that's a more effective way. You hit the person using the gun for bad purposes directly rather than the control of guns.

I think the fact that US crime rates are going down while European crime rates are going up is a very interesting set of case studies provided to us by the data. The question is, why this very different change in societies that in other respects are very closely linked? I guess they haven't been studied enough. I gave you some of my explanations before, so these are the sort of things that I think have been important. I can't say I'm up on every single study of crime that is going on. Since I haven't been working on it, I haven't followed it as closely as I might otherwise. But this is what I have concluded from what I am aware of.

Drugs and despair

We have a chapter in this book which examines addiction (specifically, illicit drug addiction). We discuss your 1977 paper with George Stigler on the relative theory of addiction and your 1988 paper with Kevin Murphy on rational addiction. What stimulated your initial interest in addictive behaviour? How have your views on addictive behaviour changed over time?

[*Laughs*] Well, I know what stimulated my interest. George Stigler and I started to write this paper on why preferences are stable and the same. Then we started thinking about examples. I remember he came to me with a quote from Alfred Marshall that the more good news that a person hears, the more they like it. I think we have that quote in our paper. I started thinking about that. I said, 'One could think that one has a stock of capital and that it influences one's desires for it'. So we wrote that section on addiction. We didn't quite get the formal analysis right in my judgement but we were in the right direction.

Then I had a student, Larry Iannaccone, who wrote a thesis on addiction. I thought it was a very good piece of work and that stimulated Murphy and me to get involved. We worked out this paper which became the 1988 paper on rational addiction which was the development of both what Stigler and I did and what Iannaccone did.

Have my views changed since then? I must say, not a lot [*laughs*]. We were lucky in stimulating a fair bit of literature. It surprised me at the time that there would be a number of papers. But a lot of economists seem to have gotten interested in that question, some of them testing the rational addiction model, including Michael Grossman and others, some supporting it, some rejecting it, other people trying to come up with alternative models based upon inconsistent behaviour over time. We even discussed some of these types of models in our 1988 paper but they have formalized them a little more in terms of hyperbolic discounting, for example.

What do you think of these extensions to the rational addiction model?

Well, I know those papers pretty well, particularly the hyperbolic discounting work and the work on happiness, such as whether addicts are more or less happy and like high taxes. I haven't been convinced that these extensions help us understand behaviour better. I have had these people out to workshops at Chicago. Gruber's done quite a bit of work on it and Laibson has done hyperbolic discounting.

I am very friendly with both of them and I look at papers of this type. But I haven't felt they have advanced if you look at the data, including people who state that they want to quit but can't. Most of these issues I think we anticipated in the discussion in the 1988 paper. I think we can do as well at explaining this data as they can. In fact, a couple of these papers (the one by Gruber, maybe one by Cutler and Glaeser) admit that from a positive point of view, rational addiction does well, but from a normative point of view, these other models have different implications. They do, but the question is, are they the right models for this behaviour?

So, I would say I like this literature. I think it's good to try to confront the rational addiction model. Eventually, it will have to be modified in some fashion, but I think it has stood up pretty well to a lot of onslaught. Empirically, it has done pretty well. Have I radically changed my views on it? No, I haven't. Rational addiction captured an important part of addictive behaviour and when the smoke clears, that will be the judgement in this literature. Though maybe it didn't capture all of it, so we will have to modify the 1988 paper in some way.

We also examine in this book the economics of drug prohibition and we look at policy alternatives. Would you legalize drugs? If so, how would you regulate a market for drugs?

Yes, I believe we should legalize drugs for a lot of reasons. For a pragmatic reason, I think it [the war on drugs] has been a very costly programme and it has had a very low benefit/cost ratio. Now, what would we do if we did legalize them? For one thing, like alcohol, we would want to have an age restriction on who gets access to it. You may want to tax it if you believe it has certain externalities on other people. People who become addicted may drive or come to work and harm others. A better way to treat that is to punish more severely those who are driving while under the influence of drugs or who are at work under the influence. They would be the main sort of things I think would be necessary. It would be a fairer system and less discriminatory against blacks and poor people. They are the ones who suffer the most under the present system.

How does that work?

Well, it works in three ways. One, if you look at the people who are sent to prison for drug convictions, a huge disproportion are blacks or other minorities in the United States. I know the data well for the US and I think it would be similar for Britain. [Under legalization] They wouldn't be there, at least not for those problems.

Second, the drug markets are usually centred in poor parts of the city, so poor neighbourhoods suffer as a result of that. You get a lot of transactions going on there. And not surprisingly when they are centred there, a lot of crime is more common in general. The police have their hands full, so it is hard to control the drugs trade.

And third, because it is concentrated there, access to drugs for poor, inner-city kids is easier than it is for rich kids. That is one reason why we have the law. I think it's really the middle-classes [*laughs*] battling against the poor and putting more of the burden on the part of the poor. It is discriminatory, maybe not intentionally, but that's the way it works out, against the poor and against the blacks, Hispanics and other minorities.

A legalized system, with taxes, would raise the price of drugs and the poor would be more responsive to a higher monetary price. The middle-classes are more responsive to a higher non-monetary price. For example, you can't get good jobs if it was known you took drugs. Look at the way [Douglas] Ginsburg lost the possibility of getting on the US Supreme Court because somebody reported that he smoked marijuana when he was at college. That was a big price at the end of the day.

So, for all those reasons, I would legalize it, I would tax it if need be, and I think that would have a lot of beneficial effects.

The economics of suicide is another topic featured in this book. Do you think economists have a role to play in understanding suicidal behaviour? For instance, do you think we can help explain the alarming rise in recent years of young male suicide in the USA and Europe or the emergence of suicide bombing in the Middle East?

I definitely think so. In fact, I have on-going work with Richard Posner on the economics of suicide. We have a way of approaching it which I think is interesting. We are collecting a fair bit of data and trying to test it against a lot of things. As you say, young males have a high suicide rate, older males are also high, older females are not so high. Females are much higher in attempts and lower in actual suicides. There are a lot of regularities that are interesting. Blacks have relatively low suicide rates even though low-income people tend to have a higher suicide rate than higher income people. It's an interesting question. I'm not sure I have all the answers but it's a challenge to try to explain that. And there are a lot of other regularities that one sees.

We have a quote from Arthur Schopenhauer and David Hume, both of whom said suicide is a rational response to circumstances. Some people's lives are miserable. You almost never see a happy person commit suicide. What causes suicide? Well, suicides are caused by severe, negative events that hit people like bad health, going to prison, losing your job, losing your money, divorce – these are all suicide stimulators. Some people get over that quickly, but for other people it is devastating to have that to overcome. Their utility levels go down, you might say, below that threshold where they begin to think they are better off dead than alive.

There are other people who, biologically, have a propensity to depression. A number of suicides are depressed individuals, some of whom have attempted suicide in the past. Now, one might say, 'we have to help these people'. We try and often we succeed. Anti-depressants I think have been an important tool, but up until the nineties we had very few tools. Psychoanalysis was not that successful in my judgement in treating highly suicidal, depressed people. These were people who go through many episodes of being really down, and then they come out of it sometime and then come into it again. They begin to think, 'Well, this is what my life is going to be like, it's going to be pretty miserable'. These people commit suicide. Is that rational? I think so.

Do you think a suicide bomber is a rational individual?

I think it's useful to interpret suicide bombers as rational in this following sense. They want to achieve a goal and they are willing to give up their life to achieve that goal. The hero in war risks and often loses his life in order to accomplish an aim. Do we call that an irrational act? Well, think of a suicide bomber as engaged in a war. They are willing to give up their lives to harm others. So, that's not on the face of it an irrational act. They may be indoctrinated, so we have to think of preferences being formed, but that's okay, that's part of economics – the formation of preferences. You've got to understand that process.

If you raise the cost of committing suicide, namely by reducing the likelihood they will succeed, you will cut down suicide bombing. Israel hasn't stamped it out, but by various tactics (some strong-arm, others by protecting various things and careful checking), they have cut it down. So, this strikes me as some evidence that you do get responses in suicide bombing to reducing the likelihood that you will succeed. And there are other approaches you can use.

When 9/11 came out, one of the problems I set on the theory course I teach was can you interpret suicide bombing in a rational framework. I think you can. It's also a useful way to help understand why young people get involved in doing it, what their goals are and how to combat it. Those things go together.

Behavioural economics and wackonomics
Does the behavioural economics approach of economists such as Thaler and Camerer limit or extend your approach to the study of human behaviour?

It does both. I think behavioural economics has been useful in economics. It is challenging some things that economists accepted too readily maybe and introducing some concepts that may turn out to be useful. Although it has certainly not provided any alternative, systematic theory to compete with neo-classical theory, it might ultimately enrich it, like hyperbolic discounting which is not Thaler or Camerer, but Laibson.

Now, Laibson formulates that within a rational choice framework. You have people who are rational but it is just that they are inconsistent over time. So, they have got to take rational actions to recognize that. I think for some problems that might be useful. But again, I haven't been convinced that for much behaviour like addiction we need hyperbolic discounting. But nor have I been convinced that it's worthless and not going to be useful. We will have to wait and see. That would enrich the theory of rational choice. Now we have different ways of discounting. For some problems we can maybe show why people are going to be hyperbolic and others maybe not. That would be the goal at least.

Similarly, in other areas, like in finance, some behaviourists have pointed out some empirical difficulties in the orthodox theory of efficient markets and the like. Do they have an alternative theory? Not really, not much of a successful one. But they have made people less theological about efficient markets, by having to see how we can amend some things and make it work better. There is good work going on both by people like Thaler and others but also by people who are much more strongly supportive.

So, my own overall evaluation of behavioural economics is that while it's been useful, it's not been a revolution. It's usually too focused at the individual level, not at markets. Economics is about markets, it's about groups. We have a theory of individuals to get at group behaviour, but we want to know what an excise tax does to behaviour or what more punishment does to crime. We are not so focused on the individual, but behavioural economics and experimental economics, much of it, not all, is focused on the individual.

This is one reason why there is a disconnect between psychology which is usually individual and economics which is group. Let me give you a reason why these differences may be huge. Most people can't make probability calculations as accurately as some behaviourists suggest. Those people don't go working for casinos and other places where these type of calculations are important. They won't survive in that kind of job. The blackjack dealer when he is playing against the players has to know when to stop. If you watch dealers, they are basically working out through experience what we would call optimal stopping rules. That's been shown. People who couldn't do that wouldn't be running blackjack tables.

That's true in a lot of other areas. You've got to look at the specialization that we observe in markets and embed a theory of individual choice within a market specialization framework. Now, when you do that you can well understand why most people might not be good at something but they don't end up being doctors or lawyers or whatever it may be. And is the market equilibrium we get close to what we think we get from a rational framework? I think it is, although it's not perfect. Behavioural economics can maybe fill in some of the edges there, but it certainly hasn't given us an alternative approach to understanding these problems in my judgement.

Finally, I think it fair to say that a number of people may see some of the topics covered in this book and believe it is a case of 'wackonomics'. Thirty years ago, Alan Blinder wrote a parody paper published in the Journal of Political Economy *entitled, 'The Economics of Brushing Teeth'. Are there any spheres of human activity where the application of economics does not belong?*

[*Laughs*]. Take Blinder's paper. I thought Blinder's paper was very cute and clever. Indeed he was probably right that waiters have a greater incentive to brush their teeth and have good breath than bus-boys or people washing the dishes. He was dealing with it in a humorous way with minor little issues. But it is true that waiters want to get tips and so on.

Are there any areas where it (economics) is not applicable? Probably. Do we know what they are? No. How do I reconcile those two statements? I'm not saying that at the moment this approach to behaviour explains everything that we see in the world. A lot of topics have been difficult, like war. When a country goes to war people become religious. There is interesting work going on in the economics of religion. But nobody, including leaders like Iannaccone, would claim that they have solved all of the problems to understand everything about religion.

So, with every area, there are still considerable gaps in our knowledge, whether it's the family or addiction. Some of the gaps may be because we haven't used the theory well enough. That's my position, but I don't know if all of the gaps are due to that. Maybe we have to modify the theory in certain ways. I have an open mind on that question.

All theories evolve over time. Look, Newtonian mechanics for certain purposes were replaced by quantum mechanics and certainly economic theory which is not at the level of Newtonian mechanics in terms of generality and power will be modified over time. That's inevitable, that's what a good, empirically-based science does. Economics is an empirical science and I am well prepared to see the theory being modified over time. Which modification, which areas, I don't think we know that yet. But I am sure there are areas out there that will need some important modifications to the theories.

Introduction
David D. Friedman

To most people, economics is the study of the economy, important but boring issues such as unemployment, economic growth and inflation. To many economists, economics is not a list of issues but a way of under-standing behaviour – all sorts of behaviour in all times and places. The economics of suicide is not about its effect on the GNP but about using the tools of economics to understand why people kill themselves. The economics of law – my current field – is not about how changes in the law affect the economy. It is about law as incentive, legal rules understood as ways of changing how it is in the interest of individuals to act. Applications of economics, across the whole range of human behaviour, share one underlying assumption: that behaviour is best understood by assuming that individuals have purposes and tend to take the actions that achieve them – are, at least in that limited sense, rational actors.

From rationality we get the economist's approach to value – the principle of revealed preference. If I act to achieve my objectives, you can deduce the objectives from the acts. If I buy an apple for a dollar but refuse to buy it for a dollar fifty, I must value the apple at more than the former amount but less than the latter. If I boast of my love for great novels but spend my time reading thrillers instead, that tells you two things about me – that I value thrillers more than great novels and that I value other people think-ing I like great novels more than other people thinking I like thrillers. Values are judged by actions. Viewed from the inside, as humans rather than as economists, rationality seems an implausible assumption. Most of us observe elements of irrationality and error in other people, occasionally even in ourselves. Viewed from the outside, as observers trying to find a pattern in the interacting choices of millions of people, it is the best clue we have. None of us is perfectly rational. But the tendency to choose on the basis of the ends we desire is a predictable element, perhaps the only predictable element, in our behaviour.

Starting with this one fundamental assumption, economists have gener-ated a useful toolkit of concepts for explaining and predicting behaviour: supply and demand, prices, sunk costs, externalities, opportunity cost, mar-ginal value, present value, risk aversion, joint products and many others.

Such concepts are usually developed in the context of explicit markets where goods and services are exchanged for money. They apply equally well

to the broader range of behaviour considered here and in the work of economists such as Gary Becker and James Buchanan. Sunk cost explains why a
firm that has already paid the cost of designing a product and building a
factory may continue to produce even after discovering that the price the
product can be sold at will never pay back the full cost – because losing part
of the cost of development and tooling is better than losing all of it, which
is what will happen if it scraps the project. It also explains why the customer
of a prostitute, having spent time and effort finding someone selling the
services he wants to buy, may go through with the deal even after he discovers that the price/quality combination he is being offered is not good enough
to repay the cost of finding it. The theory of joint products explains why
a rise in the demand for silver will tend to produce a fall in the price of gold –
the two being refined from the same ore. It also helps explain the economics
of sex, marriage and abortion, since, in a world with imperfect contraception, sexual pleasure and (probabilistic) pregnancy are jointly produced.

Or consider suicide – the subject of Chapter 8 of this book. When is it
rational to kill yourself? The simple answer was given more than 200 years
ago by David Hume, an economist as well as a philosopher: it is rational to
kill yourself when life is no longer worth living. That answer implies
predictions of who will kill him or herself and when. It also suggests a
highly controversial conclusion – that preventing suicide is not necessarily
a good thing.

Hume's explanation of suicide is incomplete; like many starting points,
it assumes away a number of possibly relevant complications. Consider the
decision to charge a machine gun, a form of suicide engaged in by a very
large number of young men early in the last century. The reason to go over
the top in World War I was not that life was no longer worth living but that
there was something to be gained by dying. It is rational to buy something
as long as its value is more than its cost.

If you are unhappy at viewing death in battle as suicide, I have another
example. One of my current interests is the legal system of Imperial China.
In that system superiors – familial as well as political – had enormous
advantages over inferiors. For a son to kill his father was one of the worst
crimes known to Chinese law, punished by death by torture. A father was
free to kill his son for what we would regard as trivial offences. A senior
relative could order a junior relative around. Punishments, even for serious
crimes, were scaled up when the victim was senior, down when junior.

The weak did have one recourse. Driving someone – even a junior relative – to suicide was a serious offence. Judging by accounts of actual cases,
it looks as though some suicides were committed in order to invoke that
legal rule. If life was not very much worth living, the prospect of getting
revenge on the person responsible might tip the balance.

This example points out an ambiguity in the economic approach to understanding behaviour. We assume that individuals have objectives and act to achieve them, but we do not know exactly what those objectives are – they might, for instance, include revenge. This is a problem because if we make no assumptions at all about objectives, economics loses all predictive power; you can make any behaviour consistent with rationality by assuming that the behaviour was itself the objective. Why do I spend all my time sitting in a chair doing nothing? Because I like sitting in a chair doing nothing.

The ambiguity is dealt with in practice by a balancing act. We assume objectives that we observe most of us actually have – money to buy goods, health and leisure to enjoy the goods, the welfare of those near and dear to us. We add in other objectives sparingly, when the addition gives a large return in our ability to make sense of the world for a small cost in increased ambiguity of the theory. And we try to avoid using ad hoc assumptions about what people want, to explain away apparent inconsistencies between what they do and what our theory predicts – in the hope that there may be more interesting explanations to be found. Better a theory whose predictions are occasionally wrong than a theory that can explain anything and predict nothing.

Suppose you agree that the economic approach as I have described it is relevant to a wide range of behaviour – that this is a potentially useful toolkit of ideas. What should we use it for?

One use is to make sense of the world around us. Important parts of that world consist of the behaviour of other people – living, dying, buying, selling, marrying, divorcing, getting pregnant or having an abortion, using or not using recreational drugs legal or illegal. The tools of economics provide one way of understanding that elaborate dance; the attempt to understand it and to test that understanding against the observed facts can be a rewarding and intellectually exciting project.

A second answer is that we use economics to figure out what we, and other people, ought to do. At the individual level that can be as simple as deciding whether to buy or rent, stay in school or go on the job market, look for a husband or wife or continue to play the field. The project of advising the rest of the world brings us to fields such as policy analysis and welfare economics, in which economics is used to help decide what laws should be passed, what policies followed by governments, how the world ought to be run.

I am, as you may have suspected, an economist. I am, at this very instant, advising someone on what to do. You are the someone, and the advice is to read this book. Why?

The economics of economics
If you are one of the first settlers on a newly discovered and previously uninhabited island you will, sensibly enough, choose the best location on

the island – the most fertile valley if you are a farmer. If you are a miner with a newly discovered prospect, you will try for the richest veins of ore. If you are one of the first entrepreneurs in a new field – making money on the Internet, say – you will try to grab the most profitable opportunities. Perhaps, if you are very clever, you will invent Google.

The same principle applies to academic fields. Economics is about, among other things, unemployment and inflation and growth rates and predicting next quarter's statistics. But it has been about those things for a very long time, long enough so that thousands of economists have made their careers trying to add just a little more to what we know about them. The island is thickly settled, the vein of ore largely worked out. It is still possible, if you are sufficiently brilliant and sufficiently lucky, to do something new, interesting and important. But the odds are not very good.

Consider, in contrast, the economics of suicide, or abortion, or drug addiction, or prostitution, or divorce. A great deal less has been done in those fields – little enough so that, as you will see in the chapters that follow, their authors can cite very nearly everything and summarize quite a lot of it. It follows that there is a lot still to be done – fertile fields lying empty, ore to be mined, puzzles to be solved, careers to be made.

As evidence I offer a short list of puzzles gathered from reading the rest of this book. All of them are implied by those chapters, none is satisfactorily answered. Solutions to some, perhaps most, should be within the power of many of the people reading these words. And finding them should be more fun than adding one more footnote to the next paper on the causes of inflation.

1   The cost of suicide

Chapter 8 cites an attempt to estimate the cost imposed on a society by suicide, based on the loss of the output that the suicide would have produced in the rest of his or her life. That approach reflects, in my view, a serious misunderstanding of what economics is about. The output I produce comes back to me as income – the payment I get for producing it. The fact that I choose to kill myself is evidence that the value to me of that income is less than the cost to me of continuing to live. From the standpoint of economics, that cost – whether the misery of rejected love or the pain of a terminal disease – is just as real as the benefit produced by growing another bushel of grain. Economics is not about stuff, it is about people.

How would you do the calculation correctly? How could one estimate, or at least set bounds on, the net cost (or benefit) produced by people killing themselves, taking into account the benefit to those people of not living as revealed by their choice not to live?

2   *The value of drugs*

Calculations of the social cost of drug addiction typically make a similar mistake – they ignore the fact that recreational drugs, like other forms of recreation, provide a benefit in pleasure to the user. Suppose you are willing to take revealed preference seriously, as economists should, and so wish to include that value in your calculations. Using available data and the usual economic approach to evaluating the benefits from production and consumption – consumer and producer surplus – how might you estimate the net cost imposed upon a society by laws making some recreational drugs illegal? In calculating benefits to be compared to that cost, what things do or do not legitimately go into the calculation?

3   *Violence and drugs: which should we punish?*

Suppose you believe that the use of some drugs can be a direct cause of violent behaviour. There are two ways the law might deal with the problem. It could penalize drug use directly or it could penalize it indirectly, by punishing violent behaviour, whether or not drug use is its cause. What are the relative advantages of the two approaches?

4   *Addiction and marriage*

Chapter 1 discusses a model of drug addiction in which current use of a drug increases the future cost of not using it. Chapter 5, in discussing cohabitation prior to marriage, treats it as an investment in information, likely to make people less likely to get into marriages they will later want to get out of. Suppose we apply the ideas of the former chapter to the content of the latter. Living with someone is addictive behaviour – breaking up is hard to do.

What are the implications for the effect of cohabitation on divorce rates? On whether norms that limit cohabitation outside of marriage make us better or worse off? How are your conclusions changed if we assume that cohabitation is addictive for only one partner – an assumption arguably justified by arguments from evolutionary biology suggesting that men have a greater taste for promiscuity than women?

5   *Sex, drugs and rock 'n' roll*

Chapter 6 argues that the consumption of pornography can be viewed as an addiction since, as with addictive drugs, the pleasure from current consumption depends in part on past consumption. By this definition quite a lot of things are addictive, including music, friendship and literature. Can you think of any economically interesting differences between 'good' addictions such as those and 'bad' addictions such as, presumably, heroin and pornography?

6   *Profit maximizing cops*

Chapter 4 discusses one issue of resource allocation in the criminal justice system – decisions that may lead to overcrowding prisons. It does not explore the wider question of what incentives police and prosecutors face and what behaviour they imply.

One example is civil forfeiture. Under existing US law, property used in the commission of certain sorts of crimes forfeits to the government even if the owner of the property has not been convicted, or even charged, with doing anything wrong. How does that affect the incentives of police and prosecutors? To what extent does it depend on where the forfeited property goes – whether to the police department responsible for the seizure or to help pay for the US public schools?

For another example, consider that being careful not to convict the innocent makes it harder to convict the guilty. In a world of limited resources, the criminal justice system faces a range of alternatives – from a policy heavily weighted against the risk of convicting an innocent defendant to a policy of going after anyone the prosecutor thinks he can convict, innocent or guilty. How do current rules affect that choice? What evidence can we find in the actual behaviour of police and prosecutors? How might one change their incentives so as to reduce the probability that an innocent will be charged and convicted?

7   *The optimal age of prostitutes*

Chapter 7 provides an interesting account of the market for sexual services, gathered from an online database of reports on British prostitutes by their customers. One puzzling feature of the data is that it implies two different numbers for the age at which a woman is most sexually desirable. One is deduced from prices: the more desirable a woman is the more, on average, she can charge for her services, so we can deduce an optimal age from the age at which the reported price is highest. The other is deduced from reports of consumer satisfaction. The two numbers are not the same.

One possibility is that this is simply a statistical aberration – that if we had enough additional data, the two figures would converge. But I can think of others. Can you? Do they explain other differences between determinants of price and determinants of satisfaction reported in the chapter?

8   *The wages of sin*

The same chapter presents a model of the market for prostitutes in which their high wages reflect the opportunity cost to them of giving up the opportunity for marriage. This assumes that the number of women who do not want to get married is insufficient to provide the prostitution services demanded at a price corresponding to the ordinary market wage, since otherwise there would be no need for wages to rise high enough to bid additional women out of (future) marriage and into prostitution.

Data provided in the chapter, along with your own observations and other information readily available, ought to be sufficient to tell you whether the explanation offered makes sense. If not, what other explanations might there be for high wages of prostitutes?

9   Prostitution as an inferior good
The author of the chapter conjectures that prostitution is more common in poorer societies and offers an explanation – that higher wages in alternative activities, including marriage, make prostitution a less attractive profession. This assumes that rising incomes have no effect on the demand for prostitutes – that richer customers are not willing to pay a higher price – which seems implausible. Can you think of features of poor societies other than their low average income that might make prostitution more common?

10   Is prostitution a victimless crime?
In most societies prostitution is either illegal, a violation of social norms, or both. Why? Who is made worse off by the existence of prostitution? Economics rejects the obvious answer: if women thought being a prostitute was worse than some other alternative available to them they would not choose to be prostitutes. Are there more plausible candidates, important groups of people made worse off by prostitution whose opposition might help explain its widespread negative image?

11   How to create a shortage
Chapter 10 mentions a shortage of children for adoption in the 1970s and 1980s. Under US law, then and now, payment by adopting parents to a child's natural mother in exchange for permission to adopt was illegal – price control at a price of zero. Under those circumstances, what would we expect to happen as supply and demand curves on the adoption market changed? What would have happened if the parties were free to negotiate on price? What benefits or costs can you see to shifting from one system to the other?

12   Do accidents cause people?
Children born out-of-wedlock are commonly viewed as accidents, an unwanted side effect of intercourse. It was therefore widely expected that better contraception and the legalization of abortion would sharply decrease the number of such children. In fact, the pattern has been the opposite. Improved contraception and increased access to abortion in developed Western societies has been associated with a sharp, perhaps

historically unparalleled, increase in out-of-wedlock births. Can you offer explanations for that consistent with the economic approach to human behaviour?

I hope that, by the time you finish this book, you will have answers for some of these questions – or further questions of your own devising, with answers for some of them. If so, you may want to consider enlisting in our enterprise, arming yourself from the economist's toolkit, and setting out to explore the vast wilderness of human behaviour – all behaviour, in all times and places.

PART I

SINS AND NEEDLES

1 Economics of drug addiction
Simon W. Bowmaker and Frank Heiland

From the concept of a double-kinked demand curve to the theory of rational addiction, economics can provide significant insights into the causes and consequences of illicit drug use. In 1890, British economist Alfred Marshall touched upon addictive behaviour in *Principles of Economics*:

> Whether a commodity conforms to the law of diminishing or increasing return, the increase in consumption arising from a fall in price is gradual; and, further, habits which have once grown up around the use of a commodity while its price is low are not so quickly abandoned when its price rises again.

Phlips (1983) notes that with this statement Marshall captures the three fundamental aspects of addiction: physical response (tolerance), irreversibility (withdrawal) and positive effects of habits (reinforcement). But most economists since Marshall have tended to view an addict as a myopic, imperfectly rational individual whose behaviour is not conducive to standard economic analysis. Thomas Schelling (1978), in describing a smoker who wishes to 'kick the habit', stated:

> Everybody behaves like two people, one who wants clean lungs and long life and another who adores tobacco . . . The two are in a continual contest for control; the 'straight' one often in command most of the time, but the wayward one needing only to get occasional control to spoil the other's best laid plan.

The purpose of this chapter is to show that the tools of economics can be employed in the study of drug addiction. We proceed as follows. Section 1 provides a brief overview of the nature and extent of global illicit drug use. Section 2 then considers various theories of addiction including the aforementioned theory of rational addiction in which addicts are shown to exhibit consistent, forward-looking and individually optimal behaviour. Next, Section 3 explores the price responsiveness of illicit drug users from a theoretical perspective. Are such individuals likely to be more concerned with a drug's 'money' price or its 'effective' price, the latter taking into account factors such as the risk of acquiring and taking the substance? Might we expect younger, lower-income individuals to be more price-sensitive than older, higher-income individuals? Is it possible for us to conceptualize a market demand curve for illicit drugs that has varying elasticities for different categories of drug users?

Section 4 provides a review of the empirical work undertaken by economists in estimating the price elasticity of demand for illicit drugs. The majority of these studies are from the USA, reflecting the greater availability and development of price data in that country. The primary conclusion from our literature review is that illicit drug users are just as, or even more, sensitive to price changes as cigarette smokers. Section 5 contains a brief analysis of the social costs of illicit drug use and shows how a welfare economics framework can be used to assess the rationale for government intervention in illicit drug markets. Section 6 concludes the chapter.

1   Illicit drug consumption statistics

A recurring theme throughout this book is the difficulty in obtaining reliable and consistent data relating to many of these subject areas. Illicit drugs are no exception. By definition, it is of course a largely 'hidden' activity, and aside from the difficulty of observing the 'market' price of an activity that does not enter the official market, the figures economists work with in this area tend to be drawn from either drug users' self-completion surveys or are derived indirectly from other data. While we will not dwell on the problems involved in collecting and interpreting data in this field, the figures reported in this section ought to be 'handled with care' (see Reuter and Greenfield, 2001).

The official source of data for global illicit drug use is the United Nations Office for Drugs and Crime (UNODC). Table 1.1 shows that over the 2003 to 2004 period, the total number of illicit drug users in the world was estimated to be 200 million people, equivalent to 3.2 per cent of the global population or 5.0 per cent of the population aged 15 to 64. The most commonly consumed substances were marijuana (around 160 million people), followed by amphetamine-type substances (26 million people using amphetamines and 8 million people using ecstasy). The numbers using opiates and cocaine were of a similar magnitude, with 14 million people using cocaine and 16 million people using opiates, of whom more than 10 million were reportedly using heroin.

Figures 1.1 and 1.2 use data from the European Monitoring Centre for Drugs and Drug Addiction (EMCDDA), the National Household Survey of Drug Abuse (NHSDA) of Australia and the National Survey on Drug Use and Health (NSDUH) of the USA. They show that marijuana is the most commonly used illicit drug in these countries. However, the figures also suggest that 'lifetime experience' of marijuana use is considerably higher than 'recent use' (last 12 months prevalence). The clear inference from this is that consumption of the substance is generally occasional or even discontinued after a certain period of time.

Figure 1.1 reveals that lifetime experience of marijuana use ranges from around 7 per cent (Portugal) to around 30–40 per cent (Australia,

Table 1.1 Global illicit drug use (annual prevalence) estimates (2003–04)

	Illicit drugs of which:	Marijuana	Amphetamines	Ecstasy	Cocaine	Opiates	Of which heroin:
Global (million people)	200	160.9	26.2	7.9	13.7	15.9	10.6
In % of global population	3.2	2.5	0.4	0.1	0.2	0.3	0.2
In % of global population age 15–64	5.0	4.0	0.6	0.2	0.3	0.4	0.2

Note: Annual prevalence is a measure of the number/percentage of people who have consumed an illicit drug at least once in the 12-month period preceding the assessment.

Source: UNODC (2005).

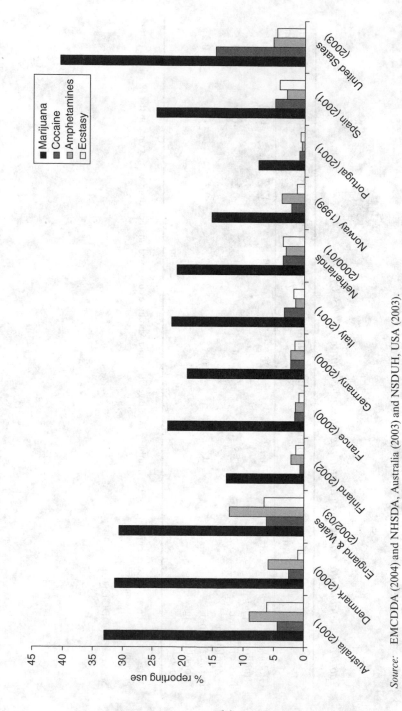

Source: EMCDDA (2004) and NHSDA, Australia (2003) and NSDUH, USA (2003).

Figure 1.1 Lifetime prevalence of illicit drug use in USA, Australia and Europe

14

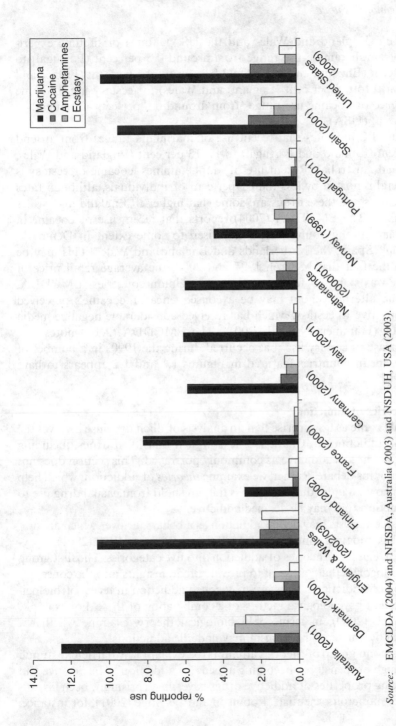

Source: EMCDDA (2004) and NHSDA, Australia (2003) and NSDUH, USA (2003).

Figure 1.2 Last year prevalence of illicit drug use in USA, Australia and Europe

15

Denmark, England and Wales and the USA). Rates of lifetime experience of amphetamine use range from around 0.5 per cent (Portugal) to 12 per cent (England and Wales) and from around 1 per cent (France and Denmark) to 6.5 per cent (England and Wales) for ecstasy use. Lifetime experience of cocaine use ranges from around 0.5 per cent (Portugal) to 15 per cent (USA).

Figure 1.2 indicates that recent use of marijuana ranges from around 3 per cent (Finland and Portugal) to 11–13 per cent (England and Wales, USA and Australia). Recent use of amphetamines, cocaine or ecstasy is in general reported by less than 1 per cent of individuals, although rates of recent use of these drugs are somewhat higher in England and Wales and Spain. The EMCDDA (2004) reports that recent use of cocaine in particular among young people has risen to some extent in Denmark, Germany, Spain, the Netherlands and England and Wales. This may be due to the fact that between 1997 and 2002, the average retail price of cocaine was stable or fell in all European Union countries (EMCDDA, 2004) or, alternatively, it may be a consequence of cocaine's perceived safety relative to ecstasy, which has received considerable negative media attention (Hammersley et al., 2001). The EMCDDA (2004) notes that the increase in ecstasy use that occurred during the 1990s in a number of the European countries featured in Figures 1.1 and 1.2 appears to have stabilized.

2   Theories of addiction

It should come as no surprise that an analysis of illicit drug use involves the issue of addiction. In Chapter 2, it is argued that illicit drugs, including heroin, are not as addictive as commonly portrayed. This section does not enter into this debate. Rather, we examine *theories* of addiction, which help explain how an individual may cross the threshold from casual drug use to consumption that may be deemed addictive.

Non-economists may define addiction as a behaviour over which an individual has impaired control with harmful consequences. West (2001), a psychologist, classifies theories of addiction into five categories. The first group involves theories that, 'attempt to provide broad insights into the conceptualization of addiction'. Thus, we may couch addiction in terms of biological, social or psychological factors, or a combination of these. For example, Betz et al. (2000), in terms of a biological theory, examine whether a common biochemical mechanism may underlie addictions.

The second group of theories attempts to, 'explain why particular stimuli have a high propensity to becoming a focus for addiction'. The positive and reinforcing properties of addictive drugs have, unsurprisingly, been investigated by numerous scientists. Robinson and Berridge (2001), for instance, suggest that these properties are enhanced rather than lessened by repeated exposure.

The third group of theories examines, 'why particular individuals are more susceptible to addiction than others'. Some persons may be especially responsive to a particular stimulus, whether biochemical, psychological or social. Cheng et al. (2000) and Cunningham et al. (1992) investigate whether this susceptibility may be genetic.

The fourth group of theories addresses, 'the environmental and social conditions which make addiction more or less likely'. An individual may find himself or herself in a particular situation that triggers the need for the effects of a stimulus, or in which those effects take on a greater significance. In such cases, addiction may well result. Kenkel et al. (2001) examine the role of economic factors in the initiation and progression of drug use in this context.

Finally, the fifth group of theories of addiction, 'focuses on recovery and relapse . . . some are broad perspectives, others focus on effects of withdrawal from particular stimuli such as drugs; still others focus on individual factors and others seek to model environmental influences'. An important contribution in this field is Prochaska and DiClemente's (1983) Transtheoretical Model, which identifies stages of change and other factors that predict treatment outcomes. Prior to the model's development, treatment for substance abuse was believed to benefit only people who were motivated to enter treatment of their own free will. However, Prochaska and DiClemente address the situation where the individual is in the process of change that allows for a more effective treatment developed for the individual rather than a 'one-size-fits-all approach'.

Economists seek to conceptualize addiction within the established framework of consumer choice. A good (or activity) is considered addictive if an increase in the stock of past consumption results in an increase in current consumption, *ceteris paribus* (Becker et al., 1994). Our principal interest is in *rationalizing* the observed behaviour of an addicted individual. Rationalizing means to propose a rule that relates an individual's objectives, preferences and constraints to his or her behaviour. A rule is illuminating if it is simple and applies broadly, that is, it predicts behaviour correctly for a large group of individuals. For instance, if we meet a fellow economist in the library basement 'chasing the dragon' (that is, inhaling the fumes from heroin as it is heated on a piece of silver foil), we will only be surprised for a few moments, if at all. We may think of the unique immediate satisfaction provided by the drug (objective and preferences), the fact that the colleague recently received promotion (less income constrained), and that the chance of bumping into a colleague in the library basement has declined greatly since the arrival of online archives (reduction in the 'effective' price of taking drugs).

Our focus for the remainder of this section is to rationalize *harmful* addiction, that is, a behavioural pattern defined by increasing consumption of a good or activity that has, for example, detrimental future effects upon one's health. However, it should be noted that theories proposed by behavioural researchers can explain not only harmful addiction, but also *beneficial* addiction within the same framework. The repetitive reading of one's favourite novel could be perceived as a beneficial addiction if a deeper understanding of the story results in even greater appreciation of its quality.

The initial step of all behavioural theories of addiction is the assumption that the amount of addictive good used or consumed in the past has lasting effects of some sort. Higher past consumption may result in a modification of the consumer's preferences, that is, the extent to which he or she 'likes' to consume the addictive good. Continuing the earlier example, this notion suggests that the fellow economist ingests more heroin when we next meet him or her since past consumption of the drug has increased their tolerance for the drug. In other words, they require larger amounts of the drug to derive the same degree of satisfaction as experienced in the past.

2.1   Relative theory of addiction

Using the tools of modern microeconomics, Stigler and Becker (1977) were among the first economists to rationalize the behaviour of increasing consumption of a good or activity. Their 'relative theory of addiction' stands in the economic tradition of the common preference approach, that is, they attempt to explain differences in behaviour across individuals by differences in economic constraints, as opposed to the individual's objectives (or preferences). Therefore, rather than assuming a relationship between previous amounts of consumption of a drug and preferences to explain addiction, Stigler and Becker present a theory that posits a feedback between consumption and its effective price as perceived by the individual.

Stigler and Becker assume that individuals have a preference for the commodity 'euphoria'. This specific state of mind is a good that the individual produces (and consumes) using other commodities such as heroin and time as inputs. Since the commodity euphoria is 'home-produced', that is, by construction not purchased in a market, its price is not readily available. However, the implicit (or full, effective or shadow) price of one unit of euphoria to the economizing individual can be derived from information on the cost of the inputs used in the production of euphoria and on the technology adopted to produce euphoria.

As the degree of euphoria obtained by the individual depends, for example, on the amount of heroin used, the price for one unit of euphoria also depends on the price of this input. It follows that the price of euphoria will therefore increase if the price of heroin increases and, similarly, a reduction in the risk of getting caught taking heroin will lead to a decrease in the shadow price of consuming euphoria.

The production of euphoria also depends on individual-specific ability to experience the sensation. Stigler and Becker (and later Becker and Murphy, 1988, in the rational addiction model) refer to this ability as 'euphoric capital' or, more generally, 'consumption capital'. The critical step in the Stigler and Becker model is the introduction of a feedback between past euphoria use and the euphoric capital stock at present: the euphoric capital depends on previous amounts of euphoria experienced ('euphoria exposure'). In the case of harmful addiction, greater past exposure to euphoria reduces the stock of euphoric capital today, implying that the implicit price of euphoria increases with past euphoria exposure. Hence, the cost of producing euphoria in the future increases if current consumption of euphoria exposure increases. In other words, it is assumed that as states of euphoria are more frequent and longer-lasting, the individual's ability to become euphoric is impaired.

The relative addiction theory predicts that under certain conditions, the demand for the inputs in the production process increases while the euphoric capital and amount of euphoria decreases. Therefore, the model can explain an individual's path of rising heroin demand while the consumption of euphoria is falling and the price of heroin remains constant. The condition for this harmful addictive behaviour to occur is a sufficiently inelastic (shadow price-insensitive) demand for euphoria, that is, there are no other goods that serve as good substitutes for the commodity euphoria.

While it is plausible that euphoria is essential to the individual, one may wonder whether there are substitutes for heroin-induced euphoria. Stigler and Becker implicitly assume that heroin is a necessary input in the production of euphoria, but addiction can arise even if there is a substitute for the addictive substance. Based on the model by Rachlin (1997), we may assume that social activity (for example, going out with friends) can produce the same kind of euphoria as heroin. Social activity can also be considered a good that exhibits positive addiction as postulated in the Stigler and Becker model, that is, the more social activity the individual was exposed to in the past, the lower the current price of social activity.

Suppose initially the shadow price of social activity is lower than the price of heroin so that only social activity is used to produce euphoria. If the price of heroin becomes cheaper relative to social activity then more heroin relative to social activity would be used to generate euphoria. As the individual's social involvement fades, the price of future social activity increases relative to the price of heroin. In turn, social activity would be further substituted by heroin use and as the exposure to euphoria increases, the shadow price of euphoria increases, stimulating demand for the inputs in the production of euphoria. Therefore, the relative theory of addiction in this framework supports a path of increasing consumption of heroin and decreasing social activity while the shadow price of euphoria and social activity increases.

2.2   Melioration theory of addiction ('primrose path')

An important step toward a theory that explicitly formalizes the transition from 'normal' levels of use of the addictive good to excessive ones results from the application of the melioration approach (Herrnstein and Vaughan, 1980). Melioration posits that choices are the result of common behavioural rules applied to specific circumstances. The behavioural rules work well for normal consumption goods and activities but 'trap' behaviour under irregular circumstances such as the addictive goods case.

Herrnstein and Prelec (1992) build on the melioration concept to explain why individuals may deliberately choose a path of increasing consumption of a harmful good or activity. To illustrate this mechanism, we refer to Figure 1.3. Point A shows the instantaneous payoff to an alternative activity ('going out with friends') if the individual has never experimented with heroin. Point B shows the payoff to using heroin if this is the individual's first experience of the drug. Given the higher payoff associated with point

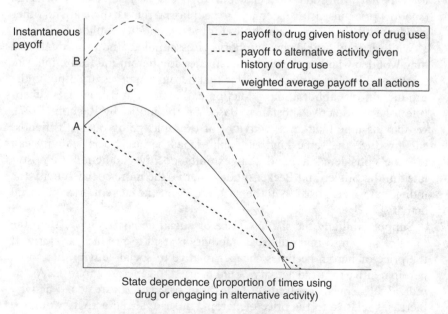

Figure 1.3   Drug user on 'primrose path' to addiction

B, it is rational for the individual to choose to use heroin for the first time and experiment with mixing the frequency of drug use and the alternative activity.

Importantly, melioration theory considers that the payoffs over time to these actions are path-dependent (that is, they depend upon the individual's history of heroin use). The dotted line illustrates the payoff to the alternative activity (going out with friends) given the individual's recent history of drug use.[1] It is drawn as a downward-sloping line to reflect the assumption that the use of heroin erodes the pleasures to be had from engaging in the alternative activity. The dashed line, meanwhile, illustrates the payoff to using heroin. Note that the individual initially enjoys increasing returns from the drug but the associated euphoria soon begins to decline rapidly. Finally, the solid line shows the weighted average payoff to all actions undertaken by the individual through time.

Point C on the solid line represents the highest possible average payoff for the individual. This economic solution occurs at the point where the marginal benefit of heroin use equals its marginal cost. However, melioration theory suggests that point D is the equilibrium solution because beyond point C, the instantaneous payoff to heroin use is still greater than the payoff to the alternative activity. In other words, the individual has an incentive to increase his or her frequency of heroin use until the payoffs from both activities are equalized (point D). Yet, at this point the individual is worse off than had he or she not started using heroin. The average payoff from both activities at point D is lower than the payoff associated with point A. The individual may be said to have ventured down a 'primrose path' of addiction, initially believing there was little danger of losing control but eventually becoming 'trapped'. Note that while each *single* decision made by the individual along this path was rational, the *sequence* of decisions was certainly not rational.

The Herrnstein–Prelec approach is criticized for assuming that the individual is unable to anticipate distant consequences of his or her activities. How increasing consumption of a harmful good is possible among individuals who are fully aware of the future consequences of their current choice is addressed by Becker and Murphy's (1988) rational addiction model, to which we now turn.

2.3   Theory of rational addiction

The rational addiction model is the most influential economic theory of addiction to date. It builds on the model by Stigler and Becker (1977) discussed earlier, but assumes that instead of consuming heroin-induced euphoria, the representative individual derives utility in each period directly from consuming the heroin. Like the Stigler and Becker model, consumption of the addictive good has lasting effects through the addictive consumption capital stock.

The main achievement of the theory of rational addiction, however, is to formally derive aspects of dynamic ('over time') consumption behaviour with respect to an addictive good. As such, it is an extension of the standard life-cycle model of consumption and saving. In this framework, an individual takes into account the consequences of his or her decisions on future outcomes. In other words, an individual is seen to be 'more rational' than previous models that assume myopic (short-sighted) behaviour. The obvious challenge in the presence of forward-looking consumers is to find illuminating conditions that guarantee addictive behaviour, that is, increasing consumption of an addictive good over the life cycle. As it turns out, the way in which past consumption affects how the individual values current consumption is crucial for addiction to occur.

The theory of rational addiction outlined below which is based on Becker et al. (1994), assumes that the individual with an infinite life maximizes his or her present value, V, of lifetime utility from consumption as follows:

$$V = \sum_{t=1}^{\infty} \beta_{t-1} U(Y_t, C_t, S_t, e_t) \tag{1.1}$$

subject to a lifetime wealth constraint,

$$A_0 = \sum_{t=1}^{\infty} \beta_{t-1}(Y_t + P_t C_t) \tag{1.2}$$

where $0 < \beta < 1$ indicates the subjective time discount factor of the individual,[2] A is the present value of wealth, P_t is the price of one unit of the addictive good, and $U(Y_t, C_t, S_t, e_t)$ denotes the individual's period utility gain from current consumption of the addictive good, C_t, and all other goods, Y_t. S_t is the addictive stock that is inversely related to period utility, and e_t represents the individual's preferences and endowments. The stock of addictive consumption capital depends on the previous period's consumption, C_{t-1}, and the non-depreciated previous consumption capital stock, δS_{t-1},

$$S_t = (1 - \delta)S_{t-1} + C_{t-1} \tag{1.3}$$

where $0 \leq \delta \leq 1$ measures how quickly the tolerance level, S_{t-1}, decays.

In this model, past consumption of the harmful good plays two roles. On the one hand, higher past consumption levels of the addictive good may increase the stock of the harmful drug, S_t, which directly reduces the utility of the individual. Thus, an individual with a larger addictive stock would need to consume relatively more of the addictive good in the current period to obtain a given level of utility, *ceteris paribus*. This is the tolerance effect.

On the other hand, a higher level of past consumption and the addictive stock may also affect the way the individual values the consumption of the drug. This is the reinforcement effect, where higher past consumption of the drug raises the marginal utility (MU) of its current consumption. Thus, an individual who consumed more drugs in the past period is positively motivated to consume relatively more drugs in the current period.

Becker and Murphy show that for addictive consumption behaviour (for example, an increasing path of drug use) to be observed it is necessary that an increase in the amount of consumption of the addictive good in the previous period boosts the marginal utility of currently consuming that good more than it raises the expected discounted stream of future marginal disutilities associated with a greater stock of addictive capital. In other words, the Becker–Murphy model requires a strong element of habit formation or 'reinforcement' in the consumption of the addictive good, that is, $\partial MU/\partial C_{t-1}$ must be large.

To illustrate these mechanisms, compare the addicted consumer of heroin to the 'social' consumer of heroin. The latter has accumulated an insignificant amount of heroin during past consumption sessions and consumes in small doses, that is, his or her level of tolerance is small. The heroin addict may be more miserable than the social consumer due to the 'side effects' of having a large stock of addictive capital (high tolerance), but the immediate relative boost from the consumption of additional units of heroin is much larger (strong reinforcement) for the heroin addict than for the non-addict.

Becker and Murphy discuss a situation where past consumption of the addictive good affects the earning power of the individual. Higher tolerance, that is, a greater S_t in equation (1.2) is assumed to depress the individual's wage rate (not incorporated in the model shown). By making income dependent on the consumption level as well, the effective (or shadow) price for the addictive good increases far beyond the simple cost of obtaining the drug.

Given the reinforcing nature of previous period's consumption on current consumption in the Becker–Murphy model, it is not surprising that those who discount future consumption heavily, that is, those who are impatient, are particularly likely to become addicted. However, the model also predicts addiction under certain conditions even if the individual cares a lot about the future. Individuals who are forward-looking and who have a tendency to experience a strong reinforcement effect of past consumption on present consumption can find themselves on the addiction path. This might explain why some young individuals are so willing to consume large amounts of addictive goods. Following a path of rising consumption and the accompanying build up of the stock of addictive consumption capital may be rational, even though the utility gain over not consuming the drug at young ages is relatively small, since the anticipated greater future gains from a stronger reinforcement effect along the addictive consumption path outweigh the costs.

As we have shown, Becker and Murphy's theory of rational addiction provides a series of insights into the dynamics of addictive behaviour. In summary, there are three main factors according to this theory that determine whether or not an individual experiences addiction:

1. How much he or she values future consumption relative to current consumption. The more heavily the future is discounted, the more likely that a consumption path is followed that leads to addiction.
2. How much the addictive capital stock depreciates over time. Individuals with higher depreciation rates are less likely to become addicted.
3. The full (or shadow or effective) price of the addictive good, that is, the price that reflects the monetary cost of the drug, preferences and the opportunity costs of consumption such as lost life cycle wages. The higher the effective price of the drug, the less likely that the individual will become addicted.

Finally, the theory of rational addiction also predicts that the long-run effect of a price change differs from the short-run effect. Becker and Murphy show that the price elasticity of demand is smaller in absolute terms in the short run than in the long run. This prediction is the result of the positive intertemporal feedback (reinforcement) effect of past consumption of addictive goods. Suppose that the price of drugs increases in the current period. This will decrease current consumption, which in turn reduces the marginal utility of consumption next period and thus also reduces future consumption. By symmetry, an anticipated increase in the price of the addictive good in the future should reduce consumption in the present because the consumer is forward-looking.

2.4   Hyperbolic discounting and other extensions to rational addiction
The standard sequential optimal choice model in economics such as the Becker–Murphy model has been criticized for assuming that an individual makes time-consistent choices. Ainslie (1975), a psychologist, and Thaler (1981), an economist, were among the first to systematically study the nature of simple choice behaviour over time and using experimental data. The former observed behavioural patterns of pigeons that were time-inconsistent, while the latter found evidence for time-inconsistent decision-making among humans.

Becker and Murphy impose time-consistent preferences by assuming that an individual discounts the value of future rewards according to an exponential function. Formally, future utilities $U(X_t)$ are discounted by a weight δ_t, which is an exponentially declining function of t (meaning that the value of future utilities will decline by a constant proportion every period). An exponential function assumes constant discount rates and presumes that an individual's relative evaluation of two rewards will depend only on the amount of delay between receiving them.

However, one way of 'rationalizing' time-inconsistent behaviour is to introduce time preferences so that the individual discounts the value of future rewards according to a hyperbolic function (for example, see Laibson, 1997) where discount rates are declining.[3] In this case, delayed rewards are weighted by $\beta\delta_t$, where β represents the preference for immediate reward and δ expresses the preference for reward delayed t periods, relative to a delay of $t+1$ periods.

Hyperbolic functions have the potential to exhibit preference reversals. For instance, in Figure 1.4 the problem for an individual is to get through

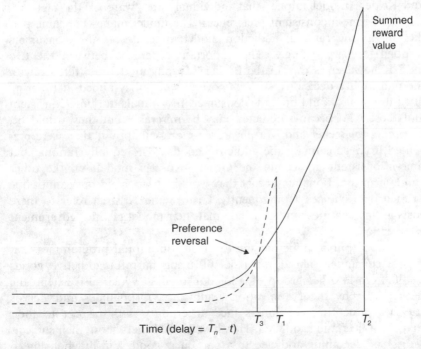

Source: Adapted from Loewenstein and Elster (1992).

Figure 1.4   Hyperbolic discounting and drug addiction

the day without using heroin. The dotted line represents the present value of scoring heroin, while the solid line is the present value of going out with his girlfriend. Point T_1 is the possibility of scoring heroin (good) and T_2 is the possibility of meeting his girlfriend (even better). Almost all day, the individual prefers the idea of meeting his girlfriend, but because of the nature of hyperbolic functions, it is possible that as the opportunity to score heroin comes closer and closer, he will begin to value it more. Indeed, at T_3, a preference reversal takes place, illustrating the idea that drug addicts tend to have a preference for 'small-early' rewards over 'later-larger' rewards. An initial preference for a 'later-larger' reward over a 'small-early' reward reverses as the latter approaches, 'with an advance choice of virtue changing to an immediate choice of vice' (Read and Van Leeuwen, 1998). This explains the surrender to temptation that is often characteristic of an addict's behaviour.

Building on the work by Laibson (1997), Gruber and Köszegi (2001) develop a version of the Becker–Murphy model, which incorporates time-inconsistent individuals. As with rational addiction, individuals are assumed to be forward-looking. Moreover, rationality in the Gruber and Köszegi model implies that individuals are aware of the fact that they have time-inconsistent preferences. The model makes the same predictions as the rational addiction model in terms of how consumers respond to price changes. The important difference between the two models, however, is that in the Becker–Murphy model interference with the individual's decisions, such as government policy aimed at lowering illicit drug use, would hurt the consumer. Individuals are time-consistent and those who became addicted may be miserable but they would be, according to Becker and Murphy, 'even more unhappy if they were prevented from consuming the addictive goods'. The equally rational but time-inconsistent addicts in the Gruber–Köszegi model, on the other hand, incur additional costs that they would like to avoid but cannot due to their own choices. Consequently, Gruber and Köszegi refer to these costs as 'internalities' and conclude that their model justifies government intervention.

A role of public policy in the form of educational programmes that inform consumers about the risks of using harmful addictive goods results from another group of addiction models, which also extend the Becker–Murphy theory of rational addiction. Orphanides and Zervos (1995) assume that consumers face uncertainty with respect to their chances of becoming addicted. They have initial beliefs about their subjective risk of becoming addicted to a particular good, and by choosing to experiment with the substance they update their beliefs. The model features individuals who choose to consume the good that is potentially addictive for them but do not realize how addictive (hence dangerous) it is before they are already addicted. The uncertainty in this framework with a possibility of learning can explain the phenomenon of addicts who regret having chosen this path, as well as withdrawal behaviour that occurs when individuals are already far along the addictive path.

Daw Namoro (2003) more generally considers the consumption behaviour of individuals when consumption may reduce life expectancy of the consumer. Assuming that higher consumption of the harmful good lowers the individual's chances of surviving to the next period, he shows that addiction is unlikely if the individual perceives the health risks to be growing at an increasing rate (for small increases in consumption).

These models show the need for policy-makers to provide consumers with more information on potentially addictive goods and their health side-effects. Policies based on Orphanides and Zervos (1995) should focus on informing individuals about the general dangers and personal risks of becoming addicted to a good. Daw Namoro (2003) suggests that aggressive advertisement towards drug users who perceive no or only a weak relationship between consumption of harmful substances and their life expectancy could reduce addiction.[4]

3　Price elasticity of demand for illicit drugs: theory

The theoretical discussion in the previous section shows how economists have contributed to the debate about the determinants of addictive behaviour. While all models point to the importance of price as a determinant of consumption behaviour, the meaning of price varies greatly between them. Moreover, the discussion so far has abstracted from any differences that may exist between actual addictive substances and the markets they are sold in. To understand the empirical evidence on the sensitivity of demand for illicit drugs to price changes presented in the next section, it is therefore helpful to elaborate on the measurement and identification issues specific to prices and markets for illicit drugs.

3.1　Effective prices

Typically, any assumption we make concerning price elasticity is likely to be based upon the notion of a simple 'money' price. However, according to Stigler and Becker's relative theory of addiction discussed earlier and work by Moore (1973, 1990), illicit drug users will be concerned with a drug's 'effective' or 'shadow' price, which includes the money price, but also other components such as the perceived risk of both acquiring and taking the drug, the probability of getting arrested, convicted, fined or imprisoned, as well as the 'search time' involved. This 'search time', which will differ from buyer to buyer, from market to market and from time to time, is essentially a measure of an illicit drug's 'availability'. As Kleiman (1992) states:

> At any given money price, some buyers who would pay that price if a particular illicit drug were easily available will not expend the effort and incur the risk involved in looking for it (and the possibility of searching unsuccessfully). Therefore, the higher the search time – again, at any given money price – the lower the quantity consumed. Search time acts as a kind of 'second price' that users pay for their illicit drugs.

While search time could be measured to a certain degree of accuracy, other non-money prices such as risk may be more difficult to measure. Nonetheless, different categories of drug users will respond in different ways, which in turn depends upon the knowledge they have to determine an effective price. Indeed, this may well be the case for recreational drug users whose greater price sensitivity reflects their limited understanding of the market (MacDonald, 2004).

Building on the rational addiction model, Becker et al. (1991) provide a further theoretical insight into the possibility of different drug users having different price sensitivity. They suggest that individuals with greater preference for the present (young, lower-income, less educated) will attach a smaller monetary value to health and other adverse effects of illicit drug use than individuals with a greater preference for the future (older, higher-income, more educated). Therefore, younger and lower-income individuals will typically react more to changes in the money price of an illicit drug, whereas older and higher-income individuals are more likely to respond to changes in future harmful effects.

Another related and consistent explanation is that how sensitive an individual is to the money price depends on what fraction of the full price is comprised of the money price. For teenagers or young adults, who have a low opportunity cost of time and may not be as future-oriented, the money price makes up a large fraction of the full price. Thus, a given change in the money price represents a relatively large change in the full price leading to a greater consumption response.

3.2   Double-kinked demand curve

We can extend the notion of different categories of drug users having different price sensitivity by reference to the concept of a double-kinked demand curve. Blair and Vogel (1973) argue that at low prices, we find recreational users as well as addicts in the illicit drugs market. If this observation holds true and should prices increase, the resulting fall in demand consists of two effects. First, there is a 'substitution effect' as the recreational users exit the market to seek other pleasures. Second, given that life cannot be sustained by drug use alone, we find addicts restraining their consumption towards maintenance levels. Beyond a specific price, however, the market consists solely of drug addicts who exhibit price insensitivity.

White and Luksetich (1983) consider the effect of very high prices on illicit drug demand, suggesting that a drug's price may eventually become so great that addicts too will have to exit the market due to a very strong 'income effect'. Perhaps, faced with such prices, addicts can only sustain their habit by committing crime and are forced to leave the market due to arrest or conviction. Alternatively, they may voluntarily choose to enrol into a drug treatment programme.

Wagstaff and Maynard (1988) combine the views of Blair and Vogel and White and Luksetich to produce a double-kinked demand curve for illicit drugs at the aggregate level. This market demand curve is depicted in Figure 1.5 and has two elastic sections, one at high prices and one at low prices, and an inelastic section for the middle range of prices. Should this be a realistic representation of the illicit drugs market, then it can be used to guide public policy. For example, we would find that price hikes, and hence punishment, would have no effect on consumption when drug users are on the vertical (inelastic) section of the demand curve. One possible problem, however, is that Wagstaff and Maynard do not suggest a range of prices at which the slope of the demand curve may change.

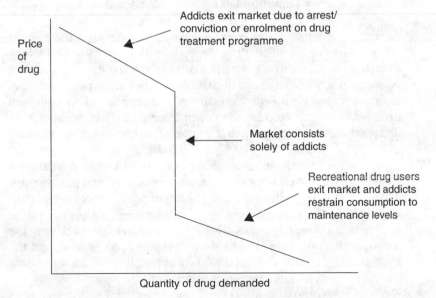

Figure 1.5   The double-kinked demand curve for illicit drugs

4   Price elasticity of demand for illicit drugs: evidence

We now turn to the empirical work undertaken by economists in estimating price elasticities for various illicit drugs. Research in this area is still somewhat hampered by poor data quality. Nevertheless, the studies reviewed in this section typically make use of two sets of data. First, illicit drug prices are derived from local purchases made by undercover drug enforcement officers in the USA. Second, these prices are combined with self-reported measures of drug use from either localized datasets or national surveys to estimate the price elasticity of demand.

The estimation procedure itself tends to involve dependent variables, which are binary indicators of whether or not a particular drug is consumed. This means that estimated price elasticities are with respect to outcomes such as past-year and past-month *participation* in drug consumption rather than actual consumption. Elasticity of participation will tell us by how much the probability of use of a drug changes given a fall in price. For a fixed population, this elasticity will also reveal the extent of the percentage increase in the number of users following the price reduction. A number of studies also produce estimates for the number of times a particular drug is used. They calculate the total price elasticity of *consumption frequency* by adding together the elasticity of drug participation and frequency conditional on participation.

The approaches to economic modelling of illicit drug use tend to fall into three main categories: conventional, myopic and rational:

1. *Conventional* – the conventional approach assumes that the current consumption of an illicit drug depends only upon current factors. Therefore, increases in current price can be expected to reduce current consumption, while increases in past price and/or anticipated increases in future price have no effect on current consumption. This approach does not take into account the dependence of current consumption decisions on past behaviour that characterizes the use of many illicit drugs.
2. *Myopic* – the myopic approach extends (1) by allowing current consumption of an illicit drug to depend upon current and *past* factors. Therefore, not only will an increase in current price reduce current consumption, but increases in past price, by reducing past consumption, also reduce current consumption. This approach predicts that the long-run effect of a permanent price change will be greater than the short-run effect, but it ignores the future implications of addictive consumption when making current consumption decisions.
3. *Rational* – in comparison to (1) and (2), the rational approach allows current consumption of an illicit drug to depend upon current, past and

future factors. We noted earlier that the rational addiction approach is the most significant theoretical contribution to the understanding of illicit drug user behaviour, and this is largely because it provides a series of testable propositions that have been investigated empirically in numerous articles on alcohol consumption (Grossman et al., 1998; Waters and Sloan, 1995), cigarette smoking (Bardsley and Olekalns, 1999), coffee drinking (Olekalns and Bardsley, 1996), the demand for cinema (Cameron, 1999), and gambling (Mobilia, 1993, see Chapter 13).

In the context of illicit drug use, the rational addiction model makes three key predictions. First, drug consumption is negatively correlated with past, current and future prices of the drug. Second, current drug consumption is positively correlated with past and future consumption. Third, as noted earlier, the long-run price elasticity of demand is greater than the short-run price elasticity.

We can illustrate the different empirical approaches found in the literature from the perspective of the rational addiction model. Assuming complete depreciation ($\delta = 1$) and a utility function that is quadratic in its arguments, the theoretical model of rational addiction presented above (equations (1.1)–(1.3)) yields the following current demand function for the illicit drug:

$$C_t = \theta_0 C_{t-1} + \beta\theta_0 C_{t+1} + \theta_1 P_t + e_{t,\,t+1} \tag{1.4}$$

where θ_0 and $\beta\theta_0$ capture the effect of past and future consumption on current consumption respectively, and θ_1 is the effect of a contemporaneous (short-run) price change on consumption. This demand function, under different assumptions about the coefficients, constitutes the basis of a number of empirical studies of addictive behaviour. The key predictions of the rational addiction model discussed above translate into the following expected signs of the coefficients: $\beta > 0$, $\theta_0 > 0$.

Myopic models of addiction, on the other hand, assume that the individual does not take the future consequences of their actions into account, which implies complete discounting of the future, that is, $\beta = 0$, while the reinforcement effect of past consumption remains, that is, $\theta_0 > 0$. Meanwhile, conventional approaches to the demand for addictive substances abstract from any reinforcement effect of consumption. Hence, conventional studies of the price elasticity of demand assume $\theta_0 = 0$.

It is clear that all three approaches predict a negative price effect, that is, $\theta_1 < 0$, but in rational addiction and myopic models, prices are more elastic in the long run than in the short run as a result of the reinforcement mechanism.

4.1   Conventional demand studies

Price data relating to marijuana is particularly unreliable and this largely explains why there is only a small number of studies estimating price elasticity for this drug. One of the earliest is by Nisbet and Vakil (1972) who used data collected from an anonymous postal questionnaire of students at the University of California, Los Angeles, USA. Students were asked to derive their individual demand functions for marijuana at current prices and after various hypothetical price changes were made. Using this information and other actual data, the authors estimated a linear and double-log demand function and produced price elasticities of demand for marijuana of between −0.36 and −1.51.

Silverman and Spruill (1977) investigated the relationship between a price index for retail heroin and monthly-recorded crimes in Detroit, USA, from November 1970 to July 1973. The assumptions underpinning their model are that heroin expenditure is a function of the retail price and quantity consumed and an addict's ability to adjust consumption as prices change is a function of tolerance build up and the availability of suitable substitutes for heroin such as methadone. Using least squares regression on a log-linear crime model, Silverman and Spruill found that property crime rates in Detroit were positively related to the price of heroin and estimated the price elasticity of demand for heroin to be −0.27. One criticism of this model, however, is the assumption that price changes are caused solely by shifts in supply.

Another small, localized dataset is used by Bretteville-Jensen and Sutton (1996) to estimate the price elasticity of demand for heroin in Oslo, Norway. Data were used on 500 individuals collected via questionnaire from attendees at a needle exchange service in the city. The objective was to distinguish between 'ordinary' drug users and 'dealer' users. The data included information on income (and its sources), heroin consumption and dealing activity, in addition to information on some of the seemingly non-measurable factors we noted earlier (such as attitudes toward risk and the effect of arrest on status) when discussing the notion of an 'effective price'.

Bretteville-Jensen and Sutton estimate the price elasticities for dealers and non-dealers to be −0.20 and −1.23 respectively. This suggests two tentative conclusions. First, non-dealers are more price-sensitive than dealers. Second, we cannot treat an individual's decision to deal in drugs as being independent of his or her decision to consume. In other words, if a dealer is a heavy consumer, he or she is likely to be less price-sensitive. Interestingly, the results of Bretteville-Jensen and Sutton's estimated spline model (which allows different sections of the demand curve to have varying elasticity) offers little empirical support for the theoretical notion of a double-kinked demand curve.

Saffer and Chaloupka (1999a) used data on over 49000 individuals aged 12 and over from the 1988, 1990 and 1991 National Household Survey on Drug Abuse (NHSDA), and drug prices from System to Retrieve Information on Drug Evidence (STRIDE) to estimate the price elasticities for cocaine and heroin in the USA. The annual participation price elasticities for cocaine and heroin were found to be −0.55 and −0.90 respectively, while monthly participation elasticities for cocaine and heroin were −0.80 and −0.36 respectively.

The same sample was used by Saffer and Chaloupka (1999b) to estimate these price elasticities separately for seven different demographic sub-groups. The cocaine price elasticity was found to be statistically insignificant for blacks and Asians, −1.83 for Native Americans, and between −0.5 and −0.8 for white males, Hispanics, women and youth. The price elasticity for heroin, meanwhile, was estimated to be −1.63 for white males, −0.62 for females, −0.36 for youth, and almost zero for all other groups.

Saffer and Chaloupka (1999a, 1999b) also estimate demand functions for cocaine, heroin and alcohol, which include the money price of each substance, with the exception of marijuana. They report negative cross-price elasticities of demand for these substances, indicating that they are complementary goods, that is, an increase in the price of cocaine, for instance, leads to a decrease in the demand for heroin.

DeSimone and Farrelly (2003) examined data from 1990–97 NHSDA and reported past-year cocaine and marijuana participation elasticities of −0.13 and −0.25 respectively for individuals aged 18 to 39, although significantly negative price effects were not reported using similar models for persons aged 12 to 17.

Chaloupka et al. (1999) used the University of Michigan's 1982 and 1989 Monitoring the Future (MTF) survey to estimate price elasticities for past-month and past-year outcomes of participation in cocaine use. The MTF asks a sample of between 15000 and 19000 high school seniors in the USA about their use of illicit drugs. Chaloupka et al. reported a price elasticity of past-year participation of −0.89, an elasticity of past-month participation of −0.98, and corresponding frequency elasticities of −0.40 and −0.45 respectively. In a similar MTF sample from 1977 to 1987, DiNardo (1993) found that past-month participation by high school seniors is insensitive to price changes.

Pacula et al. (2001) used actual price figures for marijuana combined with data from the 1985 to 1996 MTF on high school seniors and estimated past-year participation elasticities of demand of −0.33 when time effects were omitted. When time was entered quadratically into their model, however, the participation elasticity dropped to −0.06.

Another dataset used by economists to estimate price elasticities is the Drug Use Forecasting (DUF) dataset, which is maintained by the National Institute of Justice in the USA to investigate drug use levels among booked arrestees in urban areas. Its advantage is that the indicators of drug use are objectively assessed from urine specimens and therefore not subject to reporting errors that may be prevalent in survey-based data. Arrestees represent hardcore users of drugs, and therefore the elasticity estimates are interpreted as the price responsiveness of heavy use.

Caulkins (1996) combined arrest data from DUF over the period 1987 to 1991 for 24 US cities with price data from STRIDE to indirectly estimate the participation price elasticities for cocaine and heroin. He separated the price elasticities into the product of two elasticities, which includes the percentage of arrestees testing positive for either drug as an intermediate variable. In doing so, Caulkins modelled a relationship with market quantity and estimated simple equations, which included the arrests of drug users and non-users (both related and unrelated to drug use) and a function of expenditure on illicit drugs. For arrestees, the price elasticity estimates were -0.39 for cocaine and -0.28 for heroin, while general participation price elasticities were estimated to be -1.5 for heroin and -2.5 for cocaine.

4.2   Myopic demand studies

Van Ours (1995) used data on opium consumption in the Dutch East Indies (Indonesia today) during the Dutch colonial period of the 1920s and 1930s when the Dutch government monopolized the opium market in that region in an attempt to reduce criminality, guarantee purity and, ultimately, curb opium use. As part of the operation of this system (or *Opiumregie*), data on opium consumption and revenues were collected on an annual basis. Van Ours collected data on the number of users by ethnic group for 22 regions over the period 1923 to 1938 and constructed series for the real opium price and real income. His two-stage least squares estimation produced short-run and long-run price elasticities of demand for opium of -0.7 and -1.0 respectively.

Dave (2004), using DUF data from 1988 to 2000, confirms that cocaine and heroin prices have a significantly negative effect on the probability of use for arrestees. He estimated a cocaine participation price elasticity of -0.23 and a heroin participation price elasticity of -0.08 for arrestees and reported that the long-run price elasticities are about twice this magnitude for both drugs. His study also showed that heavy users respond negatively to other components of the effective price of drugs as proxied by the probability of arrest for drug possession. Like Saffer and Chaloupka (1999a, 1999b), Dave's estimated cross-price elasticities suggest that cocaine and heroin are complementary goods.

4.3   Rational demand studies

Grossman and Chaloupka (1998) applied Becker and Murphy's 1988 rational addiction model in a study of the price elasticity of demand for cocaine. They used data from panels constructed from the MTF survey responses of high school seniors between 1976 and 1985, with the last follow-up undertaken in 1989. The latter provides information about past, current and future consumption by allowing for lags and leads of the middle observation to coincide with past and current consumption respectively. Information on prices was taken from STRIDE.

They estimated the total cost of cocaine by geographic location over time and, as with consumption, employed lags and leads to generate past and future real prices of the drug. Similar measures were used for time-varying socio-economic variables and numerous estimates were presented corresponding to whether they employed either OLS or two-stage least squares and according to the different measures of drug use. They found that, irrespective of model specification, the estimated coefficient of future consumption is always positive and statistically significant, while the coefficient of past consumption is generally positive and significant. These results provide solid support for the first two predictions of the rational addiction model.

Grossman and Chaloupka's discount factor was calculated as a ratio of future consumption to the coefficient of past consumption. This reduced the robustness of the model's results. The estimated discount rates corresponded to somewhat implausible interest rates and discount factors of between −3 per cent and 4 per cent and 1.03 and 0.98 respectively. However, Grossman and Chaloupka's reported short-run and long-run elasticities of demand for cocaine of −0.96 and −1.35 respectively were consistent with the third prediction of the rational addiction model, namely that long-run price elasticities are greater than short-run price elasticities.

Table 1.3 summarizes the empirical estimates of price elasticities for illicit drugs discussed in this section. From this, we can reach the following conclusions:

1.   Contrary to popular perception, the demand for illicit drugs appears to behave according to the law of the downward-sloping demand curve. Substantial increases in money prices seem to lead to substantial falls in illicit drug use. Indeed, comparing Table 1.2 to Table 1.3 reveals that illicit drug users are just as, or even more, responsive to price changes as cigarette smokers.
2.   The price responsiveness of illicit drug users is inversely related to age, that is, young people are more sensitive to changes in price than older people. One implication of this finding could be that since most illicit

Table 1.2 Summary of price elasticity of demand for illicit drugs

Author (s)	Date	Drug (s)	Data	Elasticity estimates
Nisbet & Vakil	1972	Marijuana	Questionnaire of UCLA students	−0.36 (lower bound) −1.51 (upper bound)
Silverman & Spruill	1977	Heroin	Monthly data (1970–73) from Detroit	−0.27 (long run)
Van Ours	1995	Opium	Government data (1923-38)	−0.7 (short run) −1.0 (long run)
Caulkins	1996	Cocaine & Heroin	Drug Use Forecasting System and STRIDE	−2.5 (cocaine) −1.5 (heroin)
Brettville-Jensen & Sutton	1996	Heroin	Questionnaire of Norwegian addicts	−0.20 (dealers) −1.23 (non-dealers)
Grossman & Chaloupka	1998	Cocaine	Monitoring the Future Survey (1976–85) and STRIDE	−0.96 (short run) −1.35 (long run)
Saffer & Chaloupka	1999a	Cocaine & Heroin	National Household Survey on Drug Abuse (1988, 1990, 1991)	−0.55 & −0.80 (cocaine, past-year & past-month) −0.90 & −0.36 (heroin, past-year & past-month)
Chaloupka et al.	1999	Cocaine	Monitoring the Future Survey (1982 and 1999)	−0.89 (past-year) −0.98 (past-month)
Pacula et al.	2001	Marijuana	Monitoring the Future Survey (1985–96)	−0.33 (past-year)
DeSimone & Farrelly	2003	Cocaine & Marijuana	National Household Survey on Drug Abuse (1990–97)	−0.13 (cocaine, past-year) −0.25 (marijuana, past-year)
Dave	2004	Cocaine & Heroin	Monitoring the Future Survey (1988–2000)	−0.23 (cocaine) −0.08 (heroin)

Table 1.3   Summary of price elasticity of demand for cigarettes

	Lowest estimate	Mean estimate	Highest estimate
Aggregate consumption data (22 US studies)	−0.14	−0.387	−1.12
Aggregate consumption data (6 international studies; developed countries)	0	−0.245	−0.6
Developing countries (8 studies)	−0.1	−0.598	−1.0
Individual consumption data on adults (7 US studies)	−0.25	−0.374	−0.47
Youth prevalence (16 US studies)	0	−0.579	−1.21
Youth consumption (12 US studies)	0	−0.608	−1.44

Source: Goel and Nelson (2003).

    drug abuse begins in teenage years, large and sustained increases in price may achieve substantial long-run reductions in illicit drug abuse across the population as a whole.

3.   Estimates of the long-run effects of price on demand for illicit drugs will be biased should we overlook their addictive nature. Taking the latter into account indicates that long-run decreases in demand resulting from a permanent increase in the price of illicit drugs will be significantly greater than short-run decreases. On the other hand, the addictive nature of illicit drugs implies that temporary price changes will have little effect on demand.

4.   The demand for illicit drugs is a function of non-myopic behaviour. This suggests that increases in the future price of substances (new information on the future health consequences of illicit drug use, for instance) will lead to substantial falls in current use.

5.   More myopic individuals will be more price sensitive than will more far-sighted individuals. As suggested by Becker et al. (1991) and noted in (2), younger, less educated and lower-income persons will be more responsive to permanent changes in the money price of addictive illicit drugs than will older, more educated and higher-income individuals. Likewise, more far-sighted individuals will be more sensitive to changes in the perceived future consequences of illicit drug use and abuse.

6.   Increases in the 'effective price' of illicit drugs will also lead to reductions in their current and future use. Such increases may include increases in the expected 'punishment costs' of illicit drug use and abuse within the legal framework, and new information on the short- and long-term health consequences of illicit drug use and abuse as noted in (4).

5   Drug prohibition: the welfare economics approach

Estimating the price elasticity of illicit drug use has a potentially important role to play in the design and execution of drug policy. First, it helps confirm that drug purchases are driven by market forces. Second, it assists in evaluating the costs and benefits of drug prohibition. Governments expend resources on enforcement and apprehension to curtail illicit drug use and one may think of reductions in 'external costs' (such as accidents, crimes and neglect of responsibility) caused by illicit drug use as benefits of drug policy. In an economics framework, enforcement and apprehension work by raising the price of illicit drugs and consequently reducing consumption. If drug users are not very price responsive, however, and consumption does not change by much, perhaps the costs outweigh the benefits.

From an economist's viewpoint, the external costs of illicit drug use create a divergence, illustrated in Figure 1.6, between the marginal private

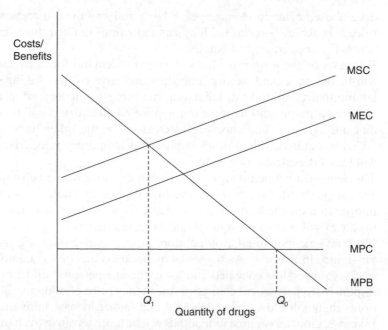

Figure 1.6   The social costs of illicit drug use

costs (MPC) of the individual decision-maker (that is, the drug user) and the marginal social costs (MSC) borne by society as a whole.[5] Given the empirical results reported in the previous section, we assume that individuals have a downward-sloping demand curve for drugs. Second, we assume a constant marginal private cost of consuming the drugs, which reflects the 'effective' costs faced by the individual drug user (such as the risk of arrest), which he or she will equate with the marginal private benefits of consumption (MPB) such as a feeling of euphoria. This yields an optimal consumption level of Q_0. The marginal external cost curve (MEC), meanwhile, reflects the external costs imposed by an individual's illicit drug use on society as a whole. In making the privately optimal choice, Q_0, the individual does not take these costs into account.

To obtain the total social costs of illicit drug use, we add the private costs to the social costs and this is represented by the marginal social cost curve (MSC). The allocation of resources resulting from the private choice of Q_0 is Pareto-inefficient from society's point of view. If we make the conventional assumption that there are no benefits to the rest of society from individual drug use, then the efficient level of consumption is Q_1, where the social costs of illicit drug use are equal to the benefits. Indeed, at any point between Q_1 and Q_0, the total costs of drug use are greater than the benefits, and efficiency can be improved by government intervention that reduces consumption from Q_0 to Q_1 (note that if the external costs are sufficiently large, Q_1 will correspond to the origin, that is, zero consumption or absolute prohibition).

Culyer (1973) examines whether society has grounds for concern over illicit drug use and proposes six principal propositions upon which prohibition arguments should be based. MacDonald (2004) summarizes them as follows:

1. One individual's use of drugs imposes costs on others in society, either through anti-social behaviour or acquisitive crime.
2. Drug users impose an additional burden on a publicly provided health service either through treatment or rehabilitation.
3. Society simply finds the use of drugs undesirable.
4. Drug users should be protected as they do not act in their own best interests.
5. An individual's choice to consume drugs may lead to an escalation in society of an undesired activity.
6. Drug users are less productive members of society.

The above propositions relate directly to the externalities and merit goods frameworks of welfare economics. Indeed, proposition (4) is the classic paternalistic case for drug prohibition, which conflicts with the traditional emphasis on consumer sovereignty in the first-year economics textbook. The main difficulty with the proposition, however, is the assumption that the rest of society is well-informed about the dangers of illicit drug use whereas the individual drug user is not. One could make a case with reference to the rational addiction model discussed earlier that this is not always true; individuals often make their choices with at least some, if not all, knowledge of the risks attached to the consumption of the good or activity. On the other hand, one could appeal to the extensions of the model that incorporate the possibility of the drug user experiencing 'learning and regret'. As we noted, such models suggest a role for policy-makers to inform individuals about the potentially negative consequences of illicit drug use and addiction.

6   Conclusion

This opening chapter has surveyed the contribution of economists in understanding perhaps one of the most notorious aspects of human deviancy: drug addiction. We have revealed the significant progress made in developing insightful theories of addictive behaviour. Also, despite having to rely upon rather imperfect data, economists have provided numerous estimates of how an illicit drug user responds to price changes. Indeed, both the theoretical and empirical advances that we have discussed have the potential to improve drug policy-making.

However, while we have demonstrated that economists have a good understanding of the determinants of the demand for illicit drugs, little is known about both the theoretical and empirical nature of the *supply* of these substances. For instance, although we can gauge from Chapter 4 the probable motivations of a drug dealer, we have only limited knowledge of what the cost structure of a typical 'firm' in this industry looks like and, importantly, how it responds to changes in market conditions and environment (see Levitt and Venkatesh, 2000). In summary, there remain rich areas of research into illicit drugs for economists to explore.

Notes

1. Recent history of drug use is measured as the proportion of total activity allocated to drug use.
2. The term discount is used here to refer to any reason to care less about a future consequence.
3. An alternative approach is to make the discount function dependent on the stock of addictive good. Orphanides and Zervos (1998) extend the Becker–Murphy model of rational addiction by assuming that individuals with a larger addictive stock ('addicts') discount future utility more heavily. In the extreme, some individuals who choose to become addicts end up being completely myopic.
4. Gruber and Mullainathan (2002) test for time-consistent versus time-inconsistent preferences by looking at the effects of cigarette taxes on a smoker's utility. With time-consistent

preferences, higher future cigarette taxes would unambiguously reduce a smoker's current utility; however, with time-inconsistent preferences, a smoker may prefer (and thus have higher current utility) to face higher future cigarette taxes to give him or herself a commitment device in the future when he or she knows that he or she will have the self-control problems. Hyperbolic discounting is also consistent with observing a positive demand for commitment devices in a variety of contexts (aids for quitting smoking, checking oneself into treatment facilities, smokers generally in favour of workplace smoking bans and so on).

5. Here we are assuming that net external costs are positive. Chapter 2 suggests that they are small and might even be negative. For example, consider individuals substituting alcohol with the, arguably, less dangerous marijuana.

References

Ainslie, G.W. (1975), 'Specious Reward: A Behavioral Theory of Impulsiveness and Impulse Control', *Psychological Bulletin*, **82**, 463–96.

Bardsley, P. and N. Olekalns (1999), 'Cigarette and Tobacco Consumption: Have Anti-Smoking Policies Made a Difference?', *The Economic Record*, **75**, 225–40.

Becker, G.S. and K.M. Murphy (1988), 'A Theory of Rational Addiction', *Journal of Political Economy*, **94** (4), 675–700.

Becker, G.S., M. Grossman and K.M. Murphy (1991), 'Rational Addiction and the Effect of Price on Consumption', *American Economic Review*, **81** (2), 237–41.

Becker, G.S., M. Grossman and K.M. Murphy (1994), 'An Empirical Analysis of Cigarette Addiction', *American Economic Review*, **84** (3), 396–418.

Becker, G.S., M. Grossman and K.M. Murphy (2004), 'The Economic Theory of Illegal Goods: The Case of Drugs', National Bureau of Economic Research Working Paper, No. W10976.

Betz, C., D. Mihalic, M.E. Pinto and R.B. Rafta (2000), 'Could a Common Biochemical Mechanism Underlie Addictions?', *Journal of Clinical Pharmacy and Therapeutics*, **25**, 11–20.

Blair, R.D. and R.J. Vogel (1973), 'Heroin Addiction and Urban Crime', *Public Finance Quarterly*, **1** (14), 457–67.

Bretteville-Jensen, A. and M. Sutton (1996), 'Gender, Heroin Consumption and Economic Behaviour', Centre for Health Economics, Discussion Paper 147, University of York.

Cameron, S. (1999), 'Rational Addiction and the Demand for Cinema', *Applied Economics Letters*, **6**, 617–20.

Caulkins, J.P. (1996), 'Estimating Elasticities of Demand for Cocaine and Heroin with Data from the Drug Use Forecasting System', School of Public Policy & Management Working Paper Series, No. 95–13, Carnegie Mellon University.

Chaloupka, F.J., M. Grossman and J.A. Tauras (1999), 'The Demand for Cocaine and Marijuana by Youth', in Frank J. Chaloupka, Michael Grossman, Warren K. Bickel and Henry Saffer (eds), *The Economic Analysis of Substance Use and Abuse: An Integration of Econometric and Behavioral Economic Research*, University of Chicago Press, pp. 133–55.

Cheng, L.S., G.E. Swan and D. Carmelli (2000), 'A Genetic Analysis of Smoking Behaviour in Family Members of Older Adult Males', *Addiction*, **95**, 427–35.

Culyer, A. (1973), 'Should Social Policy Concern Itself with Drug Abuse?', *Public Finance Quarterly*, **1**, 449–56.

Cunningham, C.L., D.R. Niehus, D.H. Malott and L.K. Prather (1992), 'Genetic Differences in the Rewarding and Activating Effects of Morphine and Ethanol', *Psychopharmacology*, **107**, 385–93.

Dave, D. (2004), 'Illicit Drug Use Among Arrestees and Drug Prices', National Bureau of Economic Research Working Paper, No. W10648.

Daw Namoro, S. (2003), 'Risk Perception and Addictive Behavior', unpublished manuscript.

DeSimone, J. and M.C. Farrelly (2003), 'Price and Enforcement Effects on Cocaine and Marijuana Demand', *Economic Inquiry*, **41** (1), 98–115.

DiNardo, J. (1993), 'Law Enforcement, the Price of Cocaine and Cocaine Use', *Mathematical and Computer Modelling*, **17**, 53–64.

European Monitoring Centre for Drugs and Drug Addiction (EMCDDA) (2004), 'The State of the Drugs Problem in the European Union and Norway', Annual Report.

Goel, R.K. and M.A. Nelson (2003), 'Controlling Use of Undesirable Goods: Survey of Effectiveness of Tobacco Control Policies', unpublished manuscript.

Grossman, M. and F.J. Chaloupka (1998), 'The Demand for Cocaine by Young Adults: A Rational Addiction Approach', *Journal of Health Economics*, **17**, 427–74.

Grossman, M., F.J. Chaloupka and I. Sirtalan (1998), 'An Empirical Analysis of Alcohol Addiction: Results from the Monitoring the Future Panels', *Economic Inquiry*, **36**, 39–48.

Gruber, J. and B. Köszegi (2001), 'Is Addiction "Rational"? Theory and Evidence', *Quarterly Journal of Economics*, **116** (4), 1261–305.

Gruber, J. and S. Mullainathan (2002), 'Do Cigarette Taxes Make Smokers Happier?', National Bureau of Economic Research Working Paper No. 8872.

Hammersley, R., F. Khan and J. Ditton (2001), *Ecstasy and the Rise of the Chemical Generation*, New York: Routledge.

Herrnstein, R.J. and D. Prelec (1992), 'A Theory of Addiction', in George Loewenstein and Jon Elster (eds), *Choice over Time*, New York: Russell Sage Foundation, pp. 331–60.

Herrnstein, R.J. and W. Vaughan, Jr. (1980), 'Melioriation and Behavioral Allocation', in John E.R. Staddon (ed.), *Limits to Action: The Allocation of Individual Behavior*, New York: Academic Press, pp. 143–76.

Kenkel, D., A.D. Mathios and R.L. Pacula (2001), 'Economics of Youth Drug Abuse, Addiction and Gateway Effects', *Addiction*, **96**, 151–64.

Kleiman, Mark A.R. (1992), *Against Excess: Drug Policy for Results*, New York: Basic Books.

Laibson, D.I. (1997), 'Golden Eggs and Hyperbolic Discounting', *Quarterly Journal of Economics*, **112** (2), 443–78.

Levitt, S.D. and S.A. Venkatesh (2000), 'An Economic Analysis of a Drug-Selling Gang's Finances', *Quarterly Journal of Economics*, **115** (3), 755–89.

Loewenstein, E. and J. Elster (eds) (1992), *Choice Over Time*, New York: Russell Sage Foundation.

Macdonald, Z. (2004), 'What Price Drug Use? The Contribution of Economics to an Evidence-Based Drugs Policy', *Journal of Economic Surveys*, **18** (2), 113–52.

Marshall, Alfred (1920) [1890], *Principles of Economics*, 8th edition, London: Macmillan and Co.

Mobilia, P. (1993), 'Gambling as a Rational Addiction', *Journal of Gambling Studies*, **9** (3), 121–52.

Moore, M.H. (1973), 'Policies to Achieve Discrimination on the Effective Price of Heroin', *American Economic Review*, **63**, 270–77.

Moore, M.H. (1990), 'Supply Reduction and Drug Law Enforcement', in Michael H. Tonry and James Q. Wilson (eds), *Drugs and Crime, A Review of Research in Crime and Justice*, Chicago: University of Chicago Press, pp. 109–57.

National Household Survey on Drug Abuse (NHSDA) (2003), 'Comparison of Substance Abuse in Australia and the United States', NHSDA.

Nisbet, C.T. and F. Vakil (1972), 'Some Estimates of Price and Expenditure Elasticities of Demand for Marihuana Among UCLA Students', *Review of Economics and Statistics*, **54**, 473–75.

Olekalns, N. and P. Bardsley (1996), 'Rational Addiction to Caffeine: An Analysis of Coffee Consumption', *Journal of Political Economy*, **104**, 1100–104.

Orphanides, A. and D. Zervos (1995), 'Rational Addiction with Learning and Regret', *Journal of Political Economy*, **103** (4), 739–58.

Orphanides, A. and D. Zervos (1998), 'Myopia and Addictive Behaviour', *Economic Journal*, **108** (1), 75–91.

Pacula, R.L., M. Grossman, F.J. Chaloupka, P.M. O'Malley, L.D. Johnston and M.C. Farrelly (2001), 'Marijuana and Youth', in Jonathon Gruber (ed.), *Risky Behavior Among Youths: An Economic Analysis*, University of Chicago Press, pp. 271–326.

Phlips, Louis (1983), *Applied Consumption Analysis*, Advanced Textbooks in Economics, Vol. 5, Revised Edition, Amsterdam: North-Holland Publishing Company.

Prochaska, J.O. and C.C. DiClemente (1983), 'Stages and Processes of Self-change of Smoking: Toward an Integrated Model of Change', *Journal of Consulting and Clinical Psychology*, **51** (3), 390–95.

Rachlin, H. (1997), 'Four Teleological Theories of Addiction', *Psychonomic Bulletin and Review*, **4** (4), 462–73.

Read, D. and B. Van Leeuwen (1998), 'Predicting Hunger: The Effects of Appetite and Delay on Choice', *Organizational Behavior and Human Decision Processes*, **76** (2), 189–205.

Reuter, P. and V. Greenfield (2001), 'Measuring Global Drug Markets: How Good are the Numbers and Why Should We Care About Them', *World Economics*, **2** (4), 159–73.

Robinson, T.E. and K.C. Berridge (2001), 'Incentive-sensitization and Addiction', *Addiction*, **96**, 103–14.

Saffer, H. and F.J. Chaloupka (1995), 'The Demand for Illicit Drugs', *Economic Inquiry*, **37** (3), 401–11.

Saffer, H. and F.J. Chaloupka (1999a), 'The Demand for Illicit Drugs', *Economic Inquiry*, **37** (3), 401–11.

Saffer, H. and F.J. Chaloupka (1999b), 'Demographic Differentials in the Demand for Alcohol and Illicit Drugs', in F.J. Chaloupka, M. Grossman, W.K. Bichel and H. Saffer (eds), *The Economic Analysis of Substance Use and Abuse*, University of Chicago Press, pp. 187–212.

Schelling, T.C. (1978), 'Ergonomics, or the Art of Self-Management', *American Economic Review*, **68** (2), 290–94.

Shane, F., G. Loewenstein and T. O'Donoghue (2002), 'Time Discounting and Time Preference: A Critical Review', *Journal of Economic Literature*, **40** (2), 351–401.

Silverman, L.P. and N.L. Spruill (1977), 'Urban Crime and the Price of Heroin', *Journal of Urban Economics*, **76**, 78–90.

Stigler, G.J. and G.S. Becker (1977), 'De Gustibus non est Disputandum', *American Economic Review*, **67**, 76–90.

Thaler, R.H. (1981), 'Some Empirical Evidence on Dynamic Inconsistency', *Economics Letters*, **8**, 201–7.

United Nations Office on Drugs and Crime (UNODC) (2005), 'World Drug Report 2005', UNODC.

Van Ours, J.C. (1995), 'The Price Elasticity of Hard Drugs: The Case of Opium in the Dutch East Indies, 1923–1938', *Journal of Political Economy*, **103**, 261–79.

Wagstaff, A. and A. Maynard (1988), 'Economic Aspects of the Illicit Drug Market and Drug Enforcement Policies in the United Kingdom', Home Office Research Study 95, London: Home Office.

Waters, T. and F. Sloan (1995), 'Why Do People Drink? Tests of the Rational Addiction Model', *Applied Economics*, **27**, 727–36.

West, R. (2001), 'Theories of Addiction', *Addiction*, **96** (1), 3–13.

White, M.D. and W.A. Luksetich (1983), 'Heroin: Price Elasticity and Enforcement Strategies', *Economic Inquiry*, **21**, 557–64.

2 Economics of drug prohibition
Jeffrey A. Miron

According to conventional wisdom, illicit drugs are responsible for a broad range of social and personal ills, including crime, diminished health and reduced productivity. Popular thinking attributes these ills mainly to the characteristics of drugs themselves. For example, standard accounts suggest that psychopharmacological effects of drugs make users commit violent and other crimes. Similarly, standard depictions suggest that mind-altering and addictive properties of drugs cause users to suffer poor health or diminished productivity.

This chapter explains that the social and personal ills typically associated with illicit drugs have little to do with drugs themselves; instead, they result from the economic incentives created by drug prohibition. This does not mean drug use is benign; drug use carries significant risks in some situations, but the magnitude of these risks is not markedly different from that of many legal goods.

Sections 1 and 2 of the chapter analyse the effect of prohibition on the price and quantity of drugs consumed. The standard defence of prohibition assumes this policy eliminates or substantially reduces the market for drugs; in this case, prohibition eliminates or substantially reduces any negative effects of drug use. The analysis here, however, shows that while price and quantity plausibly differ between a legal market and a prohibited market, both a priori reasoning and existing evidence suggest this difference is far smaller than assumed in most accounts. Thus, even if drug use itself causes the ills typically associated with drugs, prohibition has only a modest effect in reducing these ills.

Sections 3 and 4 then show that, while reducing drug use and associated ills only moderately, prohibition itself causes many of the ills usually attributed to illicit drugs. In particular, prohibition causes most of the violence in illicit drug markets, and prohibition encourages drug users to commit income-generating crimes such as theft or prostitution. The analysis further shows that prohibition causes or exacerbates the risks associated with drug use. At the same time, much of the evidence that drug use causes crime, poor health or diminished productivity is distorted, misleading or grossly exaggerated.

This chapter is not a cost–benefit evaluation of prohibition; such an evaluation must address a large number of issues that are outside the scope of the analysis here. The point of what follows is to indicate that the unusual features of drug markets result mainly from the legal status of drugs, not from the properties of drugs themselves. Rather than requiring specialized assumptions or treatment, an understanding of illicit drug markets follows readily from application of standard economic principles.

1 Price and quantity of drugs under prohibition: theory

1.1 Prohibition and the demand for drugs
Prohibition potentially reduces the demand for drugs via several mechanisms.[1] First, it can foster a social norm that drug use is wrong, thereby discouraging use. This effect is hard to quantify since norms are difficult to measure. On the other hand, prohibition might increase demand by glamorizing drugs or creating a forbidden fruit.

Prohibition can also reduce demand by those who exhibit 'respect for the law', even if such persons do not believe drug use is wrong. There is little direct evidence on this effect, but some information can be gleaned from laws that are weakly enforced, such as speeding laws, sodomy laws, and certain tax laws. In each case, violation of the law is common and the degree of non-compliance suggests caution in assuming that respect for the law, *per se*, substantially reduces the demand for drugs.

A third mechanism by which prohibition can reduce the demand for drugs, even by those who put little weight on respect for the law or on social norms that denigrate drug use, is by sanctioning the purchase or possession of drugs. These sanctions can include heavy fines, long jail terms and loss of professional licences, amongst other consequences.

The impact of these sanctions on the demand for drugs is probably modest, however. First, the actual penalties imposed for possession are typically far below the maximums allowable under law. Second, although there are many arrests for drug possession, there are also many drug users, and the number of purchases or 'possessions' is far larger than the number of users. Third, many of the arrests that do occur are incidental to the commission of other crimes, such as prostitution, theft, shop-lifting, or vagrancy. Thus, persons who are otherwise law-abiding face minimal chances of arrest for drug possession.

1.2 Prohibition and the supply of drugs
Prohibition can also affect the supply of drugs via several mechanisms. It potentially reduces supply by imposing costs that would not be borne by legal suppliers. Black market suppliers must produce, transport, distribute and store their goods secretly, or bribe law enforcement authorities to look the other way. These suppliers must compensate employees for the risk of

arrest, injury and incarceration, for the absence of fringe benefits, as well as for any stigma associated with working in a black market. Suppliers cannot use the official dispute resolution system and must therefore employ mechanisms like violence that arguably have higher costs.

Despite this tendency to raise costs, however, prohibition does not necessarily produce dramatic increases in the costs of supplying drugs (Miron, 2003a). Conditional on operating in secret, black market suppliers face low marginal costs of evading tax and regulatory policies that ordinarily add costs for legal suppliers. These policies include income taxes, excise taxes, environmental regulation, safety and health regulation, child labour laws, minimum wage laws and others. Since suppliers in a legal market can always choose to evade such laws (that is, act as though the good is prohibited), the fact that black market suppliers evade tax and regulatory costs can never cause prices to be lower in a black market than in a legal market. But the effect of prohibition in raising prices can be arbitrarily small.

Several other considerations suggest prohibition has a modest effect on the costs of supplying drugs. To begin with, prohibition can involve reduced expenditure for enforcement of the taxation and regulation policies that would otherwise exist. It might also have a modest effect on costs because the efficacy of enforcement expenditure is likely greater for taxation and regulation than for prohibition. Taxes and regulations create complainants who monitor compliance with these policies, including employees (labour market regulation), customers (false or misleading advertising), consumer watchdog groups (environmental regulation) and rival firms (most cost-increasing policies, including taxation). Prohibition creates no such complainants; indeed, prohibition prevents Pareto-improving exchanges. Thus, enforcement must rely on informants, sting operations and busts, all of which require expenditure. Moreover, the complainants vis-à-vis tax and regulatory policies are less likely to complain about violations of these policies in a black market, since they might thereby risk legal sanctions themselves. This means that, for a given level of enforcement, the costs imposed by a policy are likely higher in a legal market.

A third reason prohibition's impact on costs might be moderate is that in legal markets, advertising comprises a substantial fraction of the price of many goods. In a prohibited market, firms face increased costs of advertising, since such activities can reveal their identity or location. In monopolistically competitive models the net impact of this is ambiguous: advertising can make demand more or less elastic, so decreased advertising has an ambiguous effect on price. The plausible assumption for drugs is that advertising would enhance product differentiation, as with alcohol, cigarettes or soft drinks. In this case, advertising makes demand less elastic, so an increased price of advertising implies more elastic demand and lower goods prices.

A final factor that suggests a moderate cost effect of prohibition is its impact on market power. One view is that prohibition facilitates evasion of anti-trust laws, thereby increasing market power, or lowers the marginal costs of extreme punishments (violence), thereby enhancing the potential for collusive agreements. At the same time, certain enforcement activities appear to enhance competition. For example, efforts to prevent Peruvian coca paste (an intermediate product between coca leaf and cocaine) from being transported to Colombia for processing caused Colombian processors to develop coca-growing capabilities in Colombia.

Alternatively, the arrest and incarceration of a dominant supplier can encourage price wars among the remaining suppliers as they compete for the arrested supplier's market share. More formally, prohibition can make prices noisy, which inhibits collusion in some classes of models (for example, Green and Porter, 1984), or makes it profitable for suppliers to incur the fixed costs of new distribution networks, which then compete with pre-existing arrangements. Thus, the net effect of prohibition on market power is ambiguous and probably depends on both the level and kind of enforcement.

In summary, this section suggests that prohibition has raised costs relative to what would occur in a legal market, but by far less than asserted in many accounts. Miron (2003a) estimates that black market cocaine is currently 2–4 times, and heroin 6–19 times its price in a legalized market. In contrast, prior research had suggested that cocaine is 10–40 times, and heroin hundreds of times, its legal price. MacCoun and Reuter (1997) note that the price of marijuana in the Netherlands, which has de facto legalized marijuana, is little different from the price in the USA.

2 Price and quantity of drugs under prohibition: evidence

Theoretical reasoning therefore implies that prohibition reduces drug consumption. This reasoning also suggests, however, that the reduction in drug consumption is potentially modest. Evidence on this issue is incomplete due to lack of good data, but existing research suggests some broad conclusions.

First, the amount of drug use that occurs under prohibition suggests by itself that prohibition's impact on drug consumption is moderate. As shown in Figure 1.1 of Chapter 1, for example, roughly 40 per cent of the US population admits to having tried marijuana, and this probably understates the true frequency because some people lie or forget about their past drug use. Moreover, many of those who do not try marijuana presumably do so for reasons other than prohibition; many persons do not drink or smoke even though these activities are legal.

A second piece of evidence comes from experience in the USA with consumption of opiates before 1914, the year the Harrison Narcotics Act criminalized opiates, cocaine and other drugs.[2] Available data show that per capita consumption increased on average until the mid-1890s and then decreased steadily until 1914 (Miron, 2004). These fluctuations prior to prohibition indicate that many factors affect opiate consumption, not just its legal status. In particular, public health concerns raised by the medical profession appear to have caused the substantial decline in opiate use between the mid-1890s and 1914 (Musto, 1973).

More recent experience also fails to suggest that prohibition reduces drug consumption. Over the past 30 years in the USA, enforcement of drug prohibition has expanded dramatically, as we shall discuss further in Chapter 3. For example, the real, per capita budget of the Drug Enforcement Administration (DEA) has increased by a factor of more than three, and the drug arrest rate has increased by a factor of roughly two (see Figure 2.1).

Over the same period, however, the trends in drug production and consumption have been essentially flat, and the real, purity-adjusted prices of both cocaine and heroin in the USA have more than halved (see Figure 2.2). Measures of drug consumption in the USA that include all use show a substantial decline during the 1980s followed by a partial rebound during the 1990s, to roughly 80 per cent of the 1975 level. Measures of heavy consumption, however, show if anything an increase over this period (see Basov et al., 2001).

This evidence does not prove that increased enforcement had no effect; prices might otherwise have fallen further and drug consumption increased. But absent an explanation for why this should have occurred, this evidence constitutes a puzzle for the view that enforcement reduces consumption and increases price. DiNardo (1993) finds no evidence that enforcement, as measured by cocaine seizures, raised cocaine prices or reduced cocaine use among high school seniors during the 1980s. Similarly, Yuan and Caulkins (1998) find that a greater number of drug seizures is associated with lower black market prices of cocaine and heroin.

A further approach to estimating the impact of prohibition is to combine estimates of the effect of prohibition on demand and on costs with an estimate of the elasticity of demand. This approach is problematic for several reasons. First, it requires estimating the effect of prohibition on the demand curve itself; such estimates do not exist. Second, this approach requires estimating the effect of prohibition on costs; such estimates exist but are subject to substantial uncertainty. Third, this approach requires estimating the elasticity of the demand for drugs, which, as discussed in Chapter 1, is a difficult

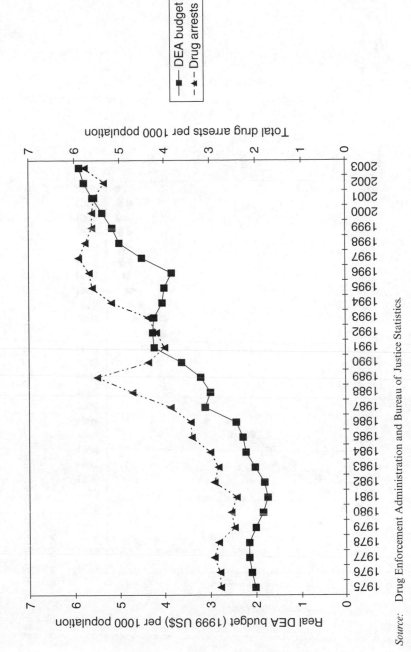

Source: Drug Enforcement Administration and Bureau of Justice Statistics.

Figure 2.1 Real DEA budget and total drug arrests per 1000 population in USA (1975–2003)

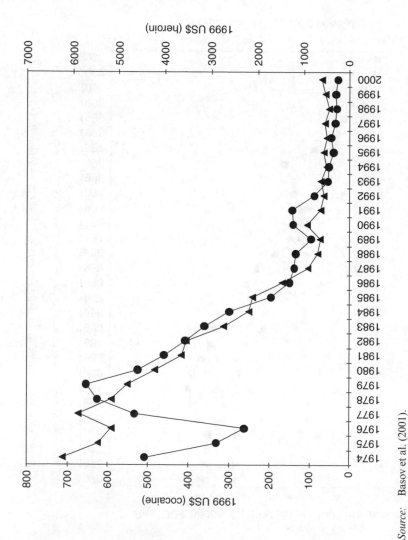

Source: Basov et al. (2001).

Figure 2.2   Median prices per pure gram of cocaine and heroin in USA (1974–2000)

50

exercise. Nevertheless, Kuziemko and Levitt (2004) use this approach to estimate that increases in enforcement since 1985 in the USA increased cocaine prices and reduced cocaine consumption by 10–15 per cent over the 1985–96 period. However, their conclusion relies on regressions of cocaine prices on drug arrest rates, commitment rates for drug arrests and other variables. They find a positive and significant effect of drug enforcement, but note that interpretation of these coefficients is difficult. Changes in drug demand might cause changes in price that would be positively correlated with drug arrest rates. Moreover, since enforcement increased substantially over this period, this conclusion is consistent with the view that prohibition has a moderate but not a dramatic effect in reducing drug consumption.

In addition to information gleaned from drug prohibition, there is also evidence from the prohibition of alcohol in the USA during the 1920–33 period (Dills and Miron, 2004). Data on alcohol consumption are not readily available for this period, but the cirrhosis death rate is a reasonable proxy. Cirrhosis was indeed lower during Prohibition than during periods before or after, but cirrhosis had reached its low, Prohibition level by the time Prohibition began, implying factors other than Prohibition caused the low level of cirrhosis. Taking into account the possible roles of state prohibitions, pre-1920 federal anti-alcohol policies, the age composition of the population and economic factors such as alcohol taxes or income, Dills and Miron (2004) estimate that national prohibition reduced cirrhosis by about 10–20 per cent.

A different kind of evidence comes from the experience of states or countries that have decriminalized marijuana. Decriminalization reduces the penalties for possession from jail terms and heavy fines to small fines only. The evidence provided by decriminalization is potentially weak; changes in the law sometimes ratify ex post what has already taken place, and changes in the law can reflect incidental factors rather than real changes in enforcement (see Pacula et al., 2003 for evidence consistent with these concerns). Nevertheless, existing evidence provides little indication that decriminalization leads to increased marijuana use.

A final piece of evidence comes from comparing drug use rates between the USA and other rich countries such as those in Western Europe, Japan or Australia. These countries have prohibition laws similar to those in the USA, especially for harder drugs such as cocaine and heroin, but, as discussed in Chapter 3, they enforce prohibition to a substantially lesser degree. Thus, if prohibition enforcement reduces drug use, these countries should have higher use rates than the USA. As shown in Figures 1.1 and 1.2 of Chapter 1, however, the use rate is little different on average in the USA compared with other rich countries; indeed, many of these countries have lower drug consumption. This fact is only suggestive, since it does not control for other determinants of drug use, but it fails to indicate that prohibition reduces use.

In summary, both theory and evidence suggest that prohibition has only a modest impact on the size of the illicit drug market. This means that, even if the ills associated with illicit drugs result from drug use, prohibition reduces them only mildly. It also means that a substantial drug market remains, although this market operates underground. This latter fact has important implications for understanding the various social and personal problems typically attributed to drugs. The following two sections of this chapter address these implications.

3   Drugs, prohibition and crime

3.1   The impact of prohibition on crime

Prohibition promotes violent crime for several reasons.[3] Most importantly, participants in illicit markets cannot resolve disputes via standard, non-violent mechanisms. Drug suppliers cannot use the legal system to adjudicate commercial disputes such as non-payment of debts. Drug traffickers risk legal penalties themselves if they report their employees for misuse of 'company' funds or property. Purchasers of illicit drugs cannot sue drug sellers for product liability, nor can drug sellers use the courts to enforce payment. Along a different line, rival traffickers cannot compete via advertising and are more likely to wage violent turf battles. Thus, participants in an illicit market for drugs resolve disagreements with violence, although it should be noted that the extent to which prohibition promotes violence depends on the degree of enforcement (see Miron, 1999, 2001b).

Prohibition may also encourage violence by increasing the profitability of drug trafficking. One model of what occurs under prohibition is that suppliers enter the illicit drug market until the total return from this activity equals the total return from legal activity, taking into account the risks of incarceration, injury or death and any stigma/glamour associated with working in a black market. Assuming everyone has the same willingness to accept these features of black market activity, prohibition does not imply excess profits in the prohibited sector. If there is heterogeneity in the willingness to work in the black market, however, those willing to do so select into this sector, earn 'rents' to this characteristic and are better off under prohibition. Such persons have more to protect under prohibition and therefore have an additional reason to use violence.

Despite these tendencies to increase violence, prohibition might reduce violence on net if prohibition reduces drug use and drug use causes violence. Existing evidence, however, suggests the net effect is to increase violence. A first piece of evidence is the behaviour of the homicide rate over the past century in the USA (Friedman, 1991; Miron, 1999). As illustrated in Figure 2.3, the murder rate rose rapidly after 1910, when many states adopted drug and alcohol prohibition laws. The rate also rose through World War I, when alcohol and drugs were first prohibited nationally, and it continued to rise during the 1920s as efforts to enforce alcohol prohibition increased. The rate then fell dramatically after alcohol prohibition's repeal in 1934 and (except for wartime) remained at modest levels for several decades. In the late 1960s, the rate increased dramatically again and stayed at historically high levels through the 1970s and 1980s, coinciding with a drastic increase in drug law enforcement. More formally, Miron (1999) shows that enforcement of drug and alcohol prohibition is strongly correlated with the homicide rate even after controlling for a broad range of other determinants.

Comparisons across cities and countries also indicate a positive relation between prohibition enforcement and violence. Brumm and Cloninger (1995) find in a sample of cities in the USA that higher drug arrest rates are associated with higher homicide rates, while Miron (2001b) and Fajnzylber et al. (1998, 1999) find a positive relation across countries between prohibition enforcement and homicide. These results must be interpreted with caution because they document correlations that might not be causal, but they are nevertheless consistent with the view that prohibition causes violence.

Micro-evidence suggests even more clearly that prohibition increases violence. Goldstein et al. (1989, 1997) find in a sample of New York City precincts during 1988 that almost three-quarters of 'drug-related' homicides were due to disputes over drug territory, drug debts and other drug trade-related issues, rather than to the psychopharmacological effects of drugs. In a substantial fraction of the cases where such effects might have been involved, the perpetrator had also consumed alcohol.

Finally, a body of evidence documents that violence is commonly used in a range of prohibited industries, independent of the characteristics of the good. Violence committed by pimps or johns against prostitutes is a well-documented feature of prostitution markets, in which prostitutes cannot easily report violence without risking legal sanctions themselves (see, for example, Lowman and Fraser, 1996 and also Chapter 7 of this volume). Similarly, violence was an important feature of the gambling industry during its early years in the USA, when entry was limited; the incidence has decreased as legal gambling has mushroomed. More broadly, violence is commonly used to resolve disputes in countries like Russia where the official dispute resolution system is ineffective.

In addition to promoting the use of violence in drug markets, prohibition promotes income-generating crime such as theft or prostitution. Prohibition raises drug prices compared with a legal market, as discussed

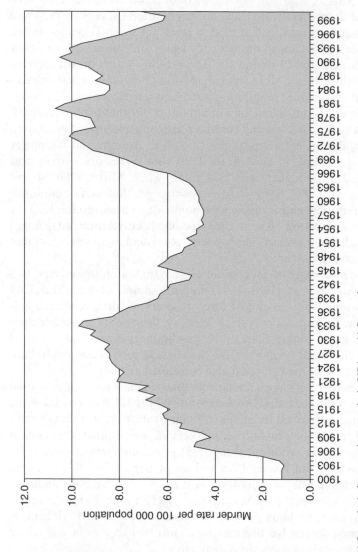

Note: 2001 figure includes terrorism attacks in USA on 11 September.

Source: National Center for Health Statistics, Vital Statistics.

Figure 2.3   Murder rate per 100 000 population in USA (1900–2001)

above, which means users require a higher real income to finance a given quantity of consumption. In many cases, such users would engage in criminal activity even if drugs sold for legal prices (many persons engage in income-generating crime to finance purchases of alcohol, TVs and the like), but prohibition appears to increase the amount of such crime. Greenberg and Adler (1974), for example, document that some individuals already inclined to commit crimes also happen to use drugs. Brown and Silverman (1974, 1980) and, as discussed in Chapter 1, Silverman and Spruill (1977) provide evidence that higher drug prices are associated with higher rates of income-generating crime.

A different kind of crime encouraged by prohibition is corruption of police, prosecutors, judges and politicians. This exists because lawsuits, lobbying and campaign contributions do not exist in a prohibited industry. In addition, drug traffickers have high profits to protect and thus added incentive to bribe or threaten those who might impede these profits. Evidence on the magnitude of corruption is difficult to obtain, but anecdotal evidence for such an effect is abundant (see, for example, US General Accounting Office, 1998).

The effects of prohibition in generating crime and corruption are especially prevalent in drug-producing countries (see, for example, Atkins, 1998; Melo, 1998 and Toro, 1998, concerning Bolivia, Columbia and Mexico respectively). Beyond the standard violence- and corruption-producing effects discussed above, prohibition promotes civil unrest by providing income to rebel groups such as the Shining Path in Peru, the FARC in Colombia, or, until recently, the Taliban in Afghanistan. Under prohibition, these groups sell protection services to drug traffickers. For instance, McClintock (1988) discusses the fact that prohibition efforts in the USA cemented a relation between Peruvian drug traffickers and the Shining Path during the 1980s.[4]

3.2 The effect of drug use on crime

The conclusion that prohibition, rather than drug use, causes most crime associated with drugs stands in contrast to the usual claim that drug use itself causes crime. Reviews of the literature have consistently concluded, however, that there is little evidence of a causal role for drugs, and to the extent that such evidence exists, it is stronger for alcohol (see, for example, Duke and Gross, 1993, pp. 37–42, 53–4, 64–6, 73–4 and US Department of Justice, 1992, p. 5). Fagan (1993) concludes: 'there is little evidence that alcohol or drugs directly cause violence' and that, 'several reviewers have concluded that alcohol is the substance most likely to lead to psychopharmacological violence' although, 'there is some evidence that cocaine, barbiturates, amphetamines, phencyclidine (PCP), and steroids also have psychopharmacological properties that can motivate violence'. He also notes that, 'the most consistent and predictable relationship between substances and violence is a result of trafficking in illicit drugs'.

The evidence usually offered as showing an effect of drug use on crime does not stand up to careful scrutiny. This evidence consists of statistics that document a high frequency of drug use among arrestees. For example, the National Institute of Justice (2000) documents that in the 34 cities monitored in 1999, at least 50 per cent of adult male arrestees tested positive for one or more illicit drugs. These statistics document that many criminals use drugs, but they do not demonstrate that drug use causes criminal behaviour.

First, the correlation between drug use and crime is contaminated by the fact that many arrests are for drug possession; the sense in which this shows drug use 'causes' crime is purely tautological. Second, these data provide no evidence that drug users were under the influence of drugs when they committed their crimes or any evidence that the influence was to make the user criminogenic. Bennet and Wright (1984) report the results of interviews with burglary offenders. Many report that they had consumed alcohol before committing their offence, and about a third said they committed their offence under the influence of alcohol. Most saw no causal relation, however. For example, these offenders suggested that they sometimes planned their offences while in drinking situations or that they just drank a lot generally. Given that a substantial percentage of criminals had consumed alcohol before commission of their crimes, at a minimum the standard evidence does not indicate which substance is implicated.[5]

In addition, the fact that many criminals are also drug users shows merely that drug use is correlated with criminal behaviour. The methodology used in these analyses would also demonstrate that consumption of fast food or wearing blue jeans causes criminal behaviour. If people from particular socio-economic groups engage in a range of illicit behaviour, then one will find this correlation independent of any effect of drug use on criminal behaviour. Thus, this kind of evidence is uninformative. Stated differently, the set of arrestees is not a random sample of the population. Data on the behaviour of arrestees do not indicate how many people consumed drugs without engaging in criminal behaviour (other than drug possession itself) and thus say nothing about the tendency of drug use to cause such behaviour.

4   Drugs, prohibition and the welfare of drug users

4.1   The impact of prohibition on drug quality

In addition to causing violence and other crime, prohibition has substantial effects on the welfare of drug users. As with crime, the usual view is that drug use itself is what damages the health or reduces the productivity of users. As with crime, however, prohibition plays a far more important role. This does not mean drug use is benign. But to the extent that drugs entail greater risk than a host of legal goods, the reason is prohibition rather than the properties of drugs themselves.[6]

The most obvious way in which prohibition may reduce the welfare of drug users is by subjecting them to legal penalties for purchasing or possessing drugs. Under prohibition, users risk arrest, fines, incarceration, loss of professional licences, public embarrassment and more, as the result of their drug use. These sanctions can be far worse than any effect of drug use per se.

A second way prohibition may harm drug users is by reducing quality control in the market for drugs. As we noted earlier, purchasers of a prohibited good cannot easily sue a seller of defective goods, while sellers of a quality product cannot easily attract business by advertising. Moreover, government agencies in the USA that monitor quality, such as the Food and Drug Administration or Federal Trade Commission, cannot easily monitor suppliers in an illicit market. While there are some instances of accidental overdoses and poisonings in a legal market and prohibition probably reduces the total amount of drug use, the evidence presented in this chapter suggests that prohibition's impact on drug consumption is modest and so accidental overdoses and poisonings are likely to be higher per unit of drug consumption under prohibition.

A number of examples illustrate this point. During Prohibition in the USA, deaths due to alcoholism rose relative to other proxies for alcohol consumption, presumably because consumption of adulterated alcohol increased (Miron and Zwiebel, 1991). Indeed, federal regulation required manufacturers of industrial alcohol to adulterate their product, knowing that much would be diverted to illicit consumption (Merz, 1932). In one case, an adulterant used by bootleggers to disguise alcohol as medicine turned out to cause permanent paralysis, victimizing thousands (Morgan, 1982). Similarly, the chemical paraquat, which the US government encouraged Mexico to spray on marijuana fields, caused sickness in many consumers (Duke and Gross, 1993).

Prohibition also creates an incentive for drugs to be marketed and consumed in the purest form possible. Suppliers prefer concentrated forms of drugs because these are easier to conceal from authorities. Consumers can dilute potent forms if they wish, but they typically lack reliable information on the purity of the drugs they purchase. This exacerbates the tendency toward accidental overdoses.

Another way that prohibition harms drug users is by raising drug prices. The direct effect is to require additional expenditure to finance a given quantity of drug consumption, which implies fewer resources for food, clothing, shelter or health care. Beyond this direct effect, however, the elevated prices caused by prohibition encourage users to employ risky consumption methods, like injection, that give the biggest bang for the buck. This harms users because of drug paraphernalia laws and prescription laws that restrict purchase of clean needles and syringes, thereby encouraging the sharing of needles contaminated with HIV and other blood-borne diseases (National Research Council, 1995).

A further way that prohibition harms drug users (and others) is by discouraging the medical use of drugs. Marijuana cannot be legally prescribed in most countries, despite evidence that it provides relief from nausea, pain and muscle spasms and alleviates symptoms of glaucoma, multiple sclerosis and migraine headaches, amongst other ailments (Grinspoon and Bakalar, 1993). Most opiates can be legally prescribed, but under prohibition doctors worry about legal or regulatory penalties and thus potentially underprescribe (*The New York Times*, 1994; Sullum, 1997).

Prohibition also harms drug users to the extent that it fosters drug-testing of employees and others. Drug-testing would exist even if drugs were legal, as argued in Chapter 3, especially for safety-sensitive or other high-skill occupations. Much drug-testing, however, results from government-mandated testing programmes that have emerged as a means of enforcing prohibition. Under these programmes, employees who test positive face sanctions like job loss even if they have never used drugs on the job.

4.2   *Drug use and addiction revisited*

The arguments above explain why prohibition causes many of the adverse consequences of drug use. In addition, the evidence suggesting that drug use itself causes reduced health, diminished productivity or other personal ills, is biased, exaggerated or misleading. One standard claim is that drug use is addictive.[7] There is some truth in this view, but drugs are far less addictive than commonly portrayed. One possible measure of addictiveness is the degree to which use continues after initial use. High continued use rates do not necessarily suggest addiction in the classic sense; if those who enjoy a particular good consume it frequently, the continued use rate will be high even if there is no addictiveness. But addiction does imply a high continued use rate, and this has been used frequently as a measure of addiction.

The data presented in Chapter 1 indicate that across all categories of drugs, at most a third of those who have ever used a drug say they have used that drug in the past year. This does not mean drugs are never addictive, but it fails to suggest a high degree of addictiveness. The fact that continued use rates for marijuana, which is not regarded as physically addictive, are similar to those for crack cocaine, which is regarded as highly addictive, also challenges the more extreme claims about addictiveness of drugs.[8] Relatedly, the continued use rates for alcohol and tobacco are even higher than those for illicit drugs, and casual observation suggests continued use rates for other legal goods are even higher (for example, chocolate, caffeine).

A different measure of addictiveness is the degree to which consumers use a particular substance casually or irregularly. The stereotypical depictions of addiction suggest that experimentation progresses inevitably into regular use and that irregular use occurs rarely. In fact, a sizeable percentage of heroin users consume only occasionally (Zinberg, 1979), and measurable withdrawal symptoms from opioids rarely occur until after several weeks of regular administration (Jaffee, 1991). Bennett (1986) discusses a literature search and interviews conducted during the 1980s with opiate users in the UK. His analysis suggests a modest degree of addictiveness. Few users are pushed into use by sellers; most start with friends or acquaintances. For most it takes months or years to become addicted. Many addicts voluntarily abstain for weeks, months or years, and many mature out of addiction. The most common reason given for using opiates is that users 'like them' and feel their lives are better on opioids. Many use opiates to self-medicate or to follow friends; few exhibited signs of compulsion.

Further evidence that addiction is less important than typical portrayals comes from the experience of returning Vietnam veterans. Robins et al. (1974) interviewed samples of veterans 8–12 months after their return from Vietnam. They found that most addicted veterans gave up their narcotic use voluntarily before departure or after a short, forced treatment period at departure. In subsequent work, Robins et al. (1980) document that although most veterans had access to cheap heroin in Vietnam, only about 35 per cent tried it and only about 19 per cent became addicted. They also conclude that heroin use does not consistently lead to daily use and addiction, that addiction frequently ceases without treatment, that maintaining recovery from heroin addiction does not require abstinence, and that the reason for high levels of social disability among heroin users is likely attributable to characteristics of the users rather than to heroin *per se*.

As with addiction, the negative health consequences of drug use are often overstated. All drugs carry some health risk, but the degree to which illicit drugs are physically detrimental is far less than generally portrayed, provided they are consumed under safe circumstances. *The Merck Manual*, a standard reference book on diagnosis and treatment of diseases (Merck & Co., Inc., 1992), states that, 'people who have developed tolerance [to heroin] may show few signs of drug use and function normally in their usual activities . . ... Many but not all complications of heroin addiction are related to unsanitary administration of the drug'. It also writes that, 'there is still little evidence of biologic damage [from marijuana] even among relatively heavy users'. Concerning cocaine, the manual does not mention effects of long-term use but emphasizes that all effects, including those that promote aggression, are short-lived. Many of the health risks discussed for all drugs result from overdoses or adulterated doses, not moderate or even heavy levels of use.

Similar evaluations appear elsewhere. These evaluations in no way imply that drug consumption is without risk; indeed, many highlight a range of adverse reactions and effects that can occur as a result of drug use. But they consistently indicate that such adverse reactions are not the norm and that even heavy, regular use can and does occur with modest or minimal negative consequences (see, in particular, Grinspoon and Bakalar, 1979 or Morgan and Zimmer, 1997 on cocaine; Grinspoon and Bakalar, 1993, Hall et al., 1994, British Medical Association, 1997 or O'Brien, 1996 on marijuana; Trebach, 1982 or Zinberg, 1979 on heroin).

A critical problem with standard depictions of the health consequences of drug use is that they rely on data sources that are biased towards those who suffer the worst consequences from drug use. One example is data from clients of drug treatment programmes. Such persons are presumably those who have had the worst experiences with drugs, but this does not demonstrate what the average or typical experience might be (just as data from alcohol treatment facilities would give a misleading impression about the typical consequences of alcohol consumption). Even a robust correlation between drug use and poor health does not indicate the effect of drug use on health, since drug use is often associated with a range of behaviours and characteristics that might be detrimental to health.

Similarly, many discussions fail to distinguish the effects of casual use from those of heavy use, or the effects that can occur for some users as opposed to those that usually occur for most users. Moderate doses of over-the-counter medications such as ibuprofen relieve pain effectively for millions of persons each day, but a large dose causes severe damage to the liver. Peanuts are an excellent food source that enhances health for most consumers, yet they can be deadly for persons who are allergic. Standard antibiotics such as penicillin provide relief from moderate to life-threatening diseases for most users but cause illness or death in persons who are allergic. These examples merely illustrate the general principle that many goods are beneficial in moderation even though potentially harmful in excess; likewise, many goods are beneficial to most persons even though they can be harmful for some persons.

4.3   Drug use and labour market outcomes

A different alleged harm of drug use is reduced income or likelihood of employment. According to this view, drug use inhibits concentration, coordination, motivation and other factors that contribute to successful job market experience. For example, widely-cited estimates of the costs of drug abuse suggest that drug use reduces productivity in the USA by tens of billions of dollars each year (Harwood et al., 1998). (See Miron, 2003b, for a critique of estimates of the costs of drug abuse.)

In fact, the existing evidence on the relation between drug use and labour market outcomes faces severe methodological difficulties. These studies utilize data on the wages and drug use of individuals, along with auxiliary information on demographic and economic characteristics such as age, education, occupation or experience. The basic analysis regresses wages on drug use plus measured individual characteristics. The problem is that drug use and wages are both plausibly correlated with unmeasured characteristics such as optimism, motivation, sociability, creativity or risk aversion. Thus, a finding that drug use and wages are correlated can reflect the influence of these omitted individual characteristics. Stated differently, the standard methodology is not experimental; it does not come from observing the behaviour of individuals who have been randomly assigned to different levels of drug use. Equivalently, there are no obvious instruments for drug use. Some analyses of this type employ two equation models, with the second having drug use as the dependent variable, but the identifying assumptions are implausible and are based mainly on non-linearities.

The results of existing studies of drug use and wages are therefore difficult to interpret at best. In addition, the results do not support the conclusion that drug use is associated with lower wages; a persistent puzzle in this literature is that the estimated relation between drug use and wages is often positive (see, for example, Kaestner, 1991, 1994a; Register and Williams, 1992; Gill and Michaels, 1992; Kenkel and Ribar, 1994, who obtain similar results for alcohol consumption).

The estimated relation between drug use and certain other labour market outcomes, such as employment status or hours worked, is more frequently negative, but even for these outcomes there are many 'paradoxical' results in the literature (see, for example, Zarkin et al., 1992; Kaestner, 1994b; Zarkin et al., 1998). Given the methodological problems that confront examination of this question, the right conclusion is that there is no evidence in either direction.

4.4 Drug use and accidents

An additional harm often attributed to drugs is automobile accidents caused by drivers under the influence. Such incidents are indeed a negative consequence of drug use, but several controlled studies indicate that marijuana has a smaller detrimental effect on driving performance than alcohol. Crancer et al. (1969) examine the simulated driving performance of subjects under the influence of marijuana and alcohol in comparison with a control group that consumed neither substance. They find that the marijuana consumers had more speedometer errors than under control conditions, but no significant difference in accelerator, brake, signal, steering or total errors. The alcohol group accumulated significantly more accelerator brake, signal, speedometer and total errors but no significant difference in steering errors (see also Smiley, 1986 or US Department of Transportation, 1993, 1999 for similar conclusions). The fact that marijuana appears to impair driving less than alcohol is especially relevant due to evidence (presented in Chapter 3) that marijuana and alcohol are substitutes in consumption.

A similar harm often linked to drug use is workplace accidents. The evidence that drugs cause a substantial number of accidents is at best mixed, and alcohol is implicated at least as often as illicit drugs (National Research Council, 1994). Kaestner and Grossman (1998) examine the relation between drug use and workplace accidents using the 1988 and 1992 National Longitudinal Survey of Youth (NLSY). For males, they find weak evidence that drug users have a higher accident rate than non-users; for females, they find no evidence of such an effect. Moreover, their evidence shows only whether drug users have elevated accident rates; it does not show in any way that drug use caused these accidents.

4.5   Drug use and the unborn fetus

A further problem potentially caused by drug use is harm to the unborn fetus. A vast literature examines the correlation between illicit drug use and adverse pregnancy outcomes such as low birth weight or shorter gestation length. There is no doubt that excessive use of certain substances can have negative effects on pregnancy outcomes, but careful evaluation of the evidence suggests the adverse effects of drugs have been drastically overstated. Many pregnant women consume legal substances like alcohol or tobacco that might also contribute to poor postnatal outcomes, but some studies do not control for legal substance use in assessing the effects of illicit drugs. Relatedly, many studies control imperfectly for other factors that affect pregnancy outcomes, including access to pre-natal care, income, presence of a father, nutrition, exercise or sleep habits. Further, as with studies of drug use and crime or drug use and productivity, even studies that control for a broad range of observed factors cannot address the unobserved differences across women that might simultaneously explain both drug use and poor pregnancy outcomes. In any event, the studies that exist do not consistently suggest substantial or necessarily persistent effects of drug use on children, and the negative effects that do occur are not obviously different from those of legal goods such as alcohol or cigarettes. (For detailed discussion of these issues, see Behnke and Eyler, 1993; Richardson, et al., 1993; US Department of Health and Human Services, 1996; Inciardi et al., 1997; LaGasse et al., 1999).

5 Conclusion

Standard accounts of drugs and drug markets often portray them as different from other goods, somehow defying the usual laws of supply and demand or requiring special economic principles or insights to become understandable. We have confirmed the findings of Chapter 1 that current drug markets do indeed exhibit characteristics that are rare or non-existent in other markets, but the main purpose of this chapter was to emphasize that these characteristics result from the legal status of drugs rather than from the characteristics of drugs themselves. Moreover, we demonstrated that a normative analysis of prohibition must distinguish between the effects of prohibition and the effects of drugs themselves and an obvious question raised by our analysis is whether prohibition is the best policy toward illicit drugs. By assessing a range of alternatives to prohibition, Chapter 3 addresses this issue.

Notes

1. The discussion in this section draws heavily on Miron and Zwiebel (1995) and Miron (1998, 1999, 2001a, 2001b, 2003a, 2004).
2. The Harrison Act did not prohibit marijuana; this resulted from the 1937 Marijuana Tax Act.
3. The discussion in this section draws heavily on Miron and Zwiebel (1995) and Miron (1998, 1999, 2001a, 2001b, 2004).
4. In addition to increasing 'drug-related' crime, prohibition can affect non-drug-related crime. Enforcement of prohibition potentially diverts resources from deterrence of other crime (Benson and Rasmussen, 1991; Benson et al., 1992; Rasmussen et al., 1993 and Sollars et al., 1994). Similarly, incarceration of drug offenders can crowd out incarceration of other criminals. Alternatively, incarceration of drug offenders might incapacitate persons who commit both drug and non-drug crime. On the last two effects, see Kuziemko and Levitt (2004).
5. Greenfeld (1998) summarizes data from the National Crime Victimization Survey, the Uniform Crime Reports, the National Incident-Based Reporting System, Bureau of Justice Statistics (BJS) surveys of probationers, jail and prison inmates, BJS censuses of prisons and jails, and the Fatal Accident Reporting System on the relation between alcohol consumption, drug use and crime of various types. The focus is mainly on alcohol; it contains less extensive data on drug use. With respect to alcohol, this review provides the standard type of data indicating an association between alcohol use and crime. For example, many victims of crime perceive that the offender had been drinking at the time of the offence.
6. The discussion in this section draws heavily on Miron and Zwiebel (1995) and Miron (1998, 2001a, 2004).
7. The discussion here takes as given that addiction *per se* is a negative consequence, but this view is open to debate (see Chapter 1 for a discussion of this issue).
8. While these data are potentially biased by under-reporting, and the degree of under-reporting with respect to recent use might be greater than with respect to lifetime use, there might be more forgetting of lifetime use than of recent use.

References

Atkins, A. (1998), 'The Economic and Political Impact of the Drug Trade and Drug Control Policies in Bolivia', in Elizabeth Joyce and Carlos Malamud (eds), *Latin America and the Multinational Drug Trade*, Great Britain: Macmillan Press Ltd.

Basov, S., M. Jacobson and J.A. Miron (2001), 'Prohibition and the Market for Illegal Drugs: An Overview of Recent History', *World Economics*, **2** (4), 133–58.

Behnke, M. and F.D. Eyler (1993), 'The Consequences of Prenatal Substance Use for the Developing Fetus, Newborn, and Young Child', *The International Journal of Addictions*, **28** (13), 1341–91.

Bennett, T.H. (1986), 'A Decision-Making Approach to Opioid Addiction', in Derek B. Cornish and Ronald V.G. Clarke (eds), *The Reasoning Criminal*, New York: Springer-Verlag, pp. 83–102.

Bennet, T. and R. Wright (1984), 'The Relationship Between Alcohol Use and Burglary', *British Journal of Addiction*, **79**, 431–7.

Benson, B.L. and D.W. Rasmussen (1991), 'The Relationship Between Illicit Drug Enforcement Policy and Property Crimes', *Contemporary Policy Issues*, **9**, 106–15.

Benson, B.L., I. Kim, D.W. Rasmussen and T.W. Zuehlke (1992), 'Is Property Crime Caused by Drug Use or by Drug Enforcement Policy?', *Applied Economics*, **24**, 679–92.

British Medical Association (1997), *Therapeutic Uses of Cannabis*, the Netherlands: Harwood Academic Publishers.

Brown, G.F. Jr. and L.P. Silverman (1974), 'The Retail Price of Heroin: Estimation and Applications', *Journal of the American Statistical Association*, **69** (347), 595–606.

Brown, G.F. Jr. and L.P. Silverman (1980), 'The Retail Price of Heroin: Estimation and Applications', in Irving Leveson (ed.), *Quantitative Explorations in Drug Abuse Policy*, New York: SP Medical and Scientific Books, pp. 25–53.

Brumm, H.J. and D.O. Cloninger (1995), 'The Drug War and the Homicide Rate: A Direct Correlation?', *Cato Journal*, **14** (3), 509–17.

Chaloupka, F.J. and A. Laixuthai (1997) 'Do Youths Substitute Alcohol and Marijuana? Some Econometric Evidence', *Eastern Economic Journal*, **23** (3), 253–76.

Crancer, A. Jr., J.M. Dille, J.C. Delay, J.E. Wallace and M.D. Haykin (1969), 'Comparison of the Effects of Marihuana and Alcohol on Simulated Driving Performance', *Science*, **164**, 851–4.

Dills, A. and J.A. Miron (2004), 'Alcohol Consumption and Alcohol Prohibition', *American Law and Economics Review*, **6** (2), 285–318.

DiNardo, J. (1993), 'Law Enforcement, the Price of Cocaine, and Cocaine Use', *Mathematical and Computer Modelling*, **17** (2), 53–64.

Duke, S.B. and A.C. Gross (1993), *America's Longest War: Rethinking Our Tragic Crusade Against Drugs*, New York: G.P. Putnam's Sons.

Fagan, J. (1993), 'Interactions Among Drugs, Alcohol, and Violence', *Journal of Health Affairs*, Winter, 65–79.

Fajnzylber, P., D. Lederman and N. Loazya (1998), 'Determinants of Crime Rates in Latin America and the World: An Empirical Assessment', Washington, DC: World Bank.

Fajnzylber, P., D. Lederman and N. Loazya (1999), 'Inequality and Violent Crime', World Bank, manuscript.

Friedman, M. (1991), 'The War We Are Losing', in Melvyn B. Krauss and Edward P. Lazear (eds), *Searching for Alternatives: Drug-Control Policy in the United States*, Stanford, California: Hoover Institution Press, pp. 53–67.

Gill, A.M. and R.J. Michaels (1992), 'Does Drug Use Lower Wages?', *Industrial and Labor Relations Review*, **45** (3), 419–34.

Goldstein, P.J., H.H. Brownstein, P.J. Ryan and P.A. Bellucci (1989), 'Crack and Homicide in New York City, 1988: A Conceptually Based Event Analysis', *Contemporary Drug Problems*, Winter, 651–87.

Goldstein, P.J., H.H. Brownstein, P.J. Ryan and P.A. Belluci (1997), 'Crack and Homicide in New York City: A Case Study in the Epidemiology of Violence', in Craig Reinarman and

Harry G. Levine (eds), *Crack in America: Demon Drugs and Social Justice*, Berkeley: University of California Press, pp. 113–30.

Green, E. and R. Porter (1984), 'Noncooperative Collusion under Imperfect Price Information', *Econometrica*, **52**, 87–100.

Greenberg, S.W. and F. Adler (1974), 'Crime and Addiction: An Empirical Analysis of the Literature, 1920–1973', *Contemporary Drug Problems*, **3**, 221–69.

Greenfeld, L.A. (1998), 'Alcohol and Crime: An Analysis of National Data on the Prevalence of Alcohol Involvement in Crime', Washington, DC: Office of Justice Programs, US Department of Justice.

Grinspoon, L. and J.B. Bakalar (1979), 'Cocaine', in Robert L. Dupont, Avram Goldstein and John O'Donnell (eds), *Handbook on Drug Abuse*, Washington, DC: NIDA.

Grinspoon, Lester and James B. Bakalar (1993), *Marihuana: The Forbidden Medicine*, New Haven: Yale University Press.

Hall, W., N. Solowij and J. Lemon (1994), 'The Health and Psychological Consequences of Cannabis Use', Canberra: Australian Government Publishing Service.

Harwood, H., D. Fountain and G. Livermore (1998), 'The Economic Costs of Alcohol and Drug Abuse in the United States, 1992', Rockville, Maryland: US Department of Health and Human Services.

Inciardi, J.A., H.L. Surratt and C.A. Saum (1997), *Cocaine-Exposed Infants: Social, Legal, and Public Health Issues*, Thousand Oaks, CA: Sage Publications.

Jaffee, J.H. (1991), 'Opiates', in Ilana Glass (ed.), *The International Handbook of Addictive Behaviors*, pp. 64–8.

Kaestner, R. (1991), 'The Effect of Illicit Drug Use on the Wages of Young Adults', *Journal of Labor Economics*, **9** (4), 381–412.

Kaestner, R. (1994a), 'New Estimates of the Effect of Marijuana and Cocaine Use on Wages', *Industrial and Labor Relations Review*, **47** (3), 454–70.

Kaestner, R. (1994b), 'The Effect of Illicit Drug Use on the Labor Supply of Young Adults', *Journal of Human Resources*, **29** (1), 126–55.

Kaestner, R. and M. Grossman (1998), 'The Effect of Drug Use on Workplace Accidents', *Journal of Labor Economics*, **5**, 267–94.

Kenkel, D.S. and D.C. Ribar (1994), 'Alcohol Consumption and Young Adults' Socioeconomic Status', *Brookings Papers: Microeconomics*, 119–75.

Kuziemko, I. and S.D. Levitt (2004), 'An Empirical Analysis of Imprisoning Drug Offenders', *Journal of Public Economics*, **88** (9–10), 2043–66.

LaGasse, L.L., R. Seifer and B.M. Lester (1999), 'Interpreting Research on Prenatal Substance Exposure in the Context of Multiple Confounding Factors', *Clinics in Perinatology*, **26** (1), 39–54.

Lerner, R. (1998), 'The Drug Trade in Peru', in Elizabeth Joyce and Carlos Malamud (eds), *Latin America and the Multinational Drug Trade*, Great Britain: Macmillan Press Ltd.

Lowman, J. and L. Fraser (1996), 'Violence Against Persons Who Prostitute: The Experience in British Columbia', Technical Report 1996–14e, Department of Justice Canada.

MacCoun, R.J. and P. Reuter (1997), 'Interpreting Dutch Cannabis Policy: Reasoning by Analogy in the Legalization Debate', *Science*, **278**, 47–52.

MacCoun, Robert J. and Peter Reuter (2001), *Drug War Heresies: Learning from Other Vices, Times, and Places*, Cambridge: Cambridge University Press.

McClintock, C. (1988), 'The War on Drugs: The Peruvian Case', *Journal of Interamerican Studies and World Affairs*, **30** (Summer/Fall), 127–41.

Melo, J.O. (1998), 'The Drug Trade, Politics, and the Economy: The Colombian Experience', in Elizabeth Joyce and Carlos Malamud (eds), *Latin America and the Multinational Drug Trade*, Great Britain: Macmillan Press Ltd.

Merck & Co., Inc. (1992), *The Merck Manual of Diagnosis and Therapy*, 16th edition, Robert Berkow (ed.), Rahway, NJ: Merck Research Laboratories.

Merz, Charles (1932), *The Dry Decade*, Garden City, NY: Doubleday, Doran and Co.

Miron, J.A. (1998), 'Drug Prohibition', in Peter Newman (ed.), *The New Palgrave Dictionary of Economics and the Law*, London: The Macmillan Press, pp. 648–52.

Miron, J.A. (1999), 'Violence and the U.S. Prohibitions of Drugs and Alcohol', *American Law and Economics Review*, 1–2 (Fall), 78–114.

Miron, J.A. (2001a), 'The Economics of Drug Prohibition and Drug Legalization', *Social Research*, **68** (3), 835–55.

Miron, J.A. (2001b), 'Violence, Guns, and Drugs: A Cross-Country Analysis', *Journal of Law and Economics*, **2** (4), 615–33.

Miron, J.A. (2002a), 'Review of Drug War Heresies: Learning from Other Vices, Times, & Places', by Robert J. MacCoun and Peter Reuter, *The Independent Review*, **7** (2), 297–300.

Miron, J.A. (2002b), 'The Effect of Marijuana Decriminalization on the Budgets of Massachusetts Governments, With a Discussion of Decriminalization's Effect on Marijuana Use', Report to the Drug Policy Forum of Massachusetts, October, 2002.

Miron, J.A. (2003a), 'Do Prohibitions Raise Prices? Evidence from the Markets for Cocaine and Heroin', *Review of Economics and Statistics*, **85** (3), 522–30.

Miron, J.A. (2003b), 'A Critique of Estimates of the Economic Cost of Drug Abuse', manuscript, Boston University, manuscript.

Miron, Jeffrey A. (2004), *Drug War Crimes: The Consequences of Prohibition*, Independent Institute.

Miron, J.A. and J. Zwiebel (1991), 'Alcohol Consumption During Prohibition', *American Economic Review*, **81**, 242–7.

Miron, J.A. and J. Zwiebel (1995), 'The Economic Case Against Drug Prohibition', *Journal of Economic Perspectives*, **9** (4), 175–92.

Morgan, J.P. (1982), 'The Jamaica Ginger Paralysis', *Journal of the American Medical Association*, **245** (15), 1864–7.

Morgan, J.P. and L. Zimmer (1997), 'The Social Pharmacology of Smokeable Cocaine: Not All It's Cracked up to Be', in Craig Reinarman and Harry G. Levine (eds), *Crack in America: Demon Drugs and Social Justice*, Berkeley: University of California Press, pp. 131–70.

Musto, David F. (1973), *The American Disease*, New Haven: Yale University Press.

National Institute of Justice (2000), '1999 Annual Report on Drug Use Among Adult and Juvenile Arrestees', Washington: US Department of Justice, Office of Justice Programs.

National Research Council (1994), 'Under the Influence? Drugs and the American Work Force', Jacques Normand, Richard O. Lempert and Charles P. O'Brien (eds), Washington, DC: National Academy Press.

National Research Council (1995), 'Preventing HIV Transmission: The Role of Sterile Needles and Bleach', Washington, DC: National Academy Press.

New York Times, The (1994), 'It Pains a Nation of Stoics to Say "No" to Pain', 3 April, p. E5.

O'Brien, C.P. (1996), 'Drug Addiction and Drug Abuse', in *Goodman and Gilman's The Pharmacological Basis of Therapeutics*, 9th edition, Joel G. Hardman, Lee E. Limbird, Perry B. Molinoff and Raymond W. Ruddon (eds), New York: McGraw-Hill.

Pacula, R.L., J.F. Chriqui and J. King (2003), 'Marijuana Decriminalization: What Does it Mean in the United States?', National Bureau of Economic Research Working Paper No. 9690.

Rasmussen, D.W., B.L. Benson and D.L. Sollars (1993), 'Spatial Competition in Illicit Drug Markets: The Consequences of Increased Drug Law Enforcement', *Review of Regional Studies*, **23** (3), 219–36.

Register, C.A. and D.R. Williams (1992), 'Labor Market Effects of Marijuana and Cocaine Use Among Young Men', *Industrial and Labor Relations Review*, **45** (3), 435–48.

Resignato, A.J. (2000), 'Violent Crime: A Function of Drug Use or Drug Enforcement?', *Applied Economics*, **32**, 681–8.

Reuter, P. (2001), 'The Limits of Supply-Side Drug Control', *Milken Institute Review*, **3** (1), 14–23.

Richardson, G.A., N.J. Day and P.J. McGauhey (1993), 'The Impact of Prenatal Marijuana and Cocaine Use on the Infant and Child', *Clinical Obstetrics and Gynecology*, **36** (2), 302–18.

Robins, L.N., D.H. Davis and D.N. Nurco (1974), 'How Permanent Was Vietnam Drug Addiction?', *American Journal of Public Health*, **64**, 38–43.

Robins, L.N., J.E. Helzer, M. Hesselbrock and E. Wish (1980), 'Vietnam Veterans Three Years After Vietnam: How Our Study Changed Our View of Heroin', in Leon Brill and Charles Winick (eds), *The Yearbook of Substance Use and Abuse*, vol. 2, New York: Human Sciences.

Silverman, L.P. and N.L. Spruill (1977), 'Urban Crime and the Price of Heroin', *Journal of Urban Economics*, 4, 80–103.

Smiley, A. (1986), 'Marijuana: On-Road and Driving Simulator Studies', *Alcohol, Drugs, and Driving*, 2 (3–4), 121–34.

Sollars, D.L., B.L. Benson and D.W. Rasmussen (1994), 'Drug Enforcement and the Deterrence of Property Crime Among Local Jurisdictions', *Public Finance Quarterly*, 22 (1), 22–45.

Sullum, J. (1997), 'No Relief in Sight', *Reason*, 28, 22–9.

Toro, M.C. (1998), 'The Political Repercussions of Drug Trafficking in Mexico', in Elizabeth Joyce and Carlos Malamud (eds), *Latin America and the Multinational Drug Trade*, Great Britain: Macmillan Press Ltd.

Trebach, Arnold S. (1982), *The Heroin Solution*, New Haven: Yale University Press.

US Department of Health and Human Services (1996), 'Behavioral Studies of Drug-Exposed Offspring: Methodological Issues in Human and Animal Research', Cora Lee Wetherington, Vincent L. Smeriglio and Loretta P. Finnegan (eds), *National Institute on Drug Abuse Research Monograph 164*, Rockville, MD: NIDA.

US Department of Justice (1992), 'Drugs, Crime and the Justice System', NCJ-133752, Washington, DC: USGPO.

US Department of Transportation (1993), 'Marijuana and Actual Driving Performance', Washington, DC.

US Department of Transportation (1999), 'Marijuana, Alcohol, and Actual Driving Performance', Springfield, VA: National Technical Information Service.

US General Accounting Office (1998), 'Law Enforcement: Information on Drug-Related Police Corruption', Report to the Honorable Charles B. Rangel, House of Representatives, Washington, DC: USGAO.

United National Office for Drug Control and Crime Prevention (2003), 'Global Illicit Drug Trends 2002', ODCCP Studies on Drugs and Crime (www.undcp.org/ global_illicit_drug_trends.html).

Yuan, Y. and J.P Caulkins (1998), 'The Effect of Variation in High-Level Domestic Drug Enforcement on Variation in Drug Prices', *Socio-Economic Planning Sciences*, 32 (4), 265–76.

Zarkin, G.A., M.T. French and J. Valley Rachal (1992), 'The Relationship Between Illicit Drug Use and Labor Supply', Research Triangle Institute, manuscript.

Zarkin, G.A., T.A. Mroz, J.W. Bray and M.T. French (1998), 'The Relationship Between Drug Use and Labor Supply for Young Men', *Journal of Labor Economics*, 5, 385–409.

Zinberg, N.E. (1979), 'Non-Addictive Opiate Use', in Robert L. Dupont, Avram Goldstein and John O'Donnell (eds), *Handbook on Drug Abuse*, Washington, DC: National Institute on Drug Abuse.

3 Economics of drug liberalization
Mark Thornton, Bruce L. Benson and
Simon W. Bowmaker

In Chapter 2, we drew attention to the many unintended consequences of drug prohibition, including violent crime and corruption, and suggested that prohibition causes or exacerbates the various risks associated with illicit drug use. Tullock and McKenzie (1985) argue that economists have always been anti-prohibition, dating back to the days of the ban on alcohol in the USA:

> In the early part of this century, many well-intentioned Americans objected to the consumption of alcoholic beverages. They succeeded in getting the Constitution amended to prohibit the sale of alcohol. By the 1930s most of them had given up because they discovered how difficult it was to enforce the law. If they had consulted economists, I'm sure they would have been told that the law would be very difficult and expensive to enforce. With this advice they might have decided not to undertake the program of moral elevation. The same considerations should, of course, be taken into account now with respect to other drugs.

There have been exceptions, however. Irving Fisher, one of the USA's greatest mathematical economists, was a leading proponent of alcohol prohibition. As late as 1927, Fisher claimed he could not find one economist to speak out against prohibition at a meeting of the American Economic Association, and in *The Noble Experiment*, published in 1930, Fisher clearly remained a strong believer in the virtues of alcohol prohibition:

> Summing up, it may be said that Prohibition has already accomplished incalculable good, hygienically, economically and socially. Real personal liberty, the liberty to give and enjoy the full use of our faculties, is increased by Prohibition. All that the wets can possibly accomplish is laxity of enforcement or nullification: in other words, enormously to increase the very disrespect for the law which they profess to deplore. Hence the only satisfactory solution lies in fuller enforcement of the law.

More recently, Thornton (1995, 2004) reports that in relation to illicit drugs, the majority of economists (in the USA at least) are relatively anti-prohibition. He reports the findings of a survey he conducted in 1995 of 117 randomly selected professional economists based on membership of the American Economic Association. Of those who offered an opinion,

58 per cent were in favour of drug policy in the USA being steered toward decriminalization of drugs. Only 16 per cent favoured complete legalization, while 71 per cent of those who gave a response other than keeping the status quo, favoured either legalization or decriminalization. Less than 2 per cent supported stronger prohibition other than longer prison sentences and increased enforcement budgets.

In a separate survey, conducted in 2004, Thornton solicited the views of US economists who are actively engaged in drug policy research. Three general conclusions emerged. First, most argued that the current policy of prohibition in the USA is fairly ineffective, very ineffective or even harmful (as suggested in Chapter 2). Second, most agreed that the current policy stance ought to be shifted. Third, most believed that this shift ought to be in the direction of liberalization. A source of disagreement, however, centred on the degree of liberalization.

Therefore, the purpose of this chapter is to examine the results of an economy shifting its drug policy away from prohibition toward some form of legalization. We begin in Section 1 with a precise description of current drug policies in both Europe and the USA. This is followed by an analysis of the following policy approaches toward illicit drugs: government monopoly (Section 2), regulation (Section 3), sin taxes (Section 4) and the free market (Section 5). Examples are given from drug and non-drug markets and the potential costs and benefits of each policy are evaluated in light of theoretical analysis as well as historical and contemporary evidence. Section 6 concludes the chapter.

1 Drug policy in Europe and the USA: an overview
In recent years, Europe has continued to move away from stereotypical US-styled 'war on drugs' ideology. The shift has been characterized by recognition that illicit drug use is a health issue (an addiction, an illness) rather than a crime issue. In view of this, alternative measures implemented and currently under debate in Europe include legalization (permitting commercial sales), decriminalization (eliminating user sanctions) and harm reduction (medical provision of heroin to addicts, for instance).

1.1 European demand-side policies
It should be noted that many European nations have had a drug policy of de facto decriminalization for many years, but it is only recently that governments have been amending their legislation to reduce or remove criminal penalties for illicit drug use and possession. In 2001, for example, Belgium, Finland, Greece, Luxembourg, Portugal and Switzerland drafted, proposed or approved legislation for the decriminalization of minor drug use and possession, in most cases for marijuana. In the UK in 2004, the

declassification of marijuana from a Class B drug to a Class C drug took effect, representing the first major change to UK drug policy since the introduction of the 1971 Misuse of Drugs Act. Under the new law, possession of marijuana remains illegal but will ordinarily not be an arrestable offence.

In the Netherlands, contrary to many perceptions, marijuana possession also remains illegal, but is tolerated by the Dutch authorities. In 1976, under the auspices of the separation of markets concept, the Dutch revised their Opium Act to separate the 'hard' drug market from the 'soft' drug market and prevent soft drug users from interacting with hard drugs. One consequence of the change in laws was the emergence of 'coffee shops' throughout the nation, offering marijuana products for sale. By 1997, there were around 1200 such shops operating in the Netherlands but this number had fallen to 782 by 2002 as Dutch authorities closed premises because of nuisance complaints and code violations[1] (Osborn, 2003).

Table 3.1 summarizes the position of a number of European countries on the issue of decriminalization of illicit drug use. It shows that while not every European country has either reduced or removed penalties for minor drug offences, all have taken steps to provide a variety of treatment and harm reduction measures. For example, Sweden, seen as one of Europe's 'hard-liners' on illicit drugs, offers a suspension of prison sentence for minor drugs offences on condition that the offender seeks treatment under a 'treatment contract' (DEA, 2002).

In the past, drug substitution programmes typically consisted of treating heroin addicts with declining doses of methadone, which was pioneered by the Swiss. Today, several European nations, including Switzerland, now offer maintenance programmes, which, like other harm reduction measures, are intended to regulate the drug use of those who are unwilling to seek traditional forms of treatment. Maintenance programmes usually relate to an opiate such as morphine or heroin, but methadone is still most common. A number of countries in Europe also offer heroin prescription. Heroin is prescribed in the UK, for instance, through general practitioners to an estimated 500 clients (EMCDDA, 2003).

It was the rapid spread of the HIV virus among intravenous drug users in the 1980s that induced many European nations to seek such measures that would reduce the harmful effects of illicit drug use for those who refused treatment. A wide variety of these so-called harm reduction measures have developed throughout Europe. The most common are needle-exchange programmes, pill testing and consumption rooms (sometimes referred to as 'shooting galleries').

Needle-exchange programmes are used widely in France (in 87 out of 100 départements) and the French government subsidizes pill-testing

Table 3.1   *European approaches to reducing drug-related crime and harm (as at 2004)*

	Substitution treatment	Heroin prescription	Pill testing	Consumption rooms	Needle exchange	Decriminalization of personal use	Decriminalization of use
Austria	Yes	No	Yes	No	Yes	Yes	All drugs
Belgium	Yes	No	Yes	No	Yes	Yes	Marijuana
France	Yes	No	Yes	No	Yes	No	
Germany	Yes	Yes	Yes	Yes	Yes	Yes	All drugs
Greece	Yes	No	No	No	Yes	No	
Italy	Yes	No	No	No	Yes	Yes	All drugs
Netherlands	Yes	Yes	Yes	Yes	Yes	Yes	All drugs
Portugal	Yes	No	No	Yes	Yes	Yes	All drugs
Spain	Yes	No	Yes	Yes	Yes	Yes	All drugs
Sweden	Yes	No	No	No	Yes	No	
Switzerland	Yes	Yes	Yes	Yes	Yes	Yes	All drugs
United Kingdom	Yes	Yes	Yes	No	Yes	Yes	Marijuana

Source: The Senlis Council (2004).

71

Table 3.2   Quantity of illicit drug seizures in Europe (1985–2000)

	Cannabis (kg)	Ecstasy (tablets)	LSD (doses)	Heroin (kg)	Cocaine (kg)	Amphetamines (kg)
1985	131 146	n.a.	52 190	1 990	1 043	277
1986	164 641	n.a.	187 076	2 076	1 925	404
1987	167 304	1 217	124 207	2 312	3 912	582
1988	263 701	9 742	119 952	2 876	6 751	486
1989	224 279	51 528	177 386	2 864	7 788	383
1990	274 874	65 479	375 147	4 666	16 439	630
1991	320 379	530 956	238 595	6 029	16 508	891
1992	372 841	661 174	809 803	5 389	17 693	1 307
1993	516 666	2 568 963	1 164 561	4 809	16 892	1 674
1994	743 473	2 593 275	401 084	5 889	29 013	2 026
1995	778 417	2 663 754	585 151	5 265	20 699	1 605
1996	674 081	9 962 120	438 275	5 542	32 304	3 534
1997	764 698	4 349 845	320 358	5 815	43 207	5 266
1998	831 074	6 235 902	152 737	4 979	31 611	4 800
1999	819 598	14 874 024	121 621	7 138	43 366	3 871
2000	758 812	19 295 458	124 373	8 811	26 242	3 218

Notes: Countries under study are Belgium, Denmark, Germany, Greece, Spain, France, Ireland, Italy, Luxembourg, Netherlands, Austria, Portugal, Finland, Sweden, UK, Norway.

Source: EMCDDA.

projects[2] (EMCDDA, 2003). About five million syringes are distributed or sold each year in Switzerland, about 25 per cent of them through pharmacies (EMCDDA, 2003). Drug consumption rooms are found in 39 European cities, where users can take drugs obtained elsewhere, under supervision, in hygienic conditions, without fear of arrest (EMCDDA, 2004).

1.2   European supply-side policies
While many European nations are focusing on treating and reducing the harm caused by illicit drug use, most are also continuing to employ substantial enforcement resources against the supply of illicit drugs. As Table 3.2 shows, the quantity of illicit drugs in Europe seized over the 1985 to 2000 period has generally been increasing.

Stricter penalties on those organizations and individuals that traffic illicit drugs in Europe are also being introduced. In countries such as Austria, France, Greece and the UK, drug trafficking can result in sentences up to life imprisonment, while in Luxembourg, supplying illicit drugs to minors carries a penalty of up to lifelong forced labour.

The UK in particular has stepped up its efforts in recent years to dismantle and punish drug trafficking organizations. In 1995, the 1994 Drug Trafficking Act was implemented, which allows the court to assume that all current assets, including any owned by the offender during the previous six years, are the result of trafficking offences. Unless the offender can prove otherwise, the court may seize these assets. Further, the 2003 Proceeds of Crime Act established an Assets Recovery Agency, which grants police and customs officers powers to seize and search for money generated from drug trafficking.

The penal procedure and the drug classification system determine the trafficking penalties in the UK. The 1971 Misuse of Drugs Act divides controlled substances into three classes: A, B and C. Class A (which includes 'hard drugs' such as cocaine and heroin) trafficking is punishable by up to life imprisonment and, in 2000, the Powers of the Criminal Courts Act established a minimum seven-year sentence for a third conviction of Class A drug trafficking. Moreover, in 2001, the Criminal Justice and Police Act empowered courts in the UK to strengthen controls on convicted traffickers. For instance, a ban can be placed on all overseas travel of a convicted trafficker for up to four years in an attempt to reduce his or her opportunity to re-engage in trafficking activities (DEA, 2002).

1.3   US demand-side policy

In Chapter 2, we noted that enforcement of drug prohibition in the USA has increased dramatically over the past 30 years. However, the widespread perception that the USA has a uniformly aggressive prohibitionist policy is actually somewhat misleading. Policy implementation clearly varies over time, across types of drugs and across enforcement jurisdictions. For instance, consider policy toward marijuana consumption. In 2000, 46.5 per cent of all drug arrests in the USA were for marijuana offences (Federal Bureau of Investigation, 2000), and possession charges accounted for almost 88 per cent of these arrests. This suggests that prohibition remains the dominant policy in the USA regarding marijuana.

Yet, there are important offsetting trends in demand-side policy that should be recognized. By some indicators at least, both the probability and severity of punishment for marijuana possession offences appear to be declining in many states, for instance, often despite increasing arrests. Also, consider the fact that during the 1970s 11 states 'decriminalized' marijuana possession and use by significantly reducing their criminal sanctions against marijuana possession.[3] While no additional decriminalization occurred in the 1980s, Arizona decriminalized in 1996,

Nevada did so in 2001 (indeed, Nevada had a referendum to legalize marijuana in 2003, and while it failed to pass, about a third of the voters supported it), and similar policies have received considerable political attention in other states.[4] A number of other states have sharply reduced penalties for marijuana possession, particularly after 1989, even though they have not fully decriminalized (Pacula et al., 2003). For instance, seven additional states have specified first-time marijuana possession as a non-criminal offence.[5] Furthermore, medical uses of marijuana have been legalized in several states during the last decade, despite strong federal resistance.

Liberalization trends for heroin and cocaine can also be detected in many states. A growing number of arrested drug users are being diverted out of traditional criminal justice punishment options into programmes focusing on treatment rather than incarceration. These treatment programmes are still backed by threats of criminal justice system sanctions, however, unlike voluntary treatment programmes or treatment programmes run through public health agencies. For instance, the first 'drug court' was established in Miami, Florida in 1989, and as of 8 January 2003 the model had been adopted, with various modifications, in 1424 jurisdictions, with at least one such programme in all 50 states, the District of Columbia, Guam, Puerto Rico and at least two Federal Court Districts.

Drug courts are judge-supervised treatment programmes, often in lieu of a criminal conviction and/or sentence, which require regular appearances before the judge, mandatory participation in treatment, frequent drug-testing (typically once per week), the potential for sanctions such as short jail terms for positive drug tests or other failures to meet the programme requirements (for example, perhaps finding and keeping a job), and the ultimate threat of diversion into regular criminal justice sanctions if the participant is judged to be not living up to the mandates of the programme. In other words, such coercive treatment programmes keep the criminal justice system at the centre of drug policy even as drug abuse is implicitly or explicitly being recognized as a medical issue.

1.4   US supply-side policy

Again, let us start with marijuana policy. The federal government continues to treat marijuana as a 'Schedule I' substance (in the same category as opiates, cocaine and other hard drugs), with significant statutory penalties for use, but the major focus is on suppliers. To illustrate the supply-side federal prohibitionist focus, and the relatively large and expanding role of marijuana in this context, consider drug seizures as an indicator of drug control effort. Table 3.3 shows federal drug seizures by drug type over the 1990 to 2002 period.

Table 3.3   *Pounds of illicit drugs seized by US federal authorities by drug type (1990–2002)*

Fiscal year	Heroin	Cocaine	Marijuana	Hashish
1990	1 704	235 885	483 353	17 062
1991	3 067	246 325	499 097	178 211
1992	2 552	303 289	783 477	4 048
1993	3 516	244 315	772 086	26 080
1994	2 898	309 710	1 041 445	1 625
1995	2 569	234 105	1 308 171	32 020
1996	3 737	253 297	1 429 786	32 096
1997	3 121	252 329	1 488 362	53 051
1998	3 499	266 029	1 777 434	596
1999	2 733	284 631	2 282 313	1 678
2000	6 640	248 827	2 614 746	23 987
2001	4 392	239 957	2 674 826	433
2002	6 900	225 122	2 412 365	193

Source: Federal-wide Drug Seizure System (FDSS).

By this measure at least, federal efforts against marijuana have become increasingly dominant over time, but because the federal focus is on supply-side enforcement (interdiction, pursuit of traffickers), not demand-side enforcement (only a very small portion of the drug offenders sentenced to federal prisons are convicted for possession), they have not increased marijuana-related arrests the way the states in aggregate have. Of course, it must be recognized that marijuana is much more difficult to hide than most other drugs, so seizure efforts should be more successful against marijuana. It should also be noted that seizure efforts are not just focused on drugs themselves. Seizures of money and other assets allegedly associated with drug market activity (for example, used in transportation or in transactions, purchased with proceeds from drug sales) are an important focus as well.

The federal emphasis on the supply-side is also illustrated in Table 3.4, which shows recent federal drug control spending by function. Note that demand-side budgets for treatment and prevention (and for treatment and prevention research) have been continually expanding, but supply-side budgets for international policy initiatives, interdiction and domestic law enforcement spending (money used for the criminal justice system, research on criminal justice policy and intelligence, which certainly could be for either demand- or supply-side enforcement, but is in fact mostly

Table 3.4 US federal drug control spending (US$ million) by function (1997–2005 fiscal years)

Function	1997[1]	1998[1]	1999[1]	2000[2]	2001[2]	2002[2]	2003[2]	2004[2]	2005[3]
Drug treatment	1823.1	1795.2	1997.4	1990.9	2086.5	2236.8	2264.6	2421.1	2494.3
Drug prevention	1106.9	1330.8	1407.6	1445.8	1540.8	1629.0	1553.6	1550.4	1139.0
Prevention research	309.6	322.2	373.5	421.6	489.0	547.8	611.4	607.2	615.4
Treatment research	206.5	219.6	249.9	280.8	326.8	367.4	382.9	412.4	423.1
Demand-side total	3446.1	3667.7	4028.4	4139.1	4443.1	4781.0	4812.4	4991.1	5079.2
Domestic law enforcement	1836.3	1937.5	2100.6	2238.3	2462.8	2794.7	2954.1	3182.9	3289.2
Interdiction	1549.3	1406.5	2155.6	1904.4	1895.3	1913.7	2147.5	2534.1	2662.9
International	389.9	464.0	746.3	1619.2	617.3	1084.5	1105.1	1159.3	1131.3
Supply-side total	3775.5	3808	5002.5	5761.9	4975.4	5792.9	6206.7	6876.3	7083.4

Notes:
[1] Actual;
[2] Final;
[3] Enacted.

Source: Office of National Drug Control Policy (ONDCP).

focused on the supply-side) is always higher and increasing in aggregate, except for the reduction in 2001. Furthermore, supply-side spending has been rising at a faster overall rate than demand-side spending, indicating that federal legislators and bureaucrats are in general agreement on enforcement focus.

At the state level, the aggregate data regarding policies against drug trafficking do not provide a clear picture of trends, for similar reasons to those that create confusion about the overall direction of demand-side policy changes. Arrests for trafficking have been falling in recent years (the opposite of possession arrests), while convictions appear to be on an upward trend (see Table 3.5). These two factors imply that the likelihood of conviction given arrest is rising. Countering this is the apparent reduction in the likelihood of imprisonment for felony trafficking convictions (see Table 3.6). Similarly, trafficking sentences are declining, although reduced sentences are largely offset by increasing portions of sentences served (see Tables 3.7 and 3.8 respectively).

In other words, in aggregate, courts appear to have a different policy agenda (reducing both the likelihood and length of prison sentences) than legislators (building prisons so the portion of sentence served increases), as with possession, while police appear to be increasing focus on possession arrests. Countering this is the increasing level of seizure activity we noted earlier. In fact, many observers of US drug policy trends suggest that the dramatic increase in enforcement that occurred in the last half of the 1980s is a result of changes in asset seizure laws, which mandated that policing agencies could keep the proceeds from their seizure effort (see Rasmussen and Benson, 1994; Benson et al., 1995), rather than placing these revenues into general fund accounts or other non-criminal justice accounts

Table 3.5 Felony drug convictions in US State Courts (1992–2002)

Year	Total drug convictions	Possession convictions	Trafficking convictions	Marijuana trafficking convictions
1992	280 232	109 426	170 806	16 376
1994	274 245	108 815	165 430	15 931
1996	347 774	135 270	212 504	20 618
1998	314 626	119 443	195 183	22 975
2000	319 700	116 300	203 400	25 300
2002	340 330	127 530	212 810	21 340

Source: Bureau of Justice Statistics, 'Felony Sentences in State Courts', 1992, 1994, 1996, 1998, 2000, 2002 (published every other year).

Table 3.6   *Percentage of felony drug convictions in US State Courts sentenced to prison, jail, and probation (1992–2002)*

Year	Possession			Trafficking		
	Prison	Jail	Probation	Prison	Jail	Probation
1992	33	29	38	48	27	25
1994	34	32	34	48	23	29
1996	29	41	30	39	33	27
1998	36	29	35	45	26	29
2000	33	31	36	41	28	31
2002	34	28	38	42	26	32

Source: Bureau of Justice Statistics, 'Felony Sentences in State Courts', 1992, 1994, 1996, 1998, 2000, 2002 (published every other year).

Table 3.7   *Mean and median sentences in months for felony drug convictions sentenced to prison, jail and probation by US State Courts (1992–2002)*

Year	Possession			Trafficking		
	Prison mean/med.	Jail mean/med.	Probation mean/med.	Prison mean/med.	Jail mean/med.	Probation mean/med.
1992	55/36	4/3	45/36	72/48	8/6	51/36
1994	50/36	4/3	37/24	66/48	7/6	40/36
1996	41/24	5/5	37/36	55/36	7/6	45/36
1998	35/24	4/3	36/25	54/36	6/4	40/36
2000	34/24	5/3	33/24	52/36	7/6	39/36
2002	33/24	5/3	32/36	51/36	8/6	39/36

Source: Bureau of Justice Statistics, 'Felony Sentences in State Courts', 1992, 1994, 1996, 1998, 2000, 2002 (published every other year).

(for example, education). The disposition of asset seizures clearly is a determinant of drug enforcement efforts at any rate (Mast et al., 2000), and total asset seizures have risen dramatically as drug enforcement has increased. There is no centralized accounting of asset seizures by all policing agencies, but examinations of available records from individual states consistently show increasing seizures.

The apparently conflicting indicators become even more confusing when we consider interstate differences. There are some fairly clear liberalization

Table 3.8 *Percentage of prison sentence served and average time served in months, for drug convictions sentenced to prison by US State Courts (1992–2002)*

Year	Possession		Trafficking	
	% sentence served	Mean time served (months)	% sentence served	Mean time served (months)
1992	27	15	34	24
1994	34	17	32	21
1996	40	16	42	23
1998	40	14	41	22
2000	49	17	49	26
2002	40	14	45	24

Source: Bureau of Justice Statistics, 'Felony Sentences in State Courts', 1992, 1994, 1996, 1998, 2000, 2002 (published every other year).

actions being taken in some states, even on the supply-side. For instance, some states are allowing production of marijuana for medical uses, although the federal government continues to oppose these policies. Further, open discussion of legalizing marijuana has actually been taking place in a few states (for example, New Mexico where the past governor openly advocated legalization and Nevada where a legalization referendum garnered over 30 per cent of the votes cast). However, the open marketing of marijuana for general consumption does not appear to be on the horizon, even in states with a long history of liberalization, and liberalization regarding the sale of other drugs (for example, prescriptions for heroin for addicts) is not even being considered.

2 Government monopoly

We now turn to an in-depth evaluation of the alternative policies available in switching from prohibition to some form of legalization. These include government monopoly, regulation, the sin tax and the free market. In turn, each of these policies represents a spectrum of possible policy choices. For example, the sin tax rate could be set at a low or high rate; government regulation could be strict or lax, on the producer, consumer or both: government might regulate production, distribution, consumption or some combination of all three. Government monopoly can be open, as in the case of state-run liquor stores in the USA, or restricted as in the case of methadone clinics. Many policy reformers advocate that policies be set with respect to specific drugs so that, for example, marijuana be left completely free from government intervention while heroin be regulated by a tightly-controlled government monopoly. (For a good discussion of the policy options and establishing policies according to specific drugs, see Nadelmann, 1992 and MacCoun et al., 1996.)

One policy that is often considered a replacement policy for prohibition is to establish a government monopoly for the distribution of drugs, particularly narcotic drugs such as heroin. This approach would place the production and distribution of drugs in the hands of the state and thus provides direct control over most aspects of the marketplace. Several US states monopolize the distribution and sale of liquor, and a few also do so for wine (see Benjamin and Anderson, 1996; Benson et al., 2003). Two other examples of these privatized government monopolies are the market for human organ transplants and state lotteries.

One consequence of this policy approach is that government can directly control the product. It can establish rules for the production, distribution and consumption of the product and therefore mandate the composition of the product (for example, potency), price, quantity limits and hours of operation. With human organ transplants the government prohibits the sale of organs and determines who gets those available. With state lotteries the government regulates what products can be sold, their price and the method of sale. Some state liquor monopolies control the wholesale distribution, choosing products and setting wholesale prices, while others monopolize retailing as well, thus determining the number, location, operating hours and practices of retail outlets, along with prices and products to sell.

Government monopolies can also establish regulations concerning who is allowed to purchase and consume the product. In the area of drugs, government-run liquor stores restrict the sale of their products to adults, although the liquor is often resold by adults to minors or obtained from government stores by minors by theft or deception. Methadone clinics have a monopoly on the distribution of narcotics, but they generally only provide the drug to registered addicts. The methadone is often provided at no charge, but the addicts are required to consume the product on the premises in order to prevent resale.

The results of government monopoly vary depending on whether it is contracted out or publicly run and whether it distributes its product at high prices or gives the product away for free to pre-determined consumers. State-run liquor monopolies and state lotteries generally provide diminished access, high prices, limited product selection and high levels of tax revenue to the government.[6] Revenues typically range from 30–50 per cent of sales but the high prices tend to encourage smuggling. Most importantly, restricting access by this means does little to distinguish (and punish) bad behaviour from good behaviour (Whitman, 2003).

Government-controlled human organ transplant organizations provide 'free' organs, but as we noted earlier, only in a limited supply that is administratively allocated, and so many patients suffer and die because of the resulting shortage. Most drug maintenance programmes remain limited to a small percentage of all addicts who do see a general improvement in terms of consuming a safer product, better economic status and lower levels of criminal activity.

For instance, in January 1994, the Swiss authorities opened the first heroin maintenance clinics, and at the end of the three-year trial, more than 800 patients had received heroin on a regular basis. MacCoun and Reuter (1999) report that the crime rate among all patients declined over the course of treatment, use of non-prescribed heroin dropped sharply and the unemployment rate among the patients fell from 44 per cent to 20 per cent. Overall, though, as currently constituted, such programmes have potential but have not demonstrated their effectiveness in reducing the many harms of prohibition (MacCoun and Reuter, 2001). They are highly restrictive, offer little in the way of access to legal drugs, and in the case of methadone clinics, diversions of the drug have been known to establish new markets for illicit methadone.

3 Government regulation

Economic analysis of regulation often focuses on price regulations. While price regulations might be applied in a legalized drug market, it is much more likely that other aspects of the market would be regulated. In fact, while price constraints are often a part of government-imposed regulations in markets, regulations actually deal with many other aspects of most markets (Benson, 2003). One need only examine the markets for prescription drugs, or various alcohol markets. (For example, see Sass and Saurman, 1993 to get an idea of the wide array of controls that government can and does impose on legal markets.)

Thus, there have been many reformers who have suggested that illicit drugs be made legally available but only through a regulated process whereby buyers and sellers meet certain government requirements. Kleiman (1992) argues that alcohol drinkers and marijuana smokers pay a high tax, have a revocable licence, and a limit on the amount they consume. Under his scheme, cocaine users would be registered and could receive a limited amount of cocaine from regulated distributors either at a high price or under therapeutic supervision. Tobacco users would be registered, sellers would be licensed, quantities would be limited and heavier taxes would be imposed. Heroin prohibition would be rigidly enforced, but addicts would be registered and placed in maintenance and treatment programmes. The cost of administering Kleiman's approach would be extremely high, of course, and violations would probably be rampant, but there are alternative approaches as well (see Kleiman, 1992; Thornton, 1994 for a critique).

The prescription-licence approach has many variations both inside and outside of drug markets. Within 'prescription' drugs markets, consumers are generally registered, licensed or given a prescription for narcotic drugs from a medical doctor or drug treatment therapist. Drugs can then be purchased from a licensed pharmacy or maintenance programme facility in limited quantities. Permission to consume could be obtained along a spectrum that runs from only for legitimate medical needs, to addiction maintenance and treatment, to any adult who the doctor determines is knowledgeable and healthy enough to consume such drugs. Drug prices can range from the highly taxed to free at government-run maintenance programmes.

In the 1920s, the UK adopted a system by which doctors could prescribe heroin to addicted patients for maintenance purposes. MacCoun and Reuter (1999) note that this worked reasonably well until the mid-1960s when, '. . . a handful of physicians began to prescribe irresponsibly and a few heroin users began taking the drug purely for recreational purposes, recruiting others like themselves'. This led to a large relative increase in heroin addiction, although MacCoun and Reuter stress that the problem was small in absolute terms (about 1500 known addicts in 1967). In response, the Dangerous Drugs Act of 1967 significantly reduced access to heroin maintenance, with long-term prescription being limited to a small number of specially licensed drug-treatment specialists. Today, as we noted in Section 1, doctors in the UK prescribe heroin to only a very small number of addicts.

Benjamin and Anderson (1996) point out that the form of alcohol control (taxation and regulation) among states in the USA clearly is a function of the cost of inducing compliance. Most states along the Canadian border where smuggling is easy employ a very different approach to alcohol control than most interior or Southern States. Similarly, alcohol control differs in the traditional 'moonshine' states in the Appalachian Region where social norms support illegal production, compared with other states.

One good example of where an illegal market was legalized and regulated is the casino gambling industry in many US states. Here casinos are licensed, regulated and taxed. Generally, the requirements and taxes are considered normal rather than strict or lax and the results have been quite positive (see Chapter 13).

4   Sin taxes

Another alternative to prohibition is to allow drugs to be sold in the market, but to impose a special tax on the product above the normal sales tax, called an excise tax. This sin tax approach is common on alcohol and tobacco products, but is also used in the case of gasoline and a variety of other products. The excise tax has also been called a 'luxury' tax when applied to luxury products, for instance, where the sin apparently is conspicuous consumption, but it is clear that such taxes have been used throughout history in order to raise revenue for the government.

Many legalization advocates explicitly combine legalization with high sin taxes, including Gary Becker (see interview in this book and Becker et al., 2004). The expectation is that such taxes will reduce consumption, although the magnitude of the reduction depends on the elasticity of demand and the size of the tax. It will also raise revenues that presumably can be used to enforce compliance. Indeed, this is Becker's preferred policy, although other advocates of a sin tax approach would direct revenues toward prevention and treatment.

One potential advantage of a sin tax approach is that it is relatively politically attractive. It provides politicians with revenues and allows them to continue to condemn the product by imposing a sin tax. Many excise taxes are also earmarked for voter-preferred government programmes such as law enforcement, road building and education. They can also be directed to addiction treatment programmes or education campaigns against drug use, as exemplified by the allocation of some of the money collected from tobacco companies in the USA. Because most revenues are fungible, however, the overall impact is to increase the purchasing power of government (Shughart, 1997).

This suggests one flaw in the sin tax approach. While many of its advocates contend that the resulting revenues can and should be earmarked for enforcement, treatment or some other specific purpose, legislators will probably reduce revenues directed at such purposes from other sources as the earmarked sin tax revenues rise. Spending on the desired activity will not rise in the way that advocates intend it to. Nonetheless, this approach is more likely to be considered by political decision-makers than a pure free market, which we discuss next, and if adopted, it may provide many of the advantages of the free market approach and avoid many of the costs of prohibition (Caputo and Ostrum, 1994). It is not likely to deliver the level of benefits that its advocates suggest, however, so voters may become dissatisfied over time.

Sin taxes are generally advocated, at least in public debate, not primarily because they are revenue sources, but because they raise the price of the taxed product and therefore reduce the quantity demanded. The political nature of the taxing decision means that this consumption-reducing impact may be mitigated, however. The level of the tax is likely to be high in a US taxing jurisdiction where many citizens do not consume the product for social, moral and/or religious reasons, for instance, because these people support efforts to reduce consumption by others as well. On the other hand, where the dominant norms of the community do not discourage consumption, most citizens may oppose a high excise tax because they consume the product. Thus, the tax will be high where consumption is already curtailed by social forces, and low where consumption is widespread.

Note in this regard that the negative correlation between excise taxes and consumption does not necessarily mean that the high taxes are the primary cause of the reduced consumption. Both tax rates and consumption levels may be caused by other factors. Mast et al. (1999) illustrate this for beer taxes across the USA: a strong negative correlation appears to hold in consumption regressions with few explanatory variables, but as more controls are added, such as those reflecting the religious make-up of the population, the coefficient on excise taxes falls, becoming quite small and statistically insignificant in a fully specified supply and demand model. This does not mean that the law of demand does not hold, but it does suggest that even relatively high excise taxes do not play nearly as an important role in demand and supply determination as other market characteristics do.

Other shortcomings of the sin tax approach also require recognition. For instance, technically, most excise taxes are paid by the seller. This creates high compliance costs for sellers. In essence, enforcement costs are shifted, at least to a degree, from the public sector under prohibition, to sellers. Naturally, sellers have incentives to avoid such costs, so if they are high (and/or if the tax is so high that it dramatically reduces their sales and revenues), illegal sales will continue, much as under prohibition. Even though selling is not *per se* illegal, many sales will be illegal because taxes are not collected. A substantial portion of the product sold in this black market may be less potent and less dangerous than the products sold under prohibition because legally produced products will simply be sold illegally. However, some illegal products may also be produced and sold (moonshiners still produce alcohol in many places in order to sell it in untaxed underground markets, for instance).

The excise tax is also a regressive tax in that it takes a larger percentage of income from low-income households who purchase the taxed product than from high-income households. In the political arena this may be seen as a benefit of the sin tax, in that it presumably reduces consumption more effectively among low-income groups. On the other hand, such taxes create relatively strong incentives for buyers, and particularly low-income individuals who want to consume the good, to turn to black market sources. Most sin tax advocates assume that raising taxes simply raises price and results in reduced consumption. They fail to see that as prices rise consumers have incentives to look for substitutes and producers have incentives to supply them. One substitute for highly taxed goods is the same good sold in an illegal market. Thus, the incentives of suppliers to avoid compliance costs, and the incentives of consumers to avoid paying high taxes create the inevitable result of an ongoing black market, with low-income consumers in particular being pushed into these 'illegal' activities. The relative sizes of the legal and illegal market is a function of the level of taxes and the expected punishment for buying and selling in the illegal market.

Consider an example, Quebec's experiences with taxes on cigarettes. An 9 August 1993 article in *Maclean's* (a leading news magazine in Canada) noted that, 'tax levels in excess of 60 percent on cigarettes have convinced many smokers that they are justified in breaking the law' (quoted in Benson and Rasmussen, 1996). At the time, roughly half of the cigarettes in Quebec (and some other Canadian provinces with similar taxes)[7] were being sold in illegal markets in order to avoid excise taxes. Tax evasion is not the only 'crime' that accompanies high excise taxes, however. Canada's illegal cigarettes were being smuggled across the border. For instance, Canada exported about 7.6 billion cigarettes to the USA in 1992, and police estimated that about 80 per cent were smuggled back into Canada. Cigarette smuggling became so lucrative that organized crime became involved. Loads of cigarettes were crossing the St Lawrence from the USA to Canada, in large boats, generally stolen for this purpose, painted black for night-time crossings, and armed with machine guns for protection against police and other criminal organizations. Rival gangs exchanged gunfire as they competed for shares of the illegal market.

As smuggling and violence increased, demands for already-pressed policing, courts, prisons and other law enforcement services increased. Canadian police were forced to become involved in the same kind of interdiction and law enforcement efforts against cigarette markets that law enforcement in the USA is involved in with drug prohibition. Revenues for enforcement did not increase sufficiently to counter the increasing criminal activities, and the flow of illegal cigarettes went unabated, undermining the ability of the provincial government to collect the excise taxes. The effort to crack down on this sin tax-induced crime meant that either additional taxes from other sources would have to be raised or a larger portion of Canada's criminal justice resources would have to be shifted away from efforts to control non-sin tax-induced property and violent crime. Quebec citizens and/or policymakers apparently recognized the tradeoffs, as a massive reduction in cigarette taxes was announced by the Quebec government in 1994.

This suggests that a major problem with the sin tax approach is the difficulty in setting the tax rate. Low tax rates would have little effect on consumption, while high tax rates can spur black markets to develop in order to avoid the taxes, so the underground production, smuggling, crime and corruption associated with prohibition also occur with significant sin taxes (see Benson and Rasmussen, 1996; Thornton, forthcoming). Becker et al. (2004) are among the minority of sin tax advocates in that they recognize that illegal markets will persist under this approach, thus necessitating continued spending on enforcement. They suggest that setting the optimal level of expected punishment for black market activities will eliminate that market. If their model and predictions are correct, it must be that the Canadian government did not set the optimal levels of expected punishment, but the same implication arises for alcohol taxes (Benjamin and Anderson, 1996) and most other highly taxed goods (see Thornton, forthcoming).

For instance, as European governments attempted to establish control over maritime trade in order to tax it, and granted franchises for numerous trading monopolies between 1500 and 1800, the 'average merchant and seaman' responded with piracy and smuggling, and a substantial part of maritime commerce was carried out in violation of the laws of some nation-state (Rosenberg and Birdzell, 1986). Furthermore, the middle and even the upper classes willingly wore, drank and ate smuggled goods (Rosenberg and Birdzell, 1986). In 1776, Adam Smith described the implications of such a policy, beginning with a characterization of the typical smuggler as:

> a person who, though no doubt highly blameable for violating the laws of his country, is frequently incapable of violating those of natural justice, and would have been, in every respect an excellent citizen, had not the laws of his country made that a crime which nature never meant to be so. In those corrupted governments where there is at least a general suspicion of much unnecessary expense, and great misapplication of the public revenue, the laws which guard it are little respected. Not many people are scrupulous about smuggling, when, without perjury, they can find any easy and safe opportunity of doing so. To pretend to have any scruple about buying smuggled goods, though a manifest encouragement to the violation of the revenue laws, and to the perjury which almost always attends it, would in most countries be regarded as one of these pedantic pieces of hypocrisy which, instead of gaining credit with any body, serves only to expose the person who affects to practice them, to the suspicion of being a greater knave than most of his neighbours. By this indulgence of the public, the smuggler is often encouraged to continue a trade which he is thus taught to consider as in some measure innocent; and when the severity of the revenue laws is ready to fall upon him, he is frequently disposed to defend with violence, what he has been accustomed to regard as just property.

The expectation that such incentives can be overcome by devoting excise tax revenues to enforcement efforts is simply not borne out by history.

Yet another drawback of a sin tax approach that corresponds to a prohibition approach is that, like prohibition, taxes are targeted against consumption in general, not the external harms that some consumption may produce. For example, the tax on red wine in the USA does have the effect of reducing the consumption of red wine over the entire economy, but this reduces the health and other benefits of red wine, and yet does little to target specifically the potential harms of wine consumption, such as automobile accidents (Mast et al., 1999).

5   Free market

Very few economists advocate a completely free market in drugs. Most favour replacing one form of government intervention (prohibition) with a different form(s) of government intervention. However, the purpose of this section is to provide a rigorous examination of how such a free market might operate.

First, of course, the supply of and demand for a drug would be determined solely on the basis of market forces. Competitive conditions would result in relatively low prices and diversified offerings of competitive products, while consumer sovereignty would dictate that the products that best satisfied consumers in terms of price, quality and so on, would dominate the market.

We would also expect a large number of suppliers to enter the market and for most suppliers to leave the underground economy. When a new drug is introduced or legalized there is usually a period of relative chaos and misinformation. Over time, however, we would observe more stability and better information as the more successful firms (generally those that establish reputations for offering uniformly good quality at a competitive price) would grow and capture a larger market share, while less successful firms would fail and exit the industry. Surviving firms would develop mass production and distribution techniques and employ advertising to promote sales and develop 'good will' amongst its customers.

It is impossible to project what a mature market would look like in terms of the precise number of firms and products, but it is safe to say that most consumption would be served by commercial production, rather than by home production. Looking at other mature industries such as soft drinks, cigarettes, toothpaste, beer and over-the-counter drugs, we find that a small number of firms supply the majority of the products sold in the marketplace. These firms each offer a variety of differentiated products that are mass-produced, heavily advertised and sold through well-developed distribution networks. The existence of a small number of firms does not mean a lack of competition or the presence of a monopoly. Indeed, competition can be very intense, as most sources of reduced competition arise through state action to limit the free market (for example, price controls, entry restrictions through licensing and other such measures, and assigned markets).

In the absence of such artificial constraints on markets, smaller firms, regional firms and firms that cater to special tastes are likely to exist alongside the large firms. For instance, consider the proliferation of small local and regional micro-breweries in the USA, which are successfully competing against the large producers of national brands. There might also be boutique firms, like brewpubs in the beer industry or vacation resorts that make and sell their own wines, although these would likely constitute a very small share of the overall market. Likewise, home production is possible (especially with marijuana), but this form would be negligible in a low-tax environment.

The underground or black market for these products would be small, but perhaps not negligible, if the market faces regulation of product distribution (for example, minimum consumption ages). The existence of a wide variety of producers, many of whom may be small, helps ensure that a wide diversity of consumers' tastes are satisfied and provides a source of product innovation and competition for the large producers, preventing them from 'dominating' the market in the sense of limiting price/quality competitions, even though they may 'dominate' in terms of market share.

The advocates of legalization are often quick to emphasize all of the costs of prohibition but often downplay or dismiss the increased consumption expected under legalization. The supporters of prohibition rest much of their case on the increase in consumption that would be experienced with legalization, but neglect to consider that legalization would remove the costs of prohibition. Indeed, some prohibitionists believe that all the problems related to drugs and drug prohibition, including crime and corruption, will simply get worse as a function of the (greatly) increased consumption of drugs, despite considerable evidence to the contrary.

Prohibitionists suggest that once the prohibition is lifted, consumption of drugs will skyrocket because of a lack of legal restriction, a significant decrease in price and the use of commercial advertising promoting their use. They feel that lower prices would increase consumption among current consumers but more importantly legalization would increase the number of consumers who currently abstain only because of the legal threats or the perceived morality of the law.

They point to the experience of the Netherlands. From the mid-1980s, Dutch drug policy developed from the simple decriminalization of marijuana to the active commercialization and promotion of it. Although legal restrictions remained as we noted in Section 1, the result was a rapid increase in the number of marijuana users. For example, in 1984, 15 per cent of 18–20-year-olds in the Netherlands reported having used marijuana at some point in their lifetime. By 1992, that figure had more than doubled to 33 per cent. Of course, this does not control for additional factors at work, but MacCoun and Reuter (1999) note that it is consistent with evidence from other markets (alcohol, tobacco and legal gambling) that commercial promotion of such activities increases consumption. However, they also emphasize that the growth in marijuana use, '. . . has not led to a worsening of the Dutch heroin problem, . . . cocaine use is not especially high by European standards, and a smaller fraction of marijuana users go on to use cocaine or heroin in the Netherlands than in the United States'.

Overall, in a free market, many abstainers would not consume the drugs, particularly hard ones such as heroin and cocaine even if they were legal because they consider the consumption of those drugs to be immoral, dangerous or repugnant. Those who only refrain because of the legal threat would probably consume the drugs responsibly for fear of running afoul of other legal threats, such as Driving Under Influence (DUI) laws or the loss of their job or reputation.

In fact, legalization reformers sometimes suggest that there will be little or no increase in consumption because illegal drugs are readily available and competitively priced against their legal counterparts. With heroin and cocaine selling for less than $5 and often available inside government prisons, a case can be made that prohibition does not really restrict the availability of illegal drugs to any significant degree (Miron, 2004). However, we cannot completely discount the impact that purchasing illegal drugs involves more than just price and availability, namely going to prison, losing your job or overdosing on drugs, and that these threats do diminish the actual number of drug consumers. Indeed, we explained in Chapter 1 that it is a drug's 'effective' price that is relevant, not necessarily its market price.

We also noted in Chapter 2 that some individuals may be affected by the 'forbidden fruit' effect, which actually increases their demand for illegal products. By making a good illegal you draw attention to it and encourage its use as a way of rebelling against society or unjust laws. If prohibition creates this forbidden fruit effect and increases sales in a black market, then demand could decrease as a result of legalization. There is some evidence for the existence of this effect, but nothing that would suggest its magnitude in the case of drugs. While it is considered to be a small component in the overall demand for illicit drugs, the primary group that this is said to impact is teenagers and young male adults. This group is a major concern in the debate, but it may be less of a positive consideration if those same risk-taking individuals simply seek out alternative hazardous behaviours, especially those more dangerous than drugs.

Moving from prohibition to a completely free market would likely lead to an increased consumption of drugs. First, current consumers would face a lower price and increased quality. Second, new consumers would enter the market due to the lifting of criminal sanctions and the improved safety of the products. Third, there would be a substitution from drugs that are currently legal and highly taxed, such as alcohol and tobacco, into newly legalized drugs, which are not. Fourth, legal products would tend to be sold in lower potency forms so that the quantity of product as measured by weight or volume sold would increase. Fifth, there would be a surge in demand for the legitimate medicinal uses of marijuana, cocaine and heroin that are currently prohibited or restricted. Indeed, marijuana also has many potential commercial uses as a fibre substitute and for the oil from its seeds. It can be successfully grown in many climates without the use of large amounts of fertilizers and insecticides.

Estimates of the projected increase in consumption of these drugs are highly speculative because they are based on inaccurate historical information and questionable assumptions about how legalization would actually affect an individual's demand. Such estimates are often constructed for political purposes or to espouse a particular policy viewpoint and are not trustworthy (see Michaels, 1987). Furthermore, increased consumption is often viewed by all sides as a negative, but scientifically it is a positive result if no 'negative externalities' are associated with that consumption (see Miron, 1991).

Normally price and quantity are overriding economic considerations, but in the movement from prohibition to legalization everything about the product and its market changes dramatically, relegating price and quantity to minor roles. What are often neglected in the drug policy debate are the real characteristics of free markets governed by the rules of private property, contract and tort, and a 'free-for-all' market without any enforceable rules of the game. The fact is that rules against fraud, duress, imposition of intentional or accidental harms, and trespass or other involuntary takings, do exist in all modern economies. Furthermore, even when these rules are not instituted by the state, various kinds of 'privately-imposed' regulations would virtually guarantee that the production, distribution and consumption of drugs such as marijuana, cocaine and heroin would be significantly different compared with black market conditions. With legalization, market behaviour will look more like Budweiser, Marlboro and Coca Cola, and less like Al Capone, Miami Vice and The Sopranos.

Even in a free market, suppliers operate in an environment of both competition and a legal framework that provides certain restrictions, guidelines to behaviour and penalties for violations, mistakes and even bad luck. This legal framework is apart from the government regulatory apparatus discussed earlier, which could add various requirements regarding product characteristics (potency, consistency), distribution (age restrictions, characteristics of actual retail outlets such as location or operating hours), marketing strategies (advertising restrictions) and so on, if the competitive market process itself does not control such factors in a way that satisfies those with political decision-making power or influence. In short, the free market for drugs would be neither a ramped-upped version of the illegal market or a free-for-all orgy of intoxication.

Forces such as competition for reputation and goodwill, and the risks to a firm's capital due to contract and tort liabilities provide much in the way of what is commonly referred to as 'consumer protection', which is almost entirely absent in black markets. Therefore, we will describe some of the major aspects of free markets that are either absent or greatly curtailed with prohibition of drugs and that will either be established or expanded with legalization and how they influence and moderate behaviour. Indeed, while 'regulation of markets' can be provided by government, it also can be provided by other organizations, both formal and informal (see Holcombe and Holcombe, 1986; Thornton, 1996; Benson, 2001).

We begin with the informal constraints on drug use and abuse that are considered to have a deterrence effect. While neither commercial nor corporate in nature, informal social sanctions such as embarrassment, expressions of disapproval, resentment, ridicule, rejection, ritual and shaming can have a powerful effect on behaviour and can even be more effective than legal sanctions, especially under the right circumstances (see Zinberg, 1987). The effectiveness of these sanctions is based on their immediacy and personal nature. Sanctions imposed by peers, mentors and guardians are particularly powerful in moderating bad behaviour. Social sanctioning can correct and prevent behaviours before they become problematic. In contrast, legal sanctions are only 'probabilistic', and when eventually enforced (that is, going to prison), can actually lead to long-term association with drugs and crime. Social sanctions would be more widely practised under legalization, because drug use is necessarily a concealed behaviour, not an open social behaviour (see MacCoun and Reuter, 2001).

There are also several constraints on the behaviour of suppliers. For example, in terms of advertising, suppliers would want to promote their products with the most cost-effective advertising, but would be prevented from making false and fraudulent claims for their products. If a supplier makes fraudulent claims, consumers can sue. This legal constraint works imperfectly, but tolerably well, in the market for other products. Even in the absence of actual lawsuits, false and misleading claims work against suppliers of products where purchases are made on an ongoing basis or where the corporation produces a wide variety of products that could all be 'tinged' by the misleading promotions. Building a reputation for reliability can be a very valuable investment in a competitive market (Benson, 2001). Much of the serious health consequences of illicit drugs are due to a lack of information and the presence of misinformation about illicit drugs. For example, the majority of heroin deaths are not due to heroin *per se*, but consuming heroin with other drugs, which unknowingly causes 'over-dose'. Legalization, competitive advertising and labelling would certainly address the most egregious aspects of this problem (see Ekelund and Saurman, 1988).

In terms of potency, purity and product quality, even an unregulated free market would work much differently from an illegal market. In an illegal market, there is an incentive and marked tendency toward higher-potency products, where purity is variable and uncertain and product quality is low. With high and variable potency, customers face high risks and many die or end up in the emergency room of the hospital due to overdoses. As we emphasized in Chapter 2, suppliers of deadly drugs face little loss or reprisals for selling dangerous products (see also Thornton, 1991, 1998).

In the market, such behaviour is controlled through the forces of competition and the increased flow of information. Any supplier who sold dangerous or deadly products is not only quickly eschewed by customers; they also are subject to multimillion dollar lawsuits for negligence. Through either means, the entire value of the company could be lost. In the market for alcohol, caffeine and tobacco we have seen trends towards lower potency products, drug-free alternatives and safer products. Other firms have introduced a large number and wide variety of products and services to help consumers break their habits. In terms of product safety, consumers will experience far less danger from legal products compared with illegal products. The two popular narcotic drug products before narcotics prohibition were both low potency and controlled dosage: Bayer's heroin pills and Coca-Cola, which contained cocaine (see Courtwright, 2001). Indeed, in a free market, there would be an incentive for firms to develop new drugs that provided the 'high' with minimal adverse effects.

As we noted earlier, a free market policy does not imply a free-for-all in drug consumption. Stores currently post signs stating such rules as 'no shoes, no service', 'no smoking permitted', and 'no alcohol beyond this point'. Would you shop at stores that allowed marijuana smoking by its customers or employees? Some people would, but others would not. We would therefore have high expectations that marijuana smoking would be largely restricted to specialized marijuana bars and the consumer's private property even in the absence of any government regulation. There are a variety of market mechanisms and alternatives to government regulation that have been demonstrated to be more effective at protecting the interests of buyers (see Poole, 1982; Benson, 2001).

Likewise, we fully expect to see employer sanctions on the use of certain drugs while working on the job. Airlines and trucking companies that restrict their pilots and drivers from consuming alcohol before or during work also restrict them from smoking marijuana and a variety of other legal and illegal drugs. Drug restrictions on workers, especially those with dangerous and sensitive jobs, would continue and possibly be strengthened if drugs were legalized (see Hartwell et al., 1998). It turns out that one of the most effective forms of drug treatment is simply having a job (see Silverman and Robles-Sotelo, 1998; Feinauer, 1990).

Indeed, businesses used drug-testing and behaviour restrictions on employees long before they were ever required by government (see McGuire and Ruhm, 1993). It is also worth noting that while much remains to be established in the relationship between drug use and economic outcomes (employment, income and wealth), it is clear that labour markets provide one of the most effective checks on and punishment for drug abuse, whether legal or illegal. Businesses do this not because they necessarily oppose using drugs, but because they have an economic incentive to do so. For comparison, while the cumulative aggregate effect of law enforcement over time is large, the probability of getting caught by law enforcement in a single act of selling or consuming illicit drugs is quite small compared with the much higher probability of being caught and swiftly punished if your alcohol or drug use threatens your employer. As we suggest in Chapter 4, the certainty and swiftness (or 'celerity') of punishment appears to have a greater deterrent effect compared with the severity of punishment (see also Norman et al., 1994).

What about the case of children? In most cases, businesses would not sell dangerous drugs to children. Businesses have reputations to uphold and the bigger the business, the more important that reputation is. It should also be noted that, under both common and civil law, businesses cannot make valid legal contracts with minors. Pharmacies generally do not sell dangerous drugs to children, auto dealers do not sell them cars, and all sorts of other companies do not do business with children, either out of concern for the children, their own reputations or their financial viability and survival. With regard to the latter, companies that sell drugs to children would face severe legal consequences if harm comes to the children. Therefore, legal liability and negligence laws would greatly discourage suppliers from selling most drugs to minors. The incentives to restrict sales of dangerous and potentially poisonous drugs to children would be particularly strong in a free market, and much stronger than they are in an illegal market. Some adults may buy drugs and sell them to children, of course, as some do with alcohol and tobacco products, and some children would obtain false identification or other means of purchasing drugs, but even then, the drug product is likely to be less potent, and safer due to reduced variability in quality.

Clearly, some problems arise or persist with a free market approach for drugs. As just suggested, drugs would still be available to children, although the products generally would be in safer forms. If adults and young adults can freely purchase the drugs there would be access to minors as there is now with minimum age requirements. Indeed, there probably would be marginal sellers who might specialize in selling to children.

A second potential problem is that drug abuse can lead to negative health consequences even if the products are legally produced. We would expect the number of deaths and emergency room visits due to drug overdose to significantly decline despite overall increases in consumption, but there would still be people who harm their health via drug abuse, just as with alcohol and tobacco products today (although probably on a much smaller scale). Something that greatly exacerbates this problem is that the bulk of medical services is paid via government and insurance. This creates a moral hazard in that individuals can place their health at greater risk (with drug abuse and other health risks) given that the government will pay for their medical and hospital expenses in the event of an overdose, accident or other health problem. In other words, if individuals could not depend on the government to provide free medical services, most would be more risk-averse in their drug use. Private insurers are less susceptible to this problem because they provide incentives (for example, lower rates for non-smokers) and reduce adverse selection problems by providing group insurance policies that include healthy and unhealthy individuals.

In addition, there is a moral hazard associated with government unemployment insurance and welfare benefits. Severe drug abuse (which is what we are most concerned about) often leads to economic consequences such as the loss of employment, the inability to find a job and, worse still, poverty (Kaestner, 1998). This form of market punishment is less threatening if individuals have state-provided unemployment insurance in the short term and welfare benefits in the longer term. Removing this safety net for health and unemployment problems associated with drug abuse would reduce, although not eliminate, risk-taking behaviour associated with drug abuse.

There are also problems associated with drug use and driving automobiles, but these problems are not unique to drugs that are currently illegal. As we revealed in Chapter 2, the effects of alcohol consumption on driving are apparently more significant than those associated with most illegal drugs. Even though marijuana, cocaine and heroin may be less intoxicating and pose less of a threat than alcohol, they still could impose negative externalities on other drivers if the overall level of intoxicated driving were to increase. This need not occur, however. If marijuana consumption increases in a free market, for instance, with no change in alcohol consumption, then the level of danger and number of accidents could increase, but if marijuana is a substitute for alcohol, the negative consequences of intoxicated driving could decline even with increased marijuana consumption. In this regard, studies by DiNardo and Lemieux (2001), Chaloupka and Laixuthai (1997) and Model (1993) suggest that marijuana and alcohol are substitutes. Indeed, Model (1993) found that the decriminalization of marijuana in some states in the USA is associated with lower numbers of emergency room episodes related to alcohol (and other illegal drugs), while Chaloupka and Laixuthai (1997) report that lower marijuana prices lead to a significant drop in the probability of automobile accidents.

Yet another potential problem is that in a free market, existing drugs and particularly new drugs could have unknown side-effects from long-term consumption. This was a problem with cigarettes because the long-term results such as lung cancer were only determined after cigarettes were popular for a long time and people started living long enough for the long-term health consequences to be readily apparent. Indeed, this can be a problem with all drugs, whether sold in free or black markets, and it is not a problem that can be easily dealt with under any policy. Government testing for a drug's effectiveness and side-effects does not screen for long-term consequences and actually worsens the potential problem by providing products with the government's seal of approval (see Higgs, 1995).

Importantly, however, as we have already suggested, this problem is likely to be more significant under prohibition. Tort liability creates relatively strong incentives for legal drug producers to consider and attempt to mitigate potential long-term effects, after all, but illegal producers do not face such liabilities. Furthermore, since such consequences can never be fully avoided, tort law does create the potential for those harmed by products purchased in legal markets to at least recover some compensation, something that is virtually impossible when the harm arises from a drug purchased from an illegal firm under prohibition.

6 Conclusion

This chapter spelled out the major forms of drug legalization that are available to policy-makers throughout the world. Government monopoly, regulation, sin taxes and the free market were all described with the help of well-developed economic models that allowed us to explore their costs and benefits. As each of these policies has been used in a variety of different industries, including drugs and other illicit markets, we also had a wealth of historical experience to draw upon in order to further understand their implications. While Chapter 2 established that drug prohibition is harmful in numerous respects, this chapter's analysis showed that many of the alternatives are certainly not perfect either. Each has its own drawbacks and costs. Given that the reader will likely face the prospects of changing drug policy in their lifetime, this should be valuable information.

Notes

1. Coffee shops are restricted under the Opium Act from advertising, selling hard drugs, admitting or selling to those under 18 years of age, selling more than 5 grams to a person at any one time and causing a nuisance. Moreover, the availability of coffee shops depends upon policy in any particular Dutch municipality, that may choose to allow them, allow them with certain restrictions, or not allow them at all (see Martineau and Gomart, 2001, for a discussion of the evolution of Dutch coffee shops). At the time of writing (May 2005), the very existence of coffee shops is being threatened by new measures including a possible ban on foreigners from buying drugs in coffee shops and an anti-smoking law stipulating that employees should not be exposed to tobacco smoke.
2. Pill testing refers to the concept of providing illicit drug users with quality assessment of their chosen drug.
3. Oregon in 1973; Colorado, Alaska and Ohio in 1975; California, Maine and Minnesota in 1976; Mississippi, New York and North Carolina in 1977 and Nebraska in 1978. Oregon recriminalized in 1996 but in 1998 voters rejected recriminalization and re-established decriminalization. Alaska also recriminalized in 1990, although it is not clear that they did so in practice, but recently decriminalized again.
4. Note that the actual characteristics of each of these 13 states' decriminalization acts differ quite substantially, and many other states have adopted at least some of the legal changes that these 13 states have (see Pacula et al., 2003 for details about what appear to be the relevant aspects of liberalization in state laws).
5. Connecticut, Louisiana, Massachusetts, New Jersey, Vermont, Wisconsin and West Virginia.
6. But see Benson et al. (2003) who find that some state liquor monopolies clearly collect less revenue than they could through a sin tax approach, perhaps due to the bureaucratic inefficiencies and/or consumer-unfriendly locations and operating practices.
7. In fact, it was estimated that about one of every nine cigarettes consumed in Canada as a whole were illegally purchased.

References

Becker, G.S., M. Grossman and K.M. Murphy (2004), 'The Economic Theory of Illegal Goods: The Case of Drugs', National Bureau of Economic Research Working Paper, No. W10976.

Benjamin, D.K. and T.L. Anderson (1996), 'Taxation, Enforcement Costs, and the Incentives to Privatize', in T.L. Anderson and P.J. Hill (eds), *The Privatization Process: a Worldwide Perspective*, Lanham, MD: Rowman & Littlefield, pp. 39–54.

Benson, B.L. (2001), 'Knowledge, Trust, and Recourse: Imperfect Substitutes as Sources of Assurance in Emerging Economies', *Economic Affairs*, **21**, 12–17.

Benson, B.L. (2003), 'Regulatory Disequilibrium and Inefficiency: The Case of Interstate Trucking', *Review of Austrian Economics*, **15**, 229–55.

Benson, B.L. and D.W. Rasmussen (1996), 'Predatory Public Finance and the Origins of the War on Drugs: 1984–1989', *The Independent Review: A Journal of Political Economy*, **1**, 163–89.

Benson, B.L., D.W. Rasmussen and D.L. Sollars (1995), 'Police Bureaucrats, Their Incentives, and the War on Drugs', *Public Choice*, **83**, 21–45.

Benson, B.L., D.W. Rasmussen and P.R. Zimmerman (2003), 'Implicit Taxes Collected by State Liquor Monopolies', *Public Choice*, **115**, 313–31.

Bureau of Justice Statistics (2003), *Sourcebook of Criminal Justice Statistics 2003*, Washington, DC: United States Department of Justice.

Caputo, M.R. and B.J. Ostrum (1994), 'Potential Tax Revenue from a Regulated Marijuana Market: A Meaningful Revenue Source', *American Journal of Sociology*, **53**, 473–90.

Chaloupka, F.J. and A. Laixuthai (1997) 'Do Youths Substitute Alcohol and Marijuana? Some Econometric Evidence', *Eastern Economic Journal*, **23** (3), 253–76.

Courtwright, David T. (2001), *Forces of Habit: Drugs and the Making of the Modern World*, Cambridge, MA: Harvard University Press.

DiNardo, J. and T. Lemieux (2001), 'Alcohol, Marijuana, and American Youth: The Unintended Consequences of Government Regulation', *Journal of Health Economics*, **20**, 991–1010.

Drug and Alcohol Services Information System (2001), 'Coerced Treatment Among Youths: 1993 to 1998', *The DASIS Report* (21 September), 1–3.

Drug Enforcement Agency (DEA) (2002), 'Drug Intelligence Brief – The Changing Face of European Drug Policy', April.

Ekelund, R.B and D.S. Saurman (1988), *Advertising and the Market Process: A Modern Economic View*, San Francisco, CA: Pacific Research Institute for Public Policy.

European Monitoring Centre for Drugs and Drug Addiction (EMCDDA) (2003), 'The State of the Drugs Problem in the European Union and Norway', Annual Report.

European Monitoring Centre for Drugs and Drug Addiction (EMCDDA) (2004), 'The State of the Drugs Problem in the European Union and Norway', Annual Report.

Executive Office of the President, Office of National Drug Control Policy (ONDCP) (2001), 'Drug Treatment in the Criminal Justice System', *ONDCP Drug Policy Information Clearing House Fact Sheet* (March), 1–6.

Executive Office of the President, Office of National Drug Control Policy (ONDCP) (2003), 'Drug Data Summary', *ONDCP Drug Policy Information Clearing House Fact Sheet* (March), 1–8.

Federal Bureau of Investigation (various years), *Uniform Crime Report*.

Feinauer, D.M. (1990), 'The Relationship Between Workplace Accident Rates and Drug and Alcohol Abuse: The Unproven Hypothesis', *Labor Studies Journal*, **15** (4), 3–15.

Fisher, Irving (1930), *The Noble Experiment*, New York: Alcohol Information Committee.

Grinspoon, Lester and James B. Bakalar (1993), *Marihuana: The Forbidden Medicine*, New Haven, CT: Yale University Press.

Hartwell, T., P.D. Steele and N. Rodman (1998), 'Workplace Alcohol-testing Programs: Prevalence and Trends', *Monthly Labor Review*, **121** (6), 27–34.

Higgs, Robert (ed.) (1995), *Hazardous to our Health: FDA Regulation of Health Care Products*, Oakland, CA: Independent Institute.

Holcombe, R.G. and L.P. Holcombe (1986), 'The Market for Regulation', *Journal of Institutional and Theoretical Economics*, **142**, 684–96.

Kaestner, R. (1998), 'Does Drug Use Cause Poverty?', Cambridge, MA: National Bureau of Economic Research Working Paper No. 6406.

Kleiman, Mark A.R. (1992), *Against Excess: Drug Policy for Results*, Basic Books, New York.

MacCoun, R.J. and P. Reuter (1999), 'Does Europe Do It Better? Lessons from Holland, Britain and Switzerland', *The Nation*, 20 September.

MacCoun, Robert J. and Peter Reuter (2001), *Drug War Heresies: Learning from Other Vices, Times, & Places*, Cambridge University Press.

MacCoun, R.J. P. Reuter and T. Schelling (1996), 'Assessing Alternative Drug Control Regimes', *Journal of Policy Analysis and Management*, **15** (3), 330–52.

Martineau, H. and E. Gomart (2001), 'Coffee Shops in the Netherlands: The Dutch Tolerance in Practice', OFDT (Observatoire François des Drogues et des Toxicomanies), www.ofdt.fr/BDD/publications/docs/tend11gb.pdf.

Mast, B.D., B.L. Benson and D.W. Rasmussen (1999), 'Beer Taxation and Alcohol-Related Traffic Fatalities', *Southern Economic Journal*, **66** (2), 214–49.

Mast, B.D., B.L. Benson and D.W. Rasmussen (2000), 'Entrepreneurial Police and Drug Enforcement Policy', *Public Choice*, **104**, 285–308.

McGuire, T.G. and C.J. Ruhm (1993), 'Workplace Drug Abuse Policy', *Journal of Health Economics*, **12** (1), 19–38.

Michaels, R.J. (1987), 'The Market for Heroin Before and After Legalization', in R. Hamowy (ed.), *Dealing with Drugs: Consequences of Government Control*, San Francisco: Pacific Research Institute for Public Policy, pp. 289–326.

Miron, J.A. (1991), 'Drug Legalization and the Consumption of Drugs: An Economist's Perspective', in Melvyn B. Krauss and Edward P. Lazear (eds), *Searching For Alternatives:*

Drug-control Policy in the United States, Stanford, CA: Hoover Institution Press, pp. 68–76.

Miron, Jeffrey A. (2004), *Drug War Crimes: The Consequences of Prohibition*, Oakland, CA: Independent Institute.

Model, K.E. (1993), 'The Effect of Marijuana Decriminalization on Hospital Emergency Room Drug Episodes: 1976–1978', *Journal of the American Statistical Association*, **88**, 737–47.

Nadelmann, E.A. (1992), 'Thinking Seriously about Alternatives to Drug Prohibition', *Daedalus*, **121** (3), 85–132.

Norman, J., R.O. Lempert and C.P. O'Brien (eds) (1994), *Under the Influence? Drugs and the American Workforce*, Washington, DC: National Academy Press.

Osborn, A. (2003), 'Joint Operation', *The Guardian*, 24 November.

Pacula, R.L., J.F. Chriqui and J. King (2003), 'Marijuana Decriminalization: What Does it Mean in the United States?', National Bureau of Economic Research Working Paper No. 9690.

Poole, R.W. (ed.) (1982), *Instead of Regulation: Alternatives to Federal Regulatory Agencies*, Lexington, MA: D.C. Heath and Company.

Rasmussen, David W. and Bruce L. Benson (1994), *The Economic Anatomy of a Drug War: Criminal Justice in the Commons*, Lanham, MD: Rowman and Littlefield.

Rosenberg, N. and L.E. Birdzell Jr. (1986), *How the West Grew Rich: The Economic Transformation of the Industrial World*, Basic Books, New York.

Sass, T.R. and D.S. Saurman (1993), 'Mandated Exclusive Territories and Economic Efficiency: An Empirical Analysis of the Malt-Beverage Industry', *Journal of Law and Economics*, **36**, 153–77.

Senlis Council (2004), Document Centre – Drug Policies Table (http://www.senliscouncil.net/modules/document_centre/drug_policy_in_europe).

Shughart, William F. (ed.) (1997), *Taxing Choice: The Predatory Politics of Fiscal Discrimination*, New Brunswick, NJ: Transaction Publishers.

Silverman, K and E. Robles-Sotelo (1998), 'Employment as a Drug Abuse Treatment Intervention: A Behavioral Economic Analysis', Cambridge, MA: National Bureau of Economic Research Working Paper No. 6402.

Smith, Adam (1937) [1776], *An Inquiry into the Nature and Causes of the Wealth of Nations*, E. Cannan (ed.), New York: Modern Library.

Thornton, Mark (1991), *The Economics of Prohibition*, Salt Lake City, UT: University of Utah Press.

Thornton, M. (1994), 'Review of *Against Excess: Drug Policy for Results*', *Review of Austrian Economics*, **7** (1), 147–50.

Thornton, M. (1995), 'Economists on Illegal Drugs', *Atlantic Economic Journal*, **23** (2), 73.

Thornton, M. (1996), 'The Market for Safety', *Business Quest: A Journal of Applied Topics in Business and Economics* (http://www.westga.edu/~bquest/1996/uwlab.html).

Thornton, M. (1998), 'The Potency of Illegal Drugs', *Journal of Drug Issues*, **28** (3), 725–40.

Thornton, M. (2004), 'Prohibition vs. Legalization: Do Economists Reach a Conclusion on Drug Policy?', *Econ Journal Watch*, **1** (1), April.

Thornton, M. (forthcoming), 'Harm Reduction and Sin Taxes: Why Gary Becker is Wrong', *Advances in Austrian Economics*.

Tullock, Gordon and Richard B. McKenzie (1985), *The New World of Economics: Explorations into the Human Experience*, 4th edition, Homewood IL: Richard D. Irwin, Inc.

United Nations Office on Drugs and Crime (UNODC) (2005), 'World Drug Report 2005', UNODC.

Whitman, Douglas G. (2003), *Strange Brew: Alcohol and Government Monopoly*, Oakland, CA: The Independent Institute.

Zinberg, N.E. (1987), 'The Use and Misuse of Intoxicants: Factors in the Development of Controlled Use', in R. Hamowy (ed.), *Dealing with Drugs: Consequences of Government Control*, San Francisco: Pacific Research Institute for Public Policy, pp. 247–79.

PART II

GUNS AND ROSES

4 Economics of crime
Bruce L. Benson and Simon W. Bowmaker

In this chapter we turn to crime. As early as 1763 in his *Lectures on Jurisprudence*, Adam Smith observed that, '. . . the disorders in any country are more or less according to the number of retainers and dependents in it'. The Scotsman was referring to the 'idle and luxurious life' enjoyed by servants, which, 'renders them altogether depraved both in mind and body', and hence unwilling and unable to survive when discarded by their masters other than by 'crimes and vices'. Moving toward a commercial economy was the solution according to Smith. Not only would this 'give the poorer sort better wages', but also an independence, which is the most effective means of protection from crime.

In the year following Smith's *Lectures*, Cesare Beccaria wrote *Essays on Crime and Punishment*. The Milanese jurist, criminologist and economist was a fervent opponent of the severities and abuses of criminal law, particularly capital punishment and torture. He argued that for punishment to be effective, it should 'never be an act of violence committed by one or many against a private citizen', and that the harshest penalties must be imposed in moderation while being both 'proportionate to the crime, and established by law'.

Beccaria's writings stimulated and provided a guide for reforms in the penal codes of many European nations and his pioneering ideas of presumption of innocence and the protection of civil liberties later impacted upon the US Constitution and especially the Bill of Rights. He also had a great influence upon Jeremy Bentham, the founding father of utilitarianism. Bentham argued that the rational choice theory proposed by Beccaria assumed that individuals commit crime because the benefit outweighs the cost. The Englishman called this thought process the 'hedonic calculus' and concluded, like Beccaria, that punishment should be designed to persuade individuals that criminal activity was not worth the price to be paid. In his review of the Hard Labour Bill in 1778, Bentham argued for a 'general plan of punishment . . . in which solitary confinement might be combined with labour'.

In 1785, Bentham's compatriot, William Paley, suggested in *The Principles of Moral and Political Philosophy* that solitary incarceration did provide the greatest opportunity of 'reform', although the length of confinement ought to be measured by the 'quantity of work' achieved by the prisoner, which would 'excite industry, and . . . render it more voluntary'.

Unlike Bentham and Beccaria, however, Paley defended the use of capital punishment. In particular, he embraced the Georgian 'Bloody Code', which incorporated the idea that this form of punishment was a more powerful tool if many different types of crime could be swept 'into the net' of capital offences. 'Paley's Net', as it came to be known, would be executed only in exceptional cases and so we would find that 'few actually suffer death, whilst the dread and danger of it hang over the crimes of many'.

Edwin Chadwick, another nineteenth-century economist and utilitarian reformer, analysed the allocation of criminal justice resources (circa 1829–41) as an evolved publicly provided good with open-access common pool characteristics (see Ekelund and Dorton, 2003). Chadwick's primary goal was crime prevention: 'A good police would be one well-organized body of men acting upon a system of precautions, to prevent crimes and public calamities; to preserve public peace and order'. Given this goal he identified the evolved criminal justice system as a common pool and presented a rationale for restructuring the institutions of the entire system to deal with common pool problems. He believed that the system misplaced incentives for crime prevention, creating dissipations due to the common access to policing and other criminal justice services, so he recommended a number of interrelated incentive alterations for both enforcement and penal systems.

Surprisingly, economists' interest in crime and criminal justice declined in the late nineteenth and early twentieth centuries. It is only during the past four decades, largely in consequence of Gary Becker's seminal 1968 contribution[1] that their interest in crime has been revived. Like his classical school predecessors, Becker argued that potential criminals respond rationally and consistently to incentives. Crime is viewed as a problem of constrained utility maximization with individuals maximizing expected utility by choosing between legal and illegal activities after considering the expected gains and costs associated with each of the alternatives. It follows, according to Becker, that potential criminals will be deterred from offending by, first, increases in the probability of being caught and punished and, second, increases in the amount of punishment if caught.

This approach to the issue was initially opposed by criminologists, before it eventually became accepted that economics could make a significant contribution to the design of legal penalties and enforcement schemes. Indeed, in the last few years, economists have directly impacted upon government penal policy, particularly in the USA. For instance, Isaac Ehrlich, whose work is discussed later in this chapter, played a leading role in the re-introduction of the death penalty option post-1976 and, more recently, the empirical work of economists such as John Lott and Steven Levitt has stimulated considerable public debate and policy change in areas ranging from gun control to punishment policy (see Lott, 1998; Levitt, 1998).

This chapter proceeds as follows. After a brief overview of the world's crime problem, Section 2 provides an illustration of the economic theory of the supply of criminal offences. In order to test the hypotheses generated by this theory, it must be recognized that the supply of offences may have to be examined simultaneously with demand for crime prevention and law enforcement services. This demand is considered in Section 3 in the context of an examination of the empirical research relating to the so-called 'deterrence hypothesis', that is, whether crime rates rise with a reduction in the opportunity costs of crime and a decline in the expected cost of crime. Then, in Section 4, we investigate how resources are allocated within the public-sector criminal justice system, why they are allocated the way they are, and what the consequences are of this allocation process. Section 5 examines possible reasons for the declining crime rates in the USA during the 1990s in light of the theoretical and empirical findings outlined in the previous sections. Finally, Section 6 provides some concluding thoughts on the economics of crime and ideas for future research in this field.

1   A criminal world

Direct comparisons of crime rates between countries are fraught with difficulties; laws are different across international boundaries, and methods of collecting crime data vary enormously, with some countries relying on administrative data collected by the police and others relying more on surveys. Further, there are problems in comparing recorded crime rates over time within countries because of changes in levels of reporting to the police and recording by them. With these caveats in mind, we now show that over the past few decades, crime has for the most part been a growth industry in many countries.

Figure 4.1, for example, reveals that in England and Wales the number of recorded crimes per 100 000 population in 1951 was 1197. By 2003/04, this figure had increased almost ten-fold to 11 309. A similar picture emerges when we observe the experience of the USA. Table 4.1 shows that the All Index Crimes rate (which includes the seven categories listed) jumped by over 115 per cent between the mid-1960s and the mid-1990s. However, the USA did enjoy an unexpected fall in crime during the 1990s.

As Table 4.1 reveals, the All Index Crimes rate dropped by 30 per cent between 1990 and 2003, with the Murder and Non-negligent manslaughter rate declining by 40 per cent. Yet, despite this sharp fall, Figure 4.2 shows that over the 2000 to 2002 period, the USA still had one of the highest murder rates in the world at 5.6 per 100 000 population. The two

Source: Home Office, UK.

Figure 4.1 Recorded crime rate per 100 000 population in England and Wales (1901–2003/04)

Table 4.1 Recorded crime rate per 100 000 population in USA (1960–2003)

	Murder and Non-negligent manslaughter	Forcible rape	Robbery	Aggravated assault	Burglary	Larceny – theft	Auto theft	All index crimes
1960	5.1	9.6	60.1	86.1	508.6	1034.7	183.0	1887.2
1965	5.1	12.1	71.7	111.3	662.7	1329.3	256.8	2449.0
1970	7.9	18.7	172.1	164.8	1084.9	2079.3	456.8	3984.5
1975	9.6	26.3	220.8	231.1	1532.1	2804.8	473.7	5298.5
1980	10.2	36.8	251.1	298.5	1684.1	3167.0	502.2	5950.0
1985	8.0	37.1	208.5	302.9	1287.3	2901.2	462.0	5207.1
1990	9.4	41.2	257.0	424.1	1235.9	3194.8	657.8	5820.3
1995	8.2	37.1	220.9	418.3	987.1	3043.8	560.4	5275.9
2000	5.5	32.0	144.9	323.6	728.4	2475.3	414.2	4124.0
2001	5.6	31.8	148.5	318.6	741.8	2485.7	430.5	4162.6
2002	5.6	33.1	146.1	309.5	747.0	2450.7	432.9	4124.9
2003	5.7	32.1	142.2	295.0	740.5	2414.5	433.4	4063.4

Source: Federal Bureau of Investigation.

Note: Data for Austria, Italy, Romania, Russia, Sweden (1999–2001).

Source: Home Office (UK).

Figure 4.2 Murder rate per 100 000 population by country (2000–02 average)

countries with the highest murder rates per 100 000 population were South Africa (48.8) and Russia (22.2). Figure 4.3 shows murder rates over the 2000 to 2002 period for selected world cities with the highest rates being found in the US cities of Washington DC (42.8), Dallas (18.8), San Francisco (8.3) and New York (8.1) and the Eastern European cities of Tallinn (Estonia, 9.4) and Vilnius (Lithuania, 8.9).

Figure 4.4, meanwhile, reveals that the US imprisonment rate of 702 per 100 000 population was the highest in the world in 2002. The latest data show that as of 30 June 2004, the number of inmates held in US state and federal prisons and jails as well as local jails totalled 2 131 180, an increase of 85 per cent from 1 148 702 in 1990 (Harrison and Karberg, 2005).

Russia, the former world leader in imprisonment rates, had reduced its imprisonment rate to 608 per 100 000 population by 2002, with this figure expected to fall further following the approval of a prisoner amnesty by the Russian parliament in 2000. England and Wales (136), Portugal (132) and Scotland (127) had fairly high rates of imprisonment compared with others in Western Europe, which partly reflects the longer sentences imposed in these countries. Higher rates of imprisonment were reported in South Africa (425) and in some Eastern European countries, including Estonia (351), Lithuania (333) and Poland (212).

One reason for the differences in crime statistics across countries is that politics is central to the criminal justice system, even in terms of defining what action is criminal. For example, Anglo-American common law has always made a distinction between customary law crimes (such as murder, robbery, theft and rape) and so-called positive-law crimes, which have become crimes exclusively because some political interest group won or lost a political battle. Of course, objectives of criminalization are often unclear because of multiple demands of special interest groups and the misleading nature of political rhetoric, but changes in criminal law are driven by political forces (see Benson, 1990).

In other words, criminal deviancy is not simply a philosophical or a moral issue; it is a political question. Which acts are defined as criminal depend on the interest of the persons with sufficient power and influence to manage to have their views prevail. Once certain acts are designated as criminal, how the laws are implemented will also reflect the political power of the various affected groups. This suggests that viewing criminals as somehow different from other people, in the sense that their behaviour is abnormal or irrational, is questionable. An individual may be on the wrong side of the law simply because he or she is not in the winning political coalition. Thus, the decision to engage in crime may be quite rational. This leads us to Gary Becker's economic theory of crime, which approaches criminal activity in a manner that differs significantly from other social science paradigms.

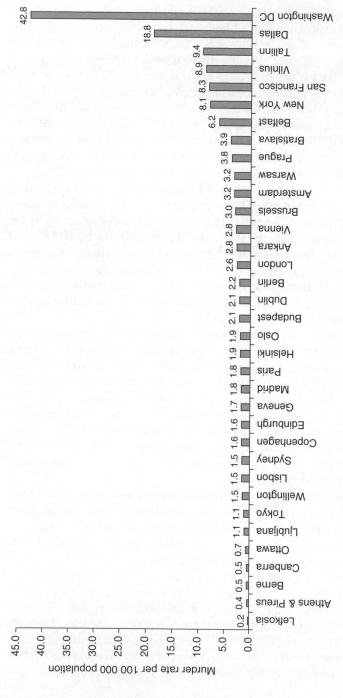

Murder rate per 100 000 population

Washington DC	42.8
Dallas	18.8
Tallinn	9.4
Vilnius	8.9
San Francisco	8.3
New York	8.1
Belfast	6.2
Bratislava	3.9
Prague	3.8
Warsaw	3.2
Amsterdam	3.2
Brussels	3.0
Vienna	2.8
Ankara	2.8
London	2.6
Berlin	2.2
Dublin	2.1
Budapest	2.1
Oslo	1.9
Helsinki	1.9
Paris	1.8
Madrid	1.8
Geneva	1.7
Edinburgh	1.6
Copenhagen	1.6
Sydney	1.5
Lisbon	1.5
Wellington	1.5
Tokyo	1.1
Ljubljana	1.1
Ottawa	0.7
Canberra	0.5
Berne	0.5
Athens & Pireus	0.4
Lefkosia	0.2

Note: Data for Vienna (1999–2001).

Source: Home Office (UK).

Figure 4.3 Murder rate per 100 000 population by city (2000–02 average)

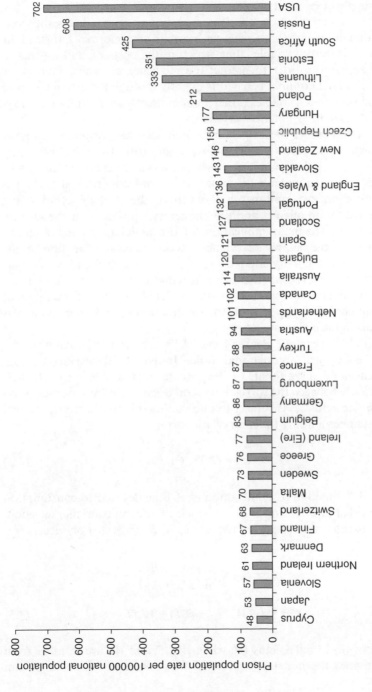

Source: Home Office (UK).

Figure 4.4 Prison population rate per 100 000 national population by country (2002)

2   The supply of criminal offences

Becker does not try to specify the ultimate causes of crime (that is, the 'preferences' that individuals have, whether 'normal' or 'abnormal'). Instead, he attempts to identify variables that structure the costs of and returns to criminal activity in order to predict the incidence of crime. That is, he explains observed criminal behaviour directly through the examination of social and economic variables rather than indirectly as a result of the psychological makeup of potential criminals.

As we noted earlier, Becker assumes that criminals respond rationally and consistently to incentives. Therefore, crime arises from the optimizing decisions of rational economic agents who maximize expected utility functions that take as arguments the expected return from criminal participation (both monetary and psychic rewards), the probability of being apprehended for an offence, and the 'monetary equivalent' of the severity of punishment. The main implications of the model are its unambiguous prediction that the 'supply of offences' is an increasing function of the return to criminal activity and a decreasing function in the level of deterrence factors. However, whether crime is reduced more by increases in the probability of apprehension or in the expected severity of punishment (given apprehension) depends on the distribution of risk aversion across individuals in the economy.

Ehrlich (1973) extends Becker's model by casting participation in the light of the theory of occupational choice. Individuals derive income from time spent in either legitimate or illegitimate (that is, criminal) activities. The difference between the two is that income generated from participation in illegitimate activities is subject to uncertainty due to deterrence factors. Ehrlich assumes a utility function of the form:

$$U^S = U(X^S, C) \tag{4.1}$$

In this utility function, C is the amount of time devoted to consumption or non-market activity and X is the stock of a composite market good. He then assumes that there are two states in S: arrest (a) or success (b), and that:

$$X^a = W^I + W_T(T) + W_L(L) \tag{4.2}$$

$$X^b = W^I + W_T(T) - F(T) + W_L(L) \tag{4.3}$$

The level of the initial asset is W^I, while W_T, F, and W_L are earnings from illegal activities, the monetary equivalent of punishment and earnings from legal activities respectively. T is time spent in illegal activities, and L is time in legal earning activities. Expected utility is given by:

$$E[U(X^S, C)] = (1-P) \, U(X^a, C) + P \, U(X^b, C) \qquad (4.4)$$

Note that P is the probability of a successful crime. Under these circumstances, the objective is to maximize expected utility over T subject to a time constraint:

$$\text{Max } E[U(X^S, C)] \text{ subject to } k = T + L + C \qquad (4.5)$$

The total hours available to the individual are given by k. The Kuhn–Tucker first-order optimality conditions are:

$$(\delta EU/\delta T) - \lambda \le 0 \qquad (4.6)$$

$$[(\delta EU/\delta T) - \lambda]T = 0 \qquad (4.7)$$

$$T \ge 0 \qquad (4.8)$$

The λ term represents the marginal utility of time spent in consumption.

If C is fixed then the optimal allocation of working time between T and L, given an interior solution (that is, the individual does not devote all of his or her time to either illegal or legal activities), is represented by:

$$-(W_T' - W_L')/(W_T' - F' - W_L') = PU'(X^a)/[(1 - P)U'(X^b)] \qquad (4.9)$$

Derivatives are indicated by the prime $(')$ symbols. The left-hand side of equation (4.9) is the slope of an opportunity boundary or the production possibility curve of the composite X between the two states of the world $[(-dX^b/dT)/(dX^a/dt)]$, as illustrated in Figure 4.5, while the right-hand side is the slope of an indifference curve defined along $dU^* = 0$. Given that T, L and $C \ge 0$, the production possibility curve is defined only between A and B in Figure 4.5. That is, A represents a point where the decision-maker specializes in illegal activities while B is a point where no illegal activities are pursued at all. C is the optimal allocation between T and L given the indifference curve shown.

Like Becker's model, Ehrlich's framework does not produce unambiguous comparative statics results with respect to the relative effectiveness of the certainty versus severity of punishment. Consideration of the second-order conditions by totally differentiating equation (4.9) demonstrates that the equilibrium position of a risk-preferrer must be to the left of that of a risk-neutral, and even further to the left of a risk-avoider, all else equal.

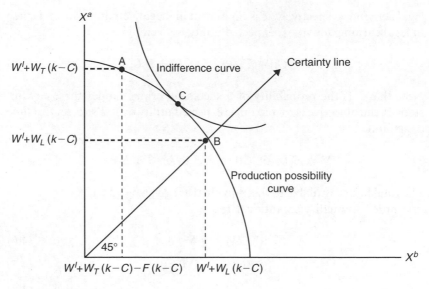

Source: Ehrlich (1973).

Figure 4.5   The allocation of time between legal and illegal activities

Furthermore, whether in equilibrium crime pays or does not pay in terms of the expected marginal returns is simply a reflection of an offender's attitude toward risk, since in equilibrium the expected marginal returns from crime would exceed, be equal to, or fall short of, the marginal returns from legitimate activity, depending on whether the offender is a risk-avoider, risk-neutral or risk-preferrer, respectively. The deterrent effect of an increase in severity of punishment also exceeds or falls short of the deterrent effect of a similar increase in the probability of punishment if the offender is a risk-avoider or a risk-preferrer, respectively.

The theoretical ambiguities arising from the Becker and Ehrlich models motivated the development of several more theoretical models. For instance, Block and Heineke (1975) show that if time spent in legitimate and illegitimate income-generating activities is allowed to enter directly into the utility function as arguments, then ambiguous comparative statics result with respect to deterrence factors, despite assumptions on the degree of risk preference of the agents. Thus, key policy implications cannot be predicted by formal theoretical models and must be examined empirically before their consequences can be anticipated. They also demonstrated that the ambiguity associated with the relative effectiveness of the certainty versus severity of punishment in Becker's model arises from the particular notion of there existing a monetary equivalent of punishment, something these authors argue may not actually exist. As such, the distribution of risk across potential offenders does not allow one to make any inference about the relative effectiveness of deterrence factors.

Critics of this economic approach to crime contend that while the model might make sense for economic crimes like robbery and burglary, the so-called 'crimes of passion' such as murder, rape and assault do not generate monetary rewards and, therefore, cannot be analysed from an economic perspective. However, this objection arises from a misunderstanding of the economist's position, which is not simply that people attempt to maximize monetary wealth. The economic model can be applied to any situation where an individual is seeking to achieve his objectives (in addition to the goods and services that can be obtained with monetary wealth, individuals may gain utility from power, security, prestige among peers, risky activities as risk-preferrers and so on), so the fact that crimes of passion often do not involve transfers of money does not mean that they cannot be explained by the economic model. Whether the model actually predicts the incidence of crimes of passion can only be determined by empirical analysis.

3   Supply of offences and demand for crime prevention
A large empirical literature explores various determinants of crime. The first empirical studies after Becker reintroduced crime to economists were undertaken by Ehrlich. In his 1973 paper discussed earlier, he examined the deterrent impact of the likelihood (and severity) of punishment on all seven of the FBI index crimes and found that these crime rates vary inversely with the probability of apprehension and punishment by imprisonment. Indeed, the so-called crimes of passion (murder, rape, assault) responded just as strongly to the expected costs of punishment as did property crimes.

3.1   Capital punishment
In this context, Ehrlich's work (1975, 1977 and Ehrlich and Gibbons, 1977) on the deterrent effect of capital punishment is probably the most well-known (and, therefore, most controversial) in the literature. In his 1975 paper, Ehrlich examined US murder and execution figures for the 1933 to 1969 period, together with measures of social factors such as unemployment and per capita income. His model revealed a statistically significant negative relationship between the murder rate and the execution rate and he noted, 'in light of these observations, one cannot reject the hypothesis that punishment, in general, and execution in particular, exert a unique deterrent effect on potential murderers'. In fact, Ehrlich suggested a 'tradeoff between executions and murders', and estimated that over the period studied, 'an additional execution per year . . . may have resulted, on average, in 7 or 8 fewer murders'.

Ehrlich's findings on capital punishment generated a storm of controversy concerning both his data and his econometric method (see Passell and Taylor, 1977; Baldus and Cole, 1975; Bowers and Pierce, 1975; Peck, 1976; Passell, 1975; Bailey, 1982; McGahey, 1980). However, as Yunker (1982) reported after examining the empirical techniques and a priori hypotheses tested in the deterrence literature, the 'hypotheses relied upon by the defenders of capital punishment possess greater inherent plausibility than those relied upon by its opponents'.

Similarly, Rubin (1978) surveyed the literature and explained that for research concluding that there was no deterrent effect:

> many of these studies were anecdotal in nature . . . But this kind of evidence cannot prove anything. We need some sort of statistical study to determine the true relationship. Many of the earlier sociological studies were statistical, but the statistics were not very sophisticated . . . The kind of study done by Ehrlich . . . is able to compensate for most differences that are thought to be significant. The results of Ehrlich's studies are very strong in indicating a deterrent effect of capital punishment.

Thus, the evidence provided by the critics of Ehrlich generally was more questionable than Ehrlich's techniques and data. Furthermore, economists have continued to explore the issues using increasingly sophisticated statistical techniques. The general result is that additional empirical support for most of Ehrlich's findings has been produced. For example, Dezhbakhsh et al. (2003), using US county-level post-moratorium panel data and a system of simultaneous equations, found that each execution results, on average, in 18 fewer murders, with a margin of error of plus or minus ten. Mocan and Gittings (2003) merge a state-level dataset, which includes crime and deterrence measures and state characteristics with information on all death sentences imposed in the USA between 1977 and 1997 and estimate that six murders are deterred per execution (see also Wolpin, 1978; Horney and Ineke, 1992; Sollars et al., 1994; Lott, 1998; Benson and Mast, 2001, for other studies of the deterrence hypothesis).

However, Levitt (2004) suggests caution in the interpretation of such figures for two reasons. First, while Figure 4.6 shows that the number of executions has generally been increasing in the USA since the restoration of the death penalty in 1976, this form of punishment is used only sparingly and the necessary legal process is often prolonged. According to Levitt, therefore, the rational criminal presented in the previous section is unlikely to be deterred by the threat of execution. Second, he argues that even if we accept the validity of these empirical estimates of the deterrent effect of the death penalty, 'the observed increase in the death penalty from 14 executions in 1991 to 66 in 2001 would eliminate between 300 and

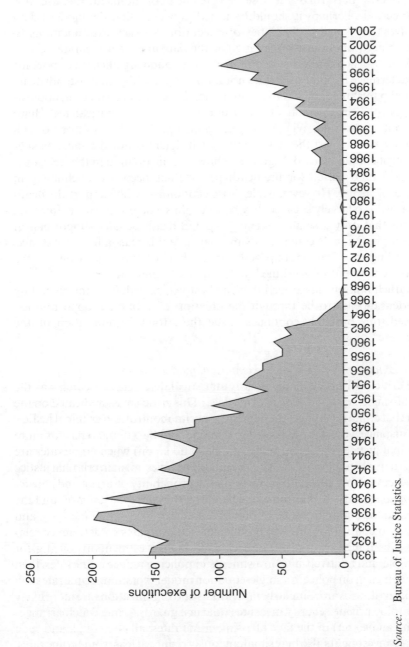

Number of executions

Source: Bureau of Justice Statistics.

Figure 4.6 Number of executions in USA (1930–2004)

400 homicides, for a reduction of 1.5 percent in the homicide rate, or less than one-twenty-fifth of the observed decline in the homicide rate over this time period'. Perhaps it should be noted, however, that the modern data involves very small probabilities of execution, so such extrapolations to probability values outside the range of the data may be inaccurate.

While Ehrlich and other economists have found significant support for the deterrence hypothesis, it does not follow that these economists advocate capital punishment or severe criminal penalties. The deterrence hypothesis is a positive implication of economic theory that empirical tests have generally supported. Whether capital punishment is desirable or not is a normative issue and the suggestion that it deters is not the same as suggesting it should be used. Figure 4.7 shows public opinion in the USA over the post-1976 period for the death penalty has been overwhelmingly in favour of its use. However, while those economists who support the death penalty do so largely because they believe it has a deterrent effect, Table 4.2 reveals that only a small percentage of US death penalty supporters (at least for individuals convicted of murder) cite this reason for their stance. According to a 2001 Gallup poll, almost half of those in favour of the death penalty put forward the 'eye for an eye' argument.

Ehrlich himself has argued that the best way to reduce crime, including murder, appears to be through the creation of economic opportunities. Indeed, this probably continues to be the strongest implication of the literature.

3.2   Extensions to the standard empirical model of crime

One criticism Ehrlich made of early statistical deterrence research was the use of single-equation statistical models.[2] This criticism is predicated on the idea that crime rates affect the demand for crime control and criminal justice. For instance, voters are expected to demand and be willing to pay for more criminal justice resources (police, prisons and so on) when crime rates are high than when they are low, all else equal. The investment in criminal justice resources in turn affects crime rates via the probability of arrest and conviction and severity of punishment. Therefore, the supply of offences and the demand for criminal justice resources are determined simultaneously, and failure to control for this will produce biased estimates of deterrence relationships. If high crime rates cause relatively high investments in policing, for example, and relatively high investments in policing reduce crime rates, then the coefficient on police in a single-equation model explaining crime rates will be biased downward. Similarly, individuals and organizations are more likely to employ private security measures (alarms, guards, crime watch arrangements and so on) in the face of rising crime rates, all else equal, and such private investments also may simultaneously reduce at least some crime rates.

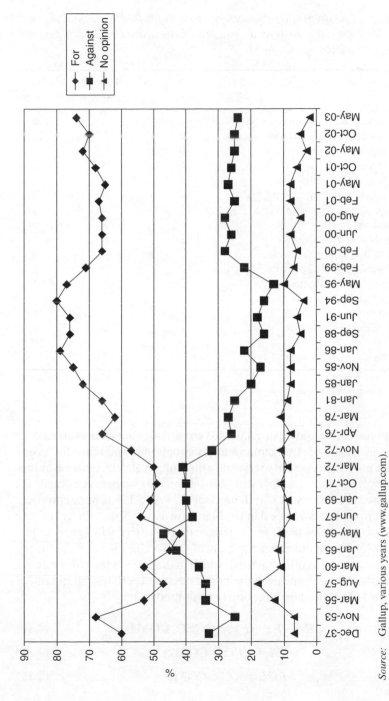

Source: Gallup, various years (www.gallup.com).

Figure 4.7 US public opinion on death penalty (selected years, 1937–2003) (Are you in favour of the death penalty for a person convicted of murder?)

117

*Table 4.2   US death penalty supporters' reasons for favouring policy
(1991–2001) (Why do you favour the death penalty for persons
convicted of murder?)*

	Feb. 2001 %	Feb. 2000 %	Jun. 1991 %
Eye for an eye/punishment fits crime	48	40	40
Save taxpayers money/prison costs	20	12	12
Acts as deterrent/sets an example	10	8	8
They deserve it	6	5	5
Support/believe in death penalty	6	0	0
Depends on type of crime committed	6	6	0
To keep them from repeating crime	6	4	4
Biblical reasons	3	3	3
Relieves prison overcrowding	2	0	0
If no doubt they committed crime	2	0	0
Life sentences don't always mean life	2	0	0
They cannot be rehabilitated	2	1	1
To serve justice	1	3	2
Fair punishment	1	6	6
It benefits families of victims	1	0	0
Other	3	10	10
No opinion	1	3	3

Source: Gallup, various years (www.gallup.com).

In response to the above, the standard empirical model has evolved over time to consist of a set of simultaneous equations explaining the crime rate(s), the probability(ies) of arrest and a measure(s) of deterrence resources (for example, police employment or budget) as dependent variables (for reviews, see Cameron, 1988; Benson, et al., 1994). The generic empirical model of crime that developed in the literature assumes that the crime rate affects the resources available to the police (that is, voters' willingness to pay for criminal justice resources such as policing and prisons is a function of the level of crime as well as other factors), which in turn affects the crime rate via the deterrence effects of the probability of arrest (and perhaps the severity of punishment). The standard equations of this model are:

$$CR = f(PA, SEV, \textbf{SOCEC}, \textbf{COM1}) \tag{4.10}$$

$$PA = g(POL, \textbf{COM2}) \tag{4.11}$$

$$POL = h(CR, \textbf{COM3}) \tag{4.12}$$

where *CR* is the jurisdiction-level crime rate being studied during a particular time period (some models have considered more than one crime rate simultaneously), *PA* is the probability of arrest in the jurisdiction in that time period (or perhaps in the previous time period, assuming that potential criminals base their expectations on the probability of arrest on past data), *POL* represents the jurisdiction's police resources in the relevant time period, and *SEV* is the severity of the sanction for the crime during the time period, which can include the probability of conviction if arrested as well as the average sentence (*SEV* may also be a function of crime rates, of course, since expenditures on punishment resources are also determined in the political arena; thus, additional equations may be added to account for the endogeneity of *SEV*). **SOCEC** is a vector of variables that reflect the socio-economic characteristics of the jurisdiction during the time period being studied. Factors such as income, unemployment, educational attainment and racial characteristics of the population are control variables or other sources of incentives and constraints for the 'rational' decision-makers who are assumed to respond to deterrents. **COM1**, **COM2** and **COM3** are vectors of other community characteristics that may influence crime, the probability of arrest and the demand for policing (for example, tax capacity, income and demographic factors). Some recent work suggests that an equation or equations to control for the demand for private security may also be important to include since private security measures may be either substitutes for or complements to public crime control efforts (see Benson, 1998; Benson and Mast, 2001).

While simultaneity bias can be an issue in some crime studies, both empirical and theoretical findings suggest that it may not be appropriate to model some individual crime rates in simultaneous equation models. After all, while the aggregate crime rate might influence the demand for policing (as well as punishment and/or private security) resources, individual crime categories may not, particularly if they constitute only a small part of overall crime activity. In this context, for instance, there is little empirical evidence of a connection between violent crime rates and police resources as implied by equation (4.12). More property crime apparently increases the demand for police resources, but violent crime is not a significant determinant of police resources.

Benson et al. (1992) provide direct evidence of this in a study of the determinants of police non-capital expenditures in Florida. They report that these outlays are significantly and positively correlated with the property crime rate (with an estimated elasticity ranging from + 0.46 to + 0.61). The effect of the violent crime rate on police expenditures, in contrast, is generally not significant and has an estimated elasticity between −0.04 and + 0.003 (see also Avio and Clark, 1976; Hakim et al., 1979; Sollars et al., 1994; Benson et al., 1994).

Second, a common finding in the literature is that a higher probability of arrest has a deterrent value but that the marginal increments in police resources do not produce a higher probability of arrest as implied by equation (4.11).[3] This result is not too surprising given that the property and violent crimes that are studied in these models often account for only a small portion of total police activity. Increases in police resources need not increase deterrence of any specific crime because those resources can be allocated to other activities. Thus, two of the three links required for a simultaneous model of at least some crime rates and the probability of punishment are very weak or non-existent: police apparently do not receive greater budgets with higher violent crime rates, although they do with higher property crime rates, and police discretion in the allocation of resources reduces the likelihood that marginal increments to police resources will alter the probability of being arrested for at least some crimes. Whether simultaneous equations should be used or not is, therefore, an issue that has to be considered in the specification of empirical models, using endogeneity tests.

The deterrence relationship is generally found by using a reported offence rate as a dependent variable, and the arrest/reported offence ratio serves as a proxy for the probability of arrest. Therefore, reported offences are explained by arrests multiplied by the inverse of reported offences, and critics of the literature note that the negative relationship could simply be a product of spurious correlation resulting from this measurement error. For instance, Brier and Fienberg's (1980) influential review (reinforced by others), concludes that there is, 'no reliable empirical support in the existing econometrics literature either for or against the deterrence hypothesis'.

In light of such criticisms, Levitt (1998) developed a model for determining the extent of measurement error. Tests of his model for the seven major Index I crime categories conclude that measurement error biases are likely to be relevant in only one of them: auto theft. Thus, Levitt's results suggest that a study focusing on the violent crime categories (murder, sexual offences, assault, robbery) or on most property crimes (burglary, larceny) will not suffer from such problems. In this context, a fixed-effects model, which is designed to deal with unobserved heterogeneity among observations in time-series cross-section pools of data, is also suggested by Levitt's findings, and this empirical device has been employed in most of the recent econometric studies of crime. By including a dummy variable for each jurisdiction, unobservable factors that do not change over time can be controlled for. After all, such unobserved heterogeneity is characteristic of jurisdictions since communities with very similar socio-economic and demographic characteristics have very different crime rates. Further, importantly, if crime reporting by victims in a jurisdiction is relatively constant over time, the use of fixed-effects models also attenuates another measurement error problem that has plagued this literature: the widely recognized inaccuracies in the number of offences known to the police arising due to the uneven reporting of victims and police departments. Thus, empirical testing of the hypotheses generated by the economic theory of crime is becoming increasingly sophisticated in order to deal with data limitations, but as the empirical literature expands and becomes more sophisticated, the robustness of certain key results suggested by Ehrlich's studies is becoming increasingly clear.

It can be concluded with considerable confidence that the opportunity cost of committing crime matters. In a strong economy with substantial opportunities for employment and high returns to labour, crime rates are relatively low, all else equal. It is also clear that the crime rates are negatively related to the probability of punishment. As the probability of punishment increases, crime rates fall, *ceteris paribus*. On the other hand, empirical inferences of the deterrence effect of the severity of punishment are less robust. Some studies, such as Ehrlich's capital punishment research and others cited above, find that relatively severe punishment deters crimes, while other studies using different data or specifications find that this is not the case. This should not be surprising, nor should it lead to the rejection of the deterrence hypothesis for at least three reasons.

First, the severity of punishment is a subjective concept. Some people may find that capital punishment is more severe than life in prison without parole, for instance, while others may feel that the opposite holds.

Second, non-measurable social sanctions (for example, loss of reputation, social ostracism, the difficulty that accused or convicted criminals have in getting a legal job or finding contractual partners) may be much more 'severe' for some types of crimes than the relatively more objectively measurable sanctions imposed by the criminal justice system. This is likely to be particularly true for individuals with significant opportunity costs in the form of high income-earning possibilities that would be sacrificed if the person is arrested (see Lott, 1987). These social sanctions may be important deterrents but because they cannot be measured, the deterrence effect cannot be observed. However, they may affect interpretation of empirical results using measurable punishment. For instance, if severity is measured by length of sentence, and unobserved social sanctions are roughly constant, then real punishment is the length of sentence plus a constant. Doubling the length of sentence will not double real punishment under these circumstances, so empirical results could suggest that criminals are risk-preferrers even if they are not.

Third, sanctions do not matter if the probability of punishment is extremely low. In fact, there is no reason to even learn about what a punishment may be if one believes that the chances of being punished are trivial. A low probability of punishment might be anticipated because an individual is a very good criminal, because of misinformation, because victims choose not to report most of the crimes of a particular type (for example, small thefts), or because very few scarce policing resources are allocated to control a particular crime.

4   The allocation of criminal justice resources

Most resources are scarce, including those allocated by the public sector. Thus, many public sector decisions, including those involved with the criminal justice system, essentially are resource allocation problems. Legislators (national or local, depending on where a budget decision is made) must decide how much funding to allocate to purchase resources for law enforcement (for example, police and policing capital like patrol cars; courts and prosecutors; prisons, parole systems) given alternative uses of tax revenues (for example, education, highways). Budgets for the purchase of law enforcement resources must then be allocated among competing uses. For example, police resources can be allocated to the control of drug markets, prostitution markets, illegal gambling; solution of robberies and burglaries; solution of rapes, assaults and murders; traffic control; crime prevention efforts and various community service and information services.

If there is political demand to increase efforts against one particular type of crime, there are two possible responses. First, a legislature may allocate more total expenditures to law enforcement so that more can be allocated to the control of that crime without sacrificing the current police efforts against other crimes. This either requires increased taxes or reduced expenditures for other publicly provided goods and services. Therefore, it is more likely that competing political demands will have to be taken into account and the resulting compromises will mean that at least part of the response will take a second form: the shifting of some law enforcement resources away from other uses. To see the consequences, let us first examine the underlying mechanisms that drive the allocation of existing law enforcement resources.

4.1   The tragedy of the criminal commons

When resources are scarce in the sense that the competing demands for their use far exceed their supply, they must be rationed among these competing uses. Many rationing techniques are possible. For instance, in a free market where resources are privately owned, those resources (as well as goods and services) are rationed by price: anyone willing to pay the market-determined price has access to the desired resources. Public law enforcement resources are not rationed by price, of course. Indeed, some would suggest that they are not rationed at all since everyone supposedly has access to them free of charge. But the fact that no money price is charged for common access resources simply means that some other rationing criteria must arise (see Chadwick, 1929; Shoup, 1964).

The implications of common access, or common pool resources, have been examined extensively in relation to publicly or commonly owned resources such as grazing land and fishing grounds, but the similarity between the problems that arise in grazing or fisheries commons and in law enforcement are striking. In the classic commons problem, for instance, when many individuals have free access to graze cattle on the same land, each has incentives to use up as much grass as possible before others with access do the same.

Free access public law enforcement resources are similarly crowded and inefficiently employed. For example, prosecutors and judges have common access to prison space. They have at best only weak incentives to limit the number of prisoners they herd into the commons when making their sentencing recommendations and decisions, or to consider alternatives to imprisonment such as fines, restitution, community service, lesser degrees of constraint like community control, treatment programmes and work release. Many such alternatives are well known to prosecutors and judges, and some are frequently employed, but the incentives to consider them are relatively weak because these decisions are made in a common pool environment.

Indeed, in as much as prosecutors have incentives to demonstrate to their local constituencies that they are tough on crime, imprisonment is a relatively attractive punishment. Even if they recognize that their actions add to the crowding problem, their private benefits (the political support they get from their tough image) may exceed their private costs (perhaps the anxiety associated with the recognition that they are crowding prisons and raising costs to society at large). Thus, imprisonment is chosen relatively frequently and the effect is that prosecutors and judges as a group crowd the common access prisons much as cattle owners crowd common access grazing land.

State legislators in the USA can also crowd the criminal justice commons since, like judges and prosecutors, they have weak incentives to conserve scarce prison resources. When passing laws that increase the penalties for certain crimes, such as mandatory minimum sentences, the legislature's action is equivalent to increasing the number of people who can use the classic grazing commons. Of course, the legislature also has the power to offset the resulting overcrowding since it can increase the number of prison beds, the equivalent of increasing the common land. But the temptation to overcrowd the commons is likely to prevail, since individual legislators are unlikely to suffer any costs from this course of action, particularly in the short run. Legislators can reap political benefits by passing longer sentences for crimes, so they appear to be tough on criminals, while ignoring the fact that the law can undermine other aspects of the criminal justice system. Since expanding criminal justice resources involves the politically unpopular task of either cutting other government functions or raising taxes, the politically astute course of action is to crowd the commons.

Crowding occurs at all levels of the criminal justice system. In fact, one reason for judges' and prosecutors' failure to consider alternatives to imprisonment is that the courts themselves are severely crowded, implying that judges may not have time to explore alternative punishments at length (Neely, 1982; Benson, 1990).

Judges must also consider other crowded conditions in their sentencing decisions as well. Probation is the most commonly used alternative sanction to imprisonment, for example, and the typical sanction for first-time offenders. In fact, roughly three times as many convicted offenders in the USA are placed on probation each year as are sentenced to prisons and jails combined. But as Byrne (1988) noted, 'Although prison crowding draws national attention and increased resources, "probation crowding" poses a more immediate threat to the criminal justice process and to community protection'. The probation population in the USA has been increasing at roughly the same rate as the prison population, severely taxing the ability of the system's limited resources to monitor and supervise probationers. All alternatives to imprisonment, other than forgiveness and release, require the use of some scarce resources for monitoring, so the potential for crowding arises even if judges do not herd criminals into the common pool prisons. Scarce police resources also see many reported crimes crowded out of the system.

But crowding is only one aspect of a commons problem. Indeed, even though crowding may be the most visible consequence of common access, it is not the most significant consequence. When grazing land is over-used, its rapid deterioration in quality means that the output of the production process that employs that land similarly deteriorates in quality. The same problem results with common access law enforcement resources. Prisons, for instance, are intended to serve several functions (produce several outputs), including punishment of convicted criminals, deterrence of potential criminals, incapacitation of dangerous criminals, and rehabilitation of criminals who can be reformed. All of these outputs of the prison system decline in quality because of the commons problem and crowding (crowding could make prisons less pleasant, thereby increasing punishment and deterrence, but in the USA, for instance, prison systems have been forced by federal court order to alleviate crowding, and this is generally done by releasing prisoners early, thereby holding the unpleasantness of prison roughly constant while reducing time served). Early release programmes mean that criminals are not punished to the degree that judges, victims and others in society feel justice requires. Potential criminals recognize that prison sentences are rarely fully served and that the portion of sentences served declines with increased admissions after capacity is reached, so deterrence may be diminished. Some non-rehabilitated and insufficiently deterred criminals are released early, despite the need for continued incapacitation, and commit more crimes. Finally, when prison budgets are consumed by efforts to accommodate overflowing prison populations, resources may not be available for rehabilitation programmes; and if they are, early release may mean that criminals are not enrolled in rehabilitation programmes long enough to benefit from them.

Individual legislators, prosecutors and judges who make the decisions that produce crowded prisons are not liable for the costs of their decisions. Instead, costs are imposed on taxpayers who face the ever-increasing cost of building more prison space; on victims who are not satisfied with the level of punishment offenders actually incur; on citizens who are victimized by prematurely released criminals and other criminals who are not sufficiently deterred; on criminals, who may have reduced opportunities for rehabilitation, face the increased violence and abuse that may accompany prison crowding, and endure additional social sanctions upon release because people do not feel that they have been sufficiently punished; and on corrections officials who must focus their efforts and resources on coping with crowded conditions rather than on other functions, such as rehabilitation and treatment.

Common access really means that many public law enforcement resources are rationed on a first-come-first-served basis. The first case of a certain type filed gets the first available slot on the court docket, for instance, and the first prisoner of a particular type sentenced gets the first open space of that type in the prison system. But rationing by first-come-first-served generally means rationing by waiting in queues, as backlogs of unmet demands build up. Thus, as noted above, there is a backlog of court cases waiting to be heard and county jails in the USA fill with prisoners waiting to be tried or to be placed in state prisons. In fact, 52 per cent of the prisoners held in local jails during 1987 were queued up, awaiting arraignment or trials, and a substantial portion of the remaining 48 per cent, who were convicted inmates, were being held until they could be transferred to another authority (US Department of Justice, 1988). Similarly, backlogs of thousands of supposedly open police cases receive little or no attention, waiting forever to be solved. In Tallahassee, Florida, for instance, there were approximately 15 900 crimes reported to police in 2001 that would require investigation to be solved. Of those, roughly 7000 had no obvious leads for investigators to follow, so no investigator was even assigned to the cases. Furthermore, another 4000 cases that actually had leads that could have been followed were not assigned to an investigator, probably because they were not considered to be important enough by the police to warrant attention. Only 5900 of the reported cases were assigned to investigative personnel.

When rationing by waiting becomes prevalent and the time cost of waiting grows, many potential demanders opt out of the queue and choose not to be served. Consequently, prosecutors and judges must expedite waiting cases by plea bargaining. Furthermore, many crime victims choose not to report crimes, either because of the low probability of satisfaction (since police facing excess demands for their services will likely be unable to solve the crime; plus the likelihood that even if the police are successful, prosecutors will drop the case or plea bargain it down to a level of punishment that is unsatisfactory from the victim's perspective) or because of the time cost associated with cooperating in prosecution. Annual Victimization Surveys conducted by the US Department of Justice suggest that over 60 per cent of the crimes against persons and property are never reported to the police.

Other rationing mechanisms also apply when there is excess demand. For one thing, suppliers generally have considerable discretion when demand exceeds supply. They can discriminate among demanders, choosing to serve some but not others. In light of the numbers reported above, for instance, the Tallahassee Police chose which crimes to investigate and which to ignore. These choices may reflect many factors, such as police officials' individual subjective evaluations of the relative merit of different crimes, political pressures (neighbourhoods with large numbers of wealthy and politically influential residents may get more patrol cars per capita and more rapid response time than those with large numbers of poor and politically powerless residents), and the self-interest motives of police. The allocation of police resources across the various crime categories reflects such decisions and essentially divides the larger common pool into smaller ones. The decision of a patrol officer to give one driver a warning while giving another a traffic ticket for the same kind of infraction (for example, because one driver was more contrite, friendlier, more attractive, politically influential, a friend) is another example.

4.2   *Allocation of resources and probability and severity of punishment*
The allocation processes in the criminal justice system determine the probability and severity of punishment for different crimes, of course. Continuing with the supply and demand analogy, these allocation decisions

result in a set of 'expected prices' of crimes in the form of expected pun-ishments that the criminal justice system sets for various criminal acts. According to the economic theory of crime outlined in Section 2, potential criminals compare these expected prices to the benefits they anticipate from criminal acts as they make their decisions to commit crimes.

The expected price of crime is not the actual sentence given to convicted criminals. Rather, the expected price is determined by the probability of punishment times the actual or average punishment. The probability of punishment involves a series of uncertain events. First, the crime or its con-sequences must be observed. When a crime has a victim this is likely to occur, of course, but the 'quality' of observations can also vary, thus influ-encing the probability of successful prosecution (for example, whether the criminal is likely to be observed in the act, producing an eye witness, or whether the crime will only be discovered after the fact, thus requiring stronger physical evidence for conviction). With consensual crimes like drug exchanges, gambling and prostitution, such observation is much less likely, of course, as it requires either that police see the transaction or that some potential reporting witness does. Not surprisingly, these crimes are often much more difficult and costly to enforce.

If the criminal act or its consequences are observed, the observation must then be reported to police, unless the observer is someone in a position to act on the observation (for example, police or private security officer). As indicated above, victims actually observe many crimes that they do not report. With consensual crimes, the problem is obviously even more signi-ficant, as witnesses almost never report them unless they are 'snitches' who exchange 'evidence' for money or some other favour, such as freedom from prosecution for crimes they have committed. Third, the criminal who committed the reported crime must be arrested. Fourth, the offender must be charged and prosecuted after being arrested. Fifth, the prosecution must be successful before a sanction is imposed. Given a conviction, the criminal can be sanctioned in one of a number of alternative ways, as sug-gested above. Possible punishments include, in the USA, the death penalty (a highly unlikely outcome except for the most heinous violent offences), prison terms, supervised release including probation, immediate release by being sentenced to time already served in jail, or a fine. Socially imposed sanctions are real alternatives that should also influence criminal decisions, but here the focus is on the 'price' of (expected punishment for) crime imposed by the public sector criminal justice system.

There is no way to determine what portion of crimes that are committed are actually observed, so the first probability listed above cannot be esti-mated. There is evidence regarding the other steps in the process, however. According to the US Department of Justice, Bureau of Justice Statistics'

Table 4.3   Expected prison time for Florida criminals in 1992

Crime	(PVR)	× (PA)	× (PP × PC × PPS)	× (APS) (years)	× (PSS) (%)	= Expected Prison Time
Homicide	1.0	0.68	0.52	21.8	38.1	2.99 years
Rape	0.53	0.56	0.52	12.9	45.8	338 days
Robbery	0.70	0.25	0.25	8.6	44.9	61.3 days
Burglary	0.60	0.15	0.30	5.5	37.3	13.2 days
Larceny	0.36	0.18	0.14	4.1	33.6	4.5 days
Auto theft	0.92	0.15	0.14	4.1	33.6	9.8 days

Victimization Survey for 1992 (this year is chosen in order to use it with other data from that year, as explained below), only about 39 per cent of all Index I crimes were reported in the USA, although reporting varies by crime type from 92 per cent for auto theft to 15 per cent for crimes of larceny resulting in losses of less than $50. Using Florida data, reported crimes cleared by arrest ranged from a high of 68 per cent for murder to a low of 15 per cent for motor vehicle theft and burglary in 1992.[4]

In Table 4.3, *PVR* is the probability of victim reporting from the Department of Justice's Annual Victimization Survey. Victims cannot report that they are victims of homicides, of course, so it is simply assumed that the probability that homicides are reported/discovered is 1.0. *PA* represents the probability of arrest given that a crime is reported, which is the clearance rate reported by the Florida Department of Law Enforcement (FDLE). *PP* is the probability of prosecution given arrest, *PC* denotes the probability of conviction given prosecution, and *PPS* is the probability of a prison sentence given conviction. These probabilities are combined into a single probability of imprisonment given arrest because the arrest data come from the FDLE while the prosecution and conviction data are from the courts and the imprisonment data are from the Florida Department of Corrections (FDOC), and the courts' reporting categories do not match with the FDLE and FDOC categories except for Robbery and Burglary. Therefore, the individual probabilities can only be directly estimated for those crimes, while the combined probabilities can be estimated for the others. *APS* represents the average prison sentence given imprisonment from the FDOC. *PSS* denotes the average portion of a sentence that is served, also from the FDOC.

The numbers in Table 4.3 might be thought of as approximations of the expected price (that is, probability-weighted prison term) the criminal justice system is charging for committing these crimes, assuming that imprisonment is the punishment that criminals consider to be most severe.

Violent crimes against persons have relatively high expected penalties, compared with property offences, but all of the probability-weighted prison
terms for most crimes committed in Florida were very low, and not surprisingly, Florida had the highest crime rates of all states in the USA at the time.

Clearly, the allocation of criminal justice resources matters, as it influences the decisions to commit various kinds of crimes. As noted in
Section 1, crime rates have been falling in the USA in the 1990s, and one
explanation is that the rapid increase in the allocation of criminal justice
resources devoted to drug enforcement ended in the early 1990s. Other
explanations, to which we now turn, are consistent with the economic
theory of crime and can also be cited.

5 Explanations for the 1990s' fall in US crime rates

As Table 1.1 shows, the FBI All Index Crime Rate was 5820.3 per 100 000
population in 1990. The crime rate dropped continuously through the
1990s, reaching 4124.0 in 2000. Why? Politicians have ready answers as they
claim credit through their support of prison construction, longer mandated
sentences, greater police funding and so on. They also claim credit for the
strong economy and low levels of unemployment, which reduce the incentives to commit property crimes. Criminologists cite many of these same
causes as well, along with the changing age distribution of the population,
as the size of the crime-prone cohort of young males has been shrinking
due to ageing and reduced birth rates. In fact, as discussed in Chapter 11,
Donohue and Levitt (2001) offer evidence that legalized abortion is an
important factor in explaining these reductions in crime.

5.1 The impact of a growing economy

The growing economy that the USA enjoyed through the 1990s had two
important impacts. First, as Ehrlich and many other economists have
stressed, crime rates fall as opportunities for legal employment improve and
wages rise. This may well be the most important factor explaining the
decline in crime during the period, although Levitt (2004) points out that
the 1960s was also a decade of strong economic growth but large increases
in crime were experienced. (Gary Becker also does not believe the strong
economy to be an important factor as his interview in this book reveals.)

Second, the rapid growth in income and wealth of the 1990s meant that
governments saw tax revenues increasing substantially without tax rate
increases. Federal, state and local legislators could increase spending on
many things, including law enforcement, and they did so. The resulting
prison construction (along with the growing funding and use of diversion-
ary programmes for drug offenders) meant that prisoners now serve
longer sentences and/or more criminals are sentenced to prison relative to

probation and other alternatives, all else equal. Thus, deterrence may be more effective due to the increased severity of punishment. Greater police funding means police can make more arrests. Of course, whether this deters Index I crimes or not depends on how police resources are allocated. As noted earlier, drug enforcement declined in the early 1990s, releasing policing (and prison) resources for other uses. With the addition of more resources in the mid-to-late 1990s, state, local and federal government increased spending on policing, so deterrence effects became stronger. In fact, these growing law enforcement budgets ultimately allowed the police to simultaneously increase drug enforcement and enforcement efforts against other crimes. For example, drug arrests in Florida reached 126 087 in 2002, up from the 1997 level of 81 846. This increase in the late 1990s and early 2000s may help explain the fact that crime rates appear to be levelling out. The 2002 drug arrest rate per 10 000 population (76) in Florida actually exceeded the 1989 rate (66.83), for instance.

5.2   The rise in private protection

There is another potential explanation for falling crime rates that has gone largely unnoticed. As early as 1968, Gary Becker (1968) observed, 'A variety of private as well as public actions also attempt to reduce the number and incidence of crimes: guards, doormen, and accountants are employed, locks and alarms installed, insurance coverage extended, parks and neighbors avoided, taxis used in place of walking or subways, and so on'. Three decades later, private citizens in the USA have responded to the fear of crime by investing increasing amounts of their own time and money in crime prevention, including crime watch and other types of neighbour-hood or building watching, patrolling and escort arrangements, installation of alarms and other detection devices, improved locks and lighting, investments in self-protection such as martial arts training and guns, and employment of private security personnel.

Information on these activities is relatively scarce, but a number of studies have been conducted over the years that indicate dramatic increases in the employment of most of these resources and services (Benson, 1998). Private security employment was roughly equal to public police personnel in 1970, for instance, but it is estimated that there are approximately three times as many private security employees today than there are public police. Spending on private security is estimated to be more than three times the level of spending on the entire public sector criminal justice system (Philipson and Posner, 1996) and this does not include the opportunity costs for individuals who alter their behaviour (for example, give up opportunities such as travel, social activities) to avoid becoming a crime target, costs that are 'likely to be substantial' (Ayres and Levitt, 1998).

It is not just numbers and expenditures that are rising. Both increasingly sophisticated labour and capital are being combined to produce ever higher levels of security where it is demanded. Indeed, some technological innovations that probably were not even motivated by fear of crime, such as the widespread ownership and use of cell phones, have probably had dramatic impacts on the incentives to commit crimes, as they have lowered the cost and increased the speed of reporting crimes. Many innovations have been directly motivated by a demand for crime control, however. The increasing level of technological sophistication for relatively low cost home alarm systems is really quite amazing, for instance, as technologies that were on the cutting edge only a short time ago are obsolete. Such technologies also lower the cost of observing and reporting crimes. Training for security personnel has had to improve dramatically in order to take advantage of the new technologies. Security personnel still do include minimum-wage night watchmen that are the stereotype of security from the 1950s and 1960s, of course, but they also include highly trained and skilled electronic-security experts and security design consultants, as growing demand for detection and deterrent equipment and technological advances that are lowering the price of such equipment stimulate demand for more educated, skilled and specialized private security labour while reducing the demand for unskilled watchmen.

Studies of the consequences of these private sector crime control activities are also scarce. However, several informative studies do exist. For example, Ayres and Levitt's (1998) empirical analysis of the impacts of Lojack, a hidden radio transmitter installed in cars, which can be remotely activated if the car is stolen, concluded that a 1 percentage point increase in installations of Lojack in a market is associated with a 20 per cent decline in auto thefts within large cities and a 5 per cent reduction in the rest of the state. These devices greatly reduce the expected loss for car owners who use them, since 95 per cent of the cars equipped with Lojack are recovered compared with 60 per cent for non-Lojack equipped cars, but this direct benefit for the individual using the device clearly is only part of the total benefit arising from its availability and use because a potential car thief does not know whether a potential target vehicle is protected by Lojack or not. This uncertainty acts as a general deterrent against auto thefts, and, 'Lojack appears to be one of the most cost-effective crime reduction approaches documented in the literature, providing a greater return than increased police, prisons, job programs, or early education interventions' (Ayers and Levitt, 1998). Lott's (1998) controversial work on concealed handguns reaches similar conclusions, finding that violent crimes, including murder, rape and robbery, are significantly deterred when potential criminals know that citizens are allowed to carry concealed handguns.

Similarly, Zedlewski' s (1992) comprehensive statistical study used data from 124 Standard Metropolitan Statistical Areas in an effort to analyse the effect of both public police and private security on the overall safety environment of communities and on offender decision-making. Greater levels of security personnel were associated with reduced levels of community crime, suggesting that investments in private security produce spillover benefits to the community at large. More recently, Benson and Mast (2001) employed a large cross-section time-series pool of data to consider the impact of private security on crime. They found robustly significant and negative relationships between rapes and private security, as well as some but less robust support for general deterrence of robbery.[5] Thus, there is growing evidence that the growth in private security helps explain the decline in crime rates through the 1990s.

Even though there have been many changes during the 1990s, the economic theory of crime probably can explain the dropping crime rates enjoyed in the USA during that decade. They generally are factors that increased legal income-earning opportunities and/or increased the probability or severity of punishment. Looking ahead, Levitt (2004) identifies the coming of age of so-called 'crack babies' in the USA and 'those who have spent their childhood years in families and neighborhoods ravaged by crack' as factors that could potentially contribute to increased crime rates over the next decade due to the 'criminogenic effect', although he suggests that the overall downward trend in crime rates experienced in the 1990s should continue.

6   Conclusion

This chapter has shown that economists have long harboured criminal interests. Our principal focus has been the examination of two specific contributions: first, the theory and empirical evidence relating to the 'deterrence hypothesis', and second, the analysis of resource allocation within the public sector criminal justice system. One topic for economists to further investigate is the impact of technology improvements on crime. In Section 5, we suggested that advances in alarms and other detection devices (together with their increased use) may also have contributed to falls in crime in the USA. Yet, it may also be true that the recent introduction of other technology such as the Internet has led to crime creation. This is particularly relevant to two topics discussed later in this book: pornography and music. In the former case, there are concerns that the Internet may have driven a rise in child pornography crimes (see Chapter 6 for an analysis of the impact of the Internet on porn consumption in general and how police authorities can enforce laws in this area). Meanwhile, Chapter 14 examines the extent to which the Internet has stimulated music piracy.

Overall, one would hope that public policy on crime can be influenced by research carried out by economists. Indeed, it is almost ten years since DiIulio (1996) appealed to the economics profession for 'help' with matters of criminal justice, while simultaneously lamenting the fact that:

> many leading experts and policymakers doubt that economic perspectives on crime have much to offer, see zero value in attempts to model the conditions under which given public policies can cut crime, and disdain efforts to measure (or, heaven forbid, quantify) the social costs and benefits of competing crime policy options.

Of course, our examination of the impact of Isaac Ehrlich's work in the 1970s on capital punishment suggests this statement may not be universally true and certainly there are signs over the past several years that the work of economists such as Steven Levitt at Chicago is stimulating policy debate. Armed with increasingly powerful tools to understand individual behaviour, the aggregation of individual choices and actions, and to establish causality, we conclude that economists are comfortably placed to make significant contributions well into the twenty-first century.

Notes

1. Becker (1968).
2. Ehrlich made this point in his 1973 article, and employed simultaneous equation techniques, but some economists continued to employ single-equation models (see Sjoquist, 1973).
3. This is emphasized in Cameron's (1988) critical review of the economics of crime and the deterrence hypothesis, but for an alternative interpretation that focuses on the allocation of policing resources, see Benson et al. (1994) and Benson et al. (1998).
4. 1992 data were gathered by one of the authors for a report prepared for the Florida Chamber of Commerce, so these data are employed here. Compiling the data is costly because much of it is not published and it must be obtained from several different sources (for example, the Florida Department of Law Enforcement, the US Department of Justice, the Florida Department of Corrections and the Florida Supreme Court). Furthermore, the data are not categorized in the same way by each agency so data must be reclassified or used in various estimation techniques in order to perform the calculations presented in the table.
5. These results are preliminary since the purpose of the analysis is to test the robustness of the Lott model, not to present a fully developed model of the influence of private security on crime rates.

References

Avio, K.L. and C.S. Clark (1976), *Property Crime in Canada: An Econometric Study*, Toronto: University of Toronto Press.

Ayres, I. and S.D. Levitt (1998), 'Measuring Positive Externalities from Unobservable Victim Precaution: An Empirical Analysis of Lojack', *Quarterly Journal of Economics*, **113** (1), 43–77.

Bailey, W. (1982), 'Capital Punishment and Lethal Assault Against Police', *Criminology*, **19**, 608–25.

Baldus, D. and J. Cole (1975), 'A Comparison of the Work of Thorstein Sellin and Isaac Ehrlich on the Deterrent Effect of Capital Punishment', *Yale Law Review*, **85**, 170–86.

Barclay, G. and C. Tavares (2003), 'International Comparisons of Criminal Justice Statistics', Home Office, Issue 12/03.

Becker, G.S. (1968), 'Crime and Punishment: An Economic Approach', *Journal of Political Economy*, **76** (2), 169–217.

Benson, Bruce L. (1990), *The Enterprise of Law: Justice Without the State*, San Francisco: Pacific Research Institute.

Benson, B.L. (1995), 'Understanding Bureaucratic Behavior: Implications from the Public Choice Literature', *Journal of Public Finance and Public Choice*, **8** (2–3), 89–117.

Benson, Bruce L. (1998), *To Serve and Protect: Privatization and Community in Criminal Justice*, New York: New York University Press.

Benson, B.L. and B.D. Mast (2001), 'Privately Produced General Deterrence', *Journal of Law and Economics*, **44** (2), 725–46.

Benson, B.L. and D.W. Rasmussen (1996), 'Predatory Public Finance and the Origins of the War on Drugs: 1984–1989', *The Independent Review: A Journal of Political Economy*, **1** (2), 163–89.

Benson, B.L., I. Kim and D.W. Rasmussen (1994), 'Estimating Deterrence Effects: A Public Choice Perspective on the Economics of Crime Literature', *Southern Economic Journal*, **61**, 161–8.

Benson, B.L., I. Kim and D.W. Rasmussen (1998), 'Deterrence and Public Policy: Tradeoffs in the Allocation of Police Resources', *International Review of Law and Economics*, **18** (1), 77–100.

Benson, B.L., I.S. Laburn and D.W. Rasmussen (2001), 'The Impact of Drug Enforcement on Crime: An Investigation of the Opportunity Cost of Police Resources', *Journal of Drug Issues*, **31** (4), 989–1006.

Benson, B.L., D.L. Sollars and D.W. Rasmussen (1995), 'Police Bureaucrats, Their Incentives, and the War on Drugs', *Public Choice*, **83** (1–2), 21–45.

Benson, B.L., I. Kim, D.W. Rasmussen and T.W. Zuehlke (1992), 'Is Property Crime Caused by Drug Use or Drug Enforcement Policy?', *Applied Economics*, **24**, 679–92.

Bentham, J. (1962) [1778], 'A View of the Hard Labour Bill', in John Bowring (ed.), *The Works of Jeremy Bentham*, Vol. IV, New York: Russell and Russell, pp. 3, 6–7, 32.

Block, M.K. and J.M. Heineke (1975), 'A Labor Theoretic Analysis of the Criminal Choice', *American Economic Review*, **65**, 314–25.

Bowers, W. and G. Pierce (1975), 'The Illusion of Deterrence in Isaac Ehrlich's Research on Capital Punishment', *Yale Law Journal*, **85**, 187–208.

Brier, S.S. and S.E. Fienberg (1980), 'Recent Econometric Modelling of Crime and Punishment: Support for the Deterrence Hypothesis?', *Evaluation Review*, **4**, 147–91.

Buchan, B. (2002), 'Punishing the Poor: Early "Liberal" Arguments for Penal and Police Reform', *International Journal of Sociology of Law*, **30**, 201–18.

Byrne, J.M. (1988), 'Probation', Washington, DC: National Institute of Justice, GPO:1.

Cameron, S. (1988), 'The Economics of Crime Deterrence: A Survey of Theory and Evidence', *Kyklos*, **41**, 301–23.

Chadwick, E. (1929), 'Preventive Police', *London Review*, **1**, 252.

Dezhbakhsh, H., P.H. Rubin and J.M. Shepherd (2003), 'Does Capital Punishment Have a Deterrent Effect? New Evidence from Postmoratorium Panel Data', *American Law and Economics Review*, **5** (2), 344–76.

DiIulio, J.J. (1996), 'Help Wanted: Economists, Crime and Public Policy', *Journal of Economic Perspectives*, **10** (1), 3–24.

Dodd, T., S. Nicholas, D. Povey and A.Walker (2004), 'Crime in England and Wales, 2004', Home Office Statistical Bulletin, 10/04, July.

Donohue, J.J. III and S.D. Levitt (2001), 'The Impact of Legalized Abortion on Crime', *Quarterly Journal of Economics*, **116**, 379–420.

Ehrlich, I. (1973), 'Participation in Illegitimate Activities: A Theoretical and Empirical Investigation', *Journal of Political Economy*, **81**, 521–65.

Ehrlich, I. (1975), 'The Deterrent Effect of Capital Punishment: A Question of Life or Death', *American Economic Review*, 397–417.

Ehrlich, I. (1977), 'Capital Punishment and Deterrence: Some Further Thoughts and Evidence', *Journal of Political Economy*, 741–88.

Ehrlich, I. and J.C. Gibbons (1977), 'On the Measurement of the Deterrent Effect of Capital Punishment and the Theory of Deterrence', *Journal of Legal Studies*, **6**, 35–50.

Ekelund, R.B. and C. Dorton (2003), 'Criminal Justice Institutions as a Common Pool: The Nineteenth Century Analysis of Edwin Chadwick', *Journal of Economic Behavior and Organization*, **50** (3), 271–94.

Hakim, S., A. Ovadia and J. Weinblatt (1979), 'Interjurisdictional Spillover of Crime and Police Expenditures', *Land Economics*, **55**, 200–212.

Harrison, P.M. and J.C. Karberg (2005), 'Prison and Jail Inmates at Midyear 2004', Bureau of Justice Statistics Bulletin, April.

Horney, J. and M. Ineke (1992), 'Risk Perceptions Among Serious Offenders: The Role of Crime and Punishment', *Criminology*, **30**, 575–93.

Levitt, S.D. (1998), 'Why Do Increased Arrest Rates Appear to Reduce Crime: Deterrence, Incapacitation or Measurement Error?', *Economic Inquiry*, **36** (3), 353–72.

Levitt, S.D. (2004), 'Understanding Why Crime Fell in the 1990s: Four Factors that Explain the Decline and Six that Do Not', *Journal of Economic Perspectives*, **18** (1), 163–90.

Lott, J.R. (1987), 'Should the Wealthy Be Able to "Buy Justice"?', *Journal of Political Economy*, **95**, 1–68.

Lott, John R. (1998), *More Guns, Less Crime: Understanding Crime and Gun-Control Laws*, Chicago: University of Chicago Press.

Manzoni, Alessandro (1964), *The Column of Infamy, Prefaced by Cesare Beccaria's 'Of Crimes and Punishments'*, Translated from the Italian by Kenelm Foster OP and Jane Grigson, with an Introduction by A.P. d'Entrêves, London: Oxford University Press.

Mast, B.D., B.L. Benson and D.W. Rasmussen (2000), 'Entrepreneurial Police and Drug Enforcement Policy', *Public Choice*, **104** (3/4), 285–308.

McGahey, R. (1980), 'Dr. Ehrlich's Magic Bullet: Econometric Theory, Econometrics, and the Death Penalty', *Crime and Delinquency*, **26**, 485–502.

Mocan, H.N. and K.J. Gittings (2003), 'Getting Off Death Row: Commuted Sentences and the Deterrent Effect of Capital Punishment', *Journal of Law and Economics*, **46** (2), 453–78.

Mocan, H.N., S.C. Billups and J. Overland (2000), 'A Dynamic Model of Differential Human Capital and Criminal Activity', National Bureau of Economic Research Working Paper No. 7584.

Myers, S.L. (1983), 'Estimating the Economic Model of Crime: Employment Versus Punishment Effects', *Quarterly Journal of Economics*, **98**, 157–66.

Neely, Richard (1982), *Why Courts Don't Work*, New York: McGraw-Hill.

Paley, William (1785), *The Principles of Moral and Political Philosophy*, London: Faulder.

Passell, P. (1975), 'The Deterrent Effect of the Death Penalty: A Statistical Test', *Stanford Law Review*, **28**, 61–80.

Passell, P. and J.B. Taylor (1977), 'The Deterrent Effect of Capital Punishment: Another View', *American Economic Review*, **67** (3), 445–51.

Peck, J. (1976), 'The Deterrence Effect of Capital Punishment: Ehrlich and His Critics', *Yale Law Journal*, **85**, 359–67.

Philipson, T. and R.A. Posner (1996), 'The Economic Epidemiology of Crime', *Journal of Law and Economics*, **39** (2), 405–33.

Rasmussen, David W. and Bruce L. Benson (1994), *The Economic Anatomy of a Drug War: Criminal Justice in the Commons*, Lanham, MD.

Rasmussen, D.W., B.L. Benson and D.L. Sollars (1993), 'Spatial Competition in Illicit Drug Markets: The Consequences of Increased Drug Enforcement', *Review of Regional Studies*, **23**, 219–36.

Reaves, B.A. (1992), 'State and Local Police Departments', Bureau of Justice Statistics Bulletin (February), 4.

Resignato, A.J. (2000), 'Violent Crime: A Function of Drug Use or Drug Enforcement?', *Applied Economics*, **32** (6), 681–8.

Rubin, P.H. (1978), 'The Economics of Crime', *Atlantic Economic Review*, July–August, 13–26.

Shoup, C. (1964), 'Standards for Distributing a Free Government Service: Crime Prevention', *Public Finance*, **19**, 383–92.

Sjoquist, D. (1973), 'Property Crime and Economic Behavior: Some Empirical Results', *American Economic Review*, **83**, 439–46.

Smith, Adam (1982) [1763], *Lectures on Jurisprudence*, R.L. Meek, D.D. Raphael and P.G. Stein (eds), Indianapolis: Liberty Fund.

Sollars, D.L., B.L. Benson and D.W. Rasmussen (1994), 'Drug Enforcement and Deterrence of Property Crime Among Local Jurisdictions', *Public Finance Quarterly*, **22**, 22–45.

US Department of Justice (1988), 'Jail Inmates 1987', Bureau of Justice Statistics Bulletin, 1.

US Department of Justice (1989), 'Prisoners in 1988', Bureau of Justice Statistics Bulletin, 5.

Wolpin, K.L. (1978), 'Capital Punishment and Homicide in England', *American Economic Review*, **68**, 422–7.

Yunker, J. (1982), 'The Relevance of the Identification Problem to Statistical Research on Capital Punishment: A Comment on McGahey', *Crime and Delinquency*, **28**, 96–123.

Zedlewski, E. (1992), 'Private Security and Controlling Crime', in G.W. Bowman, S. Hakim and P. Seidenstat (eds), *Privatizing the United States Justice System: Police Adjudication, and Corrections Services from the Private Sector*, Jefferson, NC: McFarland and Company.

5 Economics of marriage and divorce
Leora Friedberg and Steven N. Stern

Why do people get married? Love, sex, children, money. Why do they get divorced? Probably for the same reasons. While most people would, at most, want to hear what economists have to say about the financial aspects of marriage, economists (who, surprising as it may seem, marry and divorce like everyone else) have taken it on themselves to offer useful hypotheses about the rest of it too.

For example, they have studied whether divorce laws affect the divorce rate. Before 1970, many states in the USA required both spouses to agree before a divorce could take place; now, most states allow one spouse to initiate a divorce unilaterally. Under certain assumptions that economists have spelled out, the type of divorce law would not actually affect the number of divorces, even while it does affect the way that divorced couples share resources. Economists also have shown that the type of divorce law affects how married couples share resources, even if they do not divorce, and, theoretically, it might even influence how often they have sex.

In order to understand these ideas, we have to develop a model of both marriage and divorce (or, in other words, a model that allows for changes over time in the utility from marriage). In this chapter, we will set the stage for this analysis by discussing trends in marriage and divorce in Section 1. The major changes in matrimonial patterns in North America and Europe that we will highlight serve as a backdrop for the analysis we will introduce in the rest of the chapter. Then, to keep things simple, we will discuss separately the gains from marriage versus living together (Section 2), the reasons why people marry (Section 3), the nature of decision-making within marriage (Section 4), and the nature of the decisions to marry and to divorce (Section 5).[1]

1 Trends in marriage and divorce

Figures 5.1 to 5.5 illustrate trends in marriage and divorce in several industrialized countries. Figure 5.1 shows long-term trends in marriage and divorce rates in the USA, while Figures 5.2 to 5.5 compare recent trends in other industrialized countries. The figures show marriage and divorce rates by year – the number of marriages and divorces for each 1000 people in the population. It would also be interesting to know the number relative to the eligible population, that is, those available to marry (the unmarried)

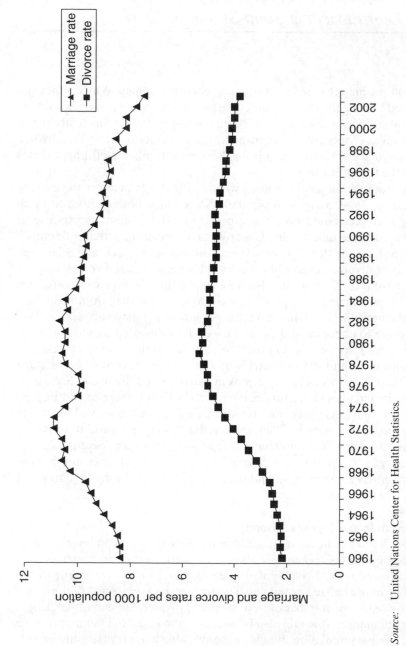

Source: United Nations Center for Health Statistics.

Figure 5.1 Marriage and divorce rates per 1000 population in USA (1960–2003)

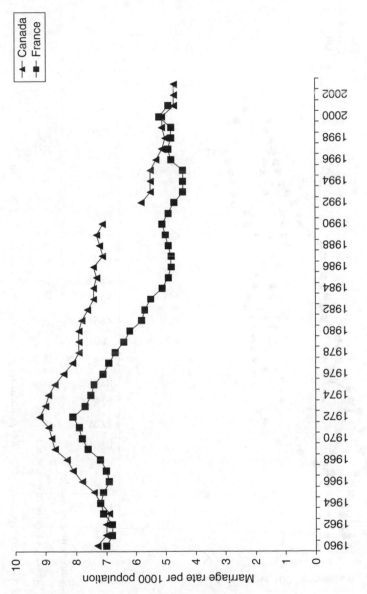

Note: Incomplete data for Canada.

Source: Statistics Canada (Canada) (www.statcan.ca) and Council of Europe (France) (www.coe.int).

Figure 5.2   Marriage rates per 1000 population in France and Canada (1960–2003)

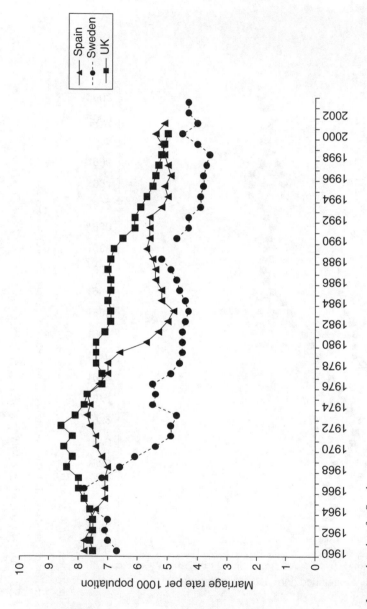

Note: Incomplete data for Sweden.

Source: Council of Europe (www.coe.int).

Figure 5.3 Marriage rates per 1000 population in Spain, Sweden and UK (1960–2003)

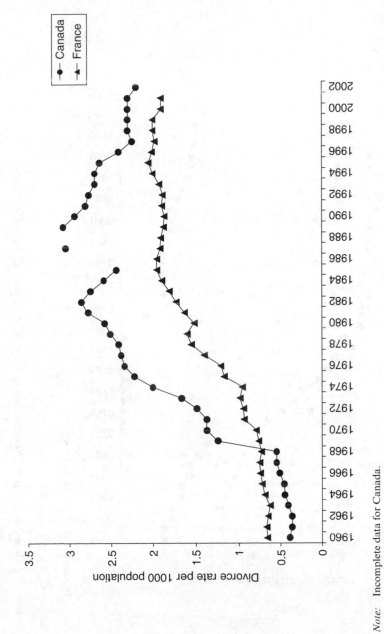

Divorce rate per 1000 population

Note: Incomplete data for Canada.

Source: Statistics Canada (Canada) (www.statcan.ca) and Council of Europe (France) (www.coe.int).

Figure 5.4 Divorce rates per 1000 population in France and Canada (1960–2002)

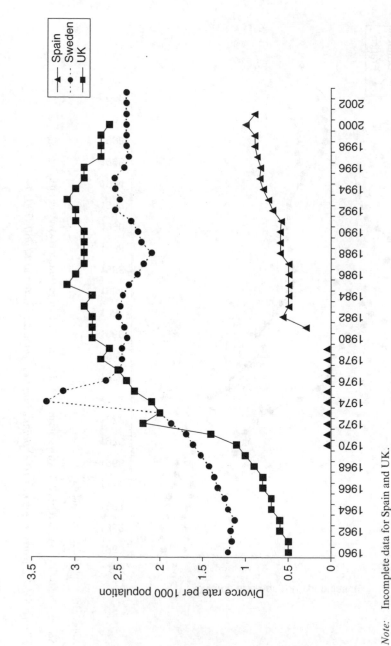

Note: Incomplete data for Spain and UK.

Source: Council of Europe (www.coe.int).

Figure 5.5 Divorce rates per 1000 population in Spain, Sweden and UK (1960–2003)

and divorce (the married). We are not able to report those statistics, however, because they are more difficult to come by and are not measured as accurately.

It is apparent from Figure 5.1 that we need to distinguish between short- and long-run patterns in the data. Over the long run, the divorce rate in the USA has steadily increased while marriage rates have bounced up and down. The recent trends have been starker, though. The divorce rate more than doubled in the recent past, rising from 2.5 per 1000 people in 1965 to 5.2 in 1980. It levelled off in the 1980s and then dropped back to 3.8 by 2003, but it remains the case that almost half of marriages end in divorce (Cherlin, 1992). More recently, marriage rates have dropped off, falling by 25 per cent from 10.5 in 1980 to 7.5 in 2003.

Looking at Figure 5.1, it is not entirely clear that these recent developments represent major breaks from past behaviour. For example, the divorce rate in the USA rose steadily in the early part of the century and then plateaued in the 1950s, making the later increase look especially sharp. In fact, if it had risen at the same annual rate as occurred between 1920 and 1950, the divorce rate would have hit 5.0 in 1990, slightly *above* the actual rate of 4.7. Similarly, the marriage rate remains above the low of 8.4 that it hit in 1958, which followed a period of very high marriage rates. What distinguishes the recent period is the same patterns – which, if anything, have been starker – occurring in other countries, along with a number of contemporaneous trends that are entirely new, including an increased frequency of cohabitation, an increase in the age at first marriage and a decline in the birth rate.

Figures 5.2 to 5.5 compare trends in marriage and divorce rates since 1960 in a selection of representative industrialized countries. Several features of the data are worth discussing.

First, the USA has had consistently higher marriage and divorce rates than other industrialized countries have. Interestingly, the number of marriages relative to divorces started out widely divergent across countries and very low in the USA but has converged to around two marriages per divorce each year in most of these countries.

Second, divorce rates in industrialized countries rose universally between 1960 and 1990. The increase started a little earlier in the USA and also flattened out sooner, around 1980. While the absolute increase was also largest in the USA, the percentage increases were higher in almost all other industrialized countries. The divorce rate more than tripled in France and more than quintupled in Canada and the UK. Moreover, the USA is somewhat unusual in the 25 per cent decline that has taken place since the divorce rate peaked. In most other countries the rate of increase has either stopped or slowed, but not turned negative.

Third, marriage rates in industrialized countries began to fall universally at some point between 1965 and 1985 and continue to drop today. These declines began after divorce rates started to rise and in many cases were preceded by a short-lived increase in marriage, perhaps reflecting remarriages among the newly divorced. The decline in marriage rates in the USA has been smaller in relative terms, at about 25 per cent from its peak, than the decline in other countries, which generally exceed 40 per cent.

2   Marriage versus cohabiting

What is the difference between shacking up and getting hitched? Marriage is a contractual arrangement, with rules determined by church or state. For example, Jewish weddings are not complete until the bride and groom sign the *ketubah*, a marriage contract which, ' . . . spells out the husband's obligations to the wife during marriage, conditions of inheritance upon his death, and obligations regarding the support of children of the marriage. It also provides for the wife's support in the event of divorce' (Anonymous, 2004a). Brides in many cultures brought (or still bring) dowries to their husbands, with religious or secular law determining the disposition of the dowry in the event of death or divorce. In other cultures, husbands must provide a bride price to the bride or her father. With some exceptions, non-marital relationships do not entail the same contractual obligations.[2] Several aspects of marriage as a contract are important.

First, marriage as a transaction may be costly in terms of time, effort and/or money to enter into and to leave. It implies that the utility from marriage must exceed the utility from being apart *as well as* the costs involved in getting married, and, possibly, divorced (although we do not emphasize this in the model of getting married, which we develop later).

Second, divorce as the dissolution of a contract entails financial obligations between the spouses. For example, one spouse may be required to pay income support to the other, and property acquired during the marriage (or even before) must be split according to some rule, perhaps depending on behaviour during the marriage. There are a few motives for these financial obligations associated with divorce. One is to provide support for children issuing from the marriage, although these rules affect childless couples as well. Another motive is to punish certain types of behaviour, which are viewed as violating the contractual obligations of marriage. An additional motive is to compensate spouses for some types of investments in the marriage, which are undertaken with the belief that the marriage will last. We will elaborate on the motives for these 'sharing rules' as we outline the reasons why people marry and subsequently divorce.

Third, the nature of the marriage contract has varied greatly across religions, countries and time periods. The Old Testament, for example, established a right of husbands to unilaterally divorce their wives, for any reason or no reason, although not without absolving all financial obligations. Subsequent Talmudic law (developed in oral form before Christ and in writing after) gave Jewish wives the right to unilateral divorce when the husband, '. . . is physically repulsive because of some medical condition or other characteristic, when he violates or neglects his marital obligations (food, clothing and sexual intercourse), or, according to some views, when there is sexual incompatibility' (Anonymous, 2004b). Jesus, in various gospels, recognized (though disapproved of) divorce, while the Roman Catholic Church forbids it. Occasionally, legal and/or religious divorce law has changed in response to demands of influential society members (for example, Henry VIII). We will discuss some reasons why the legal regime governing marriage and divorce has varied as the circumstances surrounding marriage have shifted.

3   What are the gains from marriage?
At the outset, we listed several reasons – love, sex, children and money – why people might get married. Let us consider in turn how each of them affects an individual's utility, and moreover why the impact may depend on whether the couple marries instead of just living together.

3.1   *Love and sex*
While love may be a many-splendoured thing, we will model it as a simple gain in utility from sharing your life with another. Love may matter because you enjoy being with the one you love, and it may matter because it causes you to care about the well-being of the one you love. In other words, love may be an argument of your utility function and it may change your utility function by placing weight on the utility of another person. Next, there is sex. But is sex any different from love from a modelling point of view? They both require another, and they both offer utility, given the right partner. Sex may complement love, if emotional intimacy enhances sexual satisfaction. However, there are other important characteristics of sex. One that we will ignore in this chapter is that there is a relatively well-functioning market for sex (via prostitution, discussed in Chapter 7), but not one for love, since sex is an act but love is an emotion, which is difficult to transact. Another characteristic of sex is that it involves certain risks. It may be for the latter reason that sex is often associated with marriage.

One risk of sex is disease. Monogamy reduces the risk of disease, but how does one insure monogamy? First, both marriage and cohabitation increase physical proximity and hence the ability to monitor the partner. Second, marriage, as a legal contract, often specifies penalties that raise the cost of adultery. For instance, it may provide grounds for the other partner to end the marriage or affect the distribution of income and property after divorce.

Another risk of sex is pregnancy. The risk of pregnancy explains why sex within marriage may be preferred to sex outside of marriage – because the welfare of children, and so the welfare of parents who care about their children, is enhanced by making marriage difficult to end and by the financial obligations imposed by marriage (although these obligations may be imposed for children born out of wedlock as well).

Seen in this light, one can understand why the advent of effective contraception in recent decades – by reducing the risk of pregnancy resulting from sex – has reduced the frequency of marriage and increased the frequency of living together. While condoms have been around for millennia (Youssef, 1993), the introduction of the birth control pill has had a drastic effect, especially after legal decisions in the late 1960s allowed it to be distributed widely among unmarried women. That is, because it allows women to control their fertility, and women bear more of the costs of childbearing than men do.[3]

3.2   Children

Sex naturally brings us to talk about children. There are a few reasons why people have kids besides the possibility that they are an accidental by-product of sex. One is that they feel a biological imperative. Another is that they enjoy kids. Those two reasons look the same in a simple economic model – they are things that raise an individual's utility.

What makes kids interesting for our purposes is that one kid may raise the utility of *both* parents at the same time. Thus, kids are public, not private, goods. In other words, one kid provides utility to two parents, and the utility one parent gets from spending time with the kid is not diminished by the utility the other gets from spending time with the kid – as long as the parents live together. If not, then kids are more like other private goods, for example spaghetti – if one person eats the spaghetti, the other cannot. Since kids cost about the same whether they live with one parent or both, it is efficient, from this perspective, for parents to live together. We will not have a chance to say anything about the decision of *whether* to have kids, although it may have some of the same features as other types of marital decisions, which we will discuss below. Other interesting decisions, which we will not discuss, are how many kids to have, and the trade-off between investing in child quantity (by having more kids) versus child quality (by spending more time or money on each kid).

3.3   Public goods

We already pointed out that kids are public goods. In a variety of other
ways as well, it is likely that two can live as cheaply as one. Kitchens can be
used to provide two meals about as easily as one, and larger sized bed linens
are cheaper than two sets of smaller sized bed linens. One spouse's enjoyment of heat in the winter and air conditioning in the summer is little
affected by the other's as long as their preferences over the ambient tem-
perature are not too different. The same applies to home decor (rugs and
paintings) and to home entertainment (television sets, cable service and
stereos), once again provided that tastes are relatively similar – that is, that
both spouses like to watch the same TV programme, or that one does not
mind taping the football game to watch at a later time. Moreover, if being
in love also means that your tastes are more similar, then that enhances the
'public good' aspect of many household commodities.

Suppose that *G* stands for quantity of public goods associated with
living together. We also will introduce *X* to stand for a private good, or
bundle of private goods, which individuals consume. Consider a couple
with similar incomes deciding whether to live together. If they live apart,
then each faces a budget constraint like AB in Figure 5.6. With similar

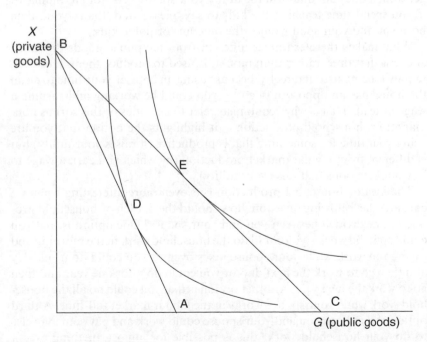

Figure 5.6   Budget constraints and indifference curves in marriage

indifference curves, the best each alone can do is reach point D where the 'best' indifference curve is tangent to the budget constraint. However, if they live together, then the cost per person of G is cut in half (because they can share it). Thus, the new budget constraint is CB, and they can pick a point like E (ignoring, for now, the possibility that they may have different preferences for G relative to X).

Kids provide a strong argument for marriage as opposed to cohabitation. Since kids require costly investments that take a long time to reach fruition, the contractual nature of marriage (the fact that it may be difficult to leave and that leaving it imposes continued financial obligations explicitly related to kids) increases one's willingness to invest in kids. The same can be said of other public goods – it is worth investing in furniture together if we are reasonably sure that the relationship will last – though with somewhat less force.

3.4   Time

There is another type of public good that is important to talk about separately. It originates with the idea that a person's *time* can be used to produce something that is a public good. For example, a clean house is a public good because both you and your spouse enjoy it, and the utility you get from it does not diminish the utility your spouse gets from it. Similarly, if you spend time teaching the kids to say 'please' and 'thank you', then both you and your spouse enjoy the outcome of polite kids.

What makes these examples different from the public goods discussed above is that time, rather than money, is used to produce them. However, money *is* being used indirectly, because using an hour of your time to clean the house has an opportunity cost – you could be working and earning a wage instead. That is why economists refer to activities of this sort as non-market or 'household production' – it highlights the notion that you are using your time for something that is productive (it raises your utility) but is different from regular market production (by which you earn a wage to buy market goods that raise your utility).

The idea of household production gets even more interesting when we consider the following question: how should the burden of household production be divided between you and your spouse? One option is that you could split the work – you could do the household work in the morning and then go to work while your spouse takes over, or you could do it one day and then go to work the next day, or you could do it for one year and then go to work the next year. Another option is that you could do all the household work while your spouse works in the labour market full-time. A third option is that both you and your spouse could work and pay someone else to do your household work; this is possible for almost anything except actually giving birth to a child.

The option that is least common is the first. There are two reasons why it is rare for both spouses to split household work and market work. One is that part-time jobs often pay much less per hour than full-time jobs. Thus, one spouse working in a full-time job will often earn considerably more than both spouses working in a half-time job. The other reason is that market work often involves a *career*, rather than simply a job. By a career, we mean a job that requires a long-term relationship with an employer or fellow workers, or a long-term investment in skills, since many skills (for example, carpentry, surgery, computer programming) take time to acquire and deteriorate or grow obsolete when they go unused. Thus, 'career' jobs typically pay more than short-term jobs.

All of this leads us to the notion of specialization – it often makes sense for one spouse to specialize in market work and the other to specialize in household work. Again, the reason is that part-time work is not highly remunerative and interrupts careers. Individuals on their own cannot specialize, but individuals in a relationship can, if one spouse provides the income (which also goes further when it is used to purchase public goods for two people) while the other spouse provides the time for household production. Moreover, marriage may be the preferred arrangement to foster specialization precisely because of the concern that, when one spouse specializes in household skills, they are giving up not just the current wage but a career and hence higher future wages. You would be more willing to do this if you receive some sort of commitment of compensation for the loss of your career in case the relationship ends. Alimony and property-sharing arrangements associated with divorce provide that commitment.

Consider a simplified model where utility depends upon consumption of potatoes as measured by X and the cleanliness of the house as measured by C, where $C = C_m + C_f$. C_m and C_f represent the proportion of time spent cleaning the house by the male and female, and $1 - C_m$ and $1 - C_f$ represent the proportion of time spent working. Let w_m be the daily wage of the male, w_f be the daily wage of the female, and p be the price of potatoes. Further, assume that the couple maximizes $U(C, X_m) + U(C, X_f)$, subject to the budget constraint,

$$\sum_{i=m,f} w_i(1 - C_i) = p(X_m + X_f)$$

when married, while each member of the couple maximizes $U(C_i, X_i)$ subject to

$$w_i(1 - C_i) = pX_i$$

for $i = m, f$ when single.

Define (X_m^*, C_m^*) and (X_f^*, C_f^*) as the optimal choices of the male and the female when single. Note that the couple, when married, can choose $(X_m^*, X_f^*, C_m^*, C_f^*)$ (the same bundle) and get utility, $U(C_m^* + C_f^*, X_m) + U(C_m^* + C_f^*, X_f)$, which is more than the sum of utilities when single. This occurs because they each benefit from the other's cleaning time as well as their own. Alternatively, the spouse with the higher wage can reduce his or her cleaning time and spend more time in the labour market allowing the couple to buy more potatoes. For example, the male could reduce his cleaning time to $C_m^{**} = \max(C_m^* - C_f^*, 0)$, which is either the difference between how much time he would spend if single (if $C_m^* > C_f^*$), or else zero. Consequently, both spouses would receive at least as much household production as when they were single, and the family would be able to buy more potatoes.

A last question arises when we consider housework. Why is it that women have historically specialized in household production and men in market production? A key reason is because women bear the children, so they have to withdraw from market work for a length of time. Another possible reason is that women are better at or care more about raising children, though this is far from being proven. In terms of the model, we could capture this idea by letting $C = aC_f + C_m$ where a now captures the productivity of women in household production relative to men. The statement that women are better at household production is equivalent to the statement that $a > 1$.

A third possibility is that men are more productive in market work as reflected in relative wage rates. In fact, the model suggests that all that really matters is the ratio of wages relative to the ratio of marginal products in the household. As w_f / w_m decreases relative to a, men will increasingly specialize in market activity and women will specialize in household production. While men's wages have historically greatly exceeded women's, the gap has narrowed in recent years. In 2002, women's average pay was 76 per cent of men's, up from 59 per cent over a 40-year period (Anonymous, 2004c). At this point, it is unclear whether women continue to be paid less for equal work (and hence choose to specialize in household production more often), or whether the wage gaps persist because women continue to specialize in household production for other reasons.

4   How do married couples make decisions?

The model we developed above showed the potential gains from getting married. Those gains are not only emotional but result from a more efficient use of time and resources enabled by two people living together. However, we have not yet said anything about how those resources are actually used. There are several sources of possible conflict. Some money will be spent on marital public goods, but some will also be spent on private goods consumed by one spouse and not the other. Spouses must also choose how to spend time on market production (work), household production (housework) and leisure. Consider, for example, three types of decisions:

1. Given a certain amount of money that is available to spend, how will couples decide whether to spend money on golf clubs or on Manolo Blahnik sandals? And what if another way to spend the money is on dinner at a nice restaurant? Or on a tricycle for the baby?
2. How will labour supply decisions by each spouse affect how much is spent on golf clubs, sandals or a tricycle? And how will spending possibilities affect each spouse's labour supply decisions?
3. How will the couple decide whether to spend money on golf clubs, sandals, a tricycle, a nice dinner – or else save for the future?

These issues involve the allocation of money between private goods (golf clubs, sandals and so on, designated X in our model above) and public goods (dinner together, a tricycle, saving for future expenses, and so on designated G). They also involve the allocation of time between working in the market ($1 - C$ in our model above, which earns a wage, w) and in household production (and producing marital public goods C, like a clean house), and taking leisure.

The available evidence, as well as introspection, tells us that individuals are not completely self-effacing or altruistic in marriage, and therefore spouses bargain over how to split shared resources. However, even as we make hard-hearted assumptions about the nature of bargaining, we can allow for the possibility that spouses get some utility from the well-being of their spouse.

4.1 How do families make decisions?
We assume that individuals maximize the utility gained from such decisions, subject to a budget constraint. Does a family act as a single decision-maker, maximizing a family utility function? If so, the family utility function depends on the total amount that the family spends on different goods regardless of who consumes them or on the utility of each family member. In these cases, we do not need to know how family members interact when these decisions are made. Interestingly, a model that yields the same outcome is one in which one member of the family is a dictator who makes all the decisions to maximize his or her own utility.

However, empirical analysis has rejected a key implication of these 'unitary' models of family decision-making: the allocation of consumption within the family should not depend on who earns what within the family. In other words, unitary models imply that we would not have to know who brings home the bacon and who fries it up in a pan in order to predict whether high-fashion sandals, high-tech golf clubs or a tricycle is purchased. However, two studies found that the share of income spent on men's versus women's and children's clothing varied in Canadian families (Browning et al., 1994) and in British families (Lundberg et al., 1997), depending on the proportion of family income earned by husbands versus wives. Another study showed that, as the share of cash income accruing to women in Côte d'Ivoire rose, the share of spending on food rose and the share on alcohol and tobacco fell (Hoddinott and Haddad, 1995).

4.2   Bargaining among family members

If families do not make decisions as a single unit, then we are back to the model of individual decision-making with which students of microeconomics are familiar. Nevertheless, being in a family still changes the way that decisions are made because family members share control over resources and are affected by actions of other family members. A natural way to model these types of interactions is using game theory.

Economists have focused on a particular type of game theory to explain family decision-making – games with cooperative bargaining between agents (or spouses, in this case). Define the value to the male of being in the relationship as R_m and the value of being separate as S_m. Similarly, assume that the value to the female of participating in the relationship is R_f and the value of not participating is S_f. R includes the benefits of relationships that we discussed earlier, and S includes the value of extra privacy and independence and the cost of loneliness along with any monetary effects. As long as spouses can agree on how to split the *surplus*, $R_m + R_f - S_m - S_f$, from being together, then they will remain together. If they cannot cooperate, then the best they can do is get utility S_m and S_f from being apart – so these are the *threat points* in the cooperative bargaining game because each individual will prefer to get S rather than to stay in the relationship and get $R < S$. Their bargaining determines how the surplus will be split, and thus the actual values of R_m and R_f. Of course, they will both walk away if there is no surplus from marriage $(R_m + R_f - S_m - S_f < 0)$, which is the same as saying that the threat points exceed the gains from marriage for both spouses $(R_m < S_m$ and $R_f < S_f)$. Manser and Brown (1980) and McElroy and Horney (1981) defined the Nash cooperative bargaining model to marriage and defined the threat points as the utility from separating.

John Nash demonstrated some important characteristics of the cooperative bargaining problem (Nash, 1950). He showed that, under relatively general conditions, cooperative bargaining will yield an allocation that maximizes the product of each spouse's surplus, $(R_m - S_m)*(R_f - S_f)$, subject to the household budget constraint. This solution is Pareto-efficient – neither spouse could be made better off without making the other worse off. As an example, suppose that the utility of each spouse when separated is, $S_m = S_f = 0$, and the utility when they are together is $R_m = U(X_m)$ and $R_f = U(X_f)$, where $U(.)$ is a standard utility function with decreasing marginal utility in X. Moreover, suppose that family income Y is going to get split so that, $Y = X_m + X_f$. The solution that maximizes

$$(R_m - S_m)*(R_f - S_f) = R_m * R_f$$
$$= U(X_m) * U(X_f)$$
$$= U(X_m) * U(Y - X_m)$$

is $X_m = X_f = Y/2$ – each spouse gets half of Y. If we changed the problem so that $S_m = S_f = 1$, the solution would not change, as long as $Y/2 > 1$; if $Y/2 < 1$, then the spouses would separate. On the other hand, if we changed the problem so that $S_m = 0$ and $S_f = 1$, then the solution is $X_m = Y/2 - a$ and $X_f = Y/2 + a$, where the value taken by a is positive (so f gets more stuff than m) and depends on the actual form of the utility function $U(.)$. It is important to note that the same results apply when $U(.)$ depends not only on private consumption X but also on marital public goods and even on the other spouse's utility, so that spouses display some altruism (that is, they are willing to give up some of their own consumption in order to increase the utility of the other spouse).

The key result, then, is that the allocation of resources to each spouse increases with their threat points. Knowing that, we can begin to answer the questions posed above. Along the way, we will also consider whether separation is the appropriate threat point in all situations of marital dispute over resources.

4.3 Decisions involving spending: golf clubs versus sandals

Suppose that all the money that the couple has is going to be spent immediately, and entirely on private goods. The choice of who gets more of the private goods (golf clubs versus sandals) depends on each spouse's bargaining power – that is, their threat points. If $S_m > S_f$, then spouse m gets more stuff.

What determines the threat points? There are a few factors involved in determining each individual's utility from being separate. One factor is how unhappy, emotionally, each partner would be when separated instead of together. If partner m would be much lonelier, while partner f has a lot of hobbies, then that reduces m's bargaining power relative to f's and hence m's ability to lay claim to private goods X_m while married. A similar outcome would be observed if f is much more likely to attract a new romantic partner than m.

A second factor affecting utility from being separate is each partner's financial resources outside of marriage. That in turn depends on their earning power and on the legal regime that governs the separation of marital assets following divorce. For example, if one partner (the wife, say) gives up a career to specialize in household production, that reduces her bargaining power over the distribution of resources within marriage. Why would she agree to this future loss in bargaining power? Perhaps she does it after extracting a large enough 'payment' up front in terms of family resources (perhaps a diamond?) that it makes up for the loss in bargaining power later on.

Another possibility is that she can find a way to bind her husband to an initial agreement not to exercise his bargaining power later on. For example, the legal regime in many states in the USA is now set up to favour the partner who specializes in household production. On the other hand, many states used to distribute property after divorce according to who had legal title to it, which at the time was generally the husband, and some states even forbade women from owning property – which gave the husband most of the bargaining power within marriage.

A third factor affecting utility from being separate involves child custody. Custody laws that favour mothers will increase their bargaining power within marriage. However, it is becoming more common to assign joint custody following divorce.

4.4   Decisions involving spending: private goods versus dinner together

When we incorporate the possibility of marital public goods, we have to reconsider whether spouses make decisions in the same way. There are a couple of possibilities. If they bargain cooperatively, then they will choose the Pareto-efficient level of marital public goods. The efficient level is dictated by adding together each partner's marginal valuation of the public good, relative to private goods (whereas the efficient level of private goods is dictated by equating the marginal valuations).

However, public goods are subject to free-rider problems when agents act non-cooperatively. The idea is that, if I know that you will provide some of the public good (by taking care of the kids, for example), then I will not bother supplying as much myself. Moreover, if you follow the same reasoning, then too little of the public good (child care) is supplied overall. Free-riding has been observed in many situations involving the private provision of public goods in non-marital settings.

Which model is correct? In the case of child care, it appears that married parents tend to act cooperatively (the first model) while divorced parents tend to act non-cooperatively (the second model) because it is difficult to monitor the other partner's contributions (Weiss and Willis, 1985). It may even be the case that the non-cooperative bargaining outcome (under-provision of the public good) is the operative threat point in a cooperative bargaining setting – it may be more realistic than considering divorce during every conflict (Bergstrom et al., 1986; Woolley, 1988; Lundberg and Pollak, 1993).

There is also evidence that mothers care more about child welfare – and hence may contribute more to the public good, either in a cooperative or free-riding setting – than fathers. For example, unearned income given to Brazilian mothers is associated not only with increased fertility but also with greater improvements in child health compared with unearned income given to fathers (Thomas, 1990).[4]

4.5   Buying stuff today versus saving
Another option is not to spend – to save resources for the future. For example, an individual will save in case of a financial emergency or to finance retirement. It will be worth doing this if the value of consumption in the future is worth more than the value today.

However, a couple may make a different decision. This may happen in a situation where some of the future uses are public (benefitting both) and some are private (benefitting only one), yet both spouses may have control over financial assets (as is common today). Therefore, there is a risk that they decide to save for the future, but then one chooses to buy private goods later on. If both fear that the other will do this, then the free-riding result from above will hold here as well – the couple will undertake too little saving because they are not confident that the other will refrain from buying private goods for themselves later. A related concern is that financial assets will be divided in the event of divorce, in which case they cease to be a public good; thus, the increase in divorce rates in the USA may be a cause of the decline in private savings rates.

5   Transitions into and out of marriage
We have discussed the gains from marriage (and cohabitation) and the nature of decision-making by couples. At this point, we will talk about how couples decide whether to enter into or leave a relationship.

5.1   Getting together
Suppose a couple is considering forming a relationship of some type. Later, we will discuss different types of relationships (cohabitation, marriage) and how couples might choose among them. For now, we can abstract away from the type and just call it a relationship.

Again, define the value to the male and female of being in the relationship as R_m and R_f and the value to them of being separate as S_m and S_f. Further, for now, assume that both the male and the female know the values of R_m, S_m, R_f, and S_f. These issues are discussed in more detail below.

Then, Becker's (1981) model of relationship formation says that a relationship will occur if and only if

$$(R_m + R_f) - (S_m + S_f) = R - S \geq 0. \tag{5.1}$$

In other words, the relationship will occur if the *total* value to the couple of forming a relationship is greater than the total value to the couple of being single. Define the left-hand side of equation (5.1) as the total net value of the relationship.

The condition defined in (5.1) is uncontroversial when both the male and female prefer being together ($R_m > S_m$ and $R_f > S_f$). Imagine, however, that

$$R_m - S_m > 0 > R_f - S_f;$$

that is, the male wants to have the relationship and the female does not. If the total net value of the relationship is positive, then there is some *side payment* or transfer p that the male can pay to the female such that

$$R_m - S_m - p > 0,$$
$$R_f - S_f + p > 0;$$

that is, both would want to form a relationship. The side payment need only satisfy the conditions that

$$R_m - S_m \geq p \geq S_f - R_f.$$

If the couple sets $p = R_m - S_m$, then the male is willing to be in the relationship because $R_m - S_m - p = 0$, and the female is willing to be in the relationship because

$$R_f - S_f + p = (R_f - S_f) + (R_m - S_m) > 0$$

(because the total net value, as defined in (5.1), is positive). Similarly, if the couple sets $p = S_f - R_f$, then the female is willing to be in the relationship because $R_f - S_f + p = 0$, and the male is willing to be in the relationship because

$$R_m - S_m - p = (R_m - S_m) - (S_f - R_f) > 0$$

(again, because the total net value is positive). On the other hand, if the total net value is negative, then there is no side payment that will induce both partners to want to form a relationship; the payment required by one of the partners with a negative value is greater than the net benefit of the relationship of the other.

In summary, any value of p between $S_f - R_f$ and $R_m - S_m$ satisfies the conditions for a relationship to occur. What determines the actual value of p? It may be the outcome of the Nash bargaining game we described earlier, so that the side payment p increases with S_f and decreases with S_m. In other words, as the wife's value of being separated increases relative to the husband's, then the payment made from the husband to the wife (if $p > 0$) grows, or the payment made from the wife to the husband (if $p < 0$) shrinks closer to zero. Even if some other form of bargaining determines p, as long as it is efficient, it will not affect whether a relationship begins.

Throughout this section, we have assumed that the couple can transfer utility from one member to the other with p. However, 'transferable utility' is a tricky concept. Bergstrom (1997) shows that, when there is no public good in the family, assuming transferable utility is not restrictive. Further, he derives a necessary and sufficient condition on utility functions for transferable utility to exist when there is a public good. We note the existence of the issue and proceed.

How does one partner make a side payment to the other? It may be in the form of allocation of household chores or relationship assets, as we discussed earlier, or it may be something less tangible like the payer being 'extra nice' to the recipient of the side payment. One might argue that, in the real world, we do not see such side payments. However, sometimes the side payments may be difficult to observe (for example, being 'extra nice'). Also, we pointed out earlier that many empirical studies have found evidence of unequal allocations of resources within families, depending upon $R_m - S_m$ relative to $S_f - R_f$. A good example of such a side payment is that Stern was so anxious to work with Friedberg on this chapter that he agreed to let her have all royalties associated with the chapter.

5.2 Breaking up

Now consider a couple in a relationship – which implies that, at the time they chose to form the relationship, the total net value of the relationship defined in (5.1) was positive. What if, for some reason, the total net value changes later on? If the total net value of the relationship is still positive, then the couple may renegotiate the side payment p so that both continue to prefer remaining in the relationship (even if one would not without the side payment). If the total net value of the relationship is now negative, then there is no side payment that will make both members of the couple better off in the relationship than apart, and the relationship ends.

The key aspects of this decision are the following. First, the couple will not break up as long as nothing about the relationship changes, because the total net value remains positive. Thus, we have to think about what may change in the relationship in order to explain why divorces occur. Second, the model we have described so far assumes that all transitions into and out of relationships are *efficient*. A couple forms a relationship if and only if the total net value is positive, and they dissolve the relationship if and only if the total net value is negative. This is a key result about bargaining that was first proposed by Coase (1960). His work made it clear that several assumptions are necessary for these transitions to occur efficiently. Later on, we will discuss the validity of these assumptions, some of which – most notably, perfect information and costless transitions – may not be reasonable when applied to marriage and divorce. Another implication of his work is that factors affecting the distribution of resources (and hence the utility of one partner relative to the other) will not influence whether a divorce occurs, as long as divorce occurs efficiently. We will also discuss specific applications of this result later on.

In the meantime, we will ask what factors may ultimately precipitate a divorce? Among economists, there have been three approaches to modelling the source of changes in the total net value of the relationship. One is to model a change in the characteristics of the relationship that determine R and S over time. A second approach is to model how partners may learn more about the true values of R and S over time. A third is to consider the possibility that actions taken by partners during marriage directly affect subsequent values of R and S. We will present evidence suggesting that, in fact, all of these probably occur.

5.3   Changes

What is it about a relationship that may change over time? We have to consider factors that affect at least one of the values R_m, S_m, R_f, and S_f. Some changes might arise because the characteristics or circumstances of one of the partners changes unforeseeably (due to, perhaps, job loss, or an inheritance, or the introduction of Viagra or Prozac) or some characteristic of the relationship itself changes (because, say, the TV breaks down, so the couple no longer spends time together watching their favourite programme).

Consider an improvement in labour market opportunities for women. This probably raises R_m, R_f, and S_f. Both R_f and S_f rise because the female has new opportunities that previously were not available, so she is better off whether she is married or not. R_m would also rise as long as the husband gets some of the benefit from his wife's good fortune, perhaps because she purchases more marital public goods. Even though R_m, R_f, and S_f all increase, however, it is likely that S_f jumps the most (because now the female is less likely to have to rely on a male for those expensive sandals); it may be the case that S_f increases by more than the sum of $R_m + R_f$ (the value of marriage). If that is the case, there will be some couples in a relationship who will now separate because the total net value of the relationship becomes negative. There will also be some couples who would have formed a relationship in the past who are no longer willing to do so, again because the total net value of the relationship is now negative. Thus, the model suggests that the observed improvements in market opportunities for women should reduce the marriage rate and, at least in the short run, increase the divorce rate, as has happened.

Consider, instead, a new divorce law that requires husbands to pay alimony to wives (or, say, the partner with more income outside of marriage to pay the partner with less income). This will raise S_f while reducing S_m by the same amount, but, under one important assumption, which we will discuss in a moment, it would *not* alter the total net value of the relationship $(R_m + R_f) - (S_m + S_f)$. Consequently, if divorces occur efficiently, then it would not precipitate a divorce. Even though it makes separation more attractive to females, it makes it less attractive to males, so males will raise their side payments p to avoid divorce, which will satisfy females. Therefore, even though it would not cause a divorce, it would alter the distribution of resources within marriage.

It is important to point out the key assumption on which this conclusion rests, since it helps illustrate the main point. We must assume that the factors determining alimony payments do not induce either ex-partner to alter their income – for example, by choosing to earn less in order to either win more or pay less alimony. If this assumption is violated, then the new divorce law *will* alter the value of divorce (by reducing it) and hence the incentive for couples to divorce.

All of these examples show that, if divorces occur efficiently, we have to draw a distinction between those changes that alter the total net value of the relationship $R - S$, and those that shift resources within the relationship without altering the total net value. As we mentioned earlier, we will discuss the assumptions necessary for divorces to occur efficiently, and we will analyse the consequences of alimony laws if divorces occur inefficiently.

5.4   Learning

What happens if the couple learns about R_m and R_f over time? Consider a model where a couple meets and receives imperfect information – a *signal* – about $R = R_m + R_f$. For example, they spend time with each other and start to learn how much they like each other. Based on the signal, the couple updates their beliefs about the value of R and then chooses whether to form a relationship. If they choose to form a relationship, then they enjoy each other's company and next period receive another signal about the relationship. Again they update their beliefs about the value of R and make a new, possibly different decision. Such a model can help explain why we observe both cohabitation and marriage. The advantages of marriage relative to cohabitation include some legal, religious or societal benefits, along with, perhaps, a greater level of commitment and intimacy; the disadvantage of marriage relative to cohabitation is the large cost associated with dissolving a marriage. Such a model suggests that couples who choose to marry without cohabiting received very good signals about the value of their match and are willing to risk a relatively small probability of future divorce to gain the advantages of marriage. Couples who choose to cohabit received a signal good enough to form a relationship but not good enough to commit to marriage. Cohabiting couples are using cohabitation as an 'option' to commit in the future if, with better information, the couple discovers that it has a very good match.

This model of learning may help explain certain facts about cohabitation and marriage. Many empirical researchers have found that cohabitation leads to higher divorce rates (Brien et al., 2006). More precisely, if we compare two apparently identical married couples, one of whom cohabited prior to marriage, then the couple who initially cohabited is subsequently more likely to divorce. This fact has led some conservative social commentators to argue that cohabitation is destroying the institution of marriage, which perhaps it does by somehow reducing the taste for marriage. The theory above suggests another story: those who marry right away received very good initial signals and, on average, have very good matches; while those who cohabit received initial weaker signals and, on average, have worse matches. Even though the ones with worse initial signals receive later signals good enough to induce them to marry, on average, they are not as good matches as those who received good enough signals to marry right away. An implication of this model is that, if everyone were forced to cohabit prior to marriage, then divorce rates would decline because the cohabitation period would have no direct effect on the quality of the subsequent marriage but it would serve as a learning period. During the learning period, some couples would discover that they are not a good match and would not marry in the first place.

5.5 Commitment

Another potentially informative fact is that, the longer a couple is in a relationship, the less likely they are to end it. There are two popular hypotheses to explain this phenomenon. One hypothesis is that it is essentially a statistical phenomenon related to *selection*. Consider the learning model outlined above, in which couples learn over time about the true value of the relationship R. Each period the couples who realize they have a negative total net value separate. Early on, all of the couples with negative match values separate. Over time, additional couples learn that they have a negative match value, but fewer do so over time because the remaining relationships have a higher average value of R. As this process continues, the separation rate for couples married at a certain point in time falls because the couples with lower values of R are selected out through divorce, even though there is no direct effect of duration on relationship quality.

The second hypothesis is that the relationship itself causes the value of the relationship to increase over time. In other words, the couple invests in their relationship as it develops. They invest by learning how to interact with each other, maybe by buying assets (such as a house) together, having children together, or in other ways intensifying their commitment to each other. Each time they invest in their relationship, they build a larger wedge between the total value of the relationship R and the total value of separating, S, thus decreasing the probability of separation.

We can take the model one step further and note that these investments are sunk in the match itself, and if the relationship dissolves, then most, if not all, of the value of the investments is lost. For example, it may be very costly to children for a married couple to divorce, or there may be large transactions costs associated with dividing up the value of a house upon separation. An implication of this point is that couples with very good matches will be more likely to invest in their relationship than those with less good matches. The couples with mediocre matches will hesitate to invest because they know there is a significant probability of dissolution in the future. Moreover, married couples will invest more than cohabiting couples because, a) they have better matches (see the discussion above) and, b) separation costs are higher for marriage than for cohabitation, so separation is less likely. The phenomenon that the level of investment depends upon the quality of the match is called *endogenous investment*. It has the feature that investment increases the variability of match quality, making the best relationships even better and not having much of an effect on mediocre relationships.

5.6   Breaking up is hard (or easy) to do

In the simple model above, we showed that all separations are efficient – they occur if and only if the total net value of the relationship $(R_m + R_f) - (S_m + S_f) = R - S$ turns negative. Most non-economists are not comfortable with this result, so it is useful to examine the underlying assumptions on which the result depends.

In this case, one offending assumption is that partners have perfect information: this requires that the male knows as much about R_f and S_f as the female, and vice versa. Consider, instead, a model where each member of a relationship has some information about his or her own preferences not observable by the other member. The couple has to bargain about the size of any side payment p from one to the other. If each had perfect information about the other's preferences, they would know the range of side payments $(S_f - R_f$ and $R_m - S_m)$ necessary to satisfy the condition that both would be better off in the relationship than not. However, if each has some unobservable information, then he or she has an incentive to lie about it to get a better deal. Knowing that, partners will still bargain, but now they will consider the trade-off between getting a bigger side payment (by exaggerating about the value of one's outside option, S) against the loss associated with a possible separation if the other partner refuses a large side payment. In such a situation, some couples break up even though the total net value of the relationship is positive (so breaking up is too easy).

Another controversial assumption is that transitions are costless. Suppose instead that the government (or perhaps a religious authority) imposes a significant monetary or non-monetary cost D on divorcing couples. The immediate effect of such a cost is to decrease S_m and S_f. For example, if the divorcing couple split the cost D equally, then the new values of being single are $S_m - \frac{1}{2}D$ and $S_f - \frac{1}{2}D$. Since S_m and S_f decline and there is no change in R_m and R_f, the total net value of the relationship increases. Thus, the effect of the divorce cost is, unsurprisingly, to decrease the number of couples who divorce (so breaking up is too hard).

It is important to note, however, that the allocation of the divorce costs between the male and female has no effect on whether a divorce occurs, since the decision to divorce depends only on the total net value (including divorce costs). A law that required the cost to be shared equally would not affect the total net value differently than a law that requires the husband, say, to pay the entire cost. All that would change would be the relative size of S_f and S_m. The husband would be willing to provide a larger side payment to stay married and avoid $S_m - D$, but the wife would only be willing to accept it if the total net value was positive. This is analogous to the result, presented above, that laws mandating alimony payments after divorce do not alter the incidence of divorce.

In the last few examples, we considered how changes in divorce laws affect the frequency of divorces (imposing a divorce cost reduces the incidence of divorce, but the allocation of the cost between partners does not). But how do they affect the marriage rate? Consider a couple *deeply in love* – they are considering marriage and not worrying about the future. Following in the footsteps of other romantic couples before them, they compute the total net value of the relationship, and, if it is positive, negotiate side payments and marry. Divorce costs and alimony rules play no role in their decision of whether to marry because they do not consider possible changes in the value of the relationship. If, in contrast, they recognize that things may change and divorces do occur, then imposing future divorce costs essentially increases the cost of marrying today, thus decreasing the total net value. Therefore, the marriage rate would decrease, but also those marriages that do occur would be stronger (in the sense that the total net value of the marriage would be higher).

5.7 Policy interventions
As we have demonstrated, if divorces occur efficiently, then divorce laws affecting the distribution of resources will not affect whether a divorce occurs. Even divorce laws that do not directly determine the distribution of resources can be interpreted in the same way. Before 1970, most states in the USA required divorcing couples to demonstrate some fault – adultery, abuse, abandonment and so on – in order to grant a divorce. This was implicitly a mutual consent divorce regime; if a couple wanted to divorce, they could lie about fault and obtain a divorce. Led by California in 1970, most states changed their law to allow both no-fault and unilateral divorce – so that one couple could instigate a divorce unilaterally and without alleging fault. This raises two questions: should this affect the divorce rate, and did it affect the divorce rate?

If divorces occur efficiently, then changing the law from mutual to unilateral divorce should not affect the divorce rate. Instead, it acts to redistribute resources from the spouse who wants to stay in the relationship (because $R_m > S_m$) to the spouse who wants to leave (because $R_f < S_f$). Under a mutual consent divorce law, the spouse who wants to leave will be willing to make a side payment that the spouse who wants to stay is willing to accept to agree to a divorce, as long as $S_m - R_m > R_f - S_f$, so the gain to spouse m from leaving the relationship exceeds the gain to spouse f from staying in the relationship. Rearranging terms, this implies that $(R_m + R_f) - (S_m + S_f) < 0$, or the total net value of the relationship is negative.

On the other hand, if the total net value is positive, then the payment that f is willing to make to obtain a divorce is smaller than the payment that m is willing to take in order to grant a divorce. Now, suppose that the divorce law changes to allow unilateral divorce – would f now go ahead and get that divorce? Because the total net value of the relationship is positive, m would now be willing to pay f to stay in the marriage, and the payment would be big enough to make f willing to stay. Thus, even though the law now allows f to leave unilaterally, f would not go unless the total net value of the relationship is negative – so the divorce rate would be unchanged, even though it looks like the law change has made divorce easier. What changes would be the direction of payments, from the spouse who wants to leave the marriage to the spouse who wants to stay.

However, empirical evidence suggests that the divorce rate rose in states in the USA after they changed their divorce laws (Friedberg, 1998). This suggests that divorces do not occur efficiently. This belief is widespread among policy-makers, who have recently reacted by discussing policies that would increase the cost of divorce. A number of states in the USA have proposed giving people a choice of two marriage types: a regular marriage or a 'covenant marriage'. A covenant marriage has extra costs associated with divorce. The Catholic Church has suggested it will approve only covenant marriages in states that provide them.

The analysis in our perfect information model suggests that such government interference will not have the intended effect because all marital separations are efficient. In this subsection, we consider various possible reasons why it might be welfare improving for the government to discourage divorce.

The most obvious possibility is the effects of divorce on children. A large empirical literature shows that children suffer in many ways when their parents divorce. If the divorcing parents do not take into account the cost of divorce to their children, then it might be appropriate for the government to increase divorce costs to simulate the costs to the children. While this argument has some merit, it also has problems. First, it is difficult to measure the effect of divorce on children. The relevant counterfactual is the welfare of the children with unhappy parents who would like to be divorced. In other words, discouraging the divorce of an unhappy couple with children does not magically create a happy couple. Second, parents do care about their children, and maybe they give equal weight to their own happiness and their children's happiness in making divorce decisions. We have no measures of how much they internalize such costs. Finally, divorce costs are imposed on couples without children when such an argument is irrelevant. In fact, if anything, such an argument should lead the government to encourage divorce among couples without children so that they do not divorce once children arrive.

Another possibility that has been discussed in the literature is that, when a couple divorces, it changes the size and the distribution of people in the marriage market. The increase in the number of single people provides a benefit for those already single, and this benefit is not internalized by the divorcing couple. The effect on the quality distribution of single people is harder to sign. In any case, because there is an externality, the government may play a role. The problem with this argument is that the externality goes the wrong way! Since divorce provides a benefit to others not internalized by the divorcing couple, the government should provide a subsidy to divorcing couples.

The final possibility is that increased divorce costs reduce divorce probabilities, causing couples to invest more and improve their relationships. Consider a case where a new husband and wife bargain over sending the wife to medical school while the husband supports her. He is more likely to agree to such a plan if he knows that she will not be able to divorce him later after she has her medical degree. Without high divorce costs, it may be difficult for her to credibly commit to not divorcing later. We can tell a similar story about the couple investing in efficient division of labour. As discussed above, it may be efficient for the wife to specialize in household production and the husband in market production. Without a commitment not to divorce, the wife may not be willing to specialize because she knows that, if they later divorce, she will need to develop market skills. The problem with this argument is that the best solution here is not an imposed divorce cost; rather it is an efficient contracting mechanism. In the first example, the husband and wife should sign a binding contract determining how the proceeds from a medical education will be shared between them if a divorce occurs. In the second example, the husband and wife should agree upon divorce-contingent alimony at the time they are bargaining about specialization. An efficient contract solves the commitment problem without causing bad marriages to remain intact.

6 Conclusion
In this chapter, we have aimed to demonstrate that economic tools can help us understand how individuals make decisions related to marriage and divorce. Economists have not only developed models to explain but also have found evidence to support several hard-hearted theories. One is that the gains to marriage are not simply from sharing love and affection but from a more efficient use of resources (both money and time). Another is that the distribution of those resources within a marriage depends at least in part on the bargaining power of each spouse. A third is that divorces may occur efficiently, so that religious or social laws governing divorce do not affect whether divorces occur but do affect the distribution of resources within marriage.

As we mentioned early on, even economists have not yet come up with definitive explanations for the recent trend away from marriage. One reason is that, as we have argued, many different factors affect decisions to marry and divorce, and these factors can interact in complicated ways. A second reason is that it is difficult to control for all of these relevant, and changing, factors when attempting to test competing theories. For example, we can write down a model showing that married women are working more because the increased probability of divorce raises the gains to investing in their careers, and another model showing that an increase in married women's labour supply raised divorce rates by augmenting friction within marriages. To test whether either, or both, explanations are valid, we need to find exogenous reasons why women are working more (to see whether that led to more divorce) and why divorce rates have risen (to see whether that led to increased labour supply). Did recent increases in women's wages exogenously cause women to work more? Perhaps, or else an increase in married women's labour supply, which boosted their investments in education and careers and their incentive and power to fight gender discrimination, raised women's wages. Did the shift in divorce laws in the early 1970s from requiring mutual agreement by spouses to divorce to allowing one spouse to leave unilaterally exogenously cause more divorce? Perhaps, or else laws were changed in response to pressure from people who increasingly wanted to exit their marriages.

In summary, challenges remain for economists who are in turn challenging researchers in other disciplines to provide coherent explanations and empirical tests of marriage and divorce behaviour.

Notes

1. In most cases, our theories apply to state-sanctioned marriage, whether between two people of different or of the same genders. Without intending any bias against homosexuals, we will sometimes use gender-specific terminology.
2. Most famously, 'palimony' (alimony for a pal) has been granted by courts under relatively stringent conditions – the cohabiting relationship had to involve, 'an express or implied contract' (http://www.palimony.com/7.html).
3. Goldin and Katz (2002) documented the consequences in terms of later marriage and increased investment by women in education and careers that followed the dissemination of the pill.
4. The indicators of child health were calorific intake, height, weight and survival probabilities. Similar outcomes were found in Côte d'Ivoire (Hoddinott and Haddad, 1995) and in Thailand (Schultz, 1990).

References

Allen, D.W. (1998), 'No-Fault Divorce In Canada: Its Cause and Effect', *Journal of Economic Behavior and Organization*, **37** (2), 129–49.
Anonymous (2004a), 'Marriage', *Judaism 101*, http://www.jewfaq.org/marriage.htm.
Anonymous (2004b), 'Divorce', *Judaism 101*, http://www.jewfaq.org/divorce.htm.
Anonymous (2004c), 'Fact Sheet: Equal Pay for Working Women', www.alfcio.org.
Becker, G.S. (1974), 'A Theory of the Allocation of Time', *Economic Journal*, **75**, 493–517.
Becker, G.S. (1981), *A Treatise on the Family*, Cambridge, MA: Harvard University Press.

Bergstrom, T. (1997), 'A Survey of Theories of the Family', in Mark Rozenzweig and Oded Stark (eds), *Handbook of Population Economics*, New York: North Holland, pp. 21–74.

Bergstrom, T., L. Blume and H. Varian (1986), 'On the Private Provision of Public Goods', *Journal of Public Economics*, **29** (1), 25–49.

Binner, J. and A. Dnes (2001), 'Marriage, Divorce, and Legal Change', *Economic Inquiry*, **39**, 298–306.

Brien, M., L. Lillard and S. Stern (2006), 'Cohabitation, Marriage, and Divorce in a Model of Match Quality', *International Economic Review*, forthcoming.

Browning, M., F. Bourguignon, P. Chiappori and V. Lechene (1994), 'Incomes and Outcomes: A Structural Model of Intra-Household Allocation', *Journal of Political Economy*, **102** (6), 1067–96.

Cherlin, A. (1992), *Marriage, Divorce, and Remarriage*, 2nd edn, Cambridge, MA: Harvard University Press.

Coase, R. (1960), 'The Problem of Social Cost', *Journal of Law and Economics*, **3** (1), 1–44.

Coelho, C. and N. Garoupa (2004), 'Did Divorce Law Reforms Raise Divorce Rates? Evidence from Portugal', Draft, Universidade Nova de Lisboa.

Friedberg, L. (1998), 'Did Unilateral Divorce Raise Divorce Rates? Evidence from Panel Data', *American Economic Review*, **88** (3), 608–27.

Goldin, C. and L. Katz (2002), 'The Power of the Pill: Oral Contraceptives and Women's Career and Marriage Decisions', *Journal of Political Economy*, **110** (4), 730–70.

Hoddinott, J. and L. Haddad (1995), 'Does Female Income Share Influence Household Expenditures? Evidence from Côte d'Ivoire', *Oxford Bulletin of Economics and Statistics*, **57** (1), 77–96.

Lundberg, S. and R. Pollak (1993), 'Separate Spheres Bargaining and the Marriage Market', *Journal of Political Economy*, **101** (6), 988–1010.

Lundberg, S., R. Pollak and T. Wales (1997), 'Do Husbands and Wives Pool their Resources? Evidence from the UK Child Benefit', *Journal of Human Resources*, **32** (3), 463–80.

Manser, M. and M. Brown (1980), 'Marriage and Household Decision Making: A Bargaining Analysis', *International Economic Review*, **21**, 31–44.

McElroy, M. and M. Horney (1981), 'Nash-Bargained Decisions: Toward a Generalization of the Theory of Demand', *International Economic Review*, **22** (2), 333–49.

Nash, J. (1950), 'The Bargaining Problem', *Econometrica*, **18** (1), 155–62.

Schultz, P.T. (1990), 'Testing the Neoclassical Model of Family Labor Supply and Fertility', *Journal of Human Resources*, **25** (4), 599–634.

Thomas, D. (1990), 'Intra-Household Resource Allocation: An Inferential Approach', *Journal of Human Resources*, **25** (4), 635–64.

United Nations (various years), *Demographic Yearbook*, New York: Department of Economic and Social Affairs, Statistical Office, United Nations.

United States National Center for Health Statistics (various years), *Vital Statistics of the United States*, Hyattsville, MD: National Center for Health Statistics, United States Center for Disease Control.

Weiss, Y. and R. Willis (1985), 'Children as Collective Goods in Divorce Settlements', *Journal of Labor Economics*, **3** (3), 268–92.

Wolfers, J. (2003), 'Did Unilateral Divorce Raise Divorce Rates? A Reconciliation and New Results', National Bureau of Economic Research Working Paper No. 10014.

Woolley, F. (1988), 'A Non-Cooperative Model of Family Decision Making', LSE Working Paper, TIDI/125.

Youssef, H. (1993), 'The History of the Condom', *Journal of the Royal Society of Medicine*, **86** (4), 226–8.

PART III

BODY AND SOUL

6 Economics of pornography
Samuel Cameron

In this chapter, we look at the contribution economics can make to analysing the behaviour of markets for pornography and to the formulation of public policy in this area. For instance, we show that economics can, through standard supply and demand models, shed light on the impact of regulatory policies on pornography and provide a framework that isolates different elements in the effect of technological change on the long-run equilibrium price and output levels of each type of pornography.

It should be noted from the outset, however, that as a general rule most academic debate and teaching on the subject of pornography is to be found within the realms of feminism, philosophy and legal theory. Economists have made scant contribution with the odd exception. Judge Richard A. Posner, for example, has repeatedly applied orthodox free market Chicago thinking to porn in several of his books (see *Economic Analysis of Law*, 1973; *Sex and Reason*, 1994; *Frontiers of Legal Theory*, 2001).

Heterodox economist David George (2001, pp. 122–4) briefly discusses porn as an instance of what he calls 'preference pollution'. In this scenario, free markets impose weakness of will upon us leading to the 'wrong choice' of consumption basket. We end up on a lower indifference curve than might otherwise have been obtained.

Yet, there are perhaps two simple areas in which debate on porn is focused, which could be summed up in these propositions:

1. There is a huge and growing amount of porn, which threatens to undermine the stability of civilization as we know it. This is a position to which the book we have just mentioned by George seems to subscribe.
2. Pornography generates extremely high profits for its entrepreneurs. This idea is to be found all over the campaigning literature by Christian groups in the USA, despite the lack of reliable statistics on the porn industry. It also inspired the witty, punning title of a book by attorney Frederick Lane III, namely, *Obscene Profits: The Entrepreneurs of Pornography in the Cyber Age*, published in 2000.

This chapter cannot hope to comprehensively answer these charges as they involve two highly contentious things: the reliability and accuracy of statistics and the rights and wrongs of the prevalence of porn in the world. The latter inevitably involves value judgements and thus any economist who claims to be providing a clear-cut proof of the matter is likely to be involved in some act of disingenuity. What we can do is provide a framework for addressing these issues, which will illustrate novel uses of economic concepts for those already used to them and, for those unused to these concepts, it will help to introduce them to their more widespread applicability.

The structure of the chapter is as follows. In Section 1, we look briefly at research outcomes on the effects of pornography. Next, in Section 2, we move on to the nature of porn as an industry just like any other industry, which requires us to consider the issue of statistical evidence. Section 3 examines Amartya Sen's argument about Paretian liberals as applied to pornography. Section 4 looks at the nature of the demand for pornography with reference to addiction and variety seeking. Section 5 outlines government approaches to regulation of porn while Section 6 uses some supply and demand analysis to illuminate the issues of the effect of the Internet on pornography and, in particular, its impact on the efficiency of enforcement efforts by the regulatory authorities. Section 7 considers the existence of possible positive externalities arising directly from both the acts of consumption and production of porn, as well as discussing whether porn should be viewed as a complementary or substitute good. Section 8 concludes the chapter.

1   Social outcomes of pornography: negative externalities

Economic research on this subject is thin. As far as I am aware, there have been no empirical studies of pornography in the major economics journals. Further, I have searched the main economics working papers (that is, a record of works in progress) websites and have not found any papers on pornography.

Evans and Winick (1996) appear to provide the only econometric study of the effects of porn. They studied the non-operation of anti-pornography statutes in four states in the USA during periods between 1973 and 1986. Since non-enforcement of pornography statutes is associated with an increase in the supply of pornographic materials, this provided an opportunity to examine the impact of statutes and pornography availability on sexual offences. They found that there were no statistically significant changes in rates for rape, prostitution or sex offences during the statute suspension. Therefore, we could perhaps conclude from this one isolated study that there is little evidence of any substantial externality effect, in terms of recorded deviant behaviour, from pornography.

Although there is a dearth of econometric studies, there have been a number of comparable statistical studies by researchers in other fields in the sense that aggregate statistics on sex crimes are correlated with some kind of measure of porn output or changes in the regulatory regime of a region (see, for example, Bryant, 2001; Gentry, 1991; Donnerstein et al., 1987; Diamond and Uchiyama, 1999; Scott 1985; Fisher and Barak, 2001). The obvious problem in such studies is eliminating factors, other than access to porn, which may be responsible for spatial or temporal fluctuations in the rates of rape and related activities.

For what it is worth, the overwhelming evidence of the above studies is that we cannot find any clear correlation between porn quantity, style/content or its regulation and the rate of sex offending. Some commentators have also pointed out that in the USA the era of increased porn supply (through VHS tapes, cable and now DVDs and the Internet) has witnessed sharp falls in rape rates. For example, the estimated total of 89 107 forcible rapes reported to law enforcement during 1999 was the lowest total since 1985 and the rate in 1999, 64 out of every 100 000 females, was 5 per cent lower than the previous year's. The latest data show that in 2003 an estimated 93 433 rapes were reported in the USA (all statistics are from FBI sources), 1.9 per cent lower than estimates for 2002. Indeed, the overall level is now extremely low in comparison with the early 1980s.

As we have already implied, one has to be cautious interpreting such statistics as there are changes in sentencing, criminal justice expenditure, police policy and user behaviour going on at the same time. Nevertheless, it cannot be avoided that the expanded prevalence of porn does not seem to be producing aggregate evidence of a negative externality effect in the form of sex crimes.

There is, of course, experimental research on the effects of porn such as the survey by Zillmann (1989), which seems to report some negative attitudinal outcomes of exposure to porn. However, mainstream positivist psychological laboratory research does face certain ethical and epistemological problems in this area. That is, researchers can only deal with willing subjects for the experiment and they cannot reasonably be allowed to test whether observed attitudinal changes would translate into actual behavioural changes of the type that has not been found in the aggregate data analysis reviewed above. Experiments also suffer from the artifactual feature of imposing a consumption style and environment on the subjects that is different from that which they would voluntarily choose in the real world. This may induce some attitudinal changes that would not otherwise occur when one is consuming in the desired way.

2 Characteristics of the industry

2.1 Production and consumption
Let us look at the scope for classification of porn as part of the economy. Although it has no such thing as an SIC (Standard Industrial Classification)

coding in censuses of industrial production, it clearly makes sense to talk of there being a 'sex economy', comprising explicitly marketed legal and illegal porn along with other activities such as prostitution (the subject of Chapter 7), lap dancing and telephone sex chat lines. Some of the legal activity, or that which takes place under the umbrella of legal production, will be partly represented in production and consumption statistics.[1]

In terms of employment, the pornography industry sees many people in categories other than simply being the actors or models. Additional employment is generated in writing scripts and literature, photography, marketing, website design, sales, legal advice and all the other ancillary services found in other forms of production.

Moreover, economics suggests that the sector will also generate standard Keynesian multiplier effects of creating additional employment in other sectors. This could be vital to local economies where there is specialization of the sector due to agglomeration and networking economies (for example, the 'sex tourism' to places such as Amsterdam and Thailand). A local specialization in porn production can also be a valuable source of export earnings (albeit untaxed) due to heavy demand in other countries, which in turn reflects major national differences in legal regulation of the definition and availability of porn.

The most reliable statistics on porn are those produced by the porn film industry, which has a publication, *Adult Video News*, which is comparable to the music industry's *Billboard*. According to a newspaper report, 'Wall Street Meets Pornography', by Timothy Egan in *The New York Times* in 2000, Americans buy or rent more than $4 billion a year worth of graphic sex videos from retail outlets and spend an additional $800 million on less explicit sexual films.

There are no trustworthy statistics on the consumption and production of porn on the Internet, although that does not stop people producing many contradictory and unreliable estimates, mainly from surveys of poor methodological content.[2] Apart from the issue of people telling lies in surveys, there are other problems with data in this area. Some 'net porn' is free and accurate statistics would require logs of the traffic to providers and this is not generally available. In addition, the same surveys are all that are available on paid net porn and we do not have access to statistics on credit card payments to these sites.

Even if one wanted to take a chance on using survey estimates on time spent visiting porn sites, there is a further problem on what this time figure really means. Everyone knows that 'pagejacking' in the form of pop-up windows attempting to take you somewhere else is a regular feature of surfing, especially for 'free' sites as the funding is likely to come from porn pay sites. Thus, time spent surfing the net for porn sites may contain a large and hard-to-measure fraction that is consumption search rather than actual consumption.

The size of the illegal porn sector (bearing in mind that what is illegal in some countries is not in others) is extremely hard to proxy. The only way to do this would be if there were a regular and consistent seizure policy by the regulatory bodies and it were fair to assume that this seized a fairly constant portion of the total supply. This requirement is not met in reality, however. For example, on the issue of consistency, recent UK policy on child porn has been to put huge resources into targeting high profile (consumer) suspects, which means small amounts detected per case compared with a strategy of spreading investigations across the sector.

2.2 Size distribution of firms

The porn sector is a very diverse one in terms of the size distribution of firms. Due to the development of technology, there are now one-person firms in the form of people who may provide still pictures, film clips or even interactive sexual performances via webcams. At the latter point, the definition is crossing over to prostitution. There are also small firms distributing what one might call almost 'home-made' porn without trained actors or scriptwriters. Traditionally, this might have been called 'amateur' porn (see O'Toole, 1998 for a discussion of amateur porn). However, the use of the word amateur to describe a product being supplied by a full-time producer and sold for a price is a little difficult to handle in terms of economic analysis. Effectively, amateur now really means one of two things:

1. A genre or style of film-making that might be seen as more 'real' than the heavily stylized products found in commercial DVDs and on 'pay' television stations.
2. Models or webcam performers who do not have any kind of agent to represent them. In some cases these may be genuine college students briefly subsidizing their education by a foray into the sex industry. In Chapter 7, we provide evidence of this phenomenon in the UK in relation to prostitution.

At the other end of the scale, we have entities such as the Playboy corporation, which is a multi-product firm supplying magazines, DVDs, its own TV channel and a website. For the traditional full-length feature-film, there are 'majors' in the same way that there are in regular movie production and they do have an annual Oscar-style award ceremony.

However, due to the restricted area of consumption these firms cannot approach the size of profits to be made in the mainstream film sector. In theory, they will nevertheless receive an implicit subsidy as some workers in the porn sector enter it to acquire relevant human capital and contacts for later use in mainstream films. This means they should be willing to accept lower wages than would otherwise be the case.

Perhaps the principal economic characteristic of the sector is that there are few entry barriers. The main obstacle to new producers of pornography is finding consumers. In the case of films, this problem has decreased due to the emergence of DVDs and pay-TV channels, which fill the gap in outlets due to the fact that in many parts of the world porn films are not allowed in conventional movie theatres and specialist porn cinemas tend to be heavily restricted. Overall, barriers to entry in pornography may in fact be lower than in some other niches of the sex industry such as prostitution, as the emphasis on depiction and suggestion of sexual acts means that 'looks' *per se* are less important.

Within the self-employed Internet-based sector we observe the interesting phenomenon of cooperation between rivals in a sector approximating perfect competition. Websites of individual models feature links to other suppliers of the same product. This seems most unusual; we would be very surprised to see plumbers, electricians or interior designers advertising the services of their rivals. The explanation for the free advertising of site links in porn could be that people are not sufficiently impressed by a website without many URL links and so all that is happening here is cooperation due to desperation. A more convincing analysis, however, requires attention to some non-standard features of consumption, which create network externality gains for those who advertise (seemingly) rival suppliers. These features in the shape of 'variety demand' and addiction are discussed in Section 4.

2.3   Profits

Let us briefly address the issue of profits that was raised in the introduction. From an economic point of view, there are a whole host of reasons why we would expect some individuals and some websites and corporations that supply hotel pay-per-view porn movies to make large profits (whether or not we regard these as super-normal profits in the textbook sense is a different matter). These are all points that apply to the sex industry in general:

1. In any industry some operators will make huge profits, whilst many other less well-known cases struggle and/or go out of business.
2. Porn is supplied in a dynamic technologically progressive industry and therefore there will be standard 'first-mover advantages' to producers who establish a niche market or perfect a delivery method.
3. Compensating differentials – whilst the pornographer is still the recipient of social opprobrium, standard labour market theory dictates that

they should be receiving higher wages to compensate for the psychic costs of being disliked.

4. Lack of non-profit motivation – whilst there may be some 'evangelical' entrepreneurs who see the supply of porn as a crusade to help humankind, it is likely that on balance the porn entrepreneur lacks some of the non-profit motives found in some other industries.

Given the above it is thus something very far from remarkable that some porn suppliers make large profits. Indeed, condemning this seems like some kind of 'moral double-counting' from those who consider porn sinful, as the act of production and consumption has already been condemned. One is left wondering if those who make the profit critique would be happier if porn profits were more evenly spread amongst the pornsters.

3 Defining pornography

3.1 The legal and philosophical perspective

We now address the thorny issue of the definition of pornography more directly, as this is an area in which everyone thinks they know what the word means, yet legal definitions have been difficult to agree upon. The original meaning of the word was as a description of the life and activities of prostitutes. This derives from the Greek, pornographos (porne = prostitutes and graphein = to write). It acquired its present meaning in the nineteenth century and seems to have two key elements, one being the obscenity of depiction of sexual acts (our principal focus for the remainder of this section) and the other, the exploitation of workers in the production of the material and/or the consumers of the material.

Therefore, analysis of pornography falls within the topic of censorship, that is, state decisions on what citizens should and should not be allowed to see. The obscenity charge includes such things as swearing and incitements to violence in cultural products like cartoons and rap and rock music records. Much legislation in the past that has dealt with pornography has also tended to be under the rubric of 'obscenity' but it has been very difficult to define pornography as a criminal offence. Instead, it has been frequently treated in legal matters as material 'with a tendency to deprave or offend' with the decision on how depraving or offensive the matter being left to a judge and/or jury.

American Supreme Court decisions have provided ample illustration of the difficulties of arriving at an obscenity definition (see Sears, 1989 for some history on this). According to Silver (1994), Justice Potter Stewart pronounced that he would know pornography 'when he saw it'. This implies either that his preferences are representative of those that should dominate social decision-making or that they represent majority social preferences. Two other judges quoted in Silver (1994), Justices White and Brennan, were particularly keen to use erect penises as a dividing line between porn and 'erotica' although they differed on how much deviation was allowed from traditional heterosexual intercourse. Justice Brennan's so-called 'limp dick' test has remained today as a dividing line in movie censorship. This is recognized by porn film-makers who insist not only on erections but ejaculation as being essential to the production of a genuine (as opposed to 'soft') porn movie (see O'Toole, 1998).

As alluded to above, lurking in the Supreme Court decisions has been the notion of an 'average person' standard, that is, the judges are agents representing the median preferences of the population. This has been a motif also of UK legal debate. For example, in the trial of D.H. Lawrence's novel, *Lady Chatterley's Lover*, as an obscene book, the judge invited the jurors to consider whether they would allow their servants to read it.

However, average person standards run into difficulties when we come to child pornography, especially when it is intertwined with claims that a work is 'erotic art'. That is, can the 'average person' know that something is a genuine work of artistic merit, particularly so if they have not invested in the 'art appreciation capital' that emerges from Beckerian models of rational addiction? This seems then to require delegation of judgement to allow some role for expert witnesses. A good example of this type of situation was reported by BBC News on 27 March 2002 when Canadian author J.R. Sharpe was found 'not guilty' of child pornography because his work had some artistic merit. Several university professors compared his work with Charles Dickens and James Joyce thereby causing the charge to fail. This is only one of numerous cases all over the world where material charged with being pornographic is defended as art.

Artistic merit is also a problematic element to bring into the definition because we still seem to be driven back to the issue of the intent of the producer rather than the nature of the product. In economic terms, we could argue that a particular book/film may have artistic merit, which is one type of output, but the porn content is a joint product. Thus, the purchaser gets two goods. Is it then acceptable to supply porn just because it is jointly supplied with another good that is deemed to be perhaps a 'merit good' by paternalistic policy advisors and governments? Even if one accepts this, it is difficult to prevent the consumer skipping to the passage of a book or a film that is deemed to be porn.

The logical response is to appoint censors to either cut out the offending segment or require it to be edited differently. If the joint outputs are neither readily separable nor divisible, then this is not so easy. In such cases, it is difficult to resolve the argument that the alleged porn component cannot be removed without effectively destroying the whole product.

3.2 The economic perspective

But, why from an economist's point of view should we be spending time trying to define porn in the first place? If individuals are rational utility maximizers, then why do they need to be barred from pornography? Furthermore, if they do, why does an exception need to be made for 'art'?

Problems arise over the optimality of individual liberty in consumption as discussed by Sen (1970) once we start to permit people's disgust at other people's consumption to be classified as a negative (consumption-on-consumption) externality. Sen posed the dilemma for the Paretian liberal in terms of permission to read *Lady Chatterley's Lover*. In itself, this indicates how the moral climate has shifted in English-speaking countries as there is now little concern about such books (Henry Miller's *Tropics* novels are another example) being published in continental Europe.

Given this, we will reformulate Sen's example in terms of the publication of a book of graphic bondage photographs, which we will assume to be with the consent of the models pictured therein and causing them no pain. However, if the people concerned were rational masochists then any physical pain they suffer may, in fact, be a source of utility to them, which would mean they will accept a lower equilibrium wage for the shoot than the non-masochist would accept.

So, let us assume there are two people, Mr 1 who wishes that no one should read the book and Ms 2 who wishes to read what we will call bob (book of bondage). There are three possible outcomes as shown in Figure 6.1: no one can be permitted to read the book or one can be made to read it and not the other. Mr 1 is a paternalistic prude who, as just noted, prefers that no one should read the book and ranks second the case where only he should read bob as Ms 2 is at risk of welfare loss from being exposed to bob (the 'demerit good' argument).

Ms 2, who might be described as an evangelical liberationist (that is, she seeks to expose others to challenges to their sexual preconceptions), has

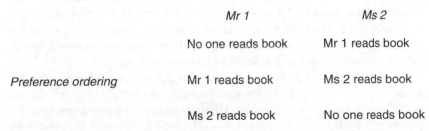

	Mr 1	Ms 2
	No one reads book	Mr 1 reads book
Preference ordering	Mr 1 reads book	Ms 2 reads book
	Ms 2 reads book	No one reads book

Figure 6.1   Sen and the impossibility of a Paretian liberal

as her least favoured option that neither should read bob. Her preferred position is that Mr 1 should have to read the book due to a utility effect from the pleasure of shocking the prude. Her second best option is for only her to read the book. According to Sen, 'liberal' society would nominate that the 'no bob' situation is the optimal choice as the other situations involve Mr 1 being forced to read the book.

This is just a simple example of a voting paradox, which would vanish if all people had the same preferences. Yet, if all people had identical preferences there would be no need for a debate about censoring pornography, but it is important to note the forced consumption element of the example given. We can always argue that people have a free choice not to consume porn. This seems to lie behind the greater tolerance of porn/obscenity in some art forms than others. For example, cinematic movie releases and live theatre tend to be less heavily censored than television provision.

The rationale for this would seem to be the differences in comparative risk of those whose preferences may need protection (for example, children, the prudish and easily shocked). Thus, although such people may not be forced to watch sado-masochism, which is not essential to a dramatic plot or an advertisement, there is clearly a cumulative risk that they may experience accidental forcing from inertia or channel hopping. The same argument applies to Internet 'pagejacking' by pop-up windows.

Some would argue (David Friedman, for example) that Sen's argument is a misreading of what 'liberal' means. He assumes the liberal wants each person to have the controlling decision between some two states of the world – where a state of the world describes everything that happens to everyone. We would more normally assume that what a liberal wants is to control certain choices relevant to her/himself only. For example, if I am a liberal I will want to have control over what book I read and I would wish that others have the same choice so long as no third party suffers.[3]

Further, there may be no conflict between liberal and Paretian outcomes in a world where there are no obstacles to efficient contracts. That is, the two individuals in the above example could come to an agreement that the prude should not read the book but the liberal can read the book. This does seem to face the problem that a prude, by definition, would not want the liberal to be allowed to read the book. It takes us into a regress of saying that it is impossible to be a Paretian liberal in a world where not everyone is a liberal, which I would assume to be the point Sen was making.

Indeed, we should pause to consider that it is questionable whether the rather restrictive concept of Pareto optimality is ever likely to be of great usefulness in analysing policy issues that are so heavily interwoven with disparate value judgements. Again, I would be inclined to think that this is the point Sen was trying to make (following on from Arrow's Impossibility

Theorem[4]) in order to provoke liberals to come up with a more convincing welfare economics.

4 Demand analysis of pornography

We now consider the demand analysis of porn within the framework of the routine assumptions of the undergraduate economics textbook, beginning with a discussion of what constitutes the 'price' of porn to the consumer. Following this, we look at some modifications to the textbook assumptions, which may provide greater insights into the economics of porn.

4.1 The price of pornography

The price of porn to the consumer could be assumed simply as the list purchase price of such a title. Generally, there is little problem with this if the porn is 100 per cent legal. However, if the porn is illegal then the market price is no longer a true reflection of the marginal cost of acquiring a unit of porn. Illegality adds some new costs to the list price:

1. Search costs of finding titles as illegality will impose transaction costs due to lack of advertising and secrecy.
2. Additional costs following from (1) in the form of restricted opportunities to consume from the need to avoid detection.
3. Explicit costs of punishment by the legal system if caught such as fines and prison sentences.
4. Punishment costs from beyond the legal system, for example, from a partner or parent or through loss of a job or restricted promotion opportunities due to consumption at work. Workers can be sacked or disciplined for wasting work time surfing pornographic websites.
5. 'Rip off' risks from unscrupulous suppliers. In the heyday of purchasing VHS videotapes from covert retail outlets in the UK, the situation arose where an individual asked for a particular title and was asked to wait. The vendor then went downstairs and wrote the desired title on the box of an entirely different film (see O'Toole, 1998). Due to the illegality of the product, the buyer does not have recourse to consumer protection legislation.

Hence, as in the case of illicit drugs discussed in Chapter 1, the effective or 'full' price of the product is higher than the price at the point of sale and so illegality would lower consumption in some proportion to the extent that it adds to the list price. This does, of course, illustrate the fact that even a zero price does not mean a free good. A rational utility-maximizing worker surfing a free site (or using a 'hack' into a pay site) on his or her work computer is not receiving a totally 'free' good.

4.2   Addiction

An additional worry about porn, aside from any 'social pollution' of negative externalities, is that it may have addictive properties in consumption. The psychological position on this is presented in Cooper et al. (1999). From an economist's perspective, addiction to porn may make any such social pollution worse and it might also be used as a case for intervention to protect the porn consumer from himself or herself.

If porn is an addiction (assuming for the moment this is the case), it is not delivered, unlike illicit drugs, in direct chemical form. Does this make any difference? According to the rational addiction model discussed in Chapter 1, the answer is no. The important thing is that some mental process creates a link between the marginal utility of consumption of units of the good in different periods. It does not matter whether chemicals directly taken into the body or produced in the mind by external stimulation of the senses forge this link.

Within this framework, fears about porn are in terms of it being a harmful addiction. This has been expressed by strict religions over all sexual activities outside of those designed to produce children within marriage (see Cameron, 2002). Such fears have, at times, given rise to claims that mental and physical deterioration will befall the sexually indulgent individual.

The addicted porn user will have low levels of social interaction in the traditional sense of face-to-face contact. Some porn consumers are in a trading network of social interaction, notably on the Internet due to its illegality, but this is not the major feature of their consumption, which has low sociability. Rather, it is the possible growth of a fantasy element where an individual seeks to control an imaginary world in which he or she is more powerful and successful than in the real one. We can illustrate this in terms of the Becker–Lancaster goods characteristics/time allocation model of household production. The aggregate fantasy production function can be written as:

Fantasy output = f (time spent fantasizing, fantasy-related goods, fantasy energy supplied, imagination, random error)

Individuals may substitute between different fantasies according to the relevant prices and the shadow prices of time. In the specific case of pornography, the goods are magazines, videos or visits to websites, all of which may be fairly time-intensive if fantasy output is to be created. One can be more than one sort of fantasist. The obsessive stalker or fan of one person demands low levels of variety as his or her utility is increased by having more items from the same category (for example, more pictures of the same person) because obsession by its nature has to be with a small set of items or people. However, it should be noted that charged obsessives are not typically porn collectors, as they may form their fantasies from collections of images that would not be deemed 'obscene' by the 'normal' person. For instance, many cases of obsessive stalking concern ordinary people, plus actors, singers and newsreaders, of whom there are no pornographic images available.

4.3   Variety-seeking

The evidence suggests that the major porn markets seem to be characterized by high levels of variety-seeking (O'Toole, 1998). As already noted, there are many overground Internet news groups in which porn consumers trade, discuss and catalogue their collections. This is comparable to what goes on in the general range of cultural products such as music and films. Our earlier observation that fantasy goods such as porn may be very time-intensive, relative to other goods, seems to imply low levels of consumption unless a person has 'idle' time available to them or, in the opposite case, high levels of income.

Fantasy may have the unusual (for a consumer choice model) property of substantial zones of increasing marginal utility, and better still (or worse still depending on your point of view) increasing returns to some of the fantasy production function inputs. This strange effect has been previously remarked upon in a piece on the phenomenon of collecting by Troilo (1999). The collector may have an increasing marginal utility for items in the collection if the sequence of acquisition is appropriately structured.

5   Regulation of porn: methods and problems

Pornography attracts attention because it is perceived as a problem requiring government action. In terms of welfare economics, the simplest case for controlling it is that it may be viewed, as mentioned earlier, as a form of 'social pollution'. Therefore, policy towards porn can be divided into the following distinct categories:

1.   Price controls.
2.   Outright quantity controls such as banning.
3.   Quantity control through licensing and regulation, in particular, through zoning by age. A notable instance of this is to be found in the 1995 Child Protection and Obscenity Enforcement Act, passed in the USA following the 1986 report of the Meese Commission. This required porn film-makers to keep detailed records proving that no under-age performers were used. In theory, this should have shifted up the cost curves of legitimate adult porn film-makers and thereby reduced equilibrium output of adult films even though that was not the ultimate aim of the policy.

4. Moral suasion possibly by encouraging the consumer to feel guilty or fearful of adverse mental and physical health consequences.
5. Product intervention via censorship. For mainstream films, producers may be required to make cuts in order to get an age certificate such as an '18' or a '12'. Without these cuts the films would be condemned to the limited circulation of the porn circuit.
6. Regulation of distribution channels. For example, a porn magazine may be required to be shrink-wrapped in an opaque cover and/or located in a position in a shop where it is not easily seen, by accident, by children or others likely to take offence. This is the origin of the phrase 'top shelf magazine'. In the case of broadcast porn, the title may be restricted to channels that are not 'free-to-air' and can therefore be blocked to inappropriate consumers.

These options differ greatly in terms of their costs of enforcement. Most of them are considerably cheaper than the outright ban. Option (1), price controls, is seldom discussed. Sex industry products in general have, unlike chemically addictive goods, not been treated with additional 'sin' taxation in the modern era. They have either been made illegal or given normal tax treatment, that is, workers pay conventional income taxes and products are taxed at standard rates.

A porn tax might seem attractive (analogous to a Pigouvian pollution tax) from an older welfare economics perspective, but in terms of more modern welfare economics, the option of selling permits, or licences, to porn merchants would seem a better price-based solution. While the sale value of the permits could be determined at a level that is social welfare maximizing, both approaches face the difficulty of being seen as dangerous due to making porn seem like a legitimate business activity rather than an 'evil' that has to be somehow contained. In view of this, porn policy in general terms veers towards the persuasion, prevention and punishment approaches, the latter two being discussed in Section 6 in relation to the impact of the Internet on pornography.

Yet, any policy faces problems of adaptive behaviour by producers and consumers. One option is smuggling of products from more tolerant nations. This flared up in the 1970s with movements of material from the Scandinavian nations to the UK and the USA, particularly after the 1969 Danish legalization of pornography, which included very liberal treatment of child porn. Physical movements of goods across borders can be prevented by systematic surveillance, particularly as videos and books are quite hard to disguise. Eventually, the liberality of legal Scandinavian child porn was curbed, however, thus reducing the burden on customs agencies abroad.

6 Supply and demand analysis of the effect of the Internet

6.1 Dirty postcards

The arrival of widespread access to pornography on the Internet can be fairly said to have sparked moral panic about the threat posed to the stability of society. It is probably worth remembering that this has happened before, albeit with a much more humble technological advance – the picture postcard. The ability to mass-market postcard images cheaply only arrived in the 1890s. Before this, porn was largely manifested in the written word and expensive non-reproducible images. It was the preserve of the wealthier classes and managed to largely escape regulation despite the pressure of organizations such as the National Vigilance Association and women's purity groups in the UK (Sigel, 2002). Even until recently it was common to refer to 'dirty postcards'.

A number of prosecutions in the UK in the 1890s brought to light the distinction between porn and erotica in terms of the fitness of the consumer. That is, the chief legal principle seemed to be that nakedness and so on were not art when consumed by those of lower income and status. They were deemed to be too easily corrupted and excited to be safe receiving such material. This takes us back to modern anxieties over digital television and now the Internet where concern is that porn is falling too readily into the wrong hands.

Of course, the global miracle of the Internet and the allied development of widespread digital copying have transformed all problems associated with international trade in cultural goods. The most obvious important innovation is the fact that the goods no longer need to be literally moved in real time in a cumbersome format across national boundaries. Rather, they can be e-mailed in compressed formats or downloaded from websites. Given a high-speed connection, an individual can rapidly download a huge collection of still pornographic images, although moving-image compression of acceptable picture quality is still much slower.

One consequence of all this is that the transaction costs of obtaining a product are greatly reduced. In addition, it is now virtually impossible to prevent the product moving from a territory where the content is legal to a consumer into one where it is illegal. This is especially germane to the issue of child porn where the age limit is 18 in the USA but much lower in many other places. This creates incentives for suppliers to locate on servers in the most tolerant countries. Even if only one person in the prohibiting nation downloads a new collection it is now fairly costless for this collection to be proliferated if the individual belongs to a covert-sharing group. The digital dimension and its accompanying cost falls have added fuel to the kind of moral panic felt in the heyday of 'dirty postcard' prosecutions.

Of course, the Internet is of considerable assistance to suppliers of illegal 'hard' porn, although the same resources are available to the policing authorities. It follows that laws can be passed and strategies formulated to regulate pornography on the Internet. This consists of two main aspects: detection and punishment and, on the other hand, prevention (for legal discussion, see Akdeniz, 1997).

6.2   Detection and punishment

Police surveillance of Internet activity includes 'cottaging' their way into an illegal porn file-sharing newsgroup and hacking into people's supposedly 'private' e-mails. This is often backed up by high-profile 'naming and shaming' and stiffer prison sentences for supplying the material. One would expect that if the consumers were rational utility maximizers that they would reduce their consumption levels as every act of transaction now carries a higher potential cost. Indeed, the important variable for deciding the optimal level of enforcement is the elasticity of porn consumption with respect to the punishment. Unfortunately, we know nothing about this.

However, we can be sure that the consumer of forbidden porn increases his or her risk of punishment greatly if he or she has an archive of porn that is not easily hidden. Once magazines have been purchased or images downloaded they have to be stored for repeat consumption (assuming that the marginal utility of gazing does not decline so rapidly that they become almost instantly valueless upon storage). The larger the collection, the greater is the risk of detection by significant disapproving others (parents, partners). Moreover, the size of the collection may also influence the size of guilt/shame punishments inflicted by these significant others as it may be easier to escape with a small punishment if a convincing case can be made that it was idle curiosity or a temporary weakness.

While a digital collection of images is much more easily hidden than a magazine, book or videocassette, cases are common of people being charged due to porn collections on the hard disk of their home or work computers. Indeed, the rapid fall in price and increase in capacity of flash memory cards, such as those used in digital cameras, provides great opportunities for evading detection as these are easily concealed. They can be read through a USB card reader attached to the machine when consumption is desired or, in an emergency, can probably be flushed down the toliet.

6.3   Prevention

Prevention of access to Internet porn requires that the would-be consumer is unable to access the site. This can be accomplished by specific software that refuses connection to a site. Such software (for example, *Cyber Patrol* and *Net Nanny*) is aimed at parents wishing to prevent children seeing porn.

Alternatively, many pay porn sites now require the purchase of an adult 'ID key' in order to prove that the consumer is legally entitled to view the material. ISP providers can also lock certain sites as unsuitable for their client base and government regulation requires that they comply with the pornography statutes in their own countries. This is not particularly difficult to overcome, however. Indeed, all prevention measures can be circumvented at some level of effort/cost by those whom they were meant to stop. The level of such costs depends essentially on the computer literacy of the person being prevented. In fact, more information technology training for schoolchildren may have the unintended by-product of making them more proficient at 'hacking' through Internet security.

6.4 Marginal productivity of porn preventers and consumers
The precise effect of the advent of the Internet depends on the relative amount by which it shifts the marginal productivity schedules of 'preventers' versus those of consumers. This is illustrated on a supply and demand-style diagram in Figure 6.2. The axes show the quantity of illegal porn and the risk of being caught and punished. The demand-style schedule (D) is downward-sloping on the assumption that the consumer treats risk as exogenous and is more willing to consume porn when risk is lower, *ceteris*

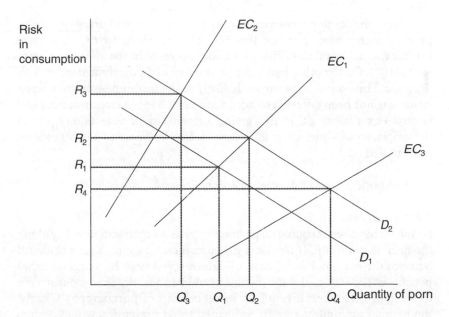

Figure 6.2   Regulation of pornography on the Internet

paribus. This curve can move due to changes in the rate of consumption by existing consumers and changes in the participation rate (that is, the fraction of people consuming). The enforcement curve (*EC*) shows the risk that enforcement agencies are able to produce. Other things being equal, they should be able to increase the number of porn arrests when there is more pornography in existence as there are more additional trades to detect. If the law becomes easier to enforce, this curve will shift upwards.

Let us suppose that the schedules D_1 and EC_1 represent the pre-Internet world in a fairly anti-porn country where there is a settled legal framework. Let us also assume that there is a fairly elastic supply of porn from the rest of the world. The model has an equilibrium risk (R_1) and volume of porn consumed (Q_1), which should be stable because a fall below R_1 will lead to excess demand, which drives the risk up to R_1 and a rise above R_1 will lead to excess supply, which drives the risk down.

Now imagine the Internet suddenly arriving in this scenario by shifting the *D* function to the right to D_2 but leaving the *EC* function unchanged. Part of this shift is due to increased participation as many who would not have overcome the obstacles to obtaining porn via other methods now have access to the Internet. This leads to a higher equilibrium consumption rate at Q_2 but also a higher equilibrium risk at R_2 and is a characterization of the very short-run impact where the authorities have not responded to the new situation.

If they can develop strategies that mean they now find arrests easier to produce then, *ceteris paribus*, the EC_1 schedule shifts to EC_2 causing a further rise in equilibrium risk (R_3) and a decrease in the volume of porn traded (Q_3). On the other hand, the productivity of punishment effort may decrease. This would be particularly likely in the medium term when legislation has not been adjusted to accommodate changed circumstances and is shown as a fall in *EC* to EC_3 giving a lower risk of detection (R_4) than the original post-Internet equilibrium and an increase in the volume of porn traded (Q_4).

7   A reconsideration of porn as an economic good

7.1   *Social benefits*
So far, we have been treating all pornography as a negative externality along the lines of pollution. If this were the case, then we simply face a trade-off between the marginal social costs of deterrence versus the marginal social benefits of reduction. But the picture would be radically changed if it were to be argued that there are, in fact, social benefits of pornography. Clearly, the optimal amount of resources devoted to its prevention would decline and, in the extreme case, we could find an optimum of legality of all porn.

Denmark was the only country where the possible positive effects of the availability of child pornography played a role in the political debate; it was suggested that child pornography could serve as an outlet for tensions that might otherwise lead to child abuse. This argument was proposed by the criminologist Berl Kutchinsky and has been reformulated in various works (Kutchinsky, 1970, 1985; Kutchinsky and Snare, 1999). He produced some evidence of correlations between availability of hard pornography and a decrease in reported cases of voyeurism and sex offences against children.

Aside from outlet benefits, it has even been argued that the demand for porn has induced the suppliers of porn to stimulate technological advances, which have brought considerable benefits to non-porn consumers. This was pointed out in an article by John Arlidge in the 3 March 2002 edition of *The Observer* (UK) newspaper entitled, 'What's Porn Done For Us?', where he lists these spin-offs:

1. Camcorder and VHS video machines were pioneered by porn produ- cers who wanted to mass-market their goods.
2. Take-up of DVD players was accelerated by pornographers and their customers because the technology enabled users to skip to and from their favourite scenes.
3. Pay-per-view cable or satellite TV movies entered the market for general movies only after porn firms introduced 'premium' services in hotels and on digital networks.
4. Interactive television, common on digital sport channels, was devel- oped by pornographers to allow users to focus on favourite actors and actresses.
5. The Internet is used for many things other than porn and the profits and scale effects generated by porn provide benefits to non-porn users.

A further point not mentioned by Arlidge is that it is likely that the con- tinuing collapse of region code protection in the DVD market is due to the widespread international trade in porn DVDs. This benefits non-porn con- sumers by expanding freedom of choice and it helps remove a barrier to international price competition. In addition, it may be argued that widely available porn can potentially improve the quality of other art/entertain- ment goods (such as mainstream Hollywood movies) by reducing the incen- tive to supply 'watered down' porn in an attempt to attract porn-rationed consumers.

7.2 Consuming porn: substitute or complement?
Returning to economic theories of consumption, we might usefully restate the case as to whether porn is most appropriately regarded as a complement

or substitute to sex industry products, or is it rather an input to a production process. Some users may regard it as complementary to their normal consumption of sexual satisfaction. Some makers (female, in particular) of softer porn movies claim that couples may use them to revive their relationships. In this situation, the negative externality seems much smaller if we rule out the non-liberal 'disapproval' factor by other people. The substitution case is where pornography provides someone with an alternative to sexual outlets involving active interaction with other people (see Cameron and Collins, 2000). This may be a positive temporary (therapeutic even) usage before they re-enter conventional relationships. Clearly, here there is the 'safety valve' benefit that can also be claimed for other sex industry products.

8   Conclusion

Pornography is a subject with wide economic ramifications. Goods that might be regarded as porn generate considerable amounts of employment, earnings and output. To the extent that this is illegal, there will be an understatement of national income. There will also be a loss of potential tax revenues from making production illegal. Where porn is legal, those who object to it are in the position of regarding it as a 'bad' (social pollution), the inclusion of which *overstates* rather than understates the true real national income. The amount of any such overstatement would be even greater if it were decided to adjust real national income to take account of utility losses from crimes, oppression and stress that might be thought to follow from the presence of porn in the economy. However, there are two problems with this that have been highlighted by the discussion in this chapter:

1.   To date there is no convincing scientific research that shows that pornography has harmful effects on its employees or consumers. Even if disturbed personality traits can be found among consumers and workers, this may simply represent a 'self-selection' bias whereby those with such problems are attracted to these products but their problems are not originated or worsened by porn output.
2.   There is immense difficulty in agreeing what constitutes 'porn'. To the person who regards anything they personally object to, of a sexual nature, as pornography, the distinction may appear obvious. However, legal action requires clear-cut criteria that can be applied. The more unclear these criteria are, the more deadweight loss is inflicted upon the economy in terms of resources used up in complex legal cases. Economics does not offer a way of resolving disputes about definition within the traditional welfare economics framework of sovereign preferences. Rather, Sen's 1970 paper on the impossibility of a Paretian

liberal shows this approach does not enable us to say much about the direction policy should take. One can attempt to break through this straitjacket by delving into the possibility of more complex preference functions. Endogenous preferences where the porn seller is creating additional wants in the buyer is one possibility and irrational addiction is another. Even so, we still face the problem that it is very hard to produce empirical evidence to support these factors as grounds for intervention.

Notes

1. Some porn production and consumption will be mixed up in the statistics for other production and consumption unless explicit attempts were made to identify it. Government household surveys may ask about spending on magazines, films and so on but not whether they were pornographic. A certain amount of the output of the leather industry, for instance, may be from inputs into the production of bondage equipment, which ends up in pornographic films or still pictures or webcam interaction. Yet, there is no way of knowing what proportion this is.
2. A good guide to all of this can be found at http://www.caslon.com.au/xcontentprofile. htm.
3. Certainly Sen's definition of liberalism under footnote 1 of his paper is one that seems to interpret liberalism as a form of dictatorship under certain pairs of alternatives. He expands on the footnote of this stating that, 'liberalism is elusive and open to alternative interpretations. Some uses of the term may not embrace the condition described here, while many uses will. I do not wish to engage in a debate on the right use of the term'.
4. Kenneth Arrow's (1951) 'impossibility theorem' suggests that no voting system can generate consistent social preferences from conflicting views about how society ought to be organized.

References

Akdeniz, Y. (1997), 'Governance of Pornography and Child Pornography on the Global Internet: A Multi-Layered Approach', in L. Edwards and C. Waelde (eds), *Law and the Internet: Regulating Cyberspace*, Hart Publishing, pp. 223–41.

Arlidge, J. (2002), 'What's Porn Done For Us? You May Disapprove of Pornography But the Spin-offs of the Industry Are All Around', *The Observer*, 3 March.

Arrow, Kenneth J. (1951), *Social Choice and Individual Values*, London: Chapman and Hall.

Becker, G.S. and K.M. Murphy (1988), 'A Theory of Rational Addiction', *Journal of Political Economy*, **96** (4), 675–700.

Bryant, P. (2001), 'Using Crime Mapping to Measure the Negative Secondary Effects of Adult Businesses in Fort Wayne, Indiana: A Quasi-Experimental Methodology', paper presented to National Institute of Justice's Crime Mapping Research Center's 2001 International Crime Mapping Research Conference: Dallas, Texas.

Cameron, Samuel (2002), *The Economics of Sin: Rational Choice or No Choice At All?*, Cheltenham, UK and Northampton, MA., US: Edward Elgar.

Cameron, Samuel and Alan Collins (2000), *Playing the Love Market: Dating, Romance and the Real World*, London: Free Association Books.

Cooper, A., C.A. Scherer, S.C. Boies and B.L. Gordon (1999), 'Sexuality on the Internet: From Sexual Exploration to Pathological Expression', *Professional Psychology: Research and Practice*, **30** (2), 154–64.

Diamond, M. and A. Uchhiyama (1999), 'Pornography, Rape, and Sex Crimes In Japan', *International Journal of Law and Psychiatry*, **22** (1), 1–22.

Donnerstein, E., D. Linz and S. Penrod (eds) (1987), *The Question of Pornography: Research Findings and Policy Implications*, The Free Press – A Division of Macmillan, Inc.

Edwards, D.M. (1992), 'Politics and Pornography: A Comparison of the Findings of the President's Commission and the Meese Commission and the Resulting Response' (http://home.earthlink.net/~durangodave/html/writing/Censorship.htm).

Egan, T. (2000), 'Wall Street Meets Pornography', *The New York Times*, 23 October.

Evans, J.T. and C. Winick (1996), 'The Relationship Between Non-enforcement of State Pornography Laws and Rates of Sex Crime Arrests', *Archives of Sexual Behavior*, **25** (5), 439–53.

Fisher, W.A. and A. Barak (2001), 'Internet Pornography: A Social Psychological Perspective On Internet Sexuality', *Journal of Sex Research*, **38** (4), 312–23.

Gentry, C. (1991), 'Pornography and Rape: An Empirical Analysis', *Deviant Behavior: An Interdisciplinary Journal*, **12**, 277–88.

George, David (2001), *Preference Pollution: How Markets Create the Desires We Dislike*, Ann Arbor: The University of Michigan Press.

Hardy, S. (1998), *The Reader, The Author, His Woman and Her Lover: Soft-core Pornography and the Heterosexual Man*, London: Cassel.

Kutchinsky, B. (1970), 'Studies on Pornography and Sex Crimes in Denmark: A Report to the US Presidential Commission on Obscenity and Pornography', Copenhagen: New Social Science Monographs, London.

Kutchinsky, B. (1985), 'Pornography and its Effects in Denmark and the United States: A Rejoinder and Beyond', in R.F. Thomasson (ed.), *Comparative Social Research*, Greenwich, CT: JAI Press, vol. 8, pp. 301–30.

Kutchinsky, Berl and Annika Snare (eds) (1999), 'Law, Pornography and Crime – The Danish Experience', *Scandinavian Studies in Criminology*, **16**, Norway: Pax Forlag.

Lane, Frederick S. III (2000), *Obscene Profits: The Entrepreneurs of Pornography in the Cyber Age*, New York: Routledge.

O'Toole, Laurence (1998), *Pornocopia: Porn, Sex, Technology, and Desire*, 2nd edition, London: Serpent's Tail.

Posner, Richard A. (1973), *Economic Analysis of Law*, Little Brown.

Posner, Richard A. (1994), *Sex and Reason*, Cambridge, MA: Harvard University Press.

Posner, Richard A. (2001), *Frontiers of Economic Theory*, Cambridge, MA: Harvard University Press.

Scott, J.E. (1985), 'Violence and Erotic Material: The Relationship Between Adult Entertainment and Rape', paper presented at the annual meeting for the American Association for the Advancement of Science, Los Angeles, California.

Sears, A.E. (1989), 'The Legal Case for Restricting Pornography', in Dolf Zillmann and Jennings B. Bryant (eds), *Pornography: Research Advances and Policy Considerations*, Lawrence Erlbaum Associates.

Sen, A.K. (1970), 'The Impossibility of a Paretian Liberal', *Journal of Political Economy*, **78**, 152–7.

Sigel, L.Z. (2002), *Governing Pleasures: Pornography and Social Change in England, 1815–1914*, New Brunswick, New Jersey and London: Rutgers University Press.

Silver, J. (1994), 'Movie Day at the Supreme Court or "I Know It When I See It": A History of the Definition of Obscenity' (http://library.lp.find law.com).

Tomkinson, M. (1982), *The Pornbrokers*, London: Virgin Books.

Troilo, G. (1999), 'Collecting', in P.E. Earl and S. Kemp (eds), *The Elgar Companion to Consumer Research And Economic Psychology*, Cheltenham, UK and Northampton, MA, US: Edward Elgar, pp. 88–92.

Zillmann, D. (1989), 'Effects of Prolonged Consumption of Pornography', in Dolf Zillmann and Jennings B. Bryant (eds), *Pornography: Research Advances and Policy Considerations*, Lawrence Erlbaum Associates.

7 Economics of prostitution
Peter G. Moffatt

This chapter applies basic principles of economics to the market for prostitution services. Section 1 attempts to identify the position taken and the role played by this market within the commercial world, paying close attention to its interactions with other markets, and to the ways in which it is evolving over time. Section 2 draws some international comparisons of legal status and industry size, and then in Section 3, the chapter examines some theoretical models of prostitution, seeking among other things to explain how equilibrium earnings are so high in a profession with only rudimentary skill and capital requirements. The distinction between the 'primary' market of marriage and the 'secondary' market of prostitution plays a central role throughout the economic analysis. Within this framework, particular attention is paid to the concepts of opportunity cost, compensating wage differentials, price discrimination, asymmetric information and welfare considerations. In Section 4, the chapter moves on to examine the empirical evidence relating to prostitution, focusing on an econometric model of the price of sexual services. Several economic concepts emerge in this empirical section, including age–earnings profiles, strategic behaviour, consumer surplus and sunk costs. Section 5 examines the issue from a policy perspective, describing and evaluating various models of legalization. Section 6 concludes the chapter.

1 Introduction
The prostitution industry is huge and operates in some form, either legally or illegally, in every corner of the world. The sheer size of this largely untaxed market makes it of considerable interest to economists. Although, as we shall see in Section 2, data sources are notoriously imperfect and it is difficult, if not impossible, to obtain accurate estimates of levels of activity in this market, a rough idea is provided by *The Economist* (Anonymous, 1998), which estimates total global income from prostitution to be in excess of US $20 billion per annum.

It is necessary to define prostitution at the outset. A dictionary definition might be, 'the undertaking of sexual actions for payment'. Edlund and Korn (2002) cite references that raise a logical problem with this type of definition: namely that some married women satisfy the definition routinely within marriage. Edlund and Korn therefore prefer a definition in terms of payment for sex that is non-reproductive from the purchaser's point of view. Such a definition is adopted here.

By far the largest part of this industry is the sale of sex by female prostitutes to male clients, and it is on this market that we shall focus in the chapter. Provision by males to homosexual male clients is a small market by comparison, as is provision by males to female clients. Provision by females to female clients appears to be virtually non-existent.

From an economist's point of view, a key feature of the prostitution market is that it is a 'secondary' market. In using this terminology, we are following the contribution of Doeringer and Piore (1971) who apply the idea to the labour market: the primary segment of the labour market is characterized by high wages, good working conditions and chances of advancement, and employment stability; the secondary segment is characterized by low pay, poor working conditions and lack of stability and advancement prospects. Here, as suggested by Cameron (2002), we are drawing an analogy in the market for sex: the 'primary' market is the market for marriage (considered in Chapter 5 of this volume), where both parties derive long-term benefits, analogous to career advancement, from a lasting relationship. In comparison, the benefits from either consuming or supplying commercial sex are strictly short term and highly superficial. By distinguishing the secondary market from the primary in this way, it is possible to develop an economic model that solves the wage differential puzzle; that is, a model that is capable of explaining the significant excess of the wage earned in the prostitution industry over that earned, with similar skill levels, in other industries. This economic model provides the focal point of this chapter, and is analysed in detail in Section 3.

Another reason why the distinction between the primary and secondary market is useful is that it allows clear explanation of the ways in which the existence of the prostitution market may be seen to enhance societal welfare, acting as the overflow mechanism necessary for the non-commercial market to function in equilibrium. These welfare considerations are discussed in Section 3, and again in Section 5, where we discuss the implications of toleration and legalization from a policy perspective.

Apart from its intimate link to the marriage market, there is no doubt that the prostitution market also has strong interdependences with other markets, for example pornography (Chapter 6), drugs (Chapters 1–3) and crime (Chapter 4). The link to pornography arises because pornographic material may be seen as a substitute for prostitution services, and the recent explosion in the availability of Internet porn may well have brought about a fall in the demand for prostitution. Indeed, a German brothel manager is quoted in *The Economist* (Anonymous, 1998) as explaining his drop in business over the previous ten years with, 'too much sex on television; why should people pay here when they can get it for free just sitting at home'.

The strong interdependences between the prostitution market and the drugs and crime markets are described in down-to-earth terms in a UK Home Office Report (May et al., 1999). This report demonstrates using case studies how each market feeds and perpetuates the others. A more recent report (Home Office, 2004) contains a survey of eight studies that investigate the relationship between prostitution and drugs: in all eight studies, more than half of the prostitutes sampled were users of Class A drugs. The conjugate existence of such markets is clearly socially undesirable, since it leads to vulnerable young people becoming trapped on a highly dangerous treadmill, often at the mercy of unsavoury and unscrupulous individuals such as drug-dealers, pimps and violent clients. Providers are also at a high risk of contracting sexually transmitted diseases (STDs) and serious diseases associated with substance abuse, and passing them to their clients. In such an environment, clients are also at risk of offences such as 'clipping',[1] which place the providers at the further risk of reprisal by infuriated clients.

In recent years, the link between prostitution and migration has taken on new levels of importance. For example, of the 500 000 prostitutes estimated to operate in Western Europe, around 250 000 are estimated to be immigrants (EUROPAP regional reports).[2] This is an especially important policy issue if it is believed that a significant proportion of such immigration is 'forced'. Although there is some recent evidence of the evil of human trafficking,[3] there is also a view, expounded in a *Spectator* article in April 2003, 'Happy hookers of Eastern Europe', by Phelim McAleer, that the problem is not nearly as severe as some campaigners claim.

Having drawn attention to the unsavoury side of the industry, a balanced treatment also requires consideration of the 'respectable' side. There is an enormous variation in the types of environment in which sexual services are provided and in the prices paid. At the bottom end of the spectrum, we see street-girls who normally deliver outdoors or in clients' cars, and might charge between US $5 and US $100 depending on geographical location. At the top end, we see high-class 'escorts' who might charge over US $1000 for a lengthy session in luxurious surroundings.

It is natural to ask why the variation in price is so much higher than that observed for other types of service such as hairdressing or restaurant meals. The answer has two parts. First, there is, as with other types of service, a good deal of variation in the quality of provision, both in terms of the physical and social attributes of the provider, and in terms of the dedication with which the service is provided. Second, high prices are used by both parties to the transaction as a 'screening' device. On the supply-side, high-class providers use their price signals to attract customers of the safest, healthiest, cleanest and most intellectually refined variety. On the demand-side, wealthy clients are attracted by high prices because they perceive them as a signal of quality. Recall the terms under which the Richard Gere character secured the services of the Julia Roberts character in the 1990 movie *Pretty Woman*. The idea here is similar to that underlying Rosen's (1981) 'Economics of superstars', where it is recognized that, for wealthy consumers, money is no object when quality of service is paramount (see Chapters 12 and 14, which explore similar ideas in the more conventional context of sporting and musical superstars). The simultaneous use of screening on both sides of the market is one of the reasons why equilibrium in the market can be maintained in the face of such enormous price variation.

One of the reasons why the prostitution industry might be looked upon differently from others is the social stigma associated with selling or purchasing sex, and the generally poor reputation of the profession. However, there is a large volume of anecdotal evidence that the 'taboo' of prostitution is being gradually lifted. A *Spectator* article in November 2002, 'Hookers at sports day', by John Gibb, describes cases of middle-class married females in the UK who have recently taken up prostitution in response to economic misfortune or in order to finance luxuries such as children's private schooling. There is also recent evidence in the UK of significant numbers of students turning to prostitution in order to finance their studies following changes in the student grant system: allegedly more than half of all sex workers in Leeds are full-time students (Chapman, 2001). Isaacs (1993, p. 204) quotes a London University philosophy undergraduate who claims proudly to earn £5000 per month in an escort agency, more than enough to support her studies. That well-educated people are prepared to enter this industry and to talk openly about their experiences in it is perhaps evidence of a softening of attitudes towards commercial sex.

An interesting issue is how high-class providers are able to attract clients in environments in which commercial sex is illegal, in ways that do not tarnish their 'clean' reputations, or make them liable to prosecution. One method is to include in their advertisement a disclaimer to the following effect (variants of which appear in many UK websites):

> NB: I am a professional independent escort and any money paid to me is for my time and companionship ONLY. Anything else that occurs between us is a matter of choice between consenting adults.

Of course, such façades do not always fool the authorities, as discovered recently by high-class 'madam' Margaret MacDonald. British-born MacDonald ran an international business with more than 400 male and female escorts, each charging around €1000 per hour, of which she took 40 per cent. In court, she admitted running the escort service, but vehemently denied being involved in prostitution in any way, claiming that her role was simply to introduce clients to escorts. The French court was unsympathetic and jailed her for four years in 2003 for, 'aggravated procuring for the purpose of prostitution'.[4]

An important development of recent years is that the supply-side has become much better organized, with sex workers' unions emerging in many countries. One union, which has been in existence since 2000, is the International Union of Sex Workers[5] (IUSW) whose terms of reference include promotion of decriminalization, access to health clinics, the promotion of re-training programmes for sex workers wishing to leave the profession and legal assistance for those wishing to sue those who exploit their labour. It also campaigns for an end to social attitudes that stigmatize those who are or have been sex workers. In March 2002, the IUSW became affiliated to one of Britain's largest unions, the GMB, perhaps a further sign that the industry is moving towards the commercial mainstream.

In Section 4, we pay attention to the demand-side of the market, principally using empirical analysis. In the past, the econometric modelling of the demand for prostitution services has been made difficult by the obstacles to data collection.[6] The problem is that both providers and clients are from 'hidden' populations and it is unrealistic to expect either group to supply reliable information on their activities when traditional data collection methods are used. This situation changed in the 1990s with the emergence of the Internet. A large number of websites have emerged as information exchanges for clients, and such sites have, albeit unintentionally, provided a rich data source for statistical analysis. One of the most famous is the Punternet site, data from which is used in our empirical analysis of Section 4.

2 Overview of world prostitution

The question of whether prostitution is legal in a given country rarely has a simple answer. As we shall see in Section 5, there are many different approaches to decriminalization and legalization, and so a wide spectrum of degrees of legalization is observed. According to information extracted from Table 10.1 of Cameron (2002), countries with the most lax policies include Austria, the Dominican Republic, Singapore and Switzerland. In these countries, not only is prostitution fully legal, but the operation of third party gainers (for example, 'pimps' or 'madams') is also permitted. Next in the spectrum we have countries where prostitution is legal, but third party gainers are not permitted. These include Australia, Germany, Honduras, Hungary and the Netherlands. Many other countries appear to have ambiguous systems, for example, China, Japan and the United

Arab Emirates, where prostitution is illegal but tolerated, and the USA, where it is legal in certain counties within the state of Nevada, but illegal everywhere else. A further complication is that countries often change their legal status, the most recent example being New Zealand, whose parliament voted narrowly for legalization in May 2003. At the harsh end of the spectrum, we have a small number of countries in which prostitution is illegal and punishable by death. To provide one recent example, in February 2001, more than 1000 people watched while two women convicted of prostitution were hanged in Afghanistan's Kandahar sports stadium.[7] Similarly, harsh penalties are evident in Iran and, until the recent regime change, in Iraq.

Whatever the legal status of prostitution, it seems to occur in some form everywhere in the world. Obtaining estimates of levels of activity in different locations is an awkward task due to the notorious unreliability of most data sources. It is particularly hard to obtain reliable data from developing countries, and although it is widely believed that they have higher levels of prostitution than the developed world (Boonchalaksi and Guest, 1998), it is hard to confirm this claim empirically. The claim is consistent with the commonly assumed positive association between poverty and

Table 7.1   Number of prostitutes in Western European countries

Country	Population (millions)	Number of prostitutes (thousands)	Population per prostitute
Austria	8	6	1333
Belgium	10	12	833
Denmark	5	6	833
France	59	40	1475
Finland	6	4	1500
Germany	80	150	533
Greece	11	12	880
Holland	16	25	640
Italy	58	60	967
Luxembourg	0.45	0.30	1500
Norway	4.5	3	1500
Sweden	8.5	2.5	3400
UK	60	80	750

Source: EUROPAP regional reports; collated by the Department of Politics at the University of Exeter (http://www.ex.ac.uk/politics/pol_data/undergrad/aac/scale.htm). The figure for Germany is extracted from Morell (1998). All figures relate to the situation pertaining at some time during the late 1990s.

prostitution. In this section of the chapter, we shall analyse some data that are available for developed countries.

Table 7.1 shows estimates of the number of prostitutes in different Western European countries, alongside figures for total population. The number of prostitutes is plotted against population size in Figure 7.1. Here, as expected, we see that larger countries have higher levels of prostitution.

Similar data for states in the USA are presented in Table 7.2. Here, the best available data are the number of arrests for prostitution and related offences in each state in a given year. This may be used as a rough proxy for the number of prostitutes operating in that state, although it is acknowledged that this measure is also influenced by such factors as the attitude of police towards prostitution. Figure 7.2 shows a plot of this variable against state populations. Again, we see a clear positive relationship.

What is most interesting about the plots shown in Figures 7.1 and 7.2 is that in both cases the number of prostitutes appears to rise more than in proportion with population size. Results from applying double logarithmic

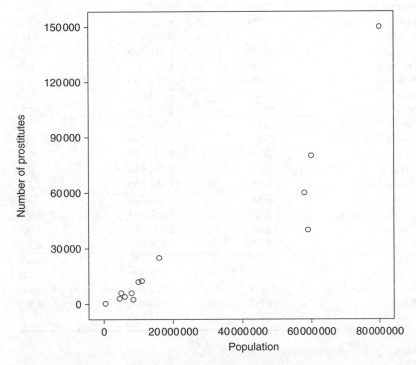

Figure 7.1   Number of prostitutes against population in European countries

Table 7.2   Number of arrests in given year for prostitution and related offences in USA

State	Year	Population	Number of arrests
Alabama	1999	4 370 000	187
Alaska	2000	626 900	117
Arizona	2000	5 130 600	2 542
Arkansas	2000	2 673 400	326
California	2000	33 871 600	12 401
Colorado	1999	4 056 000	1 366
Connecticut	2000	3 405 600	694
Delaware	2000	783 600	142
Hawaii	2000	1 211 500	469
Idaho	2000	1 294 000	6
Iowa	2000	2 926 300	266
Louisiana	1998	4 369 000	637
Maine	2000	1 274 900	23
Maryland	2000	5 296 500	989
Massachusetts	1999	6 175 000	1 818
Michigan	2000	9 938 400	1 474
Minnesota	2000	4 919 500	2 027
Nebraska	2000	1 711 300	469
Nevada	2000	1 998 300	4 177
New Jersey	2000	8 414 400	1 956
New York	1998	18 175 000	10 774
North Carolina	2000	8 049 300	1 090
North Dakota	2000	642 200	0
Oklahoma	2000	3 450 700	284
Oregon	2000	3 421 400	824
Pennsylvania	2000	12 281 100	2 338
Rhode Island	2000	1 048 300	382
South Carolina	2000	4 012 000	977
Tennessee	2000	5 690 100	1 305
Texas	2000	20 851 800	6 321
Utah	2000	2 233 200	443
Virginia	2000	7 078 500	726
West Virginia	1998	1 811 000	142
Wisconsin	1997	5 170 000	1 907
Wyoming	2000	493 800	4

Source: FBI Arrest statistics.

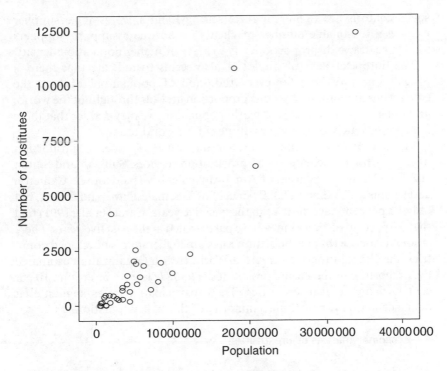

Figure 7.2 Number of prostitutes against population in US states

regressions of prostitution on population for each data set are as follows (with standard errors in parentheses):

Europe:

$$\log(prostitution) = -9.37 + 1.15 \log(population)$$
$$(se) \qquad\qquad (0.09)$$

USA:

$$\log(prostitution) = -15.5 + 1.45 \log(population)$$
$$(se) \qquad\qquad (0.19)$$

The slope coefficients in both of these regressions are significantly greater than one, confirming that a rise in the population of a country or state is expected to give rise to a *more than proportionate* increase in the number of prostitutes in that country or state. This empirical observation is loosely consistent with the reasoning of MacCoun and Reuter (2001) that since social controls are tighter in rural settings, and since a single supplier requires a reasonable number of clients for adequate support, suppliers tend to be drawn disproportionately to areas of higher population density.

The European data of Table 7.1 also seems to indicate that there is roughly one prostitute for every thousand of population. Making the courageous assumption that this proportion prevails throughout the world, and using current estimates of world population, we may deduce that there are approximately 6 million prostitutes in the world today.

Information on the demand-side is available in the form of the proportion of males who are demanders of prostitution services. Sullivan and Simon (1998) find that 17.7 per cent of American males have paid for sex. Cameron and Collins (2003) find that 4.9 per cent of UK males have paid for sex, but only 1.3 per cent have done so in the past five years. Carael et al. (1991) find that 3.3 per cent of Frenchmen have participated in the past five years. There is some evidence that participation rates are higher in less developed countries: the Global Program on AIDS/World Health Organization estimated the proportion of men using prostitutes *in a single year* to be around 10 per cent in many African countries. These participation rates suggest that demanders usually constitute a minority of the male population.

3   Economic analysis of prostitution

3.1   Overview of economic theories

As hinted in Section 1, the central question to be addressed is why earnings per hour are so high in a profession with very basic skill and capital requirements, low fixed costs, no formal training requirements and no barriers to entry such as professional organizations. Moffatt and Peters (2004) recently used UK data to estimate that the weekly earnings of a typical prostitute are roughly two times that of non-manual workers, and three times that of manual workers. There are many approaches to solving this wage differential puzzle. One approach is to focus on the demand-side of the market: Della Giusta et al. (2004) develop a theory in which the demand-side is characterized by the assumption that males are willing to pay a premium to avoid the 'hidden' costs of obtaining so-called 'unpaid' sex such as wining and dining, gifts and the longer-term consequences of attachment. Alternatively, one could focus on the supply-side, and attribute the earnings premium to the compensation necessary for the risk of violence, risk of contracting STDs and for the generally unpleasant physical experiences that prostitution entails.

A third approach, probably the most interesting to economists, is to focus on the opportunity cost of prostitution in terms of foregone marriage market opportunities. The underlying assumption here is that marriage and prostitution are incompatible for a female; one cannot be a wife and a prostitute simultaneously. While this assumption may not be universally true, there is a good deal of evidence on the difficulties faced by women attempting to do both. The assumption is particularly tenable when considering the sex industry in Victorian Britain (Fisher, 1997). After all, it is well known that in the past, even loss of virginity was considered a serious penalty in the marriage market (and still is in some societies).

One model that follows this approach is due to Edlund and Korn (2002). We shall focus on this particular model in detail later in this section, for two main reasons. First, this is the first theory of prostitution to be published by a major economics journal. Second, the model is useful because it is capable of predicting certain known features of the sex industry which other models are not.

3.2 Entry

Formal entry barriers such as required qualifications and professional organizations do not appear to exist in the prostitution market, although the International Union of Sex Workers (IUSW) is currently promoting access to training as noted earlier. One entry barrier that may be encountered is the male managers of massage parlours and escort agencies 'trying out' new employees. However, it usually transpires that this is a cheap ploy.[8] Those entering the lower end of the market may be subjected to informal barriers such as the threat of physical violence from incumbents or their associates. Under such circumstances, we might expect to see entry restricted to those who have been introduced by incumbents.

A point emphasized by Cameron (2002) is that the entry decision is completely detached from the supply decision. The supply decision may be determined in a standard neoclassical labour supply framework, depending in the usual way on non-wage earnings and the wage earned per unit supplied. The entry decision, in contrast, is heavily dependent on non-economic considerations. Many individuals in society are restricted by 'negative capital', for example, feelings of sin or social stigma, from entering this profession. Once the decision has been made to enter, however, preferences may change dramatically, and the provider may find that they experience the usual benefits from raising supply to an optimum. This two-stage decision-making process is referred to by Cameron as a 'threshold crossing' problem, and if data on number of hours supplied were available, it could be modelled econometrically using the 'double-hurdle' approach (Cragg, 1971).

3.3 Market structure

The most commonly occurring market structure in prostitution is a collection of sole traders acting independently and competitively. In fact, in many UK cities, locations from which more than two providers operate are unlawful and closed down if detected. Such incentives create the ideal conditions for a competitive market. There is, however, some anecdotal evidence of collusive behaviour with all providers operating in a particular area committing to the same prices, with (possibly violent) punishment strategies in place for deviators.

As soon as the enterprise takes on a third party gainer ('pimp') the enterprise changes status from sole trader to small firm. According to survey evidence presented in the Home Office report by May et al. (1999), the actual number of providers in the UK who are controlled by pimps is much smaller than commonly believed; the great majority claim to operate independently. This suggests that, for most prostitutes, the services provided by a pimp cost more than they are worth.

The cost structure varies according to the style of provision. At the most basic level, providers who operate on the street conduct their business outdoors or in clients' cars, and therefore do not require business premises. The only obvious fixed costs incurred are for seductive clothing, while the only variable costs are for condoms and lubricants. Providers operating in premises face the rental costs of those premises, and might well take advantage of the fixed location by investing in capital equipment such as whips, chains, handcuffs, strap-ons and uniforms of various types, in order to raise the standard of service. Providers operating in massage parlours pay fixed costs to the proprietor, detailed by O'Connell Davidson (1998).

While, for the reasons suggested in the opening paragraph of this subsection, the market in a particular locality might be described as competitive, the best description of the structure of the market as a whole is one of monopolistic competition: there is a reasonable amount of product differentiation, and this is one of the reasons why prices vary so much through the wider market. Another reason for the significant price differences is the bilateral price screening described in Section 1.

There are few large firms to talk of in the prostitution industry. However, an interesting recent development, in May 2003, was when Australia's largest brothel, Daily Planet, became the world's first brothel to float on the stock exchange. In the longer term, Daily Planet aims to expand internationally. However, it remains to be seen how successful large organizations like this one become. After all, such mega-commercialization surely has the potential to remove much of the attraction of this particular product.

The potential for large organizations to exploit monopoly power depends as always on the availability of close substitutes. One obvious substitute to commercial sex is non-commercial, non-marital sex (for example, extra-marital affairs, one-night stands, 'swingers' clubs[9]), which has undoubtedly grown in importance over the last half-century. Less obvious substitutes are magazines, videos, TV and Internet porn and 'telephone sex', which have also shown a recent surge. The continuing availability of these may be expected to act as a check on monopoly power, whether or not regulatory agencies ever choose to become involved.

3.4 Explaining the high compensating wage differential

Edlund and Korn's (2002) model considers two separate but closely related markets: the market for marriage, to which we have been referring as the 'primary' market, and the market for sex, the 'secondary' market. Use of this terminology was justified in Section 1. Market clearing conditions are derived for each market, in terms of the price of commercial sex and the number of prostitutes operating. Then, in a manner similar to IS–LM analysis in macroeconomics, a graph is used to identify the price and 'quantity' that are consistent with equilibrium in both markets simultaneously.

Here, we shall present a basic version of this model. Assume that society contains N males and N females. Of the N females, n are prostitutes, and $N - n$ are married. Note that all unmarried women are assumed to be prostitutes. This is because the only downside to marriage (in this very simple model) is foregone prostitution opportunities. Since $N - n$ is the number of married women, this is also the number of married men, implying that there are n unmarried men, equal to the number of prostitutes. However, as we shall see, the unmarried men do not match one-to-one with prostitutes for the simple reason that married men also demand the services of prostitutes; each prostitute is therefore likely to be shared between married and unmarried men.

Each female bears one child. If a female is married, both partners obtain utility from the child; if she is unmarried, only she benefits.

Everyone supplies one unit of labour. Married women are employed in some activity other than prostitution, and earn w. Married women also receive p_m from their husbands, as payment for marriage. Prostitutes earn p, the price of a unit of commercial sex. Note that one unit of commercial sex does not amount to the servicing of one client. As mentioned previously, each prostitute services more than one client in each time period, so a 'unit' is some number (not necessarily a whole number) greater than one, of encounters with clients.

Assume that each unmarried man demands $d(p)$ units of commercial sex. Note that quantity demanded depends on the price per unit, p, and by the law of demand, we expect this dependence to be negative. Further, assume that each married man demands $\lambda d(p)$ units, where $0 < \lambda < 1$. In words, married men demand a fixed fraction λ of the amount of commercial sex enjoyed by unmarried men. It is a key requirement of the model

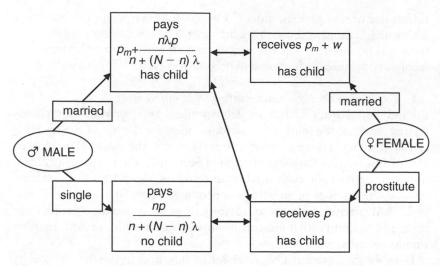

Figure 7.3   Male and female decisions, money and parenting outcomes, and the matching process

that $\lambda > 0$, that is, married men demand at least some commercial sex; if they did not, the model would break down. λ is therefore an important parameter and we shall refer to it as the 'infidelity parameter'.[10]

Each person is free to choose whether to marry. The consequences of each choice for each gender are shown in Figure 7.3, which summarizes all of the model's assumptions. Double-ended arrows represent matching.

With reference to Figure 7.3, we next derive equilibrium conditions. First, consider the female decision, and note that the return from marriage is $p_m + w$ while the return from prostitution is p. A child is enjoyed in both. For equilibrium, return from the two activities must equalize, so:

$$p^* = p_m^* + w \qquad (7.1)$$

where stars denote equilibrium values. To understand (7.1), imagine a situation in which $p < p_m + w$, so the return from marriage is greater than that from prostitution. In such a situation, there would be a transfer of women from prostitution to marriage, which would cause a rise in the price of commercial sex, p, and this process would continue until the equilibrium condition (7.1) is met. (7.1) may be interpreted as the condition for equilibrium in the marriage market.

Equation (7.1), although very simple, is very useful in that it provides the answer to the wage differential puzzle identified earlier. It shows that wages earned by prostitutes are always higher than those earned by women in alternative employment, and that the differential is given by p_m, the 'value' of marriage. Thus, equation (7.1) makes it very clear that the solution to the puzzle is in terms of the opportunity cost of prostitution, that is, the prostitute's foregone benefits from marriage. As discussed in Chapter 5, there is no doubt that the benefits of marriage are substantial. Indeed, Clark and Oswald (2002) use data on 10 000 people, together with an economic model of 'happiness', to estimate the value of marriage at £70 000 per annum.

It was mentioned earlier that the 'infidelity parameter' λ must be positive for the model to be sensible. Using Figure 7.3 and equation (7.1), we can see why this is. Imagine $\lambda = 0$, so married men demand no commercial sex. The cost to a man of being married would then be only p_m, which, by equation (7.1), is always less than the cost of being single, p. Even ignoring the additional advantage of fatherhood, every man would prefer marriage. Therefore, if $\lambda = 0$, everyone would be married, and there would be no prostitution at all.

Next, we consider the market for commercial sex. Recall that each of the n unmarried men demands $d(p)$ units of commercial sex, while each of the $N - n$ married men demands $\lambda d(p)$ units, where λ, introduced earlier, is the infidelity parameter. Market demand for commercial sex is then:

$$n \cdot d(p) + (N - n) \cdot \lambda \cdot d(p) = [n + \lambda \cdot (N - n)] \cdot d(p) \qquad (7.2)$$

Market supply of commercial sex is simply:

$$n \qquad (7.3)$$

This follows from the assumption that each of the n prostitutes supplies exactly one 'unit' of commercial sex.

We combine equations (7.2) and (7.3) in order to derive the equilibrium condition for the sex market:

$$n = [n + \lambda \cdot (N - n)] \cdot d(p) \qquad (7.4)$$

Equation (7.4) implicitly defines the market clearing price of commercial sex, p^*, as a function of the number of prostitutes, n. To make this function explicit, we need to specify a functional form for $d(p)$. For good measure, we shall do this. We assume:

$$d(p) = 2 - p \qquad (7.5)$$

which clearly satisfies the law of demand. Substituting (7.5) into (7.4) and rearranging gives:

$$p^* = 2 - \frac{n}{n + \lambda(N - n)} \qquad (7.6)$$

Equation (7.6) is the equilibrium condition in the commercial sex market. Notice that the relationship between n and p^* is negative. To verify this, set $n = 0$ in equation (7.6): if there are no prostitutes, the market clearing price is 2; then set $n = N$: if all women are prostitutes, the market clearing price is only 1.

The marriage market equilibrium condition (equation (7.1)) and the sex market equilibrium condition (equation (7.6)) are combined in Figure 7.4. The point of intersection of the two lines identifies the combination of price (p^*) and number of prostitutes (n^*), which clears both markets simultaneously. Based on the observation made from real data in Section 2, we may predict that the actual value of n^* in the context of Europe is approximately $N/500$.

The key predictions from this very basic model can be seen directly from Figure 7.4. An increase in the wage earned in alternative employment w, or alternatively an increase in the price paid to a woman for marriage p_m, both raise the position of the horizontal line in the diagram, causing both an increase in the equilibrium price of prostitution and a decrease in the number of prostitutes in the market.

These predictions might be seen as fairly obvious, but the purpose of this sub-section has been nothing more than to introduce the reader to the most basic version of the model. More useful predictions emerge when the model is generalized. To understand the technical aspects of the more general

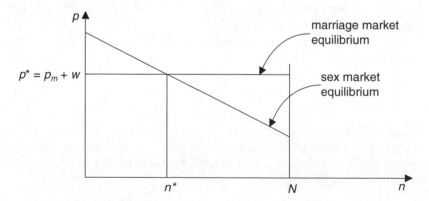

Figure 7.4   Marriage and sex market equilibrium

models, the interested reader is referred to the paper by Edlund and Korn (2002). In the sub-section that follows, we briefly outline some predictions that emerge from the more general models, avoiding technical detail.

3.5 Extensions

First, in addition to predicting that prostitution decreases in the alternative female wage w, the model can be generalized in such a way that prostitution also decreases in male income. One of the additional assumptions required for this result is that child quality depends on marital resources allocated to the child. The prediction that prostitution decreases in both male and female earnings is useful because it provides an explanation for the higher rates of prostitution in poorer countries, and for the long-term decline in prostitution seen in developed countries. Empirical evidence for these two features of the industry is documented by Edlund and Korn (2002).

Second, the assumptions that all men face identical wages, and all women in 'alternative' employment face identical wages, are relaxed. The prediction then is that higher earners of both genders are selected into marriage, while women with poor labour market possibilities are drawn towards prostitution. This too is an accurate representation of reality.

Third, the possibility of a tax on prostitution is introduced. This has the effect of reducing the number of prostitutes, since, in equilibrium, it is the prostitute's price net of tax that is now equated to the wife's earnings.

Fourth, the assumption of a closed population with equal numbers of males and females is relaxed. It is important to do this to allow for the growing phenomena of sex tourism and sexual migration. Some holiday destinations, particularly in the Far East, are popular to Western men seeking commercial sex. It is reasonable to assume that the number of males in the relevant market is greater than the number of available females. Moreover, it is reasonable to assume that the male tourists are high demanders of commercial sex (perhaps, a third category of males should be introduced to the model, with a λ value greater than 1). So, there are two reasons why the profitability of prostitution rises relative to marriage, and why we expect the number of prostitutes to be higher under such circumstances.

Sexual migration is the phenomenon of large numbers of young females migrating from developing countries to richer ones to work in the sex industry. As cited in Section 1, around one half of Europe's prostitutes are immigrants. This must have the effect of raising the number of females in the commercial sex market, and one might expect the equilibrium price to fall as a result, obviously causing great irritation to home-based providers. French prostitutes, in particular, have been heard complaining bitterly in recent years about the impact on 'their' markets of the heavy influx of Eastern European providers into French cities (see Anonymous, 2004).

3.6   The effects of asymmetric information

The Edlund and Korn model explains why the market price is so high. The presence of asymmetric information in the market means that the actual price paid may be even higher. This issue is highly relevant in markets with 'transient' consumers, for example, holidaymakers purchasing sex, since such clients may have no local knowledge of the market price. It is often the case that this market price is considerably lower than that prevailing in the client's home country, and this may clearly be exploited by local providers. Providers can maximize the consumer surplus they extract from locally inexperienced clients by engaging in first-degree price discrimination. They simply name an excessive price and then lower it until the client is in agreement.

Another sort of asymmetric information arises because advertisements appearing in newspapers, magazines, phone boxes, or on the Internet, are generally posted by the providers themselves. There is therefore a tendency for these advertisements to give a misleading description of the provider's characteristics and of the quality of the services they offer. The industry is, therefore, prone to the problems caused by informational asymmetries, as first described by Akerlof (1970). One of the negative outcomes is a version of so-called Gresham's Law: high-quality providers tend to be driven out of the market by those of lower quality.

We might at this point acknowledge the lasting effect that the emergence of the Internet may have on the prostitution industry. Obviously, providers advertise on the Internet, but equally importantly, a number of websites have appeared with the purpose of information exchanges for clients, including the Punternet site, data from which is analysed econometrically in Section 4. Since information supplied on these sites is provided by clients, and the web-managers appear vigilant in detecting and deleting false reports, there is no reason to expect it to be biased in any way. As more and more information on providers becomes available through this new medium, and as more and more clients adopt it as a routine source of information, the informational asymmetries are therefore expected to diminish substantially. In consequence, high-quality providers are likely to see their businesses flourish, while low-quality providers are likely to be driven out of the market early.

3.7   Economic welfare considerations

Cameron (2002), with the support of a number of entertaining anecdotes, presents a number of reasons why the prostitution market, in its capacity as a 'secondary' market, has the potential to raise levels of economic welfare. These welfare issues form the basis of many arguments in favour of legalization (see Section 5). Some of these ideas are summarized here.

One rather extreme perspective on the sexual climate in human societies is that male lust permeates through the community in a continuous raging torrent, with which the primary (marriage) market cannot cope. There is acute excess demand by males at all times. The secondary (prostitution) market plays the vital role of an overflow mechanism, without which equilibrium in the primary market could never be attained. The secondary market can also be seen as an externality abatement technology, since the negative externalities generated by excess male demand such as sexual harassment, cajolement and assault are likely to be reduced by its existence.

When we consider an individual with very specific, non-conformist, sexual needs and desires, it may well be the case that these demands are not able to be satisfied in the staidness of the primary market. In the secondary market, every service is available at a price, and can be obtained through specialist advertising channels. Whenever the deviant demander is matched with a cooperative supplier from the secondary market, a Pareto improvement may be said to have occurred. Indeed, we find evidence in Section 4 that the provision of 'kinky extras' not only raises the price of the service, but also significantly raises the level of satisfaction derived by the client.

Another aspect of equilibrium in the primary market relates to expectations regarding partners' sexual pasts. In some settings, there may be an expectation for the bride to be a virgin, but at the same time for the bridegroom to be highly sexually experienced. For these incongruent expectations to be realized in equilibrium, a secondary prostitution market is essential, being the only means for males to acquire the necessary experience prior to marriage without sacrificing the virginity of the pool of potential brides.

More convincingly, there may simply be an expectation on young males to have at least some experience before entering the primary market. The secondary market would again be essential in providing males with the minimal experience necessary to shed their embarrassment and enter the primary market with confidence. Perhaps the most famous fictional example is Holden Caulfield in JD Salinger's *The Catcher in the Rye* who, as a 16-year-old contemplating the loss of his virginity to a call girl, reflects: 'I figured if she was a prostitute and all, I could get in some practice on her, in case I ever get married or anything. I worry about that stuff sometimes.'

4 Empirical studies of prostitution

In this section, we move from the theoretical to the real, and consider empirical studies of the prostitution industry, which use data extracted from real markets. We also report in detail on the analysis of one particular dataset, analysed previously by Moffatt and Peters (2004).

4.1   Previous empirical work

Relatively little work has been done on the empirical analysis of the prostitution industry. One possible reason for this lies in the obvious difficulties associated with data collection. Prostitutes are unlikely to reveal information about their work since they cannot be sure that the researcher is not connected to the police or the tax department. Clients are unlikely directly to supply information on encounters with prostitutes since they may, for reasons of stigma and feelings of sexual inadequacy, prefer to keep the activity a secret unto themselves. Although data on clients have been obtained in the past, for example from self-reported surveys (Faugier and Sargeant, 1997) or from police records (Benson and Matthews, 1995), the samples are small, and the information obtained is mainly concerned with civic and health status of the individuals, rather than the economic features of the market that are of interest here.

In spite of these problems, some empirical work has been done in the past. Cameron et al. (1999) obtain data from escort advertisements extracted from gay publications in London. They then perform econometric estimation, which identifies the characteristics of the escort that make them more likely to offer particular services. They find, for example, that older prostitutes are more likely to supply deviant sexual services such as bondage and flagellation, than their younger colleagues.

Cameron and Collins (2003) focus on the demand-side, using a large UK lifestyle dataset to identify the characteristics of males that determine demand for prostitution services. The dependent variable in their model is binary: one if the respondent has purchased sex; zero otherwise. As noted in Section 2, the proportion in their sample who have done so is 4.9 per cent. They find that the most important determinants of participation are religion and risk disposition. Interestingly, age does not appear to have a significant effect on the probability of recent participation. Sullivan and Simon (1998) obtain similar results using a sample of American males, although the proportion in this sample who have purchased sex is noticeably higher, at 17.7 per cent.

Rao et al. (2003) investigate the determinants of price paid for sex in India. In particular, they focus on the impact of condom use, which they find to have a strong negative effect on price, inevitably amounting to a disincentive from the provider's point of view. This finding has far-reaching societal implications for health and education policy, not least because unprotected sex with prostitutes is one of the primary causes of the spread of HIV/AIDS in developing countries.

Moffatt and Peters (2004) carried out an empirical study of the prostitution market in the UK, using data extracted from the Punternet website (http://www.punternet.com).[11] The main purpose of this site is as an information exchange for clients. The site restricts itself to heterosexual encounters between male clients and female providers. Clients are invited to submit 'field reports' to the site on prostitutes whom they have recently encountered. The report is submitted pro-forma, and contains the location and duration of the encounter, the working name and contact details of the provider, some information about her physical attributes and personality, a description of the services rendered, and the price paid. The site is heavily used, with over 55 000 reports at August 2005.

The Punternet data were used by Moffatt and Peters (2004) to investigate the way in which the prices of prostitutes' services are determined. Therefore, they focus on the demand-side of the market, estimating the value perceived by clients of each attribute of the service, and assuming supply to be fixed. Models of this type are known as hedonic pricing models. Their most usual application is to data on property prices (for example, Hughes, 1996), but as seen in Chapter 10, they can also be applied to assisted reproduction markets.

An additional piece of information supplied in each report is whether or not the client would return to the same provider in the future. This yields a binary variable, which may be perceived as an indicator of client satisfaction. Binary data analysis of this variable may be used to identify features of the service provider and of the encounter that increase client satisfaction. It is then interesting to check whether the factors that increase client satisfaction are the same factors that attract a price premium according to the hedonic pricing analysis. After all, in a smoothly functioning market, it should be the case that any product attribute that increases customer satisfaction also increases the price.

The Punternet dataset shall be analysed here, although not at the level of sophistication of Moffatt and Peters (2004). First, the determinants of price, then the determinants of client satisfaction are identified, and a comparison is made between the two sets of results. Before this, some exploratory data analysis is reported.

4.2 Exploratory analysis of the Punternet dataset

The selected sample consists of 982 complete reports that were submitted to the site between January 1999 and July 2000. Since the focus of attention is the per-encounter price paid in pounds sterling, a histogram of this variable is shown in Figure 7.5. The price distribution has a clear mode at around £60, and shows a strong positive skew.

Figure 7.6 shows a scatter plot of price against duration of encounter in minutes, with a non-parametric regression[12] (smooth) super-imposed. From the smooth, a clear positive relationship is identifiable and, interestingly, a small degree of convexity is detected: it appears that the marginal

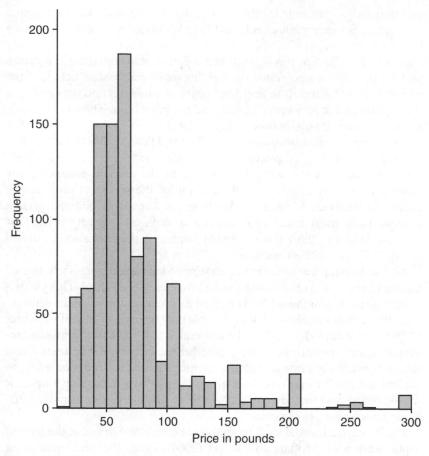

Figure 7.5   A histogram of price of prostitute's services (£)

effect of duration on price becomes higher at higher values of duration. This suggests the possibility of market segmentation, with longer durations typically being associated with a higher class of provider, namely the escort.

Figure 7.7 shows a scatter plot and smooth of price against age of provider in years. Non-linearity is again evident. The relationship is fairly level at low ages, but beyond the age of around 35, price appears to decline monotonically. This pattern calls for the use of age and age-squared, at least, as explanatory variables in the pricing model.

4.2.1 Determinants of price   An ordinary least squares regression was performed using the sample of 982 observations described earlier, with

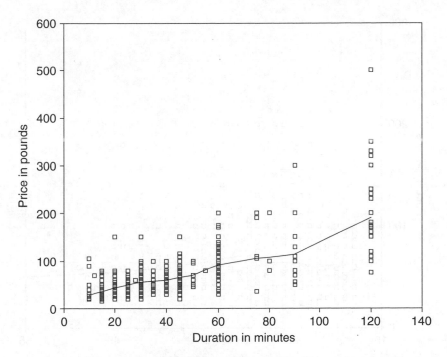

Figure 7.6   Scatter of price of prostitute's services (£) against duration in minutes, with smooth

price of encounter in pounds sterling as the dependent variable and a set of explanatory variables including duration of encounter, provider characteristics, arrangement dummies, type of service and regional dummies. The set of explanatory variables included in the model was decided using a general-to-specific model selection procedure. Results are reported in Table 7.3.

The R^2 of 0.66 reported at the end of Table 7.3 indicates that two-thirds of the variation in price is explained by this regression, which is actually quite impressive for cross-section data.

The first slope coefficient reported is for duration of the encounter in minutes. The coefficient of +1.28 indicates that an additional minute added to the duration of the encounter adds £1.28 to the price, *ceteris paribus*. Note also from the low standard error that this effect is very precisely estimated.

The next set of estimates relates to a selection of provider characteristics. To deal with the inverted U-shaped relationship between price and age of provider, we have included age-squared in addition to age. The signs of the

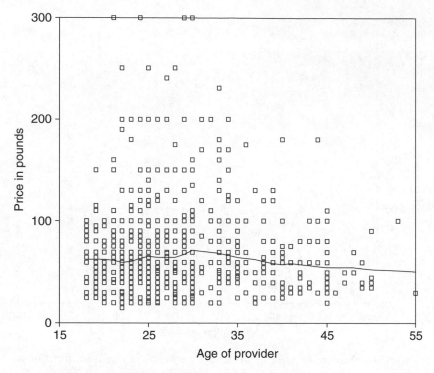

*Figure 7.7   Scatter of price of prostitute's services (£) against age of
provider in years, with smooth*

two coefficients confirm that the relationship is inverted U-shaped. The
turning point can be computed from the two coefficients as:

$$\frac{1.81}{2 \times 0.038} = 23.8$$

This implies that the highest prices are commanded by providers aged just
under 24 years and tells us something about the age–earnings profile of
prostitutes. However, it must be remembered that the payment for a single
encounter is being modelled here, not total annual earnings. In order to
discover, for example, the age at which total annual earnings are maximized, information would be required on the flow of clients for different
ages of provider. This information is not readily available, although see
Matthews (1997).

Next, a dummy variable is present indicating whether the provider is
'Very thin', according to the description supplied by the client. Note that
this variable has a significantly positive coefficient of +6.92, which

Table 7.3   OLS regression to identify the determinants of price of prostitute's services

Variable	Coeff. (standard error)
Constant	−17.03 (15.32)
Duration in minutes	1.28 (0.045)**
Provider characteristics:	
Age	1.81 (0.93)*
Age-squared	−0.038 (0.015)**
Very thin	6.92 (2.12)**
Attractive	−7.60 (5.39)
Arrangement (base: walk-up):	
Girl's home	17.75 (3.08)**
Parlour	11.74 (3.02)**
Client's home	49.13 (6.79)**
Hotel	59.65 (5.91)**
Service:	
Full sex	2.42 (3.54)
Kinky extras	4.20 (1.90)*
Region (base: rest of UK):	
Soho	9.80 (3.57)**
Central London	29.24 (3.15)**
Greater London	7.19 (2.66)**
Midlands	−3.10 (3.82)
Greater Manchester	−7.35 (3.60)*
North East	−8.89 (4.83)*
Merseyside	−27.70 (15.55)*
Scotland	−11.00 (4.58)**
Sample size	982
R^2	0.66

Notes:
Dependent variable: price of encounter in pounds.
Standard errors are given in parentheses.
* Indicates that a variable is significant at the 5% level, ** indicates significance at the 1% level.

represents the premium attracted by providers having this characteristic. The final provider characteristic is 'Attractive', another dummy variable based on subjective information supplied by the client. Note that the coefficient is negative (although insignificant), and this is counter-intuitive; it implies that attractive providers command lower prices. An explanation for this apparently strange result shall be offered later in the section.

The next set of variables are dummy variables for arrangement. The base case (that is, the excluded dummy) here is what is known as a 'walk-up'. A walk-up is a flat, usually in an apartment block, with a sign outside and a doorbell answered by a 'maid', from which sex can be purchased on a drop-in basis. Because the coefficients of the included arrangement dummies are all positive and significant, it appears that walk-up is by far the cheapest arrangement, *ceteris paribus*. This is explained by the high efficiency of such establishments and the associated low quality of the service. The most expensive arrangements are client's home and hotel, the latter commanding almost £60 more than a similar encounter in a walk-up. This is not surprising either: hotel visits are usually associated with 'escort' providers, widely acknowledged to be of the highest quality.

Next in the list are a pair of variables representing the type of service delivered. Many such variables were available in the dataset; only one appeared to be significant. The significant variable is a dummy indicating whether 'Kinky extras' are supplied. Such extras appear to add a few pounds to the price of the encounter. Another dummy is included if 'Full sex' was supplied, but this does not appear significant. The message here is that although price depends strongly on the duration of the encounter, the actual service supplied has very little effect. It seems that providers are broadly indifferent to what services they supply as long as they are paid for the time spent.

Finally, there is a set of regional dummy variables, the base case being 'Rest of UK'. Here, a clear pattern emerges: prices are by far the highest in Central London (excluding Soho, where there is a thriving walk-up market), and lowest in the North of England and Scotland. It therefore appears that distance from the capital is a key determinant of price. This is interesting because it ties in with one of Edlund and Korn's (2002) key theoretical predictions (see Section 3), namely that the price paid for prostitution services increases with the wage earned in alternative employment; it is well known that average wages are considerably higher in London than in the North of England and Scotland. In a sense this regional pattern is not at all surprising, since a similar story could be advanced in the context of any profession. However, since even the most obvious predictions are sometimes not supported by data, it is always reassuring when they are.

4.2.2   Determinants of satisfaction   As already noted, one of the pieces of information supplied in each report is whether or not the client would wish to return to the same provider in future. This is a useful piece of information because it provides an indication of whether or not the client is satisfied with the service received. While most clients appear to be satisfied, by no means all are: of the 982 reports used in this study, 202 clients reported that they would not return.

It is interesting to investigate the determinants of this satisfaction variable. Since it is a binary variable, ordinary least squares regression cannot be used. Logistic regression is used instead. Once again, a general-to-specific model selection procedure is used to decide on a set of variables. The results are presented in Table 7.4.

The coefficient of duration appears to have the expected sign: the longer the encounter lasts, the more likely the client is to be satisfied. The coefficient of price also has the expected sign: the more a client pays, *ceteris paribus*, the less likely he is to return to the same provider.

As in the price equation, there is a set of variables here that represent provider characteristics. First, an inverted U-shaped age effect is again apparent. The turning point can again be computed:

$$\frac{0.126}{2 \times 0.002} = 31.5$$

This implies that providers aged 31.5 supply the most satisfaction. This appears to contrast with the results from the price equation analysed earlier. There, we found that providers aged 23.8 charge the highest price. This contrast may partly be explained by the fact that older providers have

Table 7.4   Results from binary logit analysis of client satisfaction variable

Variable	coeff. (asy. se)
Constant	−4.25 (1.43)
Duration	0.074 (0.009)**
Price	−0.017 (0.003)**
Characteristics	
Age	0.126 (0.086)
Age-squared	−0.002 (0.001)*
Attractive	1.77 (0.51)**
Afro-Caribbean	1.82 (0.63)**
Service	
Full sex	0.75 (0.32)*
Kinky extras	0.84 (0.28)**
Sample size	982

Notes:
Dependent variable: would you return? yes = 1; no = 0.
Asymptotic standard errors are given in parentheses.
* indicates that a variable is significant at the 5% level, ** indicates significance at the 1% level.

had more opportunity to establish a regular clientele than younger providers, and regular clients are, by definition, more likely to indicate readiness to return. Another explanation may be in terms of the greater value older providers place on repeat business. Albert (2001) provides a case study of a Nevada brothel, including (pp. 156–7) an interview of two older providers who criticize the casual attitude of their younger colleagues towards clients, adding that, 'us working girls from the old school understand the value of repeat business'. The message here is that older providers are nurturing their clients with a view to regular custom, while younger colleagues are more confident of an unending stream of first-time clients and therefore pay less attention to quality of service.

The dummy variable 'Attractive' is included in the logistic regression. The strongly significant positive coefficient is as expected, indicating that attractive providers are more likely to attract a return visit. However, again we see an inconsistency with the results of the price equation; there, we found that attractive providers charge a lower price. This inconsistency is explained in terms of strategic behaviour by the provider. Unattractive providers charge a high price precisely because they do not expect a return visit, and they are extracting maximum consumer surplus from the client on the only opportunity. An obvious question that arises here is why a rational customer is willing to pay this higher price for a less desirable service. One answer might lie in the 'sunk costs' of search and travel: having already incurred these costs, and in doing so built up an expectation of sexual satisfaction, it is rational to pay once but never return.

The dummy variable 'Afro-Caribbean' also has a strongly significant positive coefficient. Apparently, providers of this ethnicity generate the most satisfaction. Ethnicity had no effect in the price equation, and was therefore not included there. So, once again we are seeing an inconsistency between the two equations. If the market were perfectly functioning, we might expect the price charged by Afro-Caribbean providers to rise, to reflect the higher levels of client satisfaction that they generate.

The last two variables in the list are service indicators. If a client has had full sexual intercourse, he is more likely to return to the same provider. This is quite obvious, but the significant effect here may partly be due to endogeneity of this explanatory variable: more enthusiastic clients are clearly more likely to opt for full sex during the current encounter.

Finally, the variable 'Kinky extras' has a strong positive effect on the likelihood of a return visit. This may be explained in terms of such services providing satisfaction. However, there is another explanation: the specialist services indicated by this variable may only be available from a small number of providers, so clients requiring such services are inevitably drawn to return to the same specialist provider.

5 Policy

Policy debate concerning prostitution usually revolves around the issue of legalization. This issue is currently of particular topical interest in the UK, with a four-month nationwide consultation on approaches to legalization launched by the Home Office in July 2004 (Home Office, 2004). This is the first thorough review of prostitution law in the UK for 50 years. Here, we state the standard cases for and against legalization, and then outline and evaluate various alternative models.

The principal argument against legalization, stated forcefully by Hughes and Roche (1999), is that it is giving societal approval to an activity that is sordid, unhealthy, dangerous, debasing to sexual relationships, associated closely with STDs, substance abuse, violence and many other socially undesirable phenomena. A related argument is that legalization is likely to encourage more people to become prostitutes. Most people agree that the activity is degrading to the individual as well as dangerous and unpleasant, and policies should be designed with the objective of minimizing the number of people who are subject to such degradation. However, it is not clear that legal restrictions meet this objective. MacCoun and Reuter (2001) have pointed out that no academic studies have ever established a link between legal availability and the extent of prostitution.

A separate set of arguments is concerned with the direct impact of the activity on the surrounding community. Communities most likely to reject prostitution are small towns or middle-class suburbs, predominantly populated by infrequently-moving homeowners and families. Their opposition to prostitution is more likely to arise from an objection to the 'visual pollution' (for example, kerb-crawlers, used condoms on the pavement, sexually explicit business cards in phone boxes) and other distasteful spillovers from the activity, than from any inherent moral objections. In the UK, the famous Wolfenden Committee Report (Wolfenden, 1957) articulated this pragmatic standpoint, asserting that the law should only be concerned with, 'the manner in which the activities of prostitutes and those associated with them offend against public order and decency, expose the ordinary citizen to what is offensive and injurious, or involve the exploitation of others'.

Most policies outlawing prostitution are directed towards providers themselves, with fines or prison sentences imposed on violators. An interesting alternative model is administered in Sweden, where, in January 1999, it became illegal to *purchase* sexual services, with violators facing up to six months in prison (Grundberg, 2003). The effect on the market was dramatic, with street prostitution falling by more than two-thirds. Moreover, it has become evident that the activity has been displaced, with the Internet now providing the principal medium for attracting clients. The Swedish policy approach, of curbing demand rather than supply, has therefore proved successful in reducing the undesirable spillovers listed in the preceding paragraph.

Some arguments in favour of legalization were presented earlier in this chapter, although those arguments all had a strictly theoretical tone. From a more pragmatic standpoint, the principal argument in favour of legalization is that the social problems associated with prostitution are likely to be greatly alleviated if the activity is overseen by the authorities. For example, free medical checks would limit the spread of STDs; keeping central registers of providers would alleviate the recent serious problems of human trafficking; support and advice available through drop-in centres may act as a check on the type of violence from pimps and clients to which many providers are otherwise subjected.

Running in parallel with arguments promoting drug legalization (see Chapter 3), some predict that legalization of prostitution would reduce the revenue, and therefore the attractiveness, of organized crime. As a further benefit to society, a portion of the revenue currently raised by criminals would instead become tax revenue for government. The number of undesirable characters on the scene, including 'pimps', would undoubtedly decrease, as would associated levels of street violence. Also, the time and money spent by the police fighting the losing battle of enforcing prostitution law could be diverted to more productive activities.

Another moral argument in favour of legalization is that it removes a restriction on freedom. At a certain level it seems strange that a society that, for example, allows a woman to end another's life through abortion, denies a woman the choice to sell her body in order to make a living.

Having made a decision on whether to support legalization in principle, we are then faced with the choice between a number of models of legalization, to which we now turn. These models have been described in detail by Reynolds (1986).

First, the 'laissez-faire' or 'tolerance' model is one in which government and police intervention is kept to a minimum, despite legislation prohibiting prostitution. Such inaction by the authorities may be the result of pressure from the courts, pressure from the public or some form of bribery. The model often occurs in large cities in which police are over-burdened with crimes of a more serious nature, or in locations whose economy relies heavily on adult tourism. A good example of the latter is Thailand, where the sex industry as a whole is thought to account for 14 per cent of GDP.[13] In such settings, police action would be called upon by the public only when limits of acceptable behaviour have been breached.

Second, the 'regulation' model is characterized by a licensing system. Such a scheme has recently been applied by the US government to prostitutes operating near the USA–Mexico border (Marizco, 2003). The licences are not intended to promote prostitution, but rather provide a means of exercising control over what is considered a socially undesirable activity. Licensing is useful for maintaining health standards, for detecting illegal trafficking of women and generally for keeping track of providers. Also, crimes against clients are likely to be reduced since offending providers become easily identifiable. However, an obvious downside is that society may well frown upon the idea of local government monitoring the provision of commercial sex.

Finally, the 'zoning' model describes a situation in which a minimum physical distance is set between residential areas and the locations where prostitution is permitted. Such regulations normally result in a concentration of activity in one location, known as a 'tolerance zone' or 'working area', and often located in an industrial area. Many European cities apply such a model, most notably in the Netherlands, and some UK cities look likely to adopt similar schemes soon (Humphries, 2003). Although such plans tend to provoke emotive negative responses from the Press, the schemes are likely to benefit all parties. The police are fully aware of the sort of activities taking place in the zone and find it easy to control the conduct of both providers and clients. Concentration of businesses can also benefit the clients and providers themselves. For clients, choice is maximized and search costs minimized. For providers, the complete market can be reached without the need for advertising, and publicly provided facilities such as night-shelters and CCTV surveillance have the potential to make life easier. Last but not least, the general public benefits from the spectacle of prostitution being eliminated from their doorsteps. (See Krugman, 1991 for a full economic theoretic explanation of the benefits of so-called 'market clustering' in a more general context.)

A question that arises is, given the apparent Pareto-optimality of the zoning model, why such schemes do not emerge spontaneously. The answer is that it is only the preferences of market participants that are reflected in the prevailing scheme. When left to the free market, no account is taken of the preferences of local residents and other members of the public whose lives are affected. In economic terms, the spillover effects of prostitution are negative externalities. The government's role is to actively enforce a zoning model in order to eliminate these externalities.

One thing that is clear from the descriptions of these various models of legalization is that it is appropriate to apply such schemes at a geographically local level. Therefore, it may be seen as more sensible for prostitution policy to be delegated to local government, where local knowledge may be exploited in designing an optimal scheme, than for national governments blindly to enforce blanket schemes.

It is well-known that sex workers themselves are generally in favour of legalization, or at least decriminalization (see, for example, the IUSW website). Some third party gainers are also in favour. Thai brothel owners, for instance, claim that it would relieve them of paying bribes to the police.[14] However, it is also interesting that wherever legalization has been adopted, for example in Nevada in the USA, sex workers claim to feel vulnerable to state control, being requested to work long hours for low pay. Many also complain of the soulnessness of legal brothels as workplaces. It is, therefore, not surprising that many opt to work outside of the legal system. As seen in Table 7.2, there were 4177 arrests in Nevada in the year 2000 for illegal prostitution.

When legalization is introduced, we also need to consider the destiny of those workers who are excluded from the legal market due, for example, to failing the obligatory health check, or to being an illegal immigrant. These rejects would naturally turn to the illegal sector, which would now consist of a high-risk 'underclass', but would nevertheless continue to attract clients since the lower costs associated with the illegal market, for example from avoiding tax, would allow undercutting. It must also be acknowledged that the most socially repugnant sectors of the market such as child prostitution will never emerge from underground, since no one is likely to propose legalization of these sectors.

Thus, we are led to the conclusion that any decision by a government to legalize a market would not overnight solve all of the social problems associated with prostitution; it would be impossible to have a legal market without having an illegal one operating alongside it.

6   Conclusion

The economic model introduced in this chapter makes an important distinction between two markets: marriage (primary) and commercial sex (secondary). One aspect of the importance of this distinction is that the effects of prostitution on economic welfare are seen clearly in this context: the presence of the secondary market is essential for the socially cherished marriage market to function in equilibrium.

The model is also capable of explaining a number of known features of the market for prostitution, for example, that the number of prostitutes falls as earnings from alternative employment rise. The key quantity appearing in the model is the opportunity cost of prostitution, being simply the financial benefits of marriage. The high price paid to prostitutes as compared with other workers with similar skill levels is explained in terms of the very high level of this opportunity cost.

A criticism of the economic model might be that it relies exclusively on economic factors. A complete model of the decision to enter the market for sexual services, either as a client or a provider, would surely incorporate the impact on self-esteem, the social stigma, the risks and so on. Also, the assumption that there are no possibilities other than marriage and prostitution was never fully tenable, least of all today, given the significant rise in non-marital, non-commercial sex observed in the second half of the twentieth century. Nevertheless, as a highly simplified version of reality, the model serves a useful purpose. Another reason for outlining the model in this chapter is, as previously mentioned, that this is the first model of prostitution to be published by a leading economics journal.

The demand-side has been analysed in some detail in Section 4. This sort of analysis has been made possible by the emergence of the Internet, first in inducing market participants to provide information, albeit through pseudonyms, of a sensitive and personal nature, and second in providing an easily accessible source of large amounts of such information. The analysis has been useful in the uncovering of certain interesting features of the market. Also, since it is a study based on actual prices paid, the results could be used to estimate the total flow of income generated by the industry (see Moffatt and Peters, 2004), which would, in turn, be useful in estimating the tax revenue that would be generated under legalization. However, it should also be remembered that the introduction of a tax would have the effect of reducing the number of providers in the industry.

The key findings in the empirical analysis are that price is driven mainly by factors such as duration of the encounter, type of arrangement and location, but not, as some might expect, by the actual services provided. This suggests that providers are indifferent to what services they perform, as long as they are paid for their time. Another interesting set of findings concern the discrepancies observed between the 'price equation' and the 'satisfaction equation'. A point made there is that, in a smoothly functioning market, any feature of a service that increases client satisfaction should attract a price premium. We noticed, however, that in many cases such a correspondence was not observed. The finding that 'unattractive' providers generate less satisfaction while charging higher prices is one example, and this was explained in terms of strategic behaviour on the part of the provider: she is exploiting the sunk cost vulnerability of first-time customers. This and other such findings suggest that market signals are not functioning perfectly and there exist unrealized profit opportunities.

Section 5 was mainly concerned with the legalization debate. This is one debate in which most people have very strong views on one side or the other. This may be because both sides of the argument are quite powerful, but it is more likely to be because people are insufficiently informed. This section was a modest attempt at a balanced treatment of the key issues in the debate. The key conclusions were that, whatever the perceived benefits from legalization, it is only appropriate to apply schemes at a geographically local level, and certain types of legalization have the potential to alleviate but not eliminate social problems. Another key point is that there is no evidence that the legal status of prostitution has ever actually influenced levels of activity in the market. Therefore, legalization can be used to alter the shape but not the size of the market.

An important point made was that societal rejection of prostitution has its roots mainly in objections to the undesirable spillovers generated by the industry, rather than in any moral objection. If these spillovers are reduced or eliminated, society is likely to become much more tolerant. The Internet is one means of reducing the visual pollution, since information on the Internet is normally seen only by those actively searching for it. There is no doubt that the use of the Internet as an advertising medium by sex workers has taken off spectacularly: typing 'escort service' into a search engine gives more than 100 000 hits! This must be seen as a benefit to society if it means that non-participants in the market are no longer exposed to it. Furthermore, if the Internet becomes the universal medium for advertising and information exchange, evils such as child prostitution become more easily detectable, since the Internet is accessible by everyone including the law enforcement authorities.

Various models of legalization and toleration were also described in Section 5. Each model clearly has attractions and limitations. On balance, the zoning model appears to strike a sensible compromise, and it is not surprising that schemes of this type are springing up in many locations in the Western world. However, one point that was not made is that legalization may change the nature of the product in the eyes of the client, and reduce the demand. Perhaps, there are some clients who are drawn to commercial sex precisely because it is illegal, sordid, slightly risky, even dangerous. Indeed, this perverse desire on the part of human males may be seen as a further explanation of the high compensating wage differential that has been a recurring theme in this chapter.

Notes

1. 'Clipping' is the practice of taking payment from a client and immediately departing without delivery of the agreed service.
2. Original source: EUROPAP regional reports; data collated by Department of Politics at the University of Exeter, http://www.ex.ac.uk/politics/pol_data/undergrad/aac/scale.htm.
3. For example, two Thai women were jailed for five years in June 2003 for running a multi-million pound prostitution racket in the UK, in which hundreds of young Thai girls were brought over to work as prostitutes and could not earn 'freedom' until they had serviced between 500 and 1000 clients. For full report, see: http://news.bbc.co.uk/1/hi/england/london/2960328.stm. Also in the UK, an Albanian asylum seeker was jailed for

ten years in December 2003 for similar offences. See: http://newsvote.bbc.co.uk/1/hi/
   uk/3340921.stm.
4. For full report see http://news.bbc.co.uk/1/hi/world/europe/3209541.stm.
5. http://www.iusw.org/start/.
6. One possible data source, which has been available for many years from sex shops in the
   UK, is *McCoy's British Massage Parlour Guide*.
7. See http://www.angelfire.com/stars/dorina/dpasiamiddleeast.html.
8. See http://www.punternet.com/saunaguide.html#The%20Dark%20Side.
9. 'Swinging' is a pastime enjoyed by consenting adults of both genders, in which couples
   congregate usually at a party at a private house, for the opportunity of temporarily swap-
   ping partners and engaging in sexual activities. The pastime is popular among couples
   wishing to spice up their sex lives without compromising their marriages.
10. Interesting empirical studies of infidelity appear in the microeconometrics literature,
    dating back to Fair (1978). Results from these studies could conceivably be used to
    obtain estimates of λ.
11. We are grateful to the web-manager 'Galahad' for permission to use the site for the
    purpose of the empirical analysis that follows, and to Sheena Louks for painstaking
    extraction of data from the site. Other sites exist that fulfil similar functions, for example,
    the international site, World Sex Guide, http://www.worldsexguide.org.
12. The procedure used to obtain the smooth is known as *lowess*, which is originally due to
    Cleveland (1979), and is now available in recent versions of SPSS.
13. See http://news.bbc.co.uk/1/hi/world/europe/3068827.stm.
14. See 'Thais mull legalising sex trade', http://newsvote.bbc.co.uk/1/hi/world/asia-pacific/
    3240824.stm.

References

Akerlof, G. (1970), 'The market for lemons: quality uncertainty and the market mechanism',
   Quarterly Journal of Economics, **84**, 488–500.
Albert, A. (2001), *BROTHEL: Mustang Ranch and Its Women*, USA: Random House.
Anonymous (1998), 'The sex industry', *The Economist*, 14 February.
Anonymous (2004), 'It's a foreigner's game', *The Economist*, 4 September.
Benson, C. and R. Matthews (1995), 'Street prostitution: ten facts in search of a policy',
   International Journal of the Sociology of Law, **23**, 395–415.
Boonchalaksi, W. and P. Guest (1998), 'Prostitution in Thailand', in L.L. Lim (ed.), *The Sex
   Sector: The Economic and Social Bases of Prostitution in Southeast Asia*, Geneva:
   International Labour Office.
Cameron, Samuel (2002), *Economics of Sin: Rational Choice or No Choice At All?*,
   Cheltenham, UK and Northampton, MA, US: Edward Elgar.
Cameron, S. and A. Collins (2003), 'Estimates of a model of male participation in the market
   for female heterosexual prostitution services', *European Journal of Law and Economics*, **16**,
   271–88.
Cameron, S., A. Collins and H. Thew (1999), 'Prostitution services: an exploratory analysis',
   Applied Economics, **31**, 1532–29.
Carael, M., J. Cleland and L. Adeokun (1991), 'Overview and selected findings of sexual
   behaviour surveys', *AIDS*, **5**, S65–S74.
Chapman, M. (2001), 'Hard up students turn to vice', BBC Internet report,
   http://news.bbc.co.uk/1/hi/education/1303782.stm.
Clark, A. and A. Oswald (2002), 'A simple statistical model for measuring how life events
   affect happiness', *International Journal of Epidemiology*, **31**, 1139–44.
Cleveland, W.S. (1979), 'Robust locally weighted regression and smoothing scatterplots',
   Journal of the American Statistical Association, **74**, 829–36.
Cragg, J.G. (1971), 'Some statistical models for limited dependent variables with application
   to the demand for durable goods', *Econometrica*, **39**, 829–44.
Della Giusta, M., M.L. di Tomasso and S. Strom (2004), 'Another theory of prostitution',
   University of Reading, Economics and Management Discussion Papers, 013-2004.

Doeringer, P. and M.J. Piore (1971), *Internal Labour Market and Manpower Analysis*, Lexington, MA.
Edlund, L. and E. Korn (2002), 'A theory of prostitution', *Journal of Political Economy*, **110**, 181–214.
Fair, R. (1978), 'A theory of extramarital affairs', *Journal of Political Economy*, **86**, 45–61.
Faugier, J. and M. Sargeant (1997), 'Boyfriends, "pimps" and clients', in G. Scrambler and A. Scrambler (eds), *Rethinking Prostitution*, London: Routledge.
Fisher, T. (1997), *Prostitution and the Victorians*, New York: St Martin's Press.
Gibb, J. (2002), 'Hookers at sports day', *The Spectator*, 23 November, 34–5.
Grundberg, K. (2003), 'Sweden's prostitutes ply their trade on the internet', *Agence France Presse*, 13 January.
Home Office (2004), *'Paying the price: a consultation paper on prostitution'*, http://news.bbc.co.uk/l/shared/bsp/hi/pdfs/16_07_04_paying.pdf.
Hughes, W.T. (1996), 'Uncertain neighbourhood effects and restrictive covenants', *Journal of Urban Economics*, **39**, 160–72.
Hughes, D.M. and C.M. Roche (1999), *Making the Harm Visible*, published by The Coalition Against Trafficking in Women.
Humphries, P. (2003), 'Green light districts', *The Guardian*, 14 March.
Isaacs, A. (1993), *Cassel Dictionary of Sex Quotations*, London: Cassell.
Krugman, Paul (1991), *Geography and Trade*, MIT Press.
MacCoun, Robert J. and Peter Reuter (2001), *Drug War Heresies: Learning From Other Vices, Times and Places*, Cambridge University Press.
Marizco, M. (2003), 'Efforts to control border prostitution ineffective, experts say', *Associated Press*, 30 April.
Matthews, R. (1997), *Prostitution in London: An Audit*, Middlesex University.
May, T., M. Edmunds, M. Hough and C. Harvey (1999), *Street Business: The Links Between Sex and Drugs Markets*, Police Research Series, Paper 118, Home Office.
McAleer, P. (2003), 'Happy hookers of Eastern Europe', *The Spectator*, 5 April, p. 25.
Moffatt, P.G. and S.A. Peters (2004), 'Pricing personal services: an empirical study of earnings in the UK prostitution industry', *Scottish Journal of Political Economy*, **51**, 675–90.
Morell, S. (1998), *Aktionsmappe gegen Frauenhandel – Frauenhandel ist Frauen-verachtung*, Tubingen, Germany: Terre des Femmes.
O'Connell Davidson, J. (1998), *Prostitution, Power and Freedom*, UK: Polity Press.
Rao, V., I. Gupta, M. Lokshin and S. Jana (2003), 'Sex workers and the cost of safe sex: the compensating differential for condom use among Calcutta prostitutes', *Journal of Development Economics*, **71**, 585–603.
Reynolds, Helen (1986), *The Economics of Prostitution*, Illinois, USA: Thomas.
Rosen, S. (1981), 'The economics of superstars', *American Economic Review*, **71**, 845–58.
Sullivan, E. and W. Simon (1998), 'The client: a social, psychological, and behavioural look at the unseen patron of prostitution', in J.E. Elias and G. Brewer (ed.), *Prostitution*, New York: Prometheus Books.
Wolfenden, J. (1957), *Report of the Committee on Homosexual Offences and Prostitution*, London: Her Majesty's Stationary Office.

8 Economics of suicide
Samuel Cameron

Résumé

Razors pain you;
Rivers are damp;
Acids stain you;
And drugs cause cramp;
Guns aren't lawful;
Nooses give;
Gas smells awful;
You might as well live.

Dorothy Parker (1863–1967)

Suicide is not a regular part of the diet of the trainee economist. It is not found in the typical microeconomics textbook so many professional economists remain unaware of the topic, 'economics of suicide'. This chapter sets out to show that it does indeed exist and why we should be interested.

There are three major factors in the field that might stimulate an economist to participate. First, microeconomic theory is founded on a rational choice model that might find the phenomenon of suicide to be an interesting challenge. Second, the marked patterns to be found in the statistics of suicide present a topic for the application of the formidable arsenal of econometric techniques. For example, sociological pioneers in the subject had noticed some degree of correlation of suicide rates with the business cycle. Third, the tools of standard microeconomic theory may also be informative in looking at policy measures toward suicide.

The chapter proceeds as follows. Section 1 begins with a brief historical overview of the study of suicide, with particular focus upon Emile Durkheim's socio-economic contribution. Next, Section 2 presents some international statistics on suicide. We show the variation in rates of suicide between countries, among different age groups and gender, as well as how these trends have changed over time. We also make reference to the difficulties involved in interpreting such statistics.

Sections 3 and 4 examine economic models of suicide. We begin with the simple notion of a demand for and supply of suicide and a discussion of the landmark economic contribution to the subject by Hamermesh and Soss in 1974. Section 4 extends the analysis by introducing more complex approaches to suicide, including a game-theoretic framework.

The empirical work undertaken by economists on suicide is presented in Section 5. We examine the results of various studies, which are mostly based at the aggregate level and include the testing of theories relating to gun availability and suicide. Section 6 investigates the potential economic costs of suicide, including 'celebrity' suicides. The death of rock star, Kurt Cobain, and its accompanying externalities, is a particular focus. Given the potential economic costs of suicide, we examine the economics of anti-suicide policy in Section 7 with an analysis of how an anti-suicide bureau might operate. Section 8 concludes the chapter.

1   An overview of the study of suicide

1.1   The Durkheim approach

Suicide is a subject that has attracted tremendous interest for thousands of years, particularly from its religious treatment and also due to the fact that its measured incidence displays very marked patterns by gender, age, nation, ethnicity, state of the economy and time period. The most famous contribution to theorizing on the subject was made in 1897 by economic sociologist, Emile Durkheim, in his book, *Le Suicide*.

Durkheim put suicide on the agenda as a subject for social scientific debate in contrast to the mainly moral and religious discussion of earlier times. He identified four categories of suicide, which are a mixture of theorizing and generalization, from his inspection of European suicide rate data:

1.1.1   Anomic suicide   Anomic derives from the Greek word, *anomie*, meaning lawlessness. *Nomos* means usage, custom or law and *nemein* means to distribute. Therefore, anomy is social instability resulting from breakdown of standards and values. Anomic suicide, according to Durkheim, is related to too low a degree of regulation or external constraint on individuals. This can occur when the 'normal form' of life is disrupted through either a dramatic change in society or in the personal situation of an individual.

Durkheim divides anomic suicide into economic and domestic anomie. The former can be generated during periods associated with economic depression or over-rapid economic expansion. Individuals experience a sense of disorientation and role confusion because of a large change in their relationship with society. Similarly, in domestic anomie, a person may not be able to cope with the change represented by the death of his or her husband or wife. In both cases, the strain of the situation may force an individual to commit suicide.

1.1.2   Fatalistic suicide   In contrast to anomic, fatalistic suicide may occur when regulation is too strong. Durkheim (1897) suggests that, 'persons with futures pitilessly blocked and passions violently choked by oppressive discipline' may commit suicide. The duress of prison life is often invoked as a situation where this might occur.

Having said that, we can observe that in situations of political confinement individuals react in the opposite way by struggling to construct reasons to continue living. It may be that such attempts are an instrumental device to self-motivate individuals who hold on to the belief that one day they will be freed from the situation.

1.1.3   Egoistic suicide   Egoistic suicide refers to the case where the individual lacks sufficient integration within society, resulting in a feeling of not belonging to any meaningful social group: 'However individualized a man may be, there is always something collective remaining – the very depression and melancholy resulting from this same exaggerated individualism' (Durkheim, 1897).

According to Durkheim, individuals who are strongly integrated into a family structure, a religious group or some other type of integrative group are less likely to experience these feelings and commit suicide. Indeed, his particular interest in this respect was the suicide rate amongst unmarried males. This is to some extent reflected in the focus on divorce in empirical work on suicide and does raise some questions about sexuality. For example, an unmarried gay male who lives in a solid and supportive community should, on Durkheim's premise, be less likely to commit suicide than a comparable unmarried or divorced heterosexual male.

1.1.4   Altruistic suicide   Integration is too great in the case of altruistic suicide and the individual sacrifices themselves for the benefit of others. One extreme of this would be suicide bombing to promote what the bomber perceives as the collective good of a nation or religious group. More generally, in societies where life is difficult and likely to be short it is not unknown for older persons to take their own lives so that they will not be a burden to their relatives. This is effectively an intergenerational transfer of utility, which would not be made if, at the margin, the would-be suicide found that his or her marginal productivity was sufficiently high to justify continuing to live.

One can find other examples of this type. For example, a mother might sacrifice her own life if this were essential to provide some type of body part to save the life of her child. Or, reversing the situation to 'assisted suicide', a person may find himself or herself in a situation of faculty loss such that they have to transfer agency to someone else to do the altruistic deed. This dilemma has been discussed extensively by economist Thomas Schelling (1978, 1983) who couches the issue in terms of a divergence of preference sets. That is, the agents of assisted suicide face a problem in deciding whether the person would now really want the termination of life he or she specified when in a state not deemed fit to trigger it.

As is clear from the above, Durkheim located the four types of suicide within a grid of social regulation. The core reason for any type arising is that the individual is unable to integrate his or her own needs adequately with those of society. Most of Durkheim's taxonomical enterprise revolves around the notion that people who do not feel they fit into society as 'normal' are at risk of suicide. At the time in which he wrote, this seemed to lead to much exaltation of marriage as a state, that would stave off suicide. Indeed, this family-oriented approach still seems to underlie much contemporary research on suicide despite the increasingly overt diversity in sexuality in developed economies. Outside the mainstream of suicide research there is a body of literature on the higher suicide rates amongst gay teen males.[1] What this phenomenon suggests is that suicide is as much a function of the hostility of society toward any apparent deviation as it is of the individual to adapt to the needs of society.

1.2   By their own (invisible) hand

Subsequent to Durkheim, there has been a great deal of writing on the subject by philosophers, psychiatrists and sociologists. There are even 'suicidologists'[2] who devote themselves entirely to the study of suicide and have regular conferences on the subject. A small but significant contribution to the field of suicide has been made by economists. As noted earlier, the pioneering work is by Hamermesh and Soss in 1974 and is discussed in Section 3. Further, Durkheim's approach has been assailed with a myriad of criticisms and there are some features he neglected, which recent developments in microeconomics seek to incorporate. One is the increasing tendency to look at conflict in preferences along the lines pursued by Schelling, and the other is the use of signalling games to explore the use of attempted suicide as a bargaining tactic to induce changes in behaviour by other people. Both developments are discussed in more detail in Section 4.

Prior to the twentieth century, however, economists had shown little interest in the subject. In 1759, Adam Smith devoted several pages to suicide in *The Theory of Moral Sentiments*. The bulk of this discussion was about ancient philosophical positions (especially Stoicism) on the matter of whether it was morally wrong to kill oneself. His own position seems to be that suicide is not a rational act but rather an outcome of some neurotic disorder.

Seventeen years earlier, Smith's fellow Scottish enlightenment pioneer of economics, David Hume in *Of Suicide*, discussed largely the same issues. Although also coming to the conclusion that suicide was not a crime to be punished, he goes on to see suicide as a rational choice, saying, 'I believe no man ever threw away life while it was worth keeping'. In fact, Hume draws attention to age and misfortune as causes of choosing to kill oneself, which turn out to be the main drivers of the decision in the modern economic theory of suicide. It is probably fair to say, however, that economists working on the empirical study of the subject, rather than the pure theory, have been somewhat more eclectic, even tending to incorporate a fair degree of Durkheim's original ideas in their reasoning (see, for example, Cameron, 2001; Lester and Yang, 1997; Brainerd, 2001).

2   Statistics of suicide

One guaranteed by-product of suicide is a large number of statistics routinely collected by national governments around the world. Figure 8.1 shows the wide variation in suicide rates across the USA and Europe over selected time periods. For example, overall suicide rates range from 21.5 per 100 000 population in Finland in 2000 to 3.26 in Greece in 1999. Sweden has experienced a 42.5 per cent fall in suicide rates between 1970 and 1999, while Spain has experienced an increase in suicide rates of 52.6 per cent between 1970 and 1998. It is worth nothing that despite the worldwide perception of the USA as being plagued by murder, in 2000 it had a suicide rate of 10.7 per 100 000 population, which is greater than its murder rate (see Figure 4.1 in Chapter 4).

Figures 8.2 and 8.3, meanwhile, clearly demonstrate the excess of male over female suicide rates in all featured nations at all levels of the suicide rate. Within the male and female population, again suicide rates vary across countries and time. For example, Finland had particularly high male and female suicide rates of 32.9 and 10.5 respectively in 2000, while Greece had very low male and female suicide rates of 6 and 1.4 respectively. Spain experienced large increases in both male and female suicide rates of 54.5 per cent and 35.6 per cent respectively over the 1970 to 1998 period.

According to McIntosh (2002), men in the USA are four times more likely to die by suicide, while women are three times more likely to *attempt* suicide. He also points out that women's attempts are more frequent but less violent and vice versa for men. (Two out of three male suicide victims in the USA die by firearm compared with one out of three for women. The most common method for female victims is overdose/poisoning.)

Table 8.1 shows the distribution of suicide rates by gender and age. The suicide rate appears to increase with age across most countries. The highest suicide rates are found among males in the 65 and over age group, while the highest female suicide rates are reported in the 45–54 age group. In terms of youth suicide, male suicide rates are greater than those among females

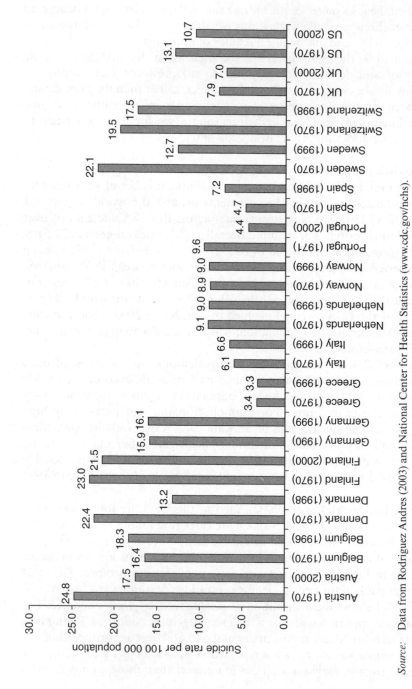

Source: Data from Rodriguez Andres (2003) and National Center for Health Statistics (www.cdc.gov/nchs).

Figure 8.1 Suicide rates per 100 000 population in USA and Europe (1970–2000)

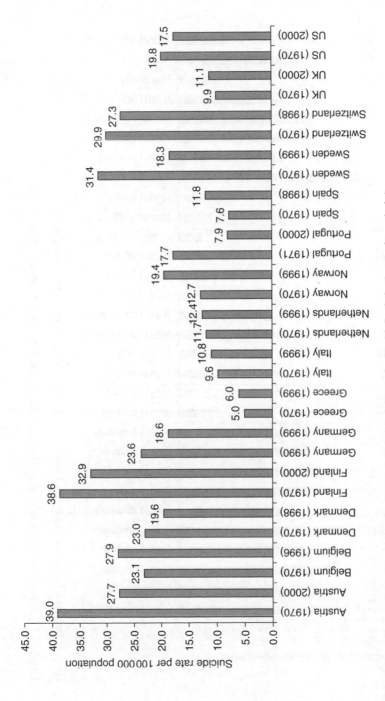

Source: Data from Rodriguez Andres (2003) and National Center for Health Statistics (www.cdc.gov/nchs).

Figure 8.2 Male suicide rates per 100 000 population in USA and Europe (1970–2000)

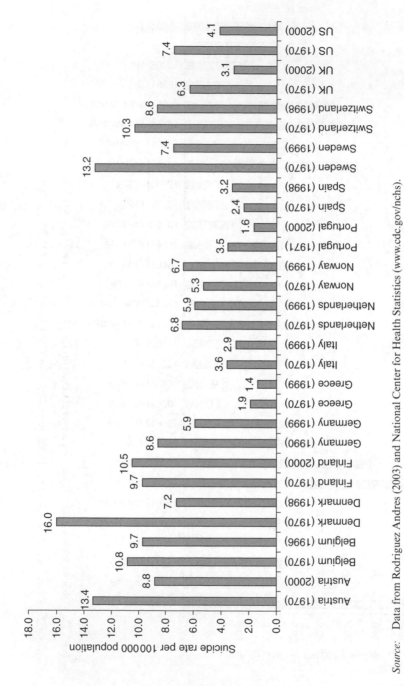

Source: Data from Rodriguez Andres (2003) and National Center for Health Statistics (www.cdc.gov/nchs).

Figure 8.3   Female suicide rates per 100 000 population in USA and Europe (1970–2000)

in the 15–24 age group. Moreover, male suicide rates for this age group have increased over time in the USA and in almost all European countries.

McIntosh (2002) notes that in 2000, suicide was the third leading cause of death of young people in the USA, whereas it was the eleventh leading cause of death overall. Cutler et al. (2001) point out that the rise in suicide in the USA among the 15–24 age group between 1950 and 1999 has been centred mainly in the country's rural states. At the time of Durkheim's writing, suicide was primarily an urban phenomenon and in fact he used this as evidence that traditional agrarian (and particularly Catholic) society played an important role in fostering a well-functioning social environment.

What the figures presented in this section do not show, however, is the massive surge in suicide rates in the Eastern European economies in transition from communism, which is perhaps a form of anomic suicide. In 2000, Estonia, Ukraine, Latvia, Belarus and Russia all had significantly higher male suicide rates per 100 000 population than any of the countries featured in Figures 8.1 to 8.3 at 45.8, 52.1, 56.6, 63.6 and 70.6 respectively. Moreover, as revealed in Chapter 4, a number of these countries, particularly Russia, have also developed a concurrent surge in the murder rate.

2.1 Problems with suicide statistics

Unfortunately, suicide data are even more subject to difficulties of interpretation and problems of error than routine economic statistics. The collection of suicide figures falls into the category of population statistics. They are classified as a cause of death along with the other causes of death and this obviously makes no attempt to harmonize differences in the recording practices across countries. For example, some countries record classified suicides only, whilst others have additional figures for death by injury where it is not possible to determine whether the death was on purpose or by accident. A classic case of this is the use of guns at home and overdosing on medication. It is not uncommon to see it reported that someone shot himself or herself by accident whilst cleaning a gun or that death was due to an overdose of prescribed medication taken by accident. Clearly, as we cannot retrospectively read the mind of the dead person it is impossible to say what the true intentions were at the time of the act.

Attempted suicides pose even greater problems of consistent data comparisons. They will not be routinely recorded in national demographic statistics. In the UK, the Samaritans quote figures for 'self-harm', which are estimates taken from the Centre for Suicide Research at the Department of Psychiatry, Warnerford Hospital, Oxford. Workers in psychiatric services will tend to ask 'at risk' individuals whether they have felt like 'harming themselves' rather than whether they are thinking of suicide.

Table 8.1 *International suicide rates by age and gender per 100 000 population*

| | | Male | | | | | | | Female | | | | | | |
| | | Age | | | | | | | Age | | | | | | |
	Year	0–14	15–24	25–34	35–44	45–54	55–64	65–74	0–14	15–24	25–34	35–44	45–54	55–64	65–74
Austria	2000	0.5	21.8	23.3	31.9	32.8	44.1	48.6	0.6	5.8	5.3	11.5	11.5	16.3	17.5
	1970	0.4	26.9	31.8	46.7	61.8	65.3	72.7	0	5.7	8.2	16.4	23	25.6	27.5
Belgium	1996	0.3	21.4	30.4	42.1	34.7	38.2	34.7	0.3	5.7	10.1	15.2	15.6	13.4	15.3
	1970	0	7.9	13.3	20.8	31.8	46.1	59.8	0	2.6	6.6	12	17.1	23.2	27.3
Denmark	1998	0.4	10.4	20.2	27	33.3	25.3	25.3	0	2.8	4	7.3	13.5	18.1	10.3
	1970	0.3	10.7	25.6	39.5	56	48.9	45.7	0	5.5	10.8	22.7	30.3	34.2	26.8
Finland	2000	0	31.2	46.1	50.4	44.3	37.3	34.1	0.4	8.1	12.2	13.6	17.4	18.1	13.3
	1970	0.78	22.4	41.3	55.5	59.6	62.4	66.6	0.2	6.8	9.8	11.3	21	16.0	12.1
France	1999	0.3	12.5	26.1	35.8	34.3	31.2	39.3	0.2	3.4	7.6	11.3	14.9	14.3	14.8
	1970	0.4	9.4	17.1	25.5	37.0	50.9	55.4	0	4.4	7.5	8	11.7	16.2	17.8
Germany	1999	0.4	12.8	17.7	23.4	24.9	25.9	30.9	0.1	3	4.4	6.8	8.7	10.5	10.9
	1970	0.3	13.6	22.3	25.2	33.7	35.7	39.0	0.1	4	6.9	7.9	12.9	14.3	19.4
Greece	1999	0	3.8	7.3	5.8	7.2	8.2	7.0	0	0.9	2	1.2	2.2	1.5	3.2
	1970	0	1.7	4.1	6.1	6.9	10.6	10.5	0.1	1.4	1.8	1.0	3.3	4.3	1.7
Italy	1999	0.3	7.2	11.5	10.4	12.2	15.3	22.2	0	1.9	2.5	3.6	3.5	4.9	6.2
	1970	0.2	3.5	5.9	7.4	11.6	18.2	24	0.1	2.3	2.7	3.5	5.4	7	7.5
Netherlands	1999	0.5	8.5	15	16.6	18.7	14.8	18.8	0.3	4.4	6.4	7.7	9.7	9.2	8.1
	1970	0.4	5.7	6.4	11.2	15.8	24	25.4	0.1	2	5.5	7.5	11.2	12.6	15

238

Norway	1999	0.2	28.1	26.1	19.2	23.2	25.4	31.2	0.2	9.1	8	9.9	11.1	5.4	9.4
	1970	0.2	5.3	15.2	17.3	19.3	24.7	19.6	0	2	4.3	10	10.4	9	6.9
Portugal	2000	0	3.6	4.9	8.7	6.4	10.8	20.7	0	0.5	1.2	1.1	2.1	3	3.8
	1971	0.3	4.2	9.2	14	22.4	35.7	50.2	0.3	1.4	3.1	3	6.3	5.9	6.3
Spain	1998	0.1	7.8	13.5	12.2	13.1	15.9	23.2	0.1	1.5	3.1	3.8	4	4.8	7.8
	1970	0.1	2	4.1	7.1	9.6	15.6	22	0	0.9	1.4	1.6	3.8	5.4	5.7
Sweden	1999	0.3	14.7	16.1	24.7	26.3	27.6	30.4	0	6.3	7.4	11.7	11.9	10	9.6
	1970	0.4	17.8	28.4	44.7	52.5	54.7	46.3	0.4	7.7	15.4	19.2	26.1	18.2	15.6
Switzerland	1998	0.5	21.8	28.5	27.6	35.3	44.3	42.7	0.3	5.6	5.4	10.5	14.5	13.6	16.7
	1970	0.5	22.6	26.6	28.7	47.7	44.6	50.5	0	5	9.9	8.2	19.3	19.5	22.2
UK	2000	0.1	10.6	17	16.8	15.8	11.7	10.4	0.1	2.9	3.9	4.4	4.9	3.8	3.6
	1970	0	5.8	8.9	11.7	13.9	17.9	19.7	0	2.4	4.6	7.4	10.7	12.9	14.1
USA	2000	1.2	17.1	19.6	22.8	22.4	19.4	22.7	0.3	3.0	4.3	6.4	6.7	54	4.0
	1970	0.5	13.5	19.8	22.1	27.9	32.7	36.0	0.2	4.2	8.6	11.9	12.6	11.4	9.0

Source: Data from Rodriguez Andres (2003) and National Center for Health Statistics (www.cdc.gov/nchs).

Notwithstanding this, a certain volume of self-harm (such as someone cutting himself or herself to get attention) may not be attempted suicide.

To the non-economist, the main worry is simple accuracy in counting of the totals. However, for the economist who is likely to draw heavily on the coefficient estimates from multiple regression equations there is the more serious problem of an inflated error variance leading to over-acceptance of null hypotheses about the relationships with the supposed determinants of suicide rates. As discussed further in Section 3, the economist will tend to model suicide as a supply function, which should show the total intended offer of suicides at the existing 'prices' of suicide. They are, in effect, allocation of time functions where the individual allocates time to suicide attempts, not all of which will be successful. So, any estimated supply curve based on recorded suicides will be distorted by two types of omission:

1. Some deaths that were due to suicide are included in the figures under 'other causes of death'. The misallocation of suicides to other sources of death is often deliberate due to the culture of a particular region. In the extreme case we find a zero number of suicides. This is the case for a country such as Egypt as it is forbidden by national law.
2. The non-inclusion of the failed attempts. The number of these massively exceeds the number of completed suicides. For example, in the USA, for every teen that commits suicide (one-hundredth of 1 per cent each year), 400 teens report attempting suicide (4 per cent per year), 100 report requiring medical attention for a suicide attempt (1 per cent per year), and 30 are hospitalized for a suicide attempt (0.3 per cent year) (Cutler et al., 2001).

Researchers can make adjustments by moving the estimated number of suicides in other death categories to the suicide category and they can add the failed attempts to the completed suicides. However, evidence suggests that the underlying correlates of these are very different. Despite all this, one can at least be confident that the total number of suicides presented in this section for all countries are an underestimate of the true number.

3   The simple microeconomics of suicide

The previous section presents a very diverse and confusing picture, which defies simple explanation in terms of social or cultural factors. What now follows is an examination of how suicidology could perhaps benefit from more of an economic focus. For instance, we outline the Hamermesh and Soss (1974) economic theory of suicide, which predicts that suicide rises with age and falls with income. But first we ask whether we can look at the issue using a simple demand and supply framework.

3.1 Demand for and supply of suicide

Lester and Yang (1997) claim that we can indeed have a supply and demand model for suicide. However, this seems rather hard to imagine without a great deal of strain. Admittedly, many economic situations in which we are accustomed to seeing textbooks apply supply and demand models are not literally applicable. Clearly, suicide is not a product that is sold in a market at a price of so much per unit and, unless it were to become mainly a spectator sport, it is hard to see how there are 'consumers' who demand it. There may be a derived demand for inputs to suicide production such as drugs for peaceful termination of life, but there is no demand for suicides as such. However, we can make a case, as we do in Section 4, that there is an implicit or derived demand for celebrity suicides.

The supply of suicide may be viewed as a 'price' response in the sense of there being a net profit or benefit from suicide in terms of the utility difference between death and life. The costs of suicide include transaction costs in the form of the money costs and time costs of effecting departure from the world. For example, as we noted in Section 2, men and women tend to choose radically different methods for committing suicide. Indeed, a suicidal individual may want to research this and might have to use up time seeking out his or her most preferred choice. On the other hand, one economic factor conducive to suicide is that low-cost methods are always available and, if he or she is at liberty and no one suspects his or her intentions, little effort will be needed to make the attempt undetected.

We can find some casual evidence to support the argument that suicides have a rational component in the shape of price responsiveness. Gassing oneself in the domestic oven was once a long-established method of suicide in England and Wales. In 1963, for instance, suicide by domestic gas accounted for more than 40 per cent of suicides in England and Wales but when the facility to do this was reduced by the falling carbon monoxide content of the gas supply (see Kreitman, 1976) there was a marked drop in the total number of suicides as shown in Figure 8.4.

Specifically, between 1963 and 1975, the annual number of suicides in England and Wales fell from 5714 to 3693 at a time when suicide continued to rise in most other European countries. Few of those prevented from using gas appear to have found some other method of killing themselves. This tale is consistent with the notion of a 'marginal suicide' who would drop out of the supply of suicide attempts if the net rate of return falls sufficiently due to a cost rise. However, the suicide rate did return to its 'typical' level after a few years, suggesting that there is a difference between the long-run and short-run price elasticities of suicide due to a lagged adjustment to equilibrium taking place.

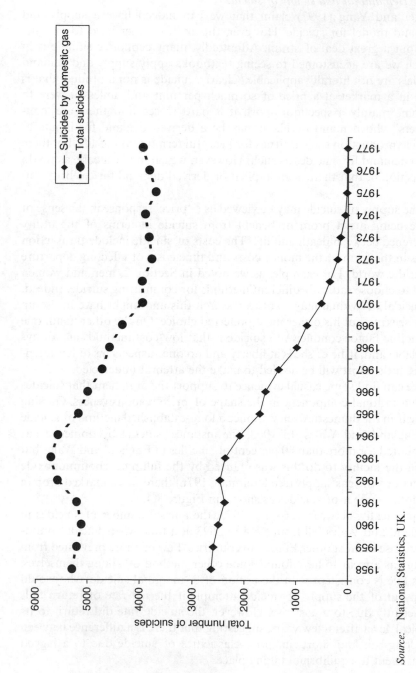

Source: National Statistics, UK.

Figure 8.4 The gas story (suicides in England and Wales, 1958–77)

Attempted and completed suicide may have explicit and implicit 'punishment' costs, for example, in religious doctrine. These may be the basis of the common treatment of suicide as a criminal offence. Suicide was only decriminalized in the UK in 1961 and in the Republic of Ireland in 1993 and it has been forbidden in many religions with the suggestion that it condemns the individual to Hell or Purgatory and can involve the loss of certain burial rights. Having said that, in some minor religions suicide has been a way of 'life' for individuals and in some cults, group suicide of members has been carried out.

Yet, standard economic models of suicide do not fully consider the role of religion in the suicide decision even though the Subjective Expected Utility model has its origin in worries about the existence of God. This is in the form of 'Pascal's Wager' wherein seventeenth-century French mathematician Blaise Pascal explored the wisdom of deciding on the existence of God by way of calling heads or tails on a coin toss, namely, a 50–50 bet (see Chapter 9). Extrapolating this to the notion that a suicide may land one in Hell, it follows that belief in God may retard suicides and, *ceteris paribus*, will do to a greater extent the more risk-averse one is. Other explicit and implicit 'punishment' costs of attempted and completed suicide arise through the effects on others, which are explored in Section 4.

3.2   The Hamermesh and Soss model

So, how can we fit suicide into an economic model? Is it not rather outside the boundaries of such an approach, as economics is so heavily premised on rational choice whereas the voluntary termination of one's life seems to be far from rational? Looking at the pioneering contribution by Hamermesh and Soss (1974), the answer to these questions seems to be 'easily' and 'no'.

Hamermesh and Soss (1974) continued the trend of 'economic imperialism' inspired by Gary Becker whereby traditional topics and problems of other disciplines were penetrated by the insights of economic models without much incorporation of the approach of the other disciplines. This strictly neoclassical economics approach was continued in a textbook on investment decisions by Dixit and Pindyck (1994) and is carried on in a paper by Mirer (1998).

The core economic model of suicide revolves around consumption and the basic premise is an individual maximizing total discounted lifetime utility. Utility is a function of consumption, which in turn is a function of age and income, and Hamermesh and Soss further assume that the individual has a given discount rate, which is known over his or her lifetime. In order for suicide to be a welfare improvement, the individual must have reached the point where any further existence brings a negative discounted utility, although it is important to note that this does not necessarily mean that all future periods have negative net utility.

Specifically, the present value of lifetime expected utility, Z, at age a, is given by:

$$Z(a, Y) = \int_a^{a*} e^{-r(m-a)} U_m P(m) dm \qquad (8.1)$$

where $a*$ denotes life expectancy or maximum attainable age, Y is permanent income, r is the discount rate, $P(m)$ is the probability of living at age m given that one is alive at age a, and U_m is utility for an individual, which, as already noted, is a function of consumption, which in turn depends upon age and income.

From equation (8.1), therefore, suicide is a straightforward investment value decision. The term on the left represents the value of the life an individual may have left. If his or her permanent income rises then, *ceteris paribus*, the value of life rises and continuing to live is preferable to committing suicide. Age enters into the lifetime utility function as a negative component, however. This is because as an individual gets older, his or her most valuable asset (life) has decreased in duration and thus must have a lower total discounted value. Formally, $e^{-r(m-a)}$ decreases because $(m-a)$ increases with age. Moreover, the lower the probability of survival, $P(m)$, the higher the probability the individual will commit suicide.

In this model, life itself does not have an independent value. Rather it is just a collection of sums of utility and the person does calculations on the time pattern of these to see whether he or she should switch off the utility generating machine that is his or her body before its current expected termination date. Dixit and Pindyck (1994) suggest that one should circumvent this limitation by allowing for 'option value' of life. Option value gives rise to 'option demand'. In the traditional cost–benefit example, we might value the pure existence of a wildlife park even though we never intend to go to see it. In the suicide example, we attach value to having a life even though we might think that it will not be worth living again in terms of its net utility benefit from the components of existence. This is consistent with certain traditions in religious teaching.

A modified version of this model could have implications for an individual's health stock and euthanasia. If life expectancy has decreased then the incentive to invest in health has decreased suggesting that one is voluntarily further reducing expected life length even though the decision is not an explicit one to perform a suicidal act. In fact, euthanasia (assisted suicide) might appear as an optimal choice in cases of decreased life expectancy.

4 Not so simple?

4.1 *Preferences and suicide*
The microeconomic model of suicide is perhaps complex in its mathematical development but is undoubtedly simple in terms of the underlying assumptions. The would-be suicide is treated as a rational individual in the sense of having a stable unified intertemporal utility function with a constant discount rate and risk perceptions based on a Von Neumann–Morgenstern utility function.

All these assumptions have been increasingly questioned in fields such as insurance and risk-taking in general. In the case of such an important decision as deciding to kill oneself, it is surely even more imperative that key assumptions be scrutinized. I will concentrate on the most philosophical of these assumptions, rather than the more technical ones, that is, there is a set of completely known, unified and stable preferences.

The standard model can be modified to allow for 'mistakes' in the sense of deciding to kill oneself due to faulty discounting or over-estimation of future periods of negative utility. Indeed, this suggests a 'public goods' role for providing useful information about such things as depression and addiction. Such mistakes are, therefore, due to market failure or individual cognitive limitations.

If we take the last insight somewhat further, namely, that the individual has a limited ability to process information in order to arrive at a rational choice, then we move into the field of 'expanded preference' models. The simplest way to expand the preference ordering approach of economics is to suppose that a person has two distinct sets of preferences. This raises two questions: (i) Which one of these *will* they try to maximize? (ii) Which one of these *should* they try to maximize? The first question covers the area of 'positive economics' whilst the second covers the area of 'normative economics', including the whole formal apparatus of welfare economics. A number of authors have written on such 'dual preference' models, which do have a long pedigree in philosophical literature. Various distinctions can be made as to the status of each set of preferences:

(i) *Long-run versus short-run preferences*
This could involve the notion of correcting 'mistakes' if individuals are involved in dynamic learning. Admittedly, a completed suicide allows no scope for such learning but, even so, someone on the margins of attempted suicide may learn from observing the conduct of others.

(ii) *Higher versus lower preferences*
The individual may wish to follow the higher preference set but succumbs to temptation and gives in to the lower. In the case of suicide, this could go

either way. An individual may regret the acting out of suicidal urges as a lower order preference that requires controls to be placed on him or her. Conversely, an individual may believe that suicide corresponds to the optimum dictated by his or her higher order preferences but regrets the possible cowardliness or recalcitrance in giving in to the temptation to stay alive. In a dual preference set-up of this type, the individual would optimize by choosing a suicide method that is harder to withdraw from part way through the attempt, provided it did not have a level of money and transactions costs that offset the gain.

(iii) Temporary versus permanent preferences

This approach was implied earlier when we discussed Schelling's papers on assisted suicide. Modern interest in it derives from the work of Jon Elster (1998, p. 70) on the neglected role of the emotions in economics. It should not be confused with category (i), long-run versus short-run preferences. In that case, the short-run preferences will turn into the long-run preferences when the individual reaches full equilibrium. Any variable change that alters the cost of suicide would promote this. Elster's temporary preference notion concerns the case of preferences that flare up in response to stimuli. In the suicide case, bad or depressing news may precipitate the temporary preference set to the level where suicide seems optimal in the current frame of mind. However, if the act is delayed long enough (which could happen due to random variation in such things as delays in the time taken to procure any necessary suicide equipment or pills) the permanent preferences will take over and greatly decrease the likelihood of completed action. This is the way the Samaritans in the UK seek to operate by providing a phone-in service for those on the margins of suicide.

A notable case of temporary preferences for suicide is 'romantic suicides'. This does not refer to the narrow 'Romeo and Juliet' scenario of lovers who face insurmountable odds to be together as this falls into the standard model. The romantic suicide, as termed here, is one where an individual wants to commit suicide because he or she feels that the current period has just delivered such a sublime experience that everything afterwards is doomed to be a comparative disappointment even though the flow of utility may be positive at all times. This has been expressed in various art forms over the years and achieved a notable popular manifestation in the song, 'There Is A Light That Never Goes Out', by The Smiths, released in 1986. In this the narrator wishes to die because he is in a state of bliss due to finally being beside the object of his unrequited love.

4.2 Para-suicide signalling games

Specialists use the term 'para-suicide' to denote a case of deliberate self-harm not intended to result in death. This raises questions about how this could be seen to bring any utility at all to the perpetrator in a strictly economic model. One form of reconciliation would be to allow a source of direct utility from self-harm. A wider explanation of para-suicide, however, would seem to require us to view it as an extreme strategy in a game-theoretic model of relationship management first developed formally by Rosenthal (1993).

Let us assume that there are two parties, the would-be para-suicide who we term AP (aggrieved party) and the person he or she sees as responsible for his or her condition, SO (significant other). The strategy of para-suicide is then a form of investment risk taken in an attempt to raise the discounted utility of staying alive by inducing changes in the behaviour of others.

The strategy is needed because the AP sees the SO as causing them negative utility and is unable to find a superior means of conveying the satisfactory degree of angst. If the SO only feels weak external effects of the negative externalities they inflict on the AP then a strategy of exaggeration is needed. In other words, if lesser strategies of exaggeration are subject to diminishing returns (due to a lessening impact on the SO's utility function), then the probable optimality of para-suicide will increase.

The showbusiness and entertainment world provides illuminating tales of the para-suicide persuasion strategy. Well-known musician Peter Gabriel experienced attempted suicides from women who wanted children he was not willing to supply. Fortunately, these people survived. On the other hand, the actress Sarah Miles details in her autobiography the repeated emotional blackmailing of suicide threats by a woman who had become dependent on her. Finally, when thrown out of Miles's house the person jumped off a building. This case resonates with us due to the implicit cost of guilt we would feel if a serial para-suicide or threatener thereof killed themselves.

4.2.1 Suicidal children

Cutler et al. (2001) use a game-theoretic framework to explain the rise in attempted suicides amongst teens in the USA, which we noted in Section 1. They suggest that a child's suicide signal may convince their parents that they are genuinely miserable so that the latter choose to allocate more resources to the child such as time and money. This is referred to as the direct value of a suicide signal. In other cases, the parents may in principle be unwilling to distribute these resources to the child, but give in due to the internal or external cost (embarrassment, for example) at having a child attempt suicide.

To illustrate this formally, Cutler et al. consider a child with a utility function $V(T, \mathbf{Z})$, where T is the amount of time or money the parents transfer to the child and Z is a vector of other factors that affect the child's happiness. The parents obtain utility both from their own consumption $[U(Y-T)]$ and the happiness of their child, $[aV(T, Z)]$. The child's happiness is assumed to be known to the child but not to the parents.

Unhappy children may want more parental input and the value of parental resources is greater when the child is exogenously less happy (that is, $d^2 V/dTdZ < 0$). As child utility is not observable to the parent, suicide attempts are a credible threat to signal this unhappiness if there is some probability that they succeed and if the utility loss from death is smaller for unhappy children. Cutler et al. show that if parents cannot observe the child's happiness, equilibrium is where children with $Z < Z^*$ attempt suicide and children with $Z > Z^*$ do not.

In summary, these results indicate that a child communicates his or her unhappiness to their parents so that more resources such as time and money are received by the child. Suicide is, therefore, one potential signal because a child who is less happy values future life less than one who is happier. However, while a suicide attempt may convince parents of their child's unhappiness, occasionally, for the signal to be transmitted, the child must die.

5   Empirical work

5.1   Alcohol, business cycles and suicide

In Section 2 we described some international statistics on suicide. Much of the literature on suicide is empirically based at an aggregate level in contrast to the highly individualistic formulation of the Hamermesh–Soss model, for instance. In their original 1974 paper, Hamermesh and Soss estimate equations using aggregate cross-section and time-series US data, which found that suicide rates tend to increase with age and decrease with income.

It is extremely unlikely, however, that the ideal database for testing the economic model of suicide could ever be obtained. This would require a large survey-based analysis using a random sample of many people over a large number of years, which included faithful recording of suicide attempts. The nearest data to this is the University of Southern Illinois' Core Institute, which conducts annual surveys of college students in the USA, focusing on drinking, drug use and outcomes associated with drinking and drug use. Markowitz et al. (2002) use the Core Institute's 1991 survey and report a causal relationship from alcohol and illicit drug consumption to suicide thoughts and attempts.

Other surveys from the USA containing information on suicide include the Youth Risk Behavior Survey (YRBS) and the National Comorbidity Survey (NCS). The YRBS samples different groups of teenagers (between

10 000 and 15 000) in grade 9–12 in the USA every two years between 1991 and 1999, while the survey respondents in the NCS are 8098 individuals aged 15 to 54 between 1990 and 1992, with the majority of interviews being conducted in 1991. Markowitz et al. (2003) combine the two surveys in a study that reports that a causal relationship between 'binge' drinking and suicide attempts among youth in the USA is very unlikely, but a causal relationship does exist between clinically defined alcohol use disorders and suicide attempts among girls.

Marcotte (2003) uses the NCS conducted in 1991 and 1992 and employs the indirect approach of estimating an earnings function with the log of annual earnings as the dependent variable and suicide-related dummies appearing as 'explanatory' variables for earnings. This provides little evidence that actual past attempts influence earnings as the relationship may well reflect a number of other factors that are associated with suicide, but it does show that *thinking* about suicide is correlated with lower later earnings.

The more typical econometric study uses aggregate statistics following in the path of Hamermesh and Soss. A paper by Rodriguez Andres (2003), for instance, investigates the determinants of suicide rates in 15 European countries, using age-standardized suicide rates for both men and women over the period 1970 to 1997 as the fluctuations to be explained. The results show that divorce, per capita income, unemployment, income inequality and alcohol consumption have significant effects on suicide rates but these results differ across age groups and gender. For instance, female suicide rates seem to be more sensitive to changes in per capita income than male suicide rates. Unemployment has a positive influence on suicide rates for both sexes. Income inequality exhibits a positive and significant effect on male suicide rates but a negative and significant effect on female suicide rates. Divorce appears to have a positive and significant effect on suicide rates and its impact declines with age. A negative and significant effect was found of alcohol consumption on suicide rates for both sexes.

The Rodriguez Andres paper focuses on a fairly stable set of economies. In contrast, the work of Brainerd (2001) looked at 22 transition economies of Eastern Europe, which indicated that male suicide rates are highly sensitive to the state of the macroeconomy. This suggests that the steep and prolonged declines in GDP in the western countries of the former Soviet Union may have been partly to blame for the suicide epidemic that we highlighted in Section 1. The evidence also indicates that the general adult male mortality crisis in the region had an epidemic or cascading quality in that the loss of a spouse or friend (or simply declining life expectancy) contributed to rising suicide rates. Female suicide rates were not statistically significantly related to the state of the macroeconomy and were more strongly related to alcohol consumption. A lesser sensitivity of female suicide rates to income movements was also found in a study of Taiwanese data by Cheung and Huang (1997) and in work reported in Lester and Yang (1997).

One response to the problem of scarce and deficient suicide data is to apply simulations to a more precisely formulated theoretical model. In these simulations the researcher traces out the probability of an event occurring in response to different combinations of the parameters and causal variables. For instance, Mirer (1998) uses a life-cycle model of retirement planning in which rational choice regarding the length of life can lead to suicide. This model is similar to the Hamermesh–Soss model, although it is couched in discrete rather than continuous terms and contains an explicit term for risk-aversion. Similarly, it ignores the bequest motive, which may appear to be relevant in actual cases of suicide.

Mirer's model is concerned with the allocation of a given level of initial wealth over an uncertain lifetime, and the critical assumption is that an individual regards the utility of living with some particular low level of consumption, C^*, as equivalent to the utility of death. In the simulations, various fractions of the sustainable level of consumption are used to approximate C^* and Mirer calculates the likelihood of suicide in some plausible economic circumstances. In essence, the model attributes suicide to a fear of poverty in old age for someone in employment, implying unemployment may also be a cause of suicide. If unemployment is perceived as long term by an individual, who does not have adequate sources of non-earned income, then it can be seen as a form of forced retirement. Similarly, sudden arrivals of a large debt problem from causes such as business collapse or gambling addiction would precipitate suicide on a rational choice basis.

However, we should not automatically jump to the conclusion that statistically significant relationships of suicide with income validate the microeconomic model of suicide, which is based essentially on substitution at the margin. Income and unemployment at the aggregate level may be indicators of stress (along with other stressors like social tension and divorce) bearing down upon individuals as per the various formulations of Durkheimian models (see Lester and Yang, 1997). For example, male–female differences in aggregate income sensitivity may represent males feeling more distress at the loss of their symbolic role as the wage earner. Falling or negative growth rates and rising unemployment may also create a social milieu in which the support networks available to help potential suicides are curtailed by lack of resources. That is, there may be restricted budgets for mental and other health service provision, but also more reluctance from family and friends to allocate time inputs to those in need.

It should also be apparent from the above discussion that the studies by economists include many variables that do not follow obviously from the economic model; that is, alcoholism and divorce are treated largely as proxies for stress. Studies by non-economists such as those surveyed in Stack (2000) and Platt and Hawton (2000) also include these variables but interpret other variables such as income and unemployment in a different way from economists. Usually these interpretations derive from some version of Durkheim's ideas.

5.2 Gun availability and suicide

Attempts to estimate a loosely formulated supply equation for suicide have tended to focus on precipitating factors (labour market conditions, alcohol, divorce and so on) rather than opportunity factors, notwithstanding the well-known UK 'gas supply effect' that we noted in Section 3. Leaving aside all other statistical problems, this could seriously bias the results found in the research studies. The most obvious opportunity factor that is likely to vary substantially across countries, and over time, is access to guns. Table 8.2 provides some evidence on this, and in doing so reflects the unfortunate fact that gun availability is not readily measured.

Surprisingly, there is no obvious simple correlation between gun availability and suicide. The small literature on the relationship is surveyed by Kleck (1997) who comes to the conclusion that guns simply create a substitution effect, in the mode of death, rather than adding to the total supply of suicides. He points out that in the USA from 1972 to 1995, the estimated stock of guns increased by 50 per cent but the aggregate suicide rate fluctuated within a fairly narrow range.

In the absence of satisfactory information on gun ownership rates, one could resort to arguments based on differences in gun legislation across countries, although Stolinsky (2000) notes that this does not help support the idea of a gun–suicide relationship as many countries with liberal gun control regimes have fairly low gun suicide rates. Ludwig and Cook (2000) examined the impact of the Brady Law in the USA on murder and suicide rates. In states where criminal background checks were not already required for gun purchases, the Brady Law mandated a background check and a five-day waiting period. When the laws were introduced in March 1994, 18 states already had laws as strict as or stricter than the Brady Law, and so Ludwig and Cook were able to categorize these as the 'control group'. The other 32 states were the 'experimental' group. They found that changes in rates of homicide and suicide for treatment and control states were not significantly different. The only category in which they found a statistically significant change caused by the Brady Law was a reduction in firearms suicides among persons aged 55 years or over. However, while firearms suicides fell significantly among this

*Table 8.2   International suicide rates and firearm suicides per 100 000
population*

Country	Year	Total suicide	Firearm suicide	% Households with guns
Estonia	1994	40.95	3.13	n/a
Hungary	1994	35.38	0.88	n/a
Slovenia	1994	31.16	2.51	n/a
Finland	1994	27.26	5.78	23.2
Brazil	1993	3.46	0.73	n/a
Denmark	1993	22.13	2.25	n/a
Austria	1994	22.12	4.06	n/a
Switzerland	1994	21.28	5.61	27.2
France	1994	20.79	5.14	22.6
Mexico	1994	2.89	0.91	n/a
Belgium	1990	19.04	2.56	16.6
Portugal	1994	14.83	1.28	n/a
United States	1993	12.06	7.35	39.0
Japan	1994	16.72	0.04	n/a
Sweden	1993	15.75	2.09	15.1
Germany	1994	15.64	1.17	8.9
Taiwan	1996	6.88	0.12	n/a
Singapore	1994	14.06	0.17	n/a
Canada	1992	13.19	3.72	29.1
Mauritius	1993	12.98	0.09	n/a
Argentina	1994	6.71	3.05	n/a
Norway	1993	13.64	3.95	32.0
N. Ireland	1994	8.41	1.34	8.4
Australia	1994	12.65	2.35	19.4
New Zealand	1993	12.81	2.14	22.3
Scotland	1994	12.16	0.31	4.7
Hong Kong	1993	10.29	0.07	n/a
Netherlands	1994	10.10	0.31	1.9
South Korea	1994	9.48	0.02	n/a
Ireland	1991	9.81	0.94	n/a
Italy	1992	8.00	1.11	16.0
England/Wales	1992	7.68	0.33	4.7
Israel	1993	7.05	1.84	n/a
Spain	1993	7.77	0.43	13.1
Greece	1994	3.40	0.84	n/a
Kuwait	1995	1.66	0.06	n/a

Source: Adapted from http://www.guncite.com/gun_control_gcgvintl.html, which gives the
original sources.

group, the overall suicide rate did not fall by a statistically significant amount because non-firearm suicides rose at the same time.

6   Economic costs of suicide for society

6.1   *Loss of human capital stock*

Given the statistics documented in Section 2, it appears that the economic costs of suicide are potentially very large. Suicide might be likened to a war that carries off a certain portion of the stock of human capital on a regular basis. Human capital can also be eroded by damage due to failed or para-suicides. If suicide is disproportionately concentrated amongst the old and variously infirm and poor/unemployed it could be argued that the economic loss is greatly diminished because of reductions in health care expenditures and social security payments.

Looking at the UK, there seems to be a selective removal of some parts of the human capital stock. National Statistics provides data on the relative statistical risk of suicides by occupation in the form of the PMR (Proportional Mortality Ratio). This shows the proportion of deaths from suicide in a group compared with the national average rate, which is set at 100. Therefore, a PMR of 200 indicates twice the average risk, while a PMR of 50 indicates half the average risk. Over the period 1991 to 1996 for men aged 20 to 64 and women aged 16 to 59, Tables 8.3 and 8.4 show a profound skew towards loss of those in caring and information professions.

American PMR figures are discussed in detail by Stack (2000) using the 1990 Population Census, but only for 21 states. This shows similarities to the UK pattern with dentists, doctors, mathematicians and scientists, artists and social workers scoring above the expected rate of suicide. His figures show only farmers not to be a high-risk group although there is a slight risk factor for farm workers. Stack's figures are not broken down by gender.

Researchers attempting to assess occupational risk of suicide face the problem of whether or not persons in so-called high-risk occupations have the said risk because of stress, economic or otherwise, associated with the occupation or because of its demographic composition. Second, there is the 'problem' of tiny samples. For instance, although dentists appear to be at high risk from suicide according to Tables 8.3 and 8.4, they only represent a small fraction of the total population, only a small fraction of them die in a given year, and only a small fraction of those deaths are by suicide. However, it does seem likely that one important factor influencing the risk in a number of the occupations featured in the tables is access to potentially lethal means of suicide (for example, shotguns in the case of farmers, and pharmaceuticals in the case of those in the caring professions). Indeed, 36 per cent of male farming-related suicides in the UK involve

Table 8.3   UK men (aged 20–64) suicide by occupation (1991–96)

Occupation	PMR	Suicides
Veterinarians	324	9
Dental practitioners	249	25
Pharmacists	171	25
Garage proprietors	155	43
Sales representatives – property and services	151	97
Medical practitioners	147	71
Farmers, horticulturists, farm managers	144	190
Publicans	128	129
Other motor drivers	124	221
Cleaners, window cleaners, road sweepers	122	204
Painters and decorators, French polishers	119	389
Builders	119	332
Shop salesmen and assistants	118	296
Gardeners, groundsmen	117	234
Carpenters and joiners	115	384

Source: Kelly and Bunting (1998).

Table 8.4   UK women (aged 20–59) suicide by occupation (1991–96)

Occupation	PMR	Deaths
Veterinarians	500	4
Medical practitioners	285	25
Domestic housekeepers	247	16
Waitresses	187	37
Professional and related in education, welfare and health	183	26
Students	139	132
Cleaners, window cleaners, road sweepers	138	95
Nurse administrators, nurses	137	240
Hospital ward orderlies	130	139

Source: Kelly and Bunting (1998).

firearms compared with only 5 per cent of all male suicides (Kelly and Bunting, 1998).

6.2 Celebrity suicides: the Kurt Cobain case

Now we discuss the consequences of celebrity suicide. Take, for example, the suicide in 1994 of Nirvana rock star, Kurt Cobain. This has two components: the suicide itself and the impact of his suicide on the value of his product (music).

Artists and celebrities can be classified into two groups. Some artists produce works that are relevant to their choice of suicide, while others do not. For example, Cobain's music and lyrics reflect the misery, despair, hopelessness and helplessness that he experienced in his own life. Thus, his death from suicide validated his artistic products (including lyrics) in the eyes of his audience. Listening to his music may result in sensations, reflections and inspirations that provide insights into one's own life (as well as that of Cobain). The products acquire iconic and increasing value for those who have already purchased the products.[3] This can be characterized as a positive externality, but different from a monopoly restriction of output, which results from the supply of works decreasing after an artist dies.

In the realm of literature, the poets Sylvia Plath and Anne Sexton wrote poems about their mental illness and their suicidality, after which they killed themselves. The writings of Ernest Hemingway, although somewhat autobiographical in nature, do not provide clues to the despair and suicidality of his old age. It could be hypothesized that the positive externality will be greater in the first group than in the latter group.

Let us examine the economic impact of Kurt Cobain's suicide. To do so, we need to compare the social benefit from his suicide with the social cost of his lost life.

6.2.1 Positive externalities of Cobain's death Among the economic gains are those mentioned above that accrue to Cobain's fans, but there are also positive externalities to the record companies that produced his compact discs and accompanying merchandise, as well as the economic gains to his widow and heirs. The headline in the weekly trade journal *Billboard* on 23 April 1994, read 'Cobain Death Spurs Rush At Retail' (Rosen and Morris, 1994). Nirvana had four albums already released, and all four made gains in the week following Cobain's suicide:

- *In Utero* (1993) jumped from number 72 to 27 in the Billboard 200, with an increase in sales from 18 000 to 40 000 units.
- *Nevermind* (1991) jumped from number 167 to 56, with an increase in sales from 7000 to 20 000 units.

- *Incesticide* (1992) re-entered the Billboard 200 at number 135, with an increase in sales from 2000 to 8000.
- *Bleach* (1989), Nirvana's debut album, entered the Top Pop Catalogue chart for the first time at number 6, with an increase in sales from 2000 to 9000 units.

Sales of posters and collectibles (such as t-shirts) also rose. However, suicide as a cause of death may have several effects on sales that may be difficult to separate:

1. Owners of intellectual property associated with the deceased artist will step up marketing once the suicide occurs, such as releasing compilations of the artist's songs. In the case of Kurt Cobain, his publishers also considered releasing unpublished tracks, and the group's album, *Unplugged In New York*, was released in 1994, after Cobain's suicide.
2. The suicide is its own advertisement, reminding people that the artist existed and, by its newsworthiness may alert hitherto non-consumers of the product to its existence.
3. The suicide may have a 'salience' effect on the consumer, which could include a 'Van Gogh romantic suffering effect' (as perpetuated in the pop song 'Vincent' recorded by Don McLean), which makes the artist somehow seem more important.
4. Associates may capitalize on the suicide (intentionally or unintentionally). For example, people who worked with the artist may enhance their own career, as perhaps New Order did when they emerged from the remains of Joy Division after lead singer Ian Curtis hanged himself. Interestingly, Cobain's suicide occurred just four days before his wife's debut album was released (*Live Through This*, by Hole, led by Courtney Love). Cobain's suicide most certainly had an impact on sales of this album too.
5. Other artists may benefit by making 'covers' of the original music by the deceased artist(s), as might the writers of the songs recorded by the deceased artist.

6.2.2 Negative externalities of Cobain's death The social cost of a suicide such as Kurt Cobain's typically consists of the potential value of his future productivity and the associated externalities. However, the life-cycle of artistic creativity and productivity must also be taken into account. Artists do not generally stay creative and productive throughout their lives. In Cobain's case, he died at an early age (27). Thus, he might have reached his peak in a few more years and then begun a downhill slide. It is generally the case in 'popular' music that artists produce their best-selling works early on as compared with visual and literary artists. Therefore, the potential productivity of Cobain's future artistic output may be much less than was generated by his suicide, even without taking into account his maladaptive lifestyle and his substance abuse. Indeed, it is possible that future mediocre works might have blighted a legacy, leading to negative reappraisals and possible lower sales of the peak-period work.

However, we may still face a problem that emulation effects are stimulated, leading to the emergence of some non-beneficial suicides. In other words, there may be negative externalities associated with Cobain's death. If these emulated suicides are in sufficient number, then this may offset the gains from the suicide of the artist. Emulation may come about due to the loss of an emotional support system for some consumers. In the case of an artist whose work is based on misery and depression, other depressed individuals may lose (after the suicide) the reassurance that here is someone 'like them' (a kind of imaginary friend) who is able to cope by expressing how he or she feels. This may reduce their reasons for continuing to live.

Does the suicide of an icon persuade or dissuade others to commit suicide? It is difficult to find examples of dissuasion. The death of Jesus Christ can be viewed as a victim-precipitated homicide, which may have been motivated in part by suicidal desires, probably unconscious (Wolfgang, 1959). In a way, Jesus Christ's death perhaps dissuaded some in subsequent years not to commit suicide. However, imitation is definitely the norm. Phillips (1974) examined the impact of newspaper stories about suicides from 1947 to 1968 and found that, in general, there was an increase in suicides in the month after the story. The more publicity devoted by the Press to the suicide, the greater the increase in the number of suicides. Stack (1990a) found that both celebrity suicides (such as Marilyn Monroe's in 1962) and suicides by high profile non-celebrities (such as Victor Kravchenko, a Russian defector to the USA, in 1966) increased the number of suicides in the following month, but the impact of celebrity suicides was much greater than the impact of non-celebrity suicides.

For example, in the month after the suicide of Marilyn Monroe in 1962 (reported on page 1 of *The New York Times*), there were 197 more suicides in the USA than expected (1838 versus 1641, which in effect captures the size of the negative externality). The suicide of James Forrestal in 1949 (a former US Secretary of Defense) was followed by an excess of 56 suicides. The self-immolation of Norma Morrison in 1965 to protest against the Vietnam War resulted in an excess of 58 suicides. However, not all suicides reported on page 1 of *The New York Times* were followed by a rise in the observed number of suicides over the number expected. For instance, the suicide of novelist Ross Lockridge in 1948 was followed by a decrease of 12 suicides in the following month over the number expected.

Stack (1990b) commented on the impact of 'star suicides', noting that stars promote a high level of mass identification among the audience since he or she represents the ordinary and the unusual at the same time. The audience identifies with the star on two levels: in the ordinary roles that the star plays (father, lover and so on) on the screen, and in the luxurious life that the star leads in real life. There is also evidence that the imitation (or suggestion) effect of celebrity suicides is greater among those who resemble the celebrity in age and sex (Schmidtke and Hafner, 1988).

There have been two preliminary studies of the impact of Kurt Cobain's suicide on suicidal behaviour. Jobes et al. (1996) noted that Cobain's suicide was met with immense public grieving:

> Radio stations played Nirvana's music around the clock; television, particularly MTV, showed concert footage, interviews, and music videos. Grieving fans gathered at Cobain's residence, leaving notes and flowers. News of his death was the lead story in the nation's press and made the front cover of major magazines such as *Newsweek* and *People* magazines; *Rolling Stone* devoted an entire issue to Cobain.

In Seattle, there was one copycat suicide (a 28-year-old male attended the candlelight vigil, went home and shot himself in the head), but no increase in suicides in the next four weeks. However, the Seattle Crisis Clinic experienced an increase in calls in the weeks following Cobain's suicide (Jobes et al., 1996). In Australia, Martin and Koo (1997) compared the change in the suicide rate for those aged 15 to 24 in the four weeks after Cobain's suicide as compared with the same period in neighbouring years. No increase was noted. In fact, there were fewer suicides than in the neighbouring years. Thus, in these two preliminary and small studies, no suggestion effect was observed.

However, across the USA as a whole, the average number of suicides per day in April 1994 (Cobain committed suicide on 8 April 1994) was 90.8. In the two previous years, the average numbers per day in April were 83.8 and 87.8; in the two subsequent years, the average numbers per day in April were 88.3 and 86.6. Thus, there was a peak in suicide in the April of the year in which Cobain committed suicide.[4]

7   Economics of anti-suicide policy

As we have seen in the previous section, suicide may involve direct loss of output from destruction of part of the human capital stock and thus could be an important economic, as well as social, problem. However, unlike murder and drug addiction, it has not attracted government appointment of a specific agency, 'tzar' or guru to deal with the issue. Instead, the major direct attention to the suicide problem comes from voluntary public goods provision. In the UK, as already noted, this comes in the shape of the Samaritans. In this final section we provide some basic analysis of how a government 'anti-suicide bureau' would operate.

If suicide and para-suicide are reflective of deeper underlying social problems that might be represented in the term 'decrease in social capital' (see Sobel, 2002, for a discussion of the social capital concept from an economist's viewpoint), then more benefits might accrue from directing policies towards these problems. As far as I am aware the only paper by an economist on the efficiency of suicide prevention is that by Medoff (1986), but there is a literature on suicide prevention centres and policies particularly focused on universities where an at-risk group is exposed to additional stress factors (see, for example, the report of University of British Columbia, 1999).

Medoff's paper presents some very interesting results, which suggest there might be some mileage in the type of analysis presented in this section. His results consist of two-stage least squares estimates of a suicide supply equation using American state data for 1979 of the usual type with an added variable for the density of suicide prevention centres per population. These are centres of the 'Samaritan' type designed to change the tastes of those contemplating suicide. The estimates suggest that one more suicide centre would have reduced suicide rates by 3.7 white males per 100 000 population and by one white female per 100 000 population.

Using some crude estimates of net worth of life saved based on earnings, Medoff concludes that the benefit–cost ratios showed a return per dollar of between 4.96 and 7.10 for suicide prevention centres. This suggests that more centres might be a highly efficient policy but one should have some caution over such an isolated study. It is notable that he obtains some unusual results for the variables that are traditionally included in such models, casting some doubt on the validity of the estimates.

Supposing that we can use public spending to reduce suicide rates then we may still face standard public finance problems of an equity–efficiency trade-off illustrated in the crudely simplified diagram of Figure 8.5.

This is a strictly equilibrium analysis as we abstract from effects on national output from the expenditure on suicide prevention. We also abstract from all demographic dimensions (wealth, residence, gender, race and so on) of suicide variability other than age and further divide the population of potential suicides into 'old' and 'young'. We assume that the total number of young is the same as the total number of old. The figure has two schedules: a social welfare function giving society's preferences over the possible combinations of old–young suicides and a transformation curve showing the suicide levels that can be obtained by allocating a fixed budget for a 'suicide prevention bureau' differently with respect to expenditure that deters the old and the young.

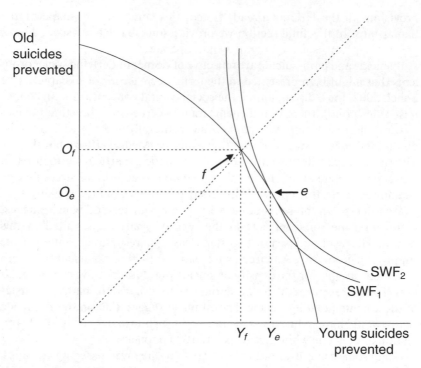

Figure 8.5   Optimal suicide reduction with choice over 'old' and 'young' suicides

The social welfare function (SWF) is negatively sloped as it reflects the trade-off between suicide of young and old. It is also very steep (that is, the marginal rate of substitution is very large) because the assumption that saving a young person is more valuable than saving an old person implies that if we give up saving a young person, we must save several more old people to leave us equally well off. The transformation curve is assumed to be downward-sloping on the grounds that there is some trade-off in deterring 'old' versus 'young' suicides and vice versa. It is drawn as concave on the assumption that the marginal rates of reduction of suicide via spending do not decrease at the same rate.

The figure shows the standard welfare optimum where the marginal rate of substitution in (social) consumption is equal to the marginal rate of transformation in production. This is point *e*, which has a very high ratio of old-to-young suicides due to the assumed shape of the two schedules. However, suppose someone objected that this is unfair. The 'fair' point in terms of equal risk is shown at point *f*, which involves a welfare loss to society equal to the utility value of the gap between SWF_1 and SWF_2. Any move to equality might be said to involve 'sacrificing' the number of young equal to $Y_e - Y_f$ in order to 'save' the number of old equal to $O_f - O_e$.

8   Conclusion

It may have come as something of a surprise to learn that economists have made serious contributions to the study of suicide. Notwithstanding, their approach to the subject is far from surprising, in that variations in suicide rates are explained from a basis of individualistic rational choice economics. The pure theory papers on the subject have been more in the nature of spin-offs of other areas like the human capital model, retirement planning and health capital models.

One thing economics brings to any topic is a degree of precision and clarity. Economic models clearly predict that rises in income and age will, respectively, decrease and increase the rate of suicide. Although this has been largely borne out in econometric work, the major features of suicide in many countries present something of a challenge. For example, suicide rates have shown a tendency to rise in some places in the face of rising average incomes and particularly within the group of younger males. If these trends persist we could delegate the explanation to other subject areas or simply write them off as mechanical statistical aberrations (namely, younger males might be getting better at completing attempted suicides and/or the reluctance to record suicides as being so might be declining suddenly). The alternative is to incorporate more external factors in the rational choice model in the form of influences of social groups and society.

Notes

1. See http://www.youth-suicide.com/gay-bisexual/ for references and abstracts of papers.
2. See, for example, the website of the American Association of Suicidologists at http://www.suicidology.org.
3. Some artists may also sing or write of misery and depression while living a life of luxury, such as James Taylor who often based his songs on his own mental ill-health, or Johnny Marr and Patrick Morrissey of The Smiths. Their deaths would probably not have such impact.
4. I would like to thank Dr John McIntosh for supplying these data.

References

Bernstein, P.L. (1996), *Against the Gods: The Remarkable Story of Risk*, New York: John Wiley and Sons.

Brainerd, E. (2001), 'Economic Reform and Mortality in the Former Soviet Union: A Study of the Suicide Epidemic in the 1990s', IZA Discussion Papers No. 243, January, Bonn.

Cameron, S. (1997), 'Economics of Preference Change: The Case of Therapy', *Journal of Economic Psychology*, **18**, 453–63.

Cameron, S. (2001), 'Self-execution, Capital Punishment and the Economics of Murder', *American Journal of Economics and Sociology*, **60** (4), 881–90.

Cheung, H. and W. Huang (1997), 'Economic Correlates of Regional Suicide Rates: A Pooled Cross-section and Time Series Analysis', *Journal of Socio-Economics*, **26**, 277–89.

Cutler, D., E.L. Glaeser and K.E. Norberg (2001), 'Explaining the Rise in Youth Suicide', in Jonathan Gruber (ed.), *Risky Behavior Among Youths: An Economic Analysis*, Chicago: University of Chicago Press, pp. 219–69.

Czapinski, J. (1995), 'Money Isn't Everything: On the Various Social Costs of Transformation', *Polish Sociological Review*, **112**, 289–302.

Dixit, Avinash K. and Robert S. Pindyck (1994), *Investment Under Uncertainty*, Princeton University Press.

Durkheim, Emile (1897), *Le Suicide*, Paris: Felix Alcan.

Elster, J. (1998), 'Emotions and Economic Theory', *Journal of Economic Literature*, **36** (1), 47–74.

Hamermesh D. and N. Soss (1974), 'An Economic Theory of Suicide', *Journal of Political Economy*, **82**, 83–98.

Hume, D. (1904) [1741–42], 'Of Suicide', in *Essays: Moral, Political and Literary*, London, Edinburgh, Glasgow, New York and Toronto: Henry Frowde.

Jobes, D.A., A.L. Berman, P.W. O'Carroll, S. Eastguard and S. Knickmeyer (1996), 'The Kurt Cobain Suicide Crisis: Perspectives from Research, Public Health and the News Media', *Suicide and Life-Threatening Behavior*, **26**, 260–71.

Kelly, S. and J. Bunting (1998), 'Trends in Suicide in England and Wales, 1982–1996', *Population Trends*, No. 92, Summer.

Kleck, Gary (1997), *Targeting Guns: Firearms and Their Control*, New York: de Gruyter.

Kreitman, N. (1976), 'The Coal Gas Story: United Kingdom Suicide Rates 1960–1971', *British Journal of Preventive Social Medicine*, **30**, 86–93.

Lester, David and Bijou Yang (1997), *The Economy and Suicide: Economic Perspectives on Suicide*, Commack, NY: Nova Science.

Ludwig, J. and P.J. Cook (2000), 'Homicide and Suicide Rates Associated with Implementation of the Brady "Handgun Violence Prevention Act"', *Journal of the American Medical Association*, **284** (5), 585–91.

Marcotte, D. (2003), 'The Economics of Suicide, Revisited', *Southern Economic Journal*, **69** (3), 628–43.

Markowitz, S., P. Chatterji, R. Kaestner and D. Dave (2002), 'Substance Use and Suicidal Behaviors Among Young Adults', National Bureau of Economic Research Working Paper No. W8810.

Markowitz, S., P. Chatterji, R. Kaestner and D. Dave (2003), 'Alcohol Abuse and Suicide Attempts Among Youth – Correlation or Causation?', National Bureau of Economic Research Working Paper No. W9638.

Martin, G. and L. Koo (1997), 'Celebrity Suicide: Did the Death of Kurt Cobain Influence Young Suicides in Australia?', *Archives of Suicide Research*, **3** (3), 187–98.

McIntosh, J. (2002), 'USA 2000 Official Data', prepared for American Association of Suicidology.

Medoff, M.H. (1986), 'An Evaluation of the Effectiveness of Suicide Prevention Centers', *Journal of Behavioral Economics*, **15**, 43–55.

Mirer, T. (1998), 'Rational Suicide and the Optimal Length of Life', State University of New York, Albany, unpublished manuscript.

Parker, Dorothy (1926), *Enough Rope: Poems by Dorothy Parker*, New York: Boni and Liveright.

Phillips, D.P. (1974), 'The Influence of Suggestion on Suicide: Substantive and Theoretical Implications of the Werther Effect', *American Sociological Review*, **39**, 340–54.

Platt, S. and K. Hawton (2000), 'Suicidal Behaviour and the Labour Market', in Keith Hawton and Kees van Heeringen, *The International Handbook of Suicide and Attempted Suicide*, Chichester, England: John Wiley and Sons, pp. 303–78.

Rodriguez Andres, A. (2003), 'Suicide Rates in European Countries: An Empirical Investigation', unpublished manuscript.

Rosen, C. and C. Morris (1994), 'Cobain Death Spurs Sales at Retail', *Billboard*, 23 April.

Rosenthal, R.W. (1993), 'Suicide Attempts and Signaling Games', *Mathematical Social Sciences*, **26**, 25–33.

Schelling, T. (1978), 'Strategic Relationships in Dying', in E. McMullin, *Death and Decision*, Boulder, Colorado: Westview Press.

Schelling, T. (1983), 'Ethics, Law and the Exercise of Self-command', in Sterling M. McMurrin (ed.), *The Tanner Lectures on Human Value* IV, Salt Lake City: University of Utah Press.

Schmitdke, A. and H. Hafner (1988), 'The Werner Effect After Television Films: New Evidence for an Old Hypothesis', *Psychological Medicine*, **18**, 665–76.

Smith, Adam (1976) [1759], *The Theory of Moral Sentiments*, Indianapolis: Liberty Classics.

Sobel, J. (2002), 'Can We Trust Social Capital?', *Journal of Economic Literature*, **40** (1), 139–54.

Stack, S. (1990a), 'A Reanalysis of the Impact of Non-celebrity Suicides', *Social Psychiatry and Psychiatric Epidemiology*, **25**, 269–73.

Stack, S. (1990b), 'Audience Receptiveness, the Media, and Aged Suicide', *Journal of Aging Studies*, **4** (2), 195–209.

Stack, S. (2000), 'Work and the Economy', Chapter 8 in Ronald W. Maris, Alan L. Berman and Morton M. Silverman (eds), *Comprehensive Textbook of Suicidology*, New York: Guilford Publications.

Stolinsky, D. (2000), 'America: The Most Violent Nation?', *The Medical Sentinel*, **5** (6), 199–201.

University of British Columbia (1999), 'Report of the Suicide Prevention Planning Committee'.

Wolfgang, M.E. (1959), 'Suicide by Means of Victim-precipitated Homicide', *Journal of Clinical and Experimental Psychopathology*, **20**, 335–49.

9   Economics of religion
Robert J. Stonebraker

Economists hold nothing too sacred to invade with supply and demand curves, not even matters of faith. Religion may not be bought and sold like fish and chips, but there are parallels. It is a differentiated commodity that is produced and consumed in a competitive marketplace. Consumers make choices about which brands of religion to consume and how much religion to consume. Some of us choose to 'believe', and others not. Some of us choose to be Catholic, others Baptist, others Muslim. What factors drive those choices? Is it the hand of God, or is it the hand of economics? Religion is supplied and marketed by firms called churches, or maybe synagogues or mosques. Each must choose production technologies, set prices and deal with free-riders. How are these choices made? They must compete among themselves as well as with secular firms for the time, attention and financial support of potential adherents. How do they compete and what determines which will prosper and which will not?

Section 1 of this chapter considers the demand for religion and how it can be analysed in terms of such traditional economic factors as scarcity, opportunity cost, prices of related goods and capital stocks. Section 2 analyses supply-side issues with a particular emphasis on how providers of religious goods and services cope with endemic free-rider issues. Section 3 explores the problems of risk and uncertainty in religious choice and Section 4 concludes by looking at how competition and government regulation shape the structure and conduct of religious markets.

1   The demand for religion
Religion took quite a bashing from nineteenth-century intellectuals. Nietzsche proclaimed that 'God is dead'. Karl Marx and Sigmund Freud predicted that religion would be crushed by the relentless march of science and rationality, and sociologists began theorizing about the dawning age of secularization. Similar claims mark much modern discourse.

Curiously, the data refuse to submit. Religious adherence and church attendance as a percentage of population have risen over time in the USA. In recent surveys more than 60 per cent of Americans claim membership in a specific religious group compared with a paltry 17 per cent in 1776 (Iannaccone et al., 1997). While religious declines have accompanied modernization in a handful of countries, recent studies indicate that religion remains remarkably robust in most areas of the world. In the Gallup International Millennium Survey almost two-thirds of respondents claimed that God is very important in their lives (see Figure 9.1) and over 80 per cent considered themselves to be a part of some religion (see Figure 9.2).

1.1   Scarcity and the benefits of religion

This continuing demand for religion should be no surprise. Economists assume that scarcity drives behaviour. We invest heavily to find new and better ways of producing more and more goods. While these efforts certainly matter, human technologies have inherent limits; limits that can be transcended by gods. Religion offers the chance that supernatural beings might supply us with rewards, both current and eternal, well beyond what we could supply ourselves. One important lure of religion is the potential increase in our collective production possibility frontiers. In this sense, religion becomes an additional technology that rational humans might use to combat scarcity. Using the terminology of sociologists Rodney Stark and William Bainbridge (1987), religion provides *compensators* that promise people rewards they could not otherwise obtain in the physical world of the 'here and now'. According to economist Laurence Iannaccone, 'the demand for supernaturalism is as basic and irrepressible as the wants it seeks to satisfy' (Iannaccone, 2002b).

Moreover, the advance of science and 'rational' thought will not necessarily undermine religion. In the world of supernaturalism Iannaccone (2002b) differentiates magic, which involves the belief in *impersonal* supernatural forces, from religion, which involves belief in supernatural *beings*. Magic can objectively be studied. For example, claims that tarot cards accurately forecast the future can be subjected to scientific analysis. Controlled experiments can be used to verify or reject such claims. However, supernatural beings elude such simple tests. It is true that we cannot prove that supernatural beings exist; but neither can we prove that they do not. Confronted with such uncertainty, rational humans might well choose to cut their risks and jump onto the religious bandwagon. As the philosopher Pascal put it long ago, 'Let us weigh the gain and loss in wagering that God is . . . If you gain, you gain all; if you lose, you lose nothing. Wager then, without hesitation that He is' (Pascal, 1660). To Pascal, investments in religious activity are perfectly rational reactions to eternal risk.

Because religion conflicts neither with science nor rational thought in this context, there is no logical reason to expect it to wither away in modern society. Magical aspects of the supernatural that can be disproved will fall prey to science, but religion will not. Indeed, among college professors, those in the 'most' scientific fields such as mathematics, chemistry, physics and biology profess the most religious faith (Iannaccone et al., 1998).

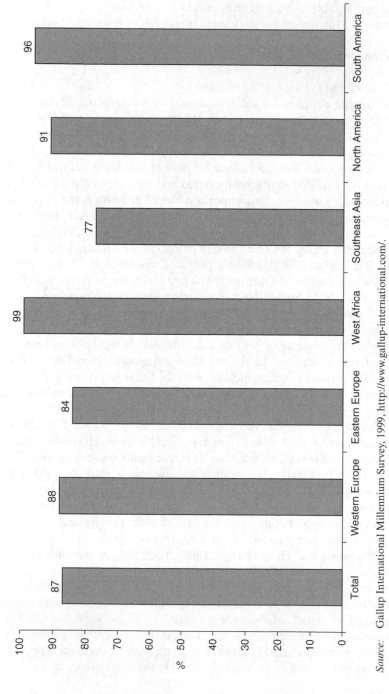

Source: Gallup International Millennium Survey, 1999, http://www.gallup-international.com/.

Figure 9.1 Respondents claiming to be part of a religion

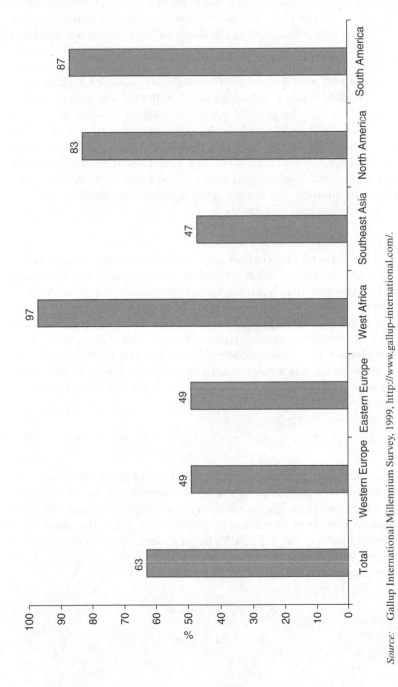

Source: Gallup International Millennium Survey, 1999, http://www.gallup-international.com/.

Figure 9.2   Respondents claiming God is very important in their lives

Many consumers emphasize the potential benefits religion might provide them in the future. Indeed, an initial economic study posited that the demand for religion springs from the demand for afterlife consumption (Azzi and Ehrenberg, 1975). However, religious activity can also offer concrete benefits in the here and now. It is one avenue, among others, that might provide consumers with a sense of affirmation and a sense of meaning or purpose. As such, it can create a sense of happiness or serenity in the present. Religion can also provide a wide assortment of other social and personal benefits. Religious activity can create improvements in both physical and emotional well-being through a variety of channels (Ellison, 1998). For example, church attendance can build stronger social networks, provide both formal and informal support systems and improve skills for coping with stress. In addition, by discouraging tobacco and alcohol, religious beliefs can promote healthier life-styles.

1.2   Determinants of demand

To model the demand for religious activity most economic studies begin with a variant of Gary Becker's (Becker, 1965) household production model. They assume that households and individuals will allocate their scarce time between secular and religious goods to maximize utility. Although initial studies emphasized the 'afterlife' value of religious activity, recent ones pay increased attention to the current benefits derived from participation (Sullivan, 1985; Sawkins et al., 1997; Heineck, 2001). In these models individuals maximize an intertemporal utility function that depends upon the consumption of secular and religious goods and services in each time period. Specifically they assume:

$$U = U(S_1, S_2, \ldots, S_t, \ldots, S_n, R_1, R_2, \ldots, R_t, \ldots, R_n) \qquad (9.1)$$

The S_t represent an individual's consumption bundles of secular goods and services in each time period t, and the R_t are consumption bundles of religious goods and services. The values of S_t depend upon the quantities of a composite secular good purchased in period t (Q_{St}) and the amount of leisure time in period t (T_{St}). Each R_t, in turn, depends upon the quantity of a composite religious good purchased (Q_{Rt}) and the amount of time spent engaging in religious activities (T_{Rt}). Or:

$$S_t = S(Q_{St}, T_{St}) \text{ and} \qquad (9.2)$$

$$R_t = R(Q_{Rt}, T_{Rt}) \qquad (9.3)$$

In these models, time is devoted either to consuming leisure (T_{St}), to consuming religious activities (T_{Rt}) or to work that provides the income needed to purchase the composite secular and religious goods.

Religious activity responds to conventional microeconomic variables in these models. For example, price should negatively affect the consumption of religious goods just as it negatively affects our willingness to buy secular items. Prices could be explicit prices for purchased religious goods or implicit prices that reflect the opportunity cost of time spent in religious activities. As a simple illustration, when inclement weather, three-day holidays or championship football games raise the opportunity cost of time, attendance at religious services falls. Statistical studies typically have examined the impacts of such traditional variables as wage rates, the price and availability of complementary and substitute goods and consumer tastes and preferences.

Wage rates can have several effects. Since higher wage rates increase the opportunity cost of time spent in religious activities, consumers might substitute toward work and away from religious activities $(T_{Rt}$ falls). On the other hand, higher wages can also raise income and release individuals from having to work as many hours. With increased income and fewer hours on the job, consumers might also decide they can better afford to invest money and time into religious involvement. In this scenario, both Q_{Rt} and T_{Rt} can rise. Thus, the theoretical impact on the quantity of religion demanded is ambiguous and statistical studies do show mixed results (Sawkins et al., 1997).

More interestingly, the models predict that wages should affect the *type* of religious involvement demanded. When wages and income rise, consumers should shift from time-intensive to money-intensive forms of religion. Using the terminology above, Q_{Rt} should rise relative to T_{Rt}. And it does. For example, studies find that consumers with higher incomes do not necessarily spend more time in religious pursuits, but they do throw more money in the offering plates. Financial contributions relative to attendance rises with income. Wealthy consumers tend to join congregations that hire professional staff to preach, to teach, to sing, to cook and to clean. Religious groups that rely upon and expect members to shoulder those responsibilities often attract members with lower wages (Iannaccone, 1998).

Complementary and substitute goods also matter. Just as a cup of tea can be enhanced by judicious amounts of lemon and sugar, the benefit of religious activity can be enhanced if it is shared by other family members. Indeed, families with mixed religious preferences experience significantly higher rates of divorce (Lehrer and Chiswick, 1993). As we would expect given these religious complementarities, people are inclined to marry within their religion or to convert to their spouse's religion in a mixed marriage.

We also find higher levels of religious activity among spouses who share the same faith (Iannaccone, 1998) and among families with children (Sawkins et al., 1997). As for substitutes, the most likely suspect is employment. Hours spent on the job are hours not available for consuming most religious activities. Employment does have the predicted effect. Historically, men have been more likely to enter religious communes such as the Shakers during periods of high unemployment (Murray, 1995) and any modern cleric can cite examples of how the influx of women into the labour market decreased the number of volunteer hours that women offered their local church.

Tastes and preferences or perceived value is a final consideration. If the benefits of religion stem from its ability to provide compensators and social support, then its perceived value might be moulded by perceived needs for these factors. For example, there is some evidence that religiosity is affected by illness and the recent death of a loved one (Miller, 1995) and, although the evidence is mixed, the tendency for adults' religious activity to increase with age might partly stem from increased concern with afterlife consumption.

1.3   Religious capital
Extending this basic model to include human capital sheds additional light on patterns of religious behaviour (Iannaccone, 1992). In the secular world, individuals routinely invest in education, training and practice to build human capital. The sacred realm is no different. Just as an athlete practises to build athletic skills and a neurosurgeon studies to build medical skills, those who study and participate in religious activities create 'religious capital' that enhances their religious skills and enjoyment.

The appreciation and enjoyment of religion, like that of music and art and literature, is a *skilled* consumption activity; it requires investments in human capital. Those who have never struggled to produce music themselves will not appreciate the full power and beauty of a Bach requiem. To be pleasurable, a stimulus must contain the right mix of redundancy and novelty. Experiences too familiar or redundant are boring; we need an element of surprise or novelty to hold our attention or interest. But experiences can be too new as well. Those we perceive as totally foreign can bewilder, even frighten. A film such as *Alien* might delight a teenager accustomed to cinematic horror, yet terrorize a younger child with no prior exposure to movie mayhem.

Movies are not alone. According to the late economist Tibor Scitovsky, art cannot be fully appreciated unless it is in a reasonably familiar style, and successful literature must portray characters and dilemmas to which we can relate. Similarly, conversation, even gossip, must be about people or places we know if it is to hold our interest (Scitovsky, 1992). In this sense, cultural capital provides the background we need to appreciate additional information; it provides the redundancy needed to appreciate additional experiences. Just as knowledge of art can increase the demand for and the benefits from additional experiences in art, religious capital can raise the demand for and benefits from additional religious activity. Those who know the liturgy and theological nuances find more meaning in church services and sermons. Those already familiar with the melodies find hymns more uplifting. Those already plugged into congregational networks find more social support.

Religious capital creates a feedback loop. Participation in religious activities creates religious capital that, in turn, raises the benefit from and demand for further participation. The fact that this capital grows over time provides an alternate explanation as to why religious participation tends to increase over an adult's lifespan. Similar to models of addiction discussed earlier in this book, increased consumption in one period raises the demand for consumption in the next. Mathematically:

$$R_t = R(Q_{Rt}, T_{Rt}, RC_t) \tag{9.4}$$

where RC_t is the amount of religious capital 'owned' by a consumer. Over time, RC_t grows with the consumer's religious consumption. Specifically:

$$\Delta RC_t = RC(Q_{Rt-1}, T_{Rt-1}, RC_{t-1}) \tag{9.5}$$

Much religious capital cannot easily be transferred across denominations or even congregations. Thirty years of faithful participation in the local Methodist congregation does nothing to prepare one for life as a Hindu. Because religious capital is *faith-specific*, brand loyalty should predominate. A sale on Pepsi will readily cause consumers to switch from Coke, but switching from Methodism to Hinduism means the costly loss of religious capital. As a result, most children follow in the religious footsteps of their parents, relatively few people switch faiths, and those who do tend to switch at earlier ages before the amount of religious capital at risk becomes too large (Iannaccone, 1992).

2 The supply of religion

While some religion can be self-supplied, most is produced and marketed through non-profit firms such as churches, synagogues or mosques. The non-profit form largely results from information imperfections. In markets for which information is easily and cheaply obtained, consumers can make efficient and informed choices. For *search goods* (those for which quality can be determined easily by inspection), the process is trivial. Selecting the correct-sized mailing envelope or the dress shirt of appropriate colour requires little stress. However, *experience goods* cannot be easily judged until after they have been consumed. For these we seek advice from others. We consult consumer reports and friends to assess which autos are likely to be most durable and which wrinkle-free slacks are truly wrinkle-free.

Information problems are most severe for *credence goods*, that is, goods whose quality we cannot objectively measure even after use. For example, suppose we take a pill our doctor prescribes and then we recover. The recovery might have been caused by the pill, but we might have recovered anyway. We cannot be sure. Crediting recovery to the pill requires a subjective leap of faith. Religion is the consummate credence good. We may never know, at least in this life, if we picked a winner. Credence goods expose consumers to increased risk and vulnerability. With no effective method of judging product quality for themselves, consumers must take some supplier claims on faith.

Can suppliers be trusted? For-profit firms might be especially prone to exploiting their information advantage with bogus claims of product quality. Non-profit firms have less of a financial stake in our choices and, therefore, might be less likely to deceive or to skimp on quality. As a result, non-profit firms are more believable and easier to trust. In addition, managers might self-select. Those primarily interested in monetary rewards might locate in proprietary firms, while those with more altruistic bents plausibly could gravitate toward non-profit employment. Given that non-profit firms often open their accounting ledgers to the public and even allow consumers a voice in how their organizations are managed, it is not surprising that they dominate markets for credence goods such as education, health care and religion (Rose-Ackerman, 1996).

Despite their non-profit nature, religious organizations and leaders are certainly not immune from financial incentives. Numerous religious entrepreneurs have parlayed evangelistic efforts into substantial personal fortunes and recent economic studies suggest that prior to the competitive entry during the Protestant Reformation, Catholic officials routinely 'controlled and manipulated doctrine and rules in order to increase its revenues' (Ekelund et al., 1996).

Although money does matter, many modern studies model religious organizations as *clubs* that produce quasi-public goods that are accessible to members, but not to outsiders or non-members. Their products include worship services, religious education opportunities, counselling and a wide array of social activities. Many of these are produced within the organizations by participating members, but others are produced by agents such as clergy and other professional staff. In club models, clergy are treated as agents of the members much as corporate managers are agents of the stockholders.

2.1 External effects and free-riding

Along with traditional principal–agent issues, clubs and religious organizations are plagued by a variety of external effect and free-rider problems. Because church members produce and consume many products jointly, their utilities are interdependent. Participation, both in terms of volunteer labour and contributions, creates positive spillover or external effects. The more one member contributes, the more others have available to them. The benefit received by one member depends on the quantity of participation by others. To modify our earlier model, a consumer's utility in period t (U_t) is given by:

$$U_t = U(S_t, R_t, Q_t) \qquad (9.6)$$

where Q_t represents the quantity and quality of religious production by other members of the group in period t.

If individual members ignore their impact on others, inefficiencies result. As with other club goods, most religious goods are non-excludable. Once produced, they are available to all members at no additional cost. Because religious goods produced by one member are available to all, the marginal benefit of religious output to the group exceeds that received by the individual producing member (see Figure 9.3).

The marginal benefits (MB) to the group cover marginal cost (MC) all the way to output R_{1t}. But members who care only about themselves will rationally balance their personal benefits with cost and produce only R_{0t},

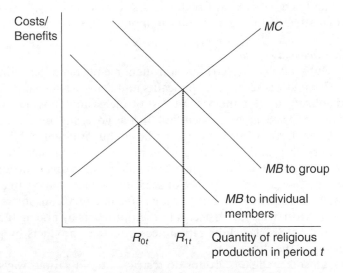

Figure 9.3 Spillover benefits and efficiency in religion

an inefficiently small amount from the perspective of the group. Of course, selfless individuals who care only about the greater good would consider the spillover benefits and produce larger quantities. Many members do voluntarily contribute generously in terms of both time and money. But many do not. Faced with the opportunity to enjoy the benefits of religious output whether or not they pay, many choose not to pay. They choose instead to free-ride on the contributions of others.

Free-riders create at least two problems for a religious congregation or group. First, free-riders can be expensive; they raise costs for the more committed members. Free-riders might avoid helping to supply religious outputs, but they are seldom shy about demanding them and often complain loudly when such goods and services are slow in coming. Clerics of every stripe can identify free-riders who rarely attend services or contribute funds, yet place disproportionate demands on their time and energy.

Second, free-riders can demoralize other members of the congregation. Worship services are chapters in a congregation's continuing and collective journey of faith. Occasional and uncommitted participants do not appreciate where the congregation has been or where it is going. They do not sing with enthusiasm because the melodies and responses are unfamiliar. They do not pray with conviction because their own commitment is marginal. They do not seek out and greet new visitors because they cannot identify which people are visitors. Committed believers add excitement to worship; free-riders often reduce it.

Of course, members can free-ride only on religious benefits provided in the 'here and now'. As David Friedman has commented privately, when it comes to matters of salvation, 'God can monitor the free-riders'.

2.2   Sacrifice and stigma
Secular clubs alleviate free-riding through membership screening and pricing. Committees scrutinize applicants and deny membership to those deemed unlikely to act in the best interest of the group. Those passing this initial test are then charged explicit fees. Just as governments levy compulsory taxes that force citizens to pay for efficient quantities of public goods, secular clubs levy initiation fees and annual dues to finance their programmes. Potential free-riders who are unwilling to pay and contribute are excluded and lose access. In the face of scarcity, we cannot allow free access to all goods and services. We must ration some potential consumers out of the market. Most firms ration access to their products by pricing the products themselves. Secular clubs ration access to their products by pricing membership in the club.

Although some religious groups do restrict entry in various ways, most consider screening committees and annual dues theologically offensive.

They need more creative ways to weed out uncommitted members likely to free-ride. Unwilling to screen potential members through explicit prices, they use implicit prices instead. These implicit prices often are charged in terms of *sacrifice and stigma* (Iannaccone, 1992).

Religious membership may not require a monetary sacrifice, but it often requires significant non-monetary ones. Hare Krishnas are expected to shave their heads and don saffron robes. Jehovah's Witnesses are expected to engage in door-to-door evangelism and forego blood transfusions. The Amish must do without cars and electricity. When religious groups impose prices this high, free-riders vanish quickly.

Sacrifice and stigma serve a second function as well. Not only do they keep free-riders out, they raise the commitment of those who remain. For example, Amish men find it difficult to interact easily in the secular world. Their beards, hats and drab black clothing set them apart and make them curiosities subject to the bemused stares of others. As a result, they avoid such interactions when possible. They prefer to remain in their own communities among those of similar beliefs. In other words, secular and sacred activities are substitute goods. By imposing heavy demands on their members, religious groups effectively raise the price to their members of interacting with people outside their own faith. By increasing the price of secular substitutes, they raise the demand for religious activities. Since the equilibrium output in a free-riding world is inefficiently low (see Figure 9.3), this increased demand for religious activity drives output closer to the optimal level for the group. As Iannaccone puts it: 'Distinctive diet, dress, grooming and social customs constrain and often stigmatize members, making participation in alternative activities more costly. Potential members are forced to choose: participate fully or not at all' (Iannaccone, 1992).

In this context, imposing harsh requirements that isolate members from other societal groups can be a rational method to discourage free-riding and build a cohesive community. High-cost or *high-tension* religious cults and sects are often accused of brainwashing their members. But there is considerable evidence that people are well aware of the costs and benefits in joining these groups and that their memberships were not coerced (Richardson, 1991; Iannaccone et al., 1998).

The high-cost strategy can work. Such groups enjoy significantly higher levels of giving and participation per member than do other religious groups. Iannaccone (1992) divided denominations into four categories: Most Churchlike, Churchlike, Sectlike and Sect. Those denominations categorized as Most Churchlike impose the lowest demands on members while Sects demand the most. For a sample of Northern Californian church members, Iannaccone found that, compared with members of the

Table 9.1　Denominational characteristics: 1963 Northern Californian data

	Most Churchlike	Churchlike	Sectlike	Sects
Size of congregation (No. of members)	939	787	335	173
Household income ($ per year)	$10 140	$9 435	$8 399	$6 944
Respondent education (years)	14.5	13.9	12.3	12.5
Sunday attendance (services/year)	33.8	38.4	44.2	49.1
Evening attendance (meetings/year)	34.5	44.9	69.0	96.8
Church contributions (% of yearly income)	2.64	3.36	4.64	8.43
Church friends (No. out of 5 closest friends)	1.32	1.51	1.80	3.15
Non-church memberships (number claimed)	3.59	3.07	2.13	1.72

Note:　Using two-tailed tests, differences between the mean values for Most Churchlike and Sects are statistically significant for all reported variables.

Source:　Raw data are from 1963 Northern Californian Church Member Study. Table is adapted from Iannaccone (1992).

Most Churchlike denominations, members of Sects attended more Sunday services per year (49.5 compared with 34.5) and more evening events per year (96.8 compared with 34.5). They also contributed significantly larger percentages of their incomes (8.43 per cent compared with 2.64 per cent) and were less likely to belong to other organizations (1.72 compared with 3.59). More complete results are listed in Table 9.1. Similar differences can be found using national data and these results persist in regressions that control for differences in such background characteristics as age, sex, education, income, marital status and geography.

Iannaccone's sacrifice and stigma thesis also explains an intriguing paradox of church growth. Conventional wisdom would predict that making membership easy would increase a group's rate of growth. However, those faiths that demand the most sacrifice and stigma are among the fastest growing. Mormons have enjoyed rapid growth, yet place heavy demands upon members in terms of expected monetary contributions and evangelistic service. On the other hand, mainstream Protestant denominations place minimal demands upon members and have been losing members and market share in recent decades. Membership is cheap, but so is free-riding. According to Berman (2003), a similar model can be used to explain the success of radical and high-cost religious militias such as the Hamas and Taliban.

Sacrifice and stigma are not foolproof strategies for enhancing church growth. Not all potential members will be persuaded, and not all current members will stay. As economists should expect, the strictest and most demanding religious groups do tend to attract those with the least attractive secular options: the less educated, the less well-to-do, the young, women and minorities (see Table 9.1). These groups also experience cyclical swings. When the economy drops into a recession and unemployment rates rise, membership in strict religious groups also tends to rise. When the economy recovers and job opportunities improve, membership in these same groups falls (Iannaccone, 1992).

2.3 Optimal firm size

Large congregations are especially vulnerable to free-rider woes. The larger the group, the easier it is to hide. Shirking one's proportionate responsibilities is tough in a group of two, but relatively easy in a group of 1000. A congregation of 1000 members might be lucky to find 300 at worship on a particular Sunday. On the other hand, being large does bring benefits. Multiple staff members support a diversified menu of programmes and interest groups that smaller congregations can only imagine. There are cost advantages as well. Attendance at liturgies, church school classes, youth groups and Bible studies rarely approaches physical capacity. Stuffing in extra participants almost always lowers the cost per person. Even when capacity is strained, constructing larger facilities often generates economies of scale. A building large enough to handle 1000 parishioners is not likely to be twice as expensive as one built to accommodate 500. Statistical studies document both effects. Within many Christian religious traditions, larger congregations attract fewer contributions per member, exactly what we would expect if proportionately more free-riders are present (Stonebraker, 1993; Zaleski and Zech, 1994). However, larger congregations also enjoy scale economies that lower operating costs per member.

For some mainline Protestant churches the size advantage dominates. As congregational size rises, average operating costs fall faster than average revenues. In these cases, the larger congregations are able to allocate disproportionately more funds for benevolence and mission projects that aid ministries beyond the congregation itself (Stonebraker, 1993). However, patterns in stricter denominations might differ. High-cost religious groups and sects that rely on sacrifice and stigma are likely to find smaller sizes more efficient. The larger the group, the more difficult and expensive it becomes to monitor and enforce behavioural standards. Theory predicts that mainline groups that impose few standards and have no significant monitoring costs will find larger sizes more efficient while high-cost sects will find smaller sizes more efficient. Interestingly, these are precisely the patterns we find. High-cost religious groups tend to be smaller than low-cost groups (see Table 9.1).

3   Religious risk

Religious suppliers must also confront risk. To Pascal, choosing to believe in God was elementary logic. If we choose not to believe, we risk eternal damnation. If we choose to believe, we risk nothing. If God does exist, believers will be rewarded. If God does not exist, believers end up in the same boat as non-believers.

But things are not so simple. Which God? Which religion? The prerequisites for salvation vary markedly among religions. Different faiths demand different and often mutually exclusive beliefs and actions. The official dogma of the Shiite Muslim and the Southern Baptist each condemns the other to an eternal hell. There is no safe belief.

Suppliers try to convince potential adherents that theirs is the one true faith. Consumers are often sceptical but, since religion is a credence good, claims cannot easily be disproved, at least in this life. Cautious buyers will seek strategies that might cut the likelihood of falling prey to religious fraud. For example, they prefer testimonials from trusted friends rather than from strangers, and testimonials from those with no financial interest at stake. Personal invitations from trusted friends and lay testimonials have proven to be successful evangelistic tools and the fact that religious professionals often earn considerably less than others with similar education and training probably contributes to their credibility as well. Nonetheless, risk remains.

In financial markets we combat risk through diversification; we spread investments over a wide variety of corporate stocks and bonds. Might religious diversification bring similar rewards? Religious diversification is not a new idea. Ancient Rome offered many potential and competing deities. Venus, the goddess of love, handled matters of the heart while Ceres, the goddess of agriculture, took care of crops and Mars, the god of war, handled military matters:

> All these existed, side by side, in an atmosphere of mutual toleration. Adherence to one did not preclude involvement in another. Citizens could, and many did, participate in multiple cults – sacrificing to several gods, worshipping the Emperor, and undertaking a variety of different rites and initiations. (Iannaccone, 1995)

More modern examples exist as well. Indians might worship a variety of Hindu gods, while Japanese families might claim both Buddhism and Shintoism, and yet rent a Catholic church for their daughter's wedding (Ono, 1998). New Age proponents mix and match tarot readings, meditation, astrological charts, trips to a mystical energy vortex, crystals, pyramids and witches' covens.

Despite its potential, religious diversification remains the exception in Western countries. Most adherents choose a specific brand of faith and consume it exclusively. Of course, no firm wants its customers to diversify. Ford prefers that its customers not diversify with General Motors and Pepsi prefers we not diversify with Coke. But secular firms rarely command the fierce customer devotion enjoyed by churches. What enables a particular religious faith to command the sole allegiance of its worshippers?

3.1 Strategies for exclusivity

Secular firms wanting exclusive consumer allegiance first must diversify themselves. They become full-line merchandisers and market themselves for one-stop shopping. Ford produces a full line of vehicles and Pepsi a full line of soft drinks. So it is in the sacred world. Because gods in the Roman panoply specialized, none could command exclusive devotion. But the Judeo-Christian God is an all-encompassing deity. Churches and synagogues in this tradition provide a full range of cradle-to-grave services; services that include a comprehensive theological system and a broad network of fellow members to meet both social and emotional needs.

Comprehensive services are necessary, but not sufficient. Consumers will grant exclusive allegiance only if firms make it efficient to do so. Developing exclusive technology is one common corporate tactic. Enthusiasts lured by Sony's PlayStation games had better buy the PlayStation game platform as well; Nintendo's are not compatible. Similar ploys succeed in religion. While the Greco-Roman gods tolerated multiple allegiances, the Judeo-Christian tradition demands exclusivity. The Ten Commandments are quite explicit. 'You shall have no other gods before me', and 'You shall not make yourself a graven image . . . you shall not bow down to them or serve them; for I the Lord your God am a jealous God' (Exodus 20:3–4). Polytheism and Christianity are not compatible.

The first two commandments forbid Christians to shop for alternative gods, but they place no restrictions on sampling different traditions within Christianity. They explain why Christians do not diversify into Hinduism, but not why Presbyterians fail to diversify into Catholicism. Perhaps such diversification is costly. Strategies that reward allegiance and/or penalize defection might build loyalty. Each November many supermarkets in the USA offer a free Thanksgiving turkey to those who spend at least $250 in the preceding month. Consumers that patronize one store exclusively can usually make the $250 level. But those that diversify and split their purchases among several stores may not. Airlines grab allegiance in the same way with frequent-flier programmes. Consumers that patronize a single carrier exclusively more easily can run up enough miles to win free trips.

Competing Christian groups pursue similar strategies. Christianity is largely a communal faith. Worship, sacred rites and other services are produced and consumed collectively within a congregation of believers. Consumers not spliced into the intricate social networks within these congregations derive few benefits. But these network connections seldom arise naturally; they must be carefully cultivated over time. And those who split their shopping among several congregations are unlikely to be successful. To drive home the point, many Christian faiths forcibly evict members who are intent on comparison shopping. The Catholic who strays into Mormonism risks ex-communication and separation from the family of faith. Mormons who regularly seek absolution from Catholic priests risk analogous penalties.

4   Religious markets

The success of a religious group might be affected by the types of demands it places upon members and by its ability to command the exclusive loyalty of those members. However, just as in the secular world, success will also hinge upon the quality of the product delivered. While religious groups certainly provide a variety of social products, their main products are *doctrines*. These doctrines vary significantly across religious traditions, yet most share a common logical structure. They contain a series of assertions, typically improvable, about what specific outcomes will result from what specific religious actions. While economists cannot prove that one doctrine is 'better' than another, we can make predictions about the types of doctrines that are most likely to succeed in a competitive marketplace (Iannaccone, 2002b).

4.1   Religious products and market competition

First, only those doctrines that offer positive expected net benefits can expect to flourish. Consumers will quickly reject religions that promise negative payoffs. Second, successful doctrines will reserve the greatest net benefits for those who are the most faithful. If they offer the same rewards to all, the marginal benefit will be zero. Consumers will expend little or no time and money pursuing religious activities if they promise no additional gain. This creates problems for many liberal Protestant denominations. According to Iannaccone, these groups often lose members to more conservative congregations 'not because they offer too much or too little, but because they cannot bring themselves to promise members substantially more than they offer non-members' (Iannaccone, 2002b). Similarly, he argues, 'with little to offer and less to withhold', it is not surprising that atheists have made little headway in religious markets (Iannaccone, 2002b).

Successful doctrines must be able to attract sellers just as they attract buyers. We cannot buy what no one is willing to sell. The fact that priests traditionally would claim a share of any sacrificial offering certainly might have affected how vigorously they touted such offerings, and the burgeoning New Age market for tarot readings, meditation lessons and channelling sessions has been helped by the variety of people willing to sell such services.

While not all doctrines are created equal, those that persist show remarkable diversity. Religious markets in many countries, including those of the USA, are characterized by many firms, differentiated products and easy entry. Like restaurants and clothing manufacturers, religious groups exhibit monopolistic competition.

Because consumers have differentiated food tastes, restaurants race to fill every available spot in their product space. Some specialize in ethnic dishes, others in seafood. Some offer drive-through service while others offer six-course, three-hour extravaganzas. Religious groups offer a similar diversity. We can find groups that offer short worship services or long ones, high liturgies or none at all, conservative theologies or liberal ones. New entrants will quickly fill unexploited market niches in religious product space. If Pentacostalists are under-served in a local market, storefront suppliers rapidly will emerge.

Although diversity and competition dominate many religious markets, such pluralism generates very different reactions. Some insist that pluralism erodes the overall demand for religiosity. They maintain that competing religious claims undercut the credibility of all. According to sociologist Steve Bruce (1992), 'Pluralism threatens the plausibility of religious belief systems by exposing their human origin . . . A chosen religion is weaker than a religion of fate because we are aware that we choose the gods rather than the gods choosing us'. In economic terms, religious pluralism raises consumer costs by increasing uncertainty and lowering the expected utility of commitment (Hull and Bold, 1998). In this view, a single monolithic faith will maximize religious faith and participation.

However, many economists disagree and suggest that pluralism might increase religiosity. Pluralism allows religious groups to specialize and differentiate their products to more accurately match up with diverse consumer tastes and preferences. Just as an ice cream parlour that offers only a single flavour will lose sales, a country that offers only one brand of faith will lose religiosity.

a: Monopoly church

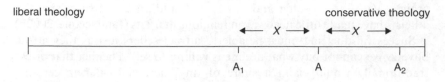

b: Competitive entry

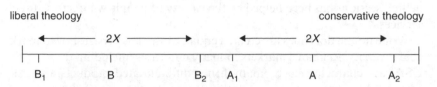

Figure 9.4   Theological product space

Economists Pedro Pita Barros and Nuno Garoupa (2002) have recently used a spatial location model to analyse the effect of religious competition. Using a simplified variant of their approach, imagine a 'theological product space' in which consumer tastes are uniformly distributed along a spectrum from conservative to liberal views. Next, assume that consumers will join a church only if the church's theology is reasonably consistent with the consumers' own tastes. For example, suppose consumers will join only if the church is located within X units of the consumers' own positions in theological product space. In Figure 9.4a, if a conservative monopoly church locates at point A, it will attract members located between A_1 and A_2 ($A \pm X$). If the church wants to attract members with more liberal tastes it can do so by moving to the theological left. But this will cause its more conservative members to drop out. Anything a single, monopoly faith does to please one market segment will alienate another.

If new churches enter the mix, they can locate in areas not served by the incumbent. For example, if a new church enters at point B (see Figure 9.4b), consumers located between B_1 and B_2 ($B \pm X$) join the fold. As new faiths emerge through time, they capture the minds and hearts of the heretofore heathen. Pluralism boosts religion participation.

Competition might also force churches to produce more efficiently. Clergy in a monopoly religion have less need to recruit members, less need to preach and teach effectively, and less need to respond and tailor their product to meet needs of their members. A lack of competitive pressure means a lack of evangelistic zeal. Monopoly power is likely to sap the evangelical fervour of the dominant faith over time. Monopolies in the sacred realm are just as prone to sloth as those in the secular world.

Pluralism proponents bolster their case by citing the example of the USA where both religious participation and religious competition are unusually high by international standards. Many statistical studies also support the positive impact of pluralism. Using appropriate control variables, they find significant positive correlations between measures of pluralism and religiosity (Iannaccone, 1991). However, many of the studies are plagued by data and statistical shortcomings and some do reach opposite conclusions (Olson and Hardaway, 1999; Voas et al., 2002).

The impact of market concentration might also depend upon its cause. For example, religious participation in Ireland, Poland and the Canadian province of Quebec has been remarkably high even though all are heavily dominated by Catholicism. However, in these areas, the church often served to galvanize opposition to outside political repression. Attending church was viewed as much an indication of nationalism as of religiosity. Interestingly, with the demise of the Soviet hegemony in Poland, religious participation has begun to wane. The same decrease in religiosity has been seen in Quebec as the French Canadians have increased their local political power (Stark and Iannaccone, 1996).

4.2 Regulated religion

While the overall impact of pluralism remains an issue, economists generally agree that artificial restrictions on religious pluralism, especially those imposed by governments, do restrict participation (Chaves and Cann, 1992).

Religious suppliers are no keener on competition than their secular counterparts. Adam Smith recognized this more than 200 years ago. He knew that if clergy are confronted by competitive pressure, 'their exertion, their zeal and industry' must rise (Smith, 1776). He knew that churches, like other producers, would fight to insulate themselves from the rigours of such competitive pressure; that, barring natural economic entry barriers, they would seek refuge in protective government regulation. They have. Religions provided divine endorsements and legitimacy to kings who, in return, granted state-endorsed monopoly privileges. The religion of the king became the national, established religion, and alternative faiths were repressed through both legislation and violence. As Iannaccone puts it, 'From Old Testament Israel to contemporary Iran, religious uniformity has arrived on the edge of the sword, and only the sword has sufficed to maintain it' (Iannaccone, 1991).

Although the American colonies were settled by refugees seeking to avoid monopoly church repression, they were intolerant themselves. They quickly set up government-backed religions of their own and used state power to erect entry barriers against new, upstart faiths. Congregational churches received revenues from colonial New England taxes, and itinerant ministers were banned from preaching without the prior approval of local clergy. Nonetheless, the constitutional separation of church and state has allowed the USA to escape the formation of a federally established church. This laid the groundwork for religious diversity that has been responsible for one of the most competitive religious markets in the world.

In many European countries state-established and state-protected churches endure. The German government still subsidizes Lutheran congregations through state-imposed membership taxes and several Scandinavian governments continue to pay Lutheran pastors as civil servants. Despite woeful attendance, the established churches of Europe display considerably less evangelistic zeal than their American counterparts:

> Europe's monopoly churches are, like its monopoly utilities, directed towards the needs of producers rather than consumers. Producer-run businesses favour technical excellence over cost-effectiveness. Compare European cathedrals with the no-frills premises of the new fundamentalists . . . Unconstrained by market forces, European churches devote energy to doctrinal niceties [that] do not interest most users. The seminaries of Southern Baptists are concerned with practical skills, just as Wal-Mart's training is directed towards minding the store, not the financial engineering of a Harvard MBA. (Kay, 2003)

The message seems clear: government-imposed entry barriers restrict competition and output.

Deregulation set the stage for several major religious shifts in the USA. The first, following the 1791 constitutional prohibition on enacting federal laws that establish an official religion, unleashed a torrent of entry in the early nineteenth century that increased consumption of religious services significantly (Olds, 1994). Changes in immigration policies helped lead to changes in the population that spurred the growth of specific religious groups. Immigrants from Ireland and Italy strengthened the competitive presence of Catholics. The relaxation of controls on Asian immigrants in the latter half of the twentieth century brought increased numbers of Buddhists and Hindus into the country. Perhaps more importantly, the new laws also enabled the entry of guru-entrepreneurs who quickly showed the ability to market their religious practices successfully among native-born Americans as well as among Asian immigrants (Iannaccone et al., 1997).

Changes in Federal Communication Commission (FCC) broadcast regulations also proved to be important. Prior to the 1960s, FCC policies pushed broadcasters to grant free airtime to religious programming. Well-heeled station owners, in turn, parcelled out the free time to the denominations to which they themselves belonged: liberal, mainline

Protestant denominations. However, when new policies no longer gave preferential treatment to broadcasters offering free airtime to religious groups, the major stations and networks quickly began shifting to paid religious programming instead. The mainline denominations hesitated at paying for access to a heretofore free resource, but conservative faiths did not. Having been denied free airtime, more conservative evangelists had been forced to buy airtime on local stations for years. They jumped quickly into the broadcasting breach. They knew the market and they knew how to cajole their audience into funding their broadcasts. Within a short period of time fundamental Christians began to dominate the American airwaves (Iannaccone et al., 1997).

Deregulation has spawned similar changes in other countries. After the Allied Occupation disestablished the Shinto religion and repealed religious regulations, Japan experienced a dramatic religious revival (Iannaccone et al., 1997). Deregulation of Catholic state-monopolies has led to the rapid growth of Protestant churches in Latin America, and the demise of Soviet control created comparable increases in Hungary and other Eastern European nations (Froese, 2001).

4.3   Competition and doctrine

In addition to its impact on religious participation, competitive pressure can also influence the nature of the product or doctrine being marketed. Barros and Garoupa (2002) consider a case in which consumers that were originally forced to join a monopoly church are suddenly given the option of not joining. Those most inclined to leave the church are likely to be those most opposed to religious strictness. As a result, an established church concerned about its power is likely to liberalize to stem the potential outflow of members. If tastes and preferences change in a way that makes the population less religious, we should observe the same liberalizing effect as the established church tries to hold onto its market.

If new faiths are allowed to enter the market, the established church should move in the direction of its new competition. Entry by conservative sects is likely to pull the established church to the right to cut off support for the new threat. Similarly, competition from more liberal faiths should pull the established church to the left. Barros and Garoupa use this theory to explain why the dominant churches in the UK and Scandinavia (where the main competitors are fairly liberal) are less strict than are the dominant faiths in Southern Europe and Brazil where the competition comes primarily from the right.

Competitive pressures might also explain the Catholic Schism of 1054. Barros and Garoupa explain that the Catholic Church enjoyed far more monopoly power in the West than in the East. Catholic rulers controlled

Western Europe and acknowledged the spiritual leadership of Rome. With no major challengers, the Western Catholic Church could afford to market a conservative doctrine. However, the Eastern Catholic Church faced significant competitive pressure from Muslims and local sects, and found itself being pulled in very different theological directions; directions that ultimately caused the split.

Competition might also explain why church officials have increasingly soft-pedalled the concept of Hell. With a near monopoly, the Catholic Church could afford to deliver a fire and brimstone message. Toe the religious line, or burn forever. According to Barros and Garoupa, increased competition, both from Protestants after the Reformation and from the 'non-church' during the Enlightenment, forced official doctrine to become more user-friendly. In addition, a doctrine that condemns non-Catholics to Hell is more viable in a world populated almost entirely by Catholics. The doctrine becomes harder to stomach in a world of religious pluralism in which many of one's best friends and relatives are non-Catholics (Iannaccone, 2002b).

5   Conclusion

Where do we stand? As we have seen throughout this book, economics is a science of choice in which people rationally consider the expected costs and benefits of their actions. It assumes that if behaviour differs across individuals or across time, it must be because perceived costs and benefits differ across individuals or across time. Such notions generate little controversy in secular enterprises and microeconomic theories consistently predict real-world behaviour with uncanny accuracy. The theory works.

Does it work equally well in the sacred world? Can we model religious behaviour with the same tools we use to analyse General Motors and Coca-Cola? For many years, social scientists considered religious choice antithetical to rationality. Religious behaviour was deemed illogical and 'scientific' analyses were often couched in terms of social and psychological pathologies.

Recent scholarship suggests otherwise. Decisions about how much and what types of religious activity to demand and supply appear remarkably consistent with traditional economic maximization behaviour. Religious choices closely mirror those made in more secular pursuits. Negatively-sloped consumer demand curves for religion shift in response to factors such as changes in tastes or price and availability of substitute and complementary goods. Suppliers of religion compete for members, search for strategies to lock in customer loyalty, and welcome government regulations that restrict competition. Religious markets evolve much like secular ones. Prices, outputs and product mixes respond to shifts in consumer tastes, technologies and competitive pressures. In the sacred world, just as in the secular world, the theory works.

References

Azzi, C. and R.G. Ehrenberg (1975), 'Household Allocation of Time and Church Attendance', *Journal of Political Economy*, **83** (1), 27–56.

Barros, P.P. and N. Garoupa (2002), 'An Economic Theory of Church Strictness', *Economic Journal*, **112** (3), 559–76.

Becker, G.S. (1965), 'A Theory of the Allocation of Time', *Economic Journal*, **75**, 493–517.

Berman, E. (2000), 'Sect, Subsidy and Sacrifice: An Economist's View of Ultra-Orthodox Jews', *Quarterly Journal of Economics*, **115** (3), 905–53.

Berman, E. (2003), 'Hamas, Taliban and the Jewish Underground: An Economist's View of Radical Religious Militias', National Bureau of Economic Research Working Paper No. w10004.

Bruce, S. (1992), 'Pluralism and Religious Vitality', in Steve Bruce (ed.), *Religion and Modernization*, Oxford: Clarendon Press, pp. 170–94.

Chaves, M. and D.E. Cann (1992), 'Regulation, Pluralism and Religious Market Structure', *Rationality and Society*, **4**, 272–90.

Ekelund, Robert B., Robert F. Hebert and Robert D. Tollison (1996), *Sacred Trust: The Medieval Church as an Economic Firm*, New York: Oxford University Press.

Ellison, C.G. (1998), 'Religion, Health and Well-Being', *Journal for the Scientific Study of Religion*, **37** (4), 692–4.

Finke, Roger and Rodney Starke (1992), *The Churching of America 1776–1990: Winners and Losers in our Religious Economy*, New Brunswick: Rutgers University Press.

Froese, P. (2001), 'Hungary for Religion: A Supply-Side Interpretation of the Hungarian Religious Revival', *Journal for the Scientific Study of Religion*, **40** (2), 251–68.

Gallup International Millennium Survey (1999), (http://www.gallup-international.com/).

Heineck, G. (2001), 'The Determinants of Church Attendance and Religious Human Capital in Germany: Evidence From Panel Data', Discussion Papers of DIW Berlin, paper no. 263, DIW Berlin, German Institute for Economic Research.

Hull, B.B. and F. Bold (1998), 'Product Variety in Religious Markets', *Review of Social Economy*, **56** (1), 1–19.

Iannaccone, L.R. (1990), 'Religious Practice: A Human Capital Approach', *Journal for the Scientific Study of Religion*, **29** (3), 297–314.

Iannaccone, L.R. (1991), 'The Consequences of Religious Market Regulation', *Rationality and Society*, **3** (2), 156–77.

Iannaccone, L.R. (1992), 'Sacrifice and Stigma: Reducing Free-Riding in Cults, Communes, and Other Collectives', *Journal of Political Economy*, **100** (2), 271–97.

Iannaccone, L.R. (1995), 'Risk, Rationality, and Religious Portfolios', *Economic Inquiry*, **33** (2), 285–96.

Iannaccone, L.R. (1998), 'Introduction to the Economics of Religion', *Journal of Economic Literature*, **36** (3), 1465–96.

Iannaccone, L.R. (2002a), 'Looking Backward: A Cross-National Study of Religious Trends', paper presented at November 2002 Meetings of the Society for the Scientific Study of Religion.

Iannaccone, L.R. (2002b), 'From Scarcity to Spirituality: The Consequences of Religious Entrepreneurship', (http://icg.harvard.edu/~ec2390d/Papers/Papers_Fall_2002/October_8_2002_Laurence_Iannaccone_Religious_Entrepreneurship.pdf).

Iannaccone, L.R., R. Finke and R. Stark (1997), 'Deregulating Religion: The Economics of Church and State', *Economic Inquiry*, **35**, 350–64.

Iannaccone, L.R., R. Stark and R. Finke (1998), 'Rationality and the "Religious Mind"', *Economic Inquiry*, **36**, 373–89.

Kay, J. (2003), 'It Pays Churches to have Faith in Markets', *Financial Times*, 10 April, p. 13.

Lehrer, E.L. and C.U. Chiswick (1993), 'Religion as a Determinant of Marital Stability', *Demography*, **30** (3), 385–404.

Miller, A.S. (1995), 'A Rational Choice Model of Religious Behavior in Japan', *Journal for the Scientific Study of Religion*, **34** (2), 234–44.

Murray, J.E. (1995), 'Determinants of Membership Levels and Duration in a Shaker Commune, 1780–1880', *Journal for the Scientific Study of Religion*, **34** (1), 35–49.

Olds, K. (1994), 'Privatizing the Church: Disestablishment in Connecticut and Massachusetts', *Journal of Political Economy*, **102** (2), 277–97.

Olson, D.V.A. and C.K. Hardaway (1999), 'Religious Pluralism and Affiliation Among Canadian Counties and Cities', *Journal for the Scientific Study of Religion*, **38** (4), 490–508.

Ono, Y. (1998), 'Here Comes the Bride All Dressed in a Kimono', *Wall Street Journal*, 9 June A25.

Pascal, Blaise (1660), *Pensees*.

Richardson, J.T. (1991), 'Cult/Brainwashing Cases and Freedom of Religion', *Journal of Church and State*, **33** (1), 55–74.

Rose-Ackerman, S. (1996), 'Altruism, Nonprofits, and Economic Theory', *Journal of Economic Literature*, **34** (2), 701–28.

Sawkins, J.W., P.T. Seaman and H.C.S. Williams (1997), 'Church Attendance in Great Britain: An Ordered Logit Approach', *Applied Economics*, **29** (2), 125–35.

Scitovsky, Tibor (1992), *The Joyless Economy* (revised edition), New York: Oxford University Press.

Smith, Adam (1776), *An Inquiry into the Nature and Causes of the Wealth of Nations*, reprinted by Modern Library, New York, 1965.

Stark, Rodney and William S. Bainbridge (1987), *A Theory of Religion*, Bern: Peter Lang.

Stark, R. and L.R. Iannaccone (1994), 'A Supply-Side Reinterpretation of the "Secularization" of Europe', *Journal for the Scientific Study of Religion*, **33** (3), 230–52.

Stark, R. and L.R. Iannaccone (1996), 'Response to Lechner: Recent Religious Declines in Quebec, Poland, and the Netherlands: A Theory Vindicated', *Journal for the Scientific Study of Religion*, **35** (3), 265–71.

Stonebraker, R.J. (1993), 'Optimal Church Size: The Bigger the Better?', *Journal for the Scientific Study of Religion*, **32** (3), 231–41.

Sullivan, D.H. (1985), 'Simultaneous Determination of Church Contributions and Church Attendance', *Economic Inquiry*, **23** (2), 309–20.

Voas, D., D.V.A. Olson and A. Crockett (2002), 'Religious Pluralism and Participation: Why Previous Research is Wrong', *American Sociological Review*, **67**, 212–30.

Zaleski, P.A. and C.E. Zech (1994), 'Determinants of Religious Giving in Urban Presbyterian Congregations', *Review of Religious Research*, **36** (2), 197–206.

PART IV

CONCEPTION AND REJECTION

10 Economics of assisted reproduction
Sherrie A. Kossoudji

Typically, when two people decide to become parents, they procreate by copulation and produce a child. What do people do if, for some reason, they cannot produce their own children but want to be parents? Until recently, if a couple wanted to have children, but was unable to do so because of fertility problems, there were limited options. They could adopt a child to become the legal parents of a child who had no legal parents, have a child who was the progeny of only one of them, or could become foster parents, the temporary (and paid) caregivers of a child who still had legal parents. Such activities are historically common and were often market exchanges. Zelizer (1985), noting the importance of the work that foster children provided for their families, claims that, 'the legitimacy of child labor was essential to early nineteenth-century substitute care arrangements'. In fact, child auctions (for fostering) were not prohibited in Sweden until 1918 (Lundberg, 2000). Zelizer also argues that the changing social value of children rendered them as, 'exclusively emotional and moral assets' who were transformed from economic assets into 'priceless' children in the early twentieth century. Children may have become recommodified: at the beginning of the twenty-first century, excess demand for children to adopt in the United States has led to an international adoption market that has greatly increased the supply of adoptable children.

A child is created when an ovum is fertilized by a sperm and together they become an embryo. The embryo must reside in a womb for approximately nine months to develop properly into a live baby. Recent developments in biotechnology have expanded the number of ways in which any of these steps can happen. Newer markets are now extensive as the ability to extract, process, freeze, transport and implant eggs, sperm and embryos becomes commonplace. Simple sperm or egg 'donation' allows a couple with one fertile partner to acquire the raw genetic material from someone of the opposite sex.[1] Artificial insemination by donor (DI) and fertilization of the ovum in vitro (IVF) are a collection of non-invasive to moderately invasive techniques to fertilize a woman's ovum with a man's sperm.[2] There are relatively few places where these techniques are illegal, although 'donation' of sperm or eggs for money is illegal in a number of places. With or without these techniques, the embryo must be able to develop in a womb.

The market in surrogate motherhood consists of a contractual arrangement where a woman agrees to carry a baby to term for a couple and to give up any parental rights she may have. The baby may or may not have any genetic components of either member of the commissioning couple, or of the surrogate mother.[3] Surrogate motherhood, although it still exists and is legal in some parts of the world, presented both legal and moral dilemmas that, as we discuss later, nearly destroyed (and significantly reduced) its market.

A final market possibility exists. Reproductive cloning for humans skips the process of uniting egg and sperm and, while still an untested possibility, has raised questions from the religious to the economic. Two sets of economics authors have considered the implications of cloning. Posner and Posner (1999) suggest that, among other impacts, cloning may accelerate the breakdown of traditional roles of men and women as marriage incentives change and as women find fewer incentives to invest in skills that are complementary to men's. Saint-Paul (2002) concludes that a *Handmaid's Tale* society will emerge under cloning, where there is, 'a reproductive class at the bottom of the distribution of ability, a productive class at intermediate levels; and a replicated class at the very top of the ability distribution'.

All of these markets, with the exception of the market for clones, exist in a number of countries. There is no consensus, though, on the legality of procedures, the enforceability of contracts, or the acceptance of commercialization. Surrogacy is legal in Spain; accepted in the UK, but not its commercialization; and its procurement is illegal in Denmark. In the United States most assisted reproduction falls under state rather than federal law, meaning that there can be 50 different legal environments for each kind of assisted reproduction. For instance, commercial surrogacy is illegal in Utah (where the law is currently being contested) but legal in neighbouring California. Table 10.1 gives a brief breakdown of current law in a number of European countries and in the United States.[4]

The economics of assisted reproduction is not well understood by economists because it is still a new and rarely studied phenomenon. For this reason, this chapter will not present a standard literature review that summarizes what economists think about the subject. Instead, we will heuristically proceed with a series of economic explorations related to assisted reproduction to gauge the scope of the issues and how economists might contribute to them. In Section 1, we show that economists do discuss the economics of the decision to have children by considering the demand for children. The traditional literature relating to this work is discussed. We briefly mention the issue of supply of children, which is not typically modelled in economics because children are assumed to be self-produced. Next, in Section 2, is an exploration of the development of markets in

Table 10.1   Assisted reproduction services in Europe and USA
            (as at 2004)

Country	IVF	DI (sperm)	DI (egg)	DI (embryo)	Surrogacy
Austria	Yes	No[a]	No[a]	No[a]	No
Germany	Yes	Yes	No	No	No
Denmark	Yes	Yes	Yes	No	No[b]
France	Yes	Yes	Yes	Yes	No
Norway	Yes	Yes	Yes	No	No
Sweden	Yes	No	No	No	No
Netherlands	Yes	Yes	Yes	Yes	Yes
Spain	Yes	Yes	Yes	Yes	Yes
United Kingdom	Yes	Yes	Yes	Yes	Yes[c]
Greece	Yes	Yes	Yes	Yes	Yes
Hungary	Yes	Yes	Yes	Yes	Yes
Italy	Yes	Yes	Yes	Yes	Yes
Poland	Yes	Yes	Yes	Yes	Yes
United States	Yes[d]	Yes[d]	Yes[d]	Yes[d]	Yes[d]

Notes:
[a] All forms of assisted conception with donated gametes are prohibited with the exception of semen donation in IVF.
[b] Surrogacy in itself is not forbidden, only its procurement. Also, surrogacy contracts are not forbidden but considered legally invalid.
[c] Surrogacy is accepted but specific regulation prohibits commercialization.
[d] Legal in at least some US states.

Source: http://www.gov.gg/childrenboard/pdf/AssistedReproduction.pdf.

assisted reproduction. Even though there is a large market in assisted reproduction services (which uses the genetic components of the couple), there will be no analysis of this medical service market in the chapter.[5] After a brief explanation of the size of the market in assisted reproduction in Section 3, the discussion in Section 4 centres on economic issues in three markets that currently exist: the markets for eggs, sperm and surrogacy. We draw out the issues of supply and demand in these markets, discuss incentives, excess demand, supply price, reservation price, risk and return, property rights and altruism. Section 5 provides a discussion of the ethics of markets in assisted reproduction. Section 6 contains some concluding thoughts.

1   Microeconomics of demand for and supply of children (before reproductive markets)

In *An Essay on the Principle of Population*, Thomas Malthus (1798) was concerned about population change but often used individual incentives to explain the demand for children: 'The labourer who earns eighteen pence a day and lives with some degree of comfort as a single man, will hesitate a little before he divides that pittance among four or five, which seems to be but just sufficient for one.' Economists have since explored in a more nuanced way how people make decisions about having children and the role of economics in such decisions. In Chapter 5, we suggested two reasons why people have children: the biological imperative and the enjoyment children provide. We noted that both factors look the same in a standard economic model because they increase an individual's utility. Let us elaborate on this idea.

In the basic microeconomic theory of the family, the demand for children (how many children and the 'quality' of children a couple desires) typically depends on the preferences of the parents, the relative price of children and income. In the simplest model, a couple will maximize a utility function, $U = f(n, q, Z)$, where n is the quantity of children, q is the quality of children (typically inferred by the time and monetary resources spent on each child for education, health care and so on), and Z is a composite of all other goods, subject to a budget constraint, which might be specified as $p_c\, qn + p_z Z = I$, where p_c is the price of each child, p_z is the price of all other goods and I is income.[6] The higher the price of children, the lower the demand, and the higher the income, the higher the demand for children (children are normal goods).[7]

In general, economists show that couples will trade off quality and quantity of children. Today, most couples choose fewer but higher quality children. Other considerations also arise in these models. For example, higher wage rates for women are negatively related to the demand for children because of the substitution effect between time raising children and time in the labour market as discussed in Chapter 5 (see also Rosenzweig and Schultz, 1985; Becker, 1981; Applebaum and Katz, 1991).

Until recently, understanding the supply of children was simple and not modelled by economists. Most men produce sperm on demand and can potentially produce millions of offspring. Women are born with all the eggs they will ever produce (up to one to two million), and release one at each ovulatory cycle. Fecundity (the probability of conceiving in any menstrual cycle) is exogenous and random. If a couple wanted to have children, then, with some probability, unprotected sexual intercourse would lead to the fertilization of a woman's egg by a man's sperm.

Rosenzweig and Schultz (1985) rue the absence of an integrated framework to analyse both the demand for and supply of children and note that: 'Economists have recognized the joint relevance of biological and behavioral factors in determining fertility . . . but this perception has not been suitably incorporated into the empirical study of fertility.'

2 The evolution of reproductive markets

Today, a prospective parent can go to the Internet, drop a vial of semen from a donor with specific selected characteristics into a 'shopping cart' and have that semen delivered in twenty-four hours. Similarly, one can sift through the profiles and pictures of women who are egg donors and select eggs from women with desired characteristics and arrange an egg delivery. These markets are two segments that loosely fall under the rubric of Assisted Reproduction Technologies (ART), which is a shorthand term for the numerous procedures aided by technology used to produce a baby.[8]

Now the cost of producing children can radically differ among people of similar incomes and values because some prospective parents pay to gain rights to the genetic components that build the child while others do not. How did we get here?

The rise of assisted reproduction is the story of need and technology changing together. The very first artificial insemination (AI) took place in 1790 in Scotland. In that case, a woman was inseminated with her husband's sperm. Until recently, male infertility was a taboo subject and donor insemination (inseminating a woman with sperm from a man who was not her husband) was a well-kept secret. The first known case of donor insemination (DI) occurred in 1884 but was not publicly admitted until 1909. According to David Plotz (2001) the delay was because the case was so shocking:

> Dr. William Pancoast, a professor at Jefferson Medical College in Philadelphia, found that a woman in his care couldn't get pregnant because of her husband's infertility. At the urging of some of his medical students and with the permission of the husband – but not the wife – Pancoast anesthetized her and impregnated her with semen taken from the 'best-looking' student in the class. She never was told what was done to her or that her husband was not her child's father. This kind of subterfuge, made-up-on-the-spot, loosey-goosey standards and reliance on overwilling medical students would become the dismal defining qualities of donor insemination (DI).

Although it was known to be practised throughout the early to mid-1900s, insemination with live sperm was conducted with discretion, or outright secrecy. Women, or couples, made arrangements privately with a doctor. Who was the father of the child? Various laws gave the babies thus produced tenuous legal standing or made them outright illegitimate in most countries. Religious leaders around the world denounced DI in the 1950s. Indeed, little may have changed if it were not for rapid changes in technology in the 1960s and 1970s: the ability to successfully freeze and use sperm later to develop an embryo and the technology to fertilize an egg outside of the body and successfully implant the embryo in a womb. These changes liberated baby production from a specific time and a specific body. Joining these technical abilities was a critical change in law in 1973 in the USA, which stated that the husband of an inseminated woman was the legal father of a DI baby as long as he knew of the treatment.[9]

These, and other rapid changes, resolved a number of issues that had relegated DI to the private arena where there was a fragmented ability to procure the components that produce a baby (we might call this an incomplete market); sperm banks could provide women and their doctors with needed sperm on demand. The public market in sperm was born along with the first sperm bank in the early 1970s. California Cryobank, the longest continuously open public sperm bank in the USA, opened in 1977. Soon after, Baby Louise, the first baby known to have been successfully born after fertilization outside of the body, 'in-vitro', was born in England in 1978. Assisted reproductive technologies, and the markets that accompanied them, took off.

Several historical facts may have sped the development of assisted reproductive technologies. The first is that the baby boom generation, the largest generation in history, reached childbearing age in the 1960s and 1970s; the second is that increasing labour force participation among women led to a delay in childbearing among baby boomers until the ages where infertility was more common; the third is that the resulting soaring demand for adoption, combined with a shortage of children available to be adopted (possibly as a result of the legality of abortion, the availability of birth control, and the illegality of market transactions for babies), left many potential parents without children. Medical procedures to eliminate, reduce or 'get around' fertility problems were guaranteed a large market if ethical and legal quandaries could be eliminated. As we have already noted, such problems were publicly illuminated in surrogacy. Early on, the surrogate's egg was implanted with a commissioning father's sperm. Fears about surrogate mothers who might fight for custody, and a number of court cases where such custody battles took place (raising such legal and ethical questions as, 'Can a baby be owned and, if so, who owns the baby?' and, 'Is surrogacy the same thing as selling a baby?') nearly destroyed the market for surrogacy. But the first known baby resulting from embryo transfer (where the egg was not from the woman in whose womb the embryo was implanted) was born in 1984 and gestational surrogacy, where the surrogate carries a baby that is not genetically hers, became popular (Mathews, 1984). This method made the parentage of the baby clearer, was contractually easier to defend and reduced the prevalence of lawsuits over custody. Indeed, gestational surrogacy, often called 'rent a womb', is now the norm.

After hundreds of court cases relating to various procedures of assisted reproduction, both the law and market regulation (which had lagged behind the market development) have begun to catch up. The Uniform Parentage Act of 2000 in the USA asserts in Article 7, Section 702, that, 'a donor is not a parent of a child conceived by means of assisted reproduction'.

3 Assessing the size of markets in assisted reproduction
How big is the potential market for assisted reproduction (AR)? In the year 2001, there were at least 421 AR laboratories in the USA and surrounding territories.[10] The medical characteristics of fecundity along with the medical, demographic and behavioural characteristics of fertility are appropriate preconditions for a potentially large demand for assisted reproduction. Medical characteristics of fertility include a woman being allergic to her husband's sperm. She is fecund, he is fecund, they just are not fertile together. Demographic characteristics include the decline of fecundity with age. Behavioural characteristics include labour market participation that may be associated with a delay in childbearing until ages when fecundity is low.

According to the Centers for Disease Control (CDC), of the 60 million women of childbearing age in 1995 in the USA, about 13 per cent received an infertility service. If each of these women were to demand some form of assisted reproduction, then, in the USA alone, there are at least 8 million potential customers of assisted reproduction. Including others who have not received infertility treatments but who may desire children (say, women without partners or gay and lesbian couples) the potential demand for assisted reproduction is even greater in the USA.

While the potential demand is large, the potential supply is even larger. Each man and woman carries millions of eggs and sperm, but only demands a few to create children for himself or herself. If each man and woman produced only enough sperm or eggs to satisfy their own demand for children, then there would be very few people willing to enter the market in assisted reproduction as suppliers. But most people have a substantial oversupply of self-produced sperm and eggs. Thus, our biological characteristics set the preconditions for large markets for eggs and sperm to exist. Further, because problems with infertility can originate with either partner or the combination of people in the couple, the size of each market (sperm, egg, surrogacy) is independently potentially large.[11]

We do know that in the USA in 2001, 107 587 procedures were performed by AR as defined by the CDC, resulting in 29 344 live births and 40 687 infants. The AR market is clearly growing. Just between 1996 and 2001, procedures increased by 66 per cent and live births by 101 per cent (CDC, 2003b). It is difficult to assess actual market size from these CDC statistics, however. They do not include pregnancies resulting from sperm donation when the egg is not handled in the laboratory (underestimating the size of the assisted reproduction market), although they do include the medical procedure of assisted reproduction, using the egg and sperm of the existing couple (overestimating the size of the market). Meanwhile, the CDC reports that there were 571 gestational carriers of fresh eggs in 2001 (CDC, 2003b). Unfortunately, there are no statistics on the size of the market in surrogate motherhood.

4 Reproductive markets: thinking about the economic issues

As with any economic analysis, we must consider the determinants of supply and demand in each market. The difference here is that there is not a long history of economic analysis of these markets. What are the main issues that have to be addressed and which economic tools may help us do so? Reproductive markets are characterized by both profit and altruistic motives of suppliers, varying levels of risk associated with both supply and demand, and prices that depend on the characteristics of suppliers and demanders. To investigate these markets, we will use the rare existent article on the subject and the fundamental tools of economics to examine the components of supply and demand. In the following discussion, it will be assumed that contracts (for eggs, sperm or surrogacy services) are traded.

4.1 Supply

Why do people supply their own eggs, sperm or wombs so that others may have a baby? What are the incentives to supply AR contracts? Many authors have written about the multiple incentives of surrogate mothers, egg and sperm donors. Although a host of reasons lie behind any person's decision, when Klock et al. (2003) evaluated nine possible motivations by querying egg donors about the motivation behind their participation, they, like other authors, found that altruism and compensation together were the primary factors.

Because of these dual motives, the markets for eggs, sperm and surrogacy share the common feature that the supply of contracts can be realized through purchase (where legal) or donation. What does the supply curve look like? For the moment, set aside ethical issues in buying and selling such contracts. If their purchase is illegal, and the 'market' supply is restricted by a price equal to zero, then only altruistic suppliers will enter the market (see Figure 10.1).[12] The supply curve (S_1) is a straight horizontal line at $P = 0$ and ends at the quantity of altruistic suppliers of contracts, Q_s. If the demand is no larger than the supply at $P = 0$ (D_1), then a price will never arise, and this 'market' is in equilibrium. Typically, however, demand is at D_2, the market is in disequilibrium, and there is excess demand for contracts.

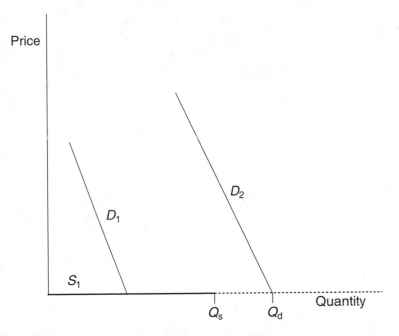

Figure 10.1   A 'market' for AR contracts with donation only

Whether or not they agree that a market is the solution, most authors agree that there is excess demand for assisted reproduction, blood supply and organs (see Ethics Committee of the American Society of Reproductive Medicine, 2000; Harris and Alcorn, 2001; Thorne, 1998). Guerin (1998) writing about sperm donation in France, where, at the time, sperm could only be donated, documents statistics showing that the number of couple candidates for AR with donor semen was six times greater than the number of sperm donors proposing a donation, and up to ten times greater than the number of donors accepted.[13]

There is a growing number of authors who argue that allowing suppliers to be compensated will increase supply, and take care of excess demand. But there is a longstanding controversy over supply behaviour in such markets. If a market emerges in an arena where altruism is an important incentive, then altruists may feel some revulsion (or derive negative utility) when the market emerges and they may refuse to participate. Titmuss (1997) derived supply change predictions when a market for human blood joins a system of donation.[14] It is possible that a market with a positive price could end up with fewer equilibrium contracts traded than one with no price at all! To see this, examine Figure 10.2. Once payment is available, some altruistic donors

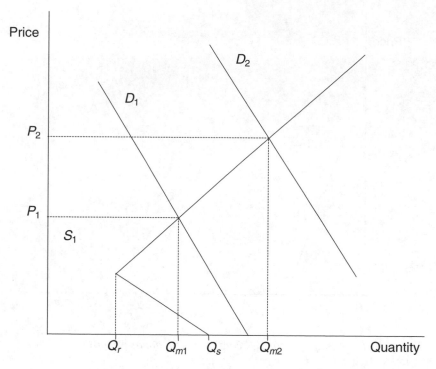

*Figure 10.2   A market for assisted reproduction contracts with a legal
positive price*

$(Q_s - Q_r)$ may withdraw from the market. Others will enter the market once
the price is positive, resulting in the supply curve S_1, that starts at $P = 0$, and
looks like a typical supply curve after the supply of altruistic donors is
exhausted. If the demand curve is D_1, then the equilibrium quantity of contracts is Q_{m1} and the equilibrium price is P_1. But the equilibrium quantity
traded is less than if the price were zero. We believe, however, that D_2 is more
representative of demand, and there is a positive equilibrium price, P_2, and
a traded quantity of contracts, Q_{m2}, that is greater than Q_s.

Hewitson (1997), in her model of surrogate motherhood, derives a supply
curve with these features. In each market (sperm, egg, surrogacy), both altruism and the profit motive are present. What other factors go into the supply
function? Ignoring risk (discussed below) each market requires varying level
of medical, emotional and physical time commitment on the part of donors:

1.   Surrogate mothers must subject themselves to initial medical and psy-
     chological exams, and to significant monitoring and restriction of their

behaviour during the pregnancy. They may experience disutility from the monitoring required in many surrogate motherhood contracts and from the elimination of behaviours that they may enjoy, but are banned through the contract period.[15] Activities that increase utility will lower the supply at each price while activities that reduce utility increase the supply at each price. Further, surrogate mothers may derive utility or disutility from gestating a fetus, birthing a child and surrendering the baby. Finally, carrying a baby to term is a time-intensive activity and, just as in the demand for children, surrogates' value of time will influence supply at every price.[16]

2. Typically, egg donors undergo a several weeks' regime of daily self-injections (hormones to bring more than one egg out during ovulation), a final injection of a different drug to release the eggs, and then an ultrasound and local anesthetic for the egg retrieval. Each of these procedures may reduce utility (and, hence, supply), although the change may be minor.

3. There seems to be little outside of altruism and compensation that determines the supply of sperm. If you think about it, this makes perfect sense. While there are some requirements to be met for sperm donors at the major clinics (for example, they must have an initial physical exam, blood draws to test for diseases, and they may have to commit to a period of participation), donating sperm is a non-invasive activity of minimal time commitment, with essentially no medical risk.

4.2 Demand

Why do people demand sperm, ova or surrogacy contracts and what determines the demand curve? Surprisingly, almost no work has been done on this issue. To the author's knowledge, as of January 2004, there are no published articles in the economics literature on assisted reproduction outside of the Hewitson (1997) article. Looking back to the older literature on the demand for children, however, we can speculate on how the couple's maximization process might be different. Remember that the utility function contains, as its arguments, the number of children, the quality of children, and other goods. In a model of the demand for children via assisted reproduction, the same features will be present with at least two additions. First, the 'quality' argument (money spent on existing children) may now have to be split into post-birth and pre-birth 'quality' considerations. Second, people derive utility from genetic continuity (see Saint-Paul, 2002; Posner and Posner, 1999) and so we might see an additional argument that is some function of the genetic makeup of the couple. Of course, genetic continuity was implicitly present before, but since children were typically self-produced, it was automatic. What that function looks like is not yet known.

However, with assisted reproduction, the level of genetic continuity (genes from both man and woman, from the woman only, from the man only, or from neither) varies as does the price of such continuity. The genetics of the mother and the father may enter the utility function separately. Further, a couple that must include the genetic makeup of another person may want to find a donor who is physically like them (that is, they may want someone of the same race, with the same hair and eye colour, and so on as one member of the couple). In other words, there may be an argument for 'look and feel' genetics. Finally, there are characteristics that are valued by society (intelligence, beauty and so on) that may enter into the utility function. This was explicit, but not exclusive to, the 'genius' sperm bank, which raised many questions about eugenics and designer babies:[17]

> Over the past decade, sperm banks have appeared around the world catering to women clients who care mostly about the physical appearance of the sperm donor. . . . Fortunately . . . a few sperm banks select sperm donors mainly based on achievements and intelligence. Their sperm donor catalogs contain extensive information about sperm donors' scientific discoveries and inventions, published papers and patents, school records, music and artistic abilities, athletic abilities, as well as the usual race and appearance information . . . Genius sperm banks select sperm donors based mainly on achievements and genetic quality rather than based solely on sperm donor appearance, race and sperm quality. They cater to clients who want to improve the intelligence of their child by selecting a sperm donor of superior intelligence and outstanding achievements. (http://www.geniusspermbank.com/)

The demand for children changes markedly under a regime of assisted reproduction when we consider the income constraint. Now, there is a price attached to the birth of each child that was not present before (the additional price of sperm, or egg, or womb and the price of the medical procedures) and there is a price variation attached to the 'quality' of the genetic components (see the discussion on price below). *Ceteris paribus*, children born from assisted reproduction are more expensive than children born the old-fashioned way.

Let us consider just a couple of the implications of these changes in the model. What used to be automatic is no longer so. Couples may now trade off genetic continuity for social value depending on the price. Also, because price can depend on the characteristics of the genetic material, both the price of having a child and the price to produce a certain quality of child at birth can be higher for AR couples (than in the old-fashioned case). Recall that quality in the old-fashioned utility function is produced by money spent on the child after birth. One potential implication of these extra costs to produce a baby is that it is possible that AR couples will have fewer children of lower post-birth quality than other couples with the same income and tastes (ignoring the fact that AR births are much more likely to produce multiple children than old-fashioned births).

4.3 Risk in demand and supply

Risk is a common attribute of reproduction. The probability that a baby will be conceived in any given reproductive cycle (called the 'take home baby rate' in assisted reproduction clinics) is only 20 per cent for couples with past proven fertility and is relatively low in all circumstances of assisted reproduction. The probabilities vary, and are higher for fresh eggs than for frozen (see Table 10.2). Even though the probability of producing a baby is low for fertile couples, in the typical case there is no cost for a couple to attempt to produce a baby in a given cycle through copulation. But every attempt to produce a child costs if using AR. Typical AR procedures include multiple stages and planned monetary payments at each stage. The CDC classifies the AR process leading to a child into five stages: cycles started, retrievals, transfers, pregnancy, childbirth. The total cost varies, but can be many thousands of dollars (and the couple may not end up with a child).

Suppose a couple requires a donor egg to conceive a child. Fertility Alternatives is one egg donor agency that posts fees (the fee structures are remarkably similar across the various agencies). Among other charges (it notes that prices will vary widely), Fertility Alternatives requires a profile fee (US $25), agency fee (US $2500 or 50 per cent of egg donor's fee, whichever is higher), egg donor's fee (US $5000–US $15000), facilitator's fee (US $250), mandatory health insurance fee (US $500), medical screening fee (US $800), attorneys' fees (US $750), and so on. Other expenses

Table 10.2   Probability of a live birth in any cycle

ART procedures	Fresh eggs	Frozen eggs
Non-donor eggs	25.4%	19.5%[a]
Donor eggs[b]	43.3%	23.5%
Gestational carriers		
Non-donor eggs	36.8%	22.6%
Donor eggs	46.1%	32.8%

Notes:
The pregnancy rate per cycle of couples with proven past fertility is approximately 20 per cent (Society for Assisted Reproductive Technology [SART], A Patient's Guide to Assisted Reproductive Technologies, p. 7, http://www.sart.org/TextPatients.htm).
[a] Per thaw.
[b] Per transfer.

Source: ART Statistics from CDC (2003a).

include egg donor travel expenses, lost wages for the donor, all medical expenses incurred by the donor and all costs of the IVF procedure (see http://www.fertilityalternatives.com/ipfeesed.html). Studies that examined various economic costs associated with a successful delivery with IVF around the world were collected in Garceau et al. (2002). Estimated costs (typically payment of fees by patients) ranged from £10 372 in Finland, to £25 499 in Canada, to £52 566 in the United States.

These fees are typically non-refundable if a baby is not produced by the contract. As a question of the economics of childbearing, this risk is critical. First, the cost to 'produce' a child is much higher for a couple that requires assisted reproduction. Second, the budget constraint is likely to have a probabilistic function of childbirth in it (a couple could pay for AR, but not end up with a child, making other payments moot). In the end, it may mean that different prospective parents with the same income and the same desired quantity and quality of children (who will face radically different costs to produce children depending on their AR needs and on the probability of child conception) will have different demands for children. Third, in the USA, all these costs are borne by the prospective parents and none by society. Health insurance still does not cover most AR procedures, and no egg or sperm purchases. In contrast, in France, IVF is fully reimbursed by the social security system; in Belgium, Denmark and Norway, the state bears almost all costs; in England and Wales, some IVF procedures are funded by the National Health System (see Garceau et al., 2002). As a result, AR contracts in the USA will only be demanded by potential parents who have substantial disposable income and who can afford to deal with the probabilistic outcome. Fourth, it is clear that high-income couples will make up the majority of demanders of AR. Since income varies by race and ethnicity, demand will subsequently reflect the race, ethnicity and the tastes of high-income people.

However, as in many markets where the outcome is risky, an insurance market is emerging. Some donor agencies in the USA now offer insurance policies, as do many IVF clinics. They are often called 'shared-risk' programmes.[18] At the moment, these insurance markets carry interesting economic and ethical questions because the insurance market is not independent of the services market. Typically, a client pays a higher fee for IVF by purchasing a policy through the agency. If the procedure is successful, then the agency keeps all fees. If not, a high proportion of the agency's fees (but not, typically, drug costs and other medical costs) is refunded. This results in a funny kind of moral hazard because the agencies themselves provide insurance: 'such programs have a built-in conflict of interest which is likely to skew clinical decision-making toward achieving pregnancy regardless of the impact on the patient in order to avoid paying a refund' (Ethics Committee of the American Society for Reproductive Medicine [ASRM], 2000).

Ethically, many believe that shared-risk programmes violate Opinion 6.01 of the American Medical Association's Code of Medical Ethics, which states that a physician's fee cannot be made contingent on the outcome (ASRM, 2000).

There are many other forms of risk in these markets, which must be considered in any economic analysis. Both surrogate mothers and egg donors face medical risks associated with the egg retrieval, implantation or pregnancy. Often, surrogate mothers lose their compensation under conditions of spontaneous abortion (taking place without any action on the part of the woman carrying the child). At this time, there is no insurance market for surrogate mothers who have gone through arduous medical and psychological testing and procedures, but fail to produce a viable baby.

Some forms of risk in the AR market can be classified as property rights risks. Who has legal rights over the baby that is conceived as a result of a contract?[19] The ways in which the property rights risk manifests itself depends on the specific market. As discussed earlier, in the past, legal disputes typically arose in surrogacy because both the commissioning couple and the surrogate mother desired custody. Sometimes, however, it is because there has been some problem with the baby's physical or mental health and no one wants custody of the baby.

Of course, property rights can get complicated both legally and ethically. In surrogacy, there are potentially five people involved in the creation of the baby: the commissioning father, his wife or partner (who must legally adopt the baby), a sperm donor, an egg donor and the surrogate. The surrogacy market, in particular, is sensitive to issues of risk and agencies spend considerable effort on risk reduction. First, agencies require the commissioning parents to pay for an independent lawyer who looks out for the interests of the surrogate mother. They also advertise whether any specific surrogate has already had a successful surrogate pregnancy (signalling a lower risk of legal disputes later). Finally, they require the commissioning father to pay for counselling sessions, either with a psychologist or in a support group of surrogate mothers. These sessions appear designed to help the surrogate see herself as a temporary caregiver rather than a mother, and this reduces the risk of a custody dispute (Kolczykiewicz, 2003). There has been no such issue for sperm donors (the Uniform Parentage Act of 2000 specifically states that the sperm donor is not the father).[20]

4.4 Putting supply and demand together

How does one think about price in AR markets? Some people may find it uncomfortable to consider prices for men's sperm and women's eggs.

However, as discussed in Chapter 7, economists often work with a concept called hedonic pricing, where an attempt is made to decompose the total price of a product into implicit prices for different traits of that product. So, what are the traits that might be valued in AR markets? Adoption markets (where formal prices are typically illegal) have always been associated with high demand for more desirable characteristics, in particular, race, looks and health (see Kossoudji, 1990). Current advertising still reflects such attitudes:

> The total expense for an adoption depends on such factors as the child's age and nationality/ethnicity, whether the child has special needs, the specific agency you work with, how long you are willing to wait, what complications arise, and (for foreign adoptions) what country you adopt from. You'll usually find that the costs involved in adopting a healthy Caucasian newborn/infant are higher than in adopting a child of other races, children with special needs, or children from other countries. (http://adoptionservices.org/adopting_families_Adoption_Cost. htm)

Assisted Reproduction markets are slightly more complicated, however. The way that firms advertise their product tells us something about what they believe customers desire (and buy). At least one egg donor agency, Tiny Treasures, advertises 'Ivy League egg donors'. Both sperm banks and egg donor agencies on the Internet offer extensive information on their donors.[21] Although each agency is unique in the specific information provided in the profiles, a host of characteristics can be found on each individual donor, related to racial or cultural characteristics (self-reported race, ethnicity, father's and mother's race or ethnicity, religion), physical traits (height, weight, eye colour, hair colour, hair texture, skin tone), health traits (blood type, personality test results, personal medical history, family medical history), and ability traits (level of education, grades, SAT scores, sometimes which university attended, occupation or major at college). Are some of these characteristics worth more than others?

Pricing operates differently in egg and sperm markets. Sperm banks do not typically price an individual donor's sperm. Instead, sperm banks may specialize in donors with particular characteristics. A review of over 30 sperm banks showed a minimum price of US $100 per vial, a maximum price of US $425 per vial, and a mean price across all sperm banks of approximately US $200 per vial.[22] In this sense, sperm banks may operate like firms in a monopolistically competitive industry. There are sperm banks based on religion, ethnicity and achievements. One sperm bank specializes in sperm from gay men and, as noted earlier, one now defunct sperm bank specialized in the sperm of Nobel Prize winners.

There is at least one sperm bank that prices broadly by education (many sperm banks select donors on the basis of education. In fact, of the 1509 donors discussed below, not a single one had not been to college). Fairfax Cryobank charges US $280 for sperm from men with (or earning) doctorates, US $215 for sperm from men without doctorates, but from whom all of the relevant personal information has been collected, and US $135, a discounted rate, for sperm from men who became donors before extensive information was gathered.[23] Given the range of prices by agency, there are two ways that men could have higher sperm prices. First, by having the broad characteristics that bring a higher price within an agency or, second, to sell sperm to an agency whose higher prices reflect a higher overall quality of donor. Without individual variation in prices, it can be difficult to tell which characteristics are desirable. So we use an alternative way to determine the desirability of a donor's sperm. Many sperm agencies publicize whether a man's sperm has already been sold (sometimes listed as resulting in a pregnancy). We will use this selection as a proxy for desirability and assess which characteristics make it more likely that a man's sperm was chosen.

It is far too early to arrive at a definitive decision about the determinants of price in these markets. However, we can present an empirical analysis that is illuminative and absolutely preliminary. As already mentioned, the author collected information on 1509 sperm donors from over 30 sperm banks that advertised on the Internet. From these, 490 had information on a previous pregnancy or selection. Not too surprisingly (given that sperm banks do not individually price sperm) there is almost no characteristic that is associated with a higher or lower sperm price (see Table 10.3). The regression on prices shows that only a graduate education (US $19.83 more than mere college) and height (US $1.91 per inch) are associated with increased prices. This is not too surprising since one sperm bank specifically prices by education.

Surprisingly (assuming selection is a good proxy for desirability), however, only race influences selection. No characteristic explains differences in selection probabilities except for being Asian or being of multiracial heritage (both negative at 5 per cent level of significance).[24] What does this tell us? Racial aspects of the market are unclear. White, African American, Latinos and Native American men are not selected at differential rates. Earlier it was noted that the income distribution may play a large role in determining the tastes of demanders. It may well be that there is racial matching for sperm (people choose sperm from individuals of their own identified race) and that there are fewer demanders of Asian or multiracial heritage (note that this could be an income effect, or a genetic effect – a lower proportion of Asian men, for example, may be infertile). It also raises the possibility, however, that the characteristics of the male do not influence desirability (or that the filters of the various agencies are strong enough to weed out any obviously

Table 10.3   Sperm donor compensation and selection effect of individual characteristics

	Compensation (US$)		Selection
Height	1.91*	(0.82)	0.985
Weight	−0.09	(0.07)	0.999
Graduate education	19.83*	(3.74)	1.283
Eye colour			
brown/black	3.48	(4.95)	1.631
green	4.37	(4.87)	1.538
Hair colour			
brown/black	−2.45	(5.42)	0.780
red	−1.61	(13.16)	1.000
Race			
Latino	−2.94	(11.65)	1.268
Asian	2.89	(6.14)	0.474*
Black	−2.44	(8.78)	1.416
Mixed	16.07	(8.75)	0.358*
N	879		438

Notes:
Standard errors in parentheses. Regression includes a constant: the omitted characteristics are a white, blue-eyed, blond, with a high school diploma. The compensation regression is OLS, and the selection regression is a binomial logit (the reported coefficients are the change in the log odds associated with that variable – a value of 1 means no change, greater (less) than 1 means increased (decreased) probability). Standard errors are not reported for these constructed numbers.
*Significant at 5% level.

undesirable characteristics, and eye and hair colour, weight, height and so on are secondary in decision-making).

Women set their own compensation request at egg donor agencies. This is known as an 'offer' price. We cannot tell how far the final price differs from the offer price because this information is not made public by agencies. In this dataset of over 2000 egg donors, the average compensation request is US $5145, the minimum is US $1800 and the maximum is US $20 000, although we cannot say for sure whether a woman will receive her compensation request. Therefore, the same technique is used for egg donors as with sperm donors (having been already selected is a proxy for desirability).

Table 10.4 shows the same regression results for women as for men. But the results for women are remarkably different. First, education plays the critical role in the compensation request and in the probability of being currently matched. A college education is worth US $448 more than a high school education and a graduate education is worth US $2365 more than a

Table 10.4   Egg donor compensation and selection effect of individual characteristics

	Compensation	Selection
Height	88.43* (34.01)	1.131*
Weight	−14.69* (5.08)	0.967*
Education		
college	448.26* (223.35)	1.499
graduate school	2384.87* (322.68)	4.740*
Eye colour		
brown/black	−263.28 (225.08)	0.669
green	−285.76 (222.70)	0.931
Hair colour		
dark	−217.39 (212.22)	1.170
Race N/A		
N	693	296

Notes:
Standard errors in parentheses. Regression includes a constant: the omitted characteristics are a white, blue-eyed, blonde, with a high school diploma. The compensation regression is OLS, and the selection regression is a binomial logit (the reported numbers are the change in the log odds associated with that variable – a value of 1 means no change, greater (less) than 1 means increased (decreased) probability). Standard errors are not reported for these constructed numbers.
*Significant at 5% level.

high school education (about 15 per cent of egg donors only have a high school education). Further, physical characteristics matter for women. Every extra inch of height brings an additional US $88 while every extra pound reduces compensation by US $15. Selection characteristics are similar: a graduate education increases the odds of being currently matched, as does height. Weight reduces the probability of a match.

Why do a woman's characteristics appear to relate so strongly to price while men's do not? A good part of this result is an artifact of the way that prices are set in the two different markets. But why is there no individual pricing for men, but women set their own price? One reason surely is that removing eggs is a more costly and risky procedure than removing sperm. At the same time, both egg and sperm are just a set of genetic components. Outside of a differential for risk, there is no obvious reason why women set their own price but there is typically undifferentiated pricing for sperm.

While it may be empowering for women to set their own compensation price, it begs the question of the determinants they use to calculate that price. Almost certainly education plays a dual role in egg pricing. It enhances the desirability of a woman's eggs because it proxies intelligence.

It also is correlated with the value of a donor's time (her opportunity cost). It is curious that for men, race appears to influence desirability, but for women, physical characteristics outside of race play a role in the price that a woman sets. Women may be more culturally sensitive to the value of looks. Selection, as a proxy for desirability, shows almost exactly the same results as the price regressions, suggesting that there are some fundamentally sound cultural reasons for setting such price differences.

5　Ethics in assisted reproduction

The previous sections of the chapter function in the realm of positive economics ('How does it work?'), but when we look at ethics, we move into the realm of normative economics ('How *should* it work?'). Ethical arguments about assisted reproduction are rich and varied. There are hundreds, if not thousands, of articles on the big and minute ethical questions raised by AR. Most arguments have to do with the proper scope of the market. Where should the market stop?

First and foremost, people argue that there should be no price put on a human being's body. The argument is against commodification of the person because this way we lose our value as humans. The Human Fertilization and Embryology Authority (HFEA, 1998) claimed just that when recommending that egg donation should be a gift and that payments should be eliminated. Radin (1996), like many, argues that we ought to be inalienable to the market and that commodification is harmful to personhood. Thus, there are 'contested commodities'. Even the language of commodification as part of the discourse is itself harmful. Surrogacy has provided fodder for a number of discussions. Anderson (1990) argues that surrogacy is women's labour, that is, the labour of carrying a baby to term, and if treated as a commodity is degraded. Further, children are reduced to commodities.

Is assisted reproduction tantamount to selling babies? Hirschman (1991) states that AR markets are, 'centered around the production and acquisition of babies – babies in the form of component sperm and eggs, babies in the form of fresh or frozen embryos, . . . and babies as full term living infants'. She argues that, in the end, although such markets are 'morally troublesome', they can be, 'ethically construed as positive if they serve the larger sacred goal of creating families'. Ethical questions often confront religious questions. What makes a family? Who can make a family? What makes a mother or a father?

6　Conclusion

In the end, these ethical questions drive us to a better understanding of ourselves. This debate is crucial to help us determine what to do about market regulations, laws about the permissibility of some markets, and the modes of market organization. At the same time, while we argue ethics, the markets go on, fed by technology, need, altruism and greed. We have outlined here some of the critical features of markets in assisted reproduction. For instance, we know that the potential size of the markets is enormous and that the actual size is growing rapidly. We also know that there are different pricing structures in egg, surrogacy, and sperm markets and that individual prices in the egg market vary markedly by the characteristics of the donor. Further, various forms of insurance have arisen to reduce the impact of risk in the markets. As relatively new markets, we can argue that they follow the basic constructs of economic theory.

What we do not know is why men do not set their own price for sperm, and why physical characteristics are important for egg donor's desirability but not sperm donor's (in either case, 50 per cent of the DNA is contributed by the donor). We also do not have a sense of the changes in social welfare that have emerged from different market organizations. In summary, we do not yet know many of the details of how these markets function, nor what stable equilibria look like in the markets for sperm, eggs and surrogacy.

Understanding the positive and normative issues of markets of today can help us figure out the social and economic consequences of the markets that are coming and the ethical arguments that may support or fall against the development of those markets. Genetic engineering and 'designer babies' are only a step away. As Francis Fukuyama (2002) states:

> even if genetic engineering on a species level remains twenty-five, fifty, or one hundred years away, it is by far the most consequential of all future developments in biotechnology. The reason is that human nature is fundamental to our notions of justice, morality, and the good life, and all of these will undergo change if this technology becomes widespread.

Notes

1. People without partners and gay and lesbian couples are also customers in the market for assisted reproduction.
2. In in-vitro (glass) fertilization, the egg and sperm are combined outside of the body, typically, in fact, in a plastic petri dish. The first baby born from in-vitro fertilization was called a 'test tube' baby.
3. The surrogate contract itself is actually between the commissioning father and the surrogate mother. The man's partner then enters into an adoption contract after the baby's birth.
4. Much of the legal and market information in this chapter focuses on the United States. Laws and regulations are changing every day in this arena and may be different from those portrayed here. Also, laws and regulations continue to differ significantly across countries as does prevalence of use of existing markets.
5. A typical example is when the egg of a woman with blocked fallopian tubes is fertilized with her partner's sperm by IVF, then inserted into her uterus. This market is a market for the medical procedure itself. Hereafter, except where noted, assisted reproduction will refer to the market where some genetic or physical component is purchased rather than the medical procedure itself.

6. There are many microeconomic models of the demand for children, some of them much more complex than this one. For a more in-depth look, *A Treatise on the Family*, by Gary Becker (1981) is a good place to start. Models often differ by whether the couple lives in a more developed or less developed economy.

7. A conundrum arose when wealthier societies began having fewer children and the relationship between income and the number of children appeared to turn negative. This problem was resolved by asserting that a couple cared not just about the number of children in the family but also about the 'quality of children' in the family.

8. The assisted reproduction literature is rife with acronyms and many of the terms do not yet have a clearly determined definition. The Centers for Disease Control (CDC) in the United States may be unique in that AR only includes techniques where both the egg and sperm are handled in the laboratory. CDC bases its definition on the 1992 law that requires it to produce an annual report on success rates at AR clinics. This means that statistics on the size of the market based on CDC success rates omit all DI or AI procedures where only the sperm is handled by the clinic. Unfortunately, CDC is the repository of clinic statistics. Statistics on sperm donation alone do not appear to exist. In this chapter, all procedures are enveloped by AR as specified above, except where specific CDC statistics are cited.

9. The Uniform Parentage Act (1973) attempted to make the laws in all states the same regarding parenthood. There were, and are today, some other conditions on determining the father of a DI baby.

10. 384 reporting to the CDC (Centers for Disease Control and Prevention) as required by law and 37 clinics known to be operating, but not reporting to CDC (see CDC, 2003b, Appendix C). This does not include sperm banks.

11. Statistics on infertility tend to be similar across nations. According to one French study, fertility problems originated with the woman in 38 cases out of 100, with the man in 20 cases, and with some combination of the two in 38 cases. In eight cases, infertility had an unknown source (de la Rochebrochard, 2001).

12. Notice that we ignore the cost of medical services, lawyers and so on. Here we concentrate on the compensation to the supplier of contracts.

13. His argument, however, is that donation could help eliminate excess demand if recruitment were improved.

14. The 1997 volume is an expanded edition of Titmuss's classic 1970 volume, *The Gift Relationship*. Market withdrawal was only one component of the argument. Changes in health risks, among other factors, also play an important role in the debate. Arrow and Titmuss argued about these outcomes. For a summary of the issues, see Thorne (1998).

15. Contracts may specify regular alcohol or drug tests, repeated psychological exams to ensure that the surrogate will willingly give up the baby, and regular medical exams. Surrogate mothers may be banned from extreme physical activity, risky vacations and smoking. A simple sample contract may be viewed at surromomsonline.com. This sample contract includes language such as: '2) The Surrogate agrees not to participate in dangerous sports or hazardous activities, and promises not to knowingly allow herself to be exposed to radiation, toxic chemicals or communicable diseases. 3) The Surrogate further agrees not to smoke any type of cigarettes, drink alcoholic beverages, or use any illegal drugs, prescription or non-prescription drugs without consent from her obstetrician or midwife.'

16. Putting much of this together, Hewitson's supply utility function is $U_i = (\alpha + \beta + \gamma - Mq^*)$ $(\theta + \epsilon R)\,(\Pi + A) - \delta\mu A + p\Pi$ where the terms in the first parentheses are parameters of the (dis)utility of gestating a fetus, birthing and surrendering a child, and the monitoring costs of the optimal child quality, the terms in the second parentheses refer to the surrogate's value of privacy and her propensity to engage in risky behaviours. All these are multiplied by either a profit ($\Pi = 1$) or altruistic ($A = 1$) contract. Both δ and μ are altruism parameters, and p is the surrogate's compensation.

17. The 'genius' sperm bank was actually called the *Repository for Germinal Choice* and was founded by Robert Graham. Only men who had won the Nobel Prize could donate

sperm. More than 200 babies were born from sperm issued by this sperm bank before it went under (see Plotz, 2001).

18. One egg donor agency offers an optional shared-risk policy. In the basic plan prospective parents receive a 50 per cent discount on the agency fee for donor matching and coordination of a subsequent egg donation cycle (US $375). In the premium plan, prospective parents will pay no agency fee for donor matching and coordination of a subsequent egg donation cycle (US $750) (see http://www.tinytreasuresagency.com).

19. In fact, one of the big ethical questions is whether rights should be thought of as property rights (which turns the baby into property – something we ought not to do).

20. My thanks to Mariusz Kolczykiewicz, a former student, for permission to use this surrogacy risk information from a paper he wrote for my class.

21. Some information is free and public on the web, and some must be purchased. The following quote is from one agency: 'California Cryobank (CCB) provides many types of information to help clients select a donor. Long donor profiles, baby photos, audio interviews, Keirsey Temperament Sorter Reports and Facial Feature Reports are available for clients to purchase. Short donor profiles and Staff Impression Reports are available for free' (http://www.cryobank.com).

22. Author's dataset of approximately 30 sperm banks and all of their donors.

23. These prices are for IUI specimens and are correct as of January 2004.

24. This dataset may contain biases that have yet to be understood. The range of information varied by agency so the selection of agencies may influence the results. Age may be a positive factor in selection, as may grades and college scores. Many firms did not advertise the same information. The chosen regression was the one with the largest sample size for men and women with the most comparable variables so that characteristics could be compared. There were not enough egg donors with information about race to construct a comparable regression. When the sperm donors' regressions were run without race, nothing was significant, indicating that race did not substitute for other characteristics. Since sperm prices do not vary by individual, the regression should be considered illustrative only. Finally, there are not reported standard errors in the selection equation because the marginals (changes in the log odds) are reported.

References

Anderson, E. (1990), 'Is Women's Labor a Commodity?', *Philosophy and Public Affairs*, **19** (1), 71–92.

Applebaum, E. and E. Katz (1991), 'The Demand for Children in the Absence of Capital and Risk Markets: A Portfolio Approach', *Oxford Economic Papers*, **43** (2), 292–304.

Becker, Gary S. (1981), *A Treatise on the Family*, Cambridge, MA: Harvard University Press.

British Broadcasting Company (1985), 'Baby for Cash' Deal', 4 January, http://news.bbc.co.uk/onthisday/hi/dates/stories/january/4/newsid_2495000/2495857.stm.

Cannell, Fenella (1990), 'Concepts of Parenthood: The Warnock Report, the Gillick Debate and Modern Myths', *American Ethnologist*, **17** (4), 667–88.

Centers for Disease Control and Prevention (CDC) (2002), 'Assisted Reproductive Technology Success Rates: National Summary and Fertility Clinic Reports', Atlanta, Georgia: US Department of Health and Human Services.

Centers for Disease Control and Prevention (CDC) (2003a), 'Surveillance Summaries', *MMWR*, **200** (3), 52 (No. SS-9).

Centers for Disease Control and Prevention (CDC) (2003b), 'Assisted Reproductive Technology Success Rates: National Summary and Fertility Clinic Reports', Atlanta, Georgia: US Department of Health and Human Services.

de la Rochebrochard, E. (2001), 'Sterility, Fecundity: What About the Men?', *Population and Societies*, Sep, **371**, 1–3.

Ethics Committee of the American Society of Reproductive Medicine (ASRM) (2000), 'Financial Incentives in Recruitment of Oocyte Donors', *Fertility and Sterility*, Aug, **74** (2), 216–20.

Fader, Sonia (1993), 'Sperm Banking: A Reproductive Resource', California Cyrobank, Inc.

Field, Martha A. (1988), *Surrogate Motherhood: The Legal and Human Issues*, Cambridge, MA: Harvard University Press.

Fukuyama, Francis (2002), *Our Posthuman Future: Consequences of the Biotechnology Revolution*, New York: Picador.

Garceau, L., J. Henderson, L.J. Davis, S. Petrou, L.R. Henderson, E. McVeigh, D.H. Barlow and L.L. Davidson (2002), 'Economic Implications of Assisted Reproductive Techniques: A Systematic Review', *Human Reproduction*, **17** (12), 3090–109.

Guerin, J.G. (1998), 'The Donation of Gametes is Possible Without Paying Donors: Experience of the French CECOS Federation', *Human Reproduction*, **13** (5), 1129–32.

Harris, C.E. and S.P. Alcorn (2001), 'To Solve a Deadly Shortage: Economic Incentives for Human Organ Donation', *Issues in Law and Medicine*, Spring, **16** (3), 213–33.

Hewitson, G. (1997), 'The Market for Surrogacy Contracts', *Economic Record*, **73** (222), 212–24.

Hirschman, E.C. (1991), 'Babies for Sale: Market Ethics and the New Reproductive Technologies', *The Journal of Consumer Affairs*, **25** (2), 358–90.

Human Fertilization and Embryology Authority (HFEA) (1998), 'Seventh Annual Report and Accounts', www. hfea.gov.uk.

Klock, S.C., J.E. Stout and M. Davidson (2003), 'Psychological Characteristics and Factors Related to Willingness to Donate Again Among Anonymous Oocyte Donors', *Fertility and Sterility*, **79** (6), 1312–16.

Kolczykiewicz, M. (2003), 'Risk and Compensation in Surrogacy Contracts', mimeo.

Kossoudji, S.A. (1990), 'Pride and Prejudice: Culture in the Labor Market and the Home', in Steven Shulman and William Darity (eds), *The Question of Discrimination: Racial Inequality in the U.S. Labor Market*, Wesleyan University Press, pp. 293–314.

Lundberg, S. (2000), 'Child Auctions in Nineteenth Century Sweden: An Analysis of Price Differences', *Journal of Human Resources*, **35** (2), 279–98.

Malthus, Thomas (1798), *An Essay on the Principle of Population*, London: J. Johnson in St Paul's Churchyard.

Mathews, Jay (1984), 'Boy's Birth is First from Embryo Transfer', *Washington Post*, 4 February, A14.

New Jersey Supreme Court (1988), 'In the Matter of Baby M, A Pseudonym for an Actual Person' (No. A-39. 109 N.J. 396; 537 A. 2d. 1227; 1988 N.J. Lexis 1; 77 A. L. R. 4th 1), 14 September, 1987, Argued, 3 February, 1988, Decided.

Plotz, D. (2001), 'The Rise of the Smart Sperm Shopper', 20 April, *Slate* website.

Posner, E.A. and R.A. Posner (1999), 'The Demand for Human Cloning', *The Hofstra Law Review*, **27** (3), 579–608.

Radin, Margaret Jane (1996), *Contested Commodities*, Cambridge, MA: Harvard University Press.

Rosenzweig, M.R. and T.P. Schultz (1985), 'The Demand and Supply of Births: Fertility and its Life Cycle Consequences', *American Economic Review*, **75** (5), 992–1015.

Saint-Paul, G. (2002), 'Economic Aspects of Human Cloning and Reprogenetics', IZA Discussion Paper No. 608.

Thorne, E.D. (1998), 'When Private Parts are Made Public Goods: the Economics of Market-inalienability', *Yale Journal on Regulation*, **15** (1), 149–75.

Tindall, Harry L. et al. (2000), 'The Uniform Parentage Act 2000', drafted by the National Conference of Commissioners on Uniform State Laws, approved and recommended for enactment by all states.

Titmuss, Richard M. (1997), 'The Gift Relationship: From Human Blood to Social Policy', expanded edition, Ann Oakley and John Ashton (eds), New Press.

Zelizer, Viviana (1985), *Pricing the Priceless Child: The Changing Social Value of Children*, New York: Basic Books.

11 Economics of abortion
Leo H. Kahane

Abortion is an old practice dating back (at least) several thousand years to ancient Egyptian, Greek and Roman civilizations. The procedure continues to be carried out in virtually all societies across the globe and in modern times has become a point of divisive, and at times explosive, social debate. The moral and emotional dimensions of abortion tend to dominate the discussion surrounding the procedure, but over the last several decades economists have carried out research on such topics as the supply of and demand for abortion, the effects of the availability of abortion on crime rates, how abortion has affected the incidence of so-called 'shotgun' marriages, as well as others. The purpose of this chapter is to describe how the methodology employed by economists has been put to work in analysing the topic of abortion in a number of interesting ways.

The layout of this chapter is as follows. Section 1 contains a brief discussion of the procedure, providing some terminology and recent statistics on trends in abortion rates throughout the world. This section is intended to give the reader a sense of the size of the 'market' for abortion services as well as prepare them for the discussion that comes later. The rest of the chapter is divided up into several sections, each devoted to a particular type of economic analysis. Section 2 focuses on the demand for and supply of abortion services and demonstrates how these fundamental tools of economic analysis can be used to understand the workings of the market. Section 3 follows with a discussion of how the availability of abortion services and their legality has had ramifications for other related issues including teen pregnancy rates, the propensity for pre-marital sexual relations, fluctuations in crime rates across time, as well as others. The chapter ends with Section 4, which contains some concluding remarks.

1 Terminology and demographics of abortion
Induced abortion can be carried out at virtually any stage of pregnancy. The earlier the procedure, the greater the variety (and simplicity) of methods available to end the pregnancy. Pregnancies that are less than nine weeks can be terminated with the relatively new drug, *mifepristone*, which was developed and made available in France in 1988 and became known as the 'RU-486' abortion pill. This drug was legalized in Great Britain in 1991, in Sweden in 1992 and in the United States in 2000. More invasive is the method

of uterine evacuation using a vacuum (typically for pregnancies up to 14 weeks in duration). Perhaps the most controversial method of abortion is that of intact dilation and extraction, often referred to as 'partial-birth' abortion in the USA, which involves dilation of the cervix, destruction and removal of the fetus (typically for pregnancies that are 13 weeks or older).

1.1   Abortion usage

As for trends, the use of abortion services varies greatly across countries. Table 11.1 presents data published by the Alan Guttmacher Institute (AGI)

Table 11.1   Worldwide estimated abortions and abortion rates (legal and illegal) (1995)

	Abortions (millions)	Abortion rate (per 1000 women aged 15–44)
World	45.5	35
Developed regions	10.0	39
Developing regions	35.5	34
Africa	5.0	33
East Africa	1.9	41
Middle Africa	0.6	35
North Africa	0.6	17
Southern Africa	0.2	19
West Africa	1.6	37
Asia	26.8	33
East Asia	12.5	36
South Central Asia	8.4	28
Southest Asia	4.7	40
West Asia	1.2	32
Europe	7.7	48
Eastern Europe	6.2	90
Northern Europe	0.4	18
Southern Europe	0.8	24
Western Europe	0.4	11
Latin America & Caribbean	4.2	37
Caribbean	0.4	50
Central America	0.9	30
South America	3.0	39
United States & Canada	1.5	22
Oceania	0.1	21

Source: The Alan Guttmacher Institute (1999, Appendix Table 3, p. 53).

for the estimated number of abortions and the abortion rate in 1995 by region.

As the table reveals, worldwide about 45.5 million abortions were performed in 1995, which translates into an abortion rate of 35 abortions per 1000 women of childbearing age (aged 15–44). Abortion rates are typically highest among women in their early 20s and lowest for women in their 40s. However, defining the *abortion ratio* as the number of abortions per 100 pregnancies, the data suggest that the relationship between this measure and a woman's age is 'U'-shaped. That is, women who are relatively young (for example, less than 20 years old) or relatively old (for example, more than 35 years old) tend to have a greater abortion ratio than those in between (AGI, 1999).

As for geographical differences, the developed regions' abortion rate of 39 is notably higher than the rate of 34 for developing regions. The African continent and Asia have the lowest abortion rates (33) whereas Europe has the highest (48), the latter being noticeably affected by the high Eastern European rate of 90 abortions per thousand women of childbearing age.[1]

Abortion trends across time differ substantially across countries. Throughout much of the world there appears to be a trend towards a lower abortion rate from 1990 to 1996 (AGI, 1999). Table 11.2 reports annual figures for abortions and the abortion rate for England and Wales and the United States and Figure 11.1 plots these abortion rates across time (and includes simple estimated quadratic trends).

As the table and associated figure show, in all locations the numbers and rates increase substantially shortly after court decisions making abortion legal nationally (the Abortion Act 1967 for England and Wales, which came into effect on 27 April 1968 and the *Roe* v. *Wade* US Supreme Court decision in 1973). In the USA, the rate peaks in 1980–81 (with a rate of 29.3) and then declines fairly steadily throughout the following years. The time path for England and Wales is quite different from that of the USA as the abortion rate, following noticeable dips from 1973 to 1977 and again from 1990 to 1995, has shown a rather consistent upward, slowly diminishing trend. It is interesting to note that the gap between the two rates appears to be narrowing.

1.2 Availability of abortion services
Regarding the availability of legal abortion services, this also varies greatly across countries and time.[2] According to Rahman et al. (1998), about 61 per cent of the world's population live in countries that have legalized abortion. Approximately 25 per cent live in countries that prohibit abortions under most circumstances. Concerning numbers of

Table 11.2   *Abortions and abortion rates: England and Wales and USA (1969–2000)*

Year	Number of abortions (thousands)		Abortion rate (abortions per 1000 women aged 15–44)	
	England & Wales*	United States**	England & Wales*	United States**
1969	49.8	–	5.3	–
1970	76.0	–	8.1	–
1971	94.6	–	10.1	–
1972	108.6	–	11.5	–
1973	110.6	744.6	11.7	16.3
1974	109.4	898.6	11.5	19.3
1975	106.2	1034.2	11.1	21.7
1976	101.9	1179.3	10.5	24.2
1977	102.7	1316.7	10.5	26.4
1978	111.9	1409.6	11.3	27.7
1979	120.6	1497.7	12.0	28.8
1980	128.9	1553.9	12.6	29.3
1981	128.6	1577.3	12.4	29.3
1982	128.6	1573.9	12.3	28.8
1983	127.4	1575	12.1	*28.5*
1984	136.4	1577.2	12.8	28.1
1985	141.1	1588.6	13.1	28.0
1986	147.6	1574	13.5	*27.4*
1987	156.2	1559.1	14.2	26.9
1988	168.3	1590.8	15.3	27.3
1989	170.5	1567	15.5	*26.8*
1990	173.9	1609	15.8	*27.4*
1991	167.4	1556.5	15.2	26.3
1992	160.5	1528.9	14.8	25.7
1993	157.8	1495	14.7	*25.0*
1994	156.5	1423	14.6	*23.7*
1995	154.3	1359.4	14.4	22.5
1996	167.9	1360.2	15.6	22.4
1997	170.1	1335	15.8	*21.9*
1998	177.9	1319	16.5	*21.5*
1999	173.7	1314.8	16.1	21.4
2000	175.5	1313.0	16.1	21.3

Sources:
*Office for National Statistics: Abortion Statistics 2001, England & Wales, series AB no. 28.
**The Alan Guttmacher Institute (2003, Table 1, p. 8). Values in italics are estimated by interpolation.

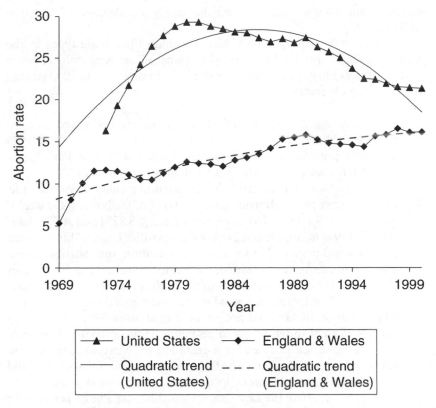

Note: Abortion rate is defined as the estimated number of abortions per 1000 women aged 15–44 years. Estimated equations for the quadratic trends are:

Abortion in US = $-194\,977 + 196.4(\text{Year}) - 0.0494(\text{Year})^2$, $R^2 = 0.765$.
Abortion in England & Wales = $-23\,228 + 23.175(\text{Year}) - 0.0058(\text{Year})^2$, $R^2 = 0.861$.

Figure 11.1   Abortion rates for England and Wales and USA (1969–2000)

providers in countries, data are scarce. However, for the USA, available data show that there has been a marked downward trend. Data for the period 1992 to 1996 show a decline in the number of providers by approximately 14 per cent, nationwide, and an 11 per cent decline from 1996 to 2000. Compared with 1982, when the number of providers in the USA was at its peak, the figure for 2000 shows a decline of approximately 37 per cent during the entire period (Finer and Henshaw, 2003a). As for the reasons for such a decline, there may be several, including greater awareness of contraception and the decreased demand and discouragement of supply due to the activities of those who oppose abortion. We discuss the effects of anti-abortion activities on the supply and demand of abortion in Section 2.

Concerning the kinds of providers, there are three basic types in the United States: hospitals, clinics and physicians' offices. According to Finer and Henshaw (2003b), a survey of 1819 abortion providers in 2000 yielded the following observations:

1. Approximately 95 per cent of all abortions are performed in non-hospital facilities.
2. The mean price for an abortion (over all types of facilities) at a gestation of ten weeks is US $468 (the median being US $370).[3]
3. The price of an abortion rises as the gestation increases. For example, the mean price for an abortion (over all types of facilities) at ten weeks' gestation is US $468, at 16 weeks' gestation is US $774 and at 20 weeks' is US $1179. The principal reason for this positive relationship between gestation and price is that for a greater gestation, the abortion procedure becomes more complicated, time-consuming and requires greater skill. Thus, these increased costs drive up the price for the procedure.
4. As the gestation increases, fewer facilities offer abortions. For example, 90 per cent of all surveyed providers offer abortion services for pregnancies of eight to ten weeks in gestation. However, only 33 per cent will offer abortion services for a gestation of 20 weeks. This inverse relationship is mostly due to the fact that as the gestation increases and the procedure then becomes more complicated (see the last point), fewer providers have the expertise and facilities capable of performing these procedures.
5. In 2001, providers with caseloads of less than 30 abortions per year had a mean charge of US $787 for an abortion whereas providers with a case load between 400 to 990 abortions per year had a mean of US $368 per abortion. The difference implies some economies to scale. These economies, however, apparently diminish rapidly as providers of 5000 or more abortions had a mean price of US $356 per abortion.
6. Approximately 8 per cent of women having abortions in non-hospital facilities had to travel more than 100 miles to the service provider. About 16 per cent travelled between 50 to 100 miles. Travel distance can be a significant barrier to the service as it adds to the overall cost of an abortion. The cost component becomes even more important if the client must make more than one trip. For example, as of 2001, four states in the USA (Louisiana, Mississippi, Utah and Wisconsin) had legislation requiring counselling between the client and the attending or referring physician at least 24 hours prior to the abortion (Finer and Henshaw, 2003b).

2 Abortion as an outcome: demand, supply and the market for abortion services

The powerful tools of economic theory and empirical methods (most notably econometrics) have been brought to bear on the topic of the incidence of abortion in essentially two ways: one with abortion on the left-hand side of the equals sign in an equation, and one on the right-hand side. In the first case, researchers have constructed theoretical models of abortion demand (and, to a lesser degree, supply). In these models, abortion demand is the dependent variable to be explained and is hypothesized to be a function of various explanatory variables. In the research where abortion appears on the right-hand side of the equals sign (that is, as an explanatory variable), researchers consider how the incidence of abortion may be a determining factor of something else. This section deals with the former, having the incidence of abortion as the dependent variable in research. The study of abortion rates as an explanatory measure is the topic of Section 3.

2.1 The basic model of demand (and supply)

The demand for and, to a lesser degree, the supply of abortion services has been researched by many authors (see, for example, Brown and Jewell, 1996; Garbacz, 1990; Haas-Wilson, 1996; Kahane, 2000; Medoff, 1988, 2000). In the case of demand, the antecedent theory draws mainly from Becker (1960, 1965), Mincer (1962, 1963) and the later work of Michael (1973). In these works, fertility control is governed by the expected net benefit of the birth of an additional child. If the net benefit of an additional child is positive, then a fecund couple may seek to increase the number of children they currently have. If the net benefit of an additional child is perceived to be negative, then a couple may seek to prevent the birth of a child using a number of birth control methods, including abortion.[4] Thus, when modelling the demand for abortion, both direct and implicit costs (or opportunity costs) are considered. The typical demand function for abortion services looks something like the following:

Abortion Demand $= f$ (Price, Income, Education, Moral
or Cultural Differences, Marital Status, Other Measures)   (11.1)

Given the lack of data on individual consumers of the service, the bulk of the empirical research considers aggregate demand, usually across time and/or regions. The most common approach is to use state-level data (a single cross-section or panel) for the USA to determine the factors explaining the differences in abortion demand across the states. Indeed, it appears that virtually all of the empirical research estimating demand has been done for the markets in the USA. An exception is one of the earliest empirical studies by Coelen and McIntyre (1978) who model abortion demand in Hungary as part of a simultaneous equations model, which includes the demand for births. Their primary conclusion regarding abortion demand is that pro-natalist policies enacted in Hungary in the late 1950s to late 1970s reduced the demand for abortion, while reductions in abortion costs increased the abortion rate.

Like the Coelen and McIntyre study, most research by economists on abortion does recognize the simultaneous determination of equilibrium price and quantity and thus treats price as endogenous and an instrumental variable method is used to estimate supply and demand simultaneously.[5] The typical equation for supply looks something like the following:

> Abortion Supply = f (Price, No. of Physicians Relative to the
> Population of Women of Child-Bearing Age, Average Hospital
> Costs, Average Wages of Employees in Physicians' Offices)   (11.2)

In equation (11.2), supply is assumed to be positively related to the price of an abortion and the availability of those capable of performing an abortion, but negatively related to input costs proxied by the average cost of a day in the hospital and the wages of employees working in physicians' offices. In some cases, average travel distance to a provider or the geographic concentration of providers is used to capture supply.

The most common measure of abortion demand and supply is the aforementioned abortion rate, equal to the number of abortions per 1000 women of childbearing age (15–44 years old). A second measure frequently used, referred to as the abortion ratio, is the number of abortions per 1000 pregnancies of women of childbearing age. There are slightly different interpretations between these two measures. In the case of the former, changes in the abortion rate may be due to a variety of factors, including greater knowledge and usage of contraception. In the latter, however, contraception is not an issue since in this case conception has already occurred. In any case, the bulk of the empirical research finds qualitatively similar results for the two measures of abortion demand.

There are several points of consistency for much of the research on abortion demand; Table 11.3 provides a summary of some selected results. All of the research finds that the law of demand (that is, there is an inverse relationship between the price of an abortion and the quantity of abortions performed) is upheld.[6] Most research finds the estimated price elasticity of demand to be less than one (in absolute terms) which, as microeconomics teaches us, is not usually consistent with profit maximization.[7] Given the nature of abortion and the kinds of institutions that provide the service, the

Table 11.3   Summary of estimated price and income elasticities of
abortion demand for selected research

Article	Price elasticity	Income elasticity
Garbacz (1990)	−0.68	0.84
Gohmann & Ohsfeldt (1993)	−0.91[*]	0.76[*]
Kahane (2000)	−0.75	1.96
Medoff (1988)	−0.81	0.79
Medoff (2000)	−0.62	1.25

Notes:
Demand is measured using the abortion rate, that is, number of abortions per 1000 women, aged 15–44.
*Gohmann and Ohsfeldt (1993) find a range of price elasticities, some greater than 1, for various models estimated. Their findings indicate that the price elasticity appears to be sensitive to model specification. The value reported in this table is for their pooled, two-stage least-squares model.

less than a profit-maximizing price is likely intended to make the service of abortion available to a wider consumer base. It should be noted, however, that a sizeable portion of the industry is not-for-profit, which includes Planned Parenthood, one of the largest groups of providers in the USA.

Income is present in most of the studies and the results are remarkably consistent: abortion is a 'normal good' (or service) as income repeatedly turns out to be positive and statistically significant. This result is consistent with the hypothesis coming from earlier theory on fertility (noted above) that women earning greater income and who become pregnant may find that the opportunity cost in terms of lost income (to them or their family) from having an additional child is too great and as such may choose to terminate a pregnancy in order to avoid those costs. Some studies (for example, Haas-Wilson, 1996; Kahane, 2000; Medoff, 1988) include women's labour force participation rates as another proxy for opportunity costs due to childbirth.

Education is also present in many studies, but in this case opposing theories exist. Education, typically measured as the percentage of women of childbearing age with a high-school degree (or perhaps college education), may serve as another proxy of opportunity costs to childbirth. Women with greater education may have more satisfying careers that may have to be put on hold in the event of childbirth. This opportunity cost may encourage women with greater education to terminate their pregnancies so as to avoid any stoppage in their career, thus we would expect the demand for abortion to be positively related to education level. On the other hand, women who are better educated are more likely to be better aware of methods of contraception and would experience fewer unwanted pregnancies, thus reducing the abortion rate. The ultimate, net effect is an empirical question. The research by Kahane (2000) and Medoff (2000) come to different conclusions with the former finding a positive yet insignificant relationship and the latter finding a negative and weakly significant relationship.[8]

In order to consider how differences in moral or cultural views of abortion affect the demand for abortion, several proxies have been employed. Two controls that are commonly used are the racial composition (for example, the percentage of a state's population that is non-white) and relative membership in certain religions that openly oppose abortion (for example, the numbers of Catholic, Southern Baptists, Evangelists and Mormons, relative to state population). The former proxy is motivated by the fact that, controlling for income differences, non-white women have historically greater abortion rates, implying some cultural differences regarding the issue of abortion. This control for race typically returns a positive and significant coefficient in abortion demand regressions. As for the control for religion, one would expect a negative coefficient. The reasoning behind this expectation has to do with the idea that individuals who are adherents to a religious faith that opposes abortion will more likely themselves have a moral aversion to, and hence a lower demand for, abortion services, all else equal. Empirical results, however, typically show insignificant effects of religious membership on abortion demand.

Last on the list of common controls is the measure of marital status. It is argued that single women are more likely to terminate a pregnancy since it is expected that single mothers would likely bear greater costs (direct and indirect) to having and caring for a child than married mothers, all else equal. This control, however, has found only weak empirical support.[9]

2.2   Public subsidies, consent laws and issues of access

One of the common variables to appear in the category of 'other measures' has to do with public subsidies for abortion. Following the 1973 *Roe* v. *Wade* US Supreme Court case, which made abortion legal in the United States, the US Congress passed the Hyde Amendment in 1976, which prohibited the use of federal funds (through the federal medical insurance programme, Medicaid) to pay for abortions under most circumstances.[10] A collection of states, however, decided to provide state funds for the procedure under most circumstances.[11] Given this 'natural experiment', a number of researchers have investigated the effects of how differing access to public funds affects abortion rates across states. The predicted effect is straightforward: public funds serve as a subsidy for the service and, *ceteris paribus*, this would increase the demand for the service. The increase would arise due to substitution effects as well as perhaps income effects. That is, the effect of the subsidy would be the possible switching of women from other contraceptive measures (including abstinence) to using abortion as a means of preventing unwanted pregnancies. In addition, the subsidy would lower costs, thus making the procedure more affordable and possibly cause an increase in demand. These predictions are borne out, albeit weakly, by the research. The results of most of the statistical analyses that control for availability of state funding of abortions find a direct relationship between states that do provide funds and the abortion rate. The statistical robustness of this result, however, is somewhat mixed: Levine et al. (1995), Medoff (1988, 2000) and Haas-Wilson (1996), for example, find a statistically significant, positive relationship, whereas Haas-Wilson (1996) and Kahane (2000) find a positive, yet statistically insignificant relationship. Given the consistency across studies of positive relationships, however, one may presume that public funds tend to increase abortion rates, all else equal.

Another issue that lands itself into the 'other measures' category has to do with legal impediments to abortion access for minors that have been put in place by state legislatures. While the 1973 *Roe* v. *Wade* decision interpreted the constitutional right to privacy to include a woman's right to terminate a pregnancy, the Supreme Court did permit states to enact various laws restricting or regulating a woman's access to abortion. The 1989 *Webster* v. *Reproductive Health Services* (492, US 490) case and the 1992 *Planned Parenthood of Southern Pennsylvania* v. *Casey* (112, S. Ct. 2791) case allowed states to enact laws requiring parental consent for minors and mandatory 24-hour waiting periods for women seeking abortions when these laws do not pose an 'undue burden' on women. As of 1993, 23 states had laws in place (NARAL, 1993).[12] The expected impact on abortion demand is obvious: the laws are intended to reduce the number of abortions by increasing the opportunity cost of an abortion both emotionally (by involving the minor's parents in the decision) and legally (in the case where a judicial bypass of the law is sought).

The empirical question presented by these access laws is whether they have been successful in significantly reducing the number of abortions performed. The results of various research papers on this issue are, for the most part, in agreement: parental consent laws do indeed reduce abortion rates. As an example, Ohsfeldt and Gohmann (1994) write, 'Parental involvement laws appear to reduce the adolescent abortion rate relative to the abortion rate of older teens or adults not subject to the laws. "Best Model" estimates imply that such laws reduce the adolescent abortion rate by about 18 percent, other things equal'. Haas-Wilson (1996) concurs, estimating a reduction between 13 to 25 per cent.

Another of the 'other measures' considered has to do with the effects of anti-abortion activities. Several of the papers cited earlier (for example,

Haas-Wilson, 1996; Gohmann and Ohsfeldt, 1993) estimate fixed-effect models in an attempt to control for 'unobservable effects' such as anti-abortion sentiment that may differ across states. Kahane (2000), however, attempts to capture these effects more directly. Using cross-section data for the 50 states in the USA in 1992, he estimates both supply and demand functions using a two-stage least-squares procedure. An independent variable included in both functions is the percentage of clinics that had experienced picketing with physical blocking or contact between clients and protestors or service providers and protestors.[13]

The hypothesized effect of anti-abortion activities is rather straight-forward: other things equal, states where clinics experience greater

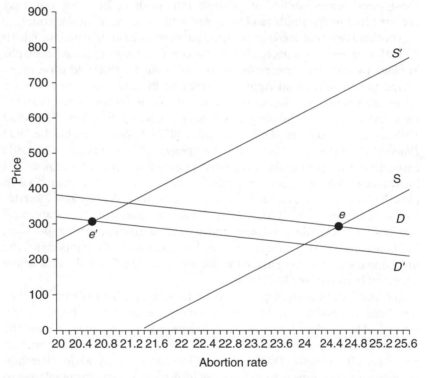

Note: The S' and D' are the location of the curves when the effects of anti-abortion activities are included in the regression. The label e' is the new equilibrium after the shifts, with e being the equilibrium before the shifts.

Source: Kahane (2000).

Figure 11.2   The estimated effects of anti-abortion activities on the supply and demand curves for abortion services

anti-abortion activities (as measured) would tend to have a reduced demand and supply. Under this assumption, both the demand and supply curve shifting left would work to reduce the equilibrium quantity of abortions performed, with the equilibrium price being indeterminate and depending on the relative size of the shifts in the supply and demand curves as well as their slopes. The estimated equations suggest that anti-abortion activities did significantly reduce both supply and demand leading to a reduction in the equilibrium quantity by about 19 per cent and raising price by about 4.3 per cent. The estimated demand and supply curves, with and without the anti-abortion effects, are shown in Figure 11.2.[14]

2.3   Other related issues of abortion demand
There are obviously a myriad of factors that govern the demand for abortion. Some of these reasons extend beyond the modelling of supply and demand considered above. For example, China in the early 1980s attempted to control population growth by mandating a one child per family policy coupled with a forced abortion policy for any woman who had an unauthorized pregnancy and sterilization for couples with two or more children (see Graham et al., 1998). Further, in some countries (for example, China, Korea, Bangladesh) male children are apparently more desirable than female children. The reasoning behind this preference is that some parents view their children as a source of support as the parents age, coupled with the notion that male children are more likely to better support their parents later in life than are female children. Furthermore, male children will carry on a family name. There is some evidence, in fact, that for these reasons abortion has been used as a means for achieving such sex preferences of children (see, for example, Bairagi, 2001). Future research that considers abortion demand across countries would need to incorporate such cultural differences into the model.

3   Abortion as a cause: the effects of abortion availability on fertility, premarital sex, shotgun weddings and crime

Another fascinating application of economics modelling using abortion is where measures of abortion (usage or availability) enter as an explanatory variable in models explaining other issues. That is, abortion appears on the right-hand side of the equals sign. This section summarizes a few of the more interesting research papers using this approach.

Key to analysis of this kind is the requirement that there be sufficient variation of abortion access (and, hence, cost) in order to examine the effects of such changes in access on various dependent variables of interest. Fortunately, from the standpoint of the researcher looking for data, a variety of policy changes affecting abortion access have occurred in the

USA over the past four decades. Furthermore, there were significant changes in abortion policy in other parts of the world, especially in Eastern Europe during the 1950s. These events have created the kind of 'natural experiment' necessary for the testing of several interesting hypotheses described below.

3.1   Abortion access and fertility

The availability of abortion services increases the options women face regarding pregnancy resolution. Faced with the reality of being pregnant, a woman who chooses to abort the pregnancy may have instead given birth had abortion services not been legally available (with illegal abortion remaining a possibility). Thus, the seemingly obvious result is that fertility rates would tend to fall in places where abortions have become legal, other things equal. Furthermore, a second consequence of legalized abortion may be that the use of contraception may decline as abortion becomes a substitute for contraception. Both of these issues were, in fact, studied in an early research paper by Frejka published in 1983.

Following the Soviet Union, where abortion was legalized in 1955, many of the countries in Eastern Europe made abortion legal a few years later. Using data on abortion rates in Eastern Europe from the mid-1950s to the late 1970s, Frejka analyses the effects of abortion liberalization on fertility rates and use of contraception. He concludes that the greater availability of abortions led to an increase in abortion use, a significant drop in fertility and a reduced usage of contraception. In one of his more striking examples, Frejka notes that for Romania the number of annual abortions increased from 578 000 to 1 115 000 between the years 1959 to 1965 (abortion was made available on demand in Romania in 1957). During the same period, the number of annual births declined by approximately 90 000.[15]

In the United States, beginning with the legalization of abortion in the state of Colorado in 1967, a total of 19 other states had followed suit by 1972 (Klerman, 1999). The 1973 *Roe* v. *Wade* US Supreme Court decision made abortion legal in all states, thus increasing overall access. The subsequent passage of the Hyde Amendment in 1976 (see Section 2 above), however, effectively allowed the decision of whether public funds will be used to subsidize the cost of an abortion to be made at the state level. This has resulted in differing restrictions on the public financing of abortions across states. Finally, the enactment of teen parental consent laws in some states, which were put in place and enforced beginning in the late 1980s to early 1990s, has led to variation in abortion access. Jacob Klerman, in his 1999 article, uses these policy changes to explore the effects of abortion access on fertility of women in the USA.

Employing individual-level birth certificate data, Klerman considers how the effects of abortion legalization and variation in Medicaid funding may have affected fertility rates across different racial and age groups. Using a 'difference-of-difference'[16] regression approach he finds some interesting results, including the following: in the case of legalization, legal access led to a moderate reduction in fertility among white women of about 2 per cent (with a greater reduction for women in their 20s as compared with women in their 30s). The data for black women revealed no statistically significant pattern resulting from abortion legalization.

With regards to the variation in Medicaid funding for abortion, Klerman finds that the changes in the availability occurring in the period 1982–92[17] led to the following effects: availability of Medicaid funding had a large, negative effect on the fertility of black women (approximately a 10 per cent reduction in births) with an even larger effect on higher-order births to women in their 20s (approximately a 15 per cent reduction). The pattern is similar for white women, yet smaller in size (for example, an estimated 3 per cent reduction for higher-order births to women in their 20s).

Finally, using his estimated model, and disaggregated data for 1992 (the last year's data in his dataset) Klerman estimates the effects of elimination of legalization and Medicaid funding on the total fertility rate (TFR). Starting with a base case of legalization and full funding he finds that for white women, ending Medicaid funding would increase the TFR by about 2 per cent and making abortion illegal would increase the TFR by an additional 3 per cent. For blacks, the numbers are considerably larger: ending Medicaid funding would lead to a predicted 10 per cent increase in the TFR and making abortion illegal would lead to an additional 5 per cent increase in the TFR.

3.2 Endogenous pregnancy

One of the implications of Frejka's 1983 work is that the variation in the availability of abortion services may lead to changes in the sexual behaviour of women, such as the usage of contraception. This idea can be extended to the very issue of pregnancy itself. That is, contrary to the perhaps more common view where pregnancy is treated as exogenous and the pregnancy resolution is then considered, pregnancy may in fact be endogenous. Thomas Kane and Douglas Staiger explored this issue in the 1996 research paper on teenage motherhood and abortion.

The hypotheses developed in Kane and Staiger (1996) are, in many ways, intuitive and are nicely summarized in the following passage from their paper:

> Our simple model assumes that women get information during the early months of pregnancy, and abort the pregnancy if the birth turns out to be unwanted

based on this new information. Given the majority of teen pregnancies are conceived out of wedlock, the father's willingness to marry is an obvious example of such information. Contraception and abstinence decisions are made only on the basis of information available before pregnancy occurs. In contrast, the abortion decision is made with the benefit of new information. Abortion (unlike contraception or abstinence) works as an insurance policy to limit the downside risk when that information is negative. Increasing the cost of abortion increases the cost of this insurance policy and discourages women from becoming pregnant. Some of these pregnancies would have resulted in births, so the model implies that an increase in the cost of abortion results in a decline of wanted births. Of course, there is a second more conventional effect as the increased cost of an abortion discourages some women from aborting unwanted pregnancies. Thus, the net effect of any restriction of abortion access on birthrates is ambiguous and, in the end, an empirical question.

The dynamics of the above hypothesis are represented diagrammatically in Figure 11.3. The figure shows a simple, sequential decision-making scheme, which begins with the question of whether a woman is involved in sexual relations. Given the woman is having sex, the possibility of pregnancy arises. If a woman having sex has become pregnant, then a decision must be made of carrying the pregnancy to full-term and giving birth or aborting the pregnancy, *if abortion is easily available* (the dashed arrow represents this latter conditionality). It is at this point in the scheme, where a decision to proceed to birth or abort the pregnancy is needed, that the woman may gain information that could affect her decision. According to Kane and Staiger, easy access to abortion gives women a low-cost 'insurance policy', which reduces the risk associated with having sex, that risk being birth from an unwanted pregnancy. This reduced risk then in fact may increase the frequency of sexual relations, represented by the dashed, curved line flowing back to the top of the diagram. Greater sexual relations would likely lead to greater unplanned pregnancies, of which some may result in birth as women, at the decision juncture for birth vs. abortion, receive new information that leads them to choose birth. Thus, we have an example of an 'insurance policy' leading to moral hazard. At the same time, if the option of abortion becomes more costly (or even eliminated), the 'encouragement' factor of abortion (that is, the dashed curve flowing back to the sex decision) is lessened (or eliminated), thus reducing sexual activity, reducing the occurrence of unplanned pregnancies and this may work to reduce the birthrate. At the same time, those unplanned pregnancies that *do* occur are now more likely to end up in birth. Thus, these two factors work in opposite directions and the end result on the birthrate is ambiguous.

In order to test the above hypotheses, Kane and Staiger use US county-level data for 14 years (1973–88) and consider the effects on the above dynamics of changes in the geographic availability of abortion (as proxied

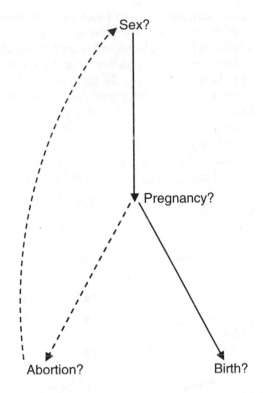

*Figure 11.3   Sequential decision-making of pregnancy and pregnancy
            resolution*

by travel distance to the nearest provider), the availability of Medicaid
funding and the imposition of parental consent laws for minors on the
birthrates of teenage mothers.[18] They find that restricting access to abortion leads to a small, but statistically significant *decline* in the teen birthrate,
with the bulk of the decline occurring for in-wedlock mothers. As an
example of their results, they find that by increasing the distance to the
nearest provider by 25 miles leads to an estimated 1 per cent reduction in
the teen birthrate among in-wedlock mothers.[19]

3.3   Abortion and shotgun weddings
The discussion in the previous section touched on the possibility that the
availability of abortion may result in the change in behaviour of women
with regard to their sexual activity. This issue is also the topic of a very
interesting (and often cited) 1996 paper by Akerlof et al. The motivation

for their paper can be understood by considering a few numbers. Between the periods 1965–69 to 1980–84, the percentage of out-of-wedlock births increased by 154 per cent for whites and by 64 per cent for blacks. Over the same periods, the incidence of 'shotgun weddings' (that is, marriage occurring after pregnancy begins, but before the birth of the child) decreased by 25 per cent for white women and by 48 per cent for blacks.[20] Figure 11.4 shows these trends over the entire period, at five-year increments. The questions that emerge are whether there is a linkage between these trends, and what might be driving these changes.

The response by Akerlof et al. to these questions is that the availability of abortion may be (at least partly) responsible. During the same periods,

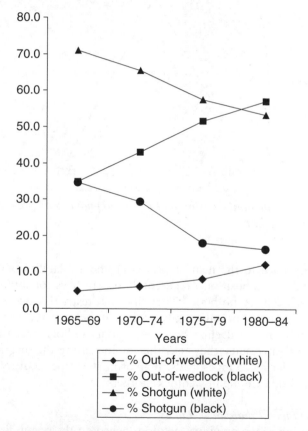

Source: Tables I and II from Akerlof et al. (1996).

Figure 11.4   Out-of-wedlock births and shotgun weddings, by race (1965–69 to 1980–84)

the number of abortions among unmarried women aged 15 to 44 increased from 88 000 in 1965–69 to 1.27 million in the period 1980–84. How may these trends be related? The relationship can be understood by viewing Figure 11.5 (which is a more elaborate version of Figure 11.3). The sequential decision-making process begins with the woman's decision of whether to engage in premarital sex or not. An affirmative answer leads us down the tree to the potential outcome where a woman has become pregnant and then must consider carrying the pregnancy to term or aborting it, *if abortion is easily available*. According to Akerlof et al., the legalization of abortion led to a change in the ability of a woman to withhold premarital sex from men. This is due to several forces. First, women who are willing to choose abortion in light of pregnancy are perhaps more willing to engage in premarital sex (here, abortion acts as the 'insurance policy' referred to by Kane and Staiger, 1996). Second, these women may be less likely to demand a promise to marry, in the event of pregnancy, as a precondition for premarital sex. Both of these possibilities then put pressure on other women because of competition from women who do not require a promise to marry. As Akerlof et al. put it, 'those women who are not willing to use contraception or obtain an abortion will also engage in [premarital] sexual activity, since they correctly fear that if they abstain their partners would seek satisfaction elsewhere'.

Adding to this, Akerlof et al. point to the possibility that a man, with the availability of abortion, may feel less compelled to marry a woman who has become pregnant. That is, according to Akerlof et al., 'the man reasons: "If she is not willing to obtain an abortion or use contraception, why should I sacrifice myself to get married?" ' Thus, their model is consistent with the observed decrease in shotgun weddings.

According to Akerlof et al., the 'technology shock' of the availability of contraceptives and particularly of abortion (shown by the dashed arrow in Figure 11.5) may have had the effect of increasing the incidence of premarital sex (shown by the dashed curve in Figure 11.5), increasing out-of-wedlock births and reducing shotgun weddings. Their model's predictions are consistent with the historical data. Furthermore, they are somewhat supported from survey results conducted with students.

3.4   *Abortion and crime*
As discussed in Chapter 4, the USA witnessed a marked drop in crime during the early 1990s. Tracking the incidence of crime from 1973 to 1991, Donohue and Levitt (2001) find that violent crime increased by about 80 per cent, property crime increased by about 40 per cent with the murder rate being essentially unchanged. Following 1991, however, these rates were dramatically reduced by about 30 per cent in the first two categories, and

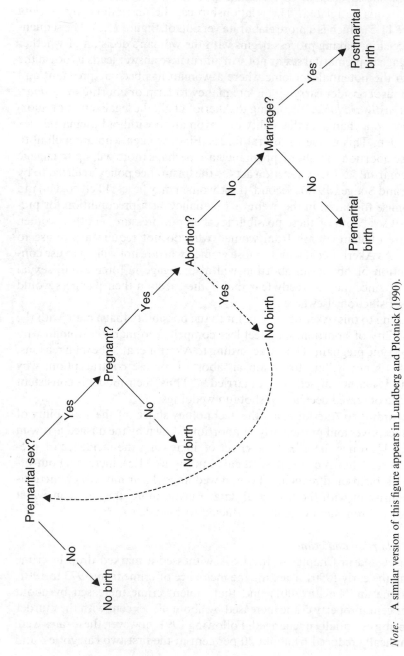

Note: A similar version of this figure appears in Lundberg and Plotnick (1990).

Figure 11.5 Sequential decision-making of premarital sex, abortion, marriage and childbirth

by approximately 40 per cent for murder. In search for a reason for this dramatic turnaround in crime rates, Donohue and Levitt (2001) postulate that a significant portion of the decrease may be due to the legalization of abortion. The mechanism by which abortion may reduce crime has two components: increased abortion may reduce the size of future cohorts of teenagers (who are more likely to commit such crimes), a sort of 'volume' effect. Second, it may reduce the birthrate of children who may be born into an environment that produces teenagers who have a greater propensity to commit crime, a sort of 'quality' effect. Their basic hypothesis on the latter effect is summarized in the following quotation from the Donohue and Levitt paper:

> children born after abortion legalization may on average have lower subsequent rates of criminality for either of two reasons. First, women who have abortions are those most at risk to give birth to children who would engage in criminal activity. Teenagers, unmarried women, and economically disadvantaged are all substantially more likely to seek abortions. Recent studies have found children born to these mothers to be at high risk for committing crime in adolescence . . . Second, women may use abortion to optimize the timing of childbearing . . . [with the result being that] children are born into better [home] environments and future criminality is likely to be reduced.

To say the least, this hypothesis has met with considerable controversy. In support of their position that in the absence of abortion, children that would have been born would have faced more difficulties, Donohue and Levitt appeal to the research of others, notably the work of Gruber et al. (1999). These authors find that the marginal child not born because of abortion would have grown up in a considerably adverse environment, in comparison with the average child. They estimate that the marginal child would have been 60 per cent more likely to be brought up in a single-parent household, would be 50 per cent more likely to be born into poverty, would be 45 per cent more likely to live in a household receiving welfare and have a 40 per cent greater chance of dying before the age of one (Gruber et al., 1999). A recent related paper by Bitler and Zavodny (2002) finds a negative relationship between legalization of abortion and incidence of child abuse.

Levitt and Donohue test their hypothesis empirically regressing state-level crime on the 'effective legalized abortion rate' (appropriately lagged) and a variety of other control variables using data for the period of 1985 to 1997.[21] This period is chosen so as to allow children born *after* legalization of abortion to have time to become teenagers, an age where the commencement of criminal activity is most common. Under their theory then, children born in 1985 or later would have faced the possibility of abortion when they were conceived. Because these pregnancies were not aborted, however, means that these children were more likely to be 'wanted' and were more likely raised in a better home environment, with the end result being lower criminal behaviour. The 'effective legalized abortion rate' is computed as a weighted average of the abortion rate across previous years with the weights being computed as the proportion of total arrests in a given year (for a given crime category) attributed to the age group of the cohort in question. Donohue and Levitt reason that such a measure is appropriate since the effects of the abortion rate on criminal activity (if any) would be gradually felt as the cohort ages and enters into the age where criminal activity typically begins.[22]

Their results are the following: in states where the abortion rate was higher in the 1970s and 1980s, the drop in crime was greater than in states where the abortion rate was lower. Further, in the five states (Alaska, California, Hawaii, New York and Washington) that made abortion legal in advance of the *Roe* v. *Wade* 1973 decision, the drop in crime commenced earlier. These results are consistent with the theory that the increase in the availability of abortion led to a drop in the crime rate. Donohue and Levitt estimate that an increase in the effective abortion rate by approximately one standard deviation reduces violent crime by about 13 per cent, reduces property crime by about 9 per cent and reduces the murder rate by about 12 per cent. Further, they note:

> Extrapolating our results out of sample to a counterfactual in which abortion remained illegal and the number of illegal abortions performed remained steady at the 1960s level, we estimate that . . . crime was almost 15–25 percent lower in 1997 than it would have been absent legalized abortion.

An impressive result that seemingly provides an answer to the question of why crime rates fell dramatically in the early 1990s.

The paper by Donohue and Levitt has come under scrutiny, however. Several authors have responded with their own research that *seems* to controvert the work of Donohue and Levitt.[23] In particular, the research by Lott and Whitley (2001) not only challenges the findings of Donohue and Levitt, but in fact finds in their own analysis that legalizing abortion has had no significant effect on crime with the exception of murder, which they estimate may have *increased* following legalization of abortion.

The centrepiece to the theoretical counter-argument in the paper by Lott and Whitley is simply an appeal to the previously discussed research of Akerlof et al. (1996). Recalling one of the theses of that paper, increased availability of abortion may have the effect of increasing the incidence of out-of-wedlock births, the opposite prediction to that proposed by Donohue and Levitt, which may thus have the effect of an *increase* in criminal activity. With competing theories, each of which may be at work at the same time, the net result is an empirical issue.

Lott and Whitley are also critical of the empirical execution of Donohue and Levitt. Specifically, they argue that Donohue and Levitt's use of aggregated data along with their 'effective abortion rate' measure, inadequately links abortion and crime to specific cohorts of individuals across time (see Note 22). Furthermore, Lott and Whitley criticize the approach of Donohue and Levitt, who implicitly assume that no abortions were being performed in states other than the early legalizers in the pre-*Roe* v. *Wade* period; Lott and Whitley provide evidence to the contrary. In their own empirical analysis, which they argue more closely links cohorts to crime and abortion[24] and which includes abortion rates of states other than the five early legalizers, they come to the following conclusion:

> There are many factors that reduce murder rates, but the legalization of abortion is not one of them. Of the over six thousand regressions that we estimated . . . only one regression implied even a small reduction in murder rates. All the other estimates implied significant if very small to modest increases in murder rates: legalizing abortion would increase murder rates by around 0.5 to 7 percent.

The work of Lott and Whitley does seem to cast doubt on the findings of Donohue and Levitt. To date, Donohue and Levitt have not issued an official written response. They have apparently, however, managed to replicate the results of Lott and Whitley. They have also discovered that the Lott and Whitley results are highly sensitive to the chosen regression model employed (Lott and Whitley estimate Poisson regressions). Using other, less restrictive regression models (for example, the negative binomial) and not lumping everyone over 30 into one group (as Lott and Whitley do) Donohue and Levitt find that they get back to their original result, that abortion had significantly reduced crime.[25] In summary, the evidence seems to weigh in favour of the Donohue and Levitt thesis, but clearly more work on this topic is warranted.

4 Conclusion

There are perhaps few social-political-economic issues more divisive than that of abortion. On 5 November 2003, President George W. Bush signed into law the Partial Birth Abortion Ban Act of 2003. The ban, which is aimed at ending a controversial type of late-term abortion described in Section 1, had earlier passed in the US House of Representatives and the Senate in lopsided votes (282 to 139 in the House and 64 to 33 in the Senate). Prior to signing the ban, President Bush noted that the bill represented, 'an important step toward building a culture of life in America'. Proponents of abortion fear that the bill moves the nation one step closer to eliminating a woman's right to seek abortion. The ban has already met with a legal challenge as the day after the signing of the bill a federal judge in New York granted a temporary restraining order that will likely delay prosecution of any cases; the bill will most likely end up in the US Supreme Court. This emotionally charged debate over abortion rights, which at times has led to drastic behaviour,[26] is likely continue on so long as there are women who seek abortion services and those who believe abortion is morally wrong.

With this backdrop, economists have applied the tools of economic analysis to the subject of abortion in much the same way they are applied to other issues in society. As this chapter has hopefully demonstrated, objective application of economics modelling and econometric methods has been successfully employed to increase the understanding of the market for abortion itself, and the affects of abortion access on other important social and economic phenomena. Given the millennia-old practice of abortion is not likely to disappear anytime soon (regardless of legal impediments), the potential work of economists on this topic will continue as well.

Notes

1. See AGI (1999), Appendix Table 4, p. 54 for a more detailed, country-by-country break-down of estimated abortion rates. Countries with particularly high estimated abortion rates include (for 1996): Vietnam (83.3), Romania (78.0) and Cuba (77.7).
2. Lack of data on the number of illegal abortions performed and the number of illegal providers precludes any reliable discussion of these services.
3. Gestation is calculated as the number of weeks since a woman's last menstrual period.
4. Note that the decision to increase the number of children born to a mother may not necessarily be a joint decision.
5. Medoff (1988, 2000), Gohmann and Ohsfeldt (1993) and Kahane (2000) use the 2SLS approach. Garbacz (1990) does not treat price as endogenous, which leaves his results somewhat in question given that Hausman tests performed by others (for example, Gohmann and Ohsfeldt, 1993) reject the null hypothesis that price is exogenous.
6. Haas-Wilson (1996) does not include price as an explanatory variable. This omission is somewhat puzzling and may be due to the unavailability of data. In any event, she estimates a fixed-effects model in which state-specific effects may, in part, control for price differentials.
7. An example where a firm (or group of firms) may find it profit maximizing to *not* price their good or service on the elastic portion of the demand curve occurs when ancillary goods or services are also sold by the same firm. For example, it has been found in professional sports that most ticket prices for sporting events are price inelastic. The reason why owners of teams may underprice tickets is that they want to increase attendance, which in turn boosts sales of ancillary goods such as concessions and parking with a final result of greater profits overall.
8. The discrepancy may be in part due to the fact that Kahane includes both education and women's labour force participation rates in the same regression, which perhaps introduces problems of high multicollinearity.
9. Mothers co-habitating with fathers (married or not) or other supportive partners could also be used to compare with single mothers. Data on such living arrangements, however, are not typically available and thus simple marital status data are used to proxy the case of single vs. non-single motherhood.
10. The Hyde Amendment was challenged in the courts. Following a series of legal decisions it ultimately went into effect in 1980 (see Levine et al., 1995, for more details). The Amendment allows for the use of federal funds in the case of rape, incest or if the mother's life is in danger.

11. According to the National Abortion Rights Action League, or NARAL, 12 states provided funds for abortions in most circumstances as of 1993: Alaska, California, Connecticut, Hawaii, Massachusetts, New Jersey, New York, North Carolina, Oregon, Vermont, Washington and West Virginia (NARAL, 1993, p. 145).

12. See Ohsfeldt and Gohmann (1994) for a more detailed discussion of the state laws restricting abortion. It is important to note that most states provide for a judicial bypass for parental consent when such consent may lead to an undue burden on the minor.

13. The measure was constructed with the help of Stanley Henshaw of the Alan Guttmacher Institute who conducted a survey of clinics inquiring about the kinds of anti-abortion activities the clinics experienced, if any.

14. A number of anti-abortion activities were considered, including simple picketing (without contact or blocking) to more drastic measures such as bomb threats. Neither of these turned out to be statistically significant. In the case of simple picketing, nearly all clinics (about 85 per cent) experienced this activity and as such there was too little variation in this measure across states. As for bomb threats, few clinics (about 25 per cent) experienced this activity, making the effect difficult to pick up in the regressions. Picketing with contact was somewhere in between (about 52 per cent) and thus had enough variation across states to be found statistically significant in the regressions.

15. The abortion figures for Romania, however, do include some spontaneous abortions along with induced abortions, thus inflating the numbers. The dramatic *relative* increase in abortions pre- and post-legalization, however, should be largely unaffected by this inclusion.

16. A 'difference-of-difference' approach considers the difference in a measure (for example, fertility rates) between two groups (for example, whites and blacks) before an event (for example, legalization of abortion) and after. Then the change in these differences before and after the event (or the 'difference of differences') is used as a dependent variable in a regression.

17. Following the 1976 Hyde Amendment a group of states stopped funding abortions immediately, however, two court cases compelled many of them to resume funding until 1980. Later, in 1982 through 1992, an additional five states changed their policy on Medicaid funding of abortions. Klerman (1999) analyses the impact of these funding changes over both periods (1977–81 and 1982–92). He finds no significant effects on fertility from funding policy changes for the earlier period.

18. A variety of other controls are implemented including controls for county economic measures, year and county-level fixed effects.

19. Similarly, negative results are found for the imposition of parental consent laws and Medicaid funding. Kane and Staiger note, however, that in these cases it may be that the results may simply reflect the already occurring downward trend in teen birthrates in states that have enacted such laws.

20. For those unfamiliar with the phrase 'shotgun wedding' it refers to the case when a woman becomes pregnant and the man responsible for the pregnancy is compelled (consider the image of the woman's father holding a shotgun as an 'incentive' for the male) to marry his pregnant partner.

21. These include the number of prisoners and police per capita, various economic measures, welfare payments, handgun control laws and per capita beer consumption. A panel data regression with fixed effects is employed.

22. Their measure is computed in the following way:

$$Effective\ Abortion = \sum_a Abortion_{t-a} * (Arrests_a / Arrests_{total})$$

where *a* indexes the age of the cohort and *t* indexes years, with *Abortion* being the number of abortions per live birth.

23. Joyce (2003) challenges the results of Donohue and Levitt. Donohue and Levitt (2004), however, respond, criticizing Joyce's work, particularly for his lack of control of the

crack epidemic, which was nearing its peak during the years 1985 through 1990, the period Joyce uses in his analysis. Donohue and Levitt demonstrate that if Joyce's approach is used, but with a lengthened dataset, their hypothesis that abortion reduced crime is once again supported.

24. They employ the Supplemental Homicide Reports, which disaggregates the number of murders by age of the perpetrator and state.
25. Steve Levitt communicated these results to the author.
26. For example, the 1993 murder of Dr David Gunn in Pensacola, Florida and John Salvi's 1994 shooting rampage that left two dead and five wounded at a clinic in Brookline, Massachusetts.

References

Akerlof, G.A., J.L. Yellen and M.L. Katz (1996), 'An Analysis of Out-Of-Wedlock Childbearing in the United States', *Quarterly Journal of Economics*, **111** (2), 277–317.

Alan Guttmacher Institute (AGI) (1999), *Sharing Responsibility: Women, Society & Abortion Worldwide*, New York: The Alan Guttmacher Institute.

Bairagi, R. (2001), 'Effects of Sex Preference on Contraceptive Use, Abortion and Fertility in Matlab, Bangladesh', *International Family Planning Perspective*, **27** (3), 137–43.

Becker, G.S. (1960), 'An Economic Analysis of Fertility', in *Demographic and Economic Change in Developed Countries*, Universities-National Bureau Conference Series 11. Princeton, NJ: Princeton University Press.

Becker, G.S. (1965), 'A Theory of the Allocation of Time', *Economic Journal*, (September), 493–517.

Bitler, M. and M. Zavodny (2002), 'Child Abuse and Abortion Availability', *American Economic Review Papers and Proceedings*, **92** (2), 363–7.

Brown, R.W. and R.T. Jewell (1996), 'The Impact of Provider Availability on Abortion Demand', *Contemporary Economic Policy*, **14** (2), 95–106.

Coelen, S.P. and R.J. McIntyre (1978), 'An Econometric Model of Pronatalist and Abortion Policies', *Journal of Political Economy*, **86** (6), 1077–101.

Donohue, J.J. III and S.D. Levitt (2001), 'The Impact of Legalized Abortion on Crime', *Quarterly Journal of Economics*, **116** (2), 379–420.

Donohue, J.J. III and S.D. Levitt (2004), 'Further Evidence that Legalized Abortion Lowered Crime: A Response to Joyce', *Journal of Human Resources*, **39** (1), 29–49.

Finer, L.B. and S.K. Henshaw (2003a), 'Abortion Incidence and Services in the United States 2000', *Perspectives on Sexual and Reproductive Health*, **35** (1), 6–15.

Finer, L.B. and S.K. Henshaw (2003b), 'The Accessibility of Abortion Services in the United States, 2001', *Perspectives on Sexual and Reproductive Health*, **35** (1), 16–24.

Frejka, T. (1983), 'Induced Abortion and Fertility: A Quarter Century of Experience in Eastern Europe', *Population and Development Review*, **9** (3), 494–520.

Garbacz, C. (1990), 'Abortion Demand', *Population Research and Policy Review*, **9**, 151–60.

Gohmann, S.F. and R.L. Ohsfeldt (1993), 'Effects of Price and Availability on Abortion Demand', *Contemporary Policy Issues*, **11** (4), 42–55.

Graham, M.J., U. Larsen and X. Xu (1998), 'Son Preference in Anhui Province, China', *International Family Planning Perspective*, **24** (2), 72–7.

Gruber, J., P. Levine and D. Staiger (1999), 'Abortion Legalization and Child Living Circumstances: Who Is the "Marginal Child"?', *Quarterly Journal of Economics*, **114** (1), 263–91.

Haas-Wilson, D. (1996), 'The Impact of State Abortion Restrictions on Minors' Demand for Abortions', *Journal of Human Resources*, **31** (1), 140–58.

Joyce, T. (2003), 'Did Legalized Abortion Lower Crime?', *Journal of Human Resources*, **38** (1), 1–37.

Kahane, L.H. (2000), 'Anti-abortion Activities and the Market for Abortion Services: Protest as a Disincentive', *American Journal of Economics and Sociology*, **59** (3), 463–85.

Kane, T.J. and D. Staiger (1996), 'Teen Motherhood and Abortion Access', *Quarterly Journal of Economics*, **111** (2), 467–506.

Klerman, J.A. (1999), 'U.S. Abortion Policy and Fertility', *American Economic Review*, **89** (2), 261–4.

Levine, P.B., A.B. Trainor and D.J. Zimmerman (1995), 'The Effect of Medicaid Abortion Funding Restrictions on Abortions, Pregnancies and Births', National Bureau of Economic Research Working Paper No. 5066.

Levine, P.B., D. Staiger, T.J. Kane and D.J. Zimmerman (1996), '*Roe* v. *Wade* and American Fertility', National Bureau of Economic Research Working Paper No. 5616.

Lott, J.R. and J.E. Whitley (2001), 'Abortion and Crime: Unwanted Children and Out-of-Wedlock Births', Yale Law and Economics Research Paper, No. 254.

Lundberg, S. and R.D. Plotnick (1990), 'Effects of State Welfare, Abortion and Family Planning Policies on Premarital Childbearing Among White Adolescents', *Family Planning Perspectives*, **22** (6), 246–51, 275.

Medoff, M.H. (1988), 'An Economic Analysis of the Demand for Abortions', *Economic Inquiry*, **26** (2), 353–9.

Medoff, M.H. (2000), 'Black Abortion Demand', *Review of Black Political Economy*, **28** (1), 29–36.

Michael, R.T. (1973), 'Education and the Derived Demand for Children', *Journal of Political Economy*, **81** (2), part 2, S128–S164.

Mincer, J. (1962), 'Labor Force Participation Rate of Married Women', in H. Gregg Lewis (ed.), *Aspects of Labor Economics*, Universities-National Bureau Conference Series 14, Princeton, NJ: Princeton University Press.

Mincer, J. (1963), 'Market Prices, Opportunity Costs and Income Effects', in C. Christ et al., *Measurement in Economics: Studies in Mathematical Economics and Econometrics in Memory of Yehuda Grunfeld*, Stanford, California: Stanford University Press.

National Abortion Rights Action League (NARAL) (1993), *Who Decides? A State-By-State Review of Abortion Rights*, 4th edition, The Naral Foundation/NARAL.

Ohsfeldt, R.L. and S.F. Gohmann (1994), 'Do Parental Involvement Laws Reduce Adolescent Abortion Rates?', *Contemporary Economic Policy*, **12** (2), 65–76.

Rahman, A., L. Katzive and S.K. Henshaw (1998), 'A Global Review of Laws on Induced Abortion, 1985–1997', *International Family Planning Perspectives*, **24** (2), 56–64.

PART V

FUN AND GAMES

12 Economics of sport
John Goddard and Peter J. Sloane

The economics of sport has proved to be an area of fascination for economists for a number of reasons, but the focus has been on the economics of professional team sports to the relative neglect of non-team sports such as golf, boxing, athletics, swimming, horse-riding and auto sports. Though these can be and have been organized on a team basis this is usually not an essential element and the teams are not generally organized into leagues that are ranked in order of playing success over the season. The same neglect is true of amateur or participant, as opposed to spectator sports, though the numbers involved in these activities are markedly greater than those who choose to watch professionals as live spectators rather than as television viewers.

There are two main reasons why economists should be interested in team sports. First, professional team sports can substitute for a laboratory for economists, since we can observe operations normally out of the public eye and also measure directly the productivity of individual employees because of the richness of the available data. Second, leagues have indulged in various forms of behaviour such as cartel behaviour, which would certainly be regarded as anti-competitive in a conventional industry and thus raise important issues for competition policy.

Such issues have come to the fore both in North America and Europe, but the means of dealing with them have differed to such a degree that reference has been made to the 'North American model' and the 'European model' of sport. In the former case, Barros et al. (2002) note that: 'Teams are organised into hermetically sealed leagues: both the number of competitors and the identity of those competitors is fixed by the members themselves, so that entry at the level of the individual team is impossible "without consent" '.

This gives rise to a number of features that are generally absent in Europe such as the entry of new franchises with financial compensation to the incumbents at a price that is agreeable to them and franchise relocation to exploit subsidies provided by city authorities. In the labour market there exist player drafts (in which the teams negotiate contracts with leading young players in reverse order to their finishing position in the league in the previous season), roster limits, salary caps and restrictions on player trading. In product markets, economic competition is limited by gate revenue-sharing of the receipts of individual games, joint merchandising and the collective sale of broadcasting rights. In the USA, the major team sports to which such arrangements apply are baseball, American rules football, basketball and ice-hockey.

In Europe, football (or soccer) dominates the other team sports, which include cricket, rugby union, rugby league and speedway, though none of these is significant in all European countries. While US sports are not entirely absent in Europe, their popularity (with one or two exceptions such as basketball in Southern Europe) is limited. Revenue-sharing is less common in Europe, while player drafts and roster limits are generally unknown and salary caps have only recently been introduced. Player trading for cash, unusual in North America, is the norm in Europe, at least in football. Furthermore, some teams are found in cities or towns with small populations, which would not be countenanced in North America. As a result there are greater imbalances in income in Europe and a greater tendency for one or two teams to dominate in their domestic leagues. There is no North American equivalent to qualification for European-wide competitions, though success in the league results in entry into the play-offs in North America. However, according to the European Commission, the key feature of the European model of sport is the system of promotion and relegation, which means the turnover of teams is at least potentially much greater than applies in North America.

US and European economists have also differed on the objectives pursued by team owners, with the profit maximization paradigm dominant in North America and non-profit objectives (such as maximization of games won subject to a profit constraint) generally considered to be more appropriate in Europe. It is possible, however, that the greatly increased income from broadcasting and the tendency for sports teams to become listed on the stock market may have led to a more commercial approach in Europe that has narrowed such differences.

In this chapter we consider the objectives followed by team and league owners (Section 1), the nature of product demand and, in particular, whether this is positively related to the uncertainty of outcome (Section 2). This is followed by an examination of the sports league's role as a cartel, including the need to impose strong anti-competitive controls to maintain competitive balance (Section 3). Finally, we examine contentious issues such as whether revenue-sharing improves competitive balance, whether salary caps are necessary and efficient and whether collective selling of broadcasting rights should be permitted (Section 4). Section 5 concludes the chapter.

1   Team and league objectives
The nature of the objectives of team owners and the leagues that control them is a key question in the economics of sport, especially given the

monopoly nature of these enterprises. The question of profit maximization versus utility maximization can be viewed at two levels: whether or not team profits are maximized and whether or not leagues attempt to maximize joint league profits. The North American literature has tended to de-emphasize utility maximization on the grounds that there is no evidence that owners, whether sports fans or publicly-traded corporations, have received less than a market rate of return on their investment. Few teams in the USA make losses in any season. In contrast, in Europe, few football, rugby or cricket teams make consistent profits, relying on donations from wealthy directors and owners or donations from supporters' clubs to continue in existence.

In principle, there are a number of ways in which one might test whether utility or profit maximization is being pursued. First, accepting long-run losses is inconsistent with profit maximizing behaviour, since such firms should only remain in business as long as short-run marginal revenue covers average variable costs and makes some contribution towards average fixed costs. Second, paying players more than the value of their marginal revenue product is inconsistent with profit maximization. Third, hiring too large a squad, defined as paying a higher salary to the last player signed than that player's expected contribution to future team revenue infringes the profit maximization rule. Fourth, building a stadium larger than needed (that is, where the marginal revenue product of capital is less than the cost of capital) is likewise inconsistent with this hypothesis. Fifth, charging prices for tickets below the marginal cost of providing the product infringes the rule. Having a waiting list for season tickets for many years would be strong evidence of behaviour inconsistent with profit maximization, as would setting prices on the inelastic segment of the demand curve, unless this generated sufficient ancillary sales to cover the implied reduction in total revenue.

There are, however, constraints on utility maximization. Many professional sports teams in North America are publicly held and holding companies will face pressures to ensure that losses are not made. Also, the fact that there are many million-plus population cities without major league teams means that the ability to relocate provides for possibilities of earning more revenue through subsidies. In general in Europe, there is an over-provision of teams, so such opportunities for revenue generation do not exist. The tendency for some European teams to become listed on the stock exchange has, however, decreased their ability to indulge in non-profit-maximizing behaviour.

While teams have individual interests, the league as a whole has a collective interest in overall profit maximization. The league as an entity has no interest in the total number of wins for each team, as each win within the league is also a loss for one of its teams. League-wide profit maximization requires, however, competitive balance. Thus, the universal problem in professional team sports leagues is to set up and police a structure that maximizes joint profits, despite the interest of individual owners in either individual profit maximization or in utility maximization. Indeed, it is not clear that a league that is made up entirely of teams whose owners were profit maximizers would behave any differently from a league that was made up entirely of utility maximizers.

2   The nature of the product

One early study (Neale, 1964) referred to the peculiar economics of professional team sports, since it is not possible to produce any output without the assistance of other producers. The essence of such sports leagues is mutual interdependence. That is, individual producers (teams) have a vested interest in the economic viability of other teams in order to maintain the interest of their fans and in turn the revenues generated from the sale of the product (the joint game). The nature of the product thus creates a requirement for uncertainty of outcome and this is the bedrock upon which a myriad of restrictions is justified.

Competitive balance can have a number of meanings. First, there is event or game uncertainty, which increases as the probability of either side winning approaches 0.5. Second, there is seasonal uncertainty over which team will eventually win the championship. Third, there is the absence of long-run domination by one or two teams, in the sense that the same or one or two teams win the league championship over a number of seasons. It is argued that more equal revenue-sharing can assist in making leagues more equal, though as we shall see this has been disputed by some economists. However, evidence that dominance has detrimental effects on attendance in terms of total league revenue is more mixed. In theory, league profits should be maximized if teams won 50 per cent of their games and cities were all of the same size. However, to the extent that the drawing power of member teams varies, more wins by teams in larger areas will likely maximize league revenues, so that there is an inherent conflict of interest between individual team owners and the interests of the league as a whole.

We can portray the relationship between an owner's preference map and the uncertainty of outcome constraint as in Figure 12.1. The proportion or probability of wins, p, is on the x-axis. The variance or uncertainty of outcome, $p(1-p)$, is on the y-axis. The theory of the distribution of a binary random variable with constant probability of success establishes a fixed relationship between the probability of winning p and $p(1-p)$, given by the inverted U shape labelled UU. We assume a conventionally shaped indifference map with I_1, I_2 and I_3 representing increasing levels of utility

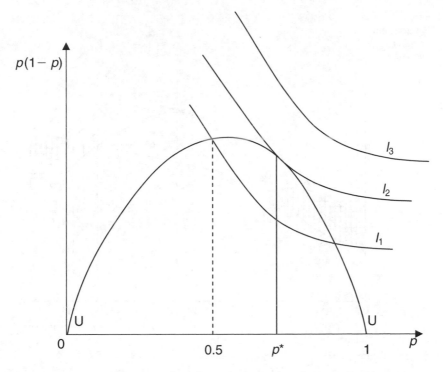

Figure 12.1   Uncertainty of outcome and owner utility

for the owner (and likely the fans too). Then, it can be seen that maximum uncertainty of outcome, where $p=0.5$, is not the level that maximizes the utility of the owner. This occurs at p^*, where the owner is prepared to trade off some uncertainty of outcome in order to have his or her own team winning more frequently and thus have a higher probability of winning the league championship. Only if there is a monotonic relationship between owner and fan utility and attendance, will p^* be the level of winning that will maximize attendance. Figure 12.1 describes a representative team, as it is not possible for all franchises to win more than 50 per cent of their games.

The above gives rise to the possibility that the sports league market is inherently unstable. Given that it is impossible for all teams to be successful in winning their games and given a positive relationship between playing success and profitability it may not be possible for all teams to be profitable at any one time. In fact, in North America even less successful teams make profits, but this does not seem descriptive of experience in Europe. Such a relationship between uncertainty of outcome, instability and mutual interdependence is illustrated in Figure 12.2.

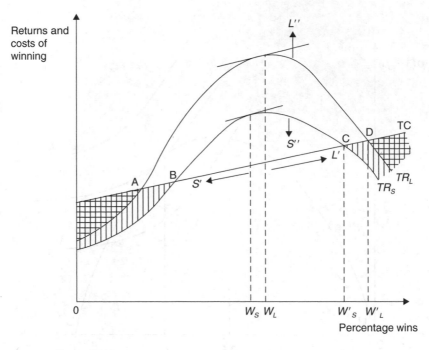

Source: Sloane (2002).

Figure 12.2   Uncertainty of outcome and mutual interdependence

We assume a two-team league consisting of a large city franchise, L, and a small city franchise, S. Further, assume that the costs (TC) of producing a winning team rise linearly and are identical for both teams, with the proviso that when one team increases its investment in acquiring a winning team, the other does not react, and that the returns to winning rise initially at an increasing rate, but then at a decreasing rate, since enthusiasm may wane if teams win too often. Let the total returns to the winning schedule of the large-market team (TR_L) be above that of the small-market team (TR_S) on the assumption that a given winning percentage will attract more spectators in the former case. Thus, there will be a unique profit maximization solution for each team. If the TR_L schedule exceeds that of the TR_S schedule by a fixed percentage, so that the slope of the former is steeper than that of the latter over the relevant range, that of the large city team will lie to the right of that of the small-market team. Instability is an inevitable consequence of the zero-sum nature of the league. Thus, if the large city team wins more often as denoted by L', this will result in the small-market team winning less often, as denoted by S'. The very success of one team drives the other into a loss-making winning percentage as shown by the shaded areas. Furthermore, the small-market team by virtue of its size is much more vulnerable to loss-making than the large-market team as it has a smaller range of winning percentages, BC, over which it is profitable, than the large-market team (AD). Finally, the pursuit of playing success subject to a break-even constraint will increase the likelihood of losses relative to the profit maximization objective, since the latter lies to the right of the former (W'_L for the large-market team and W'_S for the small-market team). Again, the zero-sum nature of the league implies greater losses for the small-market team (as well as for the large-market team) as it loses more games. In the diagram, the small-market team losses and large-market team losses are represented by the vertical-lined and hatched areas respectively.

Mutual interdependence is also influenced by the relative sizes of the markets of the two teams. If the population of team L was greater, resulting in an upward shift of the *TR* curve to *L''*, this would likely shift down the *TR* curve of team S, as the fans of the latter realized that winning the championship was even less likely than in the previous example. This emphasizes the need for leagues to keep population size differences between constituent teams as small as possible, a strategy much more successfully followed in North America than in Europe. It is also clear that far from commercialism destroying sports leagues it actually assists in maintaining competitive balance. It is the pursuit of sporting success, as opposed to profit, that imbalances leagues.

3   Cartel behaviour

According to Neale (1964), professional team sports are natural monopolies and we may consider teams simply as individual plants in a common enterprise. Others regard leagues as cartels, which impose constraints on the activities of individual teams by the imposition of various rules required to organize the league.[1] These include sporting rules to determine how games are conducted, including the determination of the fixture list, rules about the selection and employment of players by teams, as well as the number of teams in membership. Other rules are required to determine shares of revenue from games, television and other activities. Furthermore, there may be rules limiting the ability of individuals to have financial interests in more than one team in order to maintain confidence in the integrity of the competition. Such rules are unlikely to fall foul of competition policy at least in their simpler form. However, other rules are designed to influence market structure and conduct and may well raise issues for competition policy. Examples are controls on league size, on the distribution of league franchises and various forms of labour market controls.

The standard defence of these restrictions is that without such controls the wealthier teams would acquire so much player talent that they would become too dominant and kill spectator interest in the league as a whole. Some economists such as Rottenberg (1956) have used the invariance principle to argue that such restrictions will have no effect on competitive outcomes. This principle consists of two propositions. First, in the absence of transactions costs the parties to any contract will settle on the most efficient outcome. Second, the same outcome will be achieved regardless of the distribution of property rights (the invariance thesis). The implication of this thesis is that the distribution of talent would be identical regardless of whether leagues imposed limitations on the free mobility of labour. The best players would still end up in the wealthiest teams. However, this takes no account of externalities, the fact that a team signing up the best players will not likely take into account the negative effect of such a signing on other teams. This has been referred to in the literature as the Yankee Paradox (Vrooman, 1996). A further problem is that a player's talent may be team-specific (or what Vrooman refers to as the irreversibility proposition). Thus, it may be reasonable to assume that a team for whom a player has performed over a number of seasons will be better informed about the player's potential than any other team interested in signing him (the lemons phenomenon). The possibility of a winner's curse operating seems much more likely in a situation in which the maximization of playing success dominates over profit maximization considerations.

4   Current policy issues in professional team sports

According to the 'cartel' interpretation, one of the main functions of the leagues in their capacity as organizing bodies is to implement rules aimed at furthering the collective interest of their member teams. Historically, this function has in general been accepted by courts in the USA, which have permitted restrictions on the production of sporting events that would normally be regarded as anti-competitive in other fields of business and commerce. For example, in 1922 the Supreme Court granted major league baseball (MLB) exemption from the Sherman antitrust laws, and in 1961 Congress passed the Sports Broadcasting Act, entitling the leagues to sell broadcasting rights collectively on behalf of their member teams.

The North American leagues therefore impose restrictions on the operations of the teams, which seek to prevent any individual team from achieving a level of dominance that would be damaging to the interest that all teams share in maintaining some degree of competitive balance. In the early history of North American professional team sports the most important restriction of this kind was the reserve clause. Having signed a contract as a professional, the player's team retained the option to renew his contract, effectively binding the player to his present employer. The reserve clause was justified on the grounds that it was necessary to prevent the richest teams from outbidding the rest for the services of the top players, but one of its main effects was to depress players' compensation (Scully, 1974). Other restrictions on the free play of market forces in North American sports include the draft system, salary caps and revenue-sharing. The reverse-order-of-finish draft system allows the weakest teams from the previous season the first pick of rookie players moving from college (or school in the case of baseball) to professional level for the first time. Salary caps and revenue-sharing are considered in greater detail below.

4.1 Free agency and salary caps

Before discussing mechanisms for limiting the remuneration of sports professionals, it is perhaps timely to consider the level of salary payments that are found in many sports. In Table 12.1, the top 25 sports stars in terms of earnings in 2004–05 are listed, covering ten different sports. Followers of professional sports are often uneasy at the perceived large incomes that star players receive, as displayed in the table, though other groups such as film stars and musicians do not seem to attract such opprobrium. References to players' contracts being similar to those that operated under the slave trade are also difficult to swallow.

Why then do sports stars earn so much? The answer lies in the concept of a rent of ability. Real stars are few in number and possess skills that cannot be easily replicated by training the average player more intensively. Rosen (1981) referred to this as the superstar phenomenon, and illustrated how human capital interacted with production technology to magnify small differences in talent, resulting in large differences in earnings. Technology enables the product to be reproduced at low cost, since large stadia enable large numbers of spectators to consume the product at the same time, and broadcasting widens the market still further. Characteristically, wages are highly convex with respect to star quality, resulting in a highly skewed distribution of earnings with a long upper-tail to the distribution. There is good reason for this. Hausman and Leonard (1997) showed that the presence of star players can have a substantial effect on the number of television viewers. In the case of basketball, they found that superstars such as Michael Jordan, Magic Johnson and Larry Bird raised television ratings by around 30 per cent, in addition to their effect on paid attendance.

A recent study by Lucifora and Simmons (2003) tests for superstar effects on the salaries of Italian footballers. In line with Rosen's model, this study

Table 12.1   Top 25 sports star earnings in US$ (2004–05)

1	Tiger Woods (Golf) – $87.0m
2	Michael Schumacher (Motor Racing) – $60.0m
3	Oscar De La Hoya (Boxing) – $38.0m
4	Michael Vick (American Football) – $37.5m
5	Shaquille O'Neal (Basketball) – $33.4m
6	Michael Jordan (Basketball) – $33.0m
7	David Beckham (Soccer) – $32.5m
8	Kobe Bryant (Basketball) – $28.8m
9 =	Lance Armstrong (Cycling) – $28.0m
9 =	Valentino Rossi (Motor Cycling) – $28.0m
11	Alex Rodriguez (Baseball) – $27.5m
12	Phil Mickelson (Golf) – $26.8m
13	Andre Agassi (Tennis) – $26.2m
14	Derek Jeter (Baseball) – $25.5m
15	Manny Ramirez (Baseball) – $24.2m
16	Jeff Gordon (Motor Racing) – $23.4m
17	Walter Jones (American Football) – $23.2m
18	Ronaldo (Soccer) – $23.0m
19	LeBron James (Basketball) – $22.9m
20	Matt Hasselbeck (American Football) – $22.8m
21	Maria Sharapova (Tennis) – $18.2m
22	Serena Williams (Tennis) – $12.7m
23	Annika Sorenstam (Golf) – $7.3m
24	Venus Williams (Tennis) – $6.5m
25	Lindsay Davenport (Tennis) – $6.0m

Note: Earnings estimates are for June 2004 to June 2005. They include salaries, bonuses, prize money, endorsements and appearance fees. The earnings for NBA players (basketball) are net of the 10 per cent escrow tax that is withheld from their salaries as part of the league's collective bargaining agreement with the player's union.

Source: Forbes (www.forbes.com).

finds that earnings were highly convex in two goalscoring and performance measures, after controlling for personal characteristics and team effects. The implied earnings ratio for the median superstar, with a scoring record of more than 0.2 goals per game, was over four times that of the median ordinary player, with a goal scoring rate below this figure. A player located at the 99th percentile of the earnings distribution earned over ten times more than players located at the median, and 45 times more than those players located at the 10th percentile of the distribution. Only nine players in Serie A, the major Italian League, scored at a rate of 0.5 goals per game or better. The rewards for goal scoring exceeded those for supplying the final pass that created the goal. Goal scoring is clearly the most glamorous part of the sport in the eyes of the consumer.

An alternative way to represent the above is to compare the supply and demand equilibrium of sports stars with that of another occupation, for which there is a much higher demand, but at the same time a very elastic supply schedule. Fort (2003) uses the example of teachers. As constructed in Figure 12.3, the demand for teachers lies well to the right of that for sports stars. However, the supply of sports stars is much lower than that of teachers and much more inelastic, with the consequence that the earnings of sports stars, E_s, greatly exceed those of teachers at E_t, though many more teachers are employed, L_t, than is the case for sports stars, L_s.

Until the final quarter of the twentieth century, the reserve clause played a major role in restraining salary levels in North American professional sports. Baseball's reserve clause, effective since 1880, was eventually removed through collective bargaining in 1976. Subsequently, all MLB players became free agents after completing a minimum number of years of major league service (currently six years). In a settlement finalized in 1983, the National Basketball Association's (NBA) reserve clause was abolished in exchange for the introduction of a salary cap, which sought to offset the potentially harmful effects of free agency for competitive balance. The salary cap limits each team's expenditure on players' compensation to

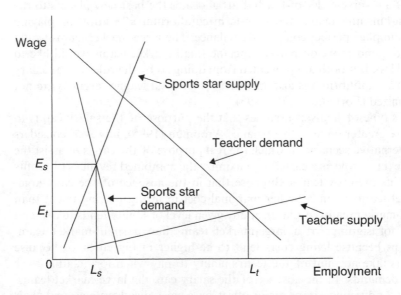

Source: Adapted from Fort (2003).

Figure 12.3   Relative supply and demand for teachers and sports stars

53 per cent of gross league revenues divided by the number of teams in the league. Several exemptions apply: for example, a team can exceed the cap in order to match an offer made to one of its first team players by a rival team. As part of its 1993 free agency settlement, the National Football League (NFL) adopted a similar arrangement, with wages limited to 67 per cent of designated revenues. An attempt to impose a salary cap in MLB resulted in a prolonged players' strike in 1994–95. The eventual settlement included a luxury tax on expenditures on wages and salaries over a certain limit, with the proceeds redistributed among the poorer teams: an arrangement that may be interpreted as a 'softer' version of a salary cap. A new version of the luxury tax was implemented in 2002.

By equalizing expenditure on players' wages and salaries throughout the league, the NBA salary cap is intended to enable the small-market teams to compete on equal terms with the large-market teams. In practice, however, the exemption clause is invoked routinely by the large-market teams and the cap has not succeeded in equalizing expenditures. Consequently total wages regularly exceed 60 per cent of revenues, and the high-spending teams' wage bills are typically more than twice those of the low-spending teams. If anything, competition in the NBA may have become slightly less balanced since the cap was introduced (Quirk and Fort, 1999).

In theory, if all teams are required to spend exactly the same on wages, and if a reverse-order-of-finish draft allocates the best new players to the lowest-finishing teams, the long-term equilibrium allocation of playing talent implies perfect competitive balance. The large-market teams would like to spend more on players and the small-market teams would like to spend less, but both are prevented from doing so by the rules of the salary cap. The equilibrium is also inefficient since total league revenues are not maximized (Fort and Quirk, 1995).

This type of analysis assumes that the purpose of the salary cap is to achieve greater competitive balance. Vrooman (1995), however, considers an alternative scenario in which the real purpose of the cap is to assist the league (in its role as a cartel) to maximize the combined revenues or profits of all its member teams. Suppose that in the absence of the cap, large-market teams incur a higher marginal cost in hiring playing talent than small-market teams. A player of any given level of ability tends to demand more for signing for a large-market team than a small-market team, perhaps because living costs tend to be higher in big cities, or because players take account of the team's ability to pay when formulating their wage demands. In the absence of the salary cap, the large-market teams' revenue advantage is partially offset by a cost disadvantage, and their tendency to dominate competition is checked to some extent. Under the rules of the salary cap, however, all teams spend the same amount on players, so the marginal cost of talent does not affect the decision to hire talent. The objective of league revenue or profit maximization requires each player to be assigned to the team for which his marginal revenue product is the greatest. In other words, revenue functions are the only determinant of the allocation of talent; cost functions are irrelevant. For this reason, the large-market teams dominate competition to a greater extent with the salary cap than in its absence.

High rates of inflation in players' wages in European football have been a serious cause for concern in recent years. In England, for example, the annual rate of wage inflation was running close to 30 per cent throughout most of the 1990s. By 2001, the average ratio of wages and salaries expend-iture to revenue in the Premier and Nationwide leagues was approaching the 70 per cent benchmark regarded by accountants Deloitte and Touche (2004) as the maximum likely to be sustainable by any team in the long term. In 2002–03, the ratio for the average Premiership club was below this benchmark at 61 per cent, but for the average Division One, Division Two and Division Three[2] clubs stood at 89 per cent, 85 per cent and 68 per cent respectively. Elsewhere in Europe, many French, Italian and Spanish foot-ball teams have recently experienced similar difficulties. In Italy, for example, all 18 Serie A teams returned an operating loss in 2001.

Rosen and Sanderson (2001) have drawn an analogy between rising expenditure on players' wages in professional sports and an arms race between nations. For an individual team (or nation) unable to influence the momentum of the spending process at the aggregate level, increasing its own expenditure may be the only rational action, given that abstention would mean losing ground. But in this zero-sum game, any expenditure by one team that achieves a relative improvement in performance imposes a negative externality on others. Teams tend to spend as much on players as their revenues (or the willingness of their owners to subsidize losses) will allow, but the benefit of the extra expenditure is largely cancelled out by others acting in the same manner. Against this background, the need for some form of collective restraint on wage expenditure in European football has been widely debated.

Given the openness of the post-Bosman footballers' labour market, it seems likely that to be effective a North American-style salary cap would have to operate Europe-wide. However, the practical and legal obstacles may well be insurmountable, especially in view of the probable scepticism of the European Commission on grounds of competition policy. Some form of voluntary restraint might be possible, however. Starting from the 2004–05 season, European football's governing body UEFA introduced a licensing scheme which imposes conditions on the financial management of football clubs and aims to promote good governance. The licensing scheme requires clubs to meet five criteria, including national financial standards, in order to be permitted to compete in the Champions League and the UEFA Cup. Meanwhile, the G14 group, comprising the leading teams from several European countries, agreed in November 2002 that each team's wage expenditure should be limited to 70 per cent of annual turnover from the 2005–06 season and are urging other clubs to follow their guidelines.

4.2   Cheating in professional team sports

A major difficulty associated with any attempt to restrain expenditure on players' salaries is that it leaves open the possibility of cheating on the part of individual teams, in the hope that they can gain an advantage over others who adhere to the rules. This can be illustrated using the prisoner's dilemma game-theoretic model. In a two-team model, assume that the league rules have capped the total size of each team's wage bill. Suppose a team that adheres to the rules of the cap earns an operating profit of +200. A team that 'cheats' and breaks the rules of the cap by overspending earns an operating profit of zero. However, there is an additional prize of +1000 for the team that wins the league. If both teams adhere to the rules of the cap or if both teams cheat, each has a 50 per cent chance of winning the prize. However, if one team cheats while the other adheres to the rules of the cap, the odds change so that the cheating team has an 80 per cent chance of winning the prize. Figure 12.4 shows the expected payoffs to each team under this structure, conditional on the actions of both teams.

If both teams adhere to the rules of the cap, combined expected proceeds are maximized (both teams earn +700). Will this joint maximizing outcome actually be attained? Consider first team A's decision. If B does not cheat, A's expected proceeds are +700 if A does not cheat, and +800 if A cheats. If B cheats, A's expected proceeds are +400 if A does not cheat, and +500 if A cheats. Whatever B does, it is therefore best for A to cheat.

		Team B	
		Cheat	Adhere
Team A	Cheat	(500, 500)	(800, 400)
	Adhere	(400, 800)	(700, 700)

Figure 12.4   The sporting prisoner's dilemma

Because the model is symmetric, B applies similar reasoning and reaches the same decision. Therefore, a sub-optimal outcome is achieved in which both parties cheat and combined expected proceeds are reduced (both teams earn +500). Both parties would be better off if they could agree to obey the rules, but neither is confident that the other party would stick to its side of the bargain. There is plenty of evidence to indicate that cheating behaviour is common when leagues impose restrictions of the kind described above.

Cricket provides another example in which the form of corruption has involved individual players accepting bribes from bookmakers or gamblers for fixing matches. The former South African captain Hansie Cronje admitted his involvement, but similar allegations have been levelled against players in Australia, England, India, New Zealand, Sri Lanka and the West Indies. It has been suggested that the cause of the problem is the low pay received by international cricketers relative to other sports, as a consequence of cricket's organizational structure, which uses the revenue from test matches and international one-day games to subsidize domestic competition. Preston et al. (2002) suggest that cheating in sports falls into two categories. Where the rewards for winning substantially exceed the rewards for finishing second or third (in terms of money or prestige), this 'winner-takes-all' structure may lead athletes to take performance-enhancing drugs or adopt other measures to gain an unfair advantage. A second form of cheating may occur where the rewards to athletes are insufficiently differentiated, as in cricket, so that the potential gains to cheating are much greater than the penalties for being caught. In this case, raising pay and increasing the penalties for being caught should help reduce the likelihood of cheating or corruption.

4.3   Revenue-sharing and the collective sale of broadcasting rights

In North American professional team sports, revenue-sharing plays an important part in offsetting inequalities in drawing power between teams. Practices concerning the distribution of gate revenues vary between sports. NFL home and away teams, historically, shared gate revenues on a 60:40 split. In January 2001, NFL owners approved a new revenue-sharing policy to begin in 2002 in which the league pools visiting teams' shares of gate receipts for all pre-season and regular season games and divides the pool equally among all 32 teams. This is much more equalizing than arrangements elsewhere. For major league baseball, the split is 95:5 in the National League and 80:20 in the American League with some modest sharing of local revenues. In the NBA and NHL, there is no sharing of gate revenues. Broadly speaking, national television revenues are shared equally between all league member teams, while the home teams keep local television revenues.

One of the best known findings of the early economics of professional team sports literature is that the existence or nature of arrangements for revenue-sharing among the members of a sports league should have no effect on competitive balance. Intuition might suggest otherwise: by narrowing the gap between the richer and poorer members of the league, revenue-sharing might be expected to allow the poorer teams to compete more effectively in the market for playing talent. In turn, this might be expected to improve competitive balance. Indeed, the aim of improving competitive balance might well be one of the main reasons for having a revenue-sharing arrangement. According to the theory, however, this intuition is misleading. The preceding argument fails to recognize the damaging effect of revenue-sharing on the incentives for teams to compete in order to attract playing talent.

Consider the two-team model introduced in Section 2. Suppose initially there is no revenue-sharing, and each team keeps all of its own revenues. At any particular allocation of playing talent between teams L and S, the marginal benefit to team L of a small increase in its win ratio brought about by hiring some incremental talent is MR_L and the marginal benefit to team S is MR_S. In accordance with the invariance principle, the profit-maximizing allocation of talent must be such that $MR_L = MR_S$. If there were any divergence between MR_L and MR_S, a trade in talent could be devised that would leave both teams better off. In this model there is an assumption of symmetry: the marginal effect on team L's revenue of an incremental increase in team L's playing talent is the same as the marginal effect of an incremental reduction in team S's talent. There is also an assumption that the total stock of playing talent is fixed, and that this fact is taken into account by both teams when making their hiring decisions. The implications of relaxing these assumptions are considered below.

Suppose now a revenue-sharing arrangement is introduced, whereby each team keeps only a proportion, say 90 per cent, of its own revenues, while the remaining 10 per cent is awarded to the other team. The marginal benefit to team L of hiring incremental talent is now 0.9 times the marginal effect on its own revenue resulting from the increase in its win ratio, plus 0.1 times the (negative) marginal effect on team S's revenue resulting from the reduction in its win ratio, or $0.9MR_L - 0.1MR_S$. Similarly, the marginal benefit to team S of hiring incremental talent is $-0.1MR_L + 0.9MR_S$.

Comparing the situation before and after the introduction of the revenue-sharing arrangement, the marginal benefit from hiring incremental talent falls by the same amount for both teams: $-0.1MR_L - 0.1MR_S$. Because the effect on both teams' marginal revenue functions is identical, the location of the profit-maximizing distribution of playing talent, and therefore the degree of competitive balance, does not alter. However, there is a reduction in the equilibrium wage: the teams do not compete as fiercely to attract talent if part of the additional revenue generated by additional talent is shared. According to this model, revenue-sharing tends to depress players' compensation, but it does not affect competitive balance.

This straightforward conclusion, that the effect of revenue-sharing on competitive balance is neutral, has been challenged by a number of economists who have developed alternative models, in which revenue sharing *does* affect the equilibrium distribution of playing talent (Atkinson et al., 1988; Rascher, 1997; Kesenne, 2000):

1. If the total supply of talent is not fixed, so it is possible for one team to increase its stock of talent without automatically depleting its competitors' stock of talent, revenue sharing may affect competitive balance.
2. If teams pursue utility-maximizing rather than profit-maximizing objectives, revenue-sharing may affect competitive balance.
3. If revenue depends not only on the relative values of each team's allocations of playing talent (which determine their win ratios) but also on the absolute values, on the grounds that spectator demand is sensitive to the overall quality of talent on view, revenue-sharing may affect competitive balance under both profit- and utility-maximizing assumptions.

Unfortunately, no consensus has so far emerged as to the direction of these effects: in some models revenue-sharing can be shown to improve competitive balance, while in others the effect is the opposite. For example, Fort and Quirk (1995) consider the effect of sharing television revenues derived from contracts between teams and local television stations. Television audience levels are assumed to be sensitive to the absolute level of talent on display, so the symmetry assumption is abandoned: the marginal effect on team L's television revenue of an incremental increase in its own playing talent is greater than the marginal effect of an incremental reduction in team S's talent, because in the first case the absolute level of talent on display increases, while in the second it declines. In this formulation the introduction of a revenue-sharing arrangement has a greater (negative) effect on the marginal revenue function of the large-market team than the small-market team. Revenue-sharing, therefore, tends to improve competitive balance.

In contrast, Szymanski and Kesenne (2004) have suggested that the conclusion that revenue-sharing has a neutral effect on competitive balance depends on a (previously unrecognized) implicit assumption about the nature of conjectural variation: the assumptions each team makes about the reactions of its competitor in response to its own actions. If team L is

considering the effect on its own revenue of an increase in its own expenditure on talent, for example, in the model described above, team L assumes
that team S will passively acquiesce in an equivalent reduction in its talent.
This is a consequence of the model's assumption that the total supply of
talent is fixed. Whether the teams would recognize their interdependence in
this way in practice is open to debate, however. An assumption about the
nature of conjectural variation more widely used in the oligopoly and game
theory literatures, known as Nash conjectures, requires each team to base
its own decisions on the assumption that its competitor will always stick to
its present position. Team L would not take into account the 'total fixed
supply of talent' constraint when evaluating the effect of an increase in its
own stock of talent, and would not assume that team S's stock of talent
would fall by an equivalent amount. In this case, the introduction of a
revenue-sharing arrangement still reduces the incentive for both teams to
spend on talent as before. But because team S has more to gain from a share
of team L's revenue than vice versa, team S reduces its expenditure by more
than team L. Revenue-sharing, therefore, causes competitive balance to
deteriorate in this formulation.

In European football, practices concerning revenue-sharing have varied
significantly, both over time and between countries. In England, for
example, until 1983, 20 per cent of the notional receipts from every league
match were paid to the visiting team. Subsequently, home teams have
retained their own gate receipts. Under another scheme, 4 per cent of all
notional receipts were paid into a pool, the proceeds from which were
distributed evenly among all league teams. The 4 per cent levy was reduced
to 3 per cent in 1986, prior to the complete withdrawal from this scheme of
the leading (Premier League) teams in 1992.

Although the general trend has been towards the erosion of arrangements for direct sharing of gate revenues, sharing of television revenues
through the collective sale of broadcasting rights is still widespread,
though not universal, throughout Europe. Among the big five European
leagues, rights are sold collectively (by the leagues and not the teams)
and exclusively (to a single broadcaster) in England and Germany. In
each case, the distribution of the proceeds between the teams is determined by formula. In France, the rights are sold collectively but there is no
exclusivity: currently the rights are shared between two broadcasters. In
Italy and Spain, the teams sell their own rights individually and retain the
proceeds.

The legality of arrangements for the collective sale of broadcasting
rights has recently been subject to scrutiny from the competition authorities at both national and European levels, and the future structure of
broadcasting rights deals is likely to be shaped in large measure by the

courts. In the UK in 1996, the Office of Fair Trading (OFT) initiated proceedings under the Restrictive Trade Practices Act, 1976 at the Restrictive Practices Court (RPC), in which the OFT argued that the Premier League acted unlawfully as a cartel in negotiating the sale of broadcasting rights on behalf of its member teams. According to the OFT, the exclusivity of the Premier League's contract with the satellite broadcaster British Sky Broadcasting (BSkyB) restricted the number of live matches screened on television, and inflated the price paid by BSkyB subscribers.

In July 1999, the RPC reached a judgement that appears to have surprised many commentators. In rejecting the OFT's case, the RPC took the view that on balance these arrangements did not operate against the public interest. The OFT's case rested partly upon the question as to whether access to exclusive live Premier League coverage conferred monopoly power upon BSkyB as sole suppliers to a distinct market for a specific programme type, or whether it merely enabled BSkyB to compete more effectively with other broadcasters for audiences as part of a wider market for television programmes in general (Cave, 2000). The RPC accepted the latter view, which implied that exclusivity could be beneficial in helping to promote competition between broadcasters through improved programme quality. From football's point of view, collectivity enabled the Premier League to market its championship as a single entity, and produced greater equality between the television revenues earned by richer and poorer teams than would be the case if the teams sold their broadcasting rights individually.

Although the outcome of the OFT's challenge settled the issue temporarily, it seems unlikely to represent the final word on this matter. In December 2002, the European Commission issued a statement of objections to the Premier League concerning the collective sale of broadcasting rights, reiterating a number of arguments aired previously at the RPC. Collective selling, especially when combined with exclusivity, excludes other broadcasters from access to live televised football, resulting in higher prices and limited choice for consumers. While the Commission accepts that some element of collectivity could be justified as a means of redistributing television revenues within football, it does not accept that the present arrangements are the only mechanism through which redistribution could be achieved. Citing arrangements for the future sale of European Champions League broadcasting rights by UEFA as an exemplar, the Commission suggested that the Premier League's broadcasting rights could be sold in smaller bundles. Some bundles might still be sold collectively, while others might be sold separately by individual teams. In July 2003, the Premier League did split its offer into three separate packages, but because BSkyB's bid was accepted for each of these packages the Commission was still not satisfied that the process was sufficient to maintain competition.

However, perhaps not all recent events suggest that the market for broadcasting rights is easily capable of diversifying in quite the way the Commission envisages. Pay-per-view transmission of live football has so far achieved only a limited foothold in the UK market. The liquidation of the terrestrial digital broadcaster ITV Digital in 2002, and the continuing financial difficulties of the two cable operators NTL and Telewest, have strengthened BSkyB's position as the most credible, and perhaps the only major bidder for pay-television rights in the foreseeable future. Meanwhile, recent turmoil in Italy, where the start of the 2002–03 season was delayed while several of the smaller Serie A teams attempted to achieve satisfactory terms for the sale of their broadcasting rights, serves ample warning as to the potentially chaotic and divisive effect of the abandonment of the collectivity principle.

5   Conclusion

The economics of sport represents an area of continuing fascination for economists. Professional sports provide fertile territory for empirical economists, who can measure the productivity of individual employees thanks to the richness of the available datasets, and for theoreticians who can observe various forms of behaviour, such as decision-making through cartels, which would either be hidden or regarded as anti-competitive in most other areas of business and commerce. Such issues have been prominent throughout the histories of professional sports in both North America and Europe, and remain so today, although the methods for dealing with them have differed, partly because of differences in the underlying structural characteristics of the North American and European models for the organization of professional team sports. North American and European economists have also differed concerning the objectives pursued by team owners, with profit maximization the dominant assumption in North America, but non-profit objectives (such as maximization of games won subject to a profit constraint) widely considered to be more realistic in a European setting.

Much of the discussion concerning the nature of professional sport's special status, which may or may not justify allowing sports leagues and teams certain exemptions from the full rigours of competition law, concerns the interdependences that exist between the interests of individual teams, and the collective interest that all share in the preservation of some degree of competitive balance (in the sporting sense) among the member teams of any league. Historically, US courts have tended to accept the argument that such considerations may indeed justify certain exemptions from competition law. More recently, the European courts, while acknowledging the principles of interdependence and collective interest at a general level, have demonstrated a certain degree of scepticism over particular issues, and have regularly questioned whether stated objectives, such as the cross-subsidization of poorer teams by their richer counterparts, could not be achieved by means other than certain specific forms of anti-competitive practice. Issues such as whether revenue-sharing improves competitive balance, whether salary caps are an effective way of restraining expenditure on players' wages and salaries, and whether the collective selling of broadcasting rights should continue, appear likely to occupy much of the policy debate for many more years to come.

Notes

1. However, a more useful approach may be to treat the league as a form of joint venture (Flynn and Gilbert, 2001). This is particularly so when there is a simple entity ownership structure as in Major League Soccer in the USA in which the league as opposed to the individual member club owns all player contracts.
2. Division 1, Division 2 and Division 3 were re-named The Championship, League 1 and League 2 respectively for the start of the 2004–05 season.

References

Atkinson, S., L. Stanley and J. Tschirhart (1988), 'Revenue Sharing as an Incentive in an Agency Problem: An Example from the National Football League', *Rand Journal of Economics*, **19** (1), 27–43.

Barros, C.P., M. Ibrahimo and S. Szymanski (eds) (2002), *Transatlantic Sport: The Comparative Economics of North American and European Sports*, Cheltenham, UK and Northampton, MA, US: Edward Elgar.

Cave, M. (2000), 'Football Rights and Competition in Broadcasting', in S. Hamil, J. Michie, C. Oughton and S. Warby (eds), *Football in the Digital Age: Whose Game is it Anyway?*, Edinburgh: Mainstream Publishing, pp. 180–90.

Deloitte and Touche (2004), *Annual Review of Football Finance*, Manchester: Deloitte and Touche.

Flynn, M.A. and R.J. Gilbert (2001), 'The Analysis of Sports Leagues as Joint Ventures', *Economic Journal*, **111** (469), F27–F46.

Fort, Rodney (2003), *Sports Economics*, New Jersey: Prentice Hall.

Fort, R. and J. Quirk (1995), 'Cross-subsidisation, Incentives and Outcomes in Professional Team Sports', *Journal of Economic Literature*, **33** (3), 1265–99.

Hausman, J. and G. Leonard (1997), 'Superstars in the National Basketball Association: Economic Value and Policy', *Journal of Labor Economics*, **15** (4), 586–624.

Kesenne, S. (2000), 'Revenue Sharing and Competitive Balance in Professional Team Sports', *Journal of Sports Economics*, **1** (1), 56–65.

Lucifora, C. and R. Simmons (2003), 'Superstar Effects in Sport: Evidence From Italian Soccer', *Journal of Sports Economics*, **4** (1), 35–55.

Neale, W.C. (1964), 'The Peculiar Economics of Professional Sports', *Quarterly Journal of Economics*, **78** (1), 1–14.

Preston, I., S.F. Ross and S. Szymanski (2002), 'Seizing the Moment: A Blueprint for the Reform of World Cricket', unpublished manuscript.

Quirk, James and Rodney Fort (1999), *Hard Ball: The Abuse of Power in Pro Team Sports*, New Jersey: Princeton University Press.

Rascher, D.A. (1997), 'A Model of a Professional Sports League', in W. Hendricks (ed.), *Advances in the Economics of Sport*, vol. 2, Greenwich, CT: JAI Press.

Rosen, S. (1981), 'The Economics of Superstars', *American Economic Review*, **71** (5), 167–83.

Rosen, S. and A. Sanderson (2001), 'Labour Markets in Professional Sports', *Economic Journal*, **111** (469), F47–F68.

Rottenberg, S. (1956), 'The Baseball Player's Labor Market', *Journal of Political Economy*, **64** (3), 242–58.

Scully, G.W. (1974), 'Pay and Performance in Major League Baseball', *American Economic Review*, **64** (6), 915–30.

Sloane, P.J. (2002), 'The Regulation of Professional Team Sports', in C.P. Barros, M. Ibrahimo and S. Szymanski (eds), *Transatlantic Sport: The Comparative Economics of North American and European Sports*, Cheltenham, UK and Northampton, MA, US: Edward Elgar, pp. 50–68.

Szymanski, S. and S. Kesenne (2004), 'Competitive Balance and Gate Revenue Sharing in Team Sports', *Journal of Industrial Economics*, **52** (1), 165–77.

Vrooman, J. (1995), 'A General Theory of Professional Sports Leagues', *Southern Economic Journal*, **61** (4), 971–90.

Vrooman, J. (1996), 'The Baseball Player's Labour Market Reconsidered', *Southern Economic Journal*, **63** (2), 339–60.

13 Economics of gambling
Robert Simmons

This chapter applies economic analysis to the growing gambling sector. Over the past 50 years, gambling has become legally recognized in all industrialized economies with an increasing variety of gambling products now on offer. Technological change, primarily via the Internet, is likely to sustain this growth path. The chapter begins with a brief summary of the scope and composition of gambling in some major jurisdictions. In Section 2, we then pose the fundamental economic question of why people gamble at all, particularly in lottery games where the probability of winning the jackpot prize is of the order of one in 14 million. Next, in Section 3 we consider economic reasons why states and governments may opt to legalize forms of gambling. A public choice approach is highlighted. In Section 4 we examine some contemporary policy issues involved in regulation and deregulation of gambling, including the social benefits and costs of gambling, the use of state and government revenues from gambling for particular purposes and the threat to government tax revenues and government regulation posed by the growth of Internet gambling. Section 5 concludes the chapter.

1   The scope of gambling worldwide

Across the world, gambling covers many products and takes both legal and illegal forms. In the USA there are presently only three states where legal gambling does not take place within their borders (Hawaii, Tennessee and Utah). The total amount wagered in 2001, termed *handle* within the industry, was estimated at US $859 billion. Deductions of winnings gives gross revenues and these were US $73 billion in 2003, more than the combined revenues from movie tickets, recorded music, theme parks, spectator sports and video games (Christiansen Capital Advisors, 2003). Market-based opportunities for gambling have grown enormously over the last decade as the Internet has made it possible for gambling transactions to be carried out quickly and easily from a home PC. Hence, Internet gaming companies advertise a range of products including casino games ('blackjack without the black tie') and betting on a wide range of sporting and political outcomes. But, although Internet gambling is a strong growth sector, it should be stressed that this represents a small proportion of gross gambling revenues (8 per cent in the USA in 2003, up from 5 per cent in 2001) as many

Table 13.1   Growth of gross wagering (handle) in Australia and USA

Year	Australia	USA
1998	100.0	100.0
1999	108.8	112.5
2000	120.4	121.8
2001	125.0	125.8
2002		132.3
2003		140.5

Note: Index numbers with base year 1998.

Source: Tasmanian Gaming Commission (Australia) and Christiansen Capital Advisors (USA).

Table 13.2   Percentage composition of handle in Australia, UK and USA (1998–2003)

	Australia		UK	USA	
	1998	2001	1998	2001	2003
Casinos & gaming machines	83.1	84.9	59.0	61.4	62.4
National & state lotteries	3.1	2.8	12.8	27.0	27.4
Betting	12.6	10.8	20.9	6.2	5.4

Sources: Tasmanian Gaming Commission (Australia), Christiansen Capital Advisors (USA), and Department for Culture, Media, and Sport (UK).

or most citizens in the USA and UK still gamble by more traditional means such as visiting casinos or buying lottery tickets in stores.

Worldwide, the most prevalent form of gambling is the purchase of lottery tickets, either as part of a draw or as 'instant' scratchcards, which reveal immediate win or loss. In the USA in 2003, 38 states plus the District of Columbia operated lotteries. Seventy-two per cent of Americans admitted to playing a lottery game at least once in the year 2000 (Gtech, 2000). In 2002, state referenda supported progress towards legislation to adopt lotteries in North Dakota and Tennessee. All Canadian provinces have lotteries, as have all European countries.

Tables 13.1 and 13.2 display the growth and composition of gross annual wagering in Australia (1998 and 2001) and the USA (2001 and 2003). Table 13.2 also shows the composition of gambling in the UK for 1998, the only year for which useful figures could be obtained. These tables reveal steady growth of wagering, together with sustained dominance of wagering in casinos and on gaming machines in both Australia and the USA. The latter has been sustained recently by the expansion of casinos in Indian reservations. In contrast, the UK has greater proportions of wagering accounted for by betting on racing and sports and by lottery wagering, with a smaller weight taken up by casino and slot machine gaming.

2 Why gamble?

A gamble is a *state-contingent claim*: an individual places a stake with the prospect of either losing this amount or having the stake returned together with some winnings. Winnings are calculated in two main ways. In *pari-mutuel* betting, associated with lotteries worldwide and horse racing in the USA and Australia, bettors' wagers are placed in a pool and winnings are shared amongst successful bettors after taxes and commissions have been deducted. The terms of the bet are not known until the lottery is drawn or the race is started.

In *fixed-odds* betting, found in Las Vegas sports betting and UK book-maker betting, a particular value of winnings for a successful stake is announced to potential bettors. In Europe most sports bettors gamble on who will win a game and the odds on the game outcome tend to be fixed. US sports betting is notable for its use of a *betting line* or *point spread*. The sports gambler bets on the result of a game compared with a predicted margin of victory for one team. If Chicago Bears are predicted to beat Detroit Lions by six points, a punter betting on Chicago will win if Chicago's margin of victory exceeds six. Conversely, a punter betting on Detroit (against Chicago) will win if Chicago's margin of victory is less than six or if Detroit wins the game. Bookmakers adjust the point spread so as to equalize amounts bet on each side of the line and hence generate a risk-free profit at the fixed odds of 10 to 11. A winning wager of $10 will return $19.09 (the $10 stake plus $10 times 10/11). The bookmaker's commission, or transactions cost from the bettor's point of view, is five cents in the dollar.

Analysis of gambling in economics usually begins with the notion of *expected utility*. Denoting utility by U, wealth by W, winnings by G, stake by S and probability of winning a wager by p, expected utility $E(U)$ is given by:

$$E(U) = pU(W + G) + (1 - p)U(W - S)$$

Economic theory of consumer behaviour typically begins with the assumption that individuals are rational and are risk-averse. In Figure 13.1,

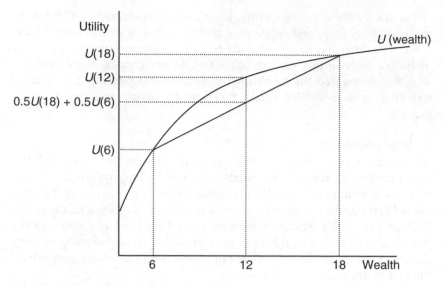

Figure 13.1   Risk aversion and gambling

risk aversion is exhibited by utility drawn as a concave relationship against wealth, with diminishing marginal utility of money. If offered a choice between the gamble in Figure 13.1, offering expected utility $E(U)$, and a 'sure thing' that pays W with certainty, where monetary returns are equal on average, a risk-averse person will always reject the gamble since $U(W) > E(U)$. A risk-averse person prefers a constant level of wealth, W, to a set of gambling opportunities in which W is the *average* level of wealth. For example, if a coin is flipped and you receive 18 cents if the coin comes up heads and six cents if it turns up tails the expected outcome is $(0.5*18) + (0.5*6) = 12$ and this will be rejected in favour of receiving 12 cents with certainty.

Risk aversion is equivalent to diminishing marginal utility of income. Essentially, a risk-averse person gains less extra satisfaction from a $100 gain compared with the drop in happiness from a $100 loss. Even a 'fair' bet, as in the example above, where the individual's expected utility is held constant over a series of wagers and there is no net loss, is rejected by the risk-averse individual. Of course, the existence of bookmaker commissions and other transactions costs (such as taxes) will usually mean that 'fair' bets are not observed in practice.

Expected utility theory is well-established in economics. Although it has been challenged theoretically and empirically (Rabin and Thaler, 2001), expected utility theory remains the economist's workhorse for dealing with difficult problems involving uncertainty. Its main advantages are simplicity and ability to generate hypotheses for empirical testing. Expected utility theory runs into some problems when trying to explain gambling behaviour. First, there is the puzzle that seemingly risk-averse individuals simultaneously gamble and buy insurance (Friedman and Savage, 1948). Only a risk-averse person would be prepared to pay a premium to reduce a risk by purchasing insurance. Someone who buys a lottery ticket effectively pays to take on risk, since the expected returns are known to be negative. This is risk-loving behaviour. So, how can a person be both risk-averse and risk-loving at the same time? One answer, which economists quickly reject, is that many people are ignorant of the terms of the bet. Irrationality is not an appealing assumption and evidence can be marshalled to demonstrate that people who gamble make the best use of available information when gambling, in accordance with the *rational expectations hypothesis*. In the case of lottery tickets, Forrest et al. (2000a) could not reject rational expectations on the part of lottery players in the UK.

Friedman and Savage proposed that people may be risk-averse when faced with the prospect of a substantial loss out of a modest asset portfolio (for example, the risk of fire or theft to one's property). Faced with a small chance of a life-changing gain, such as from winning the jackpot prize in a lottery draw, people may be risk-loving.

This resolution of the gambling–insurance puzzle leads to a further problem. If people are risk-loving with respect to lotteries, then a profit-maximizing lottery operator would only offer one prize, the jackpot. A risk-loving person offered two gambles with the same average value and different spreads would prefer the one with greater spread. He or she would be prepared to pay more for a larger spread gamble than a smaller one. Hence, lottery operators would make larger profits by offering a single large prize than by offering several large ones. Yet, lottery draws usually offer a range of prizes, not just the top jackpot prize. Horse race betting pays out winnings for second and third placed horses.

The primary difficulty with applying expected utility theory to gambling behaviour is that it views gambling as a speculative investment. But it is plausible to argue that gambling confers direct consumption benefits to the player. These benefits would comprise the fun involved in talking to friends and work colleagues about how to spend a lottery jackpot prize, and associated anticipated pleasure of giving notice to an employer, and the thrill involved with betting on a horse or sports team. Such dreams are used in lottery advertising, hence the slogan 'your ticket outta here' found in New Jersey. This thrill of gambling gives added pleasure to watching a horse race or sports fixture on television or at the venue. The 'fun' associated with gambling, even where players lose on average, has been used to motivate consumer behaviour in lotteries in a number of studies such as Forrest et al. (2002), Kearney (2002) and Farrell and Walker (1999). The emphasis in such studies is on consumption benefits from gambling rather than returns to gambling as an investment.

Many people engage in a lot of 'gambling-like' activities that do not involve real money, such as playing bridge. This is additional evidence on the associated consumption value of gambling.

Given that individuals decide to gamble, their consumer demand for particular gambling products can be couched in terms of the traditional economic variables of prices, income, price of substitute goods and market size.

The notion of a price of a gamble is subtle since it is linked to expected value of winnings. Generally, the price of a gamble can be expressed as the price paid to make a $1 wager. That is, how much should be spent on gambling, on average, to make a $1 return. This price is termed the *take-out* (one minus expected value of a gamble). In casino gaming the take-out is also the *house advantage*. Within casino gaming, Eadington (1999) shows that the lowest house advantage occurs in blackjack, baccarat and craps, while the highest house advantage accrues to keno, American roulette and slots. Within casino gaming, though, competition influences the size of house advantage and it is notable that Indian casinos placed on Indian reservations tend to offer larger house advantage than Las Vegas casinos, and are highly profitable, partly by virtue of their remote locations (Anders, 2003).

The demand for casino gambling has recently been investigated in a traditional economic formulation by Thalheimer and Ali (2003). They obtained data on slot machine wagering at 27 venues present at various times over the period 1991–98, giving 153 observations. They measure demand for slot machine gambling by amounts wagered annually on slot machines at US casinos located either on riverboats or at racetracks ('racinos') as a proportion of market area population. This measure is expressed at constant prices and in logarithms and then used as a dependent variable in a least squares regression. From their estimates, Thalheimer and Ali find that higher take-outs lead to lower amounts of slot machine wagering with elastic demand at relatively high take-out rates. Beyond US $16 500 annual per capita income, higher income is associated with greater slot machine wagering so that casino gambling is a normal good at higher income levels.

Access is an important variable determining slot machine gambling. Greater access from a market area, in terms of shorter distances travelled to casinos, raises slot machine wagering. The presence of competing riverboats or of Indian casinos, as substitutes, lowers slot machine wagering. These results are very much in accord with prior economic reasoning. The effects of regulation are pronounced as casinos with stricter loss limits and those with greater restrictions on boarding times have lower amounts of slot machine wagering.

Demand for lottery tickets has been investigated by a number of researchers (Forrest, 2003). The empirical procedure established by Gulley and Scott (1993) takes the nominal price of a lottery ticket as fixed but estimates the *effective price* of a unit stake. This is computed as one minus the expected value associated with winning the jackpot prize. In general, expected value (*EV*) is given by:

$$EV = p*JACKPOT*SHARE + \text{expected value of smaller prizes}$$

where p is the probability of winning the jackpot ($1/14\,000\,000$ in the 6/49 game operated in several jurisdictions, including the UK), *JACKPOT* is the value of the jackpot and *SHARE* is the expected share of the jackpot of a winning ticket, dependent on the distribution of number selections of other bettors. More specifically:

$$EV = [1/N][R + (1 - t)N][1 - e^{pN}] + \text{expected value of smaller prizes}$$

where N is level of sales for current drawing, R is the rollover from previous drawing, when the jackpot is not won and is carried forward, t is percentage of wagers not returned to bettors in prizes.

The empirical procedure is to estimate EV, compute $1 - EV$ as the effective price and then estimate lottery sales. The rollover value plays a critical role in the determination of expected value and hence effective price. Rollovers lower the effective price of play. The rollover is like 'free' money in the prize fund but it must be noted that the benefit of rollover is dispersed more thinly the higher are sales so, in the limit, effective price with rollover converges to (and does not fall below) take-out rate as sales increase (Forrest, 2003). When rollovers occur, demand for lottery tickets rises in response to the effective price reduction. Generally, the take-out is rather high in lottery games: a typical game will only return around 50 cents out of a $1 stake to the bettor in the form of prizes.

Various studies, summarized in Forrest (2003), have estimated the price elasticity of demand for lottery tickets, both for US states and for the UK. Results suggest that this elasticity is moderately above one in absolute value for US states and around one in the UK (Forrest et al., 2000b). A key difference between these jurisdictions is that the UK National Lottery is operated by a private franchise, whereas US state lotteries are typically run by the state authorities. In the UK case, unitary elasticity is consistent with revenue-maximizing behaviour by the operator and is therefore in accord with UK government objectives. In US state lotteries, the absolute price elasticity that maximizes revenues for the state is 1.2 and evidence of whether this is actually achieved is mixed (Gulley and Scott, 1993).

However, referring back to the consumption motive for gamble, the size of the predicted jackpot prize, rather than effective price, may be the primary economic variable affecting sales. Evidence by Forrest et al. (2002) was unable to distinguish between these two effects as the expected jackpot prize and effective price were highly correlated in UK lottery sales data.

A feature of consumer demand that has been largely ignored in the economic literature on gambling is the increased demand for variety that goes with rising incomes and rising demand for leisure. Racing, casino gaming and sports betting can be viewed as entertainment products that compete with other leisure pursuits. A night out at a casino in the USA or Britain is an alternative to a visit to the cinema or a show or a sports event. This raises the possibility of an 'option value' of gambling; I may not actually visit a nearby casino but if I tire of my normal leisure pursuits the option of casino gambling is available.

Therefore, it is reasonable to suggest that gambling products, on the whole, are normal goods. For example, Paton et al. (2004) estimate empirically that income (average earnings) has a significantly positive impact on betting demand in the UK. As consumer incomes rise, the demand for leisure will grow and the demand for gambling will continue to rise. Of course, this still leaves scope for demand variation within the sector, some of which is traceable to demographic influence. In the UK, for example, it is clear that demand for horse and greyhound betting is falling, while demand for soccer and sports betting is on a rising trend as younger gamblers prefer betting on individual and team sports. Paton et al. (2004) argue that the introduction of the UK National Lottery did not reduce demand for bookmaker betting but there was evidence of price-driven substitution between purchases of lottery tickets and bookmaker betting. However, the latter conclusion is based on use of monthly betting data, which are excessively aggregated for the purpose of the authors' study. Within the UK National Lottery, Forrest et al. (2002) find some evidence that the main lottery draws and instant scratchcard games are partial substitutes but own-game characteristics are the largest influence on sales. Hence, sales of instant scratchcards do not seriously cannibalize lottery draw sales.

A further type of substitution involving lotteries that needs to be considered is the impact on charitable giving. When the UK National Lottery was launched in 1994, various charities complained that this would result in lower charitable donations. Tanner (2002) finds that, when asked, 'Which reason most explains why you play the UK National Lottery?', only 3 per cent of respondents replied 'yes' to the option, 'to contribute to the good causes that the Lottery supports', notwithstanding the tendency of the National Lottery operator to use examples of funding for 'good causes' in television advertising. Tanner also used survey data to determine the participation and extent of charitable giving using information on peoples' age, income, education and wider macroeconomic conditions. She finds that, comparing survey responses before and after the 1994 UK National Lottery launch, neither the number of people giving to charity nor the level of donations changed significantly following the Lottery's introduction.

In the USA, Levitsky et al. (2000) offer evidence on monthly gaming revenues by source from 1988 through to 1995 from Clark County, Nevada, which contains Las Vegas. They show that although slot machines contributed to county gaming revenue at an increasing rate over time, the impact of table games on gaming revenues was declining. Siegel and Anders (2001) find evidence of revenue displacement from lotteries to casinos in Arizona, especially for games offering big prizes. Thalheimer and Ali (1995) find that the introduction of US state lotteries reduced horse betting demand.

What these empirical studies show is that when gambling is deregulated, consumers switch demand for gambling between different products. Demand for gambling as a whole tends to increase, but there are also cannibalization effects as some older gambling products tend to be displaced by new products. Hence, intra-sectoral variations in demand for gambling do occur and over time some sectors decline while others grow.

In addition to cannibalization effects, there are also conventional substitution effects as the impact of a price change in one sector spills over into demand in another sector. Such impacts are difficult to discern in gambling since the effective price of a bet for, say, fixed-odds horse racing, may not vary much over time. In the lottery sector, though, variations in effective price occur due to rollovers. Forrest et al. (2004) model daily bookmaker betting turnovers by sector and find that a lottery rollover induces substitution away from horse race, soccer and numbers betting. Paton et al. (2003) model monthly bookmaker betting and also conclude that there is strong evidence of positive cross-price elasticities across gambling products; when take-outs fall in one sector, sales will increase in that sector but demand falls in other sectors. Hence, intra-sectoral variations in demand for gambling do occur and over time some sectors decline while others grow. Against the rise in gambling revenues due to market expansion, must be offset some negative effects as take-outs fall in competing sectors. The size of these negative effects is still open for debate, particularly as some household-based evidence concludes that lottery spending does not substitute for other forms of gambling (Kearney, 2002). Kearney finds instead that household lottery gambling crowds out other household consumption by around 2 per cent. Moreover, larger proportional reductions were found among low-income households.

Overall, though, the demand for gambling is rising, as shown in Table 13.1. Given the general rise in demand for gambling, how should authorities regulate gambling? Some commentators argue that increased demand would generate social costs in excess of social benefits and further liberalization of gambling should not be encouraged. Legalization of gambling is considered next.

3   Why tolerate gambling?

Legalization of gambling typically meets with moral, religious and political opposition. In Tennessee, a referendum was carried out in November 2002 on a decision over whether to enable federal government legislature to install a state lottery. This referendum was conducted after a 17-year-long campaign by Senator Steve Cohen and resulted in a 58:42 majority approving progress towards legislation. There were several important ingredients to the successful Tennessee pro-lottery campaign. First, Tennessee is surrounded by states that already offer lotteries. It was recognized that potential state tax revenues were being shifted across state borders as lottery players travelled to buy lottery tickets and the pro-lottery campaigners made this a powerful pragmatic argument for lottery adoption. It was alleged that an annual loss of US $76 million of potential Tennessee revenues was incurred to the Kentucky lottery alone in the form of cross-border sales. Second, Tennessee had a fiscal deficit and its citizens appeared reluctant to vote for increases in sales or income tax. Hence, proceeds from lottery sales could in principle raise state revenues and alleviate any future increases in state taxes. Third, the pro-lottery campaigners drew upon the examples of Florida and Georgia and pledged that net revenues from a Tennessee state lottery would be devoted entirely to support specific educational programmes. These included university scholarships along the lines of the Georgia lottery-financed, merit-based HOPE scheme (HOPE is the acronym for Helping Outstanding Pupils Educationally). Pre-kindergarten nursery education would also benefit from lottery finance. Hence, the pro-lottery campaigners tried successfully to tap into the altruism of the Tennessee electorate, even though such altruism did not seem to extend to voting for tax raises.

This example shows some of the key economic and political influences upon lottery adoption. As shown by Kearney (2002), lottery adoption in the USA can be traced geographically from the north-east, with the first state lottery in New Hampshire in 1964, through to the west, then to the midwest and eventually to the south. A bandwagon effect on US lottery adoption seems clearly pronounced.

Sauer (2001) offers an interest group model of gambling regulation, which seems to be well-suited to the US experience of lottery and casino legalization. He notes that gambling markets are, 'the most restricted and politicised markets in the American economy'. For simplicity, Sauer's model has two groups. One has a taste for gambling and the other opposes gambling on religious and moral grounds. It is notable that vehement opposition to legalization of gambling in the USA has come from leaders of church groups, especially Baptists. The opposition group gains satisfaction (welfare) from restrictions on gambling. But state lotteries, and also casinos, offer a useful means of raising revenue. Note that the image of casinos as associated with 'hard' gambling makes legalization of casinos more difficult than legalization of lotteries, which (allegedly) represent 'soft' gambling and possibly capture a broader set of customers.

According to Sauer, states with higher tax burdens are more likely to be lottery states. Among lottery states, those with higher tax burdens get lotteries earlier than others. In equilibrium, the marginal value to the anti-gambling group of restricting gambling equals the marginal welfare cost on the pro-gambling group. A rise in the consumption value of gambling, which could come from rising incomes as argued above or a change in tastes, reduces the equilibrium level of restrictions. A rise in social costs of restrictions, for example from crime, would raise the level of restrictions.

For the anti-gambling lobby, there are some trade-offs to consider. Religious groups often solicit contributions via church bingo and lotteries. Church people like education and transport facilities just as pro-gambling citizens do and will be prepared to reduce opposition to lotteries if the opportunity cost of lottery finance rises.

The advantage to state governments of legalized gambling is that, in the context of growing demands on government revenues, removal of prohibition permits high marginal returns as new tax revenue flows in. Extra tax revenue is easier to capture from a new source than by raising existing taxes. It is notable that some states (Arizona, Colorado, California), which had large-scale property tax revolts in the 1980s subsequently passed bills to install state lotteries.

In summary, Sauer states that, 'as long as the shadow price of Government revenue remains high, political equilibrium requires that high cost revenue sources such as gambling markets will be utilised as a means of public finance'.

Empirical evidence offered by Erekson et al. (1999) is consistent with Sauer's application of public choice theory to lottery adoption. Their evidence shows that the probability of lottery adoption in 50 US states in any year over 1962 to 1990 varies positively with the size of state government deficit in the previous year, level of per capita income and the percentage of contiguous states with established lotteries. The probability of lottery adoption is lower, the greater is state education spending per pupil and the greater is the percentage of state population that is Protestant. Intriguingly, a variable representing incidence of Baptist or fundamentalist religious groups, as a sub-set of Protestants, was not included in the study although earlier studies had revealed these as being statistically negatively significant in explaining lottery adoption (Caudill et al., 1995). Alternatively, other evidence suggests that Catholics are more prone to support legalized gambling, including lottery adoption (Alm et al., 1993). Hence, legislation to adopt lotteries is likely to be passed when fiscal stress is high, particularly if neighbouring states have already adopted lotteries. These two important economic forces were clearly paramount in the majority decision by the Tennessee electorate to vote for lottery adoption.

The public choice model of gambling regulation has great appeal and force in explaining US state lottery adoption. However, gambling services are not homogeneous. In the USA, it is possible for citizens to simultaneously vote for lottery adoption yet voice fears, and reject, legalization of Internet betting. The public choice model is incomplete in that tolerance of one form of gambling (lotteries) may coexist with resistance to other forms (casino gambling on the Internet).

In the UK, progress is currently (2005) being made towards further gambling deregulation as the government has produced a White Paper outlining specific proposals. Particularly notable are proposals to relax licensing restrictions on casino openings and to permit casinos to offer entertainment and to install more slot machines than are permitted at present. Customers would have immediate access to casinos rather than facing a 24-hour wait for membership as at present. The eventual consequence is likely to be a growth in the number of casinos operating in the UK but this will take time. Unlike the USA, religious opposition has not been a strong factor in the regulation of gambling in the UK. Nevertheless, the UK government softened its initial plans to introduce a substantial number of 'resort casinos' modelled along the lines of the large Las Vegas hotel-casino leisure complexes. The number of resort casinos is initially to be limited to just one compared to 24 in earlier proposals. This is likely to confer monopoly rents to the fortunate owner of this facility. Also, the capacity for large jackpot slot machines has been substantially reduced compared to initial plans. In line with the public choice theory of Sauer (2001), noted earlier, this climbdown followed increased lobbying by groups concerned with problem gambling. Such lobbying was supported by elements of the industry likely to be adversely affected by casino deregulation, in particular, bingo operators and amusement arcade owners. UK governments have typically taken a pragmatic approach to regulation of gambling with an underlying motive to satisfy, but not induce, latent demand and, further, to extract tax revenues from gambling sources in the form of specific levies on gambling products. Until October 2001, gamblers placing bets in British retail outlets were faced with a tax of 9 per cent on winnings, part of which constituted a levy to help finance the horse race industry.

4 Issues

The growth of the gambling sector generates a number of policy issues. In this section we offer a quick review of some interesting problems of regulation facing policy-makers around the world.

4.1 Gambling as economic regenerator?

For most economists, the fact that gambling is provided to meet consumer demand is in itself welfare-enhancing in an economy, provided that consumers are not systematically misinformed. The evidence on lottery sales from Forrest et al. (2000a) and Kearney (2002) points to the likelihood that consumers of lottery products are making well-informed purchases. If purchases of gambling products add to consumer utility, for those who wish to participate, then this could be taken as sufficient reason to permit the availability of gambling.

Some would go further than the consumer welfare argument and propose that gambling facilities confer wider social benefits in the form of higher economic growth, higher employment rates and economic regeneration in previously rundown urban areas. Such claims are often wildly exaggerated. The cited expenditure and income effects consist of direct and indirect employment effects, such that total employment effects are multiplied up from the first round impact, and gains in value added. Anders (2003) points to a study paid for by the Arizona Indian Gaming Association on the economic impacts of Indian casinos in Arizona. It was proposed that these casinos generated 9300 jobs and had a total impact of US $468 million.

These numbers should be treated with caution. The sizes of these multipliers are most likely biased upwards for a number of reasons. First, consultancy reports often deliver numbers that validate the purpose for which the consultants were employed and which might facilitate repeat business for the firms involved. Beneficial estimates are thereby inflated. Second, impacts are based on predicted rather than actual gaming revenues. Third, price effects are typically ignored. Prices of local services and of property may increase. In the case of Las Vegas, wider economic benefits were obtained by synergy between gambling, tourism, hotel accommodation and the entertainment industry as large corporations developed the concept of a destination gambling resort with wider facilities than just casinos

(Eadington, 1999). The rapid growth and huge popularity of Las Vegas is testimony to the skill applied to this project, particularly as the earlier image of Las Vegas was of a crime-ridden city ruled by mob gangsters.

But Las Vegas is a hard act to follow. In Britain, local authorities and leisure companies have worked on a scheme to take advantage of forth-coming casino deregulation to set up a Las Vegas-style resort casino in Blackpool, a down-at-heel working class seaside resort on the north-west coast of England. Blackpool lacks the hot sunshine of Las Vegas but, more importantly, it also lacks the exclusivity applied to gambling in Nevada. For US citizens, Las Vegas and Atlantic City are the only resort-based gambling centres available. In England, any attempt to render Blackpool an exclusive destination for casino gambling would be met with a legitimate outcry from competitors. As noted above, the UK government has set out proposals to restrict the number of resort casinos to eight. This would most likely lead to economic rents for large casino operators with consumer welfare reduced as take-out rates are raised above levels that would be associated with greater competition.

4.2   Social costs

Social costs of gambling such as crime, bankruptcy, divorce and suicide are much cited side-effects of gambling. Grinols and Mustard (2001) claim that a county with a casino had about 8 per cent higher crime rates than a county without a casino four years after the opening of a casino. However, we should be wary of inferring too much from this claim. Additional crime is stimulated by *any* new leisure facility, not just a casino. This is because new visitors arrive and represent new targets for criminals. Also, new criminals will move into an area where new spending occurs. This will apply for a new sports stadium as much as a casino. To then impute all social costs of crime to gambling seems unreasonable, unless the investigator controls for all possible sources of crime. It is apparent that the Grinols and Mustard study is lacking in a full set of control variables. Other researchers offer more modest estimates on the relationship between gambling and crime (see Stitt et al., 2003).

The most serious social costs considered in the gambling literature relate to pathological or *problem gambling*. According to Grinols (2001), problem gamblers (defined as a broader category than pathological gamblers) represent 2.8 per cent of the US population and generate social costs in the form of bankruptcy, suicide, depression and support costs from counselling and medical services of the order of US $18 000 per problem gambler per annum.

The existence of these costs must be acknowledged. For instance, Stitt et al. (2003) compared the percentage increase of personal bankruptcies per capita for casino jurisdictions with the percentage increase in bankruptcies for paired non-casino jurisdictions over 1989 to 1998. They found that the introduction of casino gaming was associated with a significant increase in bankruptcy rates in five out of eight counties with casino openings.

But are these kinds of costs really 'social'? It is hard to see how gambling can confer social costs of the same order of magnitude as narcotics, smoking or alcoholism. The external effects such as death by secondary smoking or drunk driving are not so clear in the case of gambling. Much of the social cost element involves distress within households as problem gamblers run down household assets to support their habit and incur depression and other illnesses that impair family life. Walker and Barnett (2000) make the extra leap to argue that problem gambling does not really impose social costs. The costs of personal bankruptcy, depression and divorce amount to intra-household transfers rather than external, social costs. Of course, the costs of dealing with medical and other disorders associated with problem gambling are external to the extent that counselling and other services are provided to help problem gamblers. But most of the costs identified by Grinols as 'social' are actually transfers within households according to Walker and Barnett. On this view, the social costs of gambling are not severe enough to warrant continued opposition to new forms of gambling.

Although Walker and Barnett have a point, problem gambling is recognized by governments and industry sources as coming from a physiological addiction and various governments have set up funding to research into problem gambling. Support for problem gambling in the forms of additional research and medical and counselling facilities to help problem gamblers were identified as an essential feature of the UK government's proposals to deregulate gambling.

A strand of economics research relevant to concerns with 'problem gambling' emanates from the Becker–Murphy rational addiction theory that we discussed in Chapter 1. Recall that in this approach, consumer demand for addictive goods depends on both past consumption and expected future consumption. Consumption is affected by exogenous shocks such as changes in taxation or product market regulation. Following these shocks, two equilibria may be derived: a high use equilibrium ('addiction') and a low or zero use equilibrium ('abstention').

The rational addiction theory seems applicable to some, but not all, gambling products. The wide incidence of participation in lotto games suggests that lotto demand is not consistent with rational addiction (Forrest, 2003). Informal analysis of scratchcard purchases, however, does reveal some consumers with high rates of purchase.

Mobilia (1993) tested the rational addiction hypothesis using a large data set of racetracks in the USA over the 1950–86 period. Using take-out as the price variable and real amounts wagered by attendees she found, in line with studies of rational addiction for cigarettes, that the long-run price elasticity was –0.7, more than double the short-run elasticity. An increase in current take-out rate was observed to reduce the real amount bet per attendee in past and future years. Similarly, Nichols (1998) modelled monthly wagering in the Iowa riverboat casino industry and found that long-run price elasticity (again, using take-out as the price variable) was almost double the short-run measure.

The findings of Mobilia and Nichols may suggest that, if certain gambling products are deregulated or if take-out is reduced, that the incidence of addiction, and hence social costs, would increase. There are three important caveats, however. First, the long-run price elasticities reported in these studies are not particularly large; the largest estimate is –1.2 in the Nichols study. Second, the Becker–Murphy model posits utility-maximizing behaviour on the part of addicted consumers, regardless of any social disapproval, and if these are in some way constrained by government policy to have their pleasure denied, then consumer surplus is lost. Third, the relationship between increased incidence of addiction and social costs needs to be carefully quantified, rather than assumed, and careful empirical research is needed before welfare and policy judgements can be made.

4.3   Illegal betting

If prohibition of some forms of gambling is sustained, it does not follow that problem gambling is suppressed. The activity simply goes underground into the illegal sector where it is less easily monitored and problems such as uncontrolled debt and risk of physical violence become magnified. The scale of illegal activity in the USA is vast. With an estimated volume of wagering at US $100 billion and gross revenues of US $10 billion, the illegal sports betting market dominates the legal market. This is not surprising. The federal US government declared sports betting illegal in 1992, although Delaware, Nevada and Oregon were exempted, and now the legal sports betting market is concentrated in Las Vegas.

Strumpf (2003) provides a fascinating account of illegal sports betting in New York. His study considers betting records of six convicted, illegal bookmakers. It appears that these bookmakers operated like orthodox firms. They operated incentive contracts to regulate employee behaviour and developed relationships of trust and repeat business with their customers. These in turn gambled large sums of the order of between US $200 000 and US $400 000 per bettor in the larger operations. The bookmakers were essentially price-takers, accepting spreads and odds from Las Vegas. The bookmakers incurred substantial financial risk and could be characterized as risk-neutral or risk-averse. Bettors were subject to, and were prepared to accept, some price discrimination in that less fair prices were offered to bets on particular local teams such as the New York Yankees. Hence, sentiment was a feature of betting in this part of the illegal sector.

If this sector were legalized, nationwide operations would probably absorb small, illegal bookmakers but would, initially at least, wish to tap into the customer relationships established with the bettors involved in the illegal sector. Tax revenue would undoubtedly increase, but an illegal fringe, with tax avoidance, could persist as occurred in the alcoholic beverages sector in the USA following the end of Prohibition. The personal relationships between illegal bookmakers and their customers have recently been used by Internet bookmakers to develop information on creditworthiness and supervision of credit lines so as to offset (legal) bettor default.

The sports betting sector is surely ripe for legalization, yet there is little pressure within the USA for this to happen. Under a special legal provision, Atlantic City was offered a two-year period when casinos were opened there, so as to open sports books, but supply was not forthcoming. The sports betting market in Nevada is highly competitive and margins are very low. Hence, the pressure for legal entry into this market is weak.

4.4   The threat of the Internet?

Not all betting is about to be conducted on the Internet. According to Strumpf (2003), 'many (illegal) bettors would be unable to place an internet wager simply because they can't operate a computer'. Similarly, in the UK, traditional betting in the form of visits to a retail outlet (betting shop) will continue to be the mainstay of the bookmaking business for some time to come.

Nevertheless, the role of the Internet in shaping the gambling industry has already been substantial. The Informa Media Group predicts that Internet betting in the UK is forecast to grow to £1.4 billion in 2006 from £250 million in 2002. Gambling will be given a large boost from technological change as betting opportunities become available from computers, 3G cell phones and interactive TV. According to Datamonitor, interactive TV gambling in Europe will generate US $11 billion in revenue by 2006.

In the USA, there is no legal recourse of Internet gambling operations to bettor default. Interestingly, predictions suggest that Europe, and not North America, will take the dominant share of e-gambling business over the next few years. A key reason for this is that, in the USA, Internet gambling is essentially illegal. It is unclear whether Internet gambling is technically illegal in the USA. The Federal Wire Act, originating in 1962, prohibits the transmission of wagering information on sports across state lines. Confusion exists over the scope of this Act and whether it extends to Internet betting, rather than wireless technology. US Congress has made attempts to pass Internet prohibition acts without success. But most US credit card companies will not honour Internet gambling and this overrides any law. Internet casinos are absent in the USA and legal Internet casinos, such as those located in the Isle of Man or Australia, will refuse to accept wagers from the USA due to its confused legal status. Some locations, such as Belize, do have Internet sites that take wagers from the USA, particularly in the form of sports betting, and these will proliferate and generate increasing volumes of Internet business in the immediate future.

US Internet gambling is unlikely to be legalized in the near future. Standard concerns about problem gambling and underage gambling have been raised. Although it is clear that it would be welfare-improving to legalize and regulate Internet gambling, rather than have money flow abroad or into the illegal sector, any campaign to legalize Internet gambling in the USA would not carry the same level of support as found for lottery adoption. In part, this is due to a distaste for Internet gambling by non-participants (puritanism) and also a perception shared by the public and policy-makers that Internet gambling intrudes upon private space by permitting 'living room casinos'.

In the UK and Australia, more effort has been made to legalize and regulate Internet gambling. Indeed, the UK government explicitly recognized the legality of Internet gambling in its recent White Paper. The problem is how to harness Internet gambling to raise tax revenues. Paton et al. (2002) show how one policy response to the growth of Internet gambling may benefit consumers, producers and government in a welfare-improving manner. Prior to October 2001, the UK government levied a tax on betting as a proportion of winnings. In October 2001, this was replaced by a 15 per cent tax on bookmakers' gross revenues. The rationale for this change was that British bookmakers had shifted some parts of their operations offshore, to the Channel Islands and Gibraltar, where tax regulations were far less stringent. These bookmakers established Internet facilities for betting following the lead of Victor Chandler's bookmaking operation. As a result, the UK government was faced with potentially severe reduction in tax revenue from betting, as custom was likely to move offshore. Given Strumpf's quote above, the leakage could well have taken a long time to occur but the UK government held negotiations with leading bookmakers and agreed a switch in tax policy. In return, the bookmakers agreed to move their offshore operations back onshore. This switch of tax policy towards profits taxation rather than sales taxation could perhaps be imitated in other jurisdictions. Thus far, bookmakers have claimed increased turnover following the change in tax regime. It is worth noting that, through the period in the late 1990s when offshore Internet betting was developed, some evidence suggests that the UK fixed-odds soccer betting market moved closer to informational efficiency. Objective probabilities of game outcomes became more closely aligned with ex ante betting odds offered by leading bookmakers (Forrest and Simmons, 2002).

This new tax policy still leaves the UK government with problems. It plans to legalize online gaming, permitting punters to identify onshore and offshore sites. Online operators will be subject to approval and monitoring to ensure compliance with regulations. UK applicants for legalized online gaming must be registered as a UK company, have a UK server and a co.uk domain address. This seems fine but the government has still not addressed the issue of tax treatment of Internet gambling.

Furthermore, the UK government still faces the threat of migration of gambling business, and hence potential tax revenue, offshore. Looking at casinos, the current UK position is that profits tax and gaming duty add 7.5 per cent to overall UK tax on casino turnover. Other European locations, such as the Channel Islands, offer much lower tax rates. There, all that an offshore gambling operation has to pay to establish itself is a small licence fee. Further, Alderney in the Channel Islands has uncapped the number of gambling licences for sale (Wilding, 2002). Hence, the UK may have forestalled the movement of its established bookmaking operations offshore but there is still scope for gambling to be established in low-tax destinations.

4.5   Gambling as social engineering

Lottery revenues are essentially an implicit sales tax on consumers; players buy tickets and, after costs, revenue is returned to the government to spend as they consider appropriate. US states operate their own lotteries and in these cases the revenue goes direct to government coffers. In the UK, a private franchise operates the lottery but taxation is levied on the operator's revenue from lottery sales. Of a £1 lottery ticket, 12 pence goes directly to general tax revenue as 'lottery duty' while a further 28 pence is devoted to 'Good Causes' including promotion of sports, cultural and arts and heritage facilities.

As noted in Section 3, some US states have earmarked lottery revenues for specific purposes such as educational programmes. The Tennessee government aims to use its forthcoming lottery to promote college scholarships and to finance pre-kindergarten nurseries. Such schemes have been judged as wasteful and misdirected by several economists.

Rubenstein and Scafidi (2002) and Borg and Stranahan (2000) show that lottery taxation is highly regressive. Spending the proceeds of lottery taxation on college scholarships, as in the Georgia HOPE programme, makes this regressivity worse. The benefits of HOPE scholarships are shown to have been received disproportionately by higher income and more educated households. This is not surprising as most college students come from this type of background. Lower income and non-white households tended to have higher purchases of lottery products while receiving lower benefits as compared with higher income and white households.

Dynarski (2000) shows that Georgia's HOPE programme widened the gap in college attendance between blacks and whites and between those from low- and high-income families. Given lower marginal tax rates, both sales and income taxes would be much more efficient revenue sources than the implicit lottery tax. State income tax could be raised from 3 to 3.39 per cent or sales tax could be increased from 4 to 4.69 per cent. Either option would be less regressive than the use of lottery revenues.

The use of lottery revenues to support particular purposes violates the horizontal equity principle of public finance. It is also wasteful. Farrell and Walker (1999) estimate that the deadweight welfare loss from UK lottery taxation devoted to 'Good Causes' is of the order of 35 per cent of the revenue raised. This suggests that this means of raising money for 'Good Causes' is particularly inefficient. Since lottery products display income inelasticity this form of taxation is also regressive.

Where lottery revenues are devoted to particular projects, there is evidence from the UK National Lottery that this simply crowds out existing expenditure (Bailey and Connolly, 1997). In Florida, money formerly dedicated to education was used elsewhere and replaced by lottery revenues with no net increase in education spending. If lottery-financed public spending is indeed additional, this is itself cause for concern. Forrest and Simmons (2003) observe that expenditure on sports projects and other 'Good Causes' channelled via lottery funding escapes formal evaluation of the costs and benefits of projects. Funds may be directed towards grandiose projects (such as the Millennium Dome in London), which would not be funded if in competition with other sectors for the use of general taxation.

5   Conclusion

These are interesting times for the gambling industry. Rising incomes in advanced economies and associated rising demand for leisure has generated increased demand for gambling products. Consumers demand variety in leisure and gambling opportunities have proliferated in the last decade across the USA and Europe. Within the gambling sector, some parts have declined, such as horse racing in the USA and greyhound racing in the UK whereas others, such as legal sports betting in the UK, have grown. On the supply-side, technological change is a major factor in shaping new gambling opportunities. It appears that the USA is setting its face against legalization of Internet betting whereas other jurisdictions are permitting Internet betting opportunities to benefit consumers of gambling and, of course, to claim some part of the revenues for taxation. Gambling does confer some externalities, such as increased crime and problem gambling, and policy-makers need to identify the sources and scope of such external effects and design appropriate programmes to support individuals and communities that are adversely affected.

From a welfare economics standpoint it is surely better to legalize and regulate gambling rather than have revenues flow overseas or to illegal operators, who currently thrive in the USA. Sauer's public choice model of gambling helps us understand how and when US states adopt lotteries but does not explain why US citizens, and their politicians, can simultaneously vote for lottery adoption yet show resistance to legalization of Internet gambling.

The continued growth of demand for gambling is a sure bet. Policy-makers will need to reconsider how to manage this growth in demand for gambling as an acceptable leisure pursuit. The opportunities for researchers to investigate problems and issues in this field will grow alongside the latent demand for its various products.

References

Alm, J., M. McKee and M. Skidmore (1993), 'Fiscal pressure, tax competition and the introduction of state lotteries', *National Tax Journal*, **46** (4), 463–76.

Anders, G. (2003), 'Reconsidering the economic impact of Indian casino gambling', in Leighton Vaughan Williams (ed.), *The Economics of Gambling*, London: Routledge.

Bailey, S. and S. Connolly (1997), 'The National Lottery: a preliminary assessment of net additionality', *Scottish Journal of Political Economy*, **44** (1), 100–112.

Borg, M. and H. Stranahan (2000), 'Lottery funded merit scholarships: some lessons from the Florida Bright Futures scholarship program', University of North Florida, working paper.

Caudill, S., J. Ford, F. Mixon and T. Peng (1995), 'A discrete-time hazard model of lottery adoption', *Applied Economics*, **27** (6), 555–61.

Christiansen Capital Advisors (2003), Gross Annual Wager Data, retrieved from www.ccai.com.

Department for Culture, Media and Sport (2001), *The Gambling Review Report*, London.

Dynarski, S. (2000), 'Hope for whom? Financial aid for the middle class and its impact on college attendance', *National Tax Journal*, **53** (3), 629–61.

Eadington, W. (1999), 'The economics of casino gambling', *Journal of Economic Perspectives*, **13** (3), 173–92.

Erekson, O., G. Platt, C. Whistler and A. Ziegert (1999), 'Factors influencing the adoption of state lotteries', *Applied Economics*, **31** (7), 875–84.

Farrell, L. and I. Walker (1999), 'The welfare effects of Lotto: evidence from the UK', *Journal of Public Economics*, **72** (1), 92–120.

Forrest, D. (2003), 'Time-series modelling of Lotto demand', in Leighton Vaughan Williams (ed.), *The Economics of Gambling*, London: Routledge.

Forrest, D. and R. Simmons (2002), 'Globalisation and efficiency in the fixed-odds soccer betting market', University of Salford, working paper.

Forrest, D. and R. Simmons (2003), 'Sport and gambling', *Oxford Review of Economic Policy*, **19** (4), 598–611.

Forrest, D., O.D. Gulley and R. Simmons (2000a), 'Testing for rational expectations in the UK National Lottery', *Applied Economics*, **32** (2), 315–26.

Forrest, D., O.D. Gulley and R. Simmons (2000b), 'Elasticity of demand for UK National Lottery tickets', *National Tax Journal*, **53** (4), 853–63.

Forrest, D., O.D. Gulley and R. Simmons (2004), 'Substitution between games in the UK National Lottery', *Applied Economics*, **36** (7), 645–51.

Forrest, D., O.D. Gulley and R. Simmons (2005), 'The relationship between betting and lottery play: a high frequency time-series analysis', Lancaster University Discussion Paper.

Forrest, D., R. Simmons and N. Chesters (2002), 'Buying a dream: alternative models of demand for lotto', *Economic Inquiry*, **40** (3), 485–96.

Friedman, M. and L. Savage (1948), 'The utility analysis of choices involving risk', *Journal of Political Economy*, **56** (4), 279–304.

Grinols, E. (2001), 'Cutting the craps and cards: right thinking about gambling economics', University of Illinois, working paper.

Grinols, E. and D. Mustard (2001), 'Business profitability versus social profitability: evaluating industries with externalities – the case of casinos', *Managerial and Decision Economics*, **22** (1), 143–62.

Gtech Corporation (2000), *The Vital Signs of Legalized Gambling in America: Gtech's 8th Annual National Gaming Survey*, West Greenwich, RI.

Gulley, O.D. and F. Scott (1993), 'The demand for wagering on state-operated lottery games', *National Tax Journal*, **45** (1), 13–22.

Kearney, M.S. (2002), 'State lotteries and consumer behavior', National Bureau of Economic Research Working Paper No. 9330.

Levitsky, I., D. Assane and W. Robinson (2000), 'Determinants of gaming revenue: the extent of changing attitudes in the gaming industry', *Applied Economics Letters*, **7** (4), 155–8.

Mobilia, P. (1993), 'Gambling as a rational addiction', *Journal of Gambling Studies*, **9** (3), 121–52.

Nichols, M. (1998), 'Empirical analysis of casino gambling addiction', University of Nevada, Reno, working paper.

Paton, D., D. Siegel and L. Vaughan Williams (2002), 'A policy response to the e-commerce revolution: the case of betting taxation in the UK', *Economic Journal*, **112** (480), 296–314.

Paton, D., D. Siegel and L. Vaughan Williams (2003), 'The demand for gambling: a review', in Leighton Vaughan Williams (ed.), *The Economics of Gambling*, London: Routledge, pp. 247–63.

Paton, D., D. Siegel and L. Vaughan Williams (2004), 'A time series analysis of the demand for gambling in the United Kingdom', *National Tax Journal*, **57** (4), 847–61.

Rabin, M. and R. Thaler (2001), 'Anomalies: risk aversion', *Journal of Economic Perspectives*, **15** (1), 219–32.

Rubenstein, R. and B. Scafidi (2002), 'Who pays and who benefits? Examining the distributional consequences of the Georgia Lottery for education', *National Tax Journal*, **55** (2), 223–38.

Sauer, R. (2001), 'The political economy of gambling regulation', *Managerial and Decision Economics*, **22** (1), 5–15.

Siegel, D. and G. Anders (2001), 'The impact of Indian casinos on state lotteries: A case study of Arizona', *Public Finance Review*, **29** (2), 139–47.

Stitt, B.G., M.W. Nichols and D. Giacopassi (2003), 'Does the presence of casinos increase crime? An examination of casino and control communities', *Crime and Delinquency*, **49** (2), 253–84.

Strumpf, K. (2003), 'Illegal sports bookmakers', University of North Carolina at Chapel Hill, working paper.

Tanner, S. (2002), 'Charitable giving and the National Lottery', (www.ifs.org.uk/charities/lottery.shtml).

Thalheimer, R. and M. Ali (1995), 'The demand for pari-mutuel horserace wagering and attendance with special reference to racing quality, and competition from state lottery and professional sports', *Management Science*, **45** (1), 129–43.

Thalheimer, R. and M. Ali (2003), 'The demand for casino gaming', *Applied Economics*, **35** (8), 907–18.

Walker, D. and A. Barnett (2000), 'The social costs of gambling: an economic perspective', *Journal of Gambling Studies*, **15** (3), 213–21.

Wilding, P. (2002), 'Prospect – Cashing in on Internet gaming: El Dorado for the Channel Islands', (www.gamblingcontrol.org).

14 Economics of rock 'n' roll
Simon W. Bowmaker, Ronnie J. Phillips and Richard D. Johnson

The unique features of the music industry offer an opportunity for the economist to answer the basic questions of who gets what and why. At the level of the firm, the industry is characterized by the entrepreneurial spirit of the creative musician who seeks to produce music efficiently and of high quality in order to satisfy consumer demand. At this level, the production of music has much in common with a highly competitive market. However, the perfectly competitive model found in textbooks ultimately fails to explain the allocation of resources in the music industry because a distribution system that contains elements of monopoly stands between the producers and consumers of music. Added to this mixture is rapid technological change that promises to bring new profit opportunities for those willing to take risks and be entrepreneurial, whilst at the same time undermine the traditional way of doing business.

This final chapter proceeds as follows. Section 1 provides a brief overview of the history of the music industry, revealing how technology has always been both its friend and foe. Next, Section 2 illustrates the size and scope of today's global music market. Section 3 examines, first, the complex relationship between the major record companies (the 'Majors') and the independents (the 'Indies'), second, the economics of recording contracts, and third, how technological change is affecting the record label/artist relationship. Section 4 analyses the 'superstar phenomenon' in the music industry. Which characteristics determine the success of an artist? To what extent can superstar effects explain the recent acceleration in concert ticket prices in the USA? Section 5 investigates the economics of legal and illegal copying of music. We draw upon economic theory to show how copying does not necessarily have to be harmful to the copyright owner, before examining the empirical evidence relating to the impact of piracy on legitimate music sales. Section 6 concludes the chapter.

1 A brief history of the music industry
The rise of popular music on a global basis is essentially a post-World War II phenomenon. Despite the inventions of the radio and the phonograph, record sales remained relatively low in the first half of the twentieth century. The first significant stimulus to growth occurred in 1948 when

Columbia Records introduced the 12-inch vinylite long-playing (LP) record onto the market in the USA. LPs played at 33 revolutions per minute (rpm) and were much superior to the old 45 rpm and 78 rpm discs in terms of sound quality and durability, as well as being cheaper to produce (Strobl and Tucker, 2000). The emergence of new low-cost recording equipment in the 1950s allowed many Indies to compete with the Majors of the era (Columbia, RCA and Decca). This provided an opportunity for a greater variety of artists to release music and increased demand as consumers exploited the wider choice of music available (Strobl and Tucker, 2000).

The 1960s was a creative decade in which many of the old formulas and structures changed. Hi-fi stereo recordings were first introduced and the development of tape formats that would eventually transform the industry picked up pace in the mid-1960s with the appearance of the '4-track' and '8-track'. The 8-track achieved a dominant position over the 4-track until the cassette tape, introduced by the Philips company in 1963, eventually took over in the 1970s. Cassette tapes were smaller, more convenient, relatively cheap to produce and, in combination with the development of accompanying compatible software, transformed the production and consumption of music. The 'album' began to take precedence over the 'single' for artists and also for consumers as the growing teenage population spent much of its historically high levels of disposable income on music (Strobl and Tucker, 2000).

Growth of the industry continued until the recession of the early 1980s when the demand for music fell. Many in the industry at this time believed that the availability of home cassette recorders was responsible for much of the loss in sales and there were attempts to tax blank recording cassette tapes. Yet, some analysts suggest that the decline was predominantly related to poor quality of the recordings, inferior software, the global recession and a shortage of creative work. In addition, the difficulties may have been exacerbated by internal or X-inefficiencies and a lack of proper cost controls throughout the industry (Strobl and Tucker, 2000).

The downturn in growth only proved temporary, however, and a period of high growth followed, largely due to recording improvements and the expanded use of digital formats such as the compact disc (CD). Because of the low cost of production and strong market demand for high quality recordings, record companies focused upon low-risk opportunities for profit. This took the form of issuing CDs of back catalogues and compilations of works by established artists. At the same time, the development and growth of global satellite television channels catering for music lovers only, such as MTV, also contributed to increased demand for music (Strobl and Tucker, 2000).

By the late 1990s, a culture of 'free' music was emerging as the use of the Internet expanded. In 1999, Shawn Fanning, then an 18-year-old student at Northeastern University in Boston, USA, created a computer programme called Napster, which allowed Internet users to search for songs in MP3 format ('near' CD-quality sound) on the hard drives of other users, and then download this music to their own hard drives at no cost. Napster was an example of a peer-to-peer (P2P) network, although it did operate with a central server, listing addresses so that users could find one another.

However, within only a few months of its existence, Napster was sued by the Recording Industry Association of America (RIAA) on behalf of the major record labels for copyright infringement. A 'guilty' verdict was returned and in July 2001 it was forced to shut down, but not before it had had a significant impact on the music industry as this chapter later illustrates.

2   Size and scope of global music market

By 2004, global sales of physical recorded music (audio and video) were estimated to be worth US $33.6 billion (International Federation of the Phonographic Industry [IFPI], 2005a). This represents a fall of almost 10 per cent in constant dollar terms since 1999 (see Figure 14.1). The IFPI suggests three reasons for the recent decline in global *audio* sales; first, continued sales substitutions from downloading and CD 'burning' from unauthorized sources of music on the Internet; second, increased competition from other entertainment sectors, such as DVD videos and video games; third, the presence of adverse economic conditions.

Total global unit[1] sales in 2004 were 2.8 billion, 76 per cent of which were accounted for by sales of CDs. Figure 14.2 illustrates the spectacular growth in the popularity of the CD format in recent years and the corresponding decline in other formats, particularly vinyl and cassette.

Table 14.1 shows that in 2004, the UK had the highest per capita sales of recorded music in both volume and value terms, at 3.2 units and US $58.2 respectively, followed by the USA at 2.8 units and US $41.5 respectively.

While there has been a recent decline in sales of physical musical products, legitimate online music services (where consumers pay to download from the Internet) are experiencing significant growth. The spur to this was the success of Apple's iTunes Music Store, which was launched to Macintosh users in April 2003 and sold an average of 500 000 downloads per week over the first six months, reaching a total of 13 million by the mid-October when the service was expanded to include PC users (IFPI, 2004).

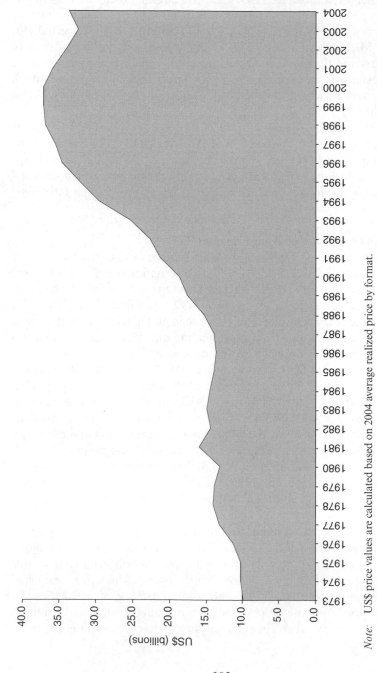

Note: US$ price values are calculated based on 2004 average realized price by format.

Source: IFPI.

Figure 14.1 Real value in US$ of global recorded music sales (1973–2004)

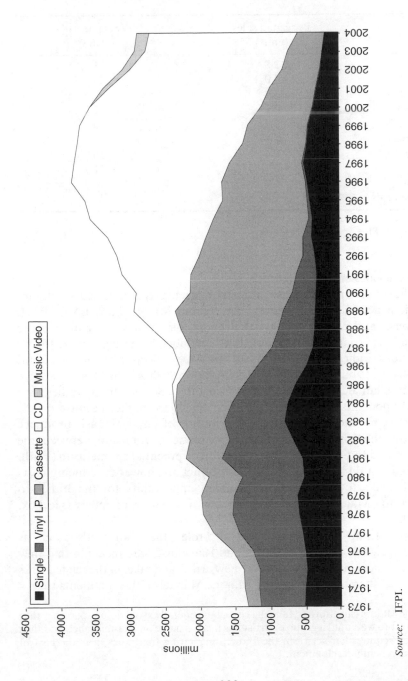

Source: IFPI.

Figure 14.2 Global recorded music sales by format (units, millions, 1973–2004)

Table 14.1   Top ten music markets (2004)

	Per capita sales (units)	Per capita sales (US$)
USA	2.8	41.5
Japan	2.0	40.6
UK	3.2	58.2
France	2.1	32.8
Germany	2.2	26.1
Canada	1.9	21.3
Australia	2.4	36.0
Italy	0.7	11.2
Spain	1.0	14.2
Netherlands	1.8	31.1

Source: IFPI.

3   Economics of record contracts

On the supply-side, the music industry has a highly concentrated, oligopolistic structure currently dominated by four Majors: Sony BMG, EMI, Universal and Warner. In 2004, they had a combined global market share of 76.2 per cent (IFPI, 2005a), the remainder being accounted for by numerous Indies whose continued presence reflects two factors. First, they have an ability to expand markets and specialize in market niches (for instance, Jamaican music and West Coast rap). Second, many Indies have relied upon the Majors to bring their music to market because of the latter's economies of scale in the distribution of physical music products. Indeed, one consequence of this symbiotic relationship between the Majors and Indies has been the reduction of potential competition (Frith, 1987). Digital technologies and the Internet are, however, reducing costs and barriers to entry and represent an opportunity for the Indies to loosen the Majors' stranglehold on the distribution of music (see Fox, 2002).

Aside from their 'market niche' role, the Indies also act as 'Schumpeterian innovators' (Silva and Ramello, 2000), meaning that they create musical innovation, discover new artists and take on the related risks of failure, thereby benefiting the Majors. Manuel (1993) comments that:

> The Majors can afford to take the risks, but generally avoid doing so; rather they prefer to wait until a group or artist has made a name on an Indie label, and then they acquire that act from the Indie, thus letting the Indies bear the cost of research and development.

The story of Sun Records, an Indie that first recorded Elvis Presley, is a classic example. Sam Phillips, the owner of Sun, sold the rights to Elvis to RCA, a Major. What RCA was able to do with Elvis was utilize its financial resources and distribution network to make Elvis a bonafide megastar. As Phillips recognized, he was unable to provide as much for Elvis as RCA could. Though some later questioned Phillips's decision, in the 1950s' environment he made the business decision that he could use the money to find another star of Elvis's stature and although he was not responsible for developing Elvis into a superstar, Phillips did play an important role in the development of the 'Memphis Sound' (Gillett, 1996).

The issue of a record company taking on risk leads us to the economics of a recording contract. What exactly is the nature of risk in signing a new artist? How does a record company (Major or Indie) spread risk? What does the incentive structure look like in a recording contract? How are contracts enforced? In answering these questions, we deal with the implications of prevailing contract practices, rather than the difference between actual and first-best contract terms. Indeed, we show that contracts in creative industries are structurally bounded far away from first-best.

3.1   Division of risk

For a record company, the decision on whether to sign a musician is complicated by the 'nobody knows' character of new musical output (Caves, 2000). Music is an example of an experience good and an individual's utility from consuming a particular piece of music is highly subjective. Record company executives and producers may have deep knowledge about what has commercially succeeded in the past but their ability to forecast the potential sales of a new artist is severely limited. The expected payoff for all parties is highly uncertain, leading Caves (2000) to suggest that the organizational problem encountered in the music industry relates to 'symmetrical ignorance', not asymmetrical information.

There is a different form of asymmetry that is important to note, however. The production of an album proceeds through a number of stages, with costs completely sunk at each stage. For example, when Artist X delivers the unfinished album to Label Y, Artist X's input to the process is sunk, but Label Y can still adjust or even withhold its input. If both parties receive new information about the album's market potential, then it is efficient for Label Y to hold decision rights about whether and how to proceed (Artist X has no more choices open). It is this asymmetry that accounts for the common use in music of the option contract, by which Label Y buys from Artist X the option to proceed with the album's production once it has digested any new information about its potential (Caves, 2000).

In practice, the artist will agree to deliver master tapes to the record company for a series of albums. The record company holds an option to distribute the albums for a specified period of time and commits to pay royalties to the artist based upon revenues generated by each recording. For each album, the record company may pay an advance to the artist to cover the cost of recording the album and a proportion of expected earnings from royalties. This advance against royalties can be viewed as absorption of risk by the record company and a guarantee of at least a minimum royalty income for the artist (Caves, 2000). However, should an album's royalties fail to cover the advance paid to the artist, this shortfall is charged against any albums that are subsequently released. This is known as 'cross-collaterization'.

Having provided an advance to the artist, the record company holds an option not to release an album should the master tape be deemed of unacceptable quality. If the record company does release the master tape as a proper album, then a contract will typically stipulate an increased future advance and royalty rate, but also a commitment for the artist to deliver another album (Caves, 2000).

Risk-averse artists are sometimes able to secure a stronger commitment from the record company to release albums even if new information about market potential is unfavourable. Highly successful, established artists often bargain for even firmer obligations for the company to release their albums; for instance, they may ask for the master tape to be only 'technically satisfactory' or 'in the artist's previous style' rather than 'commercially satisfactory' (Caves, 2000).

Overall, the options within a record contract are distinctly one-sided because the artist is bound to the label and is not permitted to quit and record for another label until the contract expires. This arrangement was recently challenged by successful musicians in California who would like to see a limit placed on the duration of record contracts (Ordonez, 2002). Due to a 1987 amendment to California labour law, musicians in this state are specifically exempt from a general seven-year limit on labour contracts.

The label seeks a long-term contract with the artist because of the high 'stiff ratio', that is, the proportion of recordings that are loss-makers. Vogel (2001) notes that only one in ten albums generate a profit, which is worse than the film industry where on average three in ten films 'make money'. Ordonez (2002) quotes SoundScan figures, which reveal that of the 6455 new albums released by major labels in the USA in 2001, only 113 were profitable.[2] So, a long-term contract is preferable for the label so that it can generate sufficient profits from the successes to cover the stiffs' losses.

In a study funded by the RIAA, Wildman (2002) examined over 6000 contracts signed over the 1994 to 2000 period between artists and the five

Majors at the time. His principal findings were that: 1) the odds of success for a new artist were very low; 2) record labels invest considerable sums of money to record and market albums by unproven artists and 3) artists who have a hit album renegotiate their contracts and require significant upfront commitments by the record company.

In particular, the Wildman study provides information on the complex and multifaceted aspects of recording contracts. There is no such thing as a 'standard' contract and there exists substantial variation in contract terms among newly signed artists. The number of albums potentially required to be delivered over the contract varied between one and ten, about three-quarters of artists signed to contracts will release albums five to seven years later, but only about 10 per cent will still be under contract after this time. The average upfront commitment (execution advance plus recording funds) for a first album in a contract in the period 1994 to 1996 was nearly $300 000 in year 2000 US dollars. For similar contracts signed in 2000, this figure had risen to over $450 000. Royalties ranged from 4 per cent to 20 per cent with a mean of 15.2 per cent. The study also found that only one contract of 244 signed from 1994 to 1996 was negotiated without the artist's legal counsel and that virtually all contracts renegotiated after a hit album added terms favouring the artist.

3.2 Incentives and enforcement

The options contract provides a strong incentive for the label to promote a new artist's first album because it secures terms of access to the artist's *future* albums. Typically, a label can contract a successful artist for long enough to recover any losses generated on earlier albums and promotion of one album may have the positive spillover effect of stimulating demand for the artist's previous works (Caves, 2000). Moreover, should the artist prove a big success, the built-in schedule of royalties specified in the contract may not rise sufficiently quickly for the artist to reap the rewards and are instead collected by the label (Caves, 2000). On the other hand, as a contract's expiration date approaches, the label's incentive to promote a successful artist fades because of the fall in expected rents picked up by the label from future albums.

The royalty contract based on the label's sales revenue is somewhat different from the terms under which authors and visual artists receive payment. Although one of the principal roles of a label is to finance physical production and distribution of an artist's album, substantial components of promotional costs (in addition to all recording costs) are recouped from the artist's royalties. If artist and label have agreed on the royalty rate schedule but not on the label's promotional efforts, then a moral hazard problem arises: the label can shift costs to the artist without being forced to renegotiate the royalty rate and this may result in the label's over-promotion of an album relative to the expenditures that would maximize both parties' combined profits (Caves, 2000). This incentive to over-promote will increase in line with the label's confidence that it can recover all costs it has advanced to the artist. It will decrease as the artist's effective royalty rate increases because the, 'higher the rate, the less of a promotion-induced extra dollar of revenue lands in the company's pocket' (Caves, 2000).

The royalty contract would appear to provide the artist with an incentive to under-invest in the amount of time spent in the studio recording an album. This is a reasonable assumption given that it is the label that collects the lion's share of additional revenue once the advanced recording costs are recouped. However, in practice, artists may have a tendency to *over*-invest in studio time because of a taste for perfectionism ('art for art's sake' [Caves, 2000]), while the album's uncertainty of success provides an economic motivation. Should the album be a 'miss', and its costs cannot be recovered, the artist does not collect any royalties but the burden of the loss falls predominantly on the label. On the other hand, should the album be a 'hit', the artist earns royalties, his or her royalty *rate* may well increase, leading to a debt–equity moral hazard problem: 'If inflating the studio costs raises the chances of a big win, while the downside loss falls entirely or mostly on the label, the artist could select a heavier investment in album production costs than the label would prefer' (Caves, 2000).

Another form of moral hazard is encountered in relation to contract enforcement. Specifically, once the contract has been agreed, it is very difficult for the artist to monitor the professional conduct of the label, particularly in terms of royalty payments. The label holds the actual sales data that determine the royalties and while most contracts allow for auditing of the label's accounting, it is a costly exercise in terms of both time and money. In response to this lack of transparency, labels have recently been reducing the scope for 'opportunistic transactions'. For instance, in 2002, BMG announced plans to adopt a 'fairer, more transparent' royalty system that would cut the length of a standard contract from 100 pages to 12. In the same year, Universal revealed that it would be adding provisions to contracts that permitted auditors previously denied access to manufacturers' records. In 2003, Warner promised revisions to simplify royalty calculations, to attach interest to royalties unearthed in audits and to reimburse audit costs when unpaid royalties exceeded 10 per cent.

Overall, Caves (2000) notes that, 'the recording contract seems peerless in the scope for governance disputes', and concludes that, 'enforcement of contracts in the creative industries depends heavily on the power of repeated interactions among parties who value their reputations for cooperative behaviour'.

3.3   Technological change and copyright ownership

How is the introduction of new information and communication technologies such as Napster affecting the relationship between artist and record label? Regner (2003) examines the relative marginal efficiency and relative indispensability of labels and artists in a pre- and post-Napster world to determine whether label or artist ownership of *copyright* is more efficient.

He argues that in the pre-Napster world, the relative marginal efficiency and indispensability are in favour of the labels because of their more efficient promotional skills and their indispensable command over the retail distribution network. Whilst established artists might have sufficient power in the production process to demand that copyrights revert back to them, for aspiring musicians without any reputation, there is no option but to rely upon the label to promote and distribute their music. Taking the market as a whole, label ownership of copyright is therefore more efficient in the pre-Napster world.

In the post-Napster world, however, information technology advances further and alternative ways to promote and distribute music emerge. Artists can promote themselves via the Internet (for example, with digital updates of their existing fan base or through the information externalities of file-sharing networks) and cheaper electronic distribution becomes possible (direct selling of music by artists in online shops or the direct distribution of MP3 files). So, marginal efficiency turns in favour of the artists in the post-Napster scenario.

Figure 14.3 depicts this technology-induced relationship change between artist (A) and record label (L). In the pre-Napster scenario, artists would generally be positioned in the lower right section of the diagram because of the high indispensability and marginal efficiency of the labels in terms of promotion and distribution. However, technological innovation and advance mean that in the post-Napster scenario, the position of artists changes and there is a movement across the ownership threshold into efficient artist ownership.

The extent of this movement depends upon the exact impact of technology and on artist type. The figure shows that established artists will find it easier to cross the threshold than new artists, typically because they are cash-endowed. Indeed, recently there have been a number of established artists releasing their music on self-owned labels, including Prince and The Eagles.

Building on Regner's model, Halonen-Akatwijuka and Regner (2004) introduce the concept of a mentor, which is an established musician who can provide new artists with an alternative to label promotion in the post-Napster scenario. A mentor 'adopts' a new artist in his or her own field who can be credibly recommended and promoted. For example, the mentor

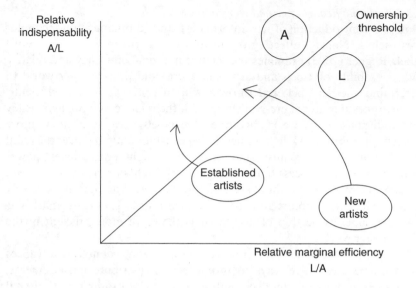

Source: Regner (2003).

Figure 14.3   Technology's impact on the record label–artist relationship

would support the aspiring artist by linking to the new artist website from his or her own frequently visited websites and endorsing him or her there. In addition, the new artist could be invited to tour with the established artist as a support act. Essentially, the mentor is acting as a venture capitalist by having faith in, promoting and financing the project of the new artist. Again, in this scenario label ownership of copyright appears less likely.

Halonen-Akatwijuka and Regner suggest that this arrangement has implications for the quality of music in the future. With a movement toward artist ownership, the relative contribution of the artist in the total value of the music increases. Therefore, the authors suggest that this will lead to an improvement in the quality of music compared with the era of label ownership, which is characterized by relatively low quality music that is well packaged and promoted.

However, they emphasize that label ownership remains feasible provided that the label retains an element of indispensability. Their model only considers the 'singer-songwriter' type who provides all the artistic input, but if this assumption is relaxed, then label ownership is reasonable. This is particularly relevant in the case of 'boygroups' where the artists only sing, with the remainder of the artistic inputs (such as songwriting and choreography) and promotion being provided by the label. Therefore, when examining the impact of technological change on copyright ownership, it is important to distinguish between music production under label ownership where label inputs are crucial and music production under artist ownership where artistic inputs are vital.

4 The winner takes it all: economics of rock superstars

4.1 Ability and record sales

In Chapter 12, with reference to Rosen's 1981 seminal contribution, we examined the 'superstar phenomenon' in sport, where small differences in ability translate into large differences in earnings.[3] Rosen concluded his paper by remarking on Alfred Marshall's reason for why a talented early nineteenth century opera singer named Elizabeth Billington earned less than a 'superstar' salary. Marshall had suggested that:

> . . . as long as the number of persons who can be reached by a human voice is strictly limited, it is not very likely that any singer will make an advance on the £10 000 said to have been earned in a season by Mrs Billington at the beginning of the last century.

In response, Rosen commented that: 'Even adjusted for 1981 prices, Mrs Billington must be a pale shadow beside Pavarotti. Imagine her income had radio and phonograph records existed in 1801! What changes in the future will be wrought by cable, video cassettes, and home computers?'

Ten years after Rosen's contribution, Hamlen (1991) tested for the presence of superstar effects in popular music. He collected data from *Billboard* ratings on 107 singers over the 1955–87 period and estimated the following log-linear equation:

$$ln\,RS = \alpha + B_1\,ln\,HAR + B_2\,ln\,DUR + B_3\mathbf{ln\,F} \qquad (14.1)$$

where *ln* denotes the natural log; *RS* is the value of total record sales; *ln HAR* is a quantitative measure of a singer's voice quality, represented by the high frequency harmonic content that vocalists use when they sing the word 'love' in one of their songs; *ln DUR* is the number of years taken for the singer to build up record sales and is a composite of the effects of rising prices and incomes during the period; **ln F** is a vector of dummy variables that represent the singer's qualitative attributes: whether the singer was female (*SX*), black (*RC*), mostly wrote his/her own songs (*SG*), was a crossover country singer rather than mainstream (*COUNTRY*), had a wide voice range (*RG*), starred in at least one movie (*MV*), was recognized for instrumental backing or a band (*BD*), and whether the singer or group had its career curtailed (*CS*) due to premature death or a group break-up at the height of its fame. The estimated demand function and associated *t*-ratios in parentheses are reported in Table 14.2.

As the table shows, Hamlen found that career longevity (*ln DUR*) is the strongest predictor of total record sales, followed by being female (*SX*). Being black (*RC*) was found to have a negative effect upon record sales, while the main measure of a singer's ability in this study, *ln HAR*, was the only other statistically significant explanatory variable. Hamlen notes that this does indicate that consumers do recognize quality in their pop singers, but because the coefficient is significantly less than one (0.14) he rejects the argument that this is the Marshall–Rosen 'superstar phenomenon' at work. Of course, it is debatable whether the harmonic content of a singer's voice is the appropriate measure of artistic quality for singers of non-classical music (Schulze, 2003).

Hamlen (1994) extended his earlier approach by incorporating the work of MacDonald (1988) and Adler (1985). MacDonald proposed a multi-market superstar model based on a dynamic 'information accumulation process', which he believed was appropriate for singers and musicians. Singers start their careers by competing in an entry-level market, where they share the revenues generated by lower-income consumers who have lower opportunity costs of time and can afford to listen to relatively poor quality singers. However, there are a small number of relatively high quality

Table 14.2   OLS regression to identify superstar effects in popular music

Dependent variable = *ln RS* (record sales) (*t*-statistics in parentheses)	
Constant	0.63871 (2.137)
ln HAR (voice quality)	0.14246 (2.826)*
ln DUR (experience)	1.22282 (13.546)*
SG (songwriter)	0.03183 (0.126)
BD (band)	0.33482 (1.205)
RG (voice range)	−0.14114 (−0.525)
RC (black)	−0.74115 (−2.295)*
SX (female)	1.00579 (3.797)*
MV (movie)	0.20500 (0.794)
CS (career curtailed)	0.04762 (0.203)
COUNTRY	0.49654 (1.622)

Notes:
$n = 107$; $F = 35.1$; $R^2 = 0.79$.
*Significant at 1% level.

Source: Hamlen (1991).

singers in the entry-level market who achieve above-average success and have the chance to compete successfully in more select, higher-level markets where consumers have higher incomes and higher opportunity costs of time. Each higher market level is characterized by consumers being willing to pay a premium to listen to only the higher quality singers who have been 'filtered out' from the lower-market levels. This multi-market process proposed by MacDonald can therefore produce the superstar phenomenon.

Hamlen notes that the work of Adler (1985) can undermine MacDonald's model. First, one assumption behind the model is that the quality filter works perfectly. Yet, in practice, we may observe some high quality singers doing poorly and some poor quality singers doing well. Second, Adler suggests that the success and failure of singers depends upon 'factors other than talent'. These other factors fall into measurable and non-measurable categories: for instance, sex or race in the former case, charisma, good looks, or luck in the latter case. It is the existence and value of these factors, according to Adler, that determine the consumer's demand for 'variety' and complicate the relationship between quality (ability) and success.

Hamlen examined the 1955–87 recorded music market within MacDonald's multi-level market superstar process and allowed for Adler's 'other factors', which lead to an imperfect filtering mechanism for quality. He divided the market into the lower-end market for singles and the higher-end market for albums, with the singles market being viewed as an entry-level quality filter for the album market. The same explanatory variables were used as in his 1991 study but with the following additions: eight different musical styles were selected to replace the *COUNTRY* variable, and variables were also included to take account of the price of singles and albums, the consumer budget on all albums, and the year in which the singer(s) released their first single or album (to allow for the fact that in the 1955–87 period some singers had more years in which to secure hit records).

Hamlen employed Tobit regressions since the number of hit singles or albums is non-negative and because it allows estimation of the interaction between singles and album markets. His single-stage reduced regression produced coefficients for quality of voice in singles and albums of 0.123 and 0.105 respectively. He suggests that because these coefficients are less than one, 'there is no evidence of the superstar phenomenon, at least as defined with respect to proportionalities'.

His two-stage and multiple-stage simultaneous Tobit regressions helped to separate the interactive influence of the singles and album markets. In the albums market, he found that voice quality is not significant but the level of endogenous hit singles is significant, providing evidence that the singles market acted as a 'quality' filter for the albums market. However, he also found support for Adler's view that this filter will be an imperfect one. For instance, some black singers who were successful in the singles market achieved, on average, one less hit record (0.857) in the albums market. While this could be offset by an additional hit single (0.758), Hamlen notes that, 'it still represents an obstacle to success and a distortion in the relationship between success and ability'. (See Chung and Cox, 1994 for another test of the theories of Rosen and Adler in relation to recorded music sales.)

4.2   Superstar concerts

Krueger (2004) examines the relevance of the superstar phenomenon to explain why concert ticket prices in the USA escalated between 1997 and 2003, and why ticket sales and the number of shows performed by top artists fell over the same period.

Figure 14.4 illustrates the average price of a concert ticket (total revenue divided by total tickets sold each year in the USA) for all concerts performed between 1981 and 2003, as well as the (ticket-weighted) average high and low price of a ticket. The figure also reveals, according to Krueger's calculations, what the average price would have been had it increased in line with the US CPI-U.

Concert ticket prices in the USA rose slightly faster than inflation from 1981 to 1986 (a compound 4.6 per cent a year compared with 3.7 per cent a year), but grew much faster than inflation from 1996 to 2003 (8.9 per cent a year compared with 2.3 per cent a year). Further, Figure 14.4 also shows that the cost of the highest priced ticket at a concert has risen even faster than the average priced ticket. Krueger estimates that weighted by total ticket sales, the average high price ticket increased by 10.7 per cent a year from 1996 to 2003, while the average price of the lowest price ticket rose by 6.7 per cent a year.

The number of concerts performed in the USA by artists featured in the *Rolling Stone Encyclopedia* increased in the 1980s, reached a peak in the first half of the 1990s, and then fell by 16 per cent from 1996 to 2003. Krueger also notes that from the late 1980s until 2000, the number of concert tickets sold by these artists fluctuated around 30 million a year, but declined to 22 million tickets by 2003. Total ticket revenue to these artists (in 2003 US dollars) increased until 2000, since which there has been a 10 per cent fall in revenue.

Krueger computes the total dollar value of ticket sales each year relative to the USA total to obtain the share of revenue captured by the top 1 per cent and top 5 per cent of all performers (ranked by their total concert revenue). Figure 14.5 reveals the increasing skewness of concert revenues in the 1980s and 1990s. In 1982, the top 1 per cent of artists received 26 per cent of concert revenue but by 2003, this figure had more than

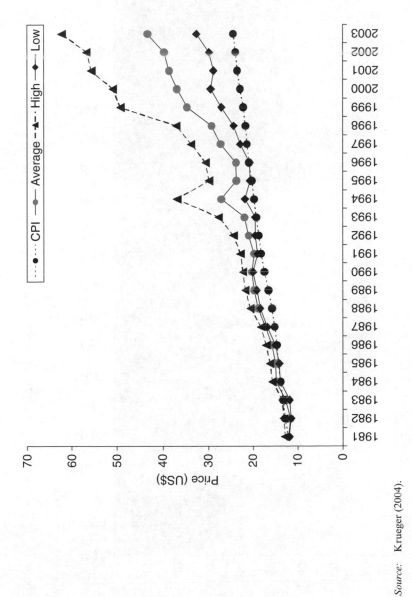

Source: Krueger (2004).

Figure 14.4 Average price per concert ticket in USA and inflation rate (1981–2003)

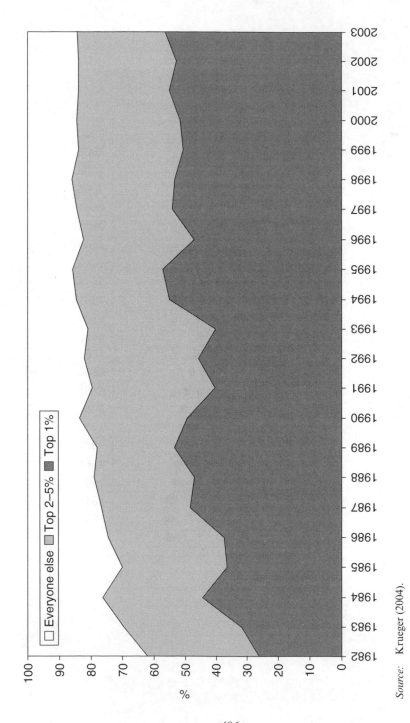

Figure 14.5   Distribution of concert ticket revenue to artists in USA (1982–2003)

doubled to 56 per cent. Similarly, the top 5 per cent generated 62 per cent of concert revenue in 1982 and 84 per cent in 2003.

Krueger also selects artists who were the highest revenue generators in the 1996 to 1999 period (and also revenues in surrounding periods) to report the revenue, number of shows performed, and average price for these top artists just prior to the price take-off (1994–95) and just after (2000–01). These figures are shown in Table 14.3. Krueger notes that the number of concerts performed by these stars dropped by 18 per cent while revenue per show rocketed by 60 per cent due to an increase in price and increase in tickets sold per show.

He suggests that for the superstar phenomenon to account for these quantity and price trends, two observations must hold: first, superstar artists have a backward-bending labour supply curve that led to a decrease in concerts despite the increase in revenues per show; second, superstar effects gained strong momentum in the post-1996 period. Krueger tests for the presence of superstar effects using two samples of data: all artists featured in a Pollstar database (containing 232 911 reports on concerts) and a subset of artists listed in the *Rolling Stone Encyclopedia of Rock & Roll* (containing information on 1786 artists, 1275 of whom having performed at least one concert represented in the Pollstar database).

For each artist (*i*) in each year (*t*), Krueger computes the following dependent variables in logarithms: the (ticket-weighted) average price, total revenue and revenue per show. The full regression model is as follows:

$$ln Y_{it} = \alpha + \beta_p S_i + X'_{it_\gamma} + \delta_t + \varepsilon_{it} \qquad (14.2)$$

where *ln* Y_{it} is the log average price (or log total revenue or log revenue per show), S_i is the measure of star quality, which Krueger captures by the number of millimetres of print columns (including photographs) devoted to each artist in the *Encyclopedia*, X'_{it_γ} is a vector of covariates (number of supporting acts, years of experience of the band, and dummies for genre and foreign status), δ_t is a set of 22 unrestricted year fixed effects, and ε_{it} is an error term.

The coefficient on star quality, β_p, has a *p* subscript, which specifies the time period (1981–96, 1987–91, 1992–96 or 1997–2003). This allows the effect of star quality to vary across time periods, which is captured in Krueger's regressions by interacting the amount of print with dummies indicating the four periods. Therefore, his 'rising-return-to-superstardom' hypothesis is essentially one of whether we observe a discrete jump in β_p after 1996.

The results for the full sample on the three models (average price, total revenue and revenue per show) reveal large and increasing superstar effects. He reports that a 200 millimetre increase in print in the *Encyclopedia* is

Table 14.3 Concert revenue and prices in USA in 1994–95 and 2000–01 for artists with highest revenue per show in 1996–99

	1994–95				2000–01				Percentage change			
	Total revenue (in thousands)	Number of shows	Rev. per show (in thousands)	Average price	Total revenue (in thousands)	Number of shows	Rev. per show (in thousands)	Average price	Total revenue	Number of shows	Rev. per show	Average price
The Eagles	$151 000	102	$1 480	$67.50	$4 837	1	$4 837	$89.22	−96.8	−99.0	226.8	32.2
Barbara Streisand	54 200	20	2 710	201.65	27 700	4	6 925	483.61	−48.9	−80.0	155.5	139.8
Reba McEntire	50 200	147	341	29.49	11 800	43	274	42.76	−76.5	−70.7	−19.6	45.0
Jimmy Buffett	35 700	64	558	31.39	49 600	62	800	39.84	39.9	−3.1	43.4	26.9
George Strait	28 600	76	376	23.73	22 500	11	2 045	48.60	−21.3	−85.5	443.5	104.8
Aerosmith	24 200	54	448	29.64	45 900	59	778	47.34	89.7	9.3	73.6	59.7
Elton John	24 200	37	654	40.66	21 800	38	574	56.70	−9.9	2.7	−12.3	39.4
Phish	23 100	141	164	23.27	21 300	40	533	30.50	−7.8	−71.6	225.0	31.0
Eric Clapton	21 500	40	538	42.65	32 900	40	823	62.46	53.0	0.0	53.0	46.4
Metallica	20 800	40	520	27.74	37 500	18	2 083	60.45	80.3	−55.0	300.6	117.9
Rod Stewart	18 500	35	529	39.46	23 900	58	412	46.12	29.2	65.7	−22.0	16.9
Janet Jackson	14 200	33	430	36.54	38 400	51	753	64.37	170.4	54.5	75.0	76.1
Dave Matthews Band	10 700	131	82	21.55	129 000	110	1 173	43.72	1 105.6	−16.0	1 335.8	102.8
Pearl Jam	9 264	33	281	23.32	8 454	18	470	28.91	−8.7	−45.5	67.3	24.0
Beastie Boys	6 196	28	221	22.99	338	2	169	50.00	−94.5	−92.9	−23.6	117.5
Luciano Pavarotti	5 410	4	1 352	88.19	10 300	9	1 144	105.78	90.4	125.0	−15.4	19.9
Bruce Springsteen	1 652	16	103	35.45	47 000	48	979	65.20	2 745.3	200.0	848.4	83.9
Ozzy Osbourne	1 516	12	126	28.86	49 100	67	733	43.37	3 139.3	458.3	480.2	50.3
Paul Simon	368	1	368	82.14	5 989	25	240	34.35	1 529.4	2 400.0	−34.8	58.2
Mariah Carey	325	1	325	27.51	6 687	8	836	59.70	1 960.5	700.0	157.6	117.0
Kiss	141	1	141	11.94	60 100	118	509	50.070	42 436.8	11 700.0	260.5	319.3
Average	23 894	48.4	494	40.41	31 196	39.5	789	50.020	30.6	−18.3	59.8	23.8

Note: Computations based on Pollstar database. All dollar figures converted to 2001 US dollars based on CPI-U.

Source: Krueger (2004).

408

associated with 5 per cent higher prices in the 1980s, 11 per cent higher prices in the early 1990s and 15 per cent higher prices over the 1997 to 2003 period. Krueger notes that while the impact of star quality upon annual revenue and revenue performance is much greater, the increase in return to star quality was much slower after 1996 than before. For instance, 200 millimetre increases in print in the 1981–86, 1987–91, 1992–96 and 1997–2003 periods were associated with increases in total revenue of 70 per cent, 90 per cent, 104 per cent and 110 per cent respectively. For the superstar phenomenon to account for the escalation in concert ticket prices after 1996, the effects need to be growing at an increasing *rate*.

Similar findings from Krueger's analysis of the sub-sample are reported. Star quality was associated with a rise in prices throughout the 1981 to 2003 periods, but the greatest increase took place in 1992–96, a period before prices sky-rocketed. Moreover, his results for total revenue and revenue per show lend even less support for the superstar explanation: the impact of print in the *Encyclopedia* on these outcomes *fell* in the 1997–2003 period compared with the 1992–96 period. Krueger concludes that, 'because revenue per performance should be the driving force in the superstar model, these results strongly suggest that accelerating returns to superstardom are not the explanation for the rapid price growth after 1996'.

4.3   David Bowie economics

One potential reason for the acceleration in the price of concert tickets in the USA after 1996 is Baumol and Bowen's Cost Disease (1966). This theory proposes that prices ought to rise faster than overall inflation in low-productivity growth sectors due to cost increases. Concerts may be viewed as a slow-productivity growth sector in the sense that it takes an artist of today as least as much time, effort and labour input to perform a particular song as it took another artist to perform it 30 years ago. However, Krueger argues that it is improbable that the concert industry underwent a 'discrete jump' in costs compared to other industries after 1996. His favoured explanation for the concert ticket price phenomenon is that musicians have experienced a large fall in their income from record sales, which are a complementary good to concerts. He terms his hypothesis Bowie Theory, after rock singer David Bowie made the following prediction in the 9 June 2002 edition of *The New York Times*:

> Music itself is going to become like running water or electricity. So it's like, just take advantage of these last few years because none of this is ever going to happen again. You'd better be prepared for doing a lot of touring because that's really the only unique situation that's going to be left. It's terribly exciting. But on the other hand it doesn't matter if you think it's exciting or not; it's what's going to happen.

While this does not necessarily provide the answer for every creative musician, it does indicate that an appropriate and innovative model is necessary to survive in the age of the Internet.

Krueger argues that a famous band has some monopoly power because of its inimitable sound and style. Therefore, he suggests that in the past when greater concert attendance converted into higher record sales, the artists had an incentive to ensure their tickets were priced below the profit-maximizing price for concerts alone. However, as already noted, new technology has emerged in recent years that allows consumers to download music without having to buy an album. This has weakened the concert/album relationship, with the result, according to Krueger, that concerts are now priced like single-market monopoly products.[4]

His hypothesis is formally explained by assuming that an artist is a firm with two complementary outputs, concert seats and albums, denoted good 1 and good 2 respectively. The artist also exerts monopoly power in both markets. The complementarity characteristic means that the artist's demand curve, $D_1 (p_1, p_2)$ and $D_2 (p_1, p_2)$, depends on both prices, while costs are assumed to be independent of each other and are a function only of each specific good produced, $C_1(D_1)$ and $C_2(D_2)$. Profit maximization is achieved by the artist choosing both prices, p_1 and p_2, as follows:

$$\underset{(p_1, p_2)}{\text{Max}} \quad p_1 D_1(p_1, p_2) + p_2 D_2(p_1, p_2) - C_1(D_1) - C_2(D_2) \qquad (14.3)$$

Meanwhile, equation (14.4) below denotes the proportionate mark-up of concert tickets over marginal cost, where the ε_{ij}'s represent the value of the own- or cross-price elasticities of demand:

$$\frac{p_1 - C_1'}{p_1} = \frac{1}{\varepsilon_{11}} - \frac{(p_2 - C_2')D_2\varepsilon_{12}}{p_1 D_1 \varepsilon_{11}} \qquad (14.4)$$

Krueger argues that the second term in equation (14.4) has fallen in recent years because, beginning in the late 1980s, an increase in concert attendance has had a much weaker effect on record sales. As a result, 'artists and their managers do not need to feel as constrained when they set concert prices'. Indeed, he finds some tentative empirical support for Bowie Theory, pointing to the observation of Oberholzer and Strumpf (2004) that jazz fans are much less likely to download music from the Internet than are pop and rock fans and from 1996 to 2003, jazz concert prices in the USA rose by only 20 per cent, while those of rock and pop concerts jumped by 99 per cent. Krueger also suggests that Bowie Theory can help explain the concert ticket price growth recently experienced in Canada and Europe.

5   Copying music: more economics of Napster and all that

We now turn to the economics of copying music and investigate how this often illegal activity, spurred by technological advances, is affecting music sales. We distinguish between three types of copying:[5]

1.   *Private copying* – where an individual makes copies on a unit scale of a CD, for instance, using home equipment such as a CD-R. In many countries private copying is not illegal provided that the copy is made for personal use and not distributed to third parties.
2.   *Commercial piracy* – involves issuing onto the market physical un-authorized copies of existing officially released music, typically at a lower price. To the best of our knowledge, this is illegal in almost every country.
3.   *Online piracy* – refers to unauthorized downloading of music from the Internet. This takes two main forms. First, the distribution of files from unlicensed Internet sites known as web and FTP sites. Second, peer-to-peer (P2P) activities on file-swapping services such as Napster, which involve direct transfers of music files between users ('peers').

5.1   Size of copying market

By definition, private copying of music is intended for private or personal use and so it seems unreasonable to speak of a 'private copying market'. Obtaining data on the extent of private copying is almost an impossible task, but the IFPI does provide figures relating to commercial piracy and online piracy.

It estimates that in 2004 the value of the global commercial piracy market was US $4.6 billion.[6] One and a half billion units of pirated music were sold, which represents an increase of over 190 per cent compared with 1991, but a fall of 35 per cent from its 1998 peak (IFPI, 2005b). CDs comprised 74 per cent of global pirate sales in 2004 with a roughly equal split between pressed discs and CD-R (38 per cent and 36 per cent respectively). Pressed discs are made on factory production lines and dominate the pirate music market in Asia and Russia, while CD-R piracy refers to the reproduction of albums using CD burning software and is most common in Latin America and Southern Europe with rapid recent growth in Eastern Europe (IFPI, 2003). The remaining 26 per cent of global pirate market unit sales in 2004 was accounted for by cassette sales (25 per cent) and DVD music video sales (1 per cent). Cassettes are the principal pirate format in the Middle East, and they are still popular in Asia, Africa and Eastern Europe (IFPI, 2002).

The IFPI estimates that in 2004 the value of the global pirate market is equal to the entire legitimate music markets of the UK, Netherlands and

Table 14.4   Domestic music piracy levels in 2004

	Over 50%	25–50%	10–24%	Less than 10%
North America				Canada, USA
Europe	Bulgaria	Croatia	Belgium	Austria
	Czech Republic	Cyprus	Finland	Denmark
	Estonia	Hungary	Netherlands	Germany
	Greece	Italy	Slovenia	Iceland
	Latvia	Poland	Spain	Ireland
	Lithuania	Portugal		Norway
	Romania	Slovakia		Sweden
	Russia			Switzerland
	Serbia/Montenegro			UK
	Turkey			
	Ukraine			
Asia	China	Philippines	Hong Kong	Japan
	India	Taiwan	South Korea	Singapore
	Indonesia		Thailand	
	Malaysia			
	Pakistan			
Latin America	Argentina			
	Brazil			
	Central America			
	Chile			
	Colombia			
	Ecuador			
	Mexico			
	Paraguay			
	Peru			
	Uruguay			
	Venezuela			
Middle East	Egypt	Israel	Bahrain	
	Kuwait	Oman	Qatar	
	Lebanon	Saudi Arabia	UAE	
Australasia				Australia
				New Zealand
Africa	Morocco	Nigeria		
		South Africa		
		Zimbabwe		

Note: Domestic music piracy levels are calculated as pirate units divided by legal units plus pirate units.

Source: IFPI.

Spain combined. It notes that there has been a marked recent increase in the number of countries whose illegal music sales exceed legal sales (see Table 14.4). A total of 31 countries had piracy levels equivalent to or greater than their legitimate music markets in 2004 compared to 23 in 2003 (IFPI, 2005b).

Silva and Ramello (2000) note that, 'unauthorized sound reproduction, in manufacturing and commercial terms, finds fertile soil in countries where per capita income is low, the market is more backward and, as a result, the legislative measures to control illegal activities are imperfect or altogether non-existent'. This is generally true for the countries featured in Table 14.4 that have domestic piracy levels in excess of 50 per cent and supports Burke's (1996) observation that, 'economic development rather than copyright legislation seems to be the most important feature distinguishing low from high piracy nations'.

In terms of online music piracy, the IFPI estimates that in January 2005, there were 870 million infringing music files on the Internet at any one time. Around 90 per cent of these were found on P2P networks, with the remainder on FTP and websites. The IFPI notes that this represents a sharp fall from the 1.1 billion unauthorized files on the Internet in April 2003 (IFPI, 2005c).

5.2   Economic theory of music copying

Unauthorized copying of music may be expected to hurt the copyright owner such as a record company because it is unable to appropriate any of the value created by its work. Prospective consumers have a reduced incentive to purchase the product (an album, for instance) when they have the option of using unauthorized copies. Economic theory does, however, provide a number of reasons why copying does not necessarily have to harm the copyright owner.

5.2.1   Indirect appropriability   The term 'indirect appropriability' was first coined by economist Stan Liebowitz in 1985 and refers to how copyright owners can collect revenue from unauthorized copiers by charging higher prices for the originals from which the copies were made. Liebowitz (2002) provides a simple example. Assume that every CD buyer makes a single audiocassette copy for use in the car. Nobody makes copies from borrowed CDs and it is impossible to prevent individuals from engaging in unauthorized copying. How would this affect the CD's copyright holder if it intends to sell prerecorded cassettes as well as CDs? Liebowitz argues that each consumer's willingness to pay for the original CD will be greater than it would otherwise be; first, each original CD will have a copy made from it, and second, each consumer will place some value on the ability to copy.

Therefore, the copyright owner is able to charge a higher price for the CD to capture some of this additional value.

Boldrin and Levine (2002) show that if the copyright holder faces an elastic demand curve, as the price of CDs falls over time due to copying technologies, output will increase more than proportionately and profits that can be indirectly appropriated in the original price will also increase. However, Klein et al. (2002) point out that this result, 'clearly conflicts with actual record-company pricing . . . if Boldrin and Levine were correct, why are record companies not pricing CDs as low as possible?' Liebowitz (2002) acknowledges that, 'just because indirect appropriability might help create profits does not mean that it will succeed in any particular case'.

Indeed, the potential for indirect appropriability to work will depend upon the variability in the number of copies made of each original. In an environment characterized by widespread copying and variability in the number of copies being made, it will be virtually impossible for the seller to identify precisely which originals should have the higher price. This is why commercial piracy and online piracy (where thousands of copies are made from an original) are viewed as more harmful to copyright holders than private copying (where only one or two copies are made from an original).

The above refers to the concept of *implicit* indirect appropriability. However, a number of countries impose a levy on copying equipment such as blank audio tapes, which is a form of *explicit* indirect appropriability. Further, in Europe, a technology named digital rights management (DRM) (see Liebowitz, 2002) is being used, which allows devices such as iPods (Digital Audio Recorders [MP3 players] with non-removable memory) to either limit copying or charge consumers a fee for each recorded work downloaded from the Internet.

5.2.2 Exposure effects, space-shifting, network externalities and price commitments   The 'exposure effect' is another means by which the copyright owner can potentially benefit from copying (or at least not be harmed by it). It refers to the process by which a consumer's online 'sampling' of individual songs will increase demand for the full album recording. In other words, this argument views online piracy as a complement to a CD purchase, rather than a substitute for it. Indeed, Robert Hall, an economist from Stanford University and one of the experts employed by Napster in its defence in court, argued: 'The exchanges of music facilitated by Napster stimulate the demand for the plaintiff's CDs by allowing consumers to sample CDs and develop an interest in CDs that they subsequently purchase.'

The exact impact of sampling may depend upon whether the album is released by a Major or Indie label. Major releases tend to receive considerable levels of promotion via radio and television, and so the sampling effect may be relatively small. By contrast, Indie releases are less likely to receive such promotion and so it is possible that they can benefit from the 'exposure effect'. It may even stimulate demand for live performances from these artists.

The 'exposure effect' argument does have certain flaws. As noted by Klein et al. (2002), a record company that sought to use Napster, for example, as an advertising platform could simply release promotional samples of its products to the Internet to distribute free. Moreover, Liebowitz (2002) points out that because better sampling reduces 'mistakes' in CD purchasing, 'consumers may discover that they do not need to purchase as many CDs since their thirst for music can be quenched with fewer of them'.

Another argument used by Napster in its defence was the 'space-shifting effect', which refers to the scenario where an individual at an office computer is merely using Napster to play a CD he or she has already purchased. This is a form of indirect appropriability and Napster drew comparisons with two similar court cases: first, the Diamond case of the late 1990s, where the court held that copying a file already stored on a computer user's hard drive to a portable listening device was non-infringing personal use, and second, the Betamax case of the early 1980s, where the activity of 'time-shifting' (taping a television programme for later viewing) was judged by the US Supreme Court to be 'fair use'. In the Napster case, however, the court rejected the analogous 'space-shifting argument'.

The concept of a network externality in relation to music piracy is relevant if the number of albums, both legitimate and illegitimate, in circulation determines an artist's fame and popularity. As with the exposure effect, information costs are reduced and new consumers are attracted to buy legitimate albums. The underlying mechanism at work here is Adler's 1985 'snowball effect', which proposes that the more people already know a particular artist, the easier it is for other people to acquire artist-specific knowledge.

Meanwhile, Takeyama (1997) argues that copying may stimulate demand for legitimate albums by allowing record companies to credibly commit to not reduce their prices in the future. Unauthorized copying at time t takes away a small proportion of the future demand for an album, enabling the record company to keep its price stable until $t + 1$, at which point the album will change in terms of its perceived quality. Then, the record company can charge a monopolistic price for its high quality albums without fostering expectations of lower prices in the short run. Takeyama shows that this strategy can increase a record company's profits and social welfare because both high and low quality demand is satisfied at time t.

In summary, the economic theory of music copying suggests that two opposing effects are in operation. On the one hand, the activity can reduce legitimate demand for albums as potential consumers substitute into pirated versions. On the other hand, copying may raise a consumer's willingness to pay and stimulate legitimate demand via various positive influences. It would appear, therefore, that the balance of these effects is an empirical issue.

5.3   Music copying and empirical evidence

Perhaps the first empirical work relating to music piracy was the evidence produced for the hearings on the preliminary injunction against Napster in the autumn of 2000. Two reports that focused on whether or not Napster was increasing or decreasing sales of CDs received particular attention: the 'Fine Report', prepared by Michael Fine, Chief Executive of Soundscan, and the 'Jay Report', prepared by Deborah Jay, a marketing consultant.

The 'Fine Report' examined CD sales in the USA from the first quarter of 1997 to the first quarter of 2000 at: 1) all 'brick-and-mortar' retailers; 2) those within one mile of any US college or university; 3) those within the top 40 most wired US universities and 4) those near universities that prohibited use of Napster after the first quarter of 2000. The underlying assumption was that students at college and university campuses were heavier users of Napster (and the Internet generally) than the average consumer, and so any significant difference between CD sales to the two groups would be due to Napster's impact.

It was found that from the first quarter of 1999 to the first quarter of 2000 (Napster actually emerged around halfway through this 12-month period), national sales of CDs grew by 6.6 per cent, sales near colleges and universities fell by 2.6 per cent, sales near the most wired colleges and universities dropped by 6.2 per cent and sales near colleges and universities where Napster was prohibited after the first quarter of 2000 fell by 8.1 per cent. From these figures, the 'Fine Report' concluded that Napster was harming sales of legitimate CDs.

However, earlier data from the report cast doubt on the validity of this conclusion. From 1998 to 1999 (a year prior to the birth of Napster), CD sales near colleges and universities dropped by around 5 per cent, while increasing elsewhere by approximately 5 per cent. These figures appeared to lend support to Napster's defence that online sales of CDs near college and university campuses were replacing 'brick-and-mortar' sales rather than illegal downloading of songs via Napster.

The 'Jay Report' presented survey evidence from college and university students to examine their reasons for using Napster and its impact on their music purchases. Aside from the usual caveats attached to survey evidence,

Liebowitz (2002) notes specific flaws in the survey design of the 'Jay Report'. For instance, two of the categories of answers, 'buy fewer CDs' and 'make my own CDs', to the question of why a student uses Napster were classified by Jay as indicating that Napster downloads are displacing CD sales. While the first answer obviously matches this description, the second is ambiguous. A student may have made a CD to sample music for later purchase, but Jay would classify that answer as an example of Napster decreasing CD sales. Unfortunately, the 'Jay Report' does not provide separate figures for each of these two answers to determine the severity of the problem, only reporting that 22 per cent of survey respondents either purchased fewer CDs or made their own CDs, while 8.4 per cent purchased more CDs. Overall, the report concluded that 41 per cent of Napster users utilized it in ways that displaced CD sales and, as noted earlier, the court took the side of the recording industry.

More recent empirical attempts by economists to measure the impact of illegal downloading on legitimate music sales include Liebowitz (2003), Oberholzer and Strumpf (2004) and Zentner (2004). Liebowitz investigates the effect of a wide variety of factors that could explain the fall in music sales in the USA between 1999 and 2002. These factors include changes in demographics, in income, in prices of albums and other entertainment substitutes, in recording format and listening equipment, in the 'quality' of music or in musical 'taste' and in music distribution. Using basic regression analysis, he found that these factors cannot fully explain the observed decline in sales and suggested that, 'downloads are causing significant harm to the record industry'.

Zentner (2004) estimates the effect of downloads on music purchases using October 2001 individual-level cross-section data of 15 000 people from seven European countries: France, Germany, Italy, Netherlands, Spain, Sweden and the UK. From a simple comparison of means, he reported a positive correlation between downloading and music purchasing, even after controlling for many individual-level characteristics. However, Zentner found difficulty in isolating the causal effect of downloads on music purchases due to the simultaneity between tastes for music and peer-to-peer usage. To overcome this, he used measures of Internet sophistication and connection speed as instruments and concluded from his results that downloading may explain a reduction in the probability of buying music of 30 per cent and a fall in music sales of 7.8 per cent in the countries under study. However, Zentner's sample omits those under 16-years-old, who are typically among the most active downloaders and heaviest buyers of music. In addition, his sample does not contain information relating to the intensity of downloading or music purchases, thus making it difficult to determine the precise impact of downloading on music sales.

Instead of using survey data, Oberholzer and Strumpf (2004) use figures taken directly from file sharing networks to estimate the impact of downloads on music sales. They analyse a dataset from the USA, which includes 0.01 per cent of the world's music downloads from the final 17 weeks of 2002. To estimate a relationship between downloading and sales, they matched downloads to the album they were released on, for which they had concurrent weekly sales figures. To establish causality, Oberholzer and Strumpf instrumented for downloads using technical features related to file sharing (such as network congestion or song length) and international school holidays, both of which are assumed to be exogenous to sales. They found that file sharing has only a limited effect on music sales. Even in their most pessimistic specification, 5000 downloads are needed to displace a single album sale.

To estimate the effect of commercial piracy on CD sales, Hui and Png (2003) examine panel data for CDs from 28 countries over the 1994 to 1998 period. Using a fixed effect specification, per capita legitimate music demand was regressed against average national CD price, personal disposable income, CD player ownership levels, worldwide MTV subscriptions and piracy levels. Due to the possible endogeneity of CD prices, Hui and Png searched for an instrument that would capture variations in CD prices while not being correlated with quantity demanded. As data on supply-side shifters were not available, they used the price of non-tradeable goods as their price instrument, arguing that the impact of music demand on the price of non-tradeable goods would be very small and their price would reflect the cost of land and labour. The latter determine the cost of retailing, which in turn influences the price of CDs.

Hui and Png argued that the quantity of pirated CDs might be endogenous as it depends on both the price of and demand for the legitimate CD. Two groups of instruments were chosen that would be correlated with the pirated quantity but not legitimate sales. The first group (piracy rates of music cassettes and business computer software) were used because they would be influenced by the same set of national characteristics such as pirated products usage and culture. The second group of instruments (unemployment rate and total consumer expenditure) were used because they are exogenous variables that shift the pirate quantity, but are not affected by the legitimate demand for CDs.

Hui and Png's two-stage least squares (2SLS) estimates indicated that, on a per capita basis, a one-unit increase in CD piracy was associated with a decline in legitimate CD sales of 0.42 units. However, they suggest that the effect of piracy is considerably less than estimated by the music industry. Assuming that the industry did not adjust CD prices, they estimate that in 1998, actual losses amounted to 6.6 per cent of sales, or 42 per cent of industry estimates. On the other hand, Hui and Png acknowledge that in reality music publishers would have reduced prices to mitigate the effect of piracy and so the true revenue loss would have been greater than 6.6 per cent.

In summary, it would appear from the empirical evidence that the negative effects of both commercial and online piracy outweigh their positive effects. In other words, piracy does lead to a fall in legitimate sales of music. However, as we have shown, the extent of the negative impact may be smaller than industry estimates. This seems a reasonable assumption given that trade groups such as the IFPI have an incentive to inflate piracy rates in order to support their position.[7]

6   Conclusion

This chapter applied economic analysis to the music industry. We showed how the industry is undergoing great change in both how music is distributed and in the tastes of the consumer, largely due to technological advances. From our investigation into the impact of music piracy, it is easy to understand why artists and record companies are at present concerned about maintaining their livelihood. However, historically, technology has been responsible for the growth of the mass consumption of music. Further, it has allowed today's superstars to earn huge sums of money compared with musicians of 200 years ago who could not even make a living through creating music unless they were lucky enough to have a patron who would commission compositions or live performances. Record companies first feared radio until they realized it could become a spur to sales. Like the invention of the recording tape and the compact disc, the Internet is more likely to ultimately result in an increase in demand for music once new business models are in place. Indeed, the success of Apple's iTunes Music Store has demonstrated that consumers are willing to pay for music downloads from the Internet. Those industries that do not innovate in a market economy, or ineffectively compete with other similar products, will decline. The same is true of music.

Notes

1. The IFPI calculates units as the total album equivalent. Three singles are counted as one album and sales of all formats are included. Multiple disc packaged products are counted as one unit, except in some countries.
2. Major album releases only become profitable after selling 500000 copies.
3. We should note that differences in talent are perhaps easier to measure in sport than in music.
4. The same result is obtained if we assume a competitive market where records and concerts are joint products. If income is lowered from one, then the other has to pay a larger share of the common cost.

5.   Space does not permit us to discuss bootlegging, the unauthorized recording and distribution of previously unreleased music. An excellent discussion and analysis of this activity can be found in Naghavi and Schulze (2001).
6.   The IFPI's value estimate is for commercial physical pirate product only. It does not include illegal downloading via the Internet and is calculated at pirate selling prices. The IFPI argues that commercial losses to the music industry from piracy are substantially greater.
7.   It should also be noted that, to the best of our knowledge, no empirical evidence exists that suggests that piracy is having an adverse effect upon artists' incentives to create music.

References

Adler, M. (1985), 'Stardom and Talent', *American Economic Review*, **75** (1), 208–12.
Adler, M. (2004), 'The Economics of Superstars: A Review with Extensions', unpublished manuscript.
Baumol, William J. and William G. Bowen (1966), *Performing Arts: The Economic Dilemma*, New York: The Twentieth Century Fund.
Boldrin, M. and D. Levine (2002), 'The Case Against Intellectual Property', *American Economic Review: Papers and Proceedings*, **92** (2), 209–12.
Burke, A.E. (1996), 'How Effective Are International Copyright Conventions in the Music Industry?', *Journal of Cultural Economics*, **20**, 51–66.
Caves, Richard E. (2000), *Creative Industries: Contracts between Art and Commerce*, Cambridge, MA: Harvard University Press.
Chung, K. and R. Cox (1994), 'A Stochastic Model of Superstardom: An Application of the Yule Distribution', *Review of Economics and Statistics*, **76**, 771–5.
Fox, M. (2002), 'Technological and Social Drivers of Change in the Online Music Industry', *First Monday* (http://www.firstmonday.dk/issues/issue7_2/fox/).
Fine, M. (2000), 'SoundScan Study on Napster Use and Loss of Sales' (http://www.riaa.com/news/filings/pdf/napster/fine.pdf).
Frith, S. (1987), 'The Industrialization of Music', in James Lull (ed.), *Popular Music and Communication*, Newbury Park: Sage.
Gillett, Charlie (1996), *The Sound of the City: The Rise of Rock and Roll*, New York: Da Capo Press.
Hall, R.E. (2000), Expert Report, *A&M Records, Inc.* v. *Napster, Inc.* 114F. Supp. 2d896 (http://newscorporate.findlaw.com/hdocs/docs/napster/napster/hall_report_final.pdf).
Halonen-Akatwijuka, M. and T. Regner (2004), 'Digital Technology and the Allocation of Ownership in the Music Industry', CMPO, University of Bristol, Working Paper, 04/096.
Hamlen, W.A. (1991), 'Superstardom in Popular Music: Empirical Evidence', *Review of Economics and Statistics*, **73** (4), 729–33.
Hamlen, W.A. (1994), 'Variety and Superstardom in Popular Music', *Economic Inquiry*, **32**, 395–406.
Hui, K. and I. Png (2003), 'Piracy and the Legitimate Demand for Recorded Music', *Contributions to Economic Analysis and Policy*, **2** (1), 1–22.
International Federation of Phonographic Industry (IFPI) (2002), 'Commercial Piracy Report 2002', IFPI.
International Federation of Phonographic Industry (IFPI) (2003), 'Commercial Piracy Report 2003', IFPI.
International Federation of Phonographic Industry (IFPI) (2004), 'Online Music Report', IFPI.
International Federation of Phonographic Industry (IFPI) (2005a), 'The Recording Industry in Numbers 2005', IFPI.
International Federation of Phonographic Industry (IFPI) (2005b), 'Commercial Piracy Report 2005', IFPI.

International Federation of Phonographic Industry (IFPI) (2005c), 'Digital Music Report', IFPI.

Jay, D.M. (2000), 'Expert Report of Deborah M. Jay', Napster Litigation.

Klein, B., A.V. Lerner and K.M. Murphy (2002), 'The Economics of Copyright "Fair Use" in a Networked World', *American Economic Review: Papers and Proceedings*, **92** (2), 205–8.

Krueger, A.B. (2004), 'The Economics of Real Superstars: The Market for Rock Concerts in the Material World', Princeton University, Working Paper.

Liebowitz, S. (2002), 'Policing Pirates in the Networked Age', *Policy Analysis*, No. 438, 15 May, Washington, DC: The Cato Institute.

Liebowitz, S. (2003), 'Will MP3 Downloads Annihilate the Record Industry?: The Evidence So Far', University of Texas, Dallas, Working Paper.

MacDonald, G. (1988), 'The Economics of Rising Stars', *American Economic Review*, **78**, 155–66.

Manuel, Peter (1993), *Cassette Culture*, Chicago, IL: University of Chicago Press.

Marshall, Alfred (1947), *Principles of Economics*, 8th edition, New York: Macmillan.

Naghavi, A.J. and G.G. Schulze (2001), 'Bootlegging in the Music Industry: A Note', *European Journal of Law and Economics*, **12** (1), 57–72.

Oberholzer, F. and K. Strumpf (2004), 'The Effect of File Sharing on Record Sales: An Empirical Analysis', Mimeo, University of North Carolina, Chapel Hill.

Ordonez, J. (2002), 'Pop Singer Fails to Strike a Chord Despite the Millions Spent by MCA', *The Wall Street Journal*, 26 February.

Pareles, J. (2002), 'David Bowie, 21st Century Entrepreneur', *The New York Times*, 31 October Issue 908, 54–6.

Regner, T. (2003), 'Innovation in Music', in Wendy J. Gordon and Richard Watt (eds), *The Economics of Copyright Developments and Research*, Cheltenham, UK and Northampton, MA, US: Edward Elgar, pp. 104–17.

Rosen, S. (1981), 'The Economics of Superstars', *The American Economic Review*, **71** (5), 845–58.

Schulze, G.G. (2003), 'Superstars', in Ruth Towse (ed.), *The Handbook of Cultural Economics*, Cheltenham, UK and Northampton, MA, US: Edward Elgar, pp. 431–6.

Silva, F. and G.B. Ramello (2000), 'Sound Recording Market: The Ambiguous Case of Copyright and Piracy', *Industrial and Corporate Change*, **9**, 415–42.

Strobl, E.A. and C. Tucker (2000), 'The Dynamics of Chart Success in the U.K. Pre-recorded Popular Music Industry', *Journal of Cultural Economics*, **24**, 113–34.

Takeyama, L. (1997), 'The Intertemporal Consequences of Unauthorized Reproduction of Intellectual Property in the Presence of Demand Network Externalities', *Journal of Law and Economics*, **40** (2), 511–22.

Vogel, Harold L. (2001), *Entertainment Industry Economics*, 5th edition, Cambridge University Press.

Wildman, S.S. (2002), 'An Economic Analysis of Recording Contracts', a study funded by the Recording Industry Association of America (RIAA).

Zentner, A. (2004), 'Measuring the Effect of Online Music Piracy on Music Sales', University of Chicago, Working Paper.

Index

ability
  record sales and, music industry
    celebrity 401–4
  rent of, free agency and salary caps,
    sport policy issues 353
abortion
  background 315
  cause, as 327–8
    access, fertility rate and 328–9
    crime and 333–7
    endogenous pregnancy 329–31
    shotgun weddings and 331–3
  demand
    anti-abortion activities effects 326
    price and income elasticities 323
  joint products and 2
  out-of-wedlock births increase and
    7–8
  outcome, as 321
    access laws 325
    anti-abortion activities 325–7
    consent laws 325
    cultural factors 327
    demand and supply, basic model
      321–4
    public subsidies 324–5
  sequential decision-making 334
  services
    availability 317–20
    usage 316–17
  terminology 315–16
  US ban on 337–8
abortion rate
  UK and USA 318, 319
  worldwide 316
access
  abortion
    fertility rate and 328–9
  laws, abortion as outcome and 325
  see also availability
accidents
  drug use and 61–2
addiction
  drug use and 58–61

'good' versus 'bad' 5
  marriage and 5
  pornography demand analysis and
    182–3
  theories 16–24
  see also drug addiction; rational
    addiction theory
Adeokun, L. 202
Adler, F. 55
Adler, M. 402, 403, 415
adoption
  market possibility for infertile couple
    291
  prices and 7
  supply and demand and 306
Adult Video News 174
advertising
  drug prohibition and 46–7
  drug prohibition and crime 55
  prostitution and 210
  prostitution, decriminalization and
    legalization 198
Africa
  abortion, service use 317
  see also South Africa
age
  prostitution and 6, 216
  suicide rate by, international 238–9
agency
  free, sport policy issues 353–8
AGI, *see* Alan Guttmacher Institute
Ainslie, G.W. 24
Akerlof, G.A. 210, 331–3, 336
Alan Guttmacher Institute (AGI)
  316–17
Albert, A. 220
alcohol, *see* drugs
Ali, M. 372, 375
Alm, J. 378
altruistic suicide
  Durkheim approach 231–2
  see also suicide
American Society for Reproductive
  Medicine (ASRM) 304–5

Anders, G. 372, 375, 379
Anderson, E. 310
Anderson, T.L. 82, 86
anomic suicide
    Durkheim approach 230
    see also suicide
antitrust, *see* competition
Apple iTunes Music Store 391, 419
appropriability
    indirect, music industry copying and
        413–14
Arizona Indian Gaming Association
    379
Arlidge, John 189
arrests
    drug offences, USA 49
    prostitution and related offences
        and, USA 200
    see also police
Arrow, Kenneth 180, 191
artificial insemination, *see* donor
    insemination
Asia
    abortion service use 317
ASRM, *see* American Society for
    Reproductive Medicine
Assane, D. 375
assisted reproduction
    contract, market for
        donation only, with 299
        legal positive price, with 300
    demand for and supply of children,
        microeconomics of before
        reproductive markets 293–4
    economic issues 298
        demand 301–3
        price 305–10, 311
        risk in demand and supply 303–5
        supply 298–301
    ethics 310
    market evolution 295–7
    market possibilities 291–3
    market size 297–8, 311
    services in Europe and USA 293
    see also birth; marriage; sex
asymmetric information
    effects, prostitution 210
Atkinson, S. 361
Australia
    drug addiction statistics 12, 16

drug prohibition 52
gambling, gross annual wagering
    368
prostitution 197, 204
suicide, celebrity 258
Austria
drug liberalization 72–3
prostitution, decriminalization and
    legalization 197
see also Europe
availability
    abortion services 317–20
    guns, suicide and 251–3
    see also access
Azzi, C. 268

Bailey, S. 386
Bainbridge, William 265
Bakalar, James B. 58
balance
    competitive, sport
        product nature 348
        revenue-sharing and collective sale
            of broadcasting rights 360–62
bankruptcy
    social costs of gambling and 380
Bardsley, P. 31
bargaining
    family members, among, decision-
        making in marriage and 152–3
Barnett, A. 381
Barros, C.P. 345
Barros, Pedro Pita 282, 285–6
baseball
    free agency and salary caps and 355
    see also sport
basketball
    free agency and salary caps and 353,
        355–6
    see also sport
Baumol and Bowen's Cost Disease 409
Beccaria, Cesare 101
Becker, Gary S.
    abortion, basic model of demand
        and supply and 321
    behavioural economics xxix–xxxi
    crime and
        capital punishment xxiii–xxiv
        economic theory of 102, 107, 110
        fear economy xxii–xxiii

terrorism xxiv–xxv
private protection against 130
criminology and xxv
discrimination and xvii–xviii
drugs and
  addiction xxvi–xxvii, 17, 18, 19, 37
  liberalization, sin taxes 83, 86
  prohibition xxvii–xxviii
family and xviii–xix
  divorce xix
  economics of xx–xxi
  inter-racial marriage xxi–xxii
  marriage contract xix–xx
  same-sex marriage xx
household production model,
    demand for religion and 268
relationship formation model 156
suicide and xxviii–xxix
  terrorism xxix
see also rational addiction theory
behaviour
  addictive, characteristics of 11
  cartel, sport 351–2
  economic principles applied to 1–3
behavioural economics
  Becker on xxix–xxxi
Belarus
  suicide, statistics 237
  see also Europe
Belgium
  assisted reproduction, risk in supply
    and demand 304
  drug liberalization 69
  see also Europe
benefits
  consumption, gambling 371–2
  marriage 145
    children 146
    love and sex 145–6
    public goods 147–8
    time 148–50
  religion
    demand and 268
    spillover 273
  social, pornography as economic
    good and 188–9
Benjamin, D.K. 82, 86
Bennet, T. 56
Bennett, T.H. 59
Benson, Bruce L.

crime and
  criminal justice system resource
    allocation 124
  police expenditure and rate of 119
  private protection 130, 132
drug liberalization and
  enforcement and asset seizures 78
  free market 91
  government regulation 81
  sin taxes 84, 85, 87
Benson, C. 212
Bentham, Jeremy 101
Bergstrom, T. 155, 157
Berman, E. 277
betting
  described 369
  illegal
    gambling policy and 382–3
    Internet 384–5
    USA 382–3
  Internet
    UK 383, 384–5
    USA 383–4
  see also gambling
The Bible 279
Billboard 255
Billington, Elizabeth 401
Birdzell, L.E. Jr. 86
birth
  live, probability in any cycle 303
  out-of-wedlock increase, abortion
    and 7–8
  sequential decision-making 334
  unborn fetus, drug use and
    62–3
  see also assisted reproduction
Bitler, M. 335
Blair, R.D. 28
Blinder, Alan xxxi
Blume, L. 155
Bold, F. 281
Boldrin, M. 414
Boonchalaksi, W. 198
Borg, M. 385
Bowie, David 409
Bowie Theory (Krueger) 409–10
Brainerd, E. 249
Bretteville-Jensen, A. 32
Brien, M. 160
Britain, *see* United Kingdom

broadcasting rights
    collective sale of, sport policy 362–4
Brown, G.F. Jr. 55
Brown, M. 152
Browning, M. 152
Bruce, Steve 281
Brumm, H.J. 53
BSkyB 363–4
budget
    constraints, indifference curves and
        in marriage 147
Burke, A.E. 413
Bush, George W. 337
business cycle
    suicide and 249–51
Byrne, J.M. 124

Cameron, Samuel
    drug addiction and, price elasticity
        of demand 31
    prostitution and
        demand for 202
        economic welfare considerations
            210
        empirical studies 212
        legalization 197
        market entry 203
        primary and secondary markets
            distinguished 194
Canada
    assisted reproduction, risk in supply
        and demand 304
    divorce trends 141, 143
    drug liberalization, taxation and 85–6
    marriage trends 139
    religion, market product and
        competition 283
Cann, D.E. 283
capital
    drug addiction and 19, 22–3
    human, stock loss, suicide and 253–5
    religious, demand and 270–71
capital punishment
    Becker on xxiii–xxiv
    demand for crime prevention and
        113–16
    number of executions, USA 115
    public opinion, USA 117
    supporters' reasons for favouring,
        USA 118

    see also punishment
Caputo, M.R. 83
Carael, M. 202
Carmelli, D. 17
cartel
    behaviour, sport 351–2
    see also competition
casinos
    economic regeneration and
        UK 380
        USA 379, 380
    reasons for gambling and, USA 372
    taxation and, UK 385
    toleration of gambling and, reasons
        for 378–9
    see also gambling
The Catcher in the Rye (Salinger) 211
Caudill, S. 378
Caulkins, J.P. 34, 48
cause
    abortion as 327–8
        access, fertility rate and 328–9
        crime and 333–7
        endogenous pregnancy 329–31
        shotgun weddings and 331–3
Cave, M. 363
Caves, Richard E. 395, 396, 397–8
CD, *see* compact disc
CDC, *see* Centers for Disease Control
celebrity
    music industry
        ability and record sales 401–4
        Bowie Theory (Krueger) 409–10
        effects in popular music, OLS
            regression identifying 402
        superstar concerts 404–9
    sport
        football, effects on salaries in Italy
            353–5
        relative demand and supply,
            teachers compared 355
    suicide 255–8
Centers for Disease Control (CDC)
    297–8
Chadwick, Edwin 102
Chaloupka, F.J. 31, 33, 34, 35, 95
Chapman, M. 196
characteristics
    addictive behaviour 11
    individual

egg donor compensation and
    selection effect of 309
sperm donor compensation and
    selection effect of 308
pornography industry
    production and consumption
        173–5
    profits 176–7
    size distribution of firms 175–6
prostitution industry 193–4
    drugs and crime link 195
    marriage link 194
    migration link 195
    pornography link 194–5
    provision 195–7
    religious denominational, USA 276
charitable giving
    gambling and 374–5
Chaves, M. 283
cheating
    sport 258–9
Cheng, L.S. 17
Cherlin, A. 143
Cheung, H. 250
childbirth, *see* birth
children
    adoption, prices and 7
    birth, out-of-wedlock increase,
        abortion and 7–8
    demand for, microeconomics before
        reproductive markets 293–4
    divorce and 164
    drug liberalization and free market
        and 93
    marriage gain, as 146
    pornography and 175, 178, 184
    suicide and 247–8
    see also family
China
    abortion, cultural factors and
        demand for 327
    prostitution, decriminalization and
        legalization 197
    suicide 2
Chiswick, C.U. 269
Chriqui, J.F. 74
Christiansen Capital Advisors 367
cigarettes, *see* drugs
Clark, A. 207
Cleland, J. 202

cloning
    market possibility for infertile couple
        292
Cloninger, D.O. 53
Coase, R. 158
Cobain, Kurt 255–8
Coelen, S.P. 322
cohabiting
    marriage compared 144–5
Cohen, Steve 376
collective sale
    broadcasting rights, sport policy and
        362–4
    see also sale
Collins, A. 202, 212
Colombia
    drug prohibition and crime 55
Columbia Records 390
commercial piracy
    defined 411
    see also music industry
commitment
    transitions into and out of marriage
        and 161
commodity
    euphoria as, relative theory of
        addiction and 18–20
    religion as 264, 286–8
compact disc (CD)
    copying market, size of 411
    copyright ownership, indirect
        appropriability and 413
    global music market, size of 391, 393
    music industry history and 390
    sales
        commercial piracy effects 418–19
        Fine report 416
        Jay report 416–17
    see also music industry
competition
    drug liberalization and free market
        and 91
    drug prohibition and 46–7
    religious market and
        doctrine 285–6
        product 280–83
    sport, cartel behaviour 351–2
    see also monopoly
competitive balance
    sport

product nature 348
revenue-sharing and collective sale
of broadcasting rights 360–62
Connolly, S. 386
consent
laws, abortion as outcome and 325
consumption
benefits, gambling 371–2
drug addiction and 20–24, 35–8
drug liberalization and free market
and 87–90
illicit drugs, statistics 12–16
pornography and 173–5
economic good, as 189–90
see also demand
contract
assisted reproduction
demand and 301–3
donation only, with 299
legal positive price, with 300
supply and 298–301
dissolution of, divorce as 144
marriage, Becker on xix–xx
marriage and 144–5
options, music industry, incentives
397
record, music industry 394–5
copyright ownership,
technological change and
399–401
enforcement 398
incentives 397–8
risk, division of 395–7
royalty, music industry, incentives
397–9
control, *see* regulation
conventional demand studies
price elasticity of demand for illicit
drugs and 32–4
see also demand
convictions
drug, USA 77
sentences to prison, jail and
probation 78
time served 79
Cook, P.J. 251
Cooper, A. 182
copying market
music industry, size 411–13
see also market

copyright
ownership, music industry
copying and, indirect
appropriability 413
record contract, technological
change and 399–401
Core Institute 248
costs
economic, suicide and 253–8
social
gambling policy and 380–82
illicit drug use 38
suicide, of 4
sunk, prostitution and 2
see also prices
Cragg, J.G. 203
Crancer, A. Jr. 61
cricket
cheating 359
see also sport
crime
abortion and 333–7
Becker on xxii–xxv
criminal justice resources allocation
122
probability and severity of
punishment and 126–9
rationing 122–6
drug prohibition and 52–5
drug use effect 55–7
drug-related, European approach to
reducing harm and 71
economists' interest in 102–3, 132
gambling and, social costs 380
music piracy
CD sales, effects on 418–19
commercial piracy defined 411
economic theory 413
empirical evidence 415–18
exposure effect 414
indirect appropriability 413–14
levels of, IFPI 'priority territories'
412
market size 411–13
network externality 415
online piracy, defined 411
price commitments 415
space-shifting effect 415
types of, defined 411
penal reform, history 101–2

pornography and 173
prostitution and 195
suicide and, USA 251
supply of offences 110–13
time allocation between legal and
    illegal activities 112
victimless, prostitution as 7
violence, of, drugs and 5
crime prevention
  demand 113
    capital punishment 113–16
    standard empirical model of
      crime, extensions 116–22
crime rate
  murder
    international 106, 108
    USA 54
  UK 104
  USA 105
    falling 129–32
  world, compared 103–9
criminal
  prison time for, USA 128
criminal justice system
  incentives for police and prosecutors
    6
  resources allocation 122
    probability and severity of
      punishment and 126–9
    rationing 122–6
criminology
  Becker on xxv
Crockett, A. 283
Cronje, Hansie 359
culture
  abortion and 324, 327
  marriage and 144
  reproductive market and 308–10
  see also ethnicity; religion
Culyer, A. 39
Cunningham, C.L. 17
Cutler, D. 237, 240, 247–8
cycle
  business, suicide and 249–51
  reproductive, probability of live
    birth in 303

Datamonitor 383
Dave, D. 34
Davidson, M. 298

Davis, D.H. 59
Daw Namoro, S. 27
DEA, *see* Drug Enforcement Agency
death penalty, *see* capital punishment
decision-making
  marriage, in 150–51
    bargaining among family
      members 152–3
    family decision-making 151–2
    spending decisions on private
      goods 153–4
    spending decisions on public
      goods 154–5
    spending versus saving 155
  relationship-making, male and
    female 206
  sequential
    pregnancy and pregnancy
      resolution 331
    premarital sex, abortion, marriage
      and childbirth 334
Della Giusta, M. 202
Deloitte and Touche 357
demand
  abortion
    anti-abortion activities effects 326
    basic model 321–4
    price and income elasticities 323
  adoption prices and 306
  assisted reproduction 301–3
    risk in 303–5
  children, for, microeconomics before
    reproductive markets 293–4
  cigarettes, price elasticity of 37
  crime prevention 113
    capital punishment 113–16
    standard empirical model of
      crime, extensions 116–22
  drug liberalization policy and
    Europe 69–72
    USA 73–4
  drug prohibition and 45
  gambling 374
  illicit drugs, price elasticity of
    36–7
    evidence 30–38
    theory 27–9
  pornography 181
    addiction 182–3
    Internet effect analysis 185–8

price 181
variety-seeking 183
relative, teachers and sports stars 355
religion 264–5
benefits 268
determinants of 268–70
religious capital 270–71
scarcity 265
suicide and 241
see also consumption
Denmark
assisted reproduction 292, 304
drug addiction statistics 16
pornography 184, 189
see also Europe
DeSimone, J. 33
detection
pornography, Internet effect and 186
see also police
di Tomasso, M.L. 202
DiClemente, C.C. 17
DiIulio, J.J. 133
Dills, A. 51
DiNardo, J. 33, 48, 95
discrimination
Becker on xvii–xviii
Ditton, J. 16
divorce
Becker on xix
contract dissolution, as 144
factors precipitating 158
relationship changes 158–9
laws, effect on 137
policy interventions and 163–5
reasons for 137
trends in 137–8, 141–4, 165–6
see also family; marriage
divorce rate
France and Canada 141
Spain, Sweden and UK 142
USA 138
Dixit, Avinash K. 243, 244
doctrine
religious, competition and 285–6
Doeringer, P. 194
Dominican Republic
prostitution, decriminalization and
legalization 197
Donohue, J.J. III 129, 333–7
donor insemination

evolution of reproductive markets
and 295–6
market possibility for infertile couple
291
supply and 299–300
double-kinked demand curve
price elasticity of demand for illicit
drugs and 28–9
see also demand
drug addiction
addiction theories 16–18
melioration 20–21
rational 21–4
relative 18–20
addictive behaviour, characteristics
11
Becker on xxvi–xxvii
demand for illicit drugs, price
elasticity of 36–7
evidence 30–38
theory 27–9
drug prohibition, welfare economics
approach 38–40
hyperbolic discounting and other
extensions to rational addiction
24–7
illicit drug consumption statistics
12–16
'primrose path' to 20
see also addiction
Drug Enforcement Agency (DEA) 48,
49, 70, 73
drug liberalization
economists and 68–9
European policy 69
demand-side 69–72
supply-side 72–3
free market 87, 95
children and 93
competition 91
constraints 91–2
consumption in 87–90
problems with 93–5
risk 91
sanctions 92–3
supply 90–91
government monopoly 79–81, 95
government regulation 81–2, 95
taxes 82–7, 95
US policy 69

demand-side 73–4
supply-side 74–9
drug prohibition
  Becker on xxvii–xxviii
  crime and 52–5
  drug use effect 55–7
  economic incentives of, problems of
    illicit drugs and 44, 63
  price and quantity of drugs under
    46–53
    demand 45
    supply 45–7
  user welfare and
    drug quality 56–8
    use and accidents 61–2
    use and addiction 58–61
    use and labour market outcomes
      60–61
    use and unborn fetus 62–3
  welfare economics approach,
    addiction and 38–40
Drug Use Forecasting (DUF) 34
drugs
  abortion 315
  alcohol
    prohibition, USA 68
    suicide and 248–9
  cigarettes, price elasticity of demand
    for 37
  control, spending, USA 76
  convictions for, USA 77
    sentences to prison, jail and
      probation 78
    time served 79
  illicit
    consumption statistics 12–16
    demand for, price elasticity of
      27–38
    global use 13
    prevalence of use in USA,
      Australia and Europe 14, 15
    problems and economic
      incentives, drug prohibition 44,
      63
    quantity seized 72, 75
    social costs of use 38
  prostitution and 195
  quality, user welfare and prohibition
    56–8
  quantity and prices, under

prohibition 45–53
suicide and 248–9
value of 5
violence and 5
DUF, *see* Drug Use Forecasting
Duke, S.B. 55, 57
Durkheim, Emile 230–31, 232
Dynarski, S. 386

Eadington, W. 372, 380
economic costs
  suicide and 253–8
economic good
  pornography as
    consumption, substitute or
      complementary goods 189–90
    social benefits 188–9
economic welfare
  prostitution and 210–11
  see also welfare
The Economist 193, 194–5
economists
  crime and, interest in 102–3, 132
  drug liberalization and 68–9
  pornography and, interest in 171–2,
    190–91
  sport and, interest in 345–6, 364
  suicide and, interest in 229, 232–3,
    261
economy
  fear, crime and, Becker on xxii–xxv
  growing, falling US crime rate and
    129–30
  regeneration of, gambling and
    379–80
Edlund, L. 193–4, 203, 205, 209, 218
education
  abortion demand and, basic demand
    and supply model 323–4
  prostitution and 196
  reproductive market and 308–9
efficiency
  religion and 273
Egan, Timothy 174
egoistic suicide
  Durkheim approach 231
  see also suicide
Ehrenberg, R.G. 268
Ehrlich, Isaac xxiv, 110–12, 113–14,
  116

Ekelund, Robert B. 272
Elster, Jon 246
EMCDDA, *see* European Monitoring
　Centre for Drugs and Drug
　Addiction
employment
　drug use and 60–61
　pornography and 174
endogenous pregnancy
　abortion and 329–31
　see also pregnancy
enforcement
　music industry record contract 398
England, *see* United Kingdom
Erekson, O. 377
Estonia
　crime rate 107
　suicide statistics 237
　see also Europe
ethics
　assisted reproduction 310
ethnicity
　inter-racial marriage, Becker on
　　xxi–xxii
　out-of-wedlock births and shotgun
　　weddings 332
　prostitution and, satisfaction
　　determinant 220
　reproductive market and 307–8
　see also culture
euphoria
　commodity, as, relative theory of
　　addiction and 18–20
Europe
　abortion, service use 317
　assisted reproduction services 293
　drug addiction statistics 12, 16
　drug liberalization policy 69
　　demand-side 69–72
　　supply-side 72–3
　drug prohibition 51–2
　drug-related crime, approach to
　　reducing harm and 71
　drugs, quantity seized 75
　Internet betting and taxation 385
　music copying 414, 417
　prostitution 195, 198, 199, 201
　sport 345–6, 347, 362–5
　suicide 233–8, 249–50
　see also individually named

countries
European Monitoring Centre for
　Drugs and Drug Addiction
　(EMCDDA) 12, 14, 15, 16, 70–72
Evans, J.T. 172
expected utility theory
　gambling and 369–71
　see also utility
exposure effect
　music industry copying and 414
externalities
　negative
　　Kurt Cobain's death 256–8
　　social outcome and, pornography
　　　172–3
　network, music industry copying
　　and 415
　positive, Kurt Cobain's death 255–6

Fajnzylber, P. 53
family
　Becker on xviii–xx, xxi–xxii
　religion and 269–70
　see also children; divorce; marriage
family economics
　Becker on xx–xxi
Fanning, Shawn 391
Farrell, L. 372, 386
Farrelly, M.C. 33
fatalistic suicide
　Durkheim approach 230–31
　see also suicide
Faugier, J. 212
FBI, *see* Federal Bureau of
　Investigation
FCC, *see* Federal Communication
　Commission
FDLE, *see* Florida Department of
　Law Enforcement
FDOC, *see* Florida Department of
　Corrections
fear economy
　crime and, Becker on xxii–xxv
Federal Bureau of Investigation (FBI)
　73
Federal Communication Commission
　(FCC) 284–5
Fertility Alternatives 303–4
fertility rate
　abortion access and 328–9

Fine, Michael 416
Finer, L.B. 319, 320
Finke, R. 264, 265, 275, 284, 285
Finland
  assisted reproduction, risk in supply
    and demand 304
  drug addiction statistics 16
  drug liberalization 69
  suicide statistics 233
  see also Europe
firearms
  availability of, suicide and 251–3
firm
  size
    distribution of, pornography and
      175–6
    optimal, supply of religion and
      277–8
Fisher, Irving 68
Fisher, T. 203
Florida Department of Corrections
  (FDOC) 128
Florida Department of Law
  Enforcement (FDLE) 128
football
  dominance in sport, Europe and
    USA compared 346
  free agency and salary caps and
    353–6, 357–8
  Internet betting and, UK 384
  revenue-sharing and collective sale
    of broadcasting rights 359,
    362–4
  see also sport
Forrest, D.
  gambling and
    consumer behaviour 371, 372
    demand 373–4
    economic regenerator, as 379, 381
    Internet threat 384–5
    social engineering, as 386
    substitution effects 375
Forrestal, James 257
Fort, Rodney 355, 356, 361
fostering, *see* adoption
Fountain, D. 61
France
  abortion, drugs for 315
  assisted reproduction, supply and
    299

divorce trends 141, 143
drug addiction statistics 16
drug liberalization 70–72, 72–3
marriage trends 139
prostitution 202, 209
sport, revenue-sharing and collective
  sale of broadcasting rights 362
see also Europe
free agency
  sport policy issues 353–8
free market
  drug liberalization and 87, 95
    children 93
    competition 91
    constraints 91–2
    consumption 87–90
    problems 93–5
    risk 91
    sanctions 92–3
    supply 90–91
Frejka, T. 328, 329
Freud, Sigmund 264
Friedberg, L. 164
Friedman, David 274
Friedman, Milton xvii, 53, 371
Frith, S. 394
Froese, P. 285
Fukuyama, Francis 311

Gabriel, Peter 247
gains, *see* benefits
Gallup International Millennium
  Survey 265, 266–7
gambling
  betting described 369
  consumption benefits 371–2
  expected utility theory and 369–71
  income and demand 374
  market size 375–6
  policy issues 386–7
    economic regenerator, as 379–80
    illegal betting 382–3
    Internet threat 383–5
    social costs 380–82
    social engineering, as 385–6
  price of a gamble 372–4
  scope worldwide 367–9
  substitute goods price 374–5
  technological change and 367, 386
  toleration of, reasons for 376–9

see also casinos; lottery
Garceau, L. 304
Garoupa, Nuno 282, 285–6
gas
    suicide and 242
gender, *see* sex
George, David 171
Germany
    drug addiction statistics 16
    prostitution 194–5, 197
    religion, regulated 284
    sport, revenue-sharing and collective
        sale of broadcasting rights 362
    see also Europe
Gibb, John 196
Gibbons, J.C. 113
Gillett, Charlie 395
Ginsburg, Douglas xxviii
Gittings, K.J. 114
Glaeser, E.L. 237, 240, 247–8
Gohmann, S.F. 325
Goldstein, P.J. 53
good
    economic, pornography as
        consumption, substitute or
            complementary goods 189–90
        social benefits 188–9
    inferior, prostitution as 7
goods
    private, spending on, decision-
        making in marriage and 153–4
    public
        marriage gain, as 147–8
        spending on, decision-making in
            marriage and 154–5
    substitute
        complementary or, pornography
            as economic good and 189–90
        euphoria commodity, relative
            theory of addiction and 19–20
        gambling and, price 374–5
        prostitution and 204–5
        religion and 269–70
government
    monopoly, drug liberalization and
        79–81, 95
    regulation, drug liberalization and
        81–2, 95
    see also policy
Greece

drug liberalization 69, 72–3
suicide statistics 233
see also Europe
Greenberg, S.W. 55
Grinols, E. 380
Grinspoon, Lester 58
Gross, A.C. 55, 57
Grossman, M.
    drug addiction and
        conventional demand studies 33
        demand, effective prices 28
        rational demand studies 31, 35, 37
        theories 17, 22
    drug liberalization and
        sin taxes 83, 86
    drug prohibition and, use and
        accidents 61–2
Gruber, J. xxvi, 26, 335
Grundberg, K. 221
Gtech Corporation 368
Guerin, J.G. 299
Guest, P. 198
Gulley, O.D.
    gambling and
        consumer behaviour 371, 372
        demand 373–4
        economic regenerator, as 379
        substitution effects 375
guns, *see* firearms

Haas-Wilson, D. 325
Haddad, L. 152
Hafner, H. 258
Halonen-Akatwijuka, M. 399–401
Hamermesh, D. 232, 243, 244, 248
Hamermesh–Soss model
    microeconomics of suicide and 243–5
Hamlen, W.A. 401–4
Hammersley, R. 16
Hardaway, C.K. 283
Harrison, P.M. 107
Harwood, H. 61
Hausman, J. 353
Hebert, Robert F. 272
Heineck, G. 268
Hemingway, Ernest 255
Henshaw, S.K. 317, 319, 320
Herrnstein, R.J. 20–21
Hewitson, G. 300, 301
HFEA, *see* Human Fertilization and

Embryology Authority
Hirschman, E.C. 310
Hoddinott, J. 152
Home Office 195, 204, 221
Honduras
  prostitution, decriminalization and
    legalization 197
HOPE (Helping Outstanding Pupils
  Educationally) 376, 385–6
Horney, M. 152
Horton, K. 251
household production
  marriage gains and 148–50
Huang, W. 250
Hughes, D.M. 221
Hui, K. 418–19
Hull, B.B. 281
human capital
  stock loss, suicide and 253–5
  see also capital
Human Fertilization and Embryology
  Authority (HFEA) 310
Hume, David xxviii, 2, 232
Humphries, P. 223
Hungary
  abortion, basic demand and supply
    model 322
  prostitution, decriminalization and
    legalization 197
  religion, regulated 284
  see also Europe
hyperbolic discounting
  rational addiction and, drug
    addiction 24–7

Iannaccone, Larry
  addiction studies xxvi
  religion and
    capital 271
    competition and doctrine 286
    demand for 264
    product and market competition
      280–81, 283
    regulated religion 284, 285
    risk 278
    sacrifice and stigma 275, 277
    scarcity and benefits of, 265, 269,
      270
Ibrahimo, M. 345
IFPI, *see* International Federation of

the Phonographic Industry
Impossibility Theorem (Arrow)
  180–81, 191
incentives
  economic, problems of illicit drugs
    and, drug prohibition 44, 63
  music industry record contract
    397–8
  police and prosecutors, for 6
income
  abortion demand and, basic demand
    and supply model 323
  drug addiction and 23
  drug use and 60–61
  gambling and 374
  prostitution and 6–7, 202, 209
    high compensating differential
      205–9
  religion and 269
  sport policy issues, caps 353–8
  suicide and 249
  see also revenue
indirect appropriability
  music industry, copying in 413–14
inferior good
  prostitution as 7
  see also good
Informa Media Group 383
information
  asymmetric, effects, prostitution and
    210
interdependence
  mutual, outcome uncertainty and,
    nature of sport product 349–51
International Federation of the
  Phonographic Industry (IFPI)
  391, 394, 411–13, 419
International Union of Sex Workers
  (IUSW) 197, 203
Internet
  gambling and
    UK 383, 384–5
    USA 383–4
    worldwide scope 367
  online piracy, defined 411
  pornography and 174–5, 176
    supply and demand analysis
      185–8
  prostitution and 210
  see also technology

Iran
　prostitution, decriminalization and
　　legalization 198
Iraq
　prostitution, decriminalization and
　　legalization 198
Ireland
　religion, market product and
　　competition 283
　suicide, supply 243
　see also Europe
Isaacs, A. 196
Italy
　sport 353–5, 362
　see also Europe
IUSW, *see* International Union of Sex
　Workers
IVF (in vitro fertilization)
　evolution of reproductive markets
　　and 296
　market possibility for infertile couple
　　291
　risk in demand and supply and 304

Jaffee, J.H. 59
jail, *see* prison
Japan
　drug prohibition 51–2
　prostitution, decriminalization and
　　legalization 197
　religion, regulated 285
Jay, Deborah 416
Jesus Christ 257
Jobes, D.A. 258
joint products
　economics of sex, marriage and
　　abortion and 2
Judaism 101 144, 145

Kaestner, R. 61, 62, 94
Kahane, L.H. 324, 325, 326
Kane, Thomas 329–31
Karberg, J.C. 107
Katz, M.L. 331–3, 336
Katzive, L. 317
Kay, J. 284
Kearney, M.S. 372, 375–6, 376, 379
Kenkel, D. 17
Kesenne, S. 361
Khan, F. 16

King, J. 74
Kleck, Gary 251
Kleiman, Mark A.R. 28, 81
Klein, B. 414, 415
Klerman, Jacob A. 328–9
Klock, S.C. 298
Kolczykiewicz, M. 305
Koo, L. 258
Korn, E. 193–4, 203, 205, 209, 218
Köszegi, B. 26
Krueger, A.B. 404–10
Kutchinsky, B. 189
Kuziemko, I. 51

labour market
　outcomes, drug use and 60–61
　see also market
Lady Chatterley's Lover (Lawrence)
　178, 179
Laibson, D.I. xxvi, xxx, 26
Laixuthai, A. 95
Latvia
　suicide, statistics 237
　see also Europe
law, *see* legislation
Lawrence, D.H. 178
learning
　transitions into and out of marriage
　　and 160–61
Lederman, D. 53
legislation
　abortion, USA 337
　access, abortion as outcome and 325
　assisted reproduction, USA 297, 305
　changes, effect on divorce 137
　competition, UK 363
　consent, abortion as outcome and
　　325
　drug liberalization
　　Netherlands 70
　　UK 70, 73, 82
　drug prohibition, USA 48
　gambling, USA 383
　gun, USA 251
　pornography, USA 183
　sport, USA 352
Lehrer, E.L. 269
Lemieux, T. 95
Leonard, G. 353
Lerner, A.V. 414, 415

Lester, David 241, 250
Levine, D. 414
Levine, P. 335
Levitsky, I. 375
Levitt, Steven D.
  crime and
    abortion xxii, xxv, 129, 333–7
    capital punishment 114–16
    measurement error extent, model
      for determining 120
    prison xxv
    private protection 130
  crime rate and, fall in US 131, 132
  drug prohibition and, price and
    quantity of drugs 51
Liebowitz, Stan 413, 414, 416, 417
Lillard, L. 160
Lithuania
  crime rate 107
  see also Europe
Livermore, G. 61
Loazya, N. 53
Lott, John R. 131, 336–7
lottery
  UK
    reasons for gambling and 373–5
    social engineering, as 385, 386
  USA
    reasons for gambling and 375
    social engineering, as 385–6
    toleration of gambling and,
      reasons for 376–8
    worldwide scope of gambling and
      368
  see also gambling
Lucifora, C. 353–5
Ludwig, J. 251
Luksetich, W.A. 29
Lundberg, S. 152, 155, 291
Luxembourg
  drug liberalization 69
  see also Europe

MacCoun, R.J.
  drug liberalization and
    free market 88–9
    government monopoly 81
    government regulation 82
  drug prohibition and, price and
    quantity of drugs 47

prostitution and
  legal availability and extent of 221
  supply and population density
    201–2
MacDonald, G. 402, 403
MacDonald, Margaret 196–7
MacDonald, Z. 28, 39
Maclean's 85
Malthus, Thomas 293–4
Manser, M. 152
Manuel, Peter 394
Manzoni, Alessandro 101
Marcotte, D. 249
Marizco, M. 222–3
market
  assisted reproduction contract, for
    donation only, with 299
    legal positive price, with 300
  free, drug liberalization 87, 95
    children and 93
    competition 91
    constraints 91–2
    consumption in 87–90
    problems with 93–5
    risk 91
    sanctions 92–3
    supply 90–91
  gambling, size 375–6
  labour, outcomes and drug use 60–61
  music, size of global 391–4
  music industry copying, size 411–13
  prostitution, structure 203–5
  religious 280
    product and competition 280–83
    competition and doctrine 285–6
    regulated religion 283–5
  reproductive, *see* assisted
    reproduction
  sex, marriage equilibrium 208
market entry
  prostitution 203
Markowitz, S. 248, 249
marriage
  addiction and 5
  budget constraints and indifference
    curves in 147
  cohabiting compared 144–5
  decision-making in 150–51
    bargaining among family
      members 152–3

family decision-making 151–2
spending decisions on private
    goods 153–4
spending decisions on public
    goods 154–5
spending versus saving 155
gains 145
    children 146
    love and sex 145–6
    public goods 147–8
    time 148–50
inter-racial, Becker on xxi–xxii
joint products and 2
prostitution and 194
    economic welfare considerations
        211
    foregone market opportunity
        202–3
    high compensating wage
        differential 205–9
reasons for 137
sequential decision-making 334
same-sex, Becker on xx
sex market equilibrium 208
shotgun, abortion and 331–3
transitions into and out of 155
    changes 158–9
    commitment 161
    learning 160–61
    policy interventions 163–5
    relationship-breaking 157–8,
        162–3
    relationship-making 155–7
trends in 137, 139–40, 165–6
see also assisted reproduction;
    divorce; family; sex
marriage contract
    Becker on xix–xx
    see also contract
marriage rate
    France and Canada 139
    Spain, Sweden and UK 140
    USA 138
Marshall, Alfred 11, 401
Martin, G. 258
Marx, Karl 264
Mast, B.D. 78, 84, 87, 132
Mathews, Jay 296
Mathios, A.D. 17
Matthews, R. 212

May, T. 195, 205
Maynard, A. 29
McAleer, Phelim 195
McElroy, M. 152
McIntosh, J. 233, 237
McIntyre, R.J. 322
McKee, M. 378
McKenzie, Richard B. 68
Medoff, M.H. 259, 324
melioration addiction theory
    drug addiction and 20–21
    see also addiction; drug addiction
Merck & Co., Inc. 59
Merz, Charles 57
Michael, R.T. 321
migration
    prostitution and 195, 209
Miles, Sarah 247
Miller, A.S. 270
Mincer, J. 321
Mirer, T. 243, 250
Miron, Jeffrey A.
    drug liberalization and, free market
        89
    drug prohibition and
        crime 52–3
        price and quantity 48, 51
        supply 47
        user welfare 57
Mobilia, P. 31, 381, 382
Mocan, H.N. 114
Model, K.E. 95
Moffatt, P.G. 202, 211, 212–13
Monitoring the Future (MTF) 33, 35
monopoly
    government, drug liberalization and
        79–81, 95
    see also competition
Monroe, Marilyn 257
Moore, M.H. 27
Morgan, J.P. 57
Morris, C. 255
Morrison, Norma 257
MTF, *see* Monitoring the Future
murder rate, *see* crime rate
Murphy, Kevin M.
    drugs and
        addiction xxvi, 17, 18, 19, 37
        liberalization, sin taxes 83, 86
    music industry copying and

exposure effects, space shifting,
network externalities and price
commitments 415
indirect appropriability 414
see also rational addiction theory
Murray, J.E. 270
music industry
copying
economic theory 413
empirical evidence 415–18
exposure effect 414
indirect appropriability 413–14
market, size of 411–13
network externality 415
price commitments 415
space-shifting effect 415
types of, defined 411
global market, size and scope 391–4
history 389–91
record contract 394–5
copyright ownership,
technological change and
399–401
enforcement 398
incentives 397–8
risk, division of 395–7
rock star
ability and record sales 401–4
Bowie Theory (Krueger) 409–10
superstar concerts 404–9
suicide and 255–8
technological change, influence of
419
unique features 389
see also compact disc
music market
global size of 391–4
see also market
Mustard, D. 380
Musto, David F. 48
myopic demand studies
price elasticity of demand for illicit
drugs and 34–5
see also demand

Napster
copyright ownership and
technological change 399
history 391
music copying and 414–17

NARAL, *see* National Abortion
Rights Action League
Nash, John 152
National Abortion Rights Action
League (NARAL) 325
National Basketball Association
(NBA) 355–6
National Comorbidity Survey (NCS)
248, 249
National Football League (NFL) 356,
359
National Household Survey of Drug
Abuse (NHSDA) 12, 33
National Longitudinal Survey of
Youth (NLSY) 62
National Research Council 58, 62
National Survey on Drug Use and
Health (NSDUH) 12
NBA, *see* National Basketball
Association
NCS, *see* National Comorbidity
Survey
Neale, W.C. 348, 351
Neely, Richard 124
Netherlands
drug addiction 16, 34
drug liberalization 70, 88–9
prostitution 197, 223
see also Europe
network externality
music industry copying and 415
The New York Times 58, 174, 257,
409
New Zealand
prostitution, decriminalization and
legalization 198
NFL, *see* National Football League
NHSDA, *see* National Household
Survey of Drug Abuse
Nichols, M. 382
Nirvana 255–6
Nisbet, C.T. 32
NLSY, *see* National Longitudinal
Survey of Youth
Norberg, K.E. 237, 240, 247–8
North America, *see* United States of
America
Norway
assisted reproduction, risk in supply
and demand 304

NSDUH, *see* National Survey on
    Drug Use and Health
Nurco, D.N. 59

Oberholzer, F. 418
The Observer 189
occupation
    suicide by, UK 254
O'Connell Davidson, J. 204
Office of Fair Trading (OFT) 363
Ohsfeldt, R.L. 325
Olds, K. 284
Olekalns, N. 31
Olson, D.V.A. 283
online piracy
    defined 411
    see also music industry
Ono, Y. 279
options contract
    music industry, incentives 397
    see also record contract
Ordonez, J. 396
Orphanides, A. 26–7
Osborn, A. 70
Ostrum, B.J. 83
Oswald, A. 207
O'Toole, Laurence 183
outcome
    abortion as 321
        access laws 325
        anti-abortion activities 325–7
        consent laws 325
        cultural factors 327
        demand and supply, basic model
            321–4
        public subsidies 324–5
    labour market, drug use and 60–61
    social, pornography and, negative
        externalities 172–3
    uncertainty, nature of sport product
        mutual interdependence and
            349–51
        owner utility and 348–9
owner
    utility and outcome uncertainty,
        nature of sport product 348–9
ownership
    copyright, music industry
        indirect appropriability and 413
        technological change and 399–401

Pacula, R.L. 17, 33, 74
Paley, William, 101–2
Parker, Dorothy 229
Pascal, Blaise 243, 265, 278
Paton, D. 374, 375, 384
Peru
    drug prohibition and crime 55
Peters, S.A. 202, 211, 212–13
Philipson, T. 130
Phillips, D.P. 257
Phlips, Louis 11
Pindyck, Robert S. 243, 244
Piore, M.J. 194
piracy
    commercial, defined 411
    online, defined 411
    see also music industry
Plath, Sylvia 255
Platt, S. 251
Plotz, David 295
Png, I. 418–19
Poland
    crime rate 107
    religion, market product and
        competition 283
    see also Europe
police
    arrests
        drug offences, USA 49
        prostitution and related offences,
            USA 200
    detection of pornography, Internet
        effect and 186
    incentives for 6
policy
    anti-suicide, economics of 258–61
    capital punishment
        public opinion, USA 117
        supporters' reasons for favouring,
            USA 118
    divorce and 163–5
    drug addiction and 26–7, 38–40
    drug liberalization
        Europe 69–73
        USA 69, 73–9
    gambling 386–7
        economic regenerator, as 379–80
        illegal betting 382–3
        Internet threat 383–5
        social costs 380–82

social engineering, as 385–6
marriage and, transitions into and
    out of 163–5
pornography regulation 183–4
prostitution 221–4
sport 352–3, 364–5
    broadcasting rights, collective sale
        of 362–4
    cheating 358–9
    free agency and salary caps 353–8
    revenue-sharing 359–62
see also government
Pollak, R. 152, 155
pornography
    defining
        economic perspective 179–81
        legal and philosophical
            perspective 177–8
    demand analysis of 181
        addiction 182–3
        price 181
        variety-seeking 183
    economic good, as
        consumption, substitute or
            complementary goods 189–90
        social benefits 188–9
    economists' interest in 171–2,
        190–91
    Internet effect, supply and demand
        analysis 185–6
        detection and punishment 186
        marginal productivity of
            preventers and consumers
            187–8
        prevention 186–7
    production and consumption 173–5
    profits 176–7
    prostitution and 194–5
    regulation
        methods 183–4
        problems 184
    size distribution of firms 175–6
    social outcomes, negative
        externalities 172–3
Portugal
    crime rate 107
    drug addiction statistics 12, 16
    drug liberalization 69
    see also Europe
Posner, E.A. 292

Posner, Richard A. xxviii, 130, 292
pregnancy
    endogenous, abortion as cause and
        329–31
    pregnancy resolution and, sequential
        decision-making 331
Prelec, D. 20–21
Presley, Elvis 395
Preston, I. 359
Pretty Woman (film) 196
prevention
    crime, demand for 113–22
    pornography, Internet effect and
        186–7
    see also regulation
prices
    abortion, basic demand and supply
        model 322–3
    adoption and 7
    assisted reproduction 305–10, 311
    drug addiction and 18–19, 24, 35–8
    drug quantity and, under
        prohibition 46–53
        demand 45
        supply 45–7
    drugs, USA 50
    effective, demand for illicit drugs
        and 27–8
    elasticity
        abortion demand and 323
        cigarette demand and 37
        illicit drug demand and 27–38
    gambling and 372–4
        substitute goods 374–5
    legal positive, market for assisted
        reproduction contract with
        300
    music industry copying and 415
    pornography demand analysis and
        181
    prostitution and 6–7, 210
        Punternet 214–18
    religion and 269
    reproductive markets and, demand
        in 302–3
    suicide and 241–3
    superstar concert, USA 404–10
    see also costs
prison
    population rate, international 109

sentences to, drug convictions, USA
        78
time
    criminals, for, USA 128
    served for drug convictions, USA
        79
private goods
    spending on, decision-making in
        marriage and 153–4
    see also goods
private protection
    crime, falling US rate and 130–32
probation
    sentences to, drug convictions, USA
        78
Prochaska, J.O. 17
product
    nature of, sport 348–51
    religious market and 280–83
    theological, space 282
production
    euphoria commodity, relative theory
        of addiction and 19
    household, marriage gains and
        148–50
    joint products, economics of sex,
        marriage and abortion and 2
    pornography 173–5
        demand analysis 182–3
        Internet effect and 187–8
profit
    pornography and 176–7
prosecutors
    incentives for 6
prostitutes
    numbers
        Europe 198, 199
        USA 201
prostitution
    age and 6
    arrests for related offences and, USA
        200
    defined 193
    economic analysis
        asymmetric information effects
            210
        economic welfare considerations
            210–11
        extensions 209
        high compensating wage

differential 205–9
    market entry 203
    market structure 203–5
    theories 202–3
economic principles, application of
    193, 224–6
empirical studies 211
    previous work 212
    Punternet 212–20
industry characteristics 193–4
    drugs and crime link 195
    marriage link 194
    migration link 195
    pornography link 194–5
    provision 195–7
inferior good, as 7
policy 221–4
prices and wages and 6–7
services, price of 214
    age of provider and 216
    determinants, OLS regression
        identifying 217
    duration in minutes and 215
sunk costs and 2
victimless crime, as 7
world, overview 197–202
see also sex
protection
    private, against crime, falling US
        crime rate and 130–32
provision, *see* supply
public goods
    marriage gain, as 147–8
    spending on, decision-making in
        marriage and 154–5
    see also goods
public subsidies
    abortion 324–5
punishment
    pornography, Internet effect and 186
    probability and severity of, criminal
        justice system resource
        allocation and 126–9
    see also capital punishment
Punternet
    background 212–13
    dataset, exploratory analysis 213–14
        price determinants 214–18
        satisfaction determinants 218–20
    see also prostitution

Quirk, James 356, 361

Rabin, M. 370
race, *see* ethnicity
Rachlin, H. 19
Radin, Margaret Jane 310
Rahman, A. 317
Ramello, G.B. 394, 413
Rao, V. 212
Rascher, D.A. 361
Rasmussen, D.W. 78, 84, 85, 87
rational addiction theory
    addictive behaviour and 24
    drug addiction and 21–4, 27–8
        hyperbolic discounting and other
            extensions 24–7
        gambling and 381–2
        pornography and 182
    see also addiction; drug addiction
rational demand studies
    price elasticity of demand for illicit
        drugs and 35–8
    see also demand
rationing
    criminal justice system resources
        122–6
Read, D. 26
record contract
    music industry 394–5
        copyright ownership,
            technological change and
            399–401
        enforcement 398
        incentives 397–8
        risk, division of 395–7
    see also contract
Recording Industry Association of
    America (RIAA) 391, 396
Regner, T. 399–401
regulation
    drug supply and 46
    drugs, USA, spending 76
    government, drug liberalization and
        81–2, 95
    pornography 183–4
        Internet and 186–7
    religion 283–5
    see also prevention
relationship
    breaking, transitions into and

    out of marriage and 157–8,
        162–3
change in
    divorce and 158–9
    transitions into and out of
        marriage and 158–9
    making, transitions into and out of
        marriage and 155–7
    see also divorce; family; marriage
relative addiction theory
    drug addiction and 18–20
    see also addiction; drug addiction
religion
    commodity, as 264, 286–7
    demand 264–5
        benefits 268
        determinants of 268–70
        religious capital 270–71
        scarcity 265
    divorce and 164
    gambling and 377
    market 280
        competition and doctrine 285–6
        product and competition 280–83
        regulated religion 283–5
    marriage and 144, 145, 164
    pornography and 182
    risk 278–9
        exclusivity strategies 279–80
    suicide and 243
    supply 271–2
        external effects and free-riding
            273–4
        optimal firm size 277–8
        sacrifice and stigma 274–7
    see also culture
rent of ability
    free agency and salary caps, sport
        policy issues 353
reproductive market, *see* assisted
    reproduction
resources
    criminal justice system, allocation of
        122
    probability and severity of
        punishment and 126–9
    rationing 122–6
Reuter, Peter
    drug liberalization and
        free market 88–9

government monopoly 81
government regulation 82
drug prohibition and, price and
quantity of drugs 47
prostitution and
legal availability and extent of 221
supply and population density
201–2
revealed preference principle
value and 1
revenue
superstar concerts, USA 408
distribution to artists 406
sharing, sport, collective sale of
broadcasting rights and 359–64
see also income
Reynolds, Helen 222
RIAA, *see* Recording Industry
Association of America
Richardson, J.T. 275
rights
broadcasting, collective sale of, sport
policy 362–4
risk
assisted reproduction demand and
supply 303–5
crime and 112
division of, music industry record
contract 395–7
drug liberalization and free market
and 91
religion and 278–9
exclusivity strategies 279–80
sex and 145–6
risk aversion
gambling and 370–71
Robins, L.N. 59
Robinson, W. 375
Roche, C.M. 221
rock 'n' roll, *see* music industry
rock star, *see* celebrity
Rodriguez Andres, A. 249
*Rolling Stone Encyclopedia of Rock &
Roll* 404, 407, 409
Romania
abortion, fertility rate and access to
328
see also Europe
Rose-Ackerman, S. 272
Rosen, C. 255

Rosen, S. 196, 353, 357, 401
Rosenberg, N. 86
Rosenthal, R.W. 247
Rosenzweig, M.R. 294
Ross, S.F. 359
royalty contract
music industry, incentives 397–9
see also record contract
Rubenstein, R. 385
Rubin, P.H. 114
Russia
crime rate 107
suicide statistics 237
see also Europe

sacrifice
religion and, supply 274–7
Saffer, H. 33, 34
Saint-Paul, G. 292
salary, *see* income
sales
CD
commercial piracy effects 418–19
Fine report 416
Jay report 416–17
collective, of broadcasting rights,
sport policy and 362–4
global recorded music by format 393
record, ability and, music industry
celebrity 401–4
Salinger, J.D. 211
Samaritans 237–40, 246, 259
Sanderson, A. 357
Sargeant, M. 212
satisfaction
prostitution and, Punternet 218–20
Sauer, R. 377, 387
Savage, L. 371
saving
spending versus, decision-making in
marriage and 155
Sawkins, J.W. 268, 269, 270
Scafidi, B. 385
scarcity
religious demand and 265
Schelling, Thomas C. 11, 231
Schmidtke, A. 258
Schopenhauer, Arthur xxviii
Schultz, T.P. 294
Schulze, G.G. 402

Scitovsky, Tibor 270
Scotland, *see* United Kingdom
Scott, F. 373, 374
Scully, G.W. 353
Seaman, P.T. 268, 269, 270
Sen, A.K. 179, 180, 190–91
services
    abortion
        availability 317–20
        usage 316–17
    assisted reproduction, Europe and
        USA 293
    prostitution
        price of 214, 215, 216, 217
sex
    joint products and 2
    love and, as marriage gain 145–6
    marriage market equilibrium 208
    premarital, sequential decision-
        making 334
    same-, marriage, Becker on xx
    suicide rate by
        Europe and USA 235–6
        international 238–9
    see also assisted reproduction;
        marriage; prostitution
Sexton, Anne 255
Sharpe, J.R. 178
Shughart, William F. 83
Siegel, D. 374, 375, 384
Sigel, L.Z. 185
Silva, F. 394, 413
Silver, J. 177–8
Silverman, L.P. 32, 55
Simmons, R.
    gambling and
        consumer behaviour 371, 372, 374
        economic regenerator, as 379
        Internet threat 384–5
        lottery 373, 375
        social engineering, as 386
    sport and, free agency and salary
        caps 353–5
Simon, W. 202, 212
Singapore
    prostitution, decriminalization and
        legalization 197
Sirtalan, I. 31
size
    firm

distribution, pornography and
    175–6
optimal, supply of religion and
    277–8
market
    assisted reproduction 297–8, 311
    copying, music industry 411–13
    gambling 375–6
    music, global 391–4
Skidmore, M. 378
Sloan, F. 31
slot machine gambling
    reasons for gambling and 372–3
    see also gambling
Smith, Adam 86, 101, 232–3, 283
The Smiths 246
Snare, Annika 189
soccer, *see* football
social benefits
    pornography as economic good and
        188–9
    see also benefits
social costs
    gambling policy and 380–82
    illicit drug use 38
    see also costs
social engineering
    gambling policy as 385–6
social outcomes
    pornography, negative externalities
        172–3
    see also outcome
Soss, N. 232, 243, 244, 248
South Africa
    crime rate 107
    see also Africa
space-shifting effect
    music industry copying and 415
Spain
    assisted reproduction, surrogate
        motherhood 292
    divorce trends 142
    drug addiction statistics 16
    marriage trends 140
    sport, revenue-sharing and collective
        sale of broadcasting rights 362
    suicide statistics 233
    see also Europe
Spectator 195, 196
spending

decision-making in marriage and
private goods, on 153–4
public goods, on 154–5
saving versus 155
sperm or egg donation, *see* donor
insemination
sport
cartel behaviour 351–2
economists' interest in, reasons for
345–6, 364
illegal betting and, USA 382–3
policy issues 352–3, 364–5
broadcasting rights, collective sale
of 362–4
cheating 358–9
free agency and salary caps 353–8
revenue-sharing 359–62
product, nature of 348–51
team and league objectives 346–8
see also individually named sports
Spruill, N.L. 32, 55
Stack, S. 251, 253, 257, 258
Staiger, Douglas 329–31, 335
Stanley, L. 361
Stark, Rodney
religion and
demand for 264
product and competition 283
regulated religion 284, 285
sacrifice and stigma 275
scarcity and benefits of 265
Stern, S. 160
Stigler, George J. xxvi, 18, 19, 21, 27
stigma
prostitution and 203
religion and, supply 274–7
Stolinsky, D. 251
Stonebraker, R.J. 277
Stout, J.E. 298
Stranahan, H. 385
STRIDE, *see* System to Retrieve
Information on Drug Evidence
Strobl, E.A. 390
Strom, S. 202
Strumpf, K. 382, 383, 418
subsidies
public, abortion and 324–5
substitute goods
complementary or, pornography as
economic good and 189–90

euphoria commodity, relative theory
of addiction and 19–20
gambling and, price 374–5
prostitution and 204–5
religion and 269–70
see also goods
suicide
alcohol and drugs and 248–9
anti-suicide policy, economics of
258–61
Becker on xxviii–xxix
business cycle and 249–51
children and 247–8
China 2
cost of 4
Durkheim approach
altruistic suicide 231–2
anomic suicide 230
egoistic suicide 231
fatalistic suicide 230–31
economic costs for society
celebrity suicides 255–8
human capital stock loss 253–5
economic principles applied to 2
economists' interest in 229, 232–3,
261
gas and 242
gun availability and 251–3
microeconomics 240–41
demand 241
Hamermesh–Soss model 243–5
supply 241–3
occupation, by, UK 254
optimal reduction, 'old' and 'young'
suicides 260
para-suicide signalling games 247
preferences 245
higher and lower 245–6
long-run and short-run 245
temporary and permanent 246
statistics 233–7, 242, 252, 254
problems with 237–40
suicide rate
Europe and USA 234
by sex 235–6
international and firearm 252
age and gender, by 238–9
Sullivan, D.H. 268
Sullivan, E. 202, 212
Sullum, J. 58

Sun Records 395
superstar, *see* celebrity
supply
  abortion
    anti-abortion activities effects 326
    basic model 321–4
  adoption prices and 306
  assisted reproduction 298–301
    risk in 303–5
  children, of, microeconomics before
      reproductive markets 293–4
  criminal offences 110–13
  donor insemination 299–300
  drug addiction and, future research
      40
  drug liberalization and
    European policy 72–3
    free market and 90–91
    US policy 74–9
  drug prohibition and 45–7
  pornography, Internet effect analysis
      185–8
  prostitution 195–7
  relative, teachers and sports stars
      355
  religion and 271–2
    external effects and free-riding
        273–4
    optimal firm size 277–8
    sacrifice and stigma 274–7
  suicide and 241–3
  surrogate motherhood and 300–301
    risk in 305
surrogate motherhood
  ethics and 310
  evolution of reproductive markets
      and 296
  market possibility for infertile couple
      292
  risk in supply and demand 305
  supply and 300–301
  see also assisted reproduction
Sutton, M. 32
Swan, G.E. 17
Sweden
  assisted reproduction, adoption 291
  abortion, drugs for 315
  divorce trends 142
  drug liberalization 70
  marriage trends 140

prostitution policy 221–2
suicide statistics 233
see also Europe
Switzerland
  drug liberalization 69, 81
  prostitution, decriminalization and
      legalization 197
  see also Europe
System to Retrieve Information on
    Drug Evidence (STRIDE) 33, 34,
    35
Szymanski, S. 345, 359, 361

Taiwan
  suicide, business cycle and 250
Takeyama, L. 415
Tanner, S. 374–5
Tauras, J.A. 33
taxation
  drug liberalization and 80–81, 82–7,
      95
  drug supply and 46
  gambling and 377–8, 384–5
  pornography and 184
  prostitution and 209, 222
technology
  change in
    copyright ownership and, music
        industry record contract
        399–401
    gambling and 367, 386
    influence on music industry 419
    record label/artist relationship,
        impact on 400
  see also Internet
terrorism
  fear economy and, Becker on
      xxiv–xxv
  suicide and, Becker on xxix
Thailand
  prostitution policy 222, 223
Thaler, R.H. 24, 370
Thalheimer, R. 372, 375
Thew, H. 212
Thomas, D. 155
Thornton, Mark 68–9
time
  allocation of, between legal and
      illegal activities 112
  marriage gains and 148–50

prison
  criminals, for, USA 128
  served for drug convictions, USA
    79
Titmuss, Richard M. 299
Tollison, Robert D. 272
Troilo, G. 183
Tschirhart, J. 361
Tucker, C. 390
Tullock, Gordon 68

UEFA 358
UK, *see* United Kingdom
Ukraine
  suicide, statistics 237
  see also Europe
unborn fetus
  drug use and 62–3
  see also birth
United Arab Emirates
  prostitution, decriminalization and
    legalization 198
United Kingdom (UK)
  abortion
    drugs for 315
    service use 317, 318, 319
  abortion rate 318, 319
  assisted reproduction
    reproductive markets, evolution of
      295
    risk in supply and demand 304
    surrogate motherhood 292
  crime rate 103, 104, 107
  divorce trends 142, 143
  drug addiction statistics 16
  drug liberalization
    demand-side policy 69–70
    government regulation 82
    supply-side policy 72–3
  drug prohibition, use and addiction
    59
  gambling
    changes in 386
    economic regenerator, as 380
    Internet 383, 384–5
    National Lottery and reasons for
      gambling 373–5
    National Lottery as social
      engineering 385, 386
    social costs of 381

  toleration of, casinos and reasons
    for 378–9
marriage trends 140
music industry, size of global market
    and 391
pornography
  child 175, 178
  defining 178
  Internet effect 185
  regulation problems 184
prostitution
  drugs and crime link 195
  market structure 204
  policy 221, 223
  provision 196–7
  Punternet 212–20
  statistics 202
sport
  free agency and salary caps 357
  revenue-sharing and collective sale
    of broadcasting rights 362,
    363–4
suicide
  economic costs 253
  occupation, by 254
  preferences 246
  statistical problems 237–40
  supply 241–3
  see also Europe
United Nations Office for Drugs and
    Crime (UNODC) 12, 13
United States of America (USA)
  abortion
    access laws 325
    access to, fertility rate and 328–9
    anti-abortion activities 326
    ban on 337–8
    crime and 333–7
    demand and supply, basic model
      321–2, 323
    endogenous pregnancy 330–31
    methods 315, 316
    public subsidies 324–5
    service availability 319–20
    service use 317, 318, 319
    shotgun weddings and 331–3
  abortion rate 318, 319
  assisted reproduction
    adoption 291
    market size 297–8

price, supply and demand and
306–7, 308–9
reproductive markets, evolution of
295, 296, 297
risk in demand and supply 303–5
services 292, 293
surrogate motherhood 292
capital punishment
number of executions 115
public opinion 117
supporters' reasons for favouring
118
crime
capital punishment 113–16,
117–18
criminal justice resources
allocation, probability and
severity of punishment and
127–9
criminal justice resources
rationing 123, 124–5, 125–6
standard empirical model of
crime, extensions 119
crime rate
fall in, 129–32
statistics 103, 105, 107
divorce
laws, effect on rate 137, 164
policy interventions 163
trends 137–8, 143–4
drug addiction
consumption statistics 12, 16
conventional demand studies 32–4
rational demand studies 35–8
drug convictions 77, 78, 79
drug liberalization
economists and 68–9
free market 88
government monopoly 79, 80
policy 69, 73–9
taxation and 83–4, 87
drug offences, arrests 49
drug prohibition
crime and 53–5
drug quality and 56–7
price and quantity of drugs under
48, 50, 51–2
use and accidents 61–2
use and addiction 59
drugs

control, spending 76
prices 50
quantity seized 75
gambling
casinos, reasons for gambling and
372
changes in 386, 387
economic regenerator, as 379, 380
gross annual wagering 368
illegal 382–3
Internet 383–4
lottery and reasons for gambling
375
lottery and reasons for toleration
of 376–8
lottery as social engineering 385–6
social costs of 380–81, 381–2
murder rate 54
music industry
global market, size of 391
history 390
music copying, empirical evidence
416–17, 417–18
record contract, division of risk
and 396–7
superstar concert prices 404–10
pornography
defining 177–8
Internet effect 185
negative externalities 172–3
regulation methods 183
regulation problems 184
statistics 174
prison
sentences to, drug convictions 78
time for criminals 128
time served, drug convictions 79
prostitutes, numbers, as percentage
of population 201
prostitution
arrests for related offences and 200
decriminalization and legalization
198
policy 222–3, 224
satisfaction determinants 220
statistics 200, 201, 202
religion
demand 264
market product and competition
283

regulated religion 283–5
risk, exclusivity strategies 279–80
supply, sacrifice and stigma 275–6
sport
  economists' interest in, Europe
    compared 345–6, 364–5
  free agency and salary caps 353,
    355–6
  policy issues generally 352–3
  revenue-sharing and collective sale
    of broadcasting rights 359
  team and league objectives,
    Europe compared 347
suicide
  alcohol and drugs and 248–9
  anti-suicide policy, economics of
    259
  celebrity 257, 258
  children and 247
  economic costs 253
  gun availability and 251–3
  statistics 233, 234–7, 240
suicide rate 234
  by sex 235–6
UNODC, *see* United Nations Office
  for Drugs and Crime
US Department of Justice 55, 125, 126,
  127–8
USA, *see* United States of America
use
  abortion services 316–17
  drug
    accidents and 61–2
    addiction and 58–61
    effect, crime and 55–7
    global 13
    labour market outcomes and 60–61
    prevalence in USA, Australia and
      Europe 14, 15
    social costs of 38
    unborn fetus and 62–3
user
  drug, 'primrose path' to addiction 20
utility
  drug addiction and, rational
    addiction theory 22–3
  owner, outcome uncertainty and,
    nature of sport product 348–9
  transferable, relationship-making
    and 157

utility function
  assisted reproduction, demand and
    301–2
  crime and 110
  religion and 268–9
  suicidal children and 247–8
utility theory
  expected, gambling and 369–71

Vakil, F. 32
value
  drugs, of 5
  relationship-breaking and 157–8
  relationship-making and 155–7
  religion and 270
  revealed preference principle and 1
Van Leeuwen, B. 26
Van Ours, J.C. 34
Varian, H. 155
variety-seeking
  pornography demand analysis and
    183
Vaughan, W. Jr. 20
Vaughan Williams, L. 374, 375, 384
victimless crime
  prostitution as 7
  see also crime
violence
  drugs and 5
  see also crime
Voas, D. 283
Vogel, Harold L. 396
Vogel, R.J. 28
Vrooman, J. 352, 356

wages, *see* income
Wagstaff, A. 29
Wales, T. 152
Walker, D. 381
Walker, I. 372, 386
Waters, T. 31
wedding, *see* marriage
Weiss, Y. 155
welfare
  drug user, prohibition and
    drug quality 56–8
    use and accidents 61–2
    use and addiction 58–61
    use and labour market outcomes
      60–61

use and unborn fetus 62–3
  economic, prostitution and 210–11
welfare economics
  drug prohibition and addiction and
    38–40
West, R. 16
White, M.D. 29
Whitley, J.E. 336–7
Whitman, Douglas G. 80–81
WHO, *see* World Health Organization
Wilding, P. 385
Wildman, S.S. 396–7
Williams, H.C.S. 268, 269, 270
Willis, R. 155
Winick, C. 172
Wolfenden, J. 221
Wolfgang, M.E. 257
Woolley, F. 155
world
  abortion rate 316
  crime rate, compared 103–9
  gambling scope 367–9
  illicit drug use 13
  murder rate 106, 108
  music market, size of 391–4
  prison population rate 109
  prostitution, overview 197–202
  recorded music sales

by format 393
  real value of 392
suicide rate 252
  age and gender, by 238–9
World Health Organization (WHO)
  202
Wright, R. 56

Yang, Bijou 241, 250
Yellen, J.L. 331–3, 336
Youssef, H.146
Youth Risk Behavior Survey (YRBS)
  248–9
YRBS, *see* Youth Risk Behavior
  Survey
Yuan, Y. 48
Yunker, J. 114

Zaleski, P.A. 277
Zavodny, M. 335
Zech, C.E. 277
Zedlewski, E. 132
Zelizer, Viviana 291
Zentner, A. 417
Zervos, D. 26–7
Zillmann, D. 173
Zinberg, N.E. 59
Zwiebel, J. 57